Teaching
DRIVER and
TRAFFIC SAFETY
Education

# Teaching DRIVER and TRAFFIC SAFETY Education

By
AMERICAN AUTOMOBILE ASSOCIATION
Washington, D.C.

McGraw-Hill Book Company
NEW YORK
ST. LOUIS, SAN FRANCISCO
TORONTO, LONDON, SYDNEY

***TEACHING DRIVER AND TRAFFIC SAFETY EDUCATION***
Copyright © 1965 by the American Automobile Association
All Rights Reserved. Printed in the United States of America. This book, or parts thereof, may not be reproduced in any form without permission of the publishers.
Library of Congress Catalog Card Number 65-19081
0 1 2 7 5
1 2 3 4 5 6 7 8 9 0   UL   7 2 1 0 6 9 8 7 6 5

# PREFACE

THE LITERATURE of driver and traffic safety education is abundant in some areas of the subject field and very sparse in others. Teacher preparation courses have customarily been well supplied with the standard high school textbooks, publications on the subject of state motor vehicle laws and regulations, and copies of the Action Program. This material is valuable and appropriate to these courses. Far less complete is professional literature composed from the viewpoint of the *teacher*. Detailed descriptions are plentiful, prescribing procedures and actions of all kinds to be performed by the *student*, yet the teacher has usually been left to his own devices for determining how to achieve the recommended student performance, learning, and behavioral effect. This obvious and long-recognized need determined the existence and the plan of this book. What does the *teacher* say, and do, to direct performance, learning, behavior? It is within this frame of reference of the *teacher* that this book views the subject field.

Another consideration which entered into the content plan of this book was identification of areas of *need* in the contemporary published body of knowledge of driver and traffic safety education. Concentration was directed to those areas in which the need was found to be greatest, as those of attitude and behavior (Chapter 4), the alcohol problem (Chapter 5), characteristics of the high school student (Chapter 3), and others. Much of this material has been taken from other, older, well-documented disciplines, but some important concepts and data are introduced into driver and traffic safety education for the first time. The experienced teacher, as well as the newcomer to the profession, will encounter new thoughts and new challenges.

No comprehensive subject field, such as ours has become today, can be covered in full by a single textbook. The course content herein is selected according to the needs of the student in the teacher preparation course and of the teacher in the field. It is enriched with post-chapter references, carefully selected for suitability to the objectives of the chapter. Also, it is recognized that the high school textbook is customarily easily available to the student in this course and to the in-service teacher. Repetition of its content in this book would have been an unnecessary expense to the purchaser, and would needlessly have displaced some of the much-needed material now contained in the following pages.

In short, the plan of this book is designed, area by area, in a mortise-and-tenon relationship with identified and carefully defined current needs in the professional field of driver and traffic safety education.

# ACKNOWLEDGMENTS

## PRINCIPAL WRITER

For his wide knowledge of and experience in driver and traffic safety education, and his skill in presenting the subject matter, special appreciation is expressed to the principal author, ARTHUR L. MAHONY, who received his doctoral degree from the Center for Safety Education of New York University. Dr. Mahony has taught safety and driver education on high school and college levels, as well as anatomy and physiology and physical and health education. He has been on the teaching staffs of Seton Hall University, the Saranac Lake (New York) and Fair Lawn (New Jersey) Public Schools, and Potsdam (New York) State Teachers College, and has served as Senior Safety Education Representative with the New Jersey Division of Motor Vehicles. The principal author of *Sportsmanlike Driving*, 4th and 5th editions, he is now Associate in Safety Education, National Commission on Safety Education, of the National Education Association.

## EDITOR

This book is a product of the vision, editorial skill, and administrative direction of W. L. ROBINSON, Associate Director, Traffic Engineering and Safety Department, American Automobile Association. As editor, he coordinated the contributions of those named herein into the basic philosophy which underlies this book.

## PIONEER

PROF. AMOS E. NEYHART, Director Emeritus, Institute of Public Safety, The Pennsylvania State University, and Consultant on Driver Education to the Association, reviewed the manuscript and contributed to the final document. The Association acknowledges deep appreciation to Professor Neyhart for this service, and for his many contributions to the subject field and to the preparation of its teaching personnel since the original professional course taught in 1936.

## ARTISANS

It would be impossible to give the credit they deserve to the many educators—college, high school, state education department, and others—who have developed the subject field to its present professional status. Their experience and their initiative underlie today's body of knowledge and our modern instructional strategy in driver and traffic safety education. Their contributions over the years form the foundation upon which both the profession and this book were created.

## SUPPORT

BURTON W. MARSH, as Director of the Traffic Engineering and Safety Department (now Executive Director, AAA Foundation for Traffic Safety), provided continuous leadership over the years to driver education, as well as to traffic safety in general. His vision was a motivating factor in the development of the concept of teacher preparation in this field, and of this book.

Since Mr. Marsh's retirement in 1964, the program in support of high school driver education and teacher preparation has been under the direction of MATTHEW C. SIELSKI, Director, Traffic Engineering and Safety Department. His review of the manuscript and special contribution to Chapter 23 is acknowledged with appreciation.

## CONTRIBUTORS

For his significant contribution to the subject field in writing Chapter 33, "The Action Program," special appreciation is due DR. RICHARD TOSSELL, Assistant Director, The President's Committee for Traffic Safety.

For their professional services in the preparation of the manuscript, much credit is due EARL ALLGAIER, Manager, Driver Education Division, and HAROLD O. CARLTON, Educational Consultant, of the staff of the Traffic Engineering and Safety Department; and to CHARLES N. BRADY, Director, Highway Department, of the American

# ACKNOWLEDGMENTS

Automobile Association. In addition, Mr. Allgaier prepared the original draft of Chapters 8, 11, 18, 27, and 35, and parts of 9 and 22; Mr. Carlton, of Chapters 10 and 16; and Mr. Brady, of Chapter 31.

Thanks are also due associates in other departments of the Association for their help on specific chapters. They include C. R. GRAY, Director, Legal Department; C. C. COLLINS, General Counsel; and MRS. SUE WILLIAMS, AAA Librarian.

For their valuable services in connection with the manuscript and illustrations, acknowledgment is also made to the following staff members: W. L. CARSON, WALTER E. MORRIS, SAM YAKSICH, JR., MRS. NORMA BUCKLIN, STUART B. HOPKINS, MISS SHIRLEY DUNN, MRS. BARBARA PIXTON, MRS. BARBARA COPELAND, and MISS DOROTHY HORN.

For valued professional and technical suggestions, and for reviewing parts of the manuscript, acknowledgment is gratefully made to the following:

WILLIAM J. BARBER, JR., Coordinator, Driver Education, Dade County Public Schools, Miami, Florida

RICHARD O. BENNETT, Secretary-Treasurer, Insurance Institute for Highway Safety, Washington, D.C.

JAMES R. BERRY, Traffic Consultant, Insurance Institute for Highway Safety, Washington, D.C.

RICHARD W. BISHOP, Associate Professor, The Florida Institute for Continuing University Studies, Tallahassee, Florida

DR. MURRAY BLUMENTHAL, Director, Research Division, National Safety Council, Chicago, Illinois

WILLIAM H. COVERT, Industrial Department, Ohio University, Athens, Ohio (on temporary assignment with Department of Traffic Safety, Michigan State University, East Lansing, Michigan)

MRS. MARJORIE C. DENNIN, Cataloguer, Virginia Theological Seminary, Arlington, Virginia

DR. GEORGE DEWEY, M.D., Washington, D.C.

A. H. EASTON, Professor of Civil and Mechanical Engineering, University of Wisconsin, College of Engineering, Madison, Wisconsin

WM. ENGLANDER, Secretary, National Committee on Films for Safety, National Safety Council, Chicago, Illinois

JUDGE SHERMAN G. FINESILVER, District Court, Denver, Colorado

HARRY D. FLETCHER, Institute of Public Safety, The Pennsylvania State University, University Park, Pennsylvania

MRS. CISSIE E. GIEDA, Safety Coordinator Department Head, Driver Education, Montgomery-Blair High School, Silver Spring, Maryland

DR. HERMAN A. HEISE, M.D., Milwaukee, Wisconsin; Former Chairman of the Committee on Medicolegal Problems of the American Medical Association

JOSEPH V. INTORRE, Supervisor, Motor Fleet and Traffic Training, Institute of Public Safety, The Pennsylvania State University, University Park, Pennsylvania

MRS. E'LISE B. KELLY, Driver Training Instructor, Los Angeles City Schools, Los Angeles, California

CAPT. R. B. KING, Safety Officer, Department of State Police, Richmond, Virginia

DR. DALIBOR W. KRALOVEC, Director, Division of Safety Education, School District of Philadelphia, The Board of Public Education, Philadelphia, Pennsylvania

D. GRANT MICKLE, Executive Director, Highway Research Board, Washington, D.C.

DR. JAY B. NASH, Former Chairman of Department of Physical Education, Health and Recreation, School of Education, New York University

RAYMOND PRINCE, Secretary, Committee on Winter Driving Hazards, National Safety Council, Chicago, Illinois

DR. OSCAR W. RICHARDS, Chief Biologist, American Optical Company, Research Division, Southbridge, Massachusetts

EDWARD SCHEIDT, Commissioner, Department of Motor Vehicles, Raleigh, North Carolina

THOMAS J. SEBURN, Associate Director, Yale Bureau of Highway Traffic, New Haven, Connecticut

GORDON H. SHEEHE, Director,
Highway Traffic Safety Center,
Michigan State University,
East Lansing, Michigan

TILTON E. SHELBURNE, State Highway
Research Engineer, Council of
Highway Investigation & Research,
Charlottesville, Virginia

GOLEY D. SONTHEIMER, Director,
Department of Safety,
American Trucking Associations, Inc.,
Washington, D.C.

QUINN TAMM, Executive Director,
International Association of
Chiefs of Police, Washington, D.C.

F. C. TURNER, Chief Engineer,
U.S. Department of Commerce, Bureau
of Public Roads, Washington, D.C.

DR. JOHN S. URLAUB, Director of Driver
Education, Berkeley High School,
Berkeley, California

KEITH E. WALLACE, Driver Education
Teacher, Burlington, Ontario,
and Driver Education Consultant to
Canadian Automobile Association

ROSS G. WILCOX, Executive Secretary,
Safe Winter Driving League,
Chicago, Illinois

ED WILLIAMSON, Consultant,
Health and Safety,
State Department of Education,
Tallahassee, Florida

## ATTITUDE AND BEHAVIOR

Chapter 4 brings to driver and traffic safety education a new concept of the phenomenon called *attitude*. The chapter is based on the doctoral dissertation "Teaching for Attitude Conducive to Safe Driving," completed at New York University in 1957 by Dr. Mahony. Appreciation is due the members of the sponsoring committee in the School of Education of New York University, DR. HERBERT J. STACK (ret.), then Director of the Center for Safety Education, DR. JOHN G. ROCKWELL (ret.), then Head of the Department of Educational Psychology, and DR. LEONARD A. LARSON, then Head of the Department of Physical Education, Health, and Recreation (now at the University of Wisconsin). Appreciation is due also DR. SHAILER U. LAWTON, M.D., F.A.C.P., for his inspirational teaching in neurology and neuroanatomy, which formed the background for the investigation, and for his review and approval of the chapter.

# CONTENTS

Preface     v
Acknowledgements     vi

## I    *A PART OF YESTERDAY IS OBSOLETE*

CHAPTER 1    The Profession—Opportunity and Challenge     3
CHAPTER 2    The Accident Problem     20
CHAPTER 3    The Student     32

## II    *HUMAN CHARACTERISTICS RELATED TO DRIVING*

CHAPTER 4    Attitude and Behavior     55
CHAPTER 5    Effects of Alcohol and Drugs     75
CHAPTER 6    Impairment of Driving Ability     91
CHAPTER 7    Aging and Driving     102

## III    *CLASSROOM INSTRUCTION*

CHAPTER 8    Teaching Aids and Equipment     115
CHAPTER 9    Simulation and the Driving Simulator     129
CHAPTER 10    Educational Television     145
CHAPTER 11    Using Psychophysical Tests     150
CHAPTER 12    Programmed Instruction     159
CHAPTER 13    Team Teaching     165

## IV    *IN-CAR INSTRUCTION*

CHAPTER 14    Teaching Techniques     173
CHAPTER 15    Winter Driving and Skid Factors     217
CHAPTER 16    Driving Ranges, Routes, and Practice Areas     231

## V    *ORGANIZATION AND ADMINISTRATION*

CHAPTER 17    Scheduling Procedures     245
CHAPTER 18    Dual-control Cars     255
CHAPTER 19    School and Teacher Liability     265
CHAPTER 20    Costs and Financing     271
CHAPTER 21    Maintaining Community Support     280

x   CONTENTS

## VI  ELEMENTS OF THE PROFESSIONAL KNOWLEDGE COMPETENCY

CHAPTER 22   Research   293
CHAPTER 23   Traffic Engineering   303
CHAPTER 24   Police Traffic Supervision   321
CHAPTER 25   Motor Vehicle Law and Administration   342
CHAPTER 26   Driver Improvement Activities   360
CHAPTER 27   Safety Features of Automobiles   369
CHAPTER 28   Automobile Maintenance   382
CHAPTER 29   Automobile Insurance   391
CHAPTER 30   The Defensive Driving Code   399
CHAPTER 31   American Highways   403
CHAPTER 32   Driving as a Profession   415

## VII  IMPROVING PROFESSIONAL LEADERSHIP

CHAPTER 33   The Action Program   425
CHAPTER 34   Traffic Safety Centers   432
CHAPTER 35   Resource Agencies   438
CHAPTER 36   Design for Tomorrow   446

Photograph Acknowledgements   459

Index   461

# Teaching DRIVER and TRAFFIC SAFETY Education

# I A PART OF YESTERDAY IS OBSOLETE

"YESTERDAY" in most of its comfortable habits is an old friend. It is usually easier to go on in the old ways—or at least it seems so. Yet in the civilized world it is *change* that is constant, and where life changes education must also change. High school driver and traffic safety education itself is a response of alert education to the changing world. This is a comforting thought to driver education people, yet there follows immediately a more disturbing thought, that the subject field itself must change if it is to profit by the experience and research which is characteristic of its own universe and of those of its contributing disciplines.

Professionally, then, yesterday is not an old friend—perhaps, metaphorically, it is more of a passing acquaintance—or, less aesthetic perhaps, more like an old shoe—familiar, comfortable, serviceable for its day, but doomed for a certainty by time. We knew "driver training" and the "safe driving course." We knew it when it was an intruder within the walls of academic respectability. We knew the two- and three-credit-hour total teaching "qualification."

Some old shoes are still with us, still wearable, and still infinitely better than no shoes at all. But we're breaking in new shoes. We have a multi-disciplined subject field which teaches, as well as absorbing data from, those disciplines. We haven't discarded the old pair. The experience and thinking of the pioneers in the field and others of yesterday hold much that is still good. But some of our driver education lore has yielded to experience and research. Improvement is the trend. The reader, experienced or new in the field, will recognize in this book, starting in this first three-chapter part, a departure from some of the thinking of yesterday—new concepts and knowledge replace some traditional beliefs—for the reader will teach *"tomorrow"*—and a part of *yesterday* is already obsolete.

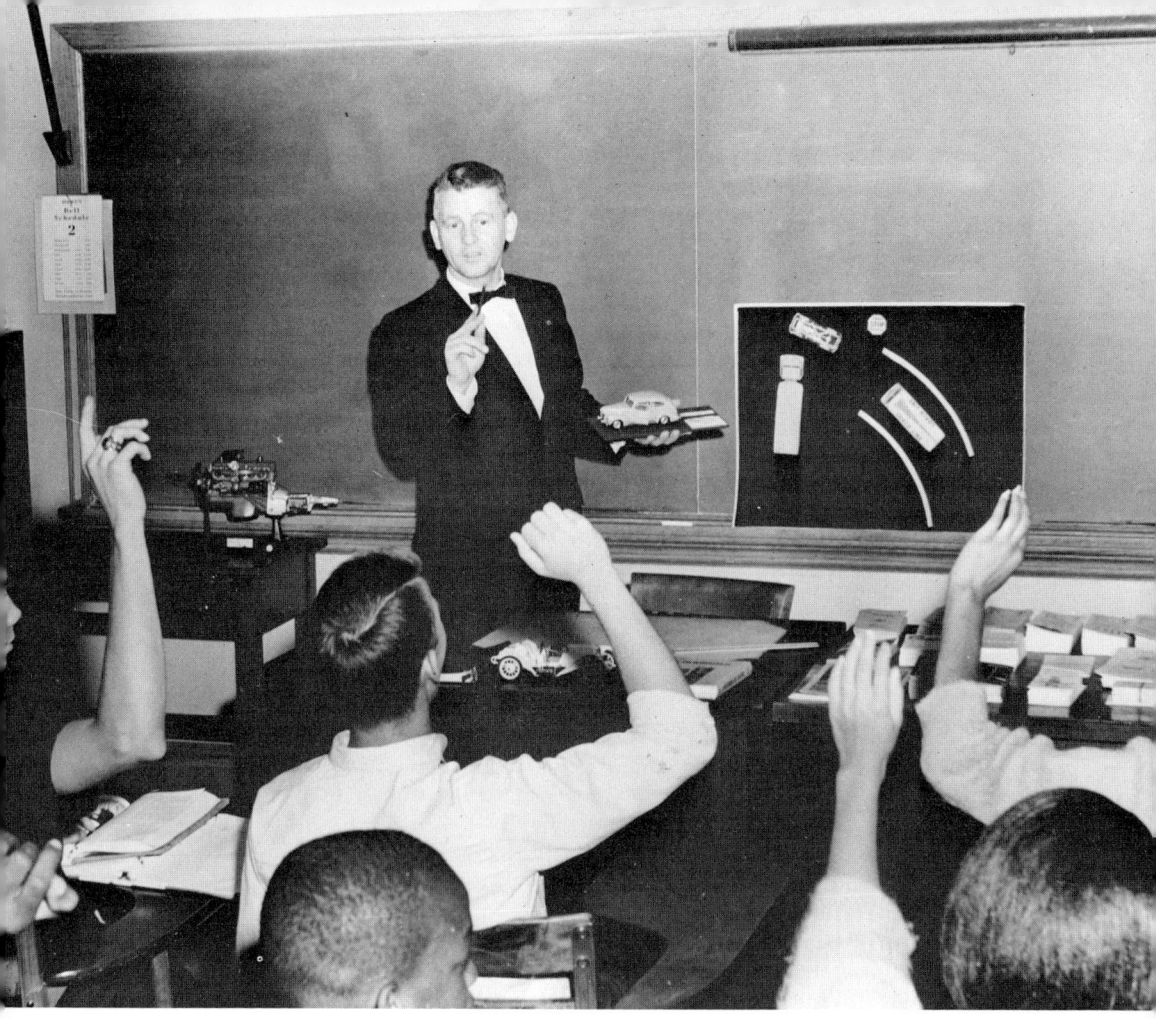

# The Profession—Opportunity and Challenge   1

THE QUALITY and success of any human endeavor hinge upon the ability of the people who conduct it. The basic characteristics of the dedicated teacher are the same in all subject fields, including driver and traffic safety education. Each area of specialization, however, requires its own characteristic qualities and competencies. The aim of our teacher qualification courses, basic and advanced, is to develop these specific qualities and competencies. This volume covers the fundamental procedures of classroom and in-car instruction, and also background preparation in the fields of mechanical and human factors, essential to effective teaching in driver education.

One could hardly be more seriously in error about driver education than to believe that it consists solely of accompanying a beginning driver and telling him what to practice. The obvious requirement of knowing what and how the learner should practice and what hazardous moves to expect comprises merely the elementary aspect of teacher preparation. They are not considered or treated as minor, but they are quite simple in comparison with the intricacies of such material as that covering the principles of conditioning attitude and human behavior. To ignore these principles would be to excise the heart of the driver education program.

## *THE TEACHER AND THE SUBJECT*

It is quite obvious that teaching the in-car instruction phase of the course requires a person who is sufficiently experienced and justly self-confident as a driver. Obviously, too, a particularly nervous or excitable individual would hardly be happy or competent in that position. Because of the factor of emotion in the student's learning process and the emotional connotation of any of his possibly hazardous errors of performance, *patience* is a prime requisite of the good driver education teacher.

Since the specially trained person, who is also a driver himself, will have his own performance behind the wheel continually observed and noted, it is essential that he accept responsibility as a public example. The teacher who drives 5 miles per hour over the speed limit or who "rolls through" instead of stopping for a stop sign would be very naïve to advise his students to observe traffic laws—and expect that they will. Needless to say, being apprehended for a traffic law violation could cause him severe embarrassment! Whatever his past driving attitude, he should finish his first teacher preparation course in driver education as a very careful observer of traffic law and regulations. We might call this the very minimum qualification.

Above all, the driver education teacher should be a *leader*. The teaching of factual material is important, of course. Critics who think only of the in-car instruction think of the course as "merely" a matter of teaching skills. Other poorly informed critics concede that knowledge teaching is involved in the classroom phase of the course, but hesitate to rank it with the tradition-defined "academic" subjects.

The fact is that the *behavior-conditioning processes* in the course are more direct, specific, and measurable than in most other areas of education. Sound methodology, based on the pertinent sciences, must be understood, applied, and kept current with advances in research. There is no known, more complex organization of form and function than that of the human brain and the human mind. The principles of that organization should be studied and understood by one who would lead others to constructive, predictable behavior.

The driver education teacher, far from being merely a "licensed" driving instructor, should have a comprehensive background including knowledge teaching, traffic safety, law, the principles of skill teaching and

FIGURE 1-1 The driver education teacher must be well-informed and versatile to effectively contribute to this new and challenging subject field.

skill learning, traffic engineering, pertinent psychophysical characteristics of drivers, and the ability to establish in his students behavior patterns which will be applied daily, resist strong environmental forces of change, and last a lifetime! Failure in any individual case may cost the student, or another, his life.

## DRIVER EDUCATION COMES OF AGE

The early development of the automobile is a familiar story to most of us, including the young. "Antique" and "classic" cars are seen at automobile shows and in parades and are photographed for newspapers, magazines, motion pictures, and television. Small, ornamental models of the different makes and styles are numerous. A great many boys enjoy the hobby of constructing models from the various kits now on the market.

During its very early days, the automobile was not taken very seriously, often being the butt of jokes and the common advice to "get a horse," whenever one of its frequent breakdowns occurred. With experience and research, the mechanical ingenuity of its makers increasingly endowed the automobile with luxury, speed, and dependability. Still to be faced after its amazing technological advances are some economic and social problems it has created. Management, labor, and government have recognized the economic problems and have been working together to solve them. All now know the automotive industry to be a major factor in the national economy. Some of the social implications became evident in a rising traffic toll over the years. This toll is, of course, both social and economic in its impact.

Traffic laws and enforcement have been steadily improved, and automotive and highway engineering have been developed into sound scientifically oriented professions.

In 1933, in the State College High School in State College, Pennsylvania, Prof. Amos E. Neyhart introduced a course in high school driver education. This new concept in traffic safety brought about acceptance of responsibility on the part of secondary education for preparing youth for life in the motor age. In 1936, Pennsylvania State College offered a course, taught by Professor Neyhart, for the preparation of teachers of driver education. The demand for teachers has increased steadily since that time until, during one recent summer alone, at least 217 teacher courses were offered in colleges. Of these, about one-third were advanced courses. The latter fact reflects the steadily improving standards in the subject field. Special courses for college instructors are now conducted also. Today, about 1 million high school students complete courses in driver education each year.

The original mimeographed text materials for the high school course, first replaced by printed pamphlets and booklets, have given way to thoroughly modern and complete textbooks with excellent supplementary aids available, such as tests, films, filmstrips, workbooks, printed guides, mechanical psychophysical testing devices, and driving simulators. Driver education has definitely come of age.

## Professional Opportunity

Though the great strides of past progress are very evident, a further, great expansion of the subject field is strongly indicated today. In spite of the rapid expansion of the past, only 47 percent of our eligible high school students are enrolled in driver education courses. Even if ours were not an expanding population, present facilities would have to be more than doubled to realize the goals of the program.

There is an observable trend toward state financial support of the program. Twenty-nine states have enacted special support legislation.[1] All the others but two have related legislation under consideration. Since the cost of the high school driver education program is a major objection of the majority of those still opposing it, the present trend toward legislative support is very significant to the future of driver education, and to the opportunities for those who are entering the field.

The actual cost of the high school driver education course is not excessive, but many school administrators and tax-paying citizens fear today to make any addition to a budget financed by local property taxation. State support from broad-based tax sources, usually (and appropriately) levied on the drivers themselves (including driver education course graduates), minimizes, as far as driver education is concerned, what many consider an inequitable method of financing public education.[2] Some states raise the support funds by a small increase in learner's permit or license fees, some from motor vehicle violation fines and bail bond forfeitures. With either method, the driving population, the main beneficiaries of the driver education program, pay this bill. Significantly, those who receive driver education

---

[1] *Special State Financial Support for Driver Education*, National Commission on Safety Education, National Education Association, Washington, D.C., 1965.

[2] *Nonproperty Taxation for Schools*, Office of Education, U.S. Department of Health, Education and Welfare, Government Printing Office, Washington, D.C., 1963.

FIGURE 1-2  The subject is a medium for developing leadership for the future.

today will contribute to its future support by paying the additional fee with each license renewal or vehicle registration.

All signs point to a continued expansion of the driver education program. This is in addition to the projected normal growth of all public education due to an expanding population. With the increases of teacher staff so indicated, corresponding increases at supervisory and administrative levels must follow.

In addition to regular teaching positions and supervisory assignments at school, district, city, and state levels, many who have completed teacher courses in driver education have found appropriate, challenging, and rewarding positions in industry and government. Their contribution to the mission of traffic safety is also a significant one.

## THE BROAD CONCEPT OF DRIVER EDUCATION

With all the highly verbalized adulation devoted to the "good old days of the three R's in the little red schoolhouse," few, if any, of the exponents of that past would favor that educational environment for their children. Music, art, home economics, business education, and health education—to name several subjects other than the three R's—make definite contributions toward achievement of the basic aims of education.

In an analysis of subject fields, one premise must be accepted. *The primary concern in design of the curriculum must be the **student**.* Each subject field should be considered as a *tool* or *device* to enable the student to achieve the full benefits for which our educational system was designed. No subject field is an end in itself. No group of subject fields should be permitted to become monopolistic unless it achieves *all* the aims of education to the greatest degree possible, and does this in an optimum manner.

It would be a rash individual who would deny that the safety and health of the student were not a responsibility of education and that teaching were not best done by the professionally educated teacher. Responsible educators concede these things, but some do not recognize driver education as a *teaching tool* as well as a factor in the future safety of the student and the population.

If the students of calculus or trigonometry, debating or Latin, finished their studies with nothing gained except specific abilities applicable to only those fields, most students—having no further use for those subjects—would have wasted their time as would the athlete with nothing gained but the specific game skills.

## THE SUBSTANTIVE IMAGE OF DRIVER EDUCATION

One of the professional goals, then, of driver education personnel should be to gain for the subject field a twofold recognition. The first phase, fairly well advanced today, is that of an area of education vital to the life and health of the student and the community and, therefore, a concern and a responsibility of education. The cogent question can be advanced: "With the life lost, of what value is all the rest of education?" The second phase of the recognition due this subject field is far less widely understood, that is, its identity as a means, a tool, or a *device of education*—in the same sense that higher mathematics, Latin, physical education, debating, and industrial arts, as opposed to vocational education, are *means to general educational objectives*.

The components of those objectives may be different values in different proportions, but there are worthwhile ends to be gained in addition to the evident value of the course content itself. Some of the less understood objectives of the course are citizenship, science, consumer education, preparation for life.

### *Citizenship*

As a framework for development of the qualities of *good citizenship*, driver education is one of the most appropriate areas in the curriculum because

1. The student *sees* the need for law, and for *voluntary observance* of law, as well as for enforcement.
2. He *sees* the effects of courtesy and cooperation—and the lack of them—among our citizenry.
3. He *sees* the tangible results of government in providing highways and devices to control their operation.

FIGURE 1-3  Good citizenship is a prime objective of driver and traffic safety education.

4. He *sees* the need for good planning for government-sponsored projects and the need for citizen interest, understanding, and support.
5. He *sees* the law violator in action and the effect of his actions on society as represented by the student and people he knows.
6. He *learns* of the very tragic results of illegal and antisocial actions.
7. He is constructively conditioned in the matter of safety in driving and pedestrian behavior, itself a not insignificant phase of citizenship in today's world.
8. He is taught a more understanding view of police and other enforcement agencies than, in many cases, he would acquire by chance and hearsay.
9. The highway environment serves him as an excellent laboratory for firsthand observation of citizenship in action, with its continuous interaction of masses of population, law and government, observance and enforcement, communication, cooperation, conflicts of movement—and occasional disaster, which brings out the urgent need for organized cooperation and proof of our interdependence.

The lessons inherent in these experiences are *taught* him by the driver education teacher, with the highway as the learning laboratory. In comparison, simple exposure alone, like that of an untaught driver, would be comparable to exposure to visual aids with no course and no teacher.

## Science

Driver education is also an area in which principles of science can be applied. The degree to which the course can involve science depends on a number of factors, the chief one of which is time. The subject field offers a distinct advantage in providing the motivating factor of young people's *interest* in cars to promote the learning process.

## Consumer Education

The same motivating factor, strong interest, applies to the study of the principles of *business* involved in buying and maintaining a car, new or used. Budgeting, time payment, loans, criteria for selection including analysis of needs, insurance, principles of the contract, depreciation and resale values, and other considerations to be studied in relation to car purchase are important items of knowledge for the future consumer. To study them under the headings of "economics," "homemaking," "family living," or "consumer education" can no doubt be motivated by a good teacher. However, there is little of the student's "distant" future that can compare with his immediate interest in that all-important purchase of *his first car*. It would be a waste of an effective instructional resource not to utilize that interest constructively.

## Preparation for Life

Although some boys practice mechanics as a hobby and some learn the principles and procedures of mechanics in industrial arts classes, it is surprising to find how many young people of high school age, especially girls, seem to have existed to date in some sort of abstract world entirely apart from material things!

A car has an "engine" (most know) and, therefore, it goes. A flat tire is something one reads about. The remedial procedure is to stand near the car and look appealingly at approaching motorists. (The possible danger of such procedure is just not apparent!) "Lubrication," whether of car, sewing machine, or any of a hundred household gadgets, is a pretty vague process and not important anyway. Carbon monoxide, loss of friction, flammable liquids, explosive vapors—these do not apply to the safe, secure world in which we live. They're *industrial!*

Farfetched? Driver education teachers have encountered surprising mechanical know-how in some high school students, and almost unbelievable naïveté in regard to their physical environment on the part of others, including many very bright ones. Just as every individual is subject to the laws of physics, chemistry, and biology, in relation to his or her life and health, he or she—however intellectually inclined—must live in a materially finite environment. Failure to adjust to this environment carries penalties varying in severity from mild frustration to death. Driver education is one of the few formal educational experiences which provide that type of adjustment for many students.

FIGURE 1-4 Understanding and appreciation of the practical is part of preparation for life.

## "TEACHABLE MOMENTS"

Some years ago, Dr. Jay B. Nash, a much-revered and prominent educator and a prolific author of professional works, wrote a book with the title, *Teachable Moments*.[3] The title itself contains an implication especially significant in assessing the values of the subject fields and their contributions to the education of high school students. It is the *inference of this title* that is important in this thought.

What is there inherent in each subject or course which intensifies the pupil's *receptiveness, impressionableness, sensitivity to learning?* The factors differ in the various fields, of course, and no doubt from day to day. We have noted the item of *interest* as widespread and strong in driver education. Another factor in conditioning the student (perhaps a precursor to interest) both for *attitude* and for *receptiveness to teaching* is *emotion*. This may first be felt in the classroom course where he has definite feelings about various aspects of driving. The competent teacher utilizes these feelings carefully and constructively (see Chapter 4, "Attitude and Behavior").

The day the student first sits behind the wheel of the driver education

---

[3] Jay B. Nash, *Teachable Moments: A New Approach to Health,* A. S. Barnes and Co., Inc., New York, 1938.

FIGURE 1-5 A "teachable moment."

car, *emotion* is a *factor* in making him *ready* to learn. Fear, excitement, desire to drive, "butterflies," "this is *it*"—whatever form the *feeling* takes, he is in a world new to him, one in which his normal feeling of adequacy in a familiar world is missing. For the driver education teacher, as for the athletic coach taking his team into a game, *this is a moment of leadership*. For stark reality, manipulation of a highly mobile ton-and-a-half of steel with human lives—including the student driver's own—in the balance cannot be duplicated in the "academic" class. Because these circumstances are *different*, we must never let them be thought less significant, in teaching or in life. The moment of emotion—even, or perhaps especially, a moment of fear—is a *teachable moment*.

## TEACHER CERTIFICATION STANDARDS

Certification of public school teachers has been traditionally a state function.[4] Whereas some agreement for at least minimum standards seems desirable, it must be remembered that the laws of supply and demand strongly affect the "market" for teachers.

[4] Some educators favor accreditation of colleges to determine the qualifications of their graduates as trained teachers, though the actual *authority* to certify or license would still remain with the state, since state legislation is the basis for the authority. Who determines the specific requirements will be a matter for educators to settle during extended conference and negotiation.

School administrators know that the amount of choice they have among candidates for teaching positions depends upon what they can offer in comparison with competing school districts. This is not to disparage the dedication of teachers but to point out that working conditions, living conditions, and standards of living are normal considerations of all workers. With no other criteria available, a person would be considered foolish to choose a poor position over a good one. As school districts compete in the free "market" for teachers, so do states, in a sense. In those states where the individual school districts have less to offer, the tendency exists to lose the better-prepared teachers and to fail to attract others from elsewhere. This fact should be presented to those who may be concerned with financing the program.

The negative side of the "offer" to teacher candidates is "requirements." The teacher must invest time and money to acquire advanced degrees, qualifications, and status. The poorer his position and pay, the less likely it is that he can manage to carry college courses. Thus a cycle is completed: the least qualified (at least in formal preparation) gravitate toward the positions which permit them the least chance of professional improvement. Even in very prosperous states, critical shortages of teacher candidates in some subject fields have forced state certification authorities to accept substandard qualifications as an emergency measure. This condition sometimes lasts for years. Mathematics and physics have been two areas of acute teacher shortage, as is girl's physical education.

**CERTIFICATION REQUIREMENTS**

Teachers of driver and traffic safety education should:

1. hold a bachelor's degree from an accredited institution of higher education
2. have a teaching certificate validated for service in secondary schools and authorizing the teaching of driver and traffic safety education (based on a total of 12 semester hours in (a) safety education, and (b) driver and traffic safety education)
3. possess physical qualities appropriate to the demands of teaching in this field as evidenced by a health certificate
4. have a valid driver license from the state in which employed
5. set a good example as evidenced by a satisfactory driving record.

FIGURE 1-6 Teacher certification standards recommended by the Fourth National Conference on Driver Education, Washington, D.C., Nov. 13-15, 1963, as published in *Policies and Practices for Driver and Traffic Safety Education.*

Another related situation that affects driver education stems partly from the newness of the field and partly from the fact that it was necessary at first to obtain teachers from other subject fields, qualifying them to teach driver education by completion of a special short course. In many cases, they were involuntarily assigned and the assignment was permitted to become permanent by a "grandfather clause" in subsequent state requirements. Many of these teachers have contributed much since the early days of driver education.

Raising certification standards, although a just cause, may be a matter of years in accomplishment since it is practical only as applied to new personnel. Many leaders in education, and many state laws, would not accept certification requirements that would be retroactive in effect. *States which have the most to offer teachers are in the best position to require high standards,* whereas many who might like to are not in so favorable a position. Another factor to consider in raising standards of teacher certification is the capability of the colleges of the state and region to accomplish the task of presenting advanced courses that would truly upgrade the level of competency of the teachers and not merely add points or credit hours. The colleges should be consulted in the planning stage of certification changes.

## *IMPLICATIONS FOR DRIVER EDUCATION*

The foregoing principles were cited to prepare the reader who may be entering the field, and the already qualified driver education teacher who is improving his own competence in an advanced course, to develop an objective view of this subject. The following data and the very human desire to improve one's own profession both naturally lead to one conclusion—*standards should be raised.* Before a firm, rigid opinion is formed, one should read and think about divergent views, or legitimate hesitancy. An objective view is then more readily achieved, and more patience and understanding of the status quo are possible—hence the preceding data on certification principles, practices, and difficulties as an introduction to the subject of *standards for teachers of driver education.* A realistic appraisal of current status is indicated, with a similar consideration of the *how* element to accompany recommendations for improvement.

### *Current Status*

With this background in mind, we find the following situation extant in the national picture: There is a wide variation among the states in the requirements for certification of driver education teachers, with several states having no specific college credit requirement in the subject field. The majority of states require only two or three semester hours. Some states require two or three credits for teaching either the in-car instruction phase of the course or the classroom phase, but permit those who taught the latter before the present requirement to continue by virtue of a "grandfather clause." This is an example of retaining past progress while raising the standards for new teachers. It is a common practice in public education, but may appear extreme in the case of driver education because many of the original teachers had no formal preparation in the subject. The newness of the field brings this group closer to us.

A few years ago, many of our industrial arts teachers were recruited from industry rather than from the college or the normal school and served to build that subject field to its present status. Before that, many of our older classroom teachers never attended school beyond high school. Obviously it is progress by evolution rather than by revolution that has been the custom in teacher education. The direction in certification requirements is toward upgrading, hopefully leading toward a college minor in driver and safety education as the minimum.[5] Progress is, however, very, very slow.

## Behind the Need

It should be obvious by now that there is urgent need for upgrading in *most* of our states. Identification of the need is too obvious to form the theme of this chapter. Rather than reiterate the so-often expressed recommendation for upgrading, driver education people face the need to *solve the problems that are now restraining the needed advance*—problems cited earlier in this chapter. Many professional meetings conclude with a resolution to recommend that the state require a certain (greater) number of college credits for teacher certification. The intent is laudable, but further suggestions to implement the action are needed. This process is comparable to consideration of the problems and needs for successful enforcement of a new traffic law when the legislation is being prepared.

State driver education associations have long pressed for betterment of the field. One of the goals of driver education people has been sound legislative support for the subject field. Financial aid from the state level has been a major point in such legislation. It is suggested here that those who initiate or assist in the formation and promotion of such legislative proposals insert a clause which will *provide funds for training teachers,* both new and in service.

The more adequately prepared teachers there are, the more feasible is any state regulation requiring adequate preparation. The better the facilities within a state for professional improvement, the more effective are efforts to raise standards for certification. A poorly planned increase in requirements could conceivably result in a serious shortage of driver education teachers, to the curtailment of the school programs. The first step, then, in raising standards is to provide means for teachers to meet those standards.

One point on which some well-meaning professional people go astray is this. Having a state certification standard of "three semester hours," they recommend raising it to six—but only in terms of "hours." Four hours should be eight, and eight should be a minor in the field. The intent is excellent, but the recommendations should be based on more specific needs than hours alone. It is suggested that driver education people who are interested in recommendations for professional standards in the subject field become familiar with *Policies and Practices for Driver and Traffic Safety Education.*[6]

---

[5] *Policies and Practices for Driver and Traffic Safety Education,* National Commission on Safety Education, National Education Association, Washington, D.C., 1964.
[6] *Ibid.*

### Implementing the Recommendations

Concluding the subject of standards for teacher certification, it is obvious that much improvement is needed in most of the country. Those who take an active part in raising standards (and all should support it) should carefully study the entire certification status in the subject state, the current teacher "market" in driver education, the *projected needs if higher standards are to be adopted,* and the experience of others who have taken similar action under approximately the same conditions in other states. Their resultant proposal should contain at least the following:

1. *Specific* recommendations as to standards.
2. Provisions for teacher preparation to conform to those standards.
3. Provision for administration of the program, if such is not provided under the present state certifying agency.
4. Provision for driver education research further to improve the subject field. (The latter may be part of support legislation if that is under consideration, and may fit into a "package" proposal. It could definitely aid graduate study in the field, as well as furnishing data from studies applied to the specific state environment.)

It is highly likely that the impetus to initiate the upgrading process will usually originate with driver education people, probably through their state associations and after consultation with their state education authorities.

## PROFESSIONAL ASSOCIATIONS

For those who are new to teaching, mention should be made of the parent professional associations of the teaching profession. Teachers in service will, of course, recognize them. They are the National Education Association (NEA) and the state education associations, its affiliates in the various states. It is doubtful if any other factor has had as great an effect in elevating teaching to professional status as this nationwide organization of teachers. At this writing, NEA (as it is generally known) has thirty-three departments affiliated with it, including the American Driver and Traffic Safety Education Association (ADTSEA). The National Commission on Safety Education of the NEA serves as secretariat for ADTSEA.

The Commission, located in the NEA Building in Washington, D.C. (1201 Sixteenth Street, N.W.), has served the field of safety education, including driver education, since 1944, in research, reporting of research, professional publications, organization and sponsorship of professional conferences, coordination and dissemination of information on advances in the field, production of instructional films and advisory services in all areas of safety education. The largest department in NEA is the Department of Classroom Teachers (DCT). There are departments in the various subject fields and administrative areas including the American Association of School Administrators (AASA).

In addition to the national association, there are education associations at state, county, and local levels. With improvement of education, as their primary general mission, state associations have been active in the advancement of favorable legislation, including provision for tenure, retirement, and minimum salary levels to benefit the teaching profession. The NEA and the state education associations are the teacher's own, and they are worthy of his membership and support. County and local associations are in a position to deal with "grass-roots" issues in education. The latter usually serve in liaison capacity between the professional staff and the local board of education. Those who will make driver and traffic safety education their life's work would be well advised to investigate their state driver education association and ADTSEA with a view toward membership.

## RESPONSIBILITIES ASSOCIATED WITH DRIVER EDUCATION

The American Driver and Traffic Safety Education Association (ADTSEA) was formerly called ADEA, but the name was changed to include the words "and Traffic Safety." It has also been called ADSEA, the American Driver and Safety Education Association. The latter concept is very significant. In some schools, where safety is concerned, the driver education teacher is almost "all things to all men," supervisor of the lower grades' safety patrols, the high school driving or traffic safety club, a community youth safety club, adviser to a student traffic court, and safety officer for school buses. Of course in larger school systems, he is more apt to be assigned as a driver education teacher with possibly one "additional duty," as all other teachers. He may, in the large high school, be free from most of the assignments mentioned. However, where one or more of the additional responsibilities concerned with safety are assigned to him, it should be accepted as quite reasonable. His professional background would make him the logical member of the teaching staff for this type of assignment.

Some administrators favor rotating assignments. Although equity may be served under this system, often the children are not—at least as far as *safety* is concerned. In some grade schools the safety patrol responsibility has been rotated among the teachers from year to year. Each year, as a new person took charge, a little of the knowledge of the job was lost. Through lack of continuity in a program, sources of information and of equipment have become lost and the activity has deteriorated. This rotation of personnel would not result in deterioration where a trained specialist is assigned charge of all safety-related activities.

It is well when being interviewed for a position as a teacher of driver education to learn what responsibilities are to be assumed. Sometimes it means attending a course in safety education during the summer, before beginning the new job. Sometimes it means looking for information on the new assignments in books and pamphlets. Many times one's colleagues are the best source of firsthand information on matters of duties in a school. If the information is not available in one's own school, it is probable that either one's fellow members of the state driver and safety education association, or of ADTSEA will know the answers. Then there is also the possibility of making inquiries at NEA or at one of the other sources of professional advice and assistance listed in Chapter 35, "Resource Agencies."

18  A PART OF YESTERDAY IS OBSOLETE

## ASSOCIATED PRIVILEGES

Lest the cited *responsibilities* of the preceding text tend to discourage the very new driver educator, it would be misleading to conclude this chapter without mentioning the *advantages* one enjoys in this subject field. A few of them are:

1. Few workers have the satisfaction enjoyed by the driver education teacher, who *knows* that, of those young people he has with him in the driver education car, he will be the means of saving some one—or many—from serious injury or death some time in the future.
2. He gets to know the young people far better in the behind-the-wheel instruction than he possibly could in the classroom, and the student-and-teacher rapport is excellent.
3. He rarely encounters disciplinary problems in the driver education car or troublesome laziness in any of his students, and "cuts" from his class are rare. The student *wants* to learn to drive.
4. Although this teacher's work calls for concentrated attention and split-second readiness while he is in the car, this part of his work doesn't involve long hours of reading themes and grading tests. If he teaches in the classroom, he has the same tasks as other classroom teachers but has a subject in which most of his students have had a growing interest for several years.
5. He is in a dynamic field which is of vital interest to all of society. Highway traffic is the lifeblood of commerce, industry, and recreation. The driver education teacher can play a very satisfying and interesting role by taking an active part in his professional associations, support groups,

FIGURE 1-7  Driver education—a self-motivated learning experience.

and police and motor vehicle authorities. In fact, in addition to being a source of personal interest and satisfaction, such liaison is highly desirable for the success of the mission of driver education.

The well-prepared driver education teacher can derive a great deal of satisfaction from success in his job. It is no less a success if he uses every available hour within the areas of responsibility of his own school or department. On the other hand, if his interest so lies and time permits, there is a world of opportunity for him to take an active part in traffic safety support work on local, state, and national levels.

## SELECTED BIBLIOGRAPHY

*Accident Facts,* National Safety Council, Chicago, Ill., annual.

*Automobile Facts and Figures,* Automobile Manufacturers' Association, Detroit, Mich., annual.

Key, Norman: *Status of Driver Education in the United States,* National Commission on Safety Education, National Education Association, Washington, D.C., 1960.

Nash, Jay B.: *Teachable Moments: A New Approach to Health,* A. S. Barnes and Co., Inc., New York, 1938.

*Policies and Practices for Driver and Traffic Safety Education,* National Commission on Safety Education, National Education Association, Washington, D.C., 1964.

*Travel Forecasting,* eight reports, *Highway Research Board,* Washington, D.C., 1963.

# The Accident Problem         2

IN ANY LOGICAL, orderly, well-organized approach to problem solving, the first step is *identification of the problem*. Is it one of mathematics? Of engineering? Ethics? Ideology? What is its true nature?

We recognize the existence of a major national problem in reading of the terrible losses suffered by the American people in highway accidents. The extent of these losses is brought home to us by frequent publication of statistical reports—reports which cite large numbers of deaths, injuries, and property losses. The numbers make a picture for us, a numerical "coloring" of a condition that exists, but are the numbers the problem itself? Numbers are useful to show the extent or severity of the problem, to give people an idea of how likely it is to touch them personally, or someone close to them, or how it definitely does affect them financially. Numbers—accident statistics—are important. But *are* numbers the problem? Or are they a symptom, a thermometer, a gauge, and is the problem of some other nature?

The heart of the accident problem is not one of mathematics but of *human factors,* mainly how much do people *care*? The actions of people which tend to increase or to aggravate or alleviate the problem, multiplied by their numbers—these are the subjects for study. Road elements and vehicle factors do enter the picture importantly, and they are reflections of human factors. Statistics, then, comprise the accident *picture,* the problem is to determine *what can be done.*

## THE HUMAN FACTOR

Assuming that the personal qualities we call "human," or "humane," are possessed by most of our people, then the potential to *care* is there. It remains for the traffic safety *education* specialist to arouse feelings associated with those qualities to cause people to *care*. To an extent, pointing to 40,000 to 50,000 motor vehicle deaths and over a million and a half disabling injuries has an effect on public understanding. Whether constant, long-term repetition of the numbers does any more to make people *care* is highly questionable. It may even be that we direct thought to the *number* and away from the meaning of the word "accident" and the *fellow-human* identity of the victims.

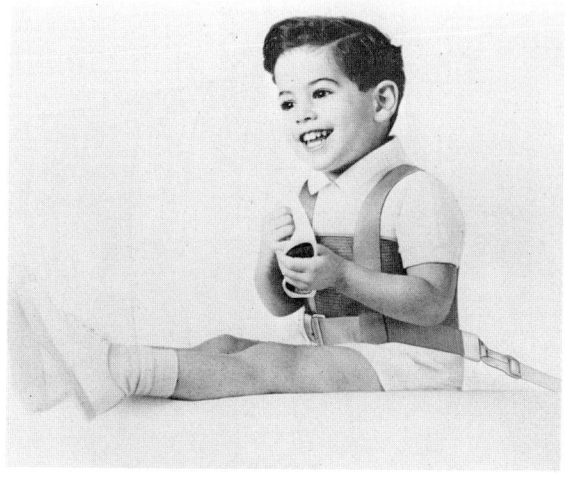

FIGURE 2-1 Accident prevention is a humane science.

When man was beset by marauding beasts of prey, the nature of the latter was a constant, beyond man's control. Today's problem, far more destructive, contains threatening elements which are well within man's control. The car, the highway, and the behavior of the driver all reflect his will. Subject number one for research, then, is Man. He cannot be expected to *care* very much if the word "accident" is made to mean a number rather than reality.

In some parts of the world, millions of people accept death as an ordinary occurrence, a definite reality. Rare is the healthy person here in our country who, in reality, *expects* his own death, though he admits its possibility as something very vague. Whether this is good or bad is not pertinent. This is the customary pattern of thinking which causes people to consider an automobile accident as:

1. Something that happens to *someone else*, usually in a newspaper story
2. A number, a unit of a statistical table

Even the word "injury" in reference to an automobile accident tends to evoke an optimistic concept, since the person "escaped" death. "One killed, three injured," the reaction is "lucky three," rather than the reality for those three people.

One problem, then, in presenting accident statistics is to avoid creating an image of infinitesimal smallness for the *accident* in a forest of impressive numbers. We should not teach about "**over 40,000** deaths," but about "over 40,000 **deaths**," or what an automobile death means to all concerned. However "nice," and however "positive" we may want to be, we will never make people really *care* about numbers, or about words that have lost the vivid meaning of reality.

There are very good professional reasons for gathering numerical data on motor vehicle and other accidents. The traffic safety specialist should

FIGURE 2–2  Statistically, an accident may be a pin on an accident spot map . . .

realize, however, that continually casting these numbers before the public is informational but not likely to have much continuous effect on behavior. This is not to discredit the work of the institutions which do gather and release these data. They perform a very useful function. This is to indicate that beyond such informational services, to a reasonable point, *much more is needed*. In short, numbers and nicely worded clichés reach a saturation point. Public education efforts must present a more meaningful concept of the *accident*, which has very nearly lost meaning in favor of being a "statistic." *The problem in the accident picture is primarily one of basic human qualities. It is intensified by numbers and affected by technology, but education is the primary approach to the human factors.*

## THE PROFESSIONAL FRAME OF REFERENCE

Here we find a different universe. The professional views the problem objectively: people sometimes do become numbers; the educator must accommodate so many driver education students; the engineer must plan for so many vehicles; budgets are based on estimates of needs which, in turn, are based upon statistical data. The ability to gather and analyze pertinent data is important to the professional. This, with his study of the human factors, is part of his professional background.

One of the handiest current references the teacher of driver and traffic

FIGURE 2–3 . . . but in life it is very real to someone.

safety education can keep at hand is a booklet titled *Accident Facts*.[1] What might be termed "the other side of the picture," the total numbers and kinds of vehicles, total mileages, data on drivers, ownership, and many other items not in direct reference to accident data are presented in *Automobile Facts and Figures*.[2] It is obvious that the data presented each year in them will be different from previous years and will be the most significant as a basis for action. This textbook presentation of the *accident problem* will make no attempt to document trends and principles with all the many, ever-changing numbers of automobile and accident statistics. For current figures, the student can refer to the latest issues of the two booklets cited above.

## *ANALYTICAL TREATMENT OF DATA*

One of the most often quoted motor vehicle accident rates is that of teen-agers. About 14.5 percent of all drivers involved in accidents are under twenty years of age. About 15.5 percent of drivers involved in accidents are in the twenty- to twenty-four-year-old group. Then there is a gradual decline in involvement percentagewise (with possible insignificant variations at times) to the highest age brackets, which include only about one percent of drivers involved in accidents. Various "reasons," perhaps rationalizations, are cited to account for the differences in accident involvement among the various age groups. Perhaps the most obvious one, not often mentioned, is the fact that the younger age groups contain by far the greatest number of beginners. It should be expected that the least amount of skill and judgment would be found among beginners. A higher-than-average accident rate would be reasonable to expect to accompany the lower ranges of skill and judgment, regardless of age.

Another point worthy of consideration is that there may be too high a value set on the "fast reaction time" and speed of movement of youth, with perhaps some lack of emphasis on degree of skill. A suitable comparison would be to *swimming*, as a skill. Many people who have excellent coordination, including many fine athletes, would drown in deep water solely because they have never practiced the skill of swimming. Also, a finely conditioned boxer or football player who was in the very early stage of learning to swim might splash almost to exhaustion trying to swim 100 yards, or even 100 feet. At the same time, an old person who had been swimming for years might leisurely swim the same distance as easily as walking it.

The accident rate of the youngest driving group is not entirely a matter of culpable behavior. Even when driving with due care, the degree of skill possessed by a driver may logically be considered a factor in the accident-involvement probability.

Perhaps the slightly higher involvement rate of the next higher age group, twenty to twenty-four, may indicate acquisition of overconfidence with increased skill, but this may not be so at all. The fact may be that the older group does more driving and has that much more *exposure* to hazards. The word "exposure" is one the safety educator should keep in mind.

[1] *Accident Facts*, National Safety Council, Chicago, Ill., annual.

[2] *Automobile Facts and Figures*, Automobile Manufacturers' Association, Detroit, Mich., annual.

## INCREASING DEPTH IN ANALYSIS

In analyzing accident statistics, a comparatively new concept should be given greater weight than heretofore. The simple *involvement* formula for determining the implications of numerical accident data can be misleading. An example is the (true) case of four cars driven by traffic safety experts who had just left a meeting. All four cars were stopped in line in a traffic lane, awaiting the change of a traffic signal. A fifth car approached from behind and struck the last car in line, forcing it forward into a chain collision involving all four of the waiting cars. The driver of the fifth car, who obviously caused the accident, was an untrained, unskilled driver with a record of irresponsible driving behavior.

Interpreted on the basis of "involvement," the effect of including this accident in accident statistics would be to weight it with a 4-to-1 probability, as evidence, that trained—in this case expert—drivers are more susceptible to accident involvement than untrained, unskilled, irresponsible drivers. How great a proportion of such misleading data exists in accident records? How close to *half* of all accident-involved drivers are in no way responsible for their accidents? Obviously inclusion of such cases contaminate the data, as far as analysis of driver characteristics is concerned. It is far more reasonable to state the logical, self-evident fact that, just as people who study mathematics are more capable of successful solution of mathematical problems than people who have not so studied and been taught, so are trained drivers better able to drive safely and well than untrained drivers.

To obtain significant numerical data, the proper course would be to remove as much of the contamination from the total data as possible prior to analysis. The new traffic safety educator should not accept a fear which exists among some, a fear that amounts to intellectual defeatism. When the word "cause" is mentioned in connection with the word "accident," clichés sometimes take the place of reason. Some of them are:

1. You can't (sometimes the word "always" is inserted here) tell the cause of an accident.
2. There may be a combination of causes.
3. There is always a combination of causes.
4. Causal relationships are difficult to establish.

None of them stand up in face of the fact that in many accidents a certain person is perfectly, *obviously* blameless. To include that person's personal characteristics or educational background in a study as a causative factor in the accident, or total of accidents, is ridiculous—yet it is often done.

Because of cliché number 1, a certain state required all drivers *involved* in two accidents within a stated period of time to attend a driver improvement clinic. No matter how *obvious* it was that a driver's own characteristics could not possibly have had anything to do with either accident, he still had to attend the clinic, take psychological, knowledge, and driving tests, and suffer considerable inconvenience. Yet, all the while this state had in its employ specialists classified as "accident analysts." Finally, accidents while *parked* were excepted, which was some improvement. Obviously this sort of "safety" measure will not bring public support to the cause of motor vehicle safety. It has caused much unnecessary dissatisfaction.

26   A PART OF YESTERDAY IS OBSOLETE

FIGURE 2-4   Some accidents are subject to analysis.

The traffic safety expert should be capable of a logical analysis of problems and should refuse to accept generalities to excuse poor research and recording procedures. *If part of the contaminated data can be removed before interpreting the statistical evidence, then the data will point—as the needle of the compensated compass—closer to the truth.*

Perhaps some of the most needed qualities among teachers of driver and traffic safety education are:

1. Ability to analyze data clearly and objectively
2. Willingness to invest the time and the cost of acquiring more than the minimum required professional background
3. Refusal to accept clichés, generalities, or conclusions based on weak research procedures, or defeatism

First, then, is the need of knowledge and the ability to analyze. When these are present, then the *accident problem* can be intelligently studied and understood.

## TOMORROW'S ACCIDENT PICTURE

In the foregoing examples of problem analysis, one important phase wasn't touched—*projection*. Today's traffic accident and motor vehicle figures are readily available in *Accident Facts* and *Automobile Facts and Figures*. A simple reading tells the story of today and offers some comparisons with "yesterday." In each yearly issue of these source references, data will differ and trends may change. The important thing is—*what of the future?* What will happen if today's procedures for traffic regulation and safety are applied to a greatly increased congestion of motor vehicles in the future? What is the outlook for the accident problem?

FIGURE 2–5 A greater number of vehicles in the future will inevitably lead to a correspondingly greater number of accidents unless—

Again, the important thing for the new driver and traffic safety educator to learn first is the matter of *principles,* and then to proceed to figures. How reliable and how desirable are prognostic figures?

If you are to plan a road network, or even a single highway for your state, you would obviously want to estimate the needs of traffic in the future. The accuracy of your estimate might determine your design not only for capacity, but also for acquiring rights-of-way through potentially high-value construction areas before improvement and condemnation proceedings would make the costs soar tremendously. Planning and design must be based on prognosis which should involve complete analysis of *all* available data.

## An Exercise in Retrospect

A review of the record of motor vehicle deaths[3] from 1913 to 1964 is shown in Table 2–1.

In 1937 there were 39,643 deaths. In 1938, there were 32,582. In spite of a trend toward steady increase, why did this considerable drop occur?

---

[3] *Accident Facts, op. cit.*

Table 2-1.  MOTOR VEHICLE DEATHS FROM 1913 TO 1964

| Year | Total motor vehicle deaths | Year | Total motor vehicle deaths |
|---|---|---|---|
| 1913–1917 avg | 6,800 | 1947 | 32,679 |
| 1918–1922 avg | 12,700 | 1948 | 32,259 |
| 1923–1927 avg | 21,800 | 1949 | 31,701 |
| 1928–1932 avg | 31,050 | 1950 | 34,763 |
| 1933 | 31,363 | 1951 | 36,996 |
| 1934 | 36,101 | 1952 | 37,794 |
| 1935 | 36,369 | 1953 | 37,955 |
| 1936 | 38,089 | 1954 | 35,586 |
| 1937 | 39,643 | 1955 | 38,426 |
| 1938 | 32,582 | 1956 | 39,628 |
| 1939 | 32,386 | 1957 | 38,702 |
| 1940 | 34,501 | 1958 | 36,981 |
| 1941 | 39,969 | 1959 | 37,910 |
| 1942 | 28,309 | 1960 | 38,137 |
| 1943 | 23,823 | 1961 | 38,091 |
| 1944 | 24,282 | 1962 | 40,804 |
| 1945 | 28,076 | 1963 | 43,600 |
| 1946 | 33,411 | 1964 | 47,800 |

Experts have cited different reasons. In one state, some traffic safety experts claimed that the corresponding drop in that state was due to the adoption of a state vehicle inspection program at just that time. This would seem logical, but there were states which took no such action but which showed a slightly greater reduction in motor vehicle deaths. The sudden drop in numbers was a nationwide phenomenon. The next significant drop came between 1941 (39,969) and 1944 (24,282). What caused that?

## A Word of Caution

Most traffic volume predictions have proved to fall short of reality. The analyst is cautioned about one pitfall, however. We have noted that prognostication should be based on complete analysis of *all* available data. Sometimes significant factors are ignored.

A common question which frequently "trips" students learning to interpret data is this: The following amounts of wheat were produced in _____ (state or country) during these years:

| | | |
|---|---|---|
| | 1920 | 200,000 bushels |
| | 1930 | 400,000 bushels |
| | 1940 | 600,000 bushels |
| | 1950 | 800,000 bushels |
| | 1960 | 1,000,000 bushels |

Based on these data, how many bushels will be produced in 1970? A com-

THE ACCIDENT PROBLEM    29

FIGURE 2–6   Less important than human casualties, the economic losses from traffic accidents are staggering.

mon answer is 1,200,000. Of course it is wrong. "Based on these data," there is no answer possible in numbers. The fallacy is one of extrapolation. One may *guess* that 1,200,000 bushels will be produced, but the data do not support this. Perhaps the full capacity of the soil was reached in 1960. There may be a drought in 1970.

Economic conditions, wars, unforeseen forces, all may have an impact on the numbers of motor vehicles in operation, the total number of miles driven, and the accident figures in 1970 and 1980. Projection of past numerical trends as the sole basis for prediction yields some indication, but must be considered only as an "educated guess." In the case of planning for new highways, it is totally inadequate. Estimation of probable urban expansion and future industrial needs and a careful study of the present traffic flow are needed, as well as consideration of any other factors that may be identifiable.

## Some Indications for the Future

Considering accident records of the past, and recognizing the limitations inherent in predicting future trends, some estimates made by specialists in reference to tomorrow's motor vehicle statistics should be noted. Traffic safety educators, engineers, and enforcement people face the task of using effective preventive measures to keep accident trends from matching the growth rate of traffic and motor vehicle volume. Some estimates are:

1. Between 1964 and 1975 there will have been an increase of about 37 percent in the number of motor vehicles, from about 85 million to about 117 million.

2. During this period the number of drivers on the road will increase by some 31 million, to a total of over 125 million.
3. Vehicle travel will increase by 60 percent, though even the most optimistic of appraisals do not see new highways and streets keeping up with the needs of the growing traffic.
4. Concentrations of population in urban and suburban areas will continue to increase. By 1975 over three-quarters of the population in the United States will be living in or near a city with a population of at least 50,000. Nearly 60 percent of the vehicle travel will be in urban areas.
5. The school-age population will include about 4 million coming of driving age each year.
6. The number of senior citizens will virtually double, with a considerable proportion still fully capable of driving.
7. Current indications point to a greater number of families having more than one car. The percentage increase in cars is even greater than the percentage increase of licensed drivers.
8. Probable shorter workweeks will mean more leisure time for driving.
9. More boat and house trailers will be used on the highways.
10. With all these, unfortunately, it appears at present that there will be a continuing lag in programs to meet traffic needs.

These are the indications for the future, based upon the conditions of yesterday and today. It is to be hoped that educators, engineers, and

FIGURE 2-7 It is hoped that research performed by specialists will successfully meet the challenge of today's accident trends.

enforcement specialists will, with necessary public and private support, accomplish so much in research and application of methods and materials that their work will successfully meet the challenges of these trends. *To accomplish this, far more effort and money will have to be devoted to solution of the accident problem than has been the case in the past, or seems likely at present. The accident problem shows no sign of abating.*

## SELECTED BIBLIOGRAPHY

*Accident Facts,* National Safety Council, Chicago, Ill., annual.

*Automobile Facts and Figures,* Automobile Manufacturers' Association, Detroit, Mich., annual.

# The Student     3

THE MOST important ingredient of our educational system is, of course, the *student*. Without him there would be no system—no need for one. Next in importance is the *teacher*, the primary catalytic agent in the learning process. His presence makes possible the use of all the educational tools, reading, writing, arithmetic—books, films, devices of all kinds. The essential phase of the educational process is the interaction of student and teacher.

    The concept of that interaction should be broader than that usually associated with the single word "instruction." Good instruction can fall on deaf ears if it is not appropriate to the specific, individually patterned, extremely complex machinery which is whirring away between those ears. A somewhat humorous criticism of the student who had difficulty with grammar was, "No, Johnny, the teacher does not 'learn' you, she *teaches* you." Oddly enough, on further thought, Johnny was at least partly right. She should do both. To teach effectively, one must *learn the student,* his capabilities, his interests, his attitudes and beliefs—what "makes him tick." This is the purpose of this chapter.

It is customary to reward the teacher for the fruits of his experience on the basis of a salary scale, usually with annual increments. This can be justified (and often is) by the fact that teaching *experience* improves the quality of the services of the teacher. Were he never to learn further about the course content of his subject field, he would still have improved his teaching potential as a result of his experience with the interaction process of pupil and teacher. It is not desirable to leave to time and to chance any more of this professional background than is necessary. No need to have today's students miss the advantage of any teacher's abilities which might or might not come in time for another school "generation."

This chapter includes facts about the student which will serve to improve the teacher-pupil interacting process, improving the quality of teaching. Items are selected primarily for their pertinency to driver education. However, if a principle will aid the driver education teacher and those in other fields as well because of its breadth of application in education, it is logical and important to include it in this book, especially if it seems unlikely to be included in that teacher's general professional preparation.

Safety education, as a mature discipline, must be considered as much as any other field a birthplace for innovation and improvement of the profession of education. It is comparatively new, vital, research-oriented, and its exponents possess backgrounds in many of the other disciplines, bringing the ingredients of an interdisciplinary interaction almost unique in our educational structure.

We conceive of education as a process of spreading the fruits of man's experience from man to contemporary man, and from generation to generation. Sometimes we forget that those fruits of man's learning exist not only in factual knowledge that increases the extent of man's control of his environment, but—much more importantly—also in man's control of his own behavior.

*Little realized as yet,* **driver and traffic safety education** *is one of the few areas in the institution of the school which is pioneering in the vital behavioral function of education.* "Behavior," in this sense, does not mean merely "Be good in school" or "Don't break the law." It means all that one does in life. The impact of the school on what the student *does,* and *will do,* is at least as important as what he *knows.* The effect should be a planned one, not merely a process of equipping him with a mass of uncoordinated knowledge which, it is rather vaguely presumed, will result in his choosing a course of constructive behavior.

Applying science to behavior, assembling man's pertinent knowledge, and applying it constructively to influence his actions in an area of crucial importance to the individual and his future—this is the mission, and in a sense the experiment, of driver education. The word "experiment" is not used in doubt of the ability of the subject field to accomplish its mission—safety and efficiency in driving a motor vehicle. Those who have been close

34   A PART OF YESTERDAY IS OBSOLETE

to the program *know* its success. Its teachers observe the results daily. The implication of experiment lies in the fact that practical and observable techniques, new to education, are being applied directly to channel human behavior constructively into patterns of good citizenship—behavioral patterns that are good for the individual and good for the community.

To reach the student effectively, it is necessary to *know* the student. Of all the subjects the teacher could study, *the student* is the most important—his characteristics, his needs, and the world in which he lives.

## THE PLASTIC CHALLENGE

The student, as he enters the driver education class the first day, is *not* a perfectly plastic, unformed (figurative) mass of clay. Neither is he a rigid, hardened, impossible-to-mold, patterned figure. He is something "in between." He has some very definite attitude patterns which he has been developing since early childhood (Chapter 4, "Attitude and Behavior"). Some of those attitude patterns concern driver behavior. He has been an interested spectator of father's and mother's driving for years. It may be that one of his favorite movie or television heroes drives a "long, low, sleek, black" something, "skillfully threading in and out of the slower moving traffic." Or it may be that his parents did a good job of making him a very responsible young man. Though the attitude pattern you recognize in him may be an undesirable one, it *is* subject to modification, depending on the

FIGURE 3-1 The high school student is a challenge to the leadership potential of the teaching profession.

time available, the strength of his existing attitude-affecting neural associations, parental and peer influences, etc.

You "can't win them all," especially within the time limits that govern. Education, medicine, law, and the great religions "lose" some individuals. No devoted exponent of any of the four, however, ever abandons a case. You equip yourself with every bit of pertinent knowledge and every technique you can acquire. Statistically, you *know* that in a short time you will turn out a "product" which is better and safer than was the raw material. Then you will be confronted by another student who is not a perfectly plastic unformed (figurative) mass of clay nor a rigid—etc. Each new student is a challenge which has already taken a definite form. Fortunately the form is still malleable. Fortunately too for that walking challenge, you are a teacher.

## *He May Seem Illogical*

The pioneers in driver education made rapid strides in advancing a very new discipline. The literature of the field thereafter kept growing continuously, founded partly on experience, partly on research, partly on the literature of other fields, and partly on reasoning. Many of the experience-based and reasoning-based conclusions were later confirmed by formal research. Occasionally a cherished belief proves false. One of the ways to start one of those false beliefs is to reason in a logical manner to account for some phenomenon of human nature, without first examining the literature of the pertinent discipline.

The physical human being has been estimated to include some 29 trillion cells, with a complexity in the nervous system alone which is far beyond man's ability to understand more than superficially. We should remember, whenever we plan to account for some phenomenon of our students' behavior, that we should at least consult man's current knowledge on the subject. Because a process seems logical to us is no reason to conclude that that is the way nature has designed it.

One of our cherished fictions makes a very convincing, "scientific" story (and a valuable lesson). It concerns the processes which enable a driver to see a danger ahead and apply the brake (and/or take other action) to avoid it, a commonly cited driving situation. There is no dispute about the seeing and recognition of a situation well ahead of the car and then taking evasive action. The fallacy enters when the "obvious" process is projected into the sudden emergency—perhaps a pedestrian steps out from behind a parked car immediately ahead. The sudden appearance is alarming. The driver hits the brake suddenly. What has happened within the nervous system of the driver?

If we credit the traditional, "logical" explanation, we will believe this:

1. The driver sees the pedestrian immediately ahead (vision) ("perception" is sometimes cited here also as following "seeing").
2. He recognizes what he sees as a hazard (cognition).
3. He decides to move his foot to the brake pedal (decision).
4. He initiates a motor impulse in his brain which will result in movement of the foot to the brake (motor initiation).

This all makes a nice little package and is certainly logical enough to be believed. Some have even assigned a *time* interval for each of the "steps" and the *distance* a car would travel at X miles per hour during each interval. The trouble with this explanation is that it is an oversimplification of the complex neural reaction that *does* occur. Our driver education student at the wheel is not only a student driver, he is also an organism with an extremely complex maze of intricate neural impulses, *multiplying* in complexity as they spread through his nervous system. What does happen in the emergency described?

The light which carries the image of the pedestrian passes through the eye of the driver and strikes the retina, the terminal expansion of the optic nerve on the posterior (rear) aspect of the eye. It triggers an electrochemical impulse which passes on through the brain stem (Chapter 4, "Attitude and Behavior") to the occipital lobe at the posterior aspect of the cerebrum. This much of the story is compatible with our classic hypothesis. However, the latter oversimplifies the facts. Rather than a simple conduction of an impulse as one conceives of a telephone wire in action, the alarming sight of the pedestrian triggers a reaction more like a star shell. More than a single circuit becomes involved.

A somewhat similar phenomenon is the long-recognized spinal reflex which follows the classic example of inadvertently touching a hand to a hot stove. The afferent (incoming) neural impulse moves upward along a nerve pathway in the posterior part of the spinal cord to the brain. However, there is some spillover on the way. Transverse connector neurons in the cord carry an overflow of the impulse from the posterior to the anterior (front) part of the cord (where the direction of impulses is downward). The impulse then spreads downward along motor neurons to muscles which move the part concerned. The original impulse goes on to reach the brain where it is recognized as pain from the burn. *There is no need for, or evidence of, recognition and "decision" preceding the action!* The spread of the impulse across the connector neurons in the spinal cord may also innervate other, vegetative, nerve pathways causing nausea or other symptoms. This spreading-of-impulse phenomenon should have been recognized when the analysis of the cited car emergency was originally made. In the latter case, the classic diagram and legend would not have been of a single, simple, "logical" pathway triggering just 1, 2, 3, and 4 in order. There should have been a diagram like a star shell.

*At the same time* that the path of the impulse transversed brain stem, occipital lobe, and cognitive and motor areas of the cerebrum, the star-shell-like spreading of the original impulse had a reflexive effect. Motor nerves operated to move the foot to the brake pedal (a "conditioned," learned reflex). Perhaps another of the spreading impulses may, in some emergency cases, blink the eyes. Sometimes innervation of the central area of the spinal cord (or other centers) triggers vegetative reactions, as some symptoms of shock, hyperadrenalization, etc.

In spite of the "logic" of a sequence of neural action including (sequentially) vision, recognition, decision, and action, there will very likely be considerable reflexive action, and the foot may start to move to the brake pedal when the mind doesn't yet understand the meaning of the situation. The learned reflex, foot to brake pedal, sometimes takes place when a person

FIGURE 3–2 Emergency! The spreading of neural impulses can be visualized as the bursting of a star shell. Though actually a photograph of a real fireworks display, this scene could have been planned to show the principles of a reflexive spread of neural impulses (lower burst) and a subsequent spread of impulses through the higher centers of the central nervous system (upper burst).

who drives is sitting beside the driver and has no brake at all in front of him! Sometimes a splash of water on the windshield, no threat at all, and no decision required, causes the driver or passenger to shut his eyes and duck.

There are two things to be learned from this situation:

1. The student can be conditioned to a reflexive response to an emergency situation, a response that is quicker than his mind can operate to cause that same response. *This does not* depend on cognitive "recognition of hazards," which is of longer range, *avoidance* significance.
2. The student is mentally, emotionally, neuromuscularly, and organically a cluster of many extremely complex universes. What may *seem* logical to account for his behavior may be wide of the truth. No analysis should be accepted unless supported by data from the pertinent discipline. *Driver and traffic safety education should not stand alone, but should utilize all that is possible from other disciplines.* There are many complex "star-shell" reactions possible in the student. A "logical" explanation is not a true one unless based on factual data. Logical analysis leads to truth only when it starts with a premise that is true!

## HE HAS OTHER LIVES TO LIVE

Driver education is a dynamic field. New and very challenging, it breeds enthusiasm among its devotees. Confronted by very limited time in which they must accomplish much, many teachers of driver education try to find more time. This is laudable and is also quite often successful. Occasionally, however, a driver education (or other) teacher will let his enthusiasm thrust aside his understanding of the total process of secondary education. He will "pile up" outside assignments, projects, and study to be completed on the student's own time. Constructive, perhaps, to the student's learning of driver education, this may throw his school life out of its normal rhythm, and may also bring opprobrium on driver education.

Remember—there is a very strong competition today for the student's time. He cannot control all the demands made upon it; so others should help him. Although it is true that some students manage to get by with a minimum of time spent in study, this is not the case with most high school students today. The student who might be intellectually able to coast through school is likely to be quite concerned with grades and college entrance requirements and choice of a college. His parents are concerned also, and he tends to work close to capacity.

Then there are many after-school activities competing psychologically for the student's after-school hours, while the course-fragmented curriculum content and some teachers compete for his evening homework time. The conscientious high school student of today would find a 40-hour workweek a very short one. In fact, it might be worth considering the possibility of giving him an hour now and then to *think* for himself.

Driver education is important. It involves a broad body of knowledge to be learned. There are projects well worth student time, *but* the teacher should be sure he doesn't unduly encroach to an unreasonable degree on the evening study time of the student. (All teachers should understand this—some do not.) Some teachers believe in an hour of homework for each hour in school. A student who takes four, five, or perhaps six subjects and may spend four, five, or six hours on regular evening homework plus additional projects assigned, term papers, study for tests, etc., is observing work hours that no labor union would condone for adults. The concept of diminishing returns should be understood by those who make assignments.

The driver education teacher should study the homework conditions that prevail, before deciding on his assignments. *Competition* among the departments of a school for students' evening time sometimes becomes quite serious. It shouldn't. Also, it should be remembered that no matter how firm a supporter of driver education a parent may be, *he is not likely to accept* driver education homework which takes the place of mathematics, science, English, etc., in the student's homework time.

## *Join Them*

Perhaps the best answer to the time problem is to get some appropriate course material integrated into other courses. This is desirable as a general policy in a school, of course, in terms of general safety education, *grades K through 12*. The teacher can also easily identify material of the driver education course content which fits nicely into science, mathematics, English, health, and other courses. In this operation, he can get *cooperation* from teachers who can be shown the strong *motivational value* of a link with the magical world of *driving a car*, magical—that is—to the teen-ager.

FIGURE 3-3 The student receives assignments from a number of teachers each day.

The ability of the driver education teacher as an exponent of his subject field (and as a leader and a salesman) will determine how much appropriate course material he can get accepted into other subject fields. Attitudinal preparation starting in the lower grades, as well as factual data of the driver education course, can be properly placed and taught to the advantage of the other course concerned and of the mission of driver education. The fact is that when one subject is used as a vehicle for teaching another which has greater appeal and motivation, *both are being taught better at the same time.* A short story, written for an English course, with the traffic accident phenomenon as an environmental setting, a science problem involving the forces affecting the starting and stopping of a car, a health education lesson in first aid at an accident scene illustrate some of the many opportunities for driver education to supply the motivation and the cooperating subject field to contribute student and teacher time to accomplish the objectives of both subject areas simultaneously.

The driver education teacher who helps other teachers to motivate their courses enhances his standing as well as that of his course and subject field. On the other hand, he who attempts to seize all extracurricular time possible by putting pressure on students may encounter trouble for himself, and for driver education and the school, from anxious parents. To the parent of a prospective college candidate, a "five-point course" is a pearl of great price. If his son writes a heartrending story of the personal tragedy that accompanies a highway accident—and gets credit in his English (five-point?) course—fine! If said son takes English homework time to read of the social and economic losses due to accidents for a driver education course credit—things are different.

The parents and the "academic subject" teacher want the very best for the student. So do you. Driver education doesn't have to *fight* them for the student's time.

"Join them."

## HIS EYES AND HIS EARS

When a saying is repeated often enough, it tends to take on an aura of truth. Moreover, it seems to expand to take in more and more "territory." Woe then to the person who dares to question its position of omniscience, especially if it has been blessed with some professional respectability! Unhappy is the teacher who has found, within his own experience, a pair of large clay feet supporting a great pronouncement. There have been many cases of teachers carrying on behind closed classroom doors with methods they *knew* to be best, but not daring to defy what "everybody says."

One of the badly battered victims of great "sayings" is the much vilified "lecture method" of teaching. Rare is the teacher who dares to admit that he simply *tells* his students some things. "Telling is not teaching," he is *told*. "A picture is worth a thousand words" is very firmly relayed from Confucius to him. He is henceforth branded as one who *lectures* to his students. Peculiarly, he may be doing the very best thing possible under the circumstances. Perhaps he merely needs to know that he is right, and *why*. Perhaps it is fitting that driver education, the newcomer to the world of education, take the courageous lead typical of pioneers the world over and defy what "they say"—and support that teacher on the basis of sound data and logic. No one should be surprised that a subject field which is so prolific in contemporary research and innovation should be found in the forefront of professional thought or that it lead in the application of new thought to its own mission in education. That this principle has implications for other subject fields makes it no less important in the teaching of driver and traffic safety education.

### *So Few Years Ago*

The high school student is not far removed in years from the young elementary school pupil who was learning to read. Reading is such a common process—one "learns to read" and thereafter one "can read." The teaching profession recognizes reading difficulty, and people sometimes speak of a "slow reader" or a "fast reader." Few people think of reading as, in effect it is, a second language.

English and other languages are a utilization of sound symbols to represent objects or ideas. These symbols have become the basis of man's unique ability to *think*, as well as to communicate. One can express the thought, "go to the store and get . . . ," without going through the motions or even drawing a picture. The hearer interprets the sound symbols, words, into the thought.

The young child learns to associate the sound of a word with an object. He acquires a vocabulary (sometimes in a manner to startle members of his family). It is a *sound-symbol* vocabulary, consisting of many word-sound-to-object associations. (Note "word symbols" and "visual symbols" in Chapter 4, "Attitude and Behavior.") Early in his school experience, a child learns to associate word sounds with letters and combinations of letters, as he learns to read.

FIGURE 3-4 The teacher communicates verbally to impart knowledge of the safety-related object.

The generally unrecognized effect here is that he is learning a *second language. The written word is not patterned on the object to which it refers but on the sound of the word.* This means a complex double translation, from written letters to sound word, and then to object, or to idea meaning. Try reading this text to get the meanings of the printed words without using the intermediate step of recognition of the sound concept of the word. This does not refer to necessarily making the sound or movement of organs of speech, although they may be unconsciously involved. This refers to the mental *concept* of the sound. Avoidance of the sound concept makes any effective reading impossible.

The primary grade pupil learns far more of his *school-taught subject matter* through hearing than by vision, once he has learned our spoken language—this in spite of some common "sayings" to the contrary. (The tool we call language, once acquired, can build knowledge and reason at a far greater rate than the visual nonverbal experience available to the child for some time *after* his first, perhaps five, years of life. *The predominance of auditory learning over visual learning continues until the "second lan-*

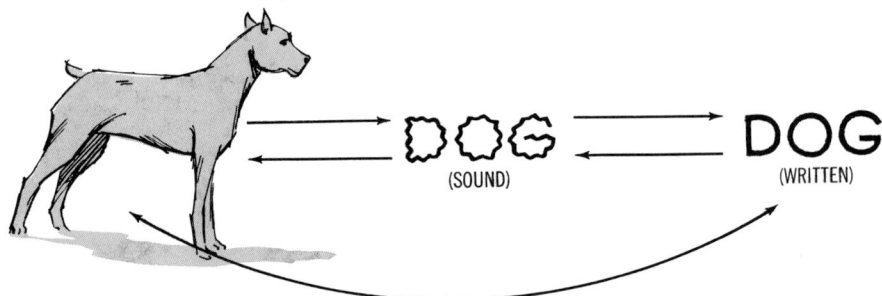

FIGURE 3-5

There is practically no shortcut which might be assumed by "whole-word" or "sight-reading" concepts of learning to read.

guage" of sound-word-symbol to printed-word-symbol translation is efficiently acquired. This latter state takes *years* to acquire, as well as a great deal of reading *practice*—more of the latter than many students have, even up to the time they complete their high school courses. Some never achieve reading efficiency. Native capacity varies widely among individuals. The boy who reads by the hour, other factors being even nearly equal, reads far more efficiently than the one who watches (and listens to) television in place of reading. The latter may have a fine vocabulary of the spoken word but may be very weak in associating sound word with printed word.

The point here is to recognize the important role the *spoken* word plays in teaching. Also, *individual variation* in ability to translate between the spoken word and the written word is great. The "poor reader" is not a very uncommon person, nor is he necessarily limited either in intelligence or vocabulary. In fact, a normal, "heterogeneous" high school class is not a group of "normal" readers with one, or two, or a few "poor readers." It is a cross section of students with an infinite number of variations of native ability to "translate," and with widely varying reading experience. It is far better to assume that your students will understand a clearly spoken sentence than that they will read the same sentence in print, translate it to sound consciousness, and then translate the sound concept into meaning. *This is not to say that verbally expressed concepts cannot be strengthened or clarified by the use of visual aids. The visual aids should be chiefly on the image, or meaning, side of the sound word, not on the printed, written-word side.*

The speaker who gives a prepared talk should first tell his audience that he will distribute copies of his talk at its conclusion. (This saves note-takers in the audience from missing parts of the talk while writing notes of their own.) Withholding the copies of the talk concentrates the audience's attention on the words he speaks. It precludes the process of the listener trying to perform the double translation (printed word to sound concept to meaning) *and trying to keep this process in exact pace with the words of the speaker.* It is, of course, extremely inefficient and unnecessary to attempt to read and listen simultaneously.

FIGURE 3-6 Verbally expressed concepts can be clarified and strengthened by the use of visual aids.

The student, then, is a person who may understand very well what you say, but not nearly so much of what you assign him to read—depending on *individual* characteristics. Check your class with quizzes on all reading assignments. *Never assume that absence of questions means that all have understood.* Detection of a reading difficulty may result in early remedial action. Undetected, however, the condition may lead to a student's becoming "lost" to the point of resigning himself to being unable to learn the subject. Constant measurement and adjusting of pace to the individual is vital in teaching. Constant checking is necessary at short intervals whenever the learning process involves *reading*, the student's "second language." Our student may understand his second language without being adept in it to the point of being "bilingual."

Probably it is partly due to time limitations in teacher preparation courses and the breadth of the material to be covered that some teachers tend to do some "textbook teaching." (In some cases it may be, in any subject field, that the teacher hasn't properly prepared for the lesson.) The teacher has the class open their textbooks to a certain place, and he reads aloud from the book while the students follow him with theirs. It would be far better, poor as this procedure is, to have them *listen* to him read to them and to be instructed *not* to look at their books. He reads at his own reading speed. If the students attempt to read with him, they perform the double translation [printed word to (silent) sound concept to meaning] while attempting to keep pace with him. The difference between the sound concept of the printed word at each instant and the simultaneously heard word of the teacher makes a very poor learning situation.

There is a tendency among girls, unconsciously perhaps, to reject knowledge of things mechanical. A reading assignment in this area may turn mild rejection to defeatism, if the girl is not a good reader. Reading is also a

FIGURE 3-7 Reading assignments can be constructive if student progress is regularly measured. Above-average students can enrich their knowledge of the subject field.

limiting factor in the use of programmed material, in attitude tests and some other psychological tests, and—with normal use of written expression—a very important part in much of the program of the school.

The power of the spoken word should also be realized in the in-car instruction, particularly in the early stages (Chapter 14, "Teaching Techniques"). When the student is learning the basic skills, devoting close attention to every facet of *performance,* mention of unrelated course content or other matters can take his attention away from his task, to the detriment of his accomplishment. The teacher's commentary should be carefully planned to strengthen the learning process rather than to distract from it.

## *A CONSTRUCTIVE ANALYSIS OF SCHOOL-STUDENT RELATIONSHIP*

One of the ways a person can achieve recognition in print is to attack the schools. So many people are genuinely concerned about them and what they do for children that any type of exposé, fact or fiction, is "news." Exposé is not the purpose of this chapter. Our schools are performing an excellent service for our society. The only justification for critical analysis of their *status quo* would be a sincere attempt at *improvement*. This school-student analysis presents the view of a comparatively new segment of American education which recognizes a need and acts to fulfill that need. Driver and traffic safety educators can recognize in this view a clear call to an important mission in education, as well as the more obvious objective of creating for the student a behavioral shield against bodily harm.

## The Fragmented Student

We have just about abandoned our faith in the self-contained classroom, and although the elementary school teacher can still command the full course content of her pupils' "subjects," the ever-expanding scope of the secondary school curriculum makes departmentalization a necessity. With it, a degree of specialization in the subject field permits a greater depth of knowledge in that field.

Few teachers in today's secondary schools have more than a one-period-per-day single-subject acquaintance with their students. The "academic subject" teacher sees a physical body, the chief characteristic of which is a learning capability. Too frequently this concept results, unconsciously of course, in a higher regard for the *value* of the brighter student. The A student makes school life more pleasant. It is hard to realize that this part of the student is only a part of even his learning ability. This same student may be quite frustrated in an industrial arts class, or in a music class, or perhaps in the art room of the school. The C or D student in English may find the satisfaction of equality with his peers in the physical education class. Although these diversified offerings of the school have great advantages, they have a great disadvantage too. Each teacher becomes acquainted with *a fragment of each student!*

The secondary school teacher is oriented to a fragmented person—the student. Majoring in a subject field in college, the teacher-to-be was separated from all other *subject fields* by the exceedingly high intercurricular walls of college organization. In service, there followed *subject-field* workshops, *subject-field* seminars, and even county, state, and national *subject-oriented* associations. Experimentation and research were carried out within that same subject-compartmentalized framework. The results show an excellent achievement in understanding, methodology, and clear-cut objectives—but all tending to be *subject-oriented*—each an excellent main-line thoroughfare, but unfortunately lacking in crossover communication.

When we piece together this fragmented-by-subject personality we call the student, we find much accomplishment in each fragment—*according to the specific objectives of each of the subjects*. But the assembled total of these fragments begins to show some blank spaces. If the objectives achieved represent the viewpoint of *each* of the subject fields, what about the objectives that apply to the whole student? Does the sum of all the subject objectives meet the full needs of the total personality—and of society? Some very famous men have praised the influence that some teacher has had on their careers, influence going back to a one-room, one-teacher, grade-1-to-8 "schoolhouse."

This is not to recommend a return to that institution, but to suggest that, to quite some extent, the opportunity for a very powerful personal influence on the part of any one teacher has been lost. We give Johnny a far more comprehensive *knowledge* background today. But do we do as much to constructively guide—not his curriculum—not his career—but what he *does,* how he *acts*? Do we *know,* aside from seeking all gifted teachers, each to stay with him for years, how we can influence his future behavior in the direction of good citizenship? In addition to *telling* him to vote and why that is his privilege and his duty, do we recognize any sound procedures for developing that behavior pattern within him? The less we know of such procedures and the more fragmented the teacher-pupil personal contacts, the less possibility we have of exerting a constructive force on his behavior.

## *The New Face of Driver Education*

Let's assume that the lifesaving function of driver education is obvious. Less understood, perhaps, is the fact that driver education is not a haphazard process of letting the student practice with a car until he learns how to drive it. It would be quite a surprise to many educators to learn the amount of sophisticated research that is performed in behavioral science to develop methods to influence constructively the actions of that citizen-driver of the future.

Although there would be no point in comparing the amount of research

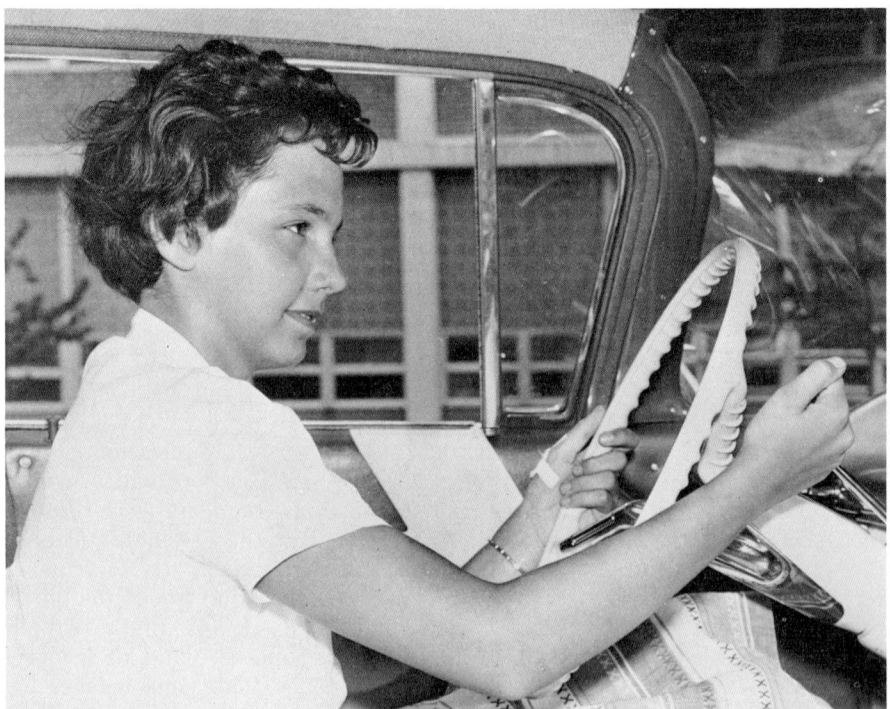

FIGURE 3–8  The student is a constant to which content and method must be adapted.

being devoted to all the various subject fields of modern secondary education, driver and traffic safety education is probably far in the lead in the study of behavioral research. Principles are emerging which apply to patterning of behavior effect in people, not only in driving a car but in other facets of life including those concerned with citizenship in community, nation, and school.

Thinking people do not assume that the granting of factual knowledge to the sensitive but yet unpatterned mind of a young child—even to the full extent of his learning capabilities—will ensure in that child—and in that adult he will become—a temporary or a lifetime behavior which will be constructive, either to society or to himself. One can be a widely informed genius, and be an enemy of society. Many of the infamous characters of history evidenced brilliance. Rarely is one called stupid.

A knowledge of this history of man will make us understand the value of freedom and equality under the law. To the person who needs no action to achieve either of them for himself, more than cold, objective knowledge is needed to cause him to *act*. He must be motivated. Such motivation should be soundly planned and given direction. Behavioral science is a potential right arm of education. More than anywhere else it is being studied for driver education.

## RECONSTRUCTING THE FRAGMENTED STUDENT

When we describe the secondary school student as a collection of subject fragments, we do not mean that he is suffering serious psychological trauma from his "condition." Actually, he is quite healthy. He doesn't even *feel* broken up. To him, it is just a lack of truly effective rapport with most of his teachers. He just doesn't know each one as well as he would if that one were the only one. They don't know him. Of course, he doesn't miss it, since that is the way he found secondary school when he entered it.

*It is the profession's view of the student that is alarming to a degree.* With the fragmented view the teacher gets in the one-period-per-day acquaintance, it sometimes takes a very long time to know just what the student is like. He doesn't "let his hair down" with most teachers, particularly with those whose necessary demands on his time and time-consuming accomplishments worry him a bit. The driver education teacher in the car gets flashes of insight into this person, sometimes quite confidential insight—such as his frank evaluation of other people! Six to twenty-four hours in the car, however, limit the acquaintance. Hence, it is not desirable for each new teacher to learn by long experience what the student is like. A description is in order:

1. "He" is bigger than his father (and she, than her mother).
2. Quite a few look formidable.
3. Except in the case of the atypical, the psychotic, he isn't. His self-confidence is quite limited in most areas.
4. *He wants to drive a car!*
5. His (or her) customs vary with place and peer group, from delightful naïveté to incredible (for the age) sophistication. Parental control is a great factor here.

FIGURE 3-9 He wants to drive a car! This desire guarantees his interest in well-prepared instructional techniques such as the stopping distance demonstration.

6. Parental control varies widely, from the very strict, through the very mild, to "teen-age control." This is something to remember when sending those "parental contact" letters home. (And don't ditto them. Make each one individual in nature.) One method of a teen-ager achieving teen-age control is to convince a parent that "all the other kids are allowed to" do something. A simultaneous attack by a number of students often results in a clear-cut victory. Occasionally a few of the more sophisticated students make contemporary complaints about a teacher. The latter are atypical cases, however.

7. With rare exceptions, the student respects fairness in his teachers above almost any other quality, and most practice fairness within their own code.

8. The "behavior problem" among students is a wise old veteran. He learns, by gradual extension of his activities, just what penalties are possible. One thing he seems to learn by instinct—he knows when a teacher fears to send him "to the office" (especially a substitute teacher), for fear of being thought unable to control a class. The teacher who succumbs to this fear in the face of problem students had better plan to change jobs and start anew somewhere else. The problem student, free of his own fears, is merciless and can usually find enough show-off friends to make a class a permanent bedlam. The word spreads from class to class like wildfire! If this timid teacher could

see other fragments of that student, as when he is with a teacher he respects (or when he is making excuses to a traffic policeman), he would appear not at all like his ferocious fragment!

9. The physical symbols of age are very important to the teen-ager. A person who has the appearance of an adult seems to him much like a different species. The appearance of youth (his age especially) gives him a feeling of rapport. In some things, he expects greater rapport with his peers than with his own parents.

10. The non-"honor student" is no less *honorable,* and no less *valuable.* The term "academic honors" is an unfortunate one. "Recognition," "credit," "acclaim," "A"—many other expressions would have been far more equitable. The average lay person has a word-meaning association with the word "honor" that isn't completely shaken by its special academic meaning. The understanding teacher sometimes sits through a commencement ceremony feeling very sorry for those students (and their parents) who are the epitome of honor, but who form only the backdrop for laudation of the intellectually gifted few.

If driver education, industrial arts, music, art, homemaking, etc., had no other value in education, their effect in spreading the opportunity *to be recognized,* even to *excel,* among so many nonhonor students would still have done a wonderful thing for the average, less-than-gifted student.

11. "He has problems." This *may* be a reason for a student's antisocial behavior. The latter may also be generated by the knowledge (quickly learned) that he has an *excuse.*

Sometimes the psychic trauma occasioned by a "problem"—a family breakup, perhaps—is lasting. Sometimes it never existed as a traumatic effect, and the behavioral pattern is unrelated. Sometimes the problem situation has long lost its effect (most old stimuli do), but a continuing "feedback" pattern exists, strengthened by the subject "dwelling upon" the past problem situation. The point is, the teacher should not assume the role of amateur psychiatrist. Many an analysis believed by an amateur to have been keenly made by himself would actually take an accomplished and gifted psychiatrist a couple of years to achieve.

"A little knowledge is a dangerous thing." The intelligent, sympathetic, fair teacher can solve many student behavioral problems on the basis of common sense and simple human understanding. Judgment should be "tempered with mercy," but too much rationalization of antisocial behavior may seriously harm "the good apples in the barrel." A principle to remember is this: Within certain—usually very wide—hereditary structural and other limiting brackets, *the mind tends to be a product of its own functioning.* In other words, *many behavioral-problem people are self-made!* This applies to teen-age students as well as adults. With the teen-ager, though, the job isn't completed and therefore lends itself better to guidance of that mind functioning to affect the pattern of the result. There usually is still hope.

12. The "fragmented-student" concept has one more very serious implication for the driver education teacher. There have been cases in which a student had some condition, mental or physical, which should have

disqualified him from driving, but which was never communicated to the driver education department. Records of the school psychologists were kept confidential. Those of the health department were available, but no check system of all individual students to be scheduled for in-car instruction was maintained. Only those teachers (if any) who had personally observed signs of the condition knew of it. In some cases, every bit of pertinent information about the students' condition was known to some people in the schools, but fragmented, never to reach those most concerned in any meaningful form. Even the elementary school-to-junior high school-to-senior high school records didn't in some cases include certain "confidential" information that would have been important in determining the fitness of the atypical student to drive.

Administratively, the total school system's recording and communication process is not normally the concern of the driver education teacher. However, should any crisis occur in the car because of some condition of the student at the wheel, there is only one member of the total school system personnel who will be sitting in the next seat!

This account of the fragmented student is not to decry the educational system nor to urge reform. It is recognized that departmentalization in secondary education is necessary and a fact of life. The elementary–junior high–senior high organization, 6-3-3 or whatever division may be best, has evolved with reason. The large secondary school, too, has many advantages of special services and equipment that might be rare among smaller school units. The concept of the fragmented student is merely a device to identify and accentuate those effects of existing organization which the driver education teacher should recognize as problems related to his area of responsibilities. Some of those cited here are especially pertinent to driver and traffic safety education. Some are solely of such nature.

Obviously, the "fragmentation" of the student is fictitious except in the concept and understanding of him that is possessed by the teacher and by the total professional staff. The student himself is not aware of it. It does not engender any kind of psychic trauma within him. The effects are all indirect, resulting from the necessarily complex organization of a great educational system. The satisfactory but very brief acquaintance of the driver education teacher with the student intensifies the need for understanding on the part of the former, especially for understanding that there is much to be known about the individual student that will not reach the teacher automatically. It must be *sought*.

The characteristics cited in this chapter are only a few of those recognized by some experienced teachers, whose knowledge of students has been accumulated over the years. The fragmenting effect of the departmental organization of the secondary school prevents satisfactory learning by the teacher of what each student is really like. The "fragmented" student doesn't really exist in nature or in his own mind. He does exist in the individual and collective minds of his teachers. When his needs are examined to serve as the basis for educative processes, it is very easy to miss one or more of the fragments which are sometimes assembled in group meetings of the teaching staff of the school. Teacher-group case studies are indicated.

THE STUDENT    51

FIGURE 3-10 Perhaps the student's greatest need is understanding. The responsibility for this lies with the teacher.

## A Further Analysis

We have observed the multifaceted person we call the student. To the professional staff of the school he is a composite of many, and sometimes divergent, individual views. Rarely do the views ever get assembled in the mind of any one person. Hence there is a need for studying the student as he really is, and to recognize his needs created by the fragmenting process.

Having considered this chance-engendered, and highly artificial, piecing of the student, the next step will be a very significant, *natural* breakdown of the subject for study. This time it will be one designed by nature, an analysis of the central nervous system as it determines his behavior, now and in years to come. This is one of those areas in education in which driver education takes the role of the pioneer. It moves, in research and in practice, into fields of study in the forefront of the parent discipline—education.

Chapter 4, "Attitude and Behavior," is a significant step in that direction.

### SELECTED BIBLIOGRAPHY

*A Look at Continuity in the School Program,* 1958 Yearbook, Association for Supervision and Curriculum Development, a Department of the National Education Association, Washington, D.C.

*Education for All American Children,* Educational Policies Commission, National Education Association and American Association of School Administrators, Washington, D.C., 1948.

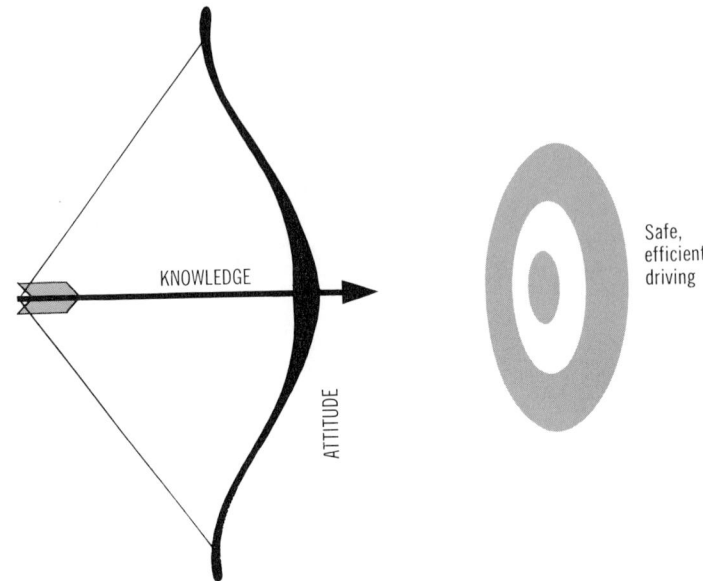

# II HUMAN CHARACTERISTICS RELATED TO DRIVING

*"KNOWLEDGE is an army with banners, marching proudly on the parade ground of consciousness. Attitude is the undercover force of law and order —or the thief in the night—its power and its danger in its anonymity."*

The accident problem is a human problem. The hammer is but an extension of the hand, the hand a servant of the mind. These are figurative, of course, for simplicity. We really mean the road, the car, the body, and the mind. Traffic safety has created its own research, but far more extensive is the great volume of pertinent data extant in other disciplines, ready to be adapted to the mission of saving lives—data in engineering in its various branches, in medicine, and in the behavioral sciences. Of the three, the engineering component of motor vehicle traffic and safety has become by far the most sophisticated. In spite of the greater complexity intrinsic to medicine and behavioral science, a more naïve, incomplete, and sometimes inaccurate translation of their data into the language and the thinking of the new lifesaving discipline has taken place.

This section on *human characteristics* presents some very critical data from other disciplines, information long overdue in the literature of traffic safety. Some of it has serious implications for general education and for the grass roots elements of life. It is recommended for study by the experienced educator as well as by the teacher-to-be. Hopefully, such study may lead future investigators into further development of this cross-discipline exchange of data, and into the very fertile areas of research exposed to view by it.

# Attitude and Behavior 4

ALTHOUGH this area may well be the most significant factor in traffic safety, there is probably less readily available documented knowledge of attitude and behavior than of any other factor. There are excellent sources of pertinent data on attitude and behavior extant today in fields other than traffic safety education. In this chapter some of this very significant knowledge will be identified, interpreted, and related to traffic safety education.

## "Folk" Knowledge

Today most people are accustomed and willing to accept conclusions derived from "scientific research." Few people realize that much of the knowledge that underlies our civilization grew out of centuries of trial and error. In some cases, this learning preceded but has been fully in accord with conclusions based on systematic research.

Man sailed the seas for centuries suffering from diseases caused by a necessarily restricted diet. Then he discovered that inclusion of certain fruits, or their derivatives (such as lime juice), in his diet could prevent the common illness known as scurvy. The beneficial effects of these fruits was discovered long before laboratory research identified the vitamin as an essential element of man's diet.

One of the forces which motivated exploration of the unknown seas, even before the time of Columbus, was a demand for shorter, more efficient sea routes for commerce. A critical item in that commerce was the trade in spices. Antedating the discovery of the nature of microorganism decay of foods, man knew that spices were effective in the preservation of foods.

For many generations man has been familiar with the symptoms of sunstroke and heat prostration. Today it is known that either extremely high body temperature or depletion of the salt (NaCl) content of body fluid can cause collapse. Although they did not know about the loss of salt from the body, athletes and people who worked in extreme heat—in hayfields or mines—learned not to drink large quantities of liquid (which tends to "wash out" salt with perspiration), no matter how thirsty they were, and even in some cases learned to add additional salt to their normal diet. This was done before the need of salt for certain body processes was known.

These are examples in which something we might call "historical" knowledge was later verified by "clinical" or "laboratory" evidence obtained by experiment.

## THE HISTORICAL-LABORATORY APPROACH

Much of the *behavioral* research in driver and traffic safety education has led to questionable conclusions, because of several factors. These are:

1. Inappropriate professional background of the investigator.
2. Failure of the investigator to recognize all factors.
3. Reliance upon statistical analysis which sometimes leads to conclusions that are not applicable to any individual human being. Faulty analysis has been especially evident in studies of attitude.
4. Failure to include information based on neuroanatomy and neurology which comprise a foundation for an understanding of human behavior.

This does not deny the value of existing driver education research, but it does point to the necessity of a new path toward understanding attitude and behavior. This new approach may be termed *historical-laboratory* in nature, citing interdependence and mutual support between the two methods of learning. It is an extension of the process herein described in reference to vitamins, salt, and spices.

### We Look at History

Millions of people living today are startling examples of the conditioning of great masses of populations to planned attitudes and resultant behavior patterns.

If we had not seen it, it would be difficult to believe that the people of great nations could accept certain others as allies and friends at one time and others as enemies—and in only a few years completely reverse their attitudes toward both. That a highly civilized people, such as that of Hitler's Germany, could be conditioned to hatred of other people and to the behavior the hatred engendered seems impossible today. Yet, history shows that it happened.

The tremendous impact of advertising on our national economy is well known. Refined over the years by trial and error, the most effective behavior-conditioning procedures have evolved and survived. Those businesses which used sound, effective techniques survived and prospered, continuing and further developing those techniques. Others with less effective methods were eliminated by the competition.

Other human activities that are based on historical examples of behavior conditioning include the great religions, propaganda, politics, and "leadership" in general.

## We Profit by History

In this section, attitude-and-behavior-conditioning principles developed in "historical" settings will be identified and compared with pertinent laboratory findings in neuroanatomy and neurology. Those principles identified and supported by both historical and laboratory criteria will be recommended for application to the program of driver and traffic safety education.

## THE FOUNDATION OF ATTITUDE AND BEHAVIOR

As our initial frame of reference, we are on firm ground in stating that the human nervous system is the physical repository or "machinery" of *attitude,* a determinant of behavior. To study the nature of attitude, we shall first study the form and function of the human "machine." This study is comparable to that of becoming familiar with the structure and parts of the automobile engine in order to be able to understand the principles of automobile propulsion. Conversely, attempts to study attitude, or even to define it, without reference to the human nervous system have often resulted in vague, tenuous, or even misleading concepts.

Figure 4–2 is not a "picture" of the actual structures (as is the silhouette, Figure 4–1), but it is a *diagram,* or a "picture of a function." It is similar to the time-exposure photograph of vehicles passing through an intersection at night in which no actual vehicle is shown but where patterns of headlight movements are seen as streaks of light. The lines of arrows represent pathways taken by the nerve impulses.

A picture, or image, strikes the retina of the eye in the form of light rays. From the retina an electrochemical nerve impulse is transmitted over the optic nerve, as shown in Figure 4–2. The nerve impulse is specific in nature, "coded" to carry a representation of the actual image seen. It passes through the brain stem to the cerebrum. Similarly, sound vibrations in the atmosphere reach the cochlea of the ear. There they initiate nerve impulses which are transmitted over the cochlear branch of the auditory nerve, reaching the brain stem and the cerebrum as shown.

## SOME PERTINENT FEATURES OF THE CENTRAL NERVOUS SYSTEM

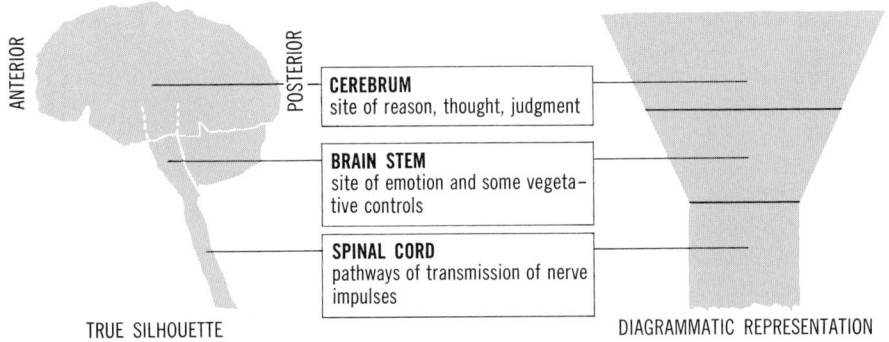

FIGURE 4-1

The significant point in seeing and hearing is this: Both types of coded nerve impulses are "read," or translated, in the cerebrum. However, the impulses pass through the brain stem first *where they are subject to possible change or distortion in taking on a new **emotional** characteristic.*

Although certain, exact localization of the emotional function is not at present possible, most neurologists believe it to be centered in the hypothalamus, an area within the brain stem. There is general agreement, however, that the brain stem does house neural tissues governing emotion.

## *THE TRIGGER IMPULSE*

Let us now consider a historical example of the development of predetermined attitudes and predictable behavior. The Hitler Youth type of training was calculated to develop an attitude toward things or people that would result in predictable behavior patterns. Initially, by stories, allegations, and appeals to already existing hatreds, fears, and prejudices, the propaganda leaders were able to associate hatred with a word or words that applied to their intended objects of hate. *This emotional association becomes firmly established in the sensitive neural tissues of the brain stem* (probably in the hypothalamus).

Now the selected words have become "trigger words." Later, when subsequent, coded, electrochemical nerve impulses which represent such words pass through the previously conditioned brain stem nerve tissues, they trigger the emotional reaction with which they have been associated. These (now emotion-biased) impulses continue on to the cerebrum where their meaning is recognized.

However, the added emotional reaction accompanies the "message." In this case, a hatred-associated response is already determined *before* the word is interpreted in the cerebrum. The word has triggered the emotional response before it can be recognized in terms of its dictionary meaning. The emotional response distorts the meaning of the coded impulse into one associated with the emotion of hatred. The Hitler Youth–trained individual could not grasp the true meaning of certain words because of the emotional response that accompanied them into the cerebrum. Some of the words were, of course, Jew, Aryan, and *der Fuehrer*.

## We All Have Some Trigger Words

Communist, Democrat, Republican, Catholic, Protestant, Jew, Negro, and many words denoting national and racial origins are examples of trigger words for some people. Other words can evoke even stronger emotional responses. Few (if any) of us do not have some common trigger word which initiates an emotional reaction.

"Selling" language also contains trigger words, words designed to give a *feeling* of value different from the true value of the product. The liquid is "golden" not "yellow." "Socialized" is used to condemn—as though implying a kinship to communism—as is the expression "welfare state," although "social" and "welfare" do not have any directly objectionable connotation. "Hospital-tested" gives a desired impression, as does the number of ways our product is "good for you." Something has a "million-dollar look." Our product is the only one with "chemicofluvium"—a copyrighted word of our own, of course.

Finally, we accent the digit which has greatest impact—$1.98 instead of $2, $9.98 instead of $10, and $29,990 for that house. Such expressions are not meant to appeal to the intellect. They give the *feel* of a bargain.

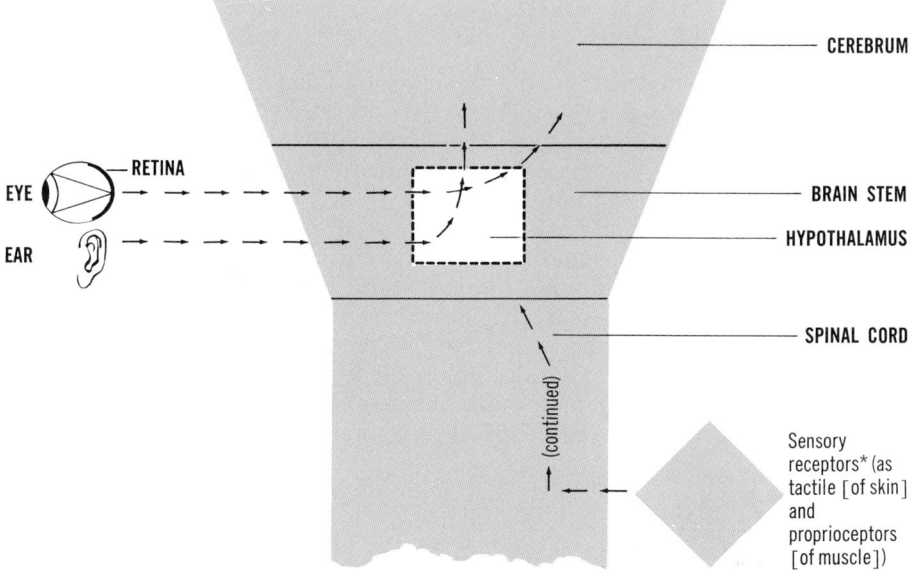

NOTE: The impulses from other (sensory) receptor organs* continue upward through the brain stem into the cerebrum, but are terminated in the diagram to avoid confusion.

FIGURE 4-2

## The Visual Image

Similarly, emotional associations with visual images exist in the brain stem. They and the word-symbol emotional associations may be purposely implanted or may be established by chance experience.

Consider the term "good looking." Have you ever heard it said (or even believed, yourself) that somebody who looked very "nice" could hardly have committed some alleged atrocious act? It just seemed incongruous. Yet there is no tangible connection between physical standards of beauty and standards of behavior. Song, story, play, motion picture, and television associate certain facial features with "good" and other "ugly" features with brutality, stupidity, and cruelty. What young person dreams of dating, or marrying, an acromegalic? Yet the latter may be the finest person of all the people he or she will ever meet.

The acquired standards of a person being "good looking" inspire pleasant emotions, such as liking and love. That such standards change according to customs, countries, races, and even styles shows that standards are acquired. The purposely elongated skull of the native of New Britain would be unlikely to inspire emotions of, or leading to, liking or love in one of our teen-agers (or oldsters). Physical "beauty" that is in accord with our conditioned standards does.

We have visual symbols emotionally associated (in the brain stem) with qualities which may or may not be truly intrinsic to the object of those visual symbols. These symbols, like the trigger-word symbols, strongly affect our behavior and our lives.

## The Billion-dollar Smile

Both the advertising industry and show business have capitalized on the trigger image of the *smile*. A smile may be accurately defined as a movement accomplished by contraction of certain facial muscles. It can be "turned on" at will. It is strongly associated in the central nervous system of the person smiled upon with an emotion of pleasure, liking, and friendliness.

The television commercial personality who smiles at you while he talks of something not at all humorous isn't merely absentminded, or happy, or pleased with you, or thinking of a funny story. He knows that you, if you're like most of us, will feel more friendly to a person who smiles at you. To him, the smile, an emotion-associated "trigger" image, is a psychological foot in the door leading to a sale. The smile is one of the techniques developed in both advertising and show business. Ever have your photograph taken? Ever been told to smile, or even to look pleasant?

## Smile and Frown

Have you ever noticed the use of the smile and frown as opposite symbols in establishing an emotional reaction to a sponsor's product? Other brands, or the absence of "our" product, are associated with a frown or unhappy facial expression. Use of the product is associated with a smile on the face of the user. *The association is a definitely planned one.*

## The Contradiction

The effect of a word-symbol emotional association may be completely countered by an accompanying visual-symbol emotional association. Witness the man who calls another by a "fighting word," that is, a trigger word. This can easily lead to further angry words or blows. Suppose, however, that the same person uses the same term, accompanied by a smile, perhaps preceded by the words, "You old. . . ." The hearer then takes the same words as a sign of friendliness! The emotion-associated visual symbol (the smile) overcomes the effect of the other emotion-associated (word) symbol.

The light, seemingly superficial nature of the advertising smile, the show person's, politician's, or propagandist's "friendly" smile should not blind us to the fact that *such trigger symbols as smiles and emotion-associated* **words** have helped build multimillion-dollar business enterprises and have set the climate in which millions have died on the battlefield or in the concentration camp. There are many other emotion-associated visual symbols in addition to those of facial beauty or ugliness, and the smile. The flag of a country is an example. The sight of blood or serious injury, as in a severe accident, is another. Some symbols have a place in the great religions.

Whether originating in chance experience, or whether purposely implanted, trigger words and trigger visual images evoke an emotional response in the brain stem even before they reach the cerebrum where they are interpreted.

## THE NEURAL BIAS MECHANISM

To return to an analogy: to comprehend the principles of automobile propulsion, we learn something of the physical structure of the engine and its parts. Without such knowledge, worded descriptions of the principles would be hopelessly vague to the learner. This has long been a weakness in our treatment of *attitude*. To form a concept of the nature of attitude which is more definitive than the "that which" definitions, a mechanistic frame of reference should be used.[1]

To help build the definitive concept, without regard to action sequence, and without further localization of function other than cerebrum, brain stem, and afferent (incoming) nerve pathways, let us group all pertinent nerve tissues as a single entity. In this group will be the cerebrum, the brain stem, and all the neural (nerve) tissues which are concerned with reception of external (chiefly auditory and visual) stimuli and with transmission of them to the cerebrum. Included also will be the corticothalamic nerve pathways which transmit impulses between the cerebral cortex and hypothalamus, providing for complex interaction of the two brain areas.

Let us call this entity the *neural bias mechanism (NBM)*[2]—"neural" referring to nerve tissue, "bias" denoting the effect on the incoming neural

---

[1] Arthur L. Mahony, "Teaching for Attitude Conducive to Safe Driving," doctoral dissertation, New York University, New York, 1957.
[2] *Ibid.*

impulses causing a biased or prejudiced reaction in the destination—the cerebrum—and "mechanism" to retain the important concept of the neural structure as an actual physical entity.

## *WHAT IS THE TRUE NATURE OF ATTITUDE?*

Nerve pathways, like the deepening bed of a swift-flowing stream (or muscle tissue developing in accordance with use), become more strongly *patterned* in their functioning with use.

Initially, a pattern is set in the neural bias mechanism by either planned indoctrination or chance experience. Appropriate neural tissues become especially sensitive to specific afferent (incoming) stimuli. These specific stimuli are the incoming coded electrochemical impulses which represent trigger words and trigger image symbols. (Even a tactile stimulus, as from touching something slimy, may be associated with an emotional reaction.) *We now have planned—or accidental—conditioned patterns in the NBM.*

When a subsequent incoming stimulus related to those specific patterns is "recognized" in the NBM, an emotional factor is added, distorting or biasing the nature of the original stimulus *on the way to* the cerebrum. This to-be-interpreted *meaning* of the stimulus is thus *biased* in the mechanism in accordance with the established patterns already in that mechanism.

*The functional patterns in the NBM are the determinant of attitude. Each incoming electrochemical, coded, neural impulse (which represents the original external impulse) is translated in the cerebral cortex* **after** *it has been affected (biased) by the brain stem patterns.* The subsequent reaction and behavior are thus also affected. The NBM is thus patterned to induce "predictable" behavior.

Figure 4–3a shows a man setting type. He is fashioning a pattern in a machine which will remain there until removed. This is somewhat like the process of setting a (functional) *pattern* in the NBM, the formation of "attitudinal" associations, chiefly on the emotional level.

Figure 4–3b shows a wide ribbon of paper passing through the printing press. From contact with the type, the paper undergoes a change. It is patterned in accordance with the previously determined arrangement of the type. This ribbon of paper corresponds to the incoming neural impulses which transverse the NBM subsequent to its being patterned. When the paper reaches its destination it is different than it was before it went through the press.

The coded (for recognition) neural impulse which came from the cochlea of the ear, generated by the vibrations of the sound of a trigger word, proceeds through the NBM like the paper through the press. Also, like the paper, it is changed, altered, biased—chiefly by having triggered an emotional reaction in transversing the conditioned or "patterned" NBM. The new changed, or biased, impulse is a *different* stimulus to the cerebral cortex than it would have been without the conditioning process—the neurological "printing," we may call it. As a different stimulus it triggers a different reaction, just as the printed sheet carries meaning that the blank paper did not.

FIGURE 4-3a    FIGURE 4-3b

Though the processes of the NBM are far more complex than our allusion would indicate, we might simplify our story to say that the printed words represent the emotional factor added to the neural impulse in the NBM, specifically in the brain stem. As a knowledge and consciousness of the printing plant provides a physical, spatial frame of reference for understanding the process of printing, and as reference to the engine and its main parts permits comprehension of the principles of automobile propulsion, so does the concept of the NBM, the *physical entity,* provide "canvas" for "painting a picture" of *attitude.*

## Impact of the Emotional Factor

We have noted that the brain stem effect, probably hypothalamic, is chiefly emotional in nature. One may ask to what degree this holds true for a highly intelligent individual, or even for one of normal intelligence. The answer is startling to many. The brain stem is phylogenetically (in the species) much older than the cerebrum. The "lower" centers of the nervous system are older than the "higher" centers. The lower (older) centers are stronger in function than the higher (newer) ones. We note this greater vitality in observing the effects of old age, alcohol, and drugs. Senility, or "second childhood," is often present while the nerve centers controlling the vegetative functions of the body are still quite efficient.

When the individual is under the influence of alcohol or other drugs (see "Effects of Alcohol and Drugs," Chapter 5), a low level of concentration in the bloodstream will affect the cerebral cortex (impairing judgment, reason, and normal inhibitions) while the "lower" neural centers of emotion and cardiac and respiratory control continue to function well. A greater (alcohol or drug) concentration is necessary to impair their function. The "truth serums" utilize this sensitivity of the higher centers to low concentrations (affecting normal inhibitions), while speech is still possible. The brain stem is then less affected than the cerebrum (cerebral cortex).

We might consider the normal interaction of cerebrocortically inhibited total brain action as a sort of balance. Under stress (as well as under drugs), it is perfectly possible for brain stem domination to produce acts of violence, and in the driver acts of hyperemotional behavior. No wonder any ensuing attempt to label a person as legally sane or insane, or as a safe or reckless driver, so often brings conflicting testimony. The sane, normal individual experiences brain stem domination at times. The behavioral results are a matter of type, circumstance, and degree—not so simple as a permanent or long-term label of good or bad, sane or insane.

### Significance of the Principle

The foregoing data were cited in support of the principle of a natural superiority *in terms of vitality of function* on the part of the lower centers as compared with the higher centers. Evidence points to a definite dominance of brain stem functioning over cerebral cortex functioning in the tremendously complex interaction which constitutes "brain" action. What we have called the "laboratory" approach supports this.

Now let us consider our own experience. We may call this our "folk" knowledge.

### The Hypothetical John Smith

John Smith is an intelligent person. He planned his high school and college curricula for a career in engineering. Upon graduation, he selected the "right" corporation for his professional future. This would give the impression that there is a definite cerebral dominance in the case of this intelligent person, would it not?

Let us consider a little further. John Smith, if he follows the general patterns of behavior of the young American male adult, probably did not make the important decision of choosing his wife on an intellectual (cerebral-dominated) basis. He didn't choose the most intelligent girl he could possibly find to improve the hereditary intellectual strain in his children and in future generations. He didn't choose the girl with the best physical heredity. If he's average, he didn't choose her for money or position either. He liked or loved her. He found her attractive. Her physical appearance was favorable. She was not physically repulsive to him. They both liked many of the same things. Sexual attraction undoubtedly played a part in deciding that he would marry, and whom. All these factors are emotional in nature, and they played a large part in the important decision to marry.

We should realize, too, that John Smith's professional career is a means to an end. He *wants* (emotion) the fruits of his labor very much. He may even be *afraid* (emotion) not to do his best on his job, because of the probable consequences. That is, even his apparently intellectually dictated career activities may, themselves, be determined by pressures of emotions of fear, need, or want. The emotional factor is not limited to the decision to marry, choice of a wife, or choice of leisure-time activities. How many highly intelligent young couples marry when "practical" considerations would require a delay of years?

## The Real You

Suppose you have your free choice of how to spend your leisure time. What will you do? What *do* you do when there are no pressures from economic needs, "wants" (emotional), or feelings of duty.

Do you always watch educational television programs, read educational books, hold extra jobs (without the pressure of needs), associate with people solely because you will derive economic or intellectual advantage from them (as opposed to going with people you like), avoid playing golf or going to the theater, or eating what you like, because the enjoyment is transitory and leaves you with less money? Or, *when you have a perfectly free choice*, do you do what you *like* to do?

## Supporting the Principles

We have plenty of "folk" experience to support our cited "laboratory" evidence which points to the *dominance* of the brain stem over the cerebral cortex. Those who may not recognize this dominance must at least concede the existence of the powerful *impact* of brain stem (emotional) function in determining human behavior. We can utilize this by recognizing and using our trigger words principle and our trigger visual symbol principle in our important mission of conditioning attitude and resultant behavior.

## THE MECHANISTIC CONCEPT OF ATTITUDE

The brain tends to be quiescent except when stimulated from "outside" (that is, outside its own structure). When it is stimulated to action, such action may be prolonged. After the stimulus a neurological "feedback," a figuratively circular pattern of impulses, may continue for a considerable time. All the "outside" word and visual image impulses pass through the brain stem before reaching the cerebrum to stimulate it into action. In traversing the nerve pathways in the brain stem, they are affected by the previously experience-established functional patterns there.

The stimuli (nerve impulses) *which are necessary to brain action* (reaction) are changed—distorted, affected, biased—in accord with those patterns, chiefly by the effect of the established association of *emotions* with the nerve impulses that represent trigger words and trigger images.

The actual physical neural structures are patterned in function to affect subsequent word and image "messages." *The act of patterning the functioning within the neural structures is the development of "attitude," "prejudice," or "bias." This is a determinant of subsequent behavior.*

## APPLYING THE PRINCIPLES OF ATTITUDE CONDITIONING

It is not our purpose in this chapter to cite all the specific procedures possible in the development of attitudes conducive to safe driving. A definitive concept of attitude has been given. Evidence, "folk," "historical," and "laboratory," was cited in support of the principles involved in attitude development. The following recommendations will serve as a general guide:

1. LEARN WHICH TRIGGER WORDS ALREADY EXIST AMONG THE STUDENTS. The driver and traffic safety education teacher should study carefully the semantic aspects of the course of study, especially in the classroom phase. He should identify those words which already have emotional or unusual significance for the *teen-agers in that area and school.*

   For instance, to many people the expression "hot rodder" means a young, irresponsible, reckless, dangerous driver. However, if one uses the term disparagingly to some audiences of young people, he arouses severe antagonism (emotion). Many young people call their car hobby "hot rodding," and yet consciously work to promote courtesy and safety on the highway. An unjust, implied accusation would be resented by them.

   An emotional block of antagonism diminishes or destroys the teacher-pupil rapport necessary for effective leadership. In this example, the term "hot rodder" would be a very unfortunate use of a trigger word. Careful study of generation-to-generation, area-to-area, and interest-group-to-interest-group differences in word meanings and implications is necessary for efficient communication.

   The teen-ager has many trigger words, not all of them directly related to his daily environment. The teacher should learn them and use them constructively in encouraging desirable behavior and in discouraging that which is objectionable. For example: A teacher might asso-

FIGURE 4-4 "Hot rodder" may be a trigger word to a teen-ager that means this (left) . . . or this (right).

ciate the much-dreaded implication of "showing off" with a certain type of driving to achieve an emotion-associated effect.

2. IMPLANT DESIRABLE TRIGGER ASSOCIATIONS. The teacher should also consciously work to vilify practices, ideas, and words which *can be made to take on an emotional association* of dislike, disapproval, perhaps hatred. This is in addition to learning and using those word-emotion associations already extant among teen-agers. Associating bad driving with danger to the *student's own family* brings in an emotional impact, constructively directed. For example: A teacher might say, "That boy who squeals his tires around the school corner drives the same way where your mother crosses the street. . . ." Here we have a combined attack. The liking, or love, for some people can be used to reinforce the induced dislike, or disapproval, or fear of the potential threat.

The student's *desire to protect those he loves* can be made one of the strongest emotional motivations. This approach has an additional advantage in being more *openly* accepted by him than talk of his own danger. Some teen-agers, especially boys, refuse to acknowledge that their concern for their own personal safety would affect their driving behavior, yet will acknowledge a strong desire to protect others. This admission has a value in discussions aimed at attitude development.

Support for driver education is usually found to be stronger among the parents of high school students than among the parents of very young children. Calling attention to the implications of safer driving by trained teen-agers and post-teen-agers *for the young children who must cross streets and who stand on corners waiting to cross* triggers a different *emotional* response in the parents of those young children. Old folks can be similarly affected. Sometimes both elementary and secondary school PTA's see driver education differently until this point is brought out. The reaction is perfectly natural—and emotional.

3. USE EMOTIONAL ASSOCIATIONS BY IMPLICATION. In traffic safety education, *implication* is a psychological device. An effective instrument might be a dual-scene poster with one picture showing a furtive figure peddling dope to young people, while the other picture shows "another deadly danger" or "a greater danger," a reckless driver threatening the lives of the same young people. Greater impact might be achieved if the former scene is near a school. In addition to relating the serious nature of the two threats, this approach is effective in reducing the tolerance of the general public toward traffic law violators which is in contrast to their attitude toward lawbreakers in general.

4. THE CHILD SHOULD BE REACHED WHILE VERY YOUNG. Driver education teachers have complained (justly) that children have acquired undesirable attitudes before they ever reach the driver education class. This is undoubtedly true. We cannot, of course, control all the child's pertinent environment. Neural patterns become more deeply seated with use. These facts indicate an urgent need for constructive action in the school environment at an early age.

The safety program of a school should be designed not only for contemporary safeguarding of the young child as a pedestrian or bus passenger, but also for guiding his development of attitude at an early age, by forming desirable patterns within the neural bias mechanism.

5. USING THE "LEADER" SYMBOL. It has been long known to the advertising business that association of a product with a popular or highly respected personality creates a receptive "feeling" for that product.

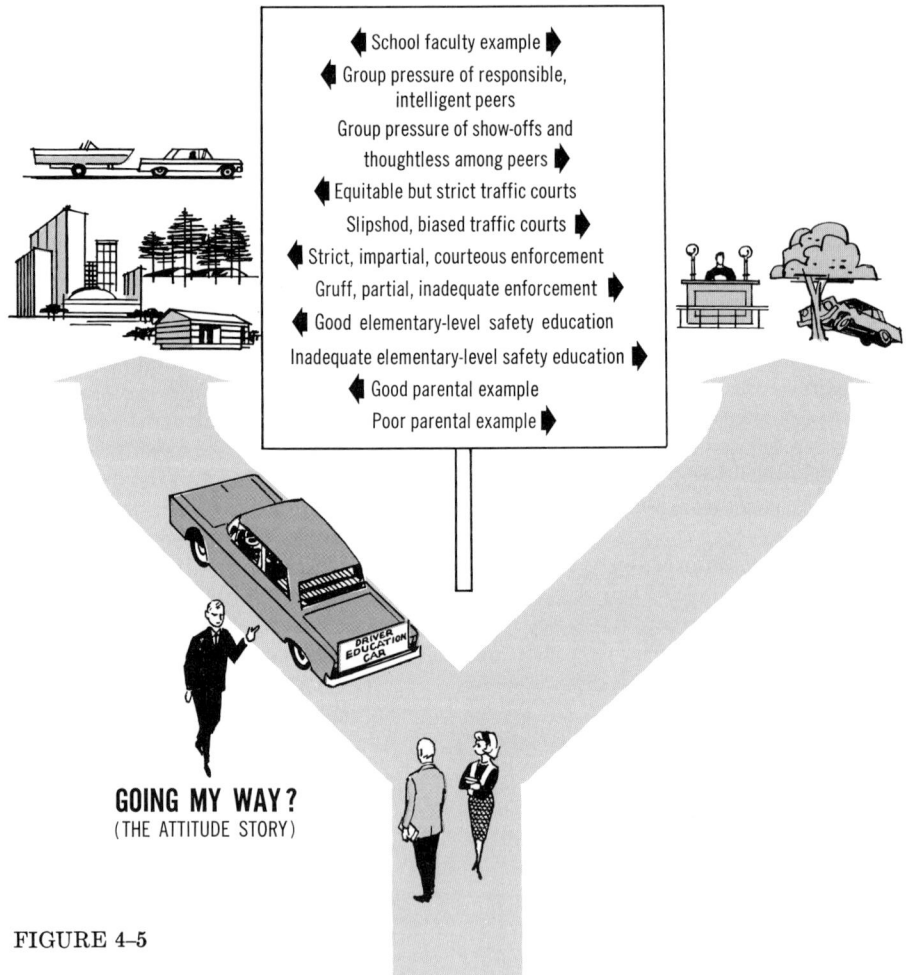

FIGURE 4–5

"Buy (so and so) and say that (so and so) sent you," says the "friendly" salesman of radio or television.

Some of the potential, popular exponents of good driving might be: the race driver who emphasizes his caution on the highway (although the impact of automobile racing on teen-age boys may be detrimental unless it is cleverly directed), acknowledged student leaders, athletic performers, well-chosen public figures, a known-to-be-respected enforcement officer who can speak well, or a successful athletic coach of college or high school. Of course the teacher must be sure that the invited personality "practices what he preaches."

6. AN EASY-TO-TEST TECHNIQUE. A simple though interesting way of testing the effect of a symbol before using it in teaching would be for a teacher in a school of sufficient enrollment to make impossible personal acquaintance with all students to try the following:

In walking through the school corridors before and after school and while classes are passing, hold a very faint expression of a smile—not a fixed "chorus-girl" type, but more a pleasant look, an invitation to a smile—giving the symbolic impression of a friendly person. It is usually quite impressive to note the number of "Hello's," "Hi's," "Good morning's," and other friendly greetings that such a facial expression evokes.

The significant point is that a facial appearance of pleasantness, friendliness, and sympathy is a psychological instrument in gaining rapport with students as well as an asset to one's personal relationships. The visual symbol can well implement the word symbols in gaining the confidence of one's students.

We have discussed the principles involved in forming patterns of emotional association in the neural bias mechanism and the effective use of those already there. It will now be a highly informative and professionally profitable practice to look for, identify, and analyze pertinent procedures observed in advertising, propaganda, politics, and in general and religious leadership.

Although in some cases the procedures originated by trial and error, the principles are consistent and can be used to develop more effective procedures in a scientifically based trial-without-error planning. Since the principles are effective and identifiable, educators can and should identify and use them constructively in their leadership mission.

## *A Caution*

One thing that has tended to confuse thinking in the matter of attitude conditioning in driver and traffic safety education is failure to distinguish between principles and methods.

A great deal is being said and written in favor of the discussion technique in driver education as a means of developing constructive attitude. It should be recognized that this is a *method* and that the same basic principles of attitude formation govern here as in any other teaching technique. Some teachers advocate "involvement" of the student in such projects as traffic surveys. This, too, is a *method* of applying principles of good teaching. In advocating the discussion technique as an instrument for attitude conditioning, the tendency common to all such movements, exaggeration, has appeared. It is a good teaching method. It is not the *only* method. The popular vilification of the "lecture" method in education often accompanies advocacy of student discussion.

It should be remembered that the principles of leadership, of conditioning attitude and behavior, apply to all methods. It is the appropriateness of the *principles* to the *subject*—the *person* to be affected—that determine the effect, not adherence to one certain method. Regardless of how one decries the "lecture" method, no one can deny the powerful effect of the skilled orator on his hearers. The inspired clergyman, the gifted politician, the great national leader, the accomplished salesman, the talented stage personality—they all apply sound principles of leadership in the lecture method. It is extremely doubtful if they could achieve the same effects in any other way.

Factors seldom mentioned in reference to method are the particular qualifications of the leader or teacher, the appropriateness of the subject matter, and the characteristics of the group to be taught. These should be considered in choosing methods, as well as the simple "change of pace" that livens a long school day. Whatever method of teaching and attitude conditioning is being used, the human nervous system is the same and responds in the same way to the same stimuli. It is up to the teacher to adapt the basic principles of affecting that nervous system to the method he chooses to use.

## A FURTHER ANALYSIS OF SOME ATTITUDE CONCEPTS

One emergent of the previously cited attitude study[3] is a new view of some of the entities that have been called "attitudes." This analysis is postulated on the basis of contemporary knowledge and informed opinion. It is true that many driver education people (as well as many others) have spoken and written of many "different" attitudes. Mentioned are "attitude toward law," "attitude toward police," "attitude toward stop signs," "attitude toward . . ."—almost anything related to traffic safety. Each one of these entities, so expressed, has received unquestioned identity as "an attitude." A more studied and informed consideration is indicated.

It seems likely that we have fallen into a semantic trap. In using the worded concept "attitude toward . . . ," the natural next step was to name an object concerned with traffic safety and then, quite naturally, to assume that the expressed entity is "an attitude" in reality. This process can be projected to "establish" the existence of a true attitude toward any object or thought that it is possible to name after the words "attitude toward. . . ."

A real analysis of each attitude entity cited in driver education has been lacking, possibly as a result of the rather vague, "that which," hazy concepts and definitions of attitude heretofore existing.

### A New Concept

There is considerable evidence that these "attitude toward . . ." entities are not, as generally believed, homogeneous attitude objects. We should realize that the interaction between cerebral cortex and brain stem in brain action is complex and that *knowledge* is necessary in relating the stop at the stop sign (for example) to actual safety needs. It is very possible that these "attitude" entities are *each a combination of the person's general attitude*

[3] *Ibid.*

*toward safety in driving (or toward self-preservation) plus the knowledge that the object, such as the stop sign, is truly related to that attitude—that the object actually is a factor in driving safely, or in preserving his life.*

We might illustrate this new concept by citing the phenomenon of conscience and specific acts related to it. Conscience may well be compared to the general attitude toward safety in driving—or toward self-preservation. The factual knowledge necessary to identify a considered act as related to one's conscience corresponds to the knowledge which gives recognition that the act, in this case stopping for the sign, is related to safety in driving or to self-preservation.

## THE KNOWLEDGE—ATTITUDE DICHOTOMIES

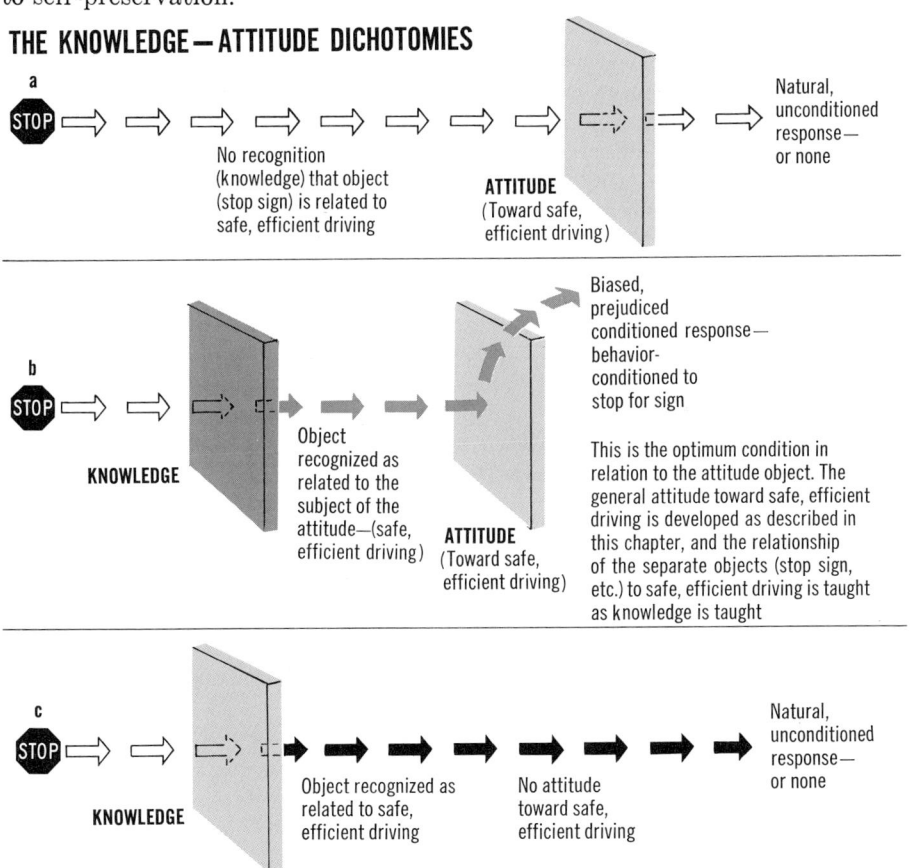

NOTE: It should be recognized that this diagram has no reference to neural structure, function, or sequence.

FIGURE 4-6 Traditionally considered a development of many "attitudes," as "toward stop signs," "toward law," "toward police," etc., the *attitude-objective* of driver and traffic safety education is shown in *b*. The *general attitude* toward safe and efficient driving is developed by application of the principles described in this chapter. The relation of the objects, *including actions*, to safe, efficient driving is taught as knowledge. In the case of each object, a dichotomy of *knowledge and attitude* is found.

## Implication for Teaching

The importance of the concept of this dichotomy in these attitude entities lies in the fact that knowledge and attitude call for different teaching techniques. Granted that we must develop in our students an attitude conducive to safe driving, we must also show how strict observance of stop-sign regulations is related to that attitude. Although much has been written in this chapter about attitude development, it is not our purpose here to describe methods of teaching the *knowledge* factor. Teachers are well equipped by professional training and experience to do this. The important point here is to identify the existence of the two separate factors, attitude and knowledge, each requiring its own separate and different treatment.

It seems highly likely that the best effect of driver education will be to achieve in its students a constructive broad attitude toward safety in driving. This can be most effectively done by application of these principles and recommendations to attitude development. In addition, the pertinent factual knowledge must be taught as such, in the manner in which teachers already know how to teach factual material. This concept of the apparent attitude entities as actual dichotomies of *a general attitude toward safety plus specific factual knowledge* contraindicates the contemporary approach, that of attempting to develop a particular attitude toward each and every item connected with traffic safety.

More research in this area is needed. Driver education teachers seeking advanced degrees might well consider the attitude-knowledge interaction to be a fertile field for study. In every case a comprehensive study of the nature of attitude and of the pertinent background sciences should be a prerequisite.

## CONCLUSIONS

1. The "mechanistic" approach of building a frame of reference by allusion to the central nervous system is highly desirable, perhaps indispensable, in understanding the nature and development of attitude, a prime determinant of behavior.
2. Principles for determining attitude-conditioning activities are identified and applied to recommended procedures.
3. Emotion plays a dominant role in attitude.
4. "Attitude" and "knowledge" in safety education are comparable to "conscience" and "knowledge of right and wrong." Further study of the relationship is indicated. A careful analysis reveals a possible change in professional thinking on the subject of safety attitude. There seems to exist a single broad attitude toward safe driving (and toward self-preservation) plus specific knowledge items which relate certain acts and objects to that attitude. This would replace the concept of an unlimited number of attitudes in driver education, each to be separately conditioned in the manner of attitude conditioning. Instead, the basic attitude would be conditioned in this way, and the numerous driving items considered and taught as matters of knowledge.
5. Attitude and resultant behavior patterns have been conditioned in great

numbers of people by national leaders, by religious leaders, and by mass advertising. The principles which guided the process have been developed in historical use and are documented in neurological research. Study and application of these principles by educators, specifically safety educators, is greatly to be desired.

6. The teacher is cautioned to require convincing documentation before fully accepting statements relating to attitude. This is particularly important in the subject of attitude measurement. The consensus of informed opinion today recognizes that although extensive use of attitude scales dates back to about 1929 (Thurstone[4] et al.), and in our field the Siebrecht Attitude Scale[5] to 1941, it is extremely doubtful that we could justify administering any driver attitude scale extant today and accept the result as a true indication of that individual's attitude in driving a motor vehicle. This is not to say that experimentation is not desirable. This is merely a caution to avoid unjust conclusions in reference to any individual on the basis of an instrument of measurement which is still in an experimental stage.

There is an implication for attitude measurement in the concept of the attitude-knowledge dichotomies. In attitude tests, or "scales," it is quite obvious that the subject's attitude toward the testing authority, toward his own driving privilege, toward getting as favorable (to him) a score in the testing procedure as possible—all tend to cause him to give the responses which appear to favor safe driving. The subject's *knowledge* of what *is* favorable makes a difference in his ability to do this.

Though in many phases of automobile driving most respondents can easily make choices which would appear to indicate a constructive attitude toward safety in driving, improving the knowledge factor improves this ability to choose—both in the person who would deceive to make a favorable score and in the sincere, constructively attitude-conditioned person. Hence pretesting and posttesting with attitude scales may (very probably) mean simply that the subjects had acquired some knowledge which enable them to answer more skillfully. There appears to be no method known today to separately measure in an individual the attitude component of the attitude-knowledge dichotomy.

For those interested in further research in the field of attitude and behavior, references may be found at the end of this chapter.

"Attitude and Behavior," the most difficult area of research in driver and traffic safety education, offers a world of opportunity for investigation by the serious educator. It is an absolute necessity, however, that the investigator first prepare himself thoroughly in driver education and in the type of science background suggested in this chapter. It should be remembered that research is a step beyond today's knowledge. Without reasonable pos-

---

[4] L. L. Thurstone, and E. J. Chave, *The Measurement of Attitudes,* The University of Chicago Press, Chicago, 1929.

[5] E. B. Siebrecht, *The Siebrecht Attitude Scale,* Center for Safety Education, New York University, New York, 1941.

session of the latter, attempts at research "study" are a waste of time, money, and effort.

The behavioral factors in the "driving task" have been the slowest to respond to research. Consequently, the most difficult segment of the driver education mission has been to develop and document principles for the constructive conditioning of attitude and behavior. In this chapter teachers are given a new and well-documented background for doing a much better job of making young people responsible, sportsmanlike drivers.

## SELECTED BIBLIOGRAPHY

The following publications were among the background reading that contributed to development of the concept of the neural bias mechanism. They are recommended for the serious student who may wish to pursue further knowledge of the nature and development of *attitude* as a determinant of behavior:

Brock, Samuel: *The Basis of Clinical Neurology,* 3d ed., The Williams & Wilkins Company, Baltimore, 1953.

Burrow, Trigant: *Science and Man's Behavior,* Philosophical Library, Inc., New York, 1953.

Eccles, Carew: *The Neurophysiological Basis of Mind,* Oxford at the Clarendon Press, 1953. Being the Waynflete Lectures delivered in the College of St. Mary, Oxford, in Hilary Term, 1952.

Elliott, H. Chandler: *Textbook of the Nervous System,* J. B. Lippincott Company, Philadelphia, 1947.

Gardner, Ernest: *Fundamentals of Neurology,* W. B. Saunders Company, Philadelphia, 1948.

Gellhorn, Ernst: *Physiological Foundations of Neurology and Psychiatry,* University of Minnesota Press, Minneapolis, Minn., 1953.

Mettler, Fred A.: *Neuroanatomy,* 2d ed., The C. V. Mosby Company, St. Louis, 1948.

Millbank Memorial Fund: *The Biology of Mental Health and Disease,* Paul B. Hoeber, Inc., New York, 1952. This is a report of a symposium held at the New York Academy of Medicine on Nov. 13–16, 1950.

Peele, Talmage Lee: *The Neuroanatomical Basis for Clinical Neurology,* McGraw-Hill Book Company, New York, 1954.

Saul, Leon J.: *Bases of Human Behavior,* J. B. Lippincott Company, Philadelphia, 1951.

Strong, Oliver S., and Adolph Elwyn: *Human Neuroanatomy,* 2d ed., The Williams & Wilkins Company, Baltimore, 1948.

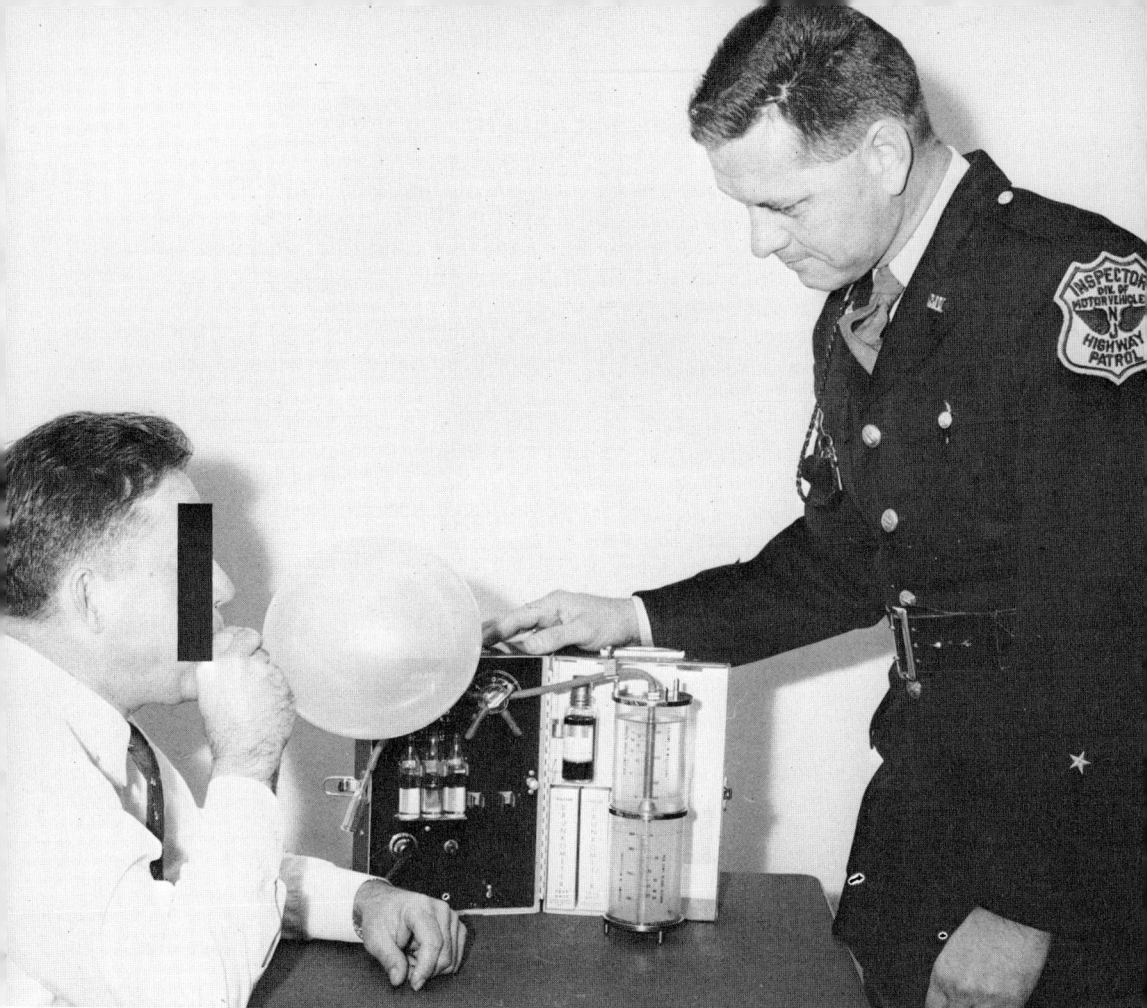

# Effects of Alcohol and Drugs[1]    5

THE SUBJECT of alcohol has long been treated in public education in a rather stereotyped manner that has been of doubtful effectiveness. Health

[1] *Editor's note.* This chapter was sent in draft form to Dr. Herman A. Heise, of Milwaukee, Wis., who was Chairman of the Committee on Medicolegal Problems of the American Medical Association from 1952 to 1962. Dr. Heise endorsed the content with the comment, "Excellent!" He also gave suggestions for additions which have been incorporated into the text. This behavior-oriented approach to treatment of the drinking-and-driving problem in driver education was introduced, with Dr. Heise's endorsement, in the student textbook, *Sportsmanlike Driving.* It has met with a great deal of highly favorable comment throughout the field.

The American Automobile Association acknowledges deep appreciation for Dr. Heise's invaluable assistance.

courses have usually included a unit on alcohol education. The customary approach featured two points of emphasis. The student was warned of the danger of becoming an alcoholic, and the condition of alcoholism was described. The other area of emphasis was the deleterious effects of alcohol on health, with particular stress on cirrhosis of the liver. Within the knowledge of the time, the material covered was appropriate. In the light of neurological data extant today, however, a major revision of the course content is indicated.

The weakness inherent in the traditional approach is the failure to achieve a *self-identification* on the part of the student. The boy or girl of sixteen is hardly likely to picture himself becoming an alcoholic. The possibility is too remote, separated from him by years and by the overindulgence that he knows precedes the condition of true alcoholism. To him, the alcoholic is the extreme, the town drunkard, the one out of many. The sixteen-year-old knows that the chance of his actually becoming a drunkard is small. Among the members of his class, he knows that there is small chance that any of them will become alcoholics. As to his liver—that's feeling fine. Health is not a problem to most teen-agers, and a person in his twenties is regarded as "old." If a teen-ager ever finds that alcohol is threatening to make him sick in that almost incomprehensible future when he's "older," he knows that he will just stop using it. Alcoholism and cirrhosis of the liver, the two traditional threats, are like accidents—they're things that happen to other people.

If teachers take a "moralistic" approach, saying that drinking is "wrong," many young people are unaffected because they see their parents and friends drink as a custom. Young people aren't going to accept a teacher's word that their parents are immoral. They are more likely to assume that the teacher is naïve and to have a lowered respect for his judgment.

When driver education entered the secondary school curriculum, it rekindled interest in alcohol education. Reliable studies had shown that one-third to one-half of all fatal motor vehicle accidents involved a drinking driver. One of the most recent studies based on autopsies showed a **57 percent** involvement. In a recent survey of hundreds of single-car accidents, which involved but one person responsible for the accident, it was found that *three out of four of the drivers had been drinking and that half of them were actually intoxicated.*

Recognizing the seriousness of the problem, many driver educators have assembled data and have taught their students about those effects of alcohol which seemed to be pertinent to driving. The main points were:

1. Alcohol impairs vision.
2. Alcohol impairs neuromuscular coordination.
3. Alcohol slows reaction time.
4. Alcohol is not a stimulant, as once believed. It is a depressant.

As far as it went, this approach was correct. The shortcoming was that the student, as well as the person who drinks and then drives, still had the following rationalization left: *He is sure that he will stop drinking just as soon as any effects are felt.* Many people believe sincerely that they "know their capacity" and merely have to stop drinking soon enough to be able to drive safely.

The common expression "drunken driver" has directed public thinking to a scapegoat and away from the statistically critical drinking-and-driving problem. The National Safety Council has stated that, "social drinkers are the big menace. Their critical judgment is impaired with a fairly low alcohol concentration. Car weavings of obvious drunks can be avoided. But the social drinker appears normal until his wits fail him in an emergency." The *social* drinker referred to is one who drinks moderately, without reaching the stage of observable impairment of his physical abilities.

This is not to discount the danger of the obviously drunken driver who should be recognized, apprehended, convicted, and removed from the highway. Such apprehension and conviction of the drunken driver are much more readily accomplished than for the social drinkers who drive. Of course, the main point of the comparison is the infinitely greater numbers of the latter on the road. Since the original driver education approach emphasized those effects which accompany a more advanced stage of drinking, it did little to affect the custom of social drinking before driving. Custom and a lack of understanding on the part of the public permit or even encourage this extremely dangerous practice.

## *A BEHAVIORAL APPROACH*

An emergent of the study[2] cited in Chapter 4, "Attitude and Behavior," indicates that teaching the true nature of the drinking-and-driving hazard is a necessity. A driver can hardly be expected to recognize and avoid a danger he doesn't even know exists.

Tested extensively in the high school situation was the ability of students to understand this comparatively new behavioral approach and its significance for them. This experience with high school students proved conclusively that they understood the significance of the behavioral approach. This approach was first published in the 4th edition of *Sportsmanlike Driving*, Chapter 5.[3] Before publication in 1961, a draft of this material was sent to Dr. Herman A. Heise, then chairman of the Committee on Medicolegal Problems of the American Medical Association. Dr. Heise approved and added some further data which were included in the chapter.

### *A Case in Point*

The basic principles of the behavioral approach can be illustrated by the story of a typical case.

Two businessmen have finished a day in their respective offices. One came to the city by train. The other drove to the office that day. They have met and are now sipping "a cocktail or two" at a hotel bar. They are not heavy drinkers and are highly intelligent individuals, accustomed to moder-

---

[2] Arthur L. Mahony, "Teaching for Attitude Conducive to Safe Driving," doctoral dissertation, New York University, New York, 1957.

[3] American Automobile Association, *Sportsmanlike Driving*, 4th ed., McGraw-Hill Book Company, New York, 1961.

ate social drinking. During the conversation, one says banteringly to the other, "You better not drink, you have to drive home." The other laughs and says, "I can finish these and still drive a good deal better than my two sons and my wife." Like most people, when he speaks of driving "better," he means more skillfully. This, of course, may be alcoholically inspired overconfidence. However, *the man may be absolutely right!* If he is normally a highly skilled, thoroughly experienced driver, his *skill* after one or two drinks may still be superior to that of members of his family who may have had hundreds of thousands of miles less driving experience. Yet one or two drinks can make him unfit to drive.

Why, then, is he the moderate, social drinker—a menace on the highway? Even if his judgment is only slightly impaired, is he less able to estimate the speed and distance of an approaching car than the other far less experienced drivers in his family? Is his driving skill at a dangerously low level? Perhaps, but not necessarily. Where, then, is the danger? Let us review some of the data in Chapter 4 on "Attitude and Behavior." Let us note certain specific neural pathways, indicated by arrows in Figure 5–1, which apply to this problem.

The "lower," "older" areas of the nervous system are more resistant to hostile chemical environment than the "higher," "newer" ones. Among possible hostile environments is the presence of alcohol in the bloodstream. When the blood-alcohol concentration is low, as it is after a person has just started to drink, only the *most* drug-sensitive areas, the higher centers, are affected.

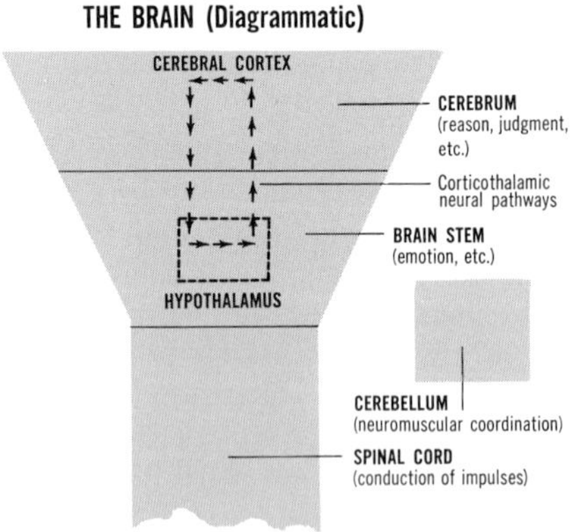

**THE BRAIN (Diagrammatic)**

CEREBRAL CORTEX

CEREBRUM (reason, judgment, etc.)

Corticothalamic neural pathways

BRAIN STEM (emotion, etc.)

HYPOTHALAMUS

CEREBELLUM (neuromuscular coordination)

SPINAL CORD (conduction of impulses)

FIGURE 5–1

Significantly, the cerebral cortex, the center of reason and judgment, is first to be impaired. *At this time, there is no appreciable effect in the brain stem to lessen emotional drives, and none in the cerebellum to impair coordination. Significantly, also, there are now no sensory neurons stimulated to give a warning "feeling" of effect.* The *time sequence* of this whole process is important to note.

Brain action, as we think of it, includes "cerebration"—a process of reasoning taking place in the cerebral cortex (the external, cell-body area of the cerebrum)—plus activity in the brain stem which affects the total brain function. The brain stem is not only a region of two-way transmission of nerve impulses between cerebrum and spinal cord, but it is also the center of such neural functions as emotion, as well as the cardiac, respiratory, and other "vegetative" controls.

The brain stem center of emotion (believed to be the hypothalamus) is linked in function with the cerebral cortex by nerve pathways we may call corticothalamic pathways ("cortico" for cerebral cortex, "thalamic" for hypothalamus). With this sensitive mechanism providing a complex interaction of cerebral and brain stem functions, both reason and emotion play their parts in total brain action and in consequent behavior.

The cerebrum, with the corticothalamic nerve pathways, normally exercises an *inhibitory* effect on brain stem (emotional) function. Because of this inhibitory effect, a person wouldn't normally give way to "blind," "unreasoning" anger. His reason warns him of the consequences.

*However, in the first (low blood-alcohol concentration) stage of drinking, the inhibitory function of the cerebral cortex and the corticothalamic pathways is impaired. These higher centers, more readily affected by alcohol and other drugs, are weakened in function. Emotion, centered in the (lower) brain stem, is as strong as ever.*

The following conditions are now present:

1. Impaired inhibitions
2. Unimpaired emotional drives
3. No sensation to warn of the condition

These describe the social-drinking driver. An emotional reaction toward another driver, perhaps sudden anger, meets with no strong inhibitory con-

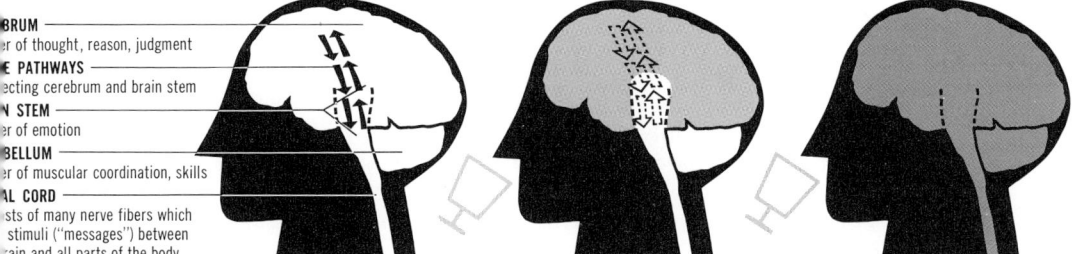

FIGURE 5–2 The basic behavior-affecting processes as progressively affected by increasing concentration of alcohol in the bloodstream. Center head: In the early stages of drinking, with a low blood-alcohol concentration, the "higher" centers of judgment and reason are impaired. Inhibitions are lessened or wiped out. Right head: With continued drinking, all parts of the nervous system are affected, impairing reaction time, skill, vision, etc. (Adapted from Figure 5–2, *Sportsmanlike Driving*, 5th edition.)

trol by the higher brain centers. The normally highly intelligent person responds to the emotional stimulus. Simply stated, normal inhibitions are gone. This is the "moderate," "social" degree of drinking.

Perhaps, under some circumstances where custom approves, social drinking may be acceptable and harmless. It should be remembered, however, that the destruction of normal inhibitions includes those which guard against phases of human behavior other than driving. The teacher of "alcohol education" should be equipped to present appropriate examples.

## An Advanced Case

A good example, which may also be used in driver education, is the young husband who leaves his job at five o'clock, planning to be home on time for the evening meal at six. Today he is a pedestrian. His way home passes the neighborhood tavern in which "some of the boys" are watching a game on television. He stops in "for a few minutes," having plenty of time before six o'clock. He buys a glass of beer and talks with the others while watching the game. They take turns at buying a few "rounds" of beer.

The game and the conversation are interesting (and appear more brilliant with each succeeding glass of beer). When he first came in, our friend had a strong inhibition against staying past six o'clock, because he did not want to arrive home late and hurt the feelings of his wife and family. Now, though his physical faculties, vision, balance, and coordination, are not yet affected, the inhibition against an unreasonable stay is pretty weak, not so important anymore, or possibly already gone from his mind. It is interesting to note that, *with each succeeding drink, the inhibition against further drinking is weakened.* Also, time sense weakens, and then practically disappears.

The result of the process is that—much later—the young husband finds himself at the bar with his friends, the game long over, and the tavern owner closing for the night. The intended six o'clock meal at home is many hours in the past. The young man didn't plan this. He didn't intend to hurt his wife and family. He merely took a drug, alcohol, and progressively lost his normal inhibitions. If the procedure were to be repeated frequently, the effect on the home would be obviously severe.

Recent investigations indicate that alcohol may have a marihuana-like effect by interfering with the ability to judge the passage of time.[4] Marihuana users, observing an object falling from a table, have had the impression that the object simply floated to the floor. Some musicians involved in "jam sessions" have discovered that marihuana allows them to crowd their drum beats and notes without effort and thus achieve "music" which races along. This phenomenon of incorrect judgment of the passage of time probably accounts for the fact that so many drinking drivers unconsciously drive at excessive speeds.

## Conclusions Drawn from Cited Cases

Perhaps if our friend's normal inhibitory neural patterns were stronger, more deeply seated in a more highly developed cerebral cortex structure, he might have had his intended "beer or two" and gone home. Many in his situation do. He, however, happens to have a nervous system so constructed, or so patterned, that he is one of those people of whom it is said, ". . . just can't drink."

---

[4] K. Joerger, "Das Erleben der Zeit und seine Veranderung durch Alkoholeinfluss: Eine Untersuchung uber den Arbeitscharakter von Schulern an Weinorten" (The experience of time and its change under the influence of alcohol: An investigation of the manner of working by school children in viticultural regions), *Exp. angew. Psychol.,* 7:126–161, 1960.

This case is offered for comparison with that of the businessman social-drinking driver. The social drinker stopped drinking at a point where his normal inhibitions were impaired, but it would take careful laboratory-type examination to detect any impairment of his vision, sense or balance, or general neuromuscular coordination or any lengthening of his reaction time. Yet, in point of potential driver behavior, he was a distinct hazard to anyone he might encounter on the road.

The young man, the advanced case, had progressed farther along the road to the state considered as drunkenness. By the time he left the tavern, his neuromuscular coordination was very poor. He either staggered or had some difficulty walking in a straight line. His reaction time would have been very much slower than normal. His ability to focus his vision was impaired, because of lack of neuromuscular control of his oculomotor muscles. He probably had the sensation of "double vision."

If this man had tried to drive, he would have been a danger to all others near him, as well as to himself. As a pedestrian in traffic in this condition, he is in danger. Oddly enough, although as a driver, he may have been more likely to have an accident than the social drinker, it is possible that he *may* have been less likely to have a fatal one. Some drinkers, *feeling* effects, drive with exaggerated caution, shunning the high speeds that often make accidents fatal. Sometimes, too, the man who leaves a tavern feeling the "physical" effects of alcohol will refuse to drive, either having a friend drive or calling a cab.

There are many possible variations of behavior while "under the influence of alcohol." That phrase is well worth remembering, since it is the legal description of the state of the drinking driver. The common expression "drunken driving" is misleading since it is not necessary to be "drunk" in order to be guilty of driving *under the influence of alcohol.*

## Sobriety Tests

Obviously the staggering drunk can be identified by his uncontrolled movements. Occasionally, police have found conviction of even *him* to be difficult, because of lack of objective standards of measurement. Eventually, chemical tests of breath, blood, or urine were devised to measure the concentration of alcohol in the blood.

In the most commonly used of these tests, a chemical analysis of the breath is made. There is a reliable relationship between the alcohol content of the breath and the alcohol content of the blood. The breath test has certain advantages, since a blood test which requires drawing a blood sample, for instance, should be done by a physician rather than a police officer. Of the three types of test, the breath test has proved to be the most acceptable. Standards of test readings are established.

The standards shown in Table 5-1 allow a considerable margin in favor of the driver. Studies indicate that there exists a measurable impairment of driving ability at a blood-alcohol concentration of 0.03 percent. How much lower than this may be the point of existing but immeasurable *behavioral* effect is not known.

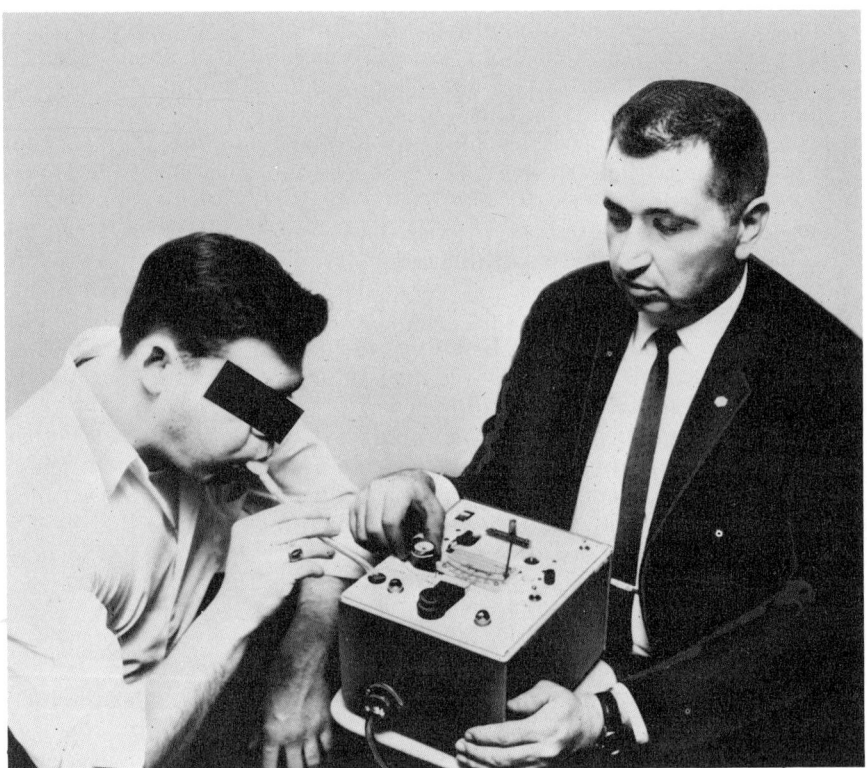

FIGURE 5-3 Running a breath test for alcohol with a Breathalyzer, one of the legally recognized testing devices. There is a reliable relationship of this analysis to alcohol in the blood.

Dr. Heise makes the following recommendation regarding teen-age drivers found to be drinking:

> Teen-agers have a particularly bad accident rate, due to inexperience and an inflated ego regarding their prowess. Alcohol further removes caution and adds to their chances of having an accident. The experienced driver has developed skills which make his driving almost automatic. He starts, steers, and stops without consciously being aware of his movements which control the car. An experienced driver can still manage to drive when paying no particular attention to his driving. Although he may be half asleep or even somewhat intoxicated, the almost automatic ability to drive, although impaired, may postpone his chance of having an accident.
> The young and inexperienced driver on the other hand, who has not as yet learned to drive automatically, is particularly susceptible to the effects of alcohol. Although there is apparently no tissue tolerance to alcohol, the novice drinker lacks experience in compensating for the effects of intoxication, and is therefore less able to cope with his handicap. His lack of experience in drinking and driving often end in disaster. It has therefore been recommended that youngsters be judged to be under the influence of alcohol when harboring

lower percentages of alcohol than those now accepted for similar impairment of adults.

Sobriety tests should be shown to be a *protection* for the driver. They help identify the dangerous drinking driver, making the highways safer for other highway users, and they guarantee against conviction of innocent persons who might mistakenly be believed to be legally "under the influence" of alcohol. Also, tests are usually used in addition to other testimony, and then only when some visible sign of alcohol effect seems evident. In any case, the breath test if negative, can offset all other, less objective evidence.

From the standpoint of the urgent need to remove the drinking driver from the highway, a rather peculiar phenomenon should be recognized. The shock of an accident or the emotional reaction of being confronted by the police when driving after drinking may temporarily overcome the symptoms of alcohol effect. It might be called a "sobering effect," although its temporary nature makes it very dangerous. A physical examination, general observation, or having such a person walk a chalk line may not truly indicate his condition. He may, for the moment, be able to answer questions fully and clearly. This "recovery" is but temporary, however, and when the cause of the situation terminates, he will relapse into his previous state. Obviously, allowing a person in such condition to proceed at the wheel of a car is to be avoided. Identification of the condition by chemical test does prevent the danger of such error.

## "Implied-consent" Provisions of Chemical Test Laws

Chemical test laws in some states have "implied-consent" provisions, which specify that any person who operates a motor vehicle upon a highway gives his consent to a chemical test when requested to submit to such a test by an arresting officer after being charged with driving while intoxicated. Failure to submit to such a test may cause his driver's license to be sus-

Table 5-1. BLOOD-ALCOHOL CONCENTRATIONS. MEDICOLEGAL INTERPRETATIONS AS TO WHETHER PERSONS TESTED ARE "UNDER THE INFLUENCE" OF AN INTOXICANT

| *Alcohol concentrations in the blood* | *Medicolegal interpretation* |
|---|---|
| 0 to 0.05% | Not evidence of being "under the influence" of an intoxicant |
| 0.05 to 0.10% | Inadequate evidence requiring further support. Possibly "under the influence" |
| 0.10% or more | Presumed to be "under the influence" |

SOURCE: Standards recognized by the American Medical Association, the American Bar Association, the National Safety Council, and other organizations. Also found in the Uniform Vehicle Code, chap. 11, sec. 11-902.

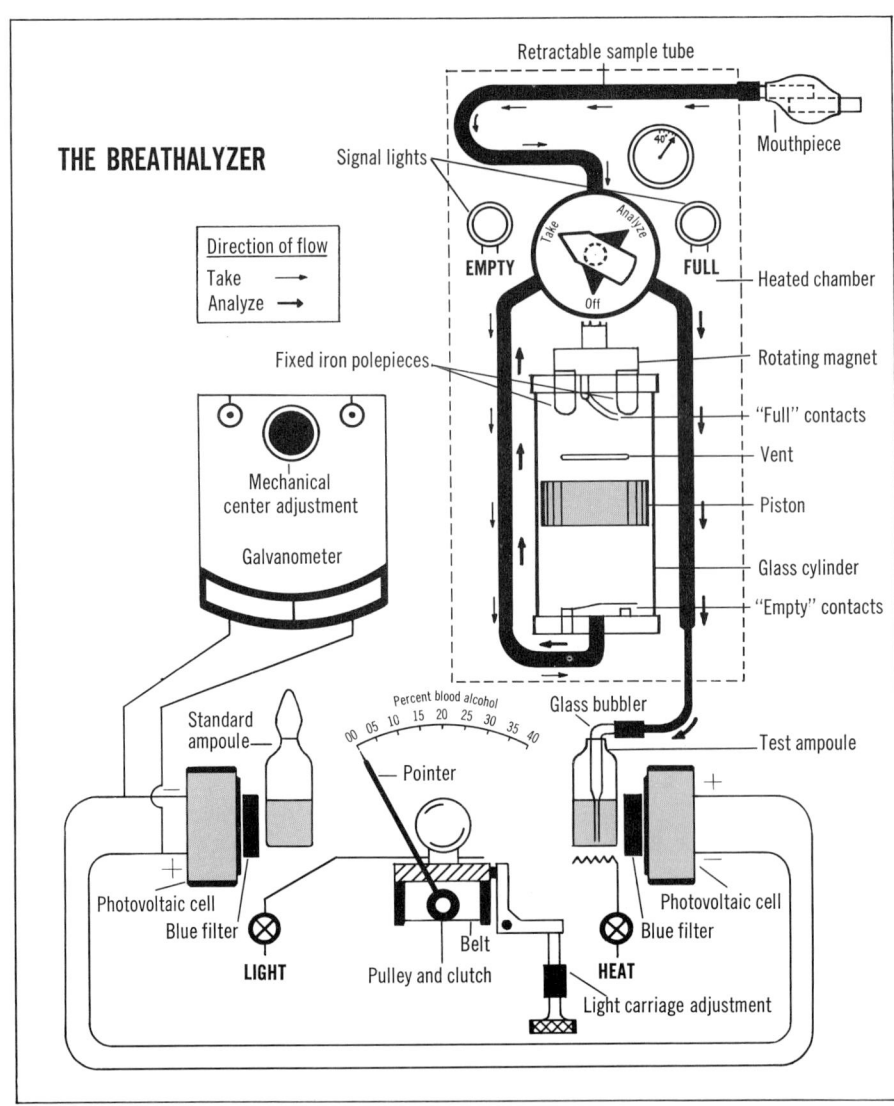

FIGURE 5-4 A schematic drawing of the Breathalyzer showing the flow of breath and the interaction of the instrument resulting in the calibrated reading of blood-alcohol content.

pended or revoked, regardless of any court action finding him innocent of the charge.

As of January, 1965, there were thirteen states whose chemical test laws contain an implied-consent provision. These states and the dates of enactment are: New York (1953), Idaho (1955), Kansas (1955), Utah (1957), Nebraska (1959), North Dakota (1959), South Dakota (1959), Vermont (1959), Minnesota (1961), Virginia (1962), Connecticut (1963), Iowa (1963), and North Carolina (1963).

The Uniform Vehicle Code, Section 6-205.1 entitled "Revocation of License in Event of Refusal to Submit to Chemical Tests," includes an implied-consent provision as described above. This particular section of the Uniform Vehicle Code was included in 1962.

## Some Common Questions

Teachers are often asked very specific questions on the subject of drinking. Probably the most common question is, "How many drinks will . . . ?" An answer giving a definite number is, of course, impossible. There are too many possible variables. Some of them are:

1. The time of the last meal and the amount of food eaten.
2. The degree of tolerance for alcohol of the individual.
3. The condition of the individual at the time.
4. The time period during which the drinks were consumed.
5. The weight of the person is a factor, since the percentage of alcohol in the body fluids varies—with a definite amount of intake—in inverse proportion to the total amount of body fluid. This does not mean that a heavy person is always less affected than a light person. There are too many other variables. Weight is but one.
6. The amount of alcohol eliminated from the system during the period of drinking, chiefly with body fluids. Oxidation of alcohol according to the metabolic rate of the body (believed by some to be increased by physical activity) is probably a factor also.

The answer is partly given in the above six items. No specific number of drinks or ounces of alcohol can be given. *The degree of effect, or "influ-*

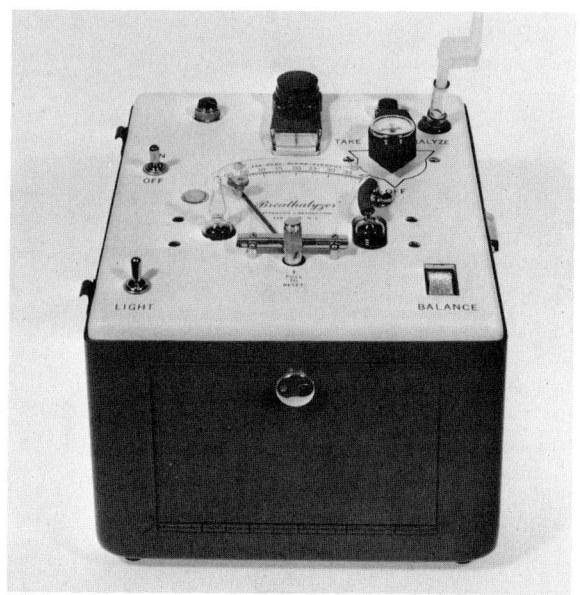

FIGURE 5-5 The Breathalyzer is used for analysis of blood alcohol by breath tests. In the field of measuring blood alcohol this portable instrument gives a direct reading on a calibrated dial by means of photoelectric cells which indicate the amount of color change caused by a person's breath as it passes through a tiny ampule of yellow potassium dichromate. Some other instruments used for the same purpose include the Drunkometer and the Intoximeter.

ence," *depends upon the concentration of alcohol in the brain.* This is measurable by determining the percentage of alcohol in the bloodstream, preferably by means of the breath test.

If the original question is rephrased to ask not how many drinks make a person "drunk," or how many he "can take," but how many will have an effect, an "influence," the answer must be "one," the first, no matter how small. The belief of building a tissue "tolerance" for alcohol is contraindicated by fact. The experienced drinker may have learned to act in such a way as to *conceal* his condition far better than the novice drinker.

The highly skilled, well-experienced driver actually *may*, even though "under the influence" to a degree, demonstrate a greater driving skill than the perfectly sober beginner. He may well know this, and it may result in his having a contempt for statements he hears and reads about drinking and driving, at least as they might apply to him. (This was illustrated in the case of the two businessmen.) He knows but part of the story, however. The fact is, of course, that his behavioral inhibitions *are* affected and that *he is driving at less than his best,* even in the matter of skill.

Regardless of experience with drinking, of ability to conceal effects, or of acquired skill, the concentration of alcohol in the arterial blood—as measured by chemical test—does determine the degree of alcohol effect.

## Dilemma of Law

In most states, taverns are located along the highways. They are legitimate businesses, licensed to sell alcoholic beverages. The conflict of law lies in the fact that every person who drinks *and then drives* is, to some degree, "under the influence." Even those whose blood-alcohol concentration is lower than the state-determined standard for being considered legally under the influence, are to some degree affected in the matter of impaired inhibitions. Again, one of the inhibitions so impaired is that against further drinking. Some people, like the young man, in our second example, are very susceptible to this effect.

It is not the purpose of this chapter to resolve this predicament. The teacher should recognize all phases of the problem and be ready to help his students to develop a pattern of thinking on the subject which will best safeguard them in the future. Concealing the difficult-to-explain aspects of the problem is not a solution. Neither is relegating it to a perfunctory and, by now, obviously ineffective process of heaping all the blame on the obviously drunken driver, who suffers from severe impairment of vision, neuromuscular coordination, speed of reaction, and something vaguely referred to as "judgment."

The new approach will not be perfectly effective in solving the problem. Custom is very strong in its generation. At the very least, teachers will have the clear, professional conscience of having told their charges the truth according to the best of today's available scientific data. At best, we may be facing a new era in alcohol education in our field. Although the data on effects are not very new, the *behavioral* approach to the problem still needs more widespread teaching, both in schools and in public information programs. Drinking and driving is still very much with us, and still not generally understood.

## DRUGS!

The common connotation of the word "drugs" brings up visions of addicts and "pushers" and stories of undercover enforcement work. There is no intent here to minimize the seriousness of that problem. The addict may be a driver, too, and therefore a subject for study in traffic safety education. However, just as in the case of the drunken driver, there is no numerical justification for concentrating study on the drug addict. The main problem lies with many thousands of people who drive while under the influence of drugs which they generally look upon as medicinal. Purchase of some of these drugs requires a doctor's prescription. Others may be purchased without a prescription, often under trade names.

The Food and Drug Administration of the U.S. Department of Health, Education and Welfare, in FDA Publication 15, lists the following drugs as potentially dangerous to drivers unless used with the advice of a doctor (who should be told of the patient's intention to drive, when the advice is sought): amphetamines (also called "bennies," "pep pills," "thrill pills," "goof balls," and "co-pilots"), barbiturates and other sedatives, tranquilizers, antihistamines, and narcotics.

The nature of the effects is usually specific to the drug taken. The users and potential users number many thousands. Each person does not always use the same type of drug. The drugs are frequently sold under trade names. In view of these variables, it would not be practical to expect the student to memorize the specific effects of each drug. Instead, the general principles which determine the effect of a driver using these drugs should be covered in the driver education course.

The following facts are important:

1. As in the case of alcohol, there is a tendency for dangerous effects to develop without any warning sensation being recognized by the user.
2. The loss of normal behavioral inhibitions is characteristic of drug use, because of the same greater susceptibility of the higher centers of the nervous system as in the case of alcohol.
3. Unrealized drowsiness, loss of coordination, hallucinations, tremors, total collapse, and even eventual addiction may be the result of using the common "driver's drugs." The dangers of these conditions when driving certainly are obvious.
4. Although some of the commonly used drugs may be legally purchased without prescription, others may not. Any person who considers purchasing drugs illegally should realize that the seller may be promoting so-called "harmless" drugs to encourage experimentation by the buyer, leading to possible future addiction. Anyone who thinks he could never be "hooked" should remember that most addicts felt this way at one time.

    Another point for the student to remember—and this might be a deterrent to the purchase by even an adventurous buyer—is this: Any person who would engage in the illegal sale of drugs wouldn't be above selling any substance as such, however contaminated or poisonous.
5. A good rule for the student to adopt is to consider drugs to be strictly in the province of the doctor. "Medicine" is the doctor's profession, and only he should prescribe. It would be well to advise students that even

when a doctor prescribes a drug, he should be consulted as to its effects on any subsequent driving.
6. The final and perhaps the most important point to be remembered is the principle of *synergy*. To the mathematician, the simple addition of 1 and 2 brings a sum total of 3. To the biologist, however, 1 plus 2 may bring $3x$. The combination of 1 and 2 may bring into being a quality which was not present in either. $3x$ may be very different from either 1 or 2, or the simple sum of 1 plus 2. In the chemistry class, the student learns that hydrogen combines with oxygen to form water. Although the first two are gases, the product is a liquid.

A person who is using one of the common drugs may at some time decide to take a drink or two. A drug or the drink may be an old story to him. For example, when he is taking a long trip in his car, he may buy an amphetamine "keep-awake" pill to avoid sleepiness when driving. He may be using an antihistamine for a cold. Although either drug alone could induce effects which might lead to an accident, he could innocently invite disaster by stopping for a glass of beer, wine, or liquor for refreshment, or even by having a cocktail or two before a meal, in addition to the drug.

*When the effects of a drug, even one which a person is accustomed to using, are combined with alcohol, the total effect is unpredictable.* It is not a case of simple addition. The results may be unbelievably severe. Perhaps the simplest allusion is to two chemicals, each an inert-appearing liquid. It is possible that, mixed together, they may produce a violent detonation. In the case of the drug and the drink, the effect would not be detonation but *synergism* which may be equally deadly in effect.

Dr. Heise warns of another phase of the drug hazard to drivers in the statement, "Not only are certain drugs and alcohol contraindicated for motorists, but the same drugs may present an even greater hazard when suddenly withdrawn. This hazard cannot be evaluated by chemical tests. The alcoholic deprived of his drinks may develop delirium tremens, the narcotic addict severe pains and mental confusion, and *it is now known that the sudden withdrawal of certain tranquilizers often causes convulsions.*"

Perhaps the best general theme to be presented to the student would be the simple one recommended by Dr. Heise: "If you're sick enough to require certain drugs, you're too sick to drive. Let your doctor make the decision. Self-medication may lead to disaster." He also warns of the constant threat of drug habituation by the use of *narcotics* for relief of sensations of pain, hunger, or fatigue.

In referring to *amphetamine*, Dr. Heise points out its value in prescriptions for the control of obesity by decreasing appetite. As a cerebral stimulant it relieves drowsiness and, prescribed by a physician, would find legitimate use in certain emergency situations, as for prolonged combat missions by military personnel. Unfortunately, though, the drug is illicitly sold to many people who use it to keep awake for long periods of time. One of the most common reasons for this practice is to permit continuous driving on extended trips, without rest or sleep. After a time, lacking the much-needed sleep, the driver performs with little realization of the traffic or other environment and lacks normal responses to external stimuli. He drives "in a daze." The danger is very obvious.

Antihistamines are very extensively used. They cause drowsiness, mental depression, and also depress the vestibular apparatus. They are used successfully today in the treatment of allergies. The patient should beware, however, of their synergistic tendency in combination with alcohol, especially if he intends to drive.

While speaking of drugs, Dr. Heise mentioned a subtle hazard of carbon monoxide (CO). The obvious source of this poisonous, colorless, odorless gas in a motor vehicle would be a leak in the exhaust system. Other cases of asphyxiation have occurred when cars were stuck in snow drifts. The less obvious hazard is excessive *smoking*. Cigarette smoke contains carbon monoxide. While asphyxiation is not the danger here, deterioration of vision, especially night vision may occur. Blood pressure is affected by carbon monoxide inhaled in smoking, and of course the union of carbon monoxide with hemoglobin to the comparative exclusion of oxygen occurs whenever carbon monoxide is inhaled. This condition is not relieved in a short period of time by merely opening the car window.

Dr. Heise tells of an incident in which he experienced the effects of asphyxiation. Trying for an underwater swimming record, he resisted the normal desire to surface and relieve the distress which accompanies the lack of oxygen until—at some point—he was quite surprised at his renewed ability to think clearly and to finish the swim with powerful strokes right up to the edge of the pool. This feat, he recalled, was followed by simply stepping up effortlessly on the pool edge without the usual process of climbing up out of the water. When he recovered, after a period of breathing air freely, he learned that the delusion of great power was just that—a delusion resulting from partial asphyxiation. Two men had towed him to the pool edge and others had carried him ashore. The effortlessness was accounted for! And so was the mental state—by asphyxiation.

Partial asphyxiation of a driver from any source can be entirely unrealized by him and, like drinking, may simply result in a (confused) sense of power, well-being, and great ability. It may never warn him to stop and seek fresh air. This, too, is a case of drugging.

## *The Teacher*

From place to place, from group to group, and from generation to generation, customs differ in the use of alcohol. Once outlawed by constitutional amendment and today illegal in many places, alcoholic beverages are a significant social and economic factor in American life. Within a single community, school, church, or even family, people have different views on the subject of drinking. It is not a mission of driver and traffic safety education to alter those views. The one area in which the driver education teacher has a mission is to build an attitudinal block in the students against drinking and driving. Of course, the use of drugs falls into the same category in connection with driving.

Methods, materials, courses, and teaching aids are important; yet the key to success or failure is the *teacher*. His image in the eyes of students and community determines, to a great extent, how much of what he teaches will be accepted. In discussing certain phases of the life of the community, he will encounter some about which people are sensitive. These concern the mores which have an emotional association in people with religion, custom, politics, patriotism, and community pride.

Since drinking customs are often considered to be a moral issue and therefore a concern of religion, emotional involvement must be anticipated if controversial statements on the subject are made. Where this type of strong attitudinal bias exists, it is highly unlikely that the driver education teacher could change it in the short period of time he has available with students. Fortunately most of the religious teachings support the "don't drink and drive" theme, directly or indirectly.

Where religion or custom is concerned, the teacher should be careful not to become "labeled" in such a way that he loses the sympathetic ear of his students and of the community. Such loss would discount in their eyes the very things he is trying to teach. It is not necessary that he alienate the clergyman or the clubman, the prohibitionist or the drinker. He can stand on the one indisputable statement that *drinking and driving* do not mix. He has statistical proof and the clear statements of leading traffic safety authorities supporting him. He now has, also, well-documented evidence of exactly what happens that makes a person who is drinking unfit to drive. He presents the evidence not as a matter of opinion, custom, or morals, just as facts—supported by historical and scientific data—and he refers to drinking and driving, and to drugs and driving.

In the neurologically based behavioral approach the following facts are considered: We live in the day of publicized science. From the objective standpoint of the scientist, by means of this approach data have been isolated and interpreted and supportable conclusions have been reached. From the viewpoint of the community, acceptance of this approach is keeping pace with the times. From the frame of reference of the teacher, with this approach thoroughly sound, tested principles can be applied in his leadership mission, advocating the *truth* to "set men free" from a destructive and dangerous custom—*drinking and driving.*

### SELECTED BIBLIOGRAPHY

Donigan, Robert L.: in *Chemical Tests and the Law,* Edward C. Fisher (ed.), Traffic Institute, Northwestern University, Evanston, Ill., 1957, 257 pp.

Mrs. John H. Sheppard Foundation, financed studies, New York:
   *Attitudes of High School Students toward Alcoholic Beverages,* Kansas University, Sociology and Anthropology Department, Lawrence, Kan., 1956, 146 pp.
   *Attitudes of High School Students toward Alcoholic Beverages,* University of Wisconsin, Bureau of Economics, Sociology and Anthropology, Madison, Wis., 1956, 87 pp.
   *Study of High School Drinking in Nassau County, A,* Hofstra College, Research Bureau, New York, 1954.

*Narcotics and Drug Addiction,* Mental Health Monogram no. 2, U.S. Department of Health, Education and Welfare, Washington, D.C., 1963, 22 pp.

*Test Your A. Q. (Alcohol Quotient),* 20 Questions on Alcohol, American Medical Association, Committee on Medicolegal Problems, Chicago, 4 pp.

# Impairment of Driving Ability 6

MOTOR VEHICLE authorities, traffic safety specialists, and research personnel are seeking all available data on the highly complex subject of driver capability. Specifically sought is well-documented information on the atypical conditions which result in impairment of driving ability.

We may assume that the normal individual of appropriate age who is free of definable impairments is capable, with proper instruction and practice, of driving an automobile safely. The task of defining such impairments and of providing a means of detecting them in the individual driver, or applicant for a license, is recognized today as vital. Perhaps the most significant advance in the accomplishment of this task has been an increasing enlistment of the services of the medical profession in an advisory capacity in connection with the problem of what to do about the impairments.

## MEDICAL ASPECTS OF DRIVER SAFETY

There are many conditions which impair driving ability, and in general, they are mainly conditions best understood by the medical profession. The logical course of action here is also the obvious one. Motor vehicle authorities who are responsible for prescribing standards for driver licensing must rely on the cooperation of medical personnel in this important area.

One of the ways of implementing this cooperative concept is the establishment of *medical advisory boards or committees*. These boards provide the professional medical knowledge, while all the administrative decisions and promulgation of regulations remain the responsibility of the motor vehicle authorities. Boards have operated in some jurisdictions, but no definite pattern or plan is used in their organization. Consequently, there are varying degrees of effectiveness in the functioning of the boards to date. The principle of utilizing medical advisory boards is important. It has received considerable attention, and it is to be hoped that further progress will be made in the not-too-distant future.

There has been considerable uncertainty throughout the field of motor vehicle administration in the matter of how to handle the problem of the medical factors related to driving ability. A definite step forward was taken in November, 1964. A National Conference on Medical Aspects of Driver Safety and Driver Licensing was held in Chicago, involving representatives of motor vehicle administration, traffic safety specialists, and a very encouraging representation of the medical profession. Not only were general, organizational, and procedural matters discussed and recommendations made, but specific pathological conditions were described and studied in relation to their effect on the ability to drive. This meeting formed a milestone in unification of our resources by *greater involvement of a pertinent "outside" discipline in the official traffic safety function of government*. It is to be hoped that the medical profession will play an ever-increasing role in cooperation with the agencies, public and private, which are devoted to accident prevention.

A previous milestone was a Committee of the American Medical Association on Medical Aspects of Automobile Injuries and Deaths, which published a booklet, *Medical Guide for Physicians in Determining Fitness to Drive a Motor Vehicle*,[1] referred to later in this chapter.

### A Reporting System

One of the stumbling blocks to application of the knowledge of the medical aspects of driver safety is the difficulty of identification by licensing authorities of drivers whose impairments make them unfit to drive. It would be unrealistic to expect that all persons whose driving ability has become impaired would recognize the condition and its implications for driving and then would report themselves for revocation of licenses.

There is no pat answer to this problem. An equitable solution which will best safeguard the public is needed. Apparently some kind of reporting

---

[1] *Medical Guide for Physicians in Determining Fitness to Drive a Motor Vehicle*, AMA Committee on Medical Aspects of Automobile Injuries and Deaths, 1959.

FIGURE 6-1 Standards for fitness to drive commercial vehicles have been recommended and are widely used.

system is needed, but details have yet to be determined. Both the medical profession and the licensing authorities are considering questions like these:

Suppose a physician recognizes a disability in a patient which he knows dangerously impairs that patient's ability to drive. What is his responsibility? Obviously he should warn the patient, but should he go further? Suppose he is doubtful of the patient's willingness to stop driving. Should he report the case to the licensing authority? What about the traditional, confidential doctor-patient relationship? Also, is the licensing authority geared to handle such cases? What about follow-up communication in cases of temporary disabilities? Should there be legislation requiring physicians to report such cases? Would enactment of such legislation condemn physicians as "irresponsible" and *would it tend to cause ill people to avoid going to a physician, for fear of losing their driving privilege?* If so, it might result in irreparable harm to them and also keep them on the road *without the benefit of medical care.*

These are a few of the problems that must be solved. They aren't simple. Conferences alone, though they can be very valuable, will not solve them. Probably the best hope is the meeting of the best-informed minds on national level as often as needed, plus organization of permanent medical advisory boards or committees, probably at state level. The latter should be recognized by licensing authorities and by state legislators as expert consultants in the matter of driver impairment.

## *PHYSICAL EXAMINATIONS*

One of the "universal cure-alls" that is occasionally advanced for solution of the driver impairment problem is to require all drivers to undergo physical examinations. The recommendations range from "vision checks" every five years to "complete physicals" every year. The usual pattern is, the more "complete" the recommendation, the less background in anatomy, physiology, and pathology is possessed by the advocate.

Like so many panaceas, the physical examination for drivers (young or old) does not stand up well under analysis. Its proponents cite a number of pathological conditions which they say might cause serious accidents. The theory is that those who have these conditions should be legally barred from driving. Usually the same very few conditions are continually stressed by well-meaning but uninformed individuals, probably because they represent the extent of the problem within the thinking of those individuals.

One difficulty is that diagnosis is not certain, and prognosis even in the very conditions so often cited is usually impossible on the basis of the routine examination. The epileptic who is so often mentioned may be identified by an electroencephalogram when a seizure is imminent, or may appear completely normal during a hundred routine medical examinations. A poll of licensing agencies found that, among some jurisdictions, eligibility for licensing of individuals suffering from epilepsy *varied from six months to three years* following the last known seizure.[2] Obviously more knowledge of the subject by those responsible for policies is needed. The oft-cited cardiac seizure may occur while driving home from a routine physical examination that gave no warning of it. The diabetic whom some want to bar from driving may be under the care of a physician who knows he is a better risk as a driver than many of his critics who may not recognize their own truly hazardous personal characteristics.

A Committee on Medical Aspects of Automobile Injuries and Deaths of the American Medical Association published the aforementioned booklet, *Medical Guide for Physicians in Determining Fitness to Drive a Motor Vehicle*.[3] Just reading this publication makes it quite obvious that routine physical examinations of all drivers and potential drivers would not be the panacea some believe it would be. For instance, in the matter of cardiovascular (heart and blood vessels) disease alone, the following procedures are recommended:

> The examination of the cardiovascular system in determining a patient's ability to drive a private, commercial, or passenger transport vehicle should consist of a complete cardiac history and physical examination. The history should establish presence or absence of edema, orthopnea, cyanosis, dyspnea, and substernal or precordial pain. Also, a *history* of rheumatic fever, congenital deformities, thyroid disease, syphilis, hypertension, and anemia should be sought.
>
> In order that the cardiovascular system be properly evaluated, the entire body must be examined, including the fundi, lungs, abdomen, and extremities. The physical examination, including palpation, percussion, and auscultation of the heart, should determine if venous congestion, cardiac enlargement, or valvular disease is present. The heart rate, rhythm, and level of blood pressure should also be ascertained.

[2] *Medical Advisory Committees,* an address by John K. Kerrick, presented at the National Conference on Medical Aspects of Driver Safety and Driver Licensing, Chicago, November, 1964.
[3] *Op. cit.*

Urinalysis, blood count, sedimentation rate, and serologic tests for syphilis should be done. Cardiac fluoroscopy, chest x-ray, and an electrocardiogram complete the examination of the cardiovascular system. In evaluating the cardiac status of an individual, it is important to ascertain the presence of cardiovascular disease and then its status according to cause, anatomic defects, physiological abnormalities, and functional capacity.

The lack of conclusive statistical data concerning the role of each cardiac condition as a potential driving hazard is recognized. However, on the basis of knowledge of pathological physiology and the clinical course of these cardiac conditions, it is believed that a medical opinion can be formulated as to the potential driving hazard.

From this it can be seen that examination procedures even when the nature of the pathologic condition is known or suspected are not a matter of a "quick checkup."

The neurological, emotional, and psychiatric disorders present some infinitely more difficult problems of diagnosis and prognosis. Also such stated criteria as the epileptic patient's not having received medication and having been seizure-free for a stated period are known if the doctor has treated the patient for that period of time. Obtaining the history of that patient, or the cardiac patient, or another in a routine license physical examination when the person wants to drive is possible only with the completely honest person. The history of the neurological, emotional, or psychiatric (or possibly other) condition has the same chance of discovery there as in the case of having it in question form on a license application, possibly with a medical certificate required when the answers are affirmative.

The point is that the physician who treats a patient for any condition which may make driving hazardous may be in a position to act for the public good as well as for that of his patient. The medical profession can be an effective force for improvement of highway safety. The matter of thinking of patients as drivers when prescribing medication is, in itself, very important. However, the routinizing of 100 million general physical examinations is an entirely different matter.

Also, since a state of health isn't guaranteed to be constant, and since many, many thousands of people become ill each year, how often would such examinations have to be given to be effective? Once or twice a year? As many as 100 million or 200 million "complete" physical examinations per year? Give them to all older drivers? To what purpose, when the disabling pathologic changes are present at all ages? We can trust the medical profession to do what is necessary without bogging it down with one-hundred-odd million "examinations" of people who are in good health, and of others with pertinent pathologic conditions which would remain unrecognized because of the limitations of the routine medical examination.

Then, the very bad effect of a program of physical examination for all drivers, aside from its ineffectiveness for safety, is what it would do to the medical services of the nation. Any person who has sat in the waiting room of a doctor's office for two, three, or even more hours, awaiting his turn, can well appreciate that effect! Accurate projection of the number of drivers in the United States in the future is, of course, impossible. Users of this edition of this book may be speaking of "our 110 million drivers," and perhaps 120 million. Now, add *110 million* callers in the offices of the general practitioners, the "family doctors," each to obtain a clean bill of health as a result of a complete physical examination (note the preceding quotation from the American Medical Association) for a driver's license, and what is to happen to the *sick* people who urgently need the services of those doctors?

What very busy, conscientious doctor would deprive his sick patients of his services to examine healthy people *for conditions he knows he probably can't in the examination period identify as hazards in driving?* (A comparative few he may.) No doubt some doctors would try to squeeze in a few extra office calls just to help their patients to obtain licenses—but 110 million! Highway safety would have little or nothing to gain. The health of the nation would have much to lose.

## *AMA Statement*

The following is the conclusion of the American Medical Association on the subject of requiring a medical examination for obtaining a driver's license:[4]

> . . . to give medical examinations initially and periodically to 91,000,000[5] drivers for the purpose of licensing to operate a motor vehicle is to use medical manpower with less than optimum effectiveness. No scientific data are available to indicate that drivers with any particular disease, including diabetes, epilepsy, color blindness, cardiovascular disease, or deafness, have higher accident rates than comparable groups not having the condition. The identification of persons with certain diseases is of little value in preventing accidents.

The statement is clear and represents the thinking of the group best informed on the subject.

## *"Do Something"*

The public should be made aware of the dangers of poorly considered "cures" for traffic problems. Periodically, individuals and groups "discover" some procedure which, they believe, would contribute greatly to traffic safety. Usually the procedures are ones that have been long known to traffic experts and were discarded as impractical or useless. Often they comprise additional requirements for drivers' licenses, imposing unwarranted burdens on motorists and on official agencies and costing money which, if available, could be used to far greater advantage in another manner.

Any organization wishing to help to improve highway safety should first seek professional advice from those reputable institutions and agencies which exist specifically in the field of highway use and safety and from the medical profession if their intended suggestions involve medical matters.

[4] Abraham J. Mirkin, M.D., Chairman, AMA Committee on Medical Aspects of Automotive Safety, *Medical Factors Related to Driving Ability*, presented at the National Conference on Medical Aspects of Driver Safety and Driver Licensing, Chicago, Nov. 16, 1964.

[5] Number of motorists estimated at time of statement.

"Remove older drivers from the road," "Don't license anyone under twenty-one," "Make the license examination 'tough,'" "Triple the traffic tickets," "Give all drivers physical examinations," "Reexamine all drivers every year (or two, or three)"—all have the same implications as the popular saying, "Don't just stand there, do push-ups." The latter have a certain value, but it is known by traffic safety experts that it is not indicated by known data that such are appropriate to the problem of traffic accidents.

## THE "TEACHER COMPETENCY"

In this area of impairment of driving ability, what should the teacher of driver and safety education know? The standard textbook coverage of the subject is usually quite comprehensive, especially in matters of vision, hearing, fatigue, and the most frequently mentioned pathologic conditions. Should he go on to study ophthalmology, optometry, etc., to be better prepared to teach? This is not indicated by the *need of the student* who will be the citizen driver of tomorrow. The latter will be better informed as a driver and as a citizen if he first learns the basic details covered in most high school textbooks, then beyond that fairly obvious content, learns what medicolegal machinery should be set up to control the licensing of impaired drivers in a manner most fair to the public and to the individuals concerned. This is a matter of informed citizenship.

With this and the specific subjects found in high school textbooks, there is one more logical area for preparation of the driver citizen to be, and consequently appropriate as part of this "teacher competency." This is an understanding of some general principles that apply to many impairments, including even the common visual and hearing defects.

### Vision and the License

Most people recognize the handicap to driving ability that may be imposed by defective vision. Licensing authorities have long been aware of this factor and have been administering vision tests in examining applicants for drivers' licenses. Whether or not today's testing procedures are the most appropriate possible for *driving* vision is a subject for more research. It may be that qualities of vision which are specific to the driving situation require different examination procedures from the simple visual acuity test usually given. Vision tests for driver licenses may take on entirely new dimensions in the future. For one thing, it may be that the very significant characteristics of *night vision* may require some new testing techniques.

One practically universal characteristic of vision is that it deteriorates with age. This imposes a dual responsibility on the licensing authority. The aging process does not group all people into a chronological age stratification (see Chapter 7, "Aging and Driving"). All changes associated with the aging process are characteristic of the individual, in the matter of degree at any given age. Expressed from the standpoint of the licensing authority, the point of efficiency of vision at which a person is capable of driving is passed retrogressively at different chronological ages in different individuals. The

FIGURE 6-2 Driving a moving vehicle requires special skills in perceiving all the necessary environmental factors.

problem is to require *correction* of driver disabling conditions of vision (or *disqualification*) and yet to impose the minimum penalty and inconvenience on all concerned. There is no conflict of principle or of objectives, but a soundly based determination of *method* is needed. Here, there may be a need for some kind of reexamination procedure. This does not conflict in any way with the statement of the American Medical Association in reference to physical examinations of drivers.

Two kinds of study are needed here. The first must determine just what constitutes the best testing procedures to evaluate *vision for driving*. The other should determine whether or not this test should be given periodically, and when, in addition to the original licensing examination. Vitally needed here too is involvement of *appropriate professional investigators to perform the research*. Like medical examination, this cannot properly be done by administrative decree or by legislation, nor can it be based on research by investigators from fields unrelated to the problem—*vision*. Motor vehicle administrators, legislators, and private citizens should be aware of these two needs.

*For the student*, perhaps the point which is most significant to appreciation of the vision problem, as in the "aging and driving" problem in general, is so simple that it is rarely stated, and certainly not realized among most young people. The problem of visual impairment in aging is not a concern of a particular "age group." The latter is merely a term of convenience, one which sometimes biases the thinking of many people and clouds their understanding of some public problems. This is a *total population* matter of serious concern to all who drive or use the public thoroughfares. Perhaps the student will have more interest, as will the young citizen-driver-voter, if he is told, "This will be *your* personal problem unless you die prematurely, *very* prematurely." This is a milestone that will be encountered by *all* drivers.

## ADJUSTMENT, TENDENCY TO COMPENSATE

A man with one eye may drive a car safely. His depth perception will not be so good, at least at some distances, as if he had two eyes. He can, however, learn to adjust, or compensate, for the condition. He learns to move his head to overcome the "tunneling" effect of having but one eye. Most people can appreciate this fact. However, suppose a driver develops a condition in one eye which calls for bandaging or a patch over the eye. It seems quite logical that he should be able to drive just as safely as a person who, perhaps, was born blind in one eye. This is not so, and he should be warned. He has not *learned to compensate* for the loss. His driving can be dangerous. Had he had but one eye functioning over a long period of time, he would have tended to develop compensating habits of performance. Because of his sudden dependence on one eye, he lacks this protective skill.

Similarly, deaf drivers have no worse driving records than others. Yet a person whose hearing is temporarily impaired (even by the sound of a loudly played car radio) may have trouble because the sound cues he has relied on are no longer present. Of course, good drivers do not *rely* on sound to warn of possible hazards. It's too easy to miss a sound, especially when a noisy vehicle is passing. However, most experienced drivers know that sound does give warning at times. Occasionally the approach of an overtaking vehicle in a "blind spot" becomes noticeable when its engine or tire

FIGURE 6–3 Night driving presents special problems not considered in customary daylight vision testing.

noise becomes audible. Yet a person who is totally deaf can be an efficient, safe driver.

A seldom-cited natural compensation possessed by the deaf driver is lack of sound distractions (like the car radio) and complete avoidance of dependence upon sound warnings such as the horns of other vehicles. Too, he is less subject to "highway hypnosis" which seems to be aided by continuous sound. Reports from Colorado, Kentucky, Oregon, Wisconsin, Virginia, Pennsylvania, Michigan, and New Jersey[6] have indicated better driving records of persons with deafness or defective hearing as compared with those with normal hearing.

The principle we identify here is that *the danger which exists in temporary sensory impairments may be inherent in their temporary or recent nature*. An acquired compensation may in time overcome the hazardous qualities of the impairing condition, but that compensation may be missing in the case of the driver who has not yet become experienced with the condition.

The principle of acquired compensation for impairments of driving ability should be considered in two ways. Persons with *recently acquired impairments* should be *warned* of the fact that they lack the compensating, or adjusting, ability of those who have had the same impairments over a significant period of time. The other implication is that this ability negates any unnecessary, broad disqualification of groups of people. At the time of the National Symposium on the Deaf Driving and Employability, President John F. Kennedy wrote of "expansion and protection of the rights of these handicapped persons to drive motor vehicles as part of their normal social and business activities." This did not refer to the principle of right versus privilege of the individual, but implied a guarantee against any unnecessary discrimination penalizing a group of drivers. It is noteworthy that many amputees have perfect driving records and that there are some who drive successfully with only their arms or only their feet!

Driver improvement schools have been operated to train deaf persons and those with hearing defects in driving procedures designed to compensate for, or adjust to, the conditions of driving with their handicaps. A leading example is a class conducted by the Denver (Colorado) Driver Improvement School for deaf drivers. The school, directed by Judge Sherman G. Finesilver, is widely known throughout the country. Driver education has been taught successfully also in schools for the deaf.

Vision and hearing are two areas in which the principle of compensation or adjustment is well illustrated.

## A CONSTRUCTIVE VIEW

It is worthy of mention here that there exists a great deal of adverse criticism of current driver license testing techniques. The teacher should make it a point to avoid unjust criticism. It is true that present examinations are a long way from being perfect. Nevertheless, two factors are operating to limit progress in this field. One is the need for research-based

---

[6] *Traffic Safety,* National Safety Council, Chicago, Ill., August, 1961.

knowledge of just what should be included in the driver license examination. The other factor is the matter of public acceptance.

People will accept testing procedures which they realize are vital to highway safety. This is true in diminishing proportion as the examination time increases. As one motor vehicle administrator expressed it, "How much of an examination will the public stand for?" This may always be a limiting factor in the driver license examining procedure. It is worth remembering when driver license examinations are criticized for their incompleteness or their brevity.

## THE BROAD VIEW OF THE SUBJECT OF IMPAIRMENTS

The foregoing are some broad, general principles to be considered in covering the subject of driver impairments. Beyond the standard, specific textbook coverage of the subject, there is a need for understanding and supporting sound principles of organization and operation of the official forces which have the responsibility of administering this important phase of accident prevention. Needed also is an understanding of general principles which apply to impairments and which are not usually recognized in the traditional approach to identifying specific impairments only.

Just as the teacher needs the "competencies" implied in an appropriate knowledge of traffic engineering, enforcement, and other phases of traffic safety, he should be sure that he possesses an understanding of the *principles* and the *machinery* involved in official control of the temporarily, or permanently, impaired driver. This should be his direction for advanced study of the subject.

## SELECTED BIBLIOGRAPHY

Kerrick, John C.: *Medical Advisory Committees,* presented at the National Conference on Medical Aspects of Driver Safety and Driver Licensing, Chicago, Nov. 16, 1964.

Mirkin, Abraham J., M.D., Chairman, AMA Committee on Medical Aspects of Automobile Safety: *Medical Factors Related to Driving Ability,* presented at the National Conference on Medical Aspects of Driver Safety and Driver Licensing, Chicago, Nov. 16, 1964.

*Medical Guide for Physicians in Determining Fitness to Drive a Motor Vehicle,* AMA Committee on Medical Aspects of Automobile Injuries and Deaths, American Medical Association, Chicago, Ill., 1959.

*Traffic Safety,* National Safety Council, Chicago, Ill., August, 1961.

# Aging and Driving           7

THE LEADERSHIP influence of the driver education teacher among teen-agers is now generally recognized. Sometimes, however, people fail to recognize this influencing as a cumulative process. Yesterday's teen-agers are today's adult citizens. Many of them today reflect the beliefs the teacher expressed in past years. In addition to this, the teacher should be a source of immediate community knowledge in his field, becoming known through newspaper accounts of the program, talks to PTA's, service clubs, and other groups. It is a distinct benefit to the community, as well as a source of professional and personal satisfaction to himself, that he be well versed in all phases of traffic safety. Some of the questions asked by genuinely interested citizens are highly significant to the community and to his mission of driver and traffic safety education.

The extended "average" life-span and the increased focus on the activities and problems of older people make the effects of age on driving a subject of growing interest. The expert who sets the pattern of community thinking on this subject accepts a serious responsibility. The views he expresses should be sound and free of the popular misconceptions that tend to penalize unfairly many of our citizens. They should be based on fact and not on opinion.

## "OLD AND FEEBLE"

This old and well-worn expression has no validity as a basis for generalizations. Most people experience some deterioration of vision in their forties and fifties. Many driver education classes study the supposed advantage the teen-ager has in "fast reaction time" and emphasize the fact that it slows down with age. Stories are told of athletes who have passed their peak (usually quite early in life) and are suffering from old age.

The concept of "old age" is usually more of an individual's idea than a definite chronological, physiological, anatomical, or pathological state. To the teen-ager, to pass the twentieth birthday is to get old. In the twenties, people tend to look at those in their thirties as past their peak.

Unfortunately, while we are confronted with the greatest concentration of rival manpower in world history, we permit ignorance and uninformed opinion to discard much of our own manpower over the age of forty the moment that chance and local industrial change separate individuals from the jobs they happen to be holding at the time.

It has been said that "there is no substitute for experience." The individual *and the nation* have a very valuable investment in the years of experience of its middle-aged and older citizens. The greater the limiting and immobilizing handicaps we place on this segment of our population, the more we all lose as a nation, and the more unwarranted restrictions *each* will meet individually in the future.

### Your Ages, Not Your Age

The lack of understanding of man's aging, whether it concerns driving, athletics, or employment, is due largely to passive mind patterns on the subject. Popular expressions such as "you're getting old," popular concepts of age as feebleness and lack of vitality, symbolic concepts of the "old" appearance—wrinkled skin, white hair, bent-over posture, etc.—making the old person different—these all contribute to a popular mental picture. Alteration of this picture would require the acquisition of accurate data with subsequent thought on the subject—but neither the data nor the thought exist in the minds of most people. Therefore, popular beliefs about aging are far from accurate. Unfortunately, such *false* concepts are sometimes permitted to form public policies.

Before looking at the record of the older person in the highway picture, let us study that person and the characteristics that make him "old."

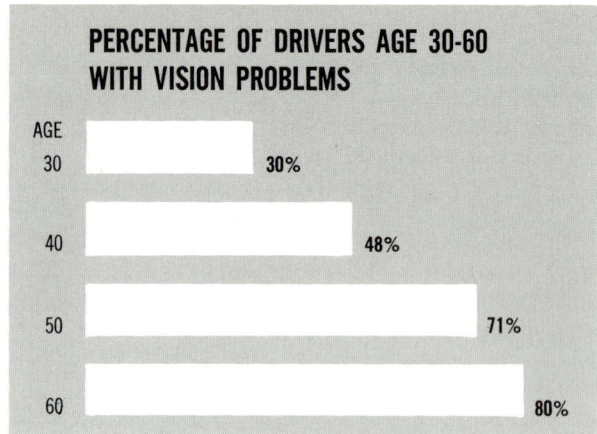

FIGURE 7-1 Vision is one characteristic in which a *trend* is discernible, but individual differences must be recognized. (Adapted from Figure 3-3, *Sportsmanlike Driving*, 5th edition.)

## *How Old Is He?*

A man drove his car to a curb and parked it. His passengers left the car. He told them he would follow shortly. He didn't "feel well." They returned some time later and found him dead. An autopsy showed that he had suffered a cerebral hemorrhage, the blood vessels in that area were sclerotic, brittle. He died a typical old-age death. The one odd note in this true story is this: He was just twenty-seven years old.

Is a man of twenty-seven an "old man?" No? Then how could he die a typical old-age death? He had no disease or injury. The blood vessels in his brain had just aged much more quickly than we consider normal.

By clock and by calendar, we measure time by the sun. Which was more significant in the case of this man, the number of times the earth had encircled the sun since he was born, or the condition his cerebral blood vessels had reached? Obviously the latter. We call the former—the number of years he has lived—his *chronological age*. The degree of deterioration of his body, commonly believed to parallel his chronological aging, is known as his *pathological age*. Pathologically, the twenty-seven-year-old man was extremely "old."

Physiologists have come to realize that the common standards of anatomy and physiology at various chronological ages, as almost universally accepted among our people, are extremely misleading.

The boy or girl who leaves high school or college for a sedentary position and engages in no further physical exercise soon becomes old physiologically. Strangely, people have passively accepted this rapid cardiovascular and muscular deterioration as an inevitable accompaniment of age. The man who sits all day and rides everywhere soon becomes incapable of strenuous—or even mild—activity. He stops all attempts to exercise because he thinks he is "too old." The fact is that in this matter most people have cause and effect reversed. They are unable to sustain activity not because they are "too old and feeble" (as some express it) in their thirties, forties, and fifties, but are old and feeble because they have ceased being active. The human body happens to be that way. People tend to generalize about all facets of aging on the basis of some rapid changes that are more correctly attributable to a degree of atrophy.

Men who have continued intense activity have remained superior athletes in their forties, fifties, and even sixties. This is a point well worth emphasizing to high school boys. Marathon runners, in the most demanding of man's physical activities, often "mature" around forty. Some have continued active in the sport in their *sixties*.

Whenever an advocate of discarding older drivers becomes unduly emphatic, an invitation for him to run 26 miles 385 yards (the Marathon distance) at a pace which most adults cannot sustain for 100 or 200 yards will give him a chance to prove his superiority over *all* old people. Some well-known professional athletes have admitted to being in their forties and fifties while still in championship competition.

## "Aging"—An Individual Characteristic

The point here is this. The *chronological age* of an individual does not tell his *pathological age*. The latter age is an *individual* characteristic. Activity plays a considerable part in the aging process. Heredity also is a factor. The aforementioned twenty-seven-year-old victim of cerebral hemorrhage was predestined to an early death by a characteristic carried to him in the genes that determined his heredity. It is worth mentioning to the uninformed that the genes don't carry warning signs by means of which a motor vehicle licensing authority can order revocation of licenses at an *individually* appropriate age—from the twenties to the nineties—and up!

The simple fact is that the number of times the earth has encircled the sun since a person was born does not tell:

1. His pathological age, including arteriosclerosis, etc.
2. His visual acuity
3. His night vision
4. His reaction time
5. Other aspects of his physical condition

It is never a certainty, but it is an indication that the more years he has lived, the more experience he has probably had. And the more experience he has had, the more opportunity to develop judgment. Judgment outweighs many other factors in driving.

## A CONCEPT FOR THE THOUGHTFUL

It is interesting to note that the "retrogressive" or "degenerative" processes that accompany chronological aging have never been established as a direct result of the passage of time. In other words, *we don't know that one's chronological age has any direct causal relationship to the physical and* (probably resultant) *mental changes that occur* as people get older in years.

The possibility is recognized that a cumulative effect of the pathologies the individual has experienced over the years may affect what we might call (for want of an accepted term) the "life force of the total organism." This effect may be the observable changes that accompany aging. It is even possible that varying pathogenic influences exist in our environment that affect us as individuals—influences which are not directly related to chronological time but which do have a cumulative effect, although they may not result in our (as yet) known, observable pathologies. One or more of such pathogenic factors may determine, for instance, the existence or the rate of increase of the sclerotic condition of blood vessels. These hypotheses do not necessarily deny the "lethal gene" concept, which is quite compatible with them.

In short, there are many things we do not know about the process of aging. Research is in progress. It is to be hoped that it will be possible to deal more intelligently with the problems of aging as more is understood about it. Meanwhile, a large segment of our population should not be penalized because of ignorance and unfounded opinion.

## IDENTIFYING THE PROBLEM

This is the first step in a logical approach. Sometimes, surprisingly, it serves to establish the fact that there is no problem. Sometimes it points to one which isn't nearly so serious or threatening as it had seemed when discussed in general terms over a period of time.

Tables 7–1 and 7–2 show a statistical picture. Statistical data are free of the prejudice that accompanies superficial opinion and guesswork. The picture is one of older drivers, including those seventy and over, the age group with the lowest accident involvement [Table 7–1, (2)].

It may be that the problem of aging drivers is the same as the problems of all drivers, and that the old person behind the wheel constitutes a visual symbol (see "Attitude and Behavior," Chapter 4) with facial features which identify his group, rather than a driver who should be subject to prejudicial restrictions.

The greatest need now in relation to older drivers, and older people in general, is research—and understanding. The next step in analysis is to interpret some additional facts pertinent to the subject.

The young and the old do not drive as many miles per year as do those in the middle ranges of the age scale. This might be a mitigating factor in favor of the driving record of the middle group as compared with young and old. On the other hand, it might be said that the amount of *exposure* in every case is an important factor in determining the seriousness of the problem. Another factor, seldom mentioned, is the hours of the day during which those in the various age categories drive. Crowded commuting hours and late-night high-fatigue hours are not characteristic of the driving of our older drivers. Another point sometimes cited is the fact that drivers in the seventy-five and over age group have a slightly higher fatality rate in accidents than those under twenty-four.

Considering that the total number of accidents involving these older drivers is so much lower, and that there is no evidence (or probability) that they drive faster (speed is a factor in the fatality rate among accidents), it appears that their resistance to, and recovery from, injury is lower. This is borne out by the fact that among pedestrians in the fifteen to twenty-four age group there is only one fatality among twenty-three injured, but in the

Table 7-1. ACCIDENTS AND VIOLATIONS

| Age group | (1) Drivers in fatal accidents, 1963* | | (2) Drivers in all accidents, 1963* | | (3) License withdrawals for intoxication † | | (4) License withdrawals for fatal accidents † | |
|---|---|---|---|---|---|---|---|---|
| | Number | Percent | 1000s | Percent | Number | Percent | Number | Percent |
| 19 and under | 7,300 | 13.5 | 2,900 | 14.5 | 8,166 | 2.2 | 347 | 13.3 |
| 20–24 | 9,500 | 17.6 | 3,100 | 15.5 | 41,491 | 11.2 | 674 | 25.8 |
| 25–29 | 6,100 | 11.3 | 2,450 | 12.3 | 44,587 | 12.0 | 446 | 17.0 |
| 30–34 | 5,300 | 9.8 | 1,950 | 9.7 | 47,502 | 12.8 | 275 | 10.5 |
| 35–39 | 4,800 | 8.9 | 2,100 | 10.5 | 54,628 | 14.7 | 258 | 9.9 |
| 40–44 | 4,800 | 8.9 | 1,800 | 9.0 | 52,338 | 14.1 | 182 | 6.9 |
| 45–49 | 4,100 | 7.6 | 1,550 | 7.8 | 44,968 | 12.1 | 125 | 4.8 |
| 50–54 | 3,200 | 5.9 | 1,250 | 6.2 | 35,038 | 9.4 | 102 | 3.9 |
| 55–59 | 2,500 | 4.6 | 1,100 | 5.5 | 21,694 | 5.9 | 57 | 2.2 |
| 60–64 | 2,100 | 3.9 | 700 | 3.5 | 11,863 | 3.2 | 51 | 1.9 |
| 65–69 | 1,700 | 3.2 | 700 | 3.5 | 5,968 | 1.6 | 39 | 1.5 |
| 70 and over | 2,600 | 4.8 | 400 | 2.0 | 2,910 | 0.8 | 59 | 2.3 |
| Total | 54,000 | 100.0 | 20,000 | 100.0 | 371,153 | 100.0 | 2,615 | 100.0 |

* National Safety Council estimates.
† License withdrawals reported to the National Driver Register Service, July 1, 1961, to Dec. 31, 1963.
The most significant data are those of column 2, in view of the chance elements inherent in determining the injury accident versus the fatal accident, including the obvious chance element in injury, the availability of medical services, the possible complications of injury, and the interval between injury and discovery and arrival at hospital—as well as the lesser resistance of the older person.

Table 7-2. Accident rates

| Age group | (1) Fatal accidents per 100,000 drivers | (2) All accidents per 100 drivers | (3) License withdrawals for intoxication per 10,000 drivers | (4) License withdrawals for fatal accidents per 1,000,000 drivers | (5) Relative fatal accident rate* based on daytime mileage | (6) Relative all accident rate* based on daytime mileage |
|---|---|---|---|---|---|---|
| 19 and under | 97 | 39 | 11 | 46 | 4.1 | 4.4 |
| 20–24 | 90 | 29 | 39 | 64 | 2.1 | 1.8 |
| 25–29 | 62 | 25 | 45 | 45 | 1.0 | 1.1 |
| 30–34 | 54 | 20 | 48 | 28 | 0.7 | 0.7 |
| 35–39 | 46 | 20 | 53 | 25 | | |
| 40–44 | 48 | 18 | 53 | 18 | 0.7 | 0.7 |
| 45–49 | 46 | 17 | 51 | 14 | | |
| 50–54 | 41 | 16 | 45 | 13 | 0.7 | 0.7 |
| 55–59 | 39 | 17 | 33 | 9 | | |
| 60–64 | 43 | 14 | 24 | 10 | 0.8 | 0.8 |
| 65–69 | 47 | 19 | 16 | 11 | | |
| 70 and over | 65 | 10 | 7 | 15 | 1.8 | 1.2 |
| Total | 58 | 21 | 39 | 28 | 1.0 | 1.0 |

* The rates include consideration of total miles driven. This may be considered as a measure of relative driving efficiency. As identification of the "accident potential," however, it is less meaningful. The individual who drives less, has less "exposure," and is less of a risk on the highway. On this basis, the data in Table 7–1 are more significant for determining the relative risk potential of the different age groups.

sixty-five and over age group one dies among every four or five injured. Since the sixty-five and over category includes even the *very oldest who are capable of driving,* the conclusion as to the cause of the high death rate per numbers of accidents appears to be one of anatomy and physiology rather than of driving proficiency, and one of effect only in relation to themselves.

## *Problem?*

Nowhere do we find convincing evidence that older drivers constitute a serious problem on our highways. Earlier in our treatment of this subject, some reasons were indicated why merely reaching a certain chronological age does not automatically make all individuals hazards on the highway. Further amplification of this thought is offered in the following statements about older drivers:

1. They drive fewer miles per year than other drivers and thus are less exposed to traffic hazards.
2. Because of years of experience, they have developed better judgment and as a result are less likely to take chances.

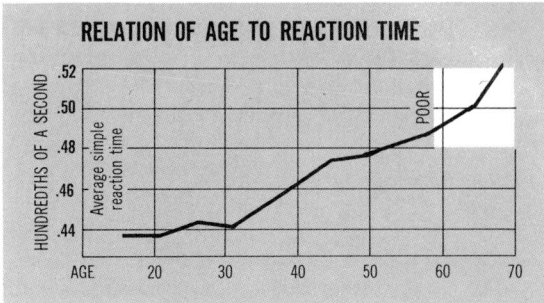

FIGURE 7-2 Older experienced drivers may compensate for deficiencies that are recognized. (Adapted from Figure 4-4, *Sportsmanlike Driving,* 5th edition.)

3. Many of them have learned of their deficiencies and have developed ways of compensating for them. Occasionally an older driver is encountered who tends to *over*compensate, perhaps to the extent of unduly impeding traffic, and to the great annoyance of other drivers. This intensifies the hazard of the "speed differential" on the highway. In cases where the driver's limitations are such that they would require this type of driving, examination procedures are in order to determine the individual's fitness to drive. (This is the opposite of the new driver whose inexperience prevents him from realizing the very limitations imposed by that inexperience.)
4. Many older drivers who develop deficiencies become aware of them and voluntarily quit driving. This tends to develop a more select group of drivers.

To a minor extent teachers are responsible for some students' exaggerated view of the limitations imposed by age. Continued emphasis on "You're young—and strong—have fast reaction time—good vision" has an effect. Unless it is tempered by emphasis on experience and judgment, it tends to lead the student into two beliefs:

1. That he is, by nature, a very competent driver
2. That older people (even older by his standards) are inferior drivers

Even when experience shows him his own limitations, he still retains the second idea. It is probable that item 2 is a common belief which sometimes takes the form of recommendations to restrict, reexamine, or remove older drivers from the highways.

One recommendation *might* have some validity if it were to apply, not to any age group, but to all drivers who had been licensed prior to establishment in their states of satisfactory standards. Opportunity might be provided for them to learn today's regulations and laws. The word "might" is used advisedly, since there is no basis other than possibility that their driving reflects a greater than normal accident incidence or traffic disruption. It may be that experience, judgment, and other factors have, after years of driving, neutralized their original source of friction with current driving conditions. Then too, although knowledge of law and good driving practices are basic, the desire to conform is also necessary. As well-experienced drivers, they may have that in abundance.

Interpreting pertinent data on aging and on its relation to driving leads to a rather obvious conclusion: that chronological age alone is not a sound criterion for appraising driver competence and that there is no justification for establishment of restrictions based on numerical age alone. Supporting this conclusion, the American Medical Association has stated: "Age per se should not be a limitation once the individual reaches licensing age; rather, the functional capacity and ability of each individual should be the determining factor."[1]

## SELECTED BIBLIOGRAPHY

Marsh, Burton W.: *Aging and Driving,* American Automobile Association, Washington, D.C., 1960.

Mirkin, Abraham J.: *"Medical Factors Related to Driving Ability,"* presented at the National Conference on Medical Aspects of Driver Safety and Driver Licensing, Chicago, Nov. 16, 1964. Dr. Mirkin is Chairman, AMA Committee on Medical Aspects of Automotive Safety.

---

[1] Abraham J. Mirken, M.D., Chairman, AMA Committee on Medical Aspects of Automotive Safety, "Medical Factors Related to Driving Ability," presented at the National Conference on Medical Aspects of Driver Safety and Driver Licensing, Chicago, Nov. 16, 1964.

# III CLASSROOM INSTRUCTION

THE GENERAL professional preparation of the teacher should orient him in his place in the insulated world of the classroom. This is a world by itself in which he controls all activity and even channels thought into subject areas. Regardless of those who would eliminate all education courses and have the teacher a master of his discipline alone, there is *much* more to teaching than remembering a body of knowledge.

The professor may present a highly successful two-hour lecture to a group of doctoral candidates; for a teacher to walk into an average secondary-school class and make the exact same presentation to those students might have some less successful and perhaps startling results. Here the "strategy of teaching," the "how to teach," is a more significant factor and the course content less complex and comprehensive. Then, place the professor or the high school teacher in complete charge of the first-grade classroom and he would have far more command of subject matter than he could possibly use. But, unless he were unusually versatile, he would be lost. Here the "how to teach" is all-important. Does the professor know a well-tested way to teach Johnny to tell time? Has he ever had a severely homesick pupil? Can he tie a child's shoelace and at the same time control a class? Not "education"? Let the critics call it what they will, somebody has taught their children, twenty and thirty at a time, and has done it ever so much better than the critics could.

TEACHING IS MORE THAN MERELY KNOWING. Aside from subject matter, we may separate the elements of teaching into two areas: the common factors of all teaching, and the specific strategies and methods intrinsic to a subject field. The former should be given every teacher-to-be in his general preparation; the latter is the responsibility of the staff of the department or center which prepares him for his specific field. There is neither need nor time for duplication.

*Classroom instruction* in this part of the book is designed specifically to present an adaptation of the general principles and procedures of teaching to the specific subject field of driver and traffic safety education—the art of teaching this subject.

# Teaching Aids and Equipment    8

DRIVER and traffic safety education is a subject field with a dual identity. Its well-known character is that of a safeguard, a protector of human life. Less visible, except to professionals in the field of education, is its alter ego, *a material, spatial universe in which conceptual, behavioral, and other quite subtle values are realized through utilization of the physical media.*

The physical, material nature of this area of education makes particularly appropriate and effective devices that can be constructed to demonstrate the "knowledge" content of the course. Mathematics teachers use plastic images to demonstrate geometric concepts, science teachers the laboratory, and teachers of English the written and printed page. Nowhere, however, are "teaching aids" more appropriate than in driver education. As in any subject field, the materials used must be kept in the role of *aids* to teaching; they are neither a substitute for it, nor ends in themselves. They should be selected to enrich the course.

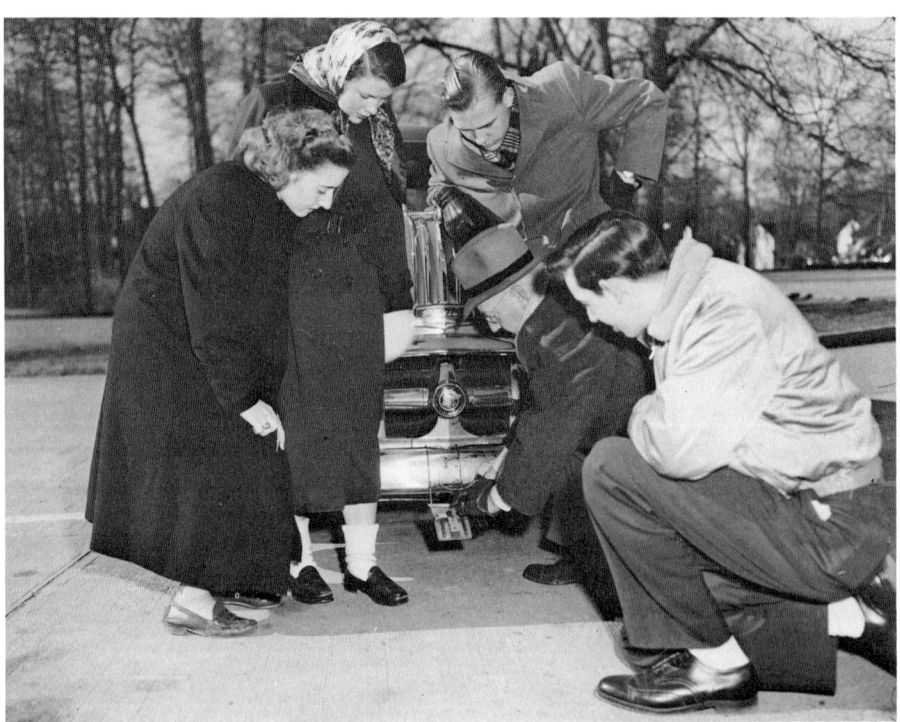

FIGURE 8–1 The detonator is a teaching aid which translates reaction, braking, and stopping distances in numbers to reality on the surface of the highway.

Teaching aids can serve several useful purposes. Whereas a picture may be worth a thousand words, a device to illustrate a mechanical principle may be worth a dozen pictures. Working models make use of the kinesthetic sense as well as the visual sense. With them, vivid and lasting impressions are easier to produce than if the instructor must rely on the spoken and written word. Properly designed films can do much to help develop proper attitudes if they depict situations in which the student can identify himself with the characters in the film.

Most teachers are aware of the value of teaching aids in the development of interest in a driver education course. However, it should be remembered that the primary purpose is to attain a specific objective, not merely to hold interest. When used for a definite purpose, teaching aids can add much to a driver education course, just as the chemistry lab adds so much to the chemistry course.

## SELECTION OF TEACHING AIDS

As in most planning, there is a right way and a wrong way. The right way is to go through the course of study, select lessons where a film or device would be helpful, and then select the best film or device for the purpose. The wrong way is to buy a supply of films and equipment and then try to fit them into the course. The major problem is not in finding a teaching aid for a particular subject, but in making all good selections from all sources.

The new teacher will do best to start with a minimum of equipment, adding to it as the need arises. A year of experience will reveal areas where aids are needed. This system will eliminate the buying of equipment for which there is little need.

Teaching aids will usually be used for a number of successive classes, and frequently they will be handled by students. For this reason, simplicity and durability should be given serious consideration. When not in use, these aids should be stored in a safe place so that they will always be ready when needed. There is always a strong inclination on the part of students to play with gadgets and devices. This interest is not limited to those in driver education. Teaching aids are most effective when used at the appropriate time, and not left around during the entire course, to become "old stuff."

### Class-constructed Aids

Visit the classroom of a teacher who is enthusiastic about the subject. You will probably find student-made posters, testing devices, and various parts of cars, possibly obtained from a junkyard. A lack of funds does not prevent the ambitious teacher from building up a set of useful teaching aids, even though they may be rather crude. Having students plan and make their own models has several advantages: there is a substantial financial saving; students will usually show a greater interest in something they have designed and built; if a model is developed by the class, it is more likely to be made to fulfill a specific need in the course. There is sometimes a tendency to obtain various teaching aids without first making a careful analysis of the objectives and the specific content of the lessons in which they are to be used.

Students will be much more enthusiastic about developing a teaching aid in which they are interested than one that is assigned to them. For this reason, students should be encouraged to suggest useful aids. Several students can be assigned to develop a device as a group project. In assigning projects of this nature, the teacher should exercise care to make sure that the project is pertinent to the subject matter under discussion. After students have given some thought to a particular project, they should discuss it with the teacher so that a clear concept will be developed of the major purpose of the device and how this purpose will be accomplished. Students should be given considerable freedom to maintain their interest, but they do need some guidance.

In constructing teaching aids, permanence should be considered. There will be greater interest in something that will be used for several classes than in something used for a single demonstration and then thrown away. This, of course, does not preclude the possibility of a later class constructing a better model, which will make the first model obsolete. The textbook, workbook, and reference material will suggest many places where a device would be useful in explaining a particular subject. No attempt is made here to develop a comprehensive list of teaching aids which might be built by students. Only a few items are suggested.

FIGURE 8-2 Charts are very useful in teaching the mechanical features of the automobile.

Large charts and diagrams are useful in depicting various parts of the car and how they function. Working models can be made to illustrate the operation of the piston, the ignition system, the lighting system, and the brake system. Most of them can be either simple or elaborate, depending on the ingenuity of the students and the facilities available. Frequently there will be boys in the class who are taking courses in industrial arts. In some cases, students will be studying automotive mechanics. These boys can make cutaway models of such items as the piston or carburetor.

Some students may have photography as a hobby. They can be encouraged to make slides to illustrate traffic signs and various highway engineering features. The alert teacher will think of many traffic situations which can be photographed for class instruction. The teacher should be careful to ascertain that no student will go to any hazardous place to take photographs. Without some guidance, a student may look for some impressively hazardous traffic situation and take some risk in attempting to get "good" pictures. The school has a definite responsibility for guiding student project activities to avoid the risk of an accident.

Models can be made from cardboard illustrating various features of modern freeways such as grade separations, acceleration lanes, ramps, etc. There are also teaching aids which are useful in the dual-control car. A simple tumbling cylinder can be made to measure smoothness of driving. Stanchions are always useful, especially when teaching parallel parking. Students who are in industrial arts classes can build a rooftop sign to identify the dual-control car. Students taking artwork can letter the sign. A miniature magnetic traffic board with cars about two inches long is useful in the car for illustrating turning movements, parallel parking, and other maneuvers.

## *PRINCIPLES AND TECHNIQUES IN THE USE OF TEACHING AIDS*

The number of films available is almost unlimited. The major problem is to select a limited number of films to accomplish specific objectives. Films should not be used as fillers but only to teach a specific lesson. The experienced teacher will try out different films from year to year to build up a selection which will be most useful. A list of available films classified by content will be found at the end of this chapter. Many films are available on a free-loan basis. The chief disadvantage here is that the film may not arrive when needed. For this reason it is desirable to build up a school library of films that have proven value.

A relatively new product is the 8-mm film cartridge. These films are short, are designed to cover a specific point, and are frequently called "single-concept films." Some single-concept films are available in both cartridge and reel form. The cartridge type has several advantages for the busy teacher: film threading is eliminated; the cartridge is simply inserted in the projector; the action can be stopped at any time; after a single showing, the film is in position for the next showing without rewinding. This makes it a simple matter to repeat the lesson when this is desirable. A number of single-concept films, each approximately four minutes in duration, are available in 16-mm, conventional-reel form, and also in 8-mm, both reel and cartridge forms.

The effect of a film depends to a large extent on how it is used. Proper planning is essential. The film should supplement what is currently being covered in the textbook. The nature of the film should be explained before it is shown. Students should be told what to look for in the film. Better still, the students may be given a list of items to watch for in the film. A written quiz after the showing, in turn followed by discussion, will add considerably to the effectiveness of the film. Knowing that a quiz will follow the film tends to motivate the lazy students in the group.

Equipment for projecting still pictures is also useful. This includes slide projectors, filmstrip projectors, and overhead projectors. It is not difficult for a teacher to have slides made covering various technical diagrams and illustrations. Overlays for overhead projectors have an important advantage in that the teacher can start with a single diagram and add to it. This is especially useful in explaining mechanical principles, such as the four-stroke cycle. Transparencies can be used on which the teacher can illustrate items with a grease pencil.

Posters and charts are useful if the class is not too large. Mounting the posters and charts so that they can be used like a flip chart will help to preserve them and will make them more convenient to use. Loose posters soon become soiled, torn, and lost. Using a standard size has many advantages. Some charts and posters can be made by students. Since most of this material can be used year after year, spending an appreciable amount of out-of-class time in developing suitable posters is justified.

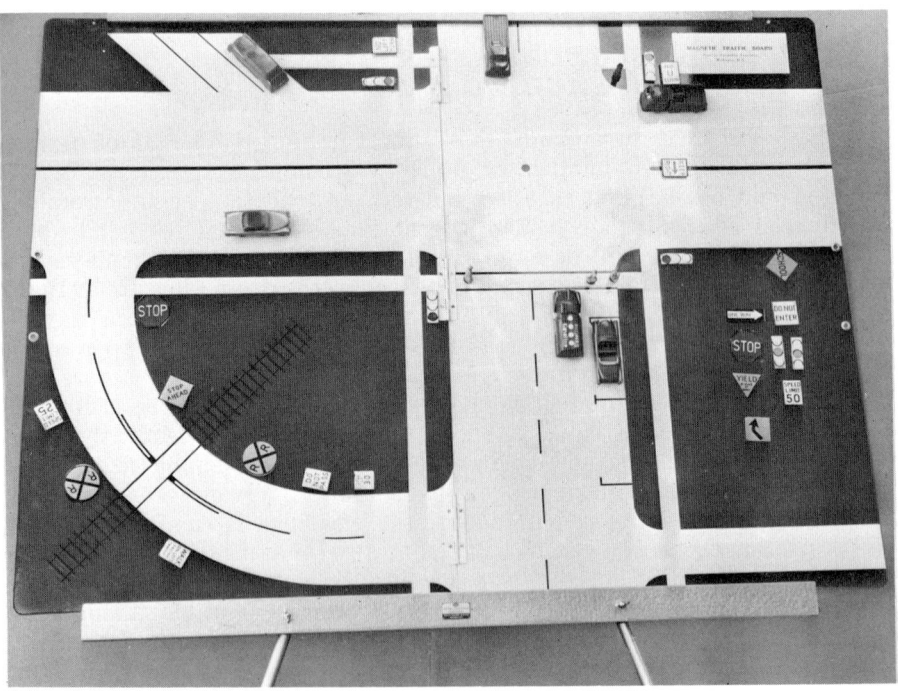

FIGURE 8-3 The magnetic board can be used to teach many items of traffic law, traffic controls, and good driving practices.

Magnetic traffic boards and flannel boards are especially useful in depicting traffic situations and special maneuvers. Local traffic problems may be illustrated by drawing an intersection on durable paper, then clipping the paper to the front of the magnetic traffic board. The features of some specially selected local intersection can be shown, adding interest to the presentation. The magnetized cars, signs, and other items can then be located in any position on the drawn intersection. The drawing itself may be preserved and used for succeeding classes.

Although training students to become mechanics is not an objective of the course, a basic understanding of some of the mechanical principles involved will develop a better understanding and appreciation of the automobile. This is where mechanical models can be especially useful. These models can be either commercially made models or parts of an actual car. Although it would seem that parts of a car would be best because of the mechanical construction, the fundamental principles are sometimes obscured. In many classes there will be boys especially interested in automobile mechanics. A teacher can capitalize on this interest. These boys can be encouraged to develop models and give demonstrations before the class. Again, it should be emphasized that the value of a teaching aid depends more on the ingenuity of the teacher than on the nature of the device.

## SOURCES OF TEACHING AIDS AND EQUIPMENT

A number of teaching aids and devices are available commercially. Before making a purchase, it is good business to evaluate carefully what is available so that the best may be obtained for the money appropriated.

American Automobile Association, 1712 G Street, N.W., Washington, D.C. 20006: working models, stanchions, vision tests, reaction time tests, car identification signs, dual controls, brake reaction detonators.

American Optical Company, Southbridge, Mass.: vision tests.

Bausch & Lomb Incorporated, Rochester, N.Y., 14602: vision tests.

Robert J. Brady Company, 130 Q Street, N.E., Washington, D.C.: transparencies.

Bumpa-Tel Sign Company, 202 N. Front Street, Mounds, Ill.: car identification signs.

Davis & Box Manufacturing Company, 3549 Bryn Mawr, Dallas 25, Tex.: stanchions.

Educational Device Company, 101 East Chicago Boulevard, Tecumseh, Mich. 49286: vision and reaction time tests.

Stanley L. Heylmun, Inc., 4945 Edgemere Avenue, Baltimore 15, Md.: reaction time tests.

Keystone View Company, Meadville, Pa. 16335: vision tests, overhead projectors, teaching machines.

Lafayette Instrument Company, Box 57, North 26th Street & 52 By-Pass, Lafayette, Ind. 47902: psychological apparatus, reaction time tests, strength tests, vision tests.

Lake Automotive Products Company, 531 Woodbine Avenue, Oak Park, Ill.: magnetic traffic boards, car identification signs.

Magno Saf-t Board, Emigsville, Pa.: magnetic traffic boards.

Marietta Apparatus Company, 118 Maple Street, Marietta, Ohio: psychological apparatus, strength tests.

J. J. McIntosh Company, 30 South Court House Avenue, Carlisle, Pa. 17013: magnetic traffic board.

Carl A. Munn, Munn Teaching Devices, 388 Lafayette Avenue, Buffalo, 13, N.Y.: model traffic signal.

Oravisual Company, Inc., Box 11150, St. Petersburg, Fla. 33733: flannel boards.

Porto-Clinic Instruments, Inc., 296 Broadway, New York, N.Y. 10007: vision tests, magnetic traffic board, overhead projector, transparencies.

Radiator Speciality Company, Charlotte, N.C.: traffic cones.

Rodgers Company, Hackensack, N.J.: traffic cones.

C. H. Stoelting Company, 424 N. Homan Avenue, Chicago, Ill. 60624: reaction time tests, strength tests, psychological apparatus.

Titmus Optical Company, Inc., Petersburg, Va.: vision tests.

Viking Company, 113 So. Edgemont Street, Los Angeles 4, Calif.: working models.

L. A. Whitney Assoc. Inc., 331 Madison Avenue, New York, N.Y. 10017: flannel boards.

## 16-MM MOTION PICTURES*

| Skill Teaching | Running time | Source† |
|---|---|---|
| Backing into a Stall and Skills on Hills | 30 min | 26 |
| City Driving | 30 min | 26 |
| City Driving (Ford Driver Education Series) | 22 min | 21 |
| Driving at Night (Ford Film Series) | 10 min | 21 |
| Driving the Super Highway | 10 min | 21 |
| Driving under Special Conditions (Ford Driver Education Series) | 19 min | 21 |
| Freeway Driving | 11 min | 20 |
| Freeway Driving Is Different | 14 min | 1 |
| Highway Driving (Ford Driver Education Series) | 17 min | 21 |
| How to Drive on Snow and Ice | 12 min | 47 |
| How to Pass Safely | 10 min | 37 |
| Parking | 30 min | 26 |
| Parking the Car (Ford Film Series) | 10 min | 21 |
| Preparing to Start | 30 min | 26 |
| Safe Driving: Advanced Skills and Problems | 17 min | 14 |
| Safe Driving: Fundamental Skills | 10 min | 48 |
| Standard Shift Driving | 30 min | 26 |
| Take It from a Champion | 27 min | 33 |
| Turns with No Regrets | 21 min | 3 |
| What's Your Driving Eye-Q? | 13 min | 2 |

*Films classified by William Englander, Secretary, National Committee on Films for Safety.
†The numbers in this column refer to the list of sources that follow this section.

## TEACHING AIDS AND EQUIPMENT 123

|  | Running time | Source |
|---|---|---|
| Winter Driving | 25 min | 37 |
| You and Your Driving | 14 min | 25 |

### *Attitudinal*

| | | |
|---|---|---|
| Last Clear Chance | 26 min | 52 |
| Last Date | 20 min | 27 |
| Look Who's Driving | 8 min | 2 |
| Mickey's Big Chance | 15 min | 1 |
| One Second to Safety | 18 min | 56 |
| Stop Driving Us Crazy | 10 min | 22 |
| Tommy Gets the Keys | 13 min | 24 |
| When You Are a Pedestrian | 12 min | 44 |

### *Driving Practices*

| | | |
|---|---|---|
| Don't Skid Yourself | 13 min | 2 |
| Emergencies in the Making | 14 min | 1 |
| The Expert Driving Series (4 films) | 10 min each | 37 |
| For Experts Only | 10 min | 37 |
| Freeway Driving Tactics | 16 min | 10 |
| League of Frightened Men | 22 min | 35 |
| Ninety-day Flash (Defensive Driving Series) | 10 min | 37 |
| The Sixth Wheel | 25 min | 46 |
| The Smith System | 8 min | 21 |
| A Professional Portrait | 28 min | 6 |
| Take a Look at the Odds (Defensive Driving Series) | 10 min | 37 |
| Ticket to Safety | 10 min | 23 |

### *Traffic Law and Enforcement*

| | | |
|---|---|---|
| Flagged for Action | 30 min | 36 |
| Accident Investigation | 15 min | 11 |
| Laws, Enforcement, and Courts | 30 min | 26 |
| Man-made Laws | 30 min | 26 |
| Procedure in the Traffic Courtroom | 20 min | 4 |
| Traffic Court, U.S.A. | 6 min | 43 |

|  | Running time | Source |
|---|---|---|
| Traffic Police | 6 min | 43 |
| Uniform Traffic Laws | 6 min | 43 |
| Using Your Traffic Records | 21 min | 32 |
| Your Highway Patrol | 13 min | 20 |

## Human Factors

|  | Running time | Source |
|---|---|---|
| Anatomy of an Accident | 26 min | 5 |
| The Bottle and the Throttle | 10 min | 48 |
| Dead Right | 11 min | 1 |
| Give a Car a Man Who Can Drive | 14 min | 45 |
| Highball Highway | 12 min | 10 |
| Home for the Holidays | 18 min | 17 |
| The Human Factor in Driving | 11 min | 44 |
| Look Alive | 15 min | 54 |
| Mr. Finley's Feelings | 10 min | 29 |
| The Mixer '53 | 10 min | 30 |
| Nightmare for the Bold | 53 min | 53 |
| None for the Road | 11 min | 10 |
| Pedestrians | 10 min | 21 |
| Seven-tenths of a Second | 6 min | 5 |
| Speed and Reflexes | 11 min | 44 |
| Theobald Faces the Facts | 16 min | 39 |
| To See Ourselves | 14½ min | 2 |

## Car Ownership (Maintenance, Insurance, Purchasing)

|  | Running time | Source |
|---|---|---|
| ABC of the Automobile Engine | 18 min | 23 |
| ABC of Internal Combustion | 13 min | 23 |
| Care of the Car (Ford Film Series) | 10 min | 21 |
| Dead End | 15 min | 34 |
| The Invisible Killer | 13 min | 9 |
| Liability and Insurance | 30 min | 26 |
| Mechanics of the Car | 30 min | 26 |
| Not around the Block | 12 min | 50 |
| The Other Guy | 12 min | 51 |
| Security Clearance | 21 min | 33 |

|  | Running time | Source |
|---|---|---|

## Multipurpose and General

| | Running time | Source |
|---|---|---|
| The Case of Officer Hallibrand | 27 min | 40 |
| The Case of the Misguided Killer | 11 min | 44 |
| A Closed Book | 26 min | 38 |
| The David Hall Story | 25 min | 19 |
| Day in Court | 29 min | 33 |
| Dick Wakes Up | 12 min | 1 |
| Millions on the Move | 27 min | 7 |
| Moral Responsibility of Safety | 6 min | 15 |
| The National System of Interstate and Defense Highways | 20 min | 42 |
| Safety Belt for Susie | 11 min | 54 |
| Safety Features | 30 min | 26 |
| Trailer Safety | 11 min | 10 |
| The Unexpected Moment | 13 min | 54 |
| Word of Honor | 30 min | 8 |
| You and Your Driving | 14 min | 25 |
| You Can't Stop on a Dime | 10 min | 48 |

## Promotional

| | | |
|---|---|---|
| According to the Record | 28 min | 31 |
| The American Road | 39 min | 21 |
| As a Matter of Fact | 5 min | 42 |
| Auto, U.S.A. | 27 min | 18 |
| The Broken Doll | 23 min | 16 |
| Broken Glass | 12 min | 10 |
| Engineering for Traffic Safety | 5 min | 43 |
| Interrupted Morning | 16 min | 54 |
| Intersection Collision | 10 min | 54 |
| Motor Vehicle Administration | 13 min | 43 |
| The Perfect Crime | 20 min | 12 |
| Right from the Start | 24 min | 41 |
| Safety through Seat Belts | 13 min | 55 |
| Signs Take a Holiday | 10 min | 37 |

126  CLASSROOM INSTRUCTION

|  | Running time | Source |
|---|---|---|
| *The Silent Witness* | 28 min | 28 |
| *Stay Alive* | 14 min | 1 |
| *The Story of Anyburg, U.S.A.* | 7 min | 57 |

## Sources

1. AAA Foundation for Traffic Safety, 1712 G Street, N.W., Washington, D.C. 20006.
2. Aetna Life Affiliated Companies, Information & Education Department, Hartford 15, Conn.
3. Allstate Insurance Company, 1610 6th Avenue, Seattle, Wash.
4. American Bar Association, 1155 East 60th Street, Chicago, Ill.
5. American Telephone & Telegraph Company, Film Division, 195 Broadway, New York 7, N.Y.
6. American Trucking Associations, Inc., 1616 P Street, N.W., Washington, D.C.
7. Association Films, Inc., 347 Madison Avenue, New York 17, N.Y.
8. Auto Industries Highway Safety Committee, 2000 K Street, N.W., Washington, D.C.
9. Automotive Exhaust-Research Institute, 20575 Center Ridge Road, Cleveland 16, Ohio.
10. Charles Cahill and Associates, 5746 Sunset Boulevard, Hollywood 28, Calif.
11. California Highway Patrol, 2490 First Avenue, P.O. Box 898, Sacramento 14, Calif.
12. Caterpillar Tractor, Peoria, Ill.
13. Citizens Traffic Safety Board of Metropolitan Chicago, 20 North Wacker Drive, Chicago 6, Ill.
14. Coronet Films, 65 East South Water Street, Chicago 1, Ill.
15. Department of the Army, Chief of Chaplains Office, The Pentagon, Washington 25, D.C.
16. Department of the Attorney General, Parliament Building, Toronto, Ontario, Canada.
17. Directorate of Aerospace Safety USAF, Norton Air Force Base, California.
18. Dynamic Films, Inc., 405 Park Avenue, New York 22, N.Y.
19. Employers Mutuals of Wausau, Wausau, Wis.
20. Fass-Levy Films, 1320 Quebec Street, Denver 20, Colo.
21. Ford Motor Company, Motion Picture Department, 3000 Schaefer Road, Dearborn, Mich.
22. General Board of Temperance of the Methodist Church, 100 Maryland Avenue, N.E., Washington 2, D.C.
23. General Motors Corporation, Film Library, General Motors Building, Detroit 2, Mich.
24. B. F. Goodrich Company, 500 South Main Street, Akron, Ohio.

25. Humble Safety Foundation, 15 West 51st Street, New York 19, N.Y.
26. Indiana University, Audio Visual Center, 1840 East 10th Street, Bloomington, Ind.
27. Lumbermen's Mutual Casualty Company, Mutual Insurance Building, Chicago 40, Ill.
28. William S. Merrell Company, Cincinnati 15, Ohio.
29. Metropolitan Life Insurance Company, 1 Madison Avenue, New York 10, N.Y.
30. M. F. A. Mutual Insurance Company, Columbia, Missouri.
31. Michigan State Police, East Lansing, Mich.
32. Michigan State University, Audio-Visual Center, East Lansing, Mich.
33. Modern Talking Pictures, Inc., 3 East 54th Street, New York 20, N.Y.
34. Monroe Auto Equipment, Monroe, Mich.
35. National Dairy Products Corporation, 260 Madison Avenue, New York 16, N.Y.
36. National Film Board of Canada, 3255 Cote de Liesse Road, Montreal 3, Quebec, Canada.
37. National Safety Council, 425 North Michigan Avenue, Chicago 11, Ill.
38. Nationwide Insurance Company, Safety Department Film Library, 246 North High Street, Columbus, Ohio.
39. National Women's Christian Temperance Union, 1730 Chicago Avenue, Evanston, Ill.
40. The Ohio Oil Company, 539 South Main Street, Findlay, Ohio.
41. Ontario Department of Transport, Highway Safety Branch, Parliament Building, Toronto, Ontario, Canada.
42. Portland Cement Association, 33 West Grand Avenue, Chicago, Ill.
43. President's Committee for Traffic Safety, 1711 H Street, N.W., Washington 25, D.C.
44. Progressive Pictures, 6351 Thornhill Drive, Oakland, Calif.
45. Richfield Oil Corporation, Richfield Building, Los Angeles, Calif.
46. Sam Orleans Film Productions, 211 West Cumberland Avenue, Knoxville 2, Tenn.
47. Seiberling Rubber Company, Akron, Ohio.
48. Sid Davis Productions, 3500 South LaBrea Avenue, Los Angeles 16, Calif.
49. Sinclair Refining Company, Merchandising Department, 5 West 48th Street, New York 20, N.Y.
50. Sullivan Bruce Productions, Inc., 707 South Brand Boulevard, Glendale 4, Calif.
51. Tyrex, Inc., Empire State Building, New York 1, N.Y.
52. Union Pacific Railroad Company, 1416 Dodge Street, Omaha 2, Nebr.
53. United States Air Force Film Library, 8900 Broadway, St. Louis 25, Mo.
54. United States Public Health Service, Division of Accident Prevention, 330 C Street, S.W., Washington 25, D.C.
55. University of California, 405 Hilgard Avenue, Los Angeles, Calif.
56. Virginia State Board of Education, Film Production Service, Richmond 16, Va.

57. Walt Disney Productions, 500 South Buena Vista Street, Burbank, Calif.

58. Washington State Patrol, State Capitol, Olympia, Wash.

## 8-MM MOTION PICTURES

"Single concept" driver education films:

Set of eight—4½ minutes each, B & W silent films, mounted on conventional reels

Set of eight—4½ minutes each, B & W silent films mounted in individual Technicolor projector cartridges

(Teacher's guide and booklet included with each set. Set of eight also available in 16 mm B & W with optical sound track mounted on individual reels.)

Source:

Public Relations Department, Room 1047, American Oil Company, 910 South Michigan Avenue, Chicago, Ill. 60680.

## FILMSTRIPS

### Ford Motor Company Time-lapse Filmstrips

1. *Freeway Maneuvers*
2. *Seeing Habits for Expert Driving*
3. *Intersection Series*
4. *Passing Series Package*

Sources:

1. and 2. Mechanical Mailing Services, Inc., 6141 Concord, Detroit, Mich. 48211.

3. and 4. National Mailing Corporation, 6201 Grand River, Detroit, Mich. 48208.

### McGraw-Hill Driver Education Filmstrip Series

Set 1
1. *Showdown with a Show-off Driver*
2. *The Eyes of the Driver*
3. *Drinking, Drugs, and Driving*
4. *Nature's Driving Laws*
5. *Traffic Clues and Cues*
6. *The Pedestrian and the Driver*

Set 2
1. *Traffic Laws Made by Man*
2. *Driving under Adverse Conditions*
3. *Driving in Cities and Towns*
4. *How the Automobile Runs*
5. *Driving on Freeways*
6. *Stopping Distances*

Source:

Text-Film Division, McGraw-Hill Book Company, 330 West 42nd Street, New York, N.Y. 10036

### Shell Better Driving Test (Filmstrip—free)

Source:

Public Relations Department, Shell Oil Company, 50 West 50th Street, New York, N.Y. 10020.

# Simulation and the Driving Simulator        9

A DRIVING simulator may be defined as a device for imitating the driving of an automobile in traffic without having either the automobile or the traffic. Simulation was given a big boost during the Second World War, especially in the Air Force, since it made possible mass training with a minimum of the combat equipment which was needed in the prosecution of the war. This demand for efficient training resulted in the development in some cases of highly sophisticated equipment. The simulators were expensive, but much less expensive than the combat equipment they replaced for training purposes. Also, of course, the accident factor was eliminated from this part of the training program.

Teaching the skills of driving is similar to teaching many of the skills involved in operating machines of war. The use of simulators in driver education appeared to be a natural progression. As a result, considerable effort in recent years has gone into the development of driving simulators which could be used to reduce the amount of time a student would normally spend behind the wheel.

Before deciding whether simulators should be used and, if used, what should be the preferred type, it is necessary to define the purposes of a simulator, and then determine if a given simulator accomplishes those purposes. No attempt will be made here to evaluate the relative effectiveness of the several devices available. Instead, information will be provided to enable the driver education teacher or school official to make a logical decision as it applies to a specific local school or school system. Many of the principles discussed here, while applying specifically to driving simulators, also apply to other skill-developing devices.

Generally, simulators are used for three major reasons:

1. ECONOMY. It is hoped that the same number of students can be given equal training at less cost, or stated in another way, more students can be given equivalent training for the same amount of money spent.
2. SAFETY. Although dual-control cars are not involved in many accidents, some accidents do occur. By giving instruction with a simulator, the hazards of traffic are eliminated.
3. RESEARCH. Because of the numerous factors involved in a real traffic situation, it is nearly impossible to measure the effect of any one factor on a driver's performance or behavior. With simulation, most factors can be controlled or kept constant while the factor under study can be varied and its effect noted.

If a simulator is to accomplish its purpose, it must enable the student to develop the same skills that he would develop behind the wheel of a car. In other words, can time on the simulator be substituted for time behind the wheel, and if so, to what extent? It is appropriate here to discuss the factors involved in skill learning.

## *SKILL LEARNING*

In considering the objectives of driver education, the one most obviously related to the simulator experience is skill achievement.

A trained gymnast can raise his arms sideward to shoulder level (for example), stop their upward motion, and hold them at that level, straight, and parallel to the ground, if he so chooses. He does not have to look right and left to *see* if they are in the desired position and to make corrections for errors of coordination. The reason he finds this so easy of accomplishment is that he has learned, through a great deal of practice, the "feel" of each movement—the *feeling* of just how much to contract each muscle, as felt through sensory nerve endings in those muscles called *proprioceptors*. When this sensation from the proprioceptors in appropriate muscles is recognized in his brain as evidence of contraction of those muscles to just the degree that his (practice) experience has associated with the movement and resultant position he wants, he simply holds that degree of contraction. This "feeling" from the proprioceptors in the muscles, which tells of the position of the body part involved, is called *kinesthetic sense*.

When a beginner is learning to play basketball, he may take a hundred shots at the basket. He sees the result of his movements in each shot, knows by feel (kinesthetic sense) how "hard" he shot, or whether too much force was applied on one side or the other—as judged by the observed result of the shot. This has been called by some an "immediate feedback or "visual feedback" of data. *He associates the contraction of certain muscles and the degree of contraction with the observed results.* By correcting in terms of contraction and degree of contraction (number of muscle fibers involved) of selected muscles, he attempts to improve his performance with each subsequent shot at the basket. This is the same skill-learning process involved in learning free gymnastics, previously cited, or in learning to drive a car.

## CRITERIA FOR EVALUATION OF SKILL-TEACHING POTENTIAL

The following factors are involved in the skill-learning process:

1. *Practice* of appropriate body movements.
2. *The kinesthetic sense*, which associates the muscle feel of an action with
3. *Immediately observed results.* By this association,
4. *Correction in subsequent practice* actions can improve performance. Then
5. *Continued practice* to develop new functional nerve pathways (see Chapter 14, "Teaching Techniques"). The practice (item 1) is guided by items 2, 3, and 4. The association of items 2 and 3 is the basis of self-improvement by practice. (Interpretation of item 3 by a trained coach, adviser, or teacher, with his guidance of practice activity is not ruled out by the term "self-improvement." The term is used to infer conscious effort at improvement, rather than mere, automatic repetition of motion.)

### Common Elements

Obviously the skill elements involved in the use of the simulator must be the same as those used in driving. Appropriate movements of the steering wheel (hand-over-hand, etc.), foot movements, and signaling—in themselves—can undoubtedly be performed with mechanical simulation. To a degree these would similarly be performed with a very simple mock-up of an automobile. This would involve item 1, practice, and item 2, kinesthetic sense. The results (item 3) of each movement, real or represented for interpretation, would be lacking. Therefore, corrective practice to achieve skill in turning a *car* would be impossible.

Practice (item 1) with the simple mock-up would improve the mechanical hand-over-hand movement (for example), but it would be similar to the parrot's improvement of his "English," disassociated from meaning—in this case from the turning behavior of the car. Although the person could improve his hand-over-hand turning of the wheel, except for the mechanics of that movement, he would not be learning to steer the car. He would not be getting the feel of how the car responds to the degree of wheel turn. If he had no way of knowing that he was oversteering, he would not learn to correct the fault, but would go on practicing it.

## *Time*

The time element in observing results (item 3) is very significant. It might be said that we have a "kinesthetic memory," inasmuch as we can repeat movements and achieve positions (as the trained gymnast cited earlier) after an interval which followed the learning of a skill. However, like any ability to recall, it has limits.

If a beginner learning to play basketball *were unable to observe the result after each shot,* but had to await completion of his hundred shots, he would not be able to recall the kinesthetic feeling of the force used with each. To be told that he had overshot on 18, undershot on 26, shot 13 to the left of the basket and 29 to the right of it, and scored on 14 shots would give him no "feeling" (kinesthetic recall) to know what to do to correct his shots.

The shorter the time interval between a practice movement and observation of results (visual feedback) and the fewer the intervening movements (if any), the better the "climate" for correction. The same implication holds true between observation of results and subsequent practice.

## *"Kinesthetic Feedback"*

In addition to the time factor in *seeing* results, practice of skills in which the result is normally *felt* should also include that feeling as *accompanying* the result. When you pick up an object from the table, your kinesthetic sense gives you a measure of the resistance of gravity and you exert just enough upward pressure to lift it—not 50 pounds more. (In the latter case the object would rise high and abruptly.) The same is true in closing a drawer and in turning the steering wheel of a car.

The actual movement of the wheel accomplished by the muscular contraction not only is observed by the eyes, but is *felt* through the proprioceptors. The *observed* movement of the car is accompanied by that *felt* movement in the muscles. The two are associated, with practice. There is a "feedback" of (associated) kinesthetic feeling to go with the observed reaction of the car. The feeling comes from contraction of muscles. When learned through practice, this contraction of muscles which is associated with a desired movement can be performed correctly at will to accomplish that car movement.

In practice, therefore, it is important that the appropriate feeling and the observed result accompany each other, so that they become firmly associated. [Lack of this "feel," from not having the hands in different (appropriate) positions, is why "walking the wheel" causes the car to "wander" (see Chapter 14, "Teaching Techniques"). Complete dependence is then placed upon vision of car movements off course, and the advantage of the kinesthetic sense in steering is lost.] Practice movements, then, should be accompanied by observed results in terms of car movement (visual feedback) and kinesthetic feeling (kinesthetic feedback) in order to associate the two in the central nervous system of the learner. If they are not, then the skill being learned is merely that of turning the steering wheel—the observed result not associated by such practice with the kinesthetic feeling. *In developing new functional neural pathways* (see Chapter 14, "Teaching Techniques"), *movement that is correct in terms of the desired result is necessary—if the new pathway pattern is to be the correct one.*

## PSYCHOLOGICAL ELEMENTS OF DRIVING

Here, measurement becomes more tenuous. Claims have been made of successful accomplishment of teaching of various psychological elements of driving through use of simulators. Evaluation of the degree of effectiveness of the procedure must be made separately in the case of each of those elements.

### Simulation of Environment

Interpretation of environment is necessary to determine choice and degree of driver response. The quality of reproduction of the highway environment by the simulator is undoubtedly an important factor in affecting the psychological elements of driving.

The environment the driver observes should be the same, or capable of being readily interpreted, as that in which he will operate on the road. Also, his actions should affect him, through affecting his "car" in his environment, in the same way as they would on the road. (The quality of environmental effect applies also in the matter of the visual feedback as a factor in skill learning.) Both the degree of realism in the simulated highway environment and the existence of effective interaction among driver, car, and environment are important factors in the psychological impact of the simulator.

### Emotion

The emotional factor in driving has been mentioned in connection with driving simulation and is considered by some to be possible of duplication in this laboratory situation. Some individual teachers added this touch years ago by disturbing the concentration of students who were performing some specific driving-connected coordination, by producing loud, unexpected traffic and other noises in the classroom. These may have produced some effect in teaching the student to concentrate on his task. Most of the immediate reactions to such sounds are reflexive in nature. Continued repetition of the sounds causes, in the normal individual, a lessening of effect. (In individuals who do not so adjust, the reaction is unpredictable.) The lessening of effect, however, tends to be very temporary.

There is little doubt that the laboratory cannot duplicate the emotion-inspiring nature of actual practice driving on the road. No amount of "duplication" of environment will convince the student to the point of intense hypothalamic involvement (Chapter 4, "Attitude and Behavior") that he is on the road, with its hazards, and with a "this-is-it" feeling.

## *Attitude*

An attitude effect has been claimed by some proponents of simulator training. If the environmental situations involved in the training evoked discussion, and if the discussion was directed in accord with sound attitude-conditioning principles (Chapter 4, "Attitude and Behavior"), there may well have been some attitude effect. The degree of effect would depend, of course, on the quality and quantity of the attitude-affecting discussion and/or instruction.

There have also been claims that simulator use has produced attitude-conditioning superior to that achieved in in-car instruction. The lesser emotional involvement of the former would tend to contradict this. There is the possibility that more time was taken for discussion and conditioning by the teacher and that this had such a result. This would indicate, of course, that the simulator was used in lieu of procedures of the classroom phase of the course rather than of in-car instruction.

Conclusions indicating superior attitude effect must be considered highly subjective, however, in view of the limitations of instruments for testing attitude (Chapter 4, "Attitude and Behavior"). Also, if the simulator were being considered for use in lieu of normal classroom procedures, it should then be compared in all its aspects with customary classroom equipment, such as that usually termed "audiovisual aids." There is no convincing evidence of the driving simulator being an appropriate instrument for attitude development.

## *Caution*

When an instrument such as the simulator is developed and put into use, experimentation is desirable. However, enthusiasm sometimes breeds rationalizations. The teacher who would investigate the potentials of a teaching device should keep in mind that unforeseen values may exist and should be recognized and communicated throughout the profession. However, values are much more likely to be realized as the result of planning for them when designing the machine. Apparent emergence of values beyond those inherent in the design should be met with very critical analysis. The burden of proof should be on those claiming such values.

## *Choice of Reaction*

The concept of "reaction" here means the driver's reaction to the highway environment. The more *realistically* the environment is reproduced in the simulator, the more significant is the driver's reaction to it. Similarly, the more *comprehensive* the simulation of environment (within the limits of realism), the greater the opportunities for choice of reaction.

Within the area of choice of reaction, one other quality of the instrument is important, the potential for *measurement* of the reaction which indicates choice. For example, does the driver choose to steer when the choice was offered too late to brake? If so, does he steer correctly, or does he understeer or oversteer, and how much? These details of reaction are important in practice as well as the over-all "either-or" choice. Also, to be effective, the simulator must feed back an accurate, timely interpretation of the driver's reactions.

## Timing of Reaction

Practice in driver reaction should also develop efficient timing of reaction if the "feedback" from the machine is effective. For sustained driver reaction, beyond the instantaneous, the machine must react as would a car presenting the driver with the *changing* environment as it is altered by his actions.

# THE TESTING FUNCTION

The simulator has been considered also an instrument for testing. Depending upon the characteristics of the machine, testing for ability in some of the elements of driving is undoubtedly possible. Basically, the question is, "How well does the machine show the results of the driver's movements in terms of car response and environmental effect?"

A characteristic of testing in road (and simulator) instruction which is very important to recognize is that instruction and testing are usually *concurrent aspects of the same procedures.* When a teacher instructs a student in performance of a driving maneuver, he is also observing the student's progress and achievement. Unless the student has additional practice time before the end of the course *without the teacher,* instruction and testing are performed *simultaneously.* This method differs from the traditional classroom procedures of teaching for a time, and then devoting a set time for testing only. The strength of this custom may lead some driver education teachers to follow the separate, end-of-the-course testing procedure, divorced from instruction, to a degree that unduly penalizes the student of valuable instruction time. This can be done with the simulator as well as in in-car instruction.

The simulator qualities concerned with visual feedback are significant also in using the machine for testing. Those concerned with kinesthetic feedback are similarly significant, since they are a determinant of the quality of the student's movements. Evaluation of the individual model of simulator for testing, as well as for teaching, should include analysis of those qualities.

The above discussion should help an instructor evaluate the effectiveness of driving simulators in general and any specific simulator in particular. The next step for interested instructors will be to gather data on the equipment that is available. In some cases, studies have been made comparing the driving performance of students trained entirely in a car with that of students receiving part of their instruction in a simulator.

136 CLASSROOM INSTRUCTION

In the following paragraphs, four simulators are briefly described. The source is also given so that further details may be obtained.

1. AETNA DRIVOTRAINER (Drivo Division, Rockwell Manufacturing Co., The Rockwell Building, Pittsburgh, Pa.). A number of films have been prepared, taken from a vehicle moving in traffic. These are projected in the classroom in front of a number of students, each in a "car" equipped with standard controls such as steering wheel, brake, etc. The number of units in a classroom varies, but usually is about twelve. As the film progresses, the student is to drive his "car" in a manner appropriate to the scenes before him. The response of each student in the use of his controls is recorded on a master record so that at the end of the film the instructor has a record of the performance of each student in reacting to a number of traffic situations. This is a programmed trainer since the action of the student has no effect on the program presented.

FIGURE 9-1 The Aetna Drivotrainer.

2. ALLSTATE GOOD DRIVER TRAINER (Evans Industries, 9756 Wilshire Boulevard, Beverly Hills, Calif.). This simulator is quite similar to the Aetna Drivotrainer in that films are used to project highway scenes and students manipulate regular automobile controls. The one added feature is a set of dials immediately in front of each student so that the student can check to see if he made the correct response to the scene being shown at the time. This is a programmed trainer since the traffic scenes presented are in no way controlled by the responses of the student.

FIGURE 9-2   Allstate Good Driver Trainer.

3. SIM-L-CAR (Link Division, General Precision, Inc., Binghamton, N.Y.). In this device miniature roadways, vehicles, and a landscape are built on a transparent disk about three feet in diameter. A fixed point source of light projects shadows of this landscape on the back of a translucent screen several feet in front of the driver. The student sits behind the wheel of a regular car. The control devices of the car are connected to the transparent disk so that the driver controls the motion of the disk and in turn the view of the roadway projected on the screen. This enables the driver to select the path he wishes to take and the speed at which he wishes to drive. This is a nonprogrammed simulator for a single student. The scene presented the student is determined by the roadway he decides to follow.

4. AAA AUTO TRAINER (American Automobile Association, 1712 G Street, N.W., Washington, D.C.). The Auto Trainer, which has the regular controls of an automobile, features the principle of instantaneous feedback, accurately depicting the result of each movement of the driver. The student operates the machine as an unprogrammed simulator since each of its responses conforms to a specific action by the driver.

## Use of Simulators

Driving simulators are relatively new and are still being developed and improved. During the 1963–1964 school year, an estimated 457 schools in 35 states used simulators for giving instruction to some 141,000 students.

It is considered advisable that when simulator instruction is used it be

FIGURE 9-3  Sim-L-Car.

assigned a 4-to-1 time ratio in the laboratory phase of the course, that is, four hours with the simulator to substitute for one hour behind the wheel of the dual-control car.[1]

## Deciding on the Use of Simulators

As a specialist in driver education, the teacher will be looked upon to advise the school authorities if and when the purchase of such equipment is being considered. A careful analysis of all available data is indicated, taking into consideration all the elements of effective simulation previously discussed in this chapter. If, after careful analysis, it is decided that simulator training can be substituted for some of the behind-the-wheel instruction, the next step is to determine a suitable location for installation of simulation equipment.

Once these matters are decided upon, the factor of economics should be considered, taking into account all local conditions. In other words, having a given number of students to instruct, what are the costs per year with and

[1] *Policies and Practices for Driver and Traffic Safety Education,* National Commission on Safety Education, National Education Association, Washington, D.C., 1964, pp. **8, 23**.

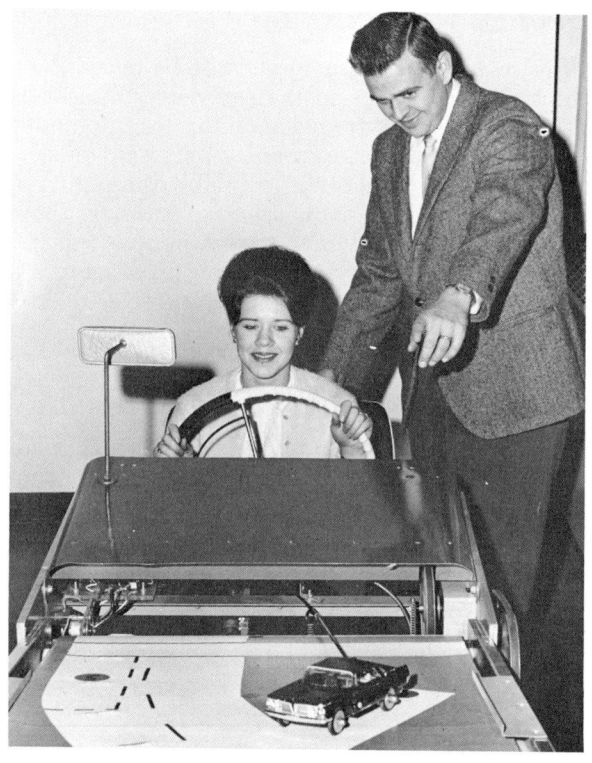

FIGURE 9-4 AAA Auto Trainer.

without simulators? In making this comparison, the following costs should be considered:

1. Teacher's salary
2. Dual-control car costs
3. Depreciation and maintenance of simulators
4. Classroom space required

If it is decided that the use of simulators will reduce the cost of instruction without affecting the quality, then the selection of a specific simulator should be based on the previous discussion in this chapter.

## RESEARCH IN DRIVING SIMULATION

There is a great deal yet to be learned about driving simulation. Some research has been performed, chiefly to determine the degree of carry-over, or "transfer of training," from learning on a simulator to driving performance in an automobile. Though some conclusions highly favorable to the use of simulators in driver education have been reported, further research and some refinement of research procedures are needed. The teacher would be well advised to regard the results of investigations thus far conducted as inconclusive.

## Transfer of Training

In reading reports of this research, certain terms will be encountered frequently. One, "transfer of training," refers to the carry-over of learned abilities from one situation to another, as from simulator to automobile. The learned qualities favorable to carry over, or transfer, are said to show *positive transfer*. If, on the other hand, they seem to inhibit the ability to perform in the new situation, they are said to show *negative transfer*. Showing no effect either way, they are said to show *no transfer*, or *zero transfer*.

Although these terms have been accepted and used by investigators in these studies, there is some naïveté in their composition. Negative transfer, for instance, is merely a term of convenience which really signifies a *positive* transfer of some learned element or elements of the task which inhibit, are unfavorable to, or oppose performance of the task in the new situation. One does not learn a negative or "minus" quantity of ability to perform a task, and carry over that minus, "owed," quantity into a new situation, "subtracting" a mathematical deficit from the ability to perform in the new situation. This point is not of great concern at the moment unless (1) investigators interpret this term to carry the mathematical meaning of "negative" or "minus," and base their research procedures on it, or (2) it conceals, and prevents identification of, the factors which, learned in the original environment, inhibit performance of the task in the new one. Since one encounters little or no attempt to identify them, item 2 may be the case.

## Significance of Kinesthetic Feedback

This is a *feeling* originating in the proprioceptors (sensory nerve endings) in the muscles, which enables a person to know the degree of contraction of those muscles. Interpreted, it tells the person the position of the body parts concerned and the force applied in the movement of these parts. It is often accompanied by visual *feedback*. Without kinesthetic feedback, movements would be as poorly coordinated and controlled as those of a person with a neurological disorder which destroyed the function of the sensory neurones in the posterior horns of the spinal cord, as in the locomotor ataxia. This condition is an example of dependence on visual feedback. Even the walk is characteristic. Investigators who minimize the significance of kinesthetic feedback in skill learning appear to miss or ignore this evidence long known to neurologists, in reliance on the investigator's own limited observation.

Some interpret kinesthetic feedback as only a matter of the "feel" of the machine. Some are concerned only with the *resistance* of the instrument, without regard to the essential "feel" of the position of the body part concerned—the selection of muscles and the degree of contraction of each, both in learning the movement and in reproducing it—the latter depending upon what we might call "kinesthetic memory." Without this kinesthetic memory we would have to watch both hand and shift lever until they touched, no matter how long we practiced the move.

Obviously, if practice directed the hand to a certain spot to contact the lever, and if we later reversed the position of the lever in another (car) situation, there would be some tendency to "use the wrong hand." This is common among drivers who change from one car to another with the parking brake on the opposite side of the steering column. This tendency is a case of "kinesthetic memory" with "negative transfer." Of course, it is more subtle when the skilled movement appears to be practically the same in the original and in the new situation. Perhaps the greater subtlety obscures its significance. The "wrong-hand" phenomenon is similar to the effect of steering part of the time with the top of the wheel and at other times with the hands at the "lazy" position at the bottom of the wheel—*opposite* movements to achieve the same machine response—a poor skill-learning (and maintaining) practice.

## *"Procedural and Adjustive"*

*Procedural* responses, or acts, are said to be of the "all-or-none" variety. You either turn the ignition key to "on" or you don't. *Adjustive* responses are identified as requiring a continuous adjustment in response to the condition encountered by performing the movement. In moving the foot to the brake pedal, the movement is termed "procedural." The continuing adjustment of brake pressure to bring the vehicle to a smooth stop properly is said to be an "adjustive" response. One can see here evidence of roughness of definition, terms of convenience but without difference in fact.

This concept of "procedural" versus "adjustive" evidences a degree of naïveté inasmuch as the difference is fictional, existing as defined in the minds of its proponents, rather than in reality. "Simple" acts such as lifting a cup to the lips or turning the ignition key have the same adjustive qualities as braking to a stop. When you lift a cup of coffee in a restaurant, a cup of different design, capacity, and weight than those you may be accustomed to at home, you do not lift it as high as your nose or eyes because you contracted certain muscles too strongly. You do not fail to lift it off the table because you underestimated its weight. You feel the weight of the cup at the very first of the lifting movement. Guided by visual and kinesthetic feedback, you make an infinite number of "adjustments" during the movement.

Motor innervation (a complex world in itself) was combined with proprioceptive (kinesthetic) feedback and visual feedback in an inconceivably intricate interaction coordinated under cerebellar control (see Skill Learning in Chapter 14, "Teaching Techniques"). Lacking kinesthetic feedback as in certain neurological disorders, vision would compensate to a degree and the movement could be accomplished, but clumsily. Without either feedback, the attempt to handle the cup would be a pitiful failure.

The coordination of factors comprises an extremely fine "adjustive" process from the beginning of the act to the end. The characteristic of that act which appears to have misled many research investigators is the fact that it takes place in so short a time with less consciousness of the continuing kinesthetic control. Movements that were not "adjustive" would resemble those of the spastic case. Unless you know these facts, you don't recognize them by "reasoning out" what you observe. Intensive preparation in the pertinent disciplines is basic to research, and future investigators in driving simulation may have to abandon some of the old concepts inherited from past study procedures of other fields.

*A detailed analysis of the skill elements in the individual driving simulator with a parallel analysis of those in the driving task, based on sound knowledge extant in pertinent disciplines is one thing that is urgently needed.* We don't really know the true potential of the simulator, or which of its components may be successful and to what degree, and which may not be.

As in the case of some other new teaching media, we have evaluated the simulator against the traditional in-car teaching with the same classic criteria each time and we almost inevitably arrive at the same classic conclusion: "No significant differences." It becomes increasingly evident that these criteria are not sufficiently sensitive to the qualities to be measured, with the possible exception of the knowledge factor.

## A Closer Look Is Needed

Statements have been made that the movements requiring continuous adjustment to perceptual feedback information tend not to transfer (in the positive sense) from typical driving simulators to actual driving. This is probably true, accepting the common concept of *adjustive response*. Since kinesthetic feedback is involved in all of them (one couldn't control muscular contraction without it, even if the response of the machine were learned by visual feedback), the belief of others that realistic kinesthetic feedback is not necessary in simulation is not supported. Rather than the existence of a *basic difference* between "procedural" and "adjustive" actions, a different degree of transfer may be due to the nature of the former being more accurately reproduced in simulation than are the feedback elements of the latter.

To get a clearer picture, the investigator should first discard the narrow concept of "learning" as taking place in a simulator or car, under instruction. Most neuromuscular coordinations are learned informally, without instruction. Then, if he will ask himself why the individual with a neurological condition which prevents proprioceptive stimuli from reaching the brain cannot perform a complex skill movement, or why he can't "learn" to do it, the important point becomes obvious: "because he lacks kinesthetic feedback." In simulation this phenomenon may be present in sufficient degree and place for one movement to be learned adequately, but in the same mechanical environment it may be missing in the case of another movement.

Steering is considered by investigators to be an "adjustive" response which surprisingly shows definite positive transfer from simulator to car. It is not surprising on analysis, since a simple mock-up would accomplish some skill learning, as the hand-and-arm movements in hand-over-hand turning of the wheel. These movements comprise one element of steering, as the parrot's sounds are one element of talking. The carry-over, or "positive transfer" should be expected—to a degree.

FIGURE 9-5 Some simple elements can be learned with the simple mock-up.

*Summary*

The purpose of this treatment of research in simulation is not to deny its value, nor to discourage simulation or further research. It is to make the teacher familiar with research in the field and its terminology and concepts. Also, it should show something of the limits of research today—how much we still have to learn—and that one should not accept the conclusions of any one study as final. The teacher should become well-informed on the subject and the principles involved, including those of skill learning (Chapter 14, "Teaching Techniques"), before deciding whether or not simulation is desirable—fits his program—and if so, what type would be best.

## THE SIMULATOR AS AN INSTRUMENT FOR RESEARCH

There is another implication of the term "research" in relation to the driving simulator. It can be employed as an *instrument* or a *device* for research in the matter of learning about the driving task itself. For some investigative procedures, both safety and economy are best served by the use of a simulator. In addition, some conditions are more susceptible to control.

Major research projects are under way in which simulators will be developed for use in research programs. The RCA Data Systems Center, Bethesda, Maryland, was awarded an $180,000 contract to build a driving simulator. The subject will be seated at the controls of a simulated automobile. He will be faced with highway situations coming toward him on moving belts. The roadway will be twenty feet long, made up of five endless belts with two lanes of the roadway, two shoulders of the road, and one center strip. The Goodyear Aerospace Corporation was awarded a smaller contract to build a driving simulator. This will involve a model of a roadway and surrounding terrain. A television camera will move along the roadway picking up the scene and projecting it on a screen in front of a driver behind the regular controls of a car. These controls in turn will guide the television camera over the miniature roadway.

## THE CONTROLLING FACTOR

It has not been the intent of this chapter to quote the specifications of the various makes of driving simulators, nor to recommend them for purchase by school districts. It is believed that the function of a teacher preparation textbook on this subject is to present data upon which the teacher can base his pertinent decisions in the future in light of the specific needs of his situation and of the equipment available at that time. This chapter has been designed as a study of the *human factors* in driving simulation. The various machines of present and future may be matched with them by the teacher in making his decisions. Human factors, and not machines, must be the constant element.

## SELECTED BIBLIOGRAPHY

*Driver Education and Driving Simulators,* National Commission on Safety Education, National Education Association, Washington, D.C., 1960.

*New Horizons for Highway Safety through Driving Simulation,* Automotive Safety Foundation, Washington, D.C., 1961.

*Policies and Practices for Driver and Traffic Safety Education,* National Commission on Safety Education, National Education Association, Washington, D.C., 1964, pp. 8, 23.

# Educational Television            10

A NUMBER of years ago, New York University introduced a television version of a course in literature. Scheduled as the "sunrise semester," it met with enthusiastic reception by the viewing public. Other courses followed, somewhat on the principle of "live" correspondence courses. College credit was given, and the results in terms of learning were found to be excellent. These courses were broadcast from a regular commercial broadcasting station. Many similar offerings are presented on the commercial wavelengths throughout the country.

Special broadcasting facilities now exist for educational programs. This new branch of the television medium is known as *educational television* (ETV). Depending on the type of broadcast service, the programs may or may not be viewed on the ordinary receiving set. On some sets, special attachments can be used to bring educational television programs to the home viewer.

Educational television may become a significant factor in driver education. Depending upon the development of the medium for general education, it is possible that driver and traffic safety education may acquire its share of TV time. This may depend also on the availability of teachers in the various subject fields, and it may be affected by beliefs in the matter of which subjects will gain most from applying the concept of the "master teacher."

There are three methods of broadcasting educational television programs:

1. Open ETV from commercial stations
2. Closed system ETV, used internally in a school system or on a college campus
3. Microwave, used for schools and colleges, a combination of closed and open broadcast

Television programs that broadcast only to schools are now called *instructional television* (ITV). The development of instructional television since its origin in Houston, Texas, in 1953, has been extensive. There are now twelve station networks, with eight more in the process of development. Many cities have two educational television stations.

Educational television can be used for broadcasting programs from schools, such as:

1. Telecourses
2. Public information broadcasts
3. School board meetings
4. Showing school programs

The full potential of educational television has yet to be explored. Employed by a skillful teacher, it is an instrument which brings his skill to many more students than he could reach in the conventional teaching situation.

We have heard much in late years of the rapidly expanding school enrollment in many suburban areas. In reality, we have been involved in three areas of rapid expansion:

1. School enrollment
2. Subject matter content in the total curriculum
3. Technology

Many schools have availed themselves of the TV medium to gain greatest advantage from the services of superior teachers. Many local school systems and some state education departments are experimenting with educational television as a method of offering a higher quality of instruction to more students than ever before.

There are strengths and weaknesses in instructional television, just as there are in the traditional visual aids. A careful analysis of both will lead to a more effective use of this new educational medium. An inescapable weakness of educational television is the lack of personal relationship between the student and the TV teacher. The lack of opportunity to adjust to individual differences of rate of learning and needs and the absence of interaction between pupil and teacher and among pupils are weaknesses of the media. Another obvious weakness is the inability of the students to engage in discussion of the subject matter under the direction of the TV teacher.

There are advantages in educational television that are worthy of note. They are:

1. A master teacher presents every subject.
2. In-service training of the class teacher is possible by observing superior presentations.
3. The same instructional services are available to small schools as to the large centralized schools.
4. Visual aids not readily available can be used in the broadcast lessons.
5. The class teacher can devote more time to individual attention to each student, having been relieved of the pressure of major presentations.

The success of television instruction depends primarily upon close cooperation between studio and professional staff in preparation, presentation, and follow-up activities.

## Educational Television in Driver and Traffic Safety Education

Interest in this unique form of instruction in driver education has been evident since 1957, when Cincinnati, Ohio, evolved a plan for using kinescopes for thirty minutes of TV presentation, to be followed by twenty minutes of class discussion. All instructors involved were qualified teachers of driver education. Evaluation of the instructional TV program indicated that brighter students tended to show greater achievement with its use, whereas there was no significant difference for slower students.

In 1959, Dade County, Florida, instituted and has continued a program of live broadcasts of fifteen minutes each. They are scheduled three times per week, for a total of twelve telecast hours. Eighteen hours of conventional classroom instruction is also provided by qualified driver education teachers. The program is coordinated so that the normal classroom work is motivated by the telecast. The open broadcast form of educational television is used, and all lessons can be received on home TV sets. The medium is serving as a form of adult education.

New York State developed a plan of providing a complete classroom course of driver education on educational television. Evaluation was not completed. Because of circumstances not related to driver education, the plan has been suspended.

South Carolina organized a series of lesson plans for thirty half-hour telecasts, using the Cincinnati kinescopes as a foundation and integrating lessons of local interest. The lesson plans were developed by a group of driver education teachers and distributed throughout the state by the TV station to schools requesting them. The local driver education teacher could plan his lessons on the prepared outline in advance of the educational

FIGURE 10-1 Regular channel television can extend the doctrine of driver education to almost unlimited audiences outside the school. High school teams competing in a statewide tournament share the benefits of their driver education experience with the public.

television lesson. This test project has been used to determine interest in the program. If the demand proves to be high, a series appropriate to the state will be prepared.

Texas developed its first edition of an educational television program of driver education during the summer of 1964, under the leadership of the Texas Education Agency, and with the cooperation of driver education teachers, school administrators, and outside consultants.

Because of many variables involving time, schedules, and numbers of students, various plans are suggested for implementation of the program. In general, the plan operates within the framework of team teaching, with the "master teacher" giving the televised presentations. Schools may utilize the telecasts as an enrichment device, a new medium of audiovisual instruction.

## Evaluation Studies Are Needed

Because of the comparative newness of television as an educational medium, it is necessary to proceed slowly and evaluate carefully. The problems of scheduling, continuity, and course content are sometimes difficult to overcome because of differences in community patterns. However, because of the growing trend of states and communities in adopting uniform motor vehicle laws and ordinances, it appears that driver education may soon provide an educational TV series to be used throughout the country. It would be supplemented by live telecasts to relate local differences to the whole program.

Television has a place in the instructional program of driver and traffic safety education as well as in other school subjects. Experience will determine the extent and methods.

## SELECTED BIBLIOGRAPHY

"Educational Television and Classroom Instruction," panel discussion, *Seventh Annual Conference Proceedings,* American Driver and Traffic Safety Education Association, National Education Association, Washington, D.C., pp. 36–38, 1963.

*Professional Rights and Responsibilities of Television Teachers,* National Education Association, Washington, D.C., 1963.

*Washington County Closed Circuit Television Report,* Board of Education, Washington County, Hagerstown, Md., 1963.

Williamson, Ed.; "Teaching Driver Education by Television," *Rockwell Safety News,* vol. II, no. 1, Winter, 1964, Rockwell Manufacturing Co., Pittsburgh, Pa.

# Using Psychophysical Tests 11

PSYCHOPHYSICAL tests are those designed to measure certain human factors concerned in the driving task. A driver, through his visual sense sees a hazard and through appropriate neural pathways in his nervous system activates the muscles which move his foot from the accelerator to the brake. With psychophysical tests we can measure a person's ability to perceive his environment through the various senses, and his ability to react. Most commonly measured are various phases of vision and reaction time under different conditions.

If properly used, psychophysical tests serve several important purposes. They make the student aware of personal characteristics which affect his driving. This awareness will encourage the student to make more effective use of his senses which help him perceive the traffic situation. By learning to appreciate the value of the tests in the classroom, the student will have a more favorable attitude toward tests when given him to qualify for a driver's license. When the student becomes a voting citizen, he is more likely to support sound licensing procedures if he has some understanding of the nature and purpose of the tests proposed.

In the classroom, one of the major purposes of testing is to point out any deficiency that a student may have. Care must be exercised in doing this so as not to offend the student. It should be explained that individuals may vary greatly in many characteristics. Not all people are of the same height and weight, and it is no disgrace to vary from the average. What is important to point out to a student scoring below average is that this deficiency may affect his driving and that he may either correct it or compensate for it. It should be emphasized that even persons with rather serious deficiencies can still be safe drivers if they know their weaknesses and drive accordingly.

One important point is sometimes overlooked. What do you tell the student who makes excellent scores? Do you tell him that because of the high scores he is sure to be a safe driver? On the contrary, you tell him he has the *potential* to become a safe driver, but a little carelessness on his part can easily result in an accident. It should be pointed out to the student who makes high scores that he must make allowances for the people with low scores who will be sharing the same highway. Although our topnotch student with fast reaction time may be able to stop quickly enough to avoid hitting the car ahead, such a sudden stop may be the indirect cause of a rear-end collision by a driver following him. The following driver may be a person with very slow reaction time. He may not be able to stop soon enough.

The young driver who is not bothered by glare may be careless in depressing his headlights. Although he may be able to see well enough in the face of glare, he may blind an oncoming driver and cause an accident. A person with 20/20 vision may fail to spot a hazard soon enough because of inattention. A person with perfect color vision may fail to see a red traffic signal because he is looking elsewhere.

## *Tests Available*

Psychophysical tests are used in various degrees in different schools. Some schools use a fairly complete set of tests, others use one or two tests, and still others use no tests other than those given by the school health department. A program in this area should not be judged by the number of devices available but by the use made of whatever equipment is on hand.

The following tests have been quite generally used in high school driver education courses:

1. VISION TESTS.
    a. Visual acuity: the ability to see details under good illumination, such as the ability to read road signs at a distance under daylight conditions
    b. Field of vision: the ability to see to the sides while looking straight ahead

152    CLASSROOM INSTRUCTION

FIGURE 11-1  The Driver Evaluator measures four important characteristics: visual acuity, depth perception, field of vision, and color vision.

   c. Depth perception: the ability to judge relative distances when looking down the highway
   d. Color vision: the ability to distinguish the colors used in traffic signals and warning lights
   e. Night vision: the ability to see under night driving conditions including the ability to see under low illumination, while faced with glaring lights, and immediately after the glaring lights have passed (threshold vision, glare resistance, and glare recovery)
2. REACTION TIME TESTS
   a. Simple reaction time: the time required to move the foot from the accelerator to the brake pedal on signal
   b. Choice, or complex, reaction time: the time required to make the correct response when several responses are possible
3. OTHER TESTS LESS FREQUENTLY USED
   a. Hand dynamometer for measuring strength
   b. Audiometer for testing hearing
   c. Muscular coordination

*Securing Equipment*

   Sources for various psychophysical devices are listed in Chapter 8, "Teaching Aids and Equipment." Complete descriptive catalogs are available from the manufacturers listed. The school principal depends upon the driver education teacher for advice on the equipment to be obtained. It is, therefore, incumbent on the teacher to be thoroughly familiar with the equipment available and to have worked out a detailed plan for its use. It does not help the teacher's reputation to have a room full of equipment gathering dust because he does not know what to do with it. Neither does that equipment help the students.

The instructor who is teaching a driver education course for the first time is wise to start with two or three tests. After he has learned to make effective use of them, he can add additional tests from time to time. The following guidelines will be helpful to the teacher setting up a testing program for the first time. A priority list should be made so that the most practical and useful tests will be obtained. Tests which should be high on the list include: (1) visual acuity, (2) simple reaction time, (3) depth perception, and (4) night vision.

In some cases, space is an important factor. If a separate room for a laboratory is available, then space is usually not a problem. However, in most cases, the classroom designed for twenty-five or thirty students will have to be used. Tests will have to be placed on tables along the walls. In such cases space may limit the number of tests which can be used. It may be necessary to use only the smaller pieces of equipment which require a minimum of space.

The time required to administer the test is also an important factor. Although it is desirable to do a thorough testing job, many teachers are confronted with the problem of having inadequate time to test a large number of students. Because of this very practical problem, use of complicated and elaborate testing devices should generally be avoided.

Simplicity is another important factor in selecting a test. It is obvious that an instructor cannot personally test all his students. He must act as a supervisor and have the actual testing performed by students with their limited training. To retain respect for the testing program, the test scores

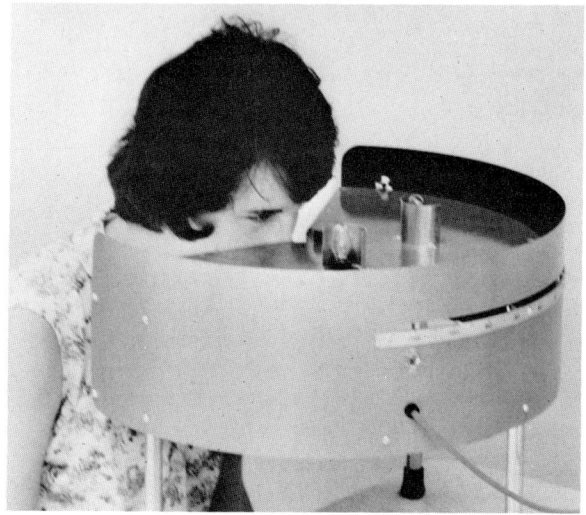

FIGURE 11-2 The field of vision test measures the ability to see objects on either side while looking straight ahead.

should be as reliable as possible. Since the tests will not be given by experts, the simpler the test, the more reliable and consistent are the scores likely to be.

Practically all tests will have certain mechanical and electrical features which are subject to wear and possible breakdown. Since these devices will usually be operated by students, it is doubly important that they be simple and durable mechanically. The more complicated tests are more likely to get out of adjustment and give different scores at different times.

## Integration with Class Activities

Psychophysical testing should not be considered as an end in itself. Rather it should be treated as an integral part of classroom instruction. Too often the tests are treated as interesting devices unrelated to the main purpose of the course. The tests should be given only after they have been thoroughly discussed in class and the students understand their relationship to driving. For example, the test of vision should be administered as soon as practicable after the subject of vision has been discussed in class. The same is true of reaction time. Although not always possible, it would be desirable to discuss reaction time in class, give the reaction time test in the classroom, and give the detonator test during the same part of the course. If this is done, the students will have a better understanding of the relationship of reaction time to actual driving.

Although the teacher is primarily responsible for instruction, the course can be enriched by enlisting outside help, provided that certain safeguards are observed. A teacher with limited knowledge of the subject of vision may wish to call in an ophthalmologist or optometrist when this subject is being covered. If this is done, the specialist should know in advance what is

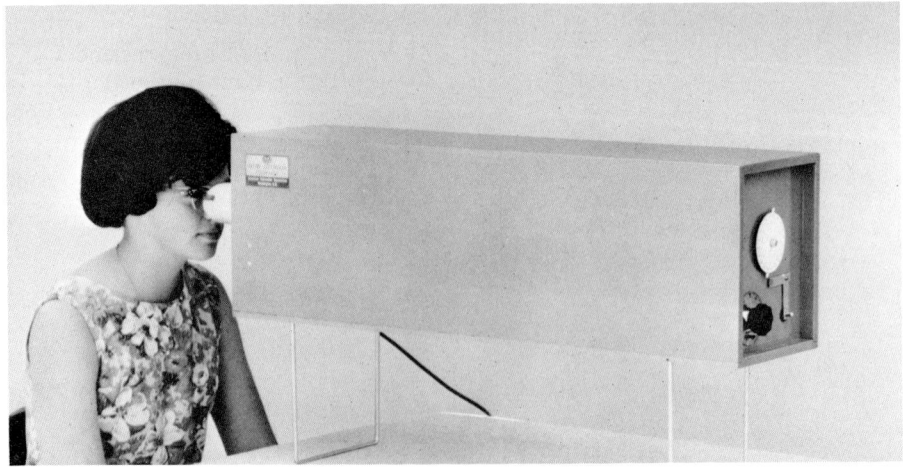

FIGURE 11-3 The Night Sight Meter measures three important abilities to see at night: (1) the ability to see under low levels of illumination; (2) the ability to see while faced with glaring lights; and (3) the ability to see immediately after the glaring lights have passed.

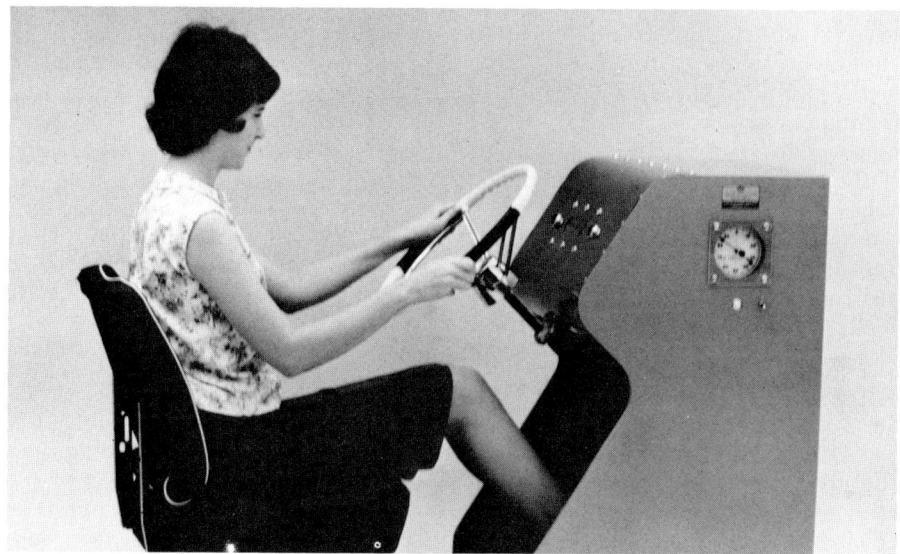

FIGURE 11–4 The complex reaction time test measures the time required for a driver to make a correct response to three different signals which come on in random order: a red light, a right-turn arrow, and a left-turn arrow.

covered in the textbook. In his talk he should stress the relationship of good vision to safe driving. Students should be encouraged to ask questions, which the average driver education teacher would not be expected to be able to answer. Because of the great amount of material to be covered in the course, the guest speaker should be given a definite time limit. Embarrassment can be avoided by scheduling the speaker for the latter part of the period. In this way the school bell will automatically limit the length of his discussion.

## *Physical Arrangements*

The old, established laboratory courses such as physics, chemistry, and biology are usually given in well-equipped laboratories. Driver education being a relatively new course is usually not so fortunate. In a few of the new buildings, special space is provided for testing devices and training aids. However, in most cases the only space available is in the typical classroom. The driver education classroom may even be used for other subjects during certain periods of the day.

If space in the classroom is limited, it may be necessary to store the tests and to set them up in the classroom only during the period when they will be used. In any case, when the tests are used they should be placed on sturdy tables along the sides or back of the classroom at ample intervals so that the operation of one test will not interfere with the operation of another. (Excepted, of course, is the floor-mounted brake reaction test.)

Vision tests should be kept away from windows where bright sunlight would interfere with the test results. If mirrors are used with vision tests to give the effect of greater distance, they should be properly lined up, and care should be taken to make sure that they do not get out of adjustment. If space permits, there is considerable merit in permanently mounting the equipment on tables. This saves the time and confusion which result when equipment is set up and taken down each time it is used. On the other hand, if the equipment is left set up during the entire semester there is a tendency for students to play with it when it is not in use.

The location of the equipment will also depend on the availability of 115-volt outlets. Care must be taken to locate all lead cords where people will not trip over them. This is one reason for placing the tests along the walls of the classroom.

## Administration of Tests

While testing is in progress, order or bedlam can exist, depending upon the preparation made by the instructor. Assume that a class of twenty-five students is to be given a battery of five tests. How can this be done most efficiently and effectively? Although there are several ways the tests may be given, here is one suggestion. Select two of the better students to be responsible for each test. These students should study the instructions thoroughly a week or two before the day for testing. The teacher should give these "examiners" additional instruction before school, during a free period, or after school. If time can be arranged, the two people on a given test should practice testing each other prior to the day assigned for testing.

When the day for testing arrives, the examiners should take their places at the equipment assigned to them. This leaves fifteen of the twenty-five students in the class to be divided among the five tests, or three for each test. In the actual testing, one examiner can give the test while the other records the scores. The persons tested should rotate around the room in cafeteria style, taking the tests in order. This distributes the students around the room and avoids congestion. During the latter part of the period, the examiners should take turns giving a test so that the free examiner can take the other tests. To expedite the testing, the examiners should record only the raw scores on the score sheet. They should not take time to compute averages or ratings.

While administering the tests, the teacher should be free to go from one test to another to make sure that each is given properly and to provide help where needed. Students should be encouraged to take the tests in order and to sit down and study their textbooks while awaiting their turns.

Most tests come with complete instructions for administering them. These should be carefully observed. The following general instructions will help to obtain reliable scores:

1. Keep the equipment clean and in good mechanical condition. Where distances are involved, measure them accurately.
2. Test all persons under the same conditions of light, noise, and distractions.
3. Give the same clear, concise instructions to all persons tested. New examiners should read the instructions.

4. Each person should be encouraged to do his very best.
5. Practice trials should be given where necessary to provide a complete understanding of the test. A sufficient number of regular trials should be given to obtain a stable average. Giving only three trials on a reaction time test is almost like pulling a number out of a hat.

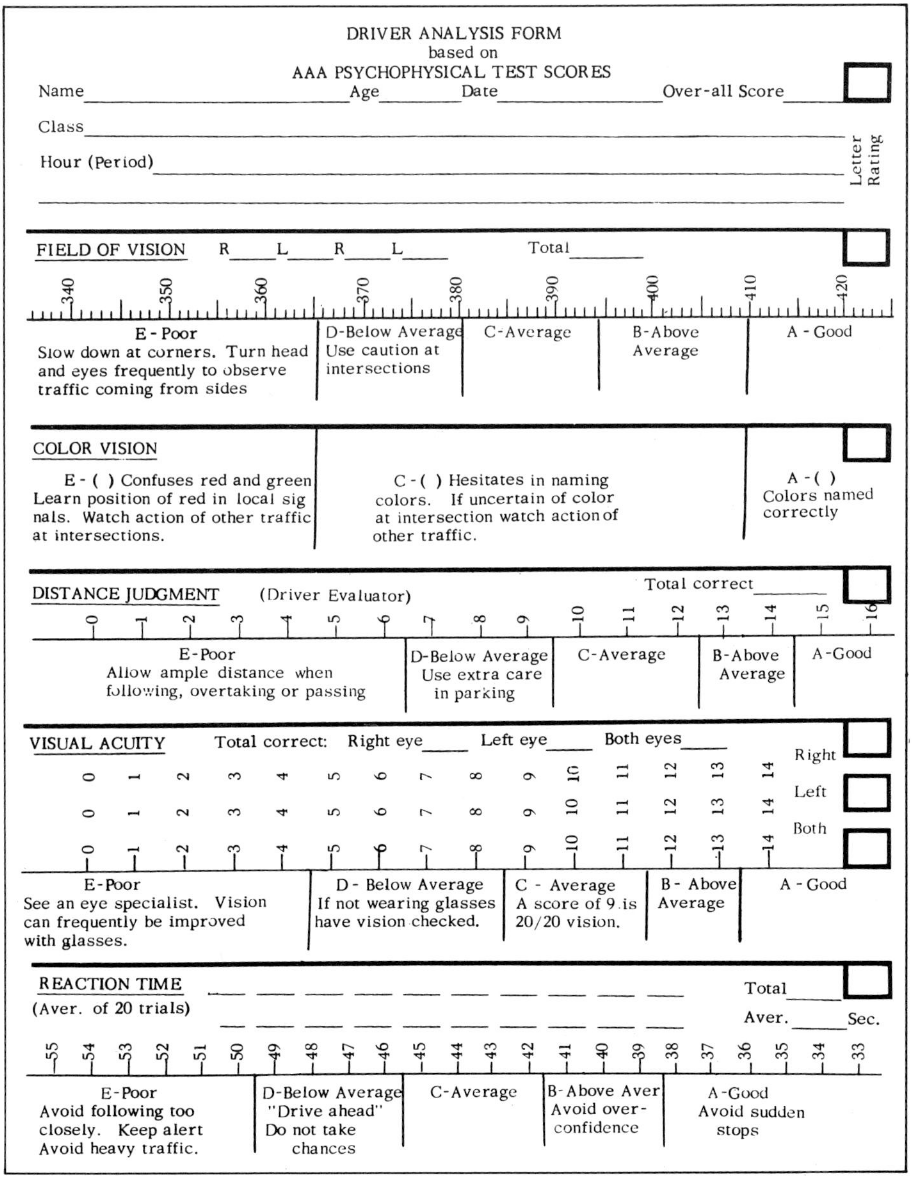

DRIVER ANALYSIS FORM
based on
AAA PSYCHOPHYSICAL TEST SCORES

Name______ Age______ Date______ Over-all Score______

Class______

Hour (Period)______

Letter Rating

FIELD OF VISION R____ L____ R____ L____ Total______

340 350 360 370 380 390 400 410 420

| E - Poor | D-Below Average | C-Average | B-Above Average | A - Good |
|---|---|---|---|---|
| Slow down at corners. Turn head and eyes frequently to observe traffic coming from sides | Use caution at intersections | | | |

COLOR VISION

| E - ( ) Confuses red and green | C - ( ) Hesitates in naming colors. | A - ( ) |
|---|---|---|
| Learn position of red in local signals. Watch action of other traffic at intersections. | If uncertain of color at intersection watch action of other traffic. | Colors named correctly |

DISTANCE JUDGMENT (Driver Evaluator) Total correct______

0 1 2 3 4 5 6 7 8 9 10 11 12 13 14 15 16

| E-Poor | D-Below Average | C-Average | B-Above Average | A-Good |
|---|---|---|---|---|
| Allow ample distance when following, overtaking or passing | Use extra care in parking | | | |

VISUAL ACUITY Total correct: Right eye____ Left eye____ Both eyes____

Right 0 1 2 3 4 5 6 7 8 9 10 11 12 13 14

Left 0 1 2 3 4 5 6 7 8 9 10 11 12 13 14

Both 0 1 2 3 4 5 6 7 8 9 10 11 12 13 14

| E-Poor | D - Below Average | C - Average | B - Above Average | A - Good |
|---|---|---|---|---|
| See an eye specialist. Vision can frequently be improved with glasses. | If not wearing glasses have vision checked. | A score of 9 is 20/20 vision. | | |

REACTION TIME (Aver. of 20 trials) Total______ Aver.______ Sec.

55 54 53 52 51 50 49 48 47 46 45 44 43 42 41 40 39 38 37 36 35 34 33

| E-Poor | D-Below Average | C-Average | B-Above Aver | A-Good |
|---|---|---|---|---|
| Avoid following too closely. Keep alert. Avoid heavy traffic. | "Drive ahead" Do not take chances | | Avoid over-confidence | Avoid sudden stops |

FIGURE 11-5 The test scores are interpreted in terms of some things they indicate that the subject, a future driver, should do.

## Interpretation of Test Scores

Some teachers consider testing an end in itself and overlook the most important aspect, the meaning of the scores to the student in relation to his future driving. After all testing is completed and each student has his score sheet, the instructor should discuss each test in detail with the entire class.

Where several trials on a test are involved, each student should compute his total or average score. Most students will want to know if they passed or failed, and how they compare with the average. Here is a good opportunity to point out that there are no pass or fail scores. Rather, there are various degrees of ability. Here is an opportunity to illustrate a normal distribution of scores. Students may report their average reaction time scores while the teacher makes a tabulation on the blackboard. The teacher may then assign an A to the top 6 percent of the scores, B to the next 25 percent, C to the middle 38 percent, D to the next 25 percent, and E to the lowest 6 percent. Each student can then give himself a letter-grade rating. In the interest of saving time, the teacher can list established norms on the blackboard, and each student can then rate himself on each test. These are not class grades.

After all scores have been computed, each test should be discussed in detail, explaining its practical application to driving. In each case, an explanation should be made of what a student with a low score can do to correct the deficiency or compensate for it. This information will be found in most high school textbooks and in the instructions for individual tests.

## Special Student Projects

If time permits, special projects making use of the test information can be assigned to groups of students. Following are a few possibilities:

1. Test students wearing glasses for visual acuity with and without glasses, and compare the scores.
2. Compute the average of a person's first five scores on a reaction time test, and compare with the last five to see if there has been any improvement.
3. Compare the average reaction times of the boys with the average for the girls.
4. Compute how far a stop sign can be read for persons with various visual acuity ratings.

### SELECTED BIBLIOGRAPHY

*Instruction Manual for Driver Tests,* American Automobile Association, Washington, D.C., 1964, 8 pp.

# Programmed Instruction — 12

*PROGRAMMED instruction is a teaching aid.* This is the most important single-sentence statement that can be made on the subject at this time. The same description can be applied to educational television, driving simulation, driving ranges, motion picture films, filmstrips, tape recorders, and textbooks. They are all *aids to teaching.* None of them, including the "teaching machines" sometimes associated with programmed instruction, is a valid *substitute* for the teacher. Each has its place—some a more important place than others—in the repertoire of the modern school and teacher.

The driver education teacher-to-be should have some acquaintance with programmed instruction in his general professional preparation, the "education courses," in the teacher-education curriculum. A detailed coverage of the technique and the mechanics of programmed instruction should not be necessary in the specialized subject field courses, such as driver education. Directions for administering the programmed lesson are simple to read and to follow. Deeper, though, are concerns about how well this medium serves in driver education. Do research reports show its value? How well does it compare with conventional teaching procedures? Is programmed material available in driver education?

Starting with the latter question, yes, programmed material is available in driver education. Some of it is coordinated with a standard driver education textbook. In fact, the subject field has its full share of what has been termed "cross-media packaged materials,"[1] filmstrips, films, booklets, supplies, and manipulative or practice materials.

## Research

Reports from many studies show a tendency to support programmed instruction as an acceptable method of teaching. As in the evaluation of other teaching aids and methods, the trend in evaluative research in this field is to instruct an *experimental* group with this technique and another, a *control* group, with traditional teaching methods. Achievement tests are given and the results interpreted as favoring one method over the other. Obviously, there are many possibilities of error and bias.

Reports of studies on programmed instruction in comparison with traditional teaching methods to date exhibit some inconsistency, with some showing no significant superiority in either the experimental or the control group, some showing the group using programmed instruction better, and an occasional one showing the control (conventionally taught) group having better results. This might seem to "average out" in favor of the programmed instruction. However, "averaging" differing conclusions such as these would be similar to finding ten witnesses who thought a car was red and another ten who remembered it as blue, and then deciding it must have been purple, or violet, or lavender, or possibly some other color, depending on whether one was thinking of paints or lights. Obviously, the only logical answer is that the witnesses did not agree and that no conclusion is possible, based on existing evidence. This is what we must accept, as yet, in comparing programmed instruction with conventional teaching in driver education—*we must judge for ourselves*, since research does not yield the answer.

One of the factors that is believed to favor the new and novel, as the "teaching machine," or even the programmed textbook, is the element of *interest* generated in the student by the novelty of the device itself—a new challenge as opposed to a common chore. This may be heightened when the programmed technique is first introduced. On the other hand, some advocates of programmed instruction, especially in reference to the machine, claim that teachers who are attitude-biased against the process tend to hinder its success. Whether this claim is valid or not is not known.

---

[1] Althea Beery, *Individualizing Instruction*, 1964 Yearbook Committee of the Association for Supervision and Curriculum Development, National Education Association, Washington, D.C.

| | |
|---|---|
| heat | 84. You can detect heat near the brake drums shortly after braking and coming to a stop. This is because the kinetic energy (or energy of motion) of the car has been changed to _____. |
| kinetic | 85. Through friction. brakes rapidly change _____ energy to heat. |
| decreases | 86. When you change a car's kinetic energy in order to slow down or stop. the kinetic energy of the car _____ (increases. decreases). |
| kinetic heat | 87. When an automobile is being stopped. _____ energy is changed to _____. which is radiated into the surrounding atmosphere. |

### THE EFFECT OF GRAVITY ON DOWNGRADES

A         B

| | |
|---|---|
| A | 88. In which case, A or B. must the stopping force overcome the pull of gravity in addition to overcoming the energy of the moving car? _____ |
| gravity | 89. Stopping a car on a downgrade requires a stopping force which will overcome kinetic energy and the pull of _____. |
| greater | 90. The steeper the hill. the _____ (greater. smaller) the pull of gravity. |
| greater | 91. When a driver tries to stop a car moving on a downgrade. part of the stopping force is needed to overcome the pull of gravity. Therefore, the braking distance on a downgrade is _____ (greater. smaller) than the braking distance on a level surface. |

### FORCE OF IMPACT

| | |
|---|---|
| impact | 92. The force with which moving objects meet is called force of impact.' When two cars collide. the force with which they collide is called force of _____. |

FIGURE 12–1 Sample page of programmed material in driver education from *Programmed Topics from Sportsmanlike Driving* (McGraw-Hill).

One point raised against the teaching machine is a claimed tendency to break down, frustrating both pupil and teacher and wasting time. This, if true, can probably be overcome and may have, if it ever has been the case in a significant proportion of the machines in use. A working trial seems to be highly desirable before purchase of any brand of machine. A possibly important point arose in one study in which the majority of teachers reported having to spend "50 percent or more" of the weekly instructional time with the machine-user group because of student requests for assistance in operating the machines.[2] This, of course, would not apply to the use of programmed material in printed form, although special instruction in the use of this new medium would be necessary at first.

Perhaps the most significant point about today's literature on programmed instruction, like that on educational television, simulators, driving ranges, etc., is that its authorship is predominantly employed in those very subject fields. One would not expect the professional baseball player to prefer cricket, nor would one expect complete objectivity, no matter how honest the intent. On one hand, we do need the direction of the expert specialist. On the other, we need thoroughly impartial research. The teacher should evaluate the authorship of any professional advocacy of any new device, in addition to judging the device objectively himself.

A related problem arises. Programming specialists and psychologists write the programmed material. At first thought, this seems quite logical. Yet, each subject field has a semantic world of its own and a body of knowledge intrinsic to it. The textbook author is traditionally one who knows the subject of the book he writes. This may not be so in the case of the programming specialist or the psychologist.

## *What Can I Believe?*

This is a question the teacher must ask himself at times, when flooded with reports, articles, recommendations, and sales literature on the various innovations in the teaching field. Here are a few points to note about programmed instruction:

1. In fairness to itself, as well as to education, it should be evaluated in every case as an *aid* to teaching—part of an instructional package—and not as a sort of automated robot-teacher intended to replace an "obsolete" human leader and counselor.
2. It should be evaluated for a specific task in a specific subject field. It may be far more appropriate to some fields than to others.
3. Certain aspects of it are fairly obvious. It does permit the individual student to pursue his task of learning at his own rate of speed; so it has this provision for individual differences. On the other hand, it does not provide for originality of response. On consideration, this point is an

---

[2] John F. O'Toole, Jr., "Teachers' and Principals' Attitudes Toward Programmed Instruction in the Elementary School," *AV Communication Review*, 1964, Department of Audio-Visual Instruction, National Education Association, Washington, D.C.

important one. There are many areas in the educative process in which we want the student's own reaction. We don't want everything to be a predictable "regurgitation" of facts he has memorized. The opportunity for originality, creativity, in programmed instruction is very limited.
4. Although student response may be individually self-paced in point of time, the programmed material which might hold one student's interest with simple, oft-repeated points to be learned would be extremely boring to a brighter student. The repeated, extremely simple frames in some of the steps appear ludicrous to students whose level of learning is average or higher.
5. There is always the danger that persons unfamiliar with the reasonable concept of programmed instructional material as an aid to the teacher may misuse it to replace him, at least to a degree. The driver and traffic safety education teacher should constantly be aware of this. His subject field is highly (and unjustifiably—see Chapter 20, "Costs and Financing") cost-conscious. It would not be out of line to state that a disproportionate amount of the impetus to research has pushed in the direction of finding methods and/or devices to cut costs of instruction. Usually a sometimes weak-sounding postscript is added, "without loss of quality of instruction." *This is not a frame of reference which would lead to improvement of instruction.*

Still more unfortunate has been the fact that, *after reliance upon extremely weak evaluative criteria,* investigators have been willing to accept "happy" conclusions that no loss of teaching efficiency was shown (negatively or positively) and that therefore the money-saving teaching processes are highly successful. The evaluative criteria should be very critically reconsidered.

In recognizing these facts, we face a clear implication for programmed instruction. Some schools having both classroom and in-car driver education will face pressure to replace the classroom teacher with programmed text material, with or without machines. This has already happened in the case of educational television. Driver education people should be prepared for such pressures and should be ready to resist them. Knowledge of their subject field and an understanding of the nature—the strengths and weaknesses—of the media proposed to replace the teacher are needed.

The well-prepared teacher neither accepts nor rejects the new media, programmed instruction, simulation, the multiple-car driving range, educational television, etc., until he has studied each. He neither fears nor fights the use of any new medium—only its *misuse.* He doesn't generalize, grouping all content of a medium as homogeneous. The "programmed text" is comparable to the "textbook"—the concept is only the cover. The *content* is critical.

The exact place of programmed instruction (as of the other teaching aids mentioned) *isn't known today*—and it won't be for some years. More research is needed on its effectiveness and its place in driver education. The best advice is, "Keep an open mind. Keep informed. Read research reports *up to* the conclusion of each, and then form your own conclusions." Better still, do your own research also!

## SELECTED BIBLIOGRAPHY

American Automobile Association: *Programmed Topics from Sportsmanlike Driving,* 5th ed., McGraw-Hill Book Company, New York, 1965.

*AV Communication Review,* Department of Audio Visual Instruction, National Education Association, Washington, D.C., 1964.

Lumsdaine, A. A., and Robert Glaser: *Teaching Machines and Programmed Learning: A Source Book,* National Education Association, Washington, D.C., 1960.

Ofiesh, Gabriel D., and Wesley C. Meierhenry: *Trends in Programmed Instruction: Papers from the First Annual Convention of the National Society for Programmed Instruction,* National Education Association, Washington, D.C., 1964.

O'Toole, John F., Jr.: "Teachers' and Principals' Attitudes Toward Programmed Instruction in the Elementary School," *AV Communication Review,* 1964, Department of Audio-Visual Instruction, National Education Association, Washington, D.C.

Schramm, Wilbur: *The Research on Programmed Instruction, An Annotated Bibliography,* U.S. Department of Health, Education and Welfare, Office of Education, Washington, D.C., 1964.

Yearbook of the Association for Supervision and Curriculum Development of the National Education Association, Washington, D.C., 1964.

# Team Teaching      13

TEAM TEACHING, like programmed instruction and other techniques, is part of the repertoire of the well-prepared teacher. It is not intrinsic to any one subject field and is logically placed in the area of his general professional preparation. The treatment of the subject here will refer to application of the team teaching concept to driver education.

    The technique is not a new one, except in its application below college level. The "master teacher" concept brings back memories of college life to generations of graduates. Many will recall the "full professor" who gave the inspiring lecture, the laboratory assistants, teaching fellows, readers, and others who "teamed up" to make the instructional team. Recently, educational television has adopted the concept of the master teacher and the team.

In driver and traffic safety education the technique has two quite different potentials. It can be used to take fullest advantage of the strengths of each member of the teaching staff, or it can be misused to defeat the professional standards that have been achieved over the years since the subject field began. It would be far less than realistic to laud each new technique or device blindly without full and frank discussion of how it will be used, or misused. A clear realization of the full scope of all the possibilities is required to enable professional people to direct their efforts toward constructive application of the medium.

## *Concentration of Teaching Strength*

Driver and traffic safety education, contrary to the belief of the uninformed, is a highly complex subject. From the physical forces involved in movement and control of the motor vehicle, to the vitally important behavior-conditioning mission of driver education, competent teaching of this subject requires a good knowledge of the physical and behavioral sciences and of other pertinent disciplines. The breadth of knowledge required fully justifies the eventual requirement, already recommended, of a minor in the field.[1] Although not yet universally accepted, the obvious extension of that concept of the minor as the minimum is recognition of a need for a full four-year course with safety education, including driver education, as the basic preparation of the teacher. There are now, of course, many individuals in the field with advanced degrees in safety education.

Here is another sensitive area in the subject field where frankness and a realistic appraisal can make the difference between complaisant mediocrity and maximum efficiency. Here are implications for the *team teaching* concept. An objective appraisal of our teacher resource brings out the following facts:

1. Of all driver education teachers in service today, a comparatively few have completed teaching minors in the field. Some have but two or three college credit hours of specific preparation in addition to their certification in some other subject field. A comparatively few, teaching in states which have had no specific driver education requirements for teaching, have had no special preparation at all.
2. Those who teach high school driver education today have had widely divergent professional preparation. They came from industrial arts, physical education, science, and other areas of the curriculum.

A potential weakness of the subject field, the condition cited in 2, can in favorable circumstances be turned into a strong asset by application of the team teaching concept. "Favorable circumstances" refers to local school conditions which concern availability of teachers, space, cooperation, etc.

For example: A high school driver education department which numbers among its teachers one who has a strong mechanical background, possibly an industrial arts major, and one who has majored in science can combine some of its classes to good effect. The science-and-driver education

---

[1] *Policies and Practices in Driver and Traffic Safety Education,* National Commission on Safety Education, National Education Association, Washington, D.C., 1964.

teacher can serve as master teacher during that part of the classroom course which deals with nature's laws governing inertia, friction, etc. The other teacher can address both classes when on the subjects of car maintenance and the basic principles of automobile propulsion. Obviously the teacher who is not addressing the double class group would not take a free period, but would assist and at the same time learn from the presentation. This would be a very simple application of the principle of concentrating teaching strength(s) on appropriate subject materials to reach all students most effectively.

Many variations of this principle can be devised, involving members of the department and those of other departments where schedules and subject matter permit. The complete theory, philosophy, and organization of team teaching should be covered in the general professional preparation of the driver education teacher and is suggested here only for supplementary reading (see Selected Bibliography at the end of the chapter). The purpose of this chapter is to call attention to the technique as a valuable one in driver education when local conditions permit.

In cases where scheduling or space prevents doubling or tripling classes, an occasional exchange of teachers may be advantageous, to make full use of teaching strengths. Where it is possible to combine classes, however, the teacher exchange is not usually advisable, since the impact of the "master teacher" in each competency is not then effective in improving the backgrounds of the others. Also, the teachers who form a team to work with the "master teacher" in any phase of the course are in a position to follow up that lesson or lessons with integration of the material covered with other phases of the course, strengthening of the concepts, and testing and remedial follow-up.

## *To Share the Fruits of Experience*

In a school where the team teaching principle is practiced in other subject fields and thus understood and accepted, the driver education department can, without calling attention to it, perform another mission in improvement of instruction. Ostensibly to take advantage of strengths in the various competencies, the team teaching technique can be adapted to permit demonstration by experienced teachers which will improve the competencies of new teachers. The latter can take their turns in assuming the role of the "master teacher," with the expressed understanding that they will privately receive from the more experienced members of the staff any hints that may be indicated by their performance.

It is worthy of mention here that educators are well aware that age doesn't guarantee teaching ability, and that youth doesn't preclude it. Nevertheless, one does learn from teaching experience. Simple examples are these: If one addresses questions to a class as a group, he learns in time that if he names a student *before* framing the question, he loses part of his audience, and they lose the question. On the other hand, he learns also that if he asks the question first and names the student to answer it at the last moment, he holds the attention of all since anyone may be the one named to respond.

Sometimes a new teacher permits low-voiced talking while he is taking the roll. It may take quite some time, possibly experience with a number of classes, for him to learn that low-voiced student communication doesn't last. It gains volume. A hundred admonitions are likely to precede a hundred and one repetitions of the crescendo tendency. A required *silence* while taking the roll, however, is *definable*. It is far easier to maintain than a "reasonable" level of sound. Students need definable rules. These are but two of a myriad of facts that a teacher learns with experience.

The very heart of the process we call *education* is *learning from the experience of others*. It is no disgrace nor a degradation of one's ability. It makes sense and it benefits the students who, because of it, will not have to suffer all the learning processes of the teacher who profits only by *his own* experience. Team teaching can be a valuable learning process for the teacher, especially the new teacher—but by no means excluding the experienced one. For the student, it concentrates the strengths of the driver and traffic safety education staff to his best advantage.

## SELECTED BIBLIOGRAPHY

*And No Bells Ring,* Team Teaching Film, Parts I and II, two 16-mm color films of team teaching in action, 26 minutes each, National Association of Secondary School Principals, National Education Association, Washington, D.C.

Blair, Nedill, and Richard G. Woodward: *Team Teaching in Action,* Houghton Mifflin Company, Boston, 1964.

Davis, Harold S., Dr., *Team Teaching Bibliography,* Director, Staff Utilization Project, Educational Research Council of Greater Cleveland, Cleveland, Ohio, 1964.

*NEA Journal,* National Education Association, Washington, D.C., March and April, 1961.

*Policies and Practices in Driver and Traffic Safety Education,* National Commission on Safety Education, National Education Association, Washington, D.C., 1964.

# IV  IN-CAR INSTRUCTION

THE LITERATURE of driver and traffic safety education is replete with excellent directions concerning the correct way to perform each driving movement as the student sees it and does it. Although directed to the student, this approach has helped teachers to *tell* the student *what to do*. The student driver education textbook has been a right arm to learning and perhaps a left arm to teaching.

Long missing, however, has been the *how* to tell it, the *teaching* element. How can a teacher tell a student to avoid striking the curb with his right rear wheel on right turns when the student can't seem to judge the distances? What must the teacher be ready for when being passed by vehicles on the left? What should he warn the student not to do (in spite of the current popular fear of "negatives")? How many students must pass through a teacher's in-car classes before that teacher knows by experience what to teach in the car and how best to teach it? How long would it take a teacher to learn by experience what has been similarly learned by many teachers? In-car instruction *from the teacher's point of view* is a long overdue item in our professional literature.

In presenting the subject from this new frame of reference, there are no implications for discarding the long-used high school textbooks from the teacher preparation courses. Properly available to college students in these courses and, of course, to driver education teachers in the high schools and colleges, those textbooks offer a major contribution to the professional background of the teacher. The key word is "contribution." Much more is needed. The most significant gap in the in-car instruction phase of driver education has been a guide directed to the teacher.

Perhaps the simplest account of the relationship between the high school textbook presentation of this subject and that herein is that the former is written from, and for, the left side of the front seat. This book sees through the eyes of the occupant of the right front seat—a person who, through directing the mind of another, directs the highly complex reactions of that other's body—and does it in such a way that when he stops, that other mind keeps directing that other body in just that way for life. There is no place here for trial and error!

# Teaching Techniques                                   14

TEACHING is a profession. Whereas a knowledge of course content is needed to teach in each of the various subject fields, all have common elements which respond to qualities possessed by the teacher. It is to these qualities that we refer when we say, "He knows how to teach."

The subject fields have as their objectives the specific values to be gained by the students. The values vary in nature and in emphasis among the subjects in the curriculum. Two of them, stressed in driver and traffic safety education, require special knowledge on the part of the teacher. One is the attitude objective of the course, developed both in the classroom and on the road. The other is that combination of qualities needed to operate the car skillfully, taught during the in-car instruction phase of the course. The special knowledge of attitude formation is the subject of "Attitude and Behavior," Chapter 4. Achievement of the other value objective is the theme of this chapter. Here, too, is the picture of what lies ahead for the new teacher when he takes charge of the dual-control car and what he can do to give his students maximum value in their so-limited time.

## FIRST DAY IN THE CAR

Introductory procedures vary somewhat, depending on whether the same teacher has had these students in the classroom, whether they have all had classroom instruction, whether they have covered this introduction to the in-car phase of the course, and just what was taught in the classroom.

Experienced teachers know the value to the student of just *minutes* of driving instruction. They know that the more of the introduction to the car and the course that can be taught in the classroom, the more of that valuable time in the car will be saved. When it is necessary to give a complete orientation in the car, having four students in a group costs each one only fifteen minutes of potential driving time for the introductory lesson. One student in the car would lose a whole period for the same coverage. This is also true of the necessary verbal instructions throughout the course. Some are fairly time-consuming. Four students in a car group can be given such instructions in as little car time and teacher time as a single student in the car. This is, of course, a matter for department organization.

It is worthy of note here that all members of the staff who teach in the car should be thoroughly familiar with the textbook in use in the classroom. *Practice Driving Guides*[1] may be used by students during the in-car instruction phase of the course.

### *You're New?*

For the new teacher on his first day, in any class in any school, here is a point to consider. Although this is a new experience to you, your students are veterans! They have probably had all kinds of teachers over the years, and probably a variety at one time. They know that different teachers require different class conditions. Consciously or unconsciously, on the first day with a new teacher they estimate just what that teacher will require in the matter of control. Will he be fair? Is he firm? How much work does he require? And occasionally a few wonder just how far they can go to impress their classmates, without suffering dire consequences. This is the "average" class—classroom size. There is less variety in each car group, of course, but any kind of student may be present. In general, because of the nature of the subject, real disciplinary problems in the car are comparatively rare. *Under normal circumstances, the teacher sets the pattern from the beginning of the first period. A pattern once set may be quite difficult to change later. If in doubt, lean in the direction of firmness—it is easier to slack off later than to tighten up.*

[1] American Automobile Association, *Practice Driving Guides for Use with Sportsmanlike Driving,* 4th and 5th eds., McGraw-Hill Book Company, New York, 1965.

# PRACTICE DRIVING GUIDE  3

**TOPICS:**
  I. Putting the Car in Motion
  II. Stopping the Car
  III. Using the Selector Low Position in Automatic Transmission Cars

## I. PUTTING THE CAR IN MOTION

### AUTOMATIC TRANSMISSION

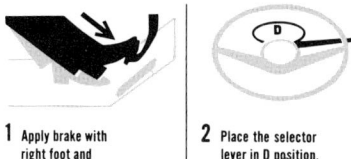

**1** Apply brake with right foot and hold through Step 5.

**2** Place the selector lever in D position.

**3** Release parking brake.

**4** Check rear-view mirror.

**5** Signal and check traffic to left and to rear.

**6** Accelerate.

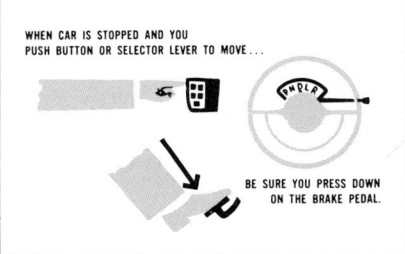

WHEN CAR IS STOPPED AND YOU PUSH BUTTON OR SELECTOR LEVER TO MOVE...
BE SURE YOU PRESS DOWN ON THE BRAKE PEDAL.

### MANUAL GEARSHIFT

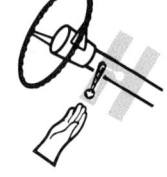

**1** Depress clutch.

**2** Shift to low gear.

**3** Release parking brake.

**4** Check rear-view mirror.

CLUTCH AT FRICTION POINT

**5** Signal before you move. Look back, check blind spot to left rear.

**6** Press accelerator. Release clutch to friction point.

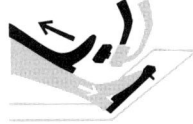

**7** Slowly let clutch pedal come up. At the same time,
**8** Increase pressure slightly on accelerator.

FIGURE 14–1  Typical lesson from a *Practice Driving Guide*.

Conceding the value in the professional advice about creating interest, this truly applies to the typical high school student. However, we also have the atypical student. Probably the most effective and easiest form of control is to convey the impression that anything other than good order in your class is unthinkable. It just isn't done. A minor break is met with a silent, "stony" look and a momentary pause. Some teachers who strive for strict discipline "blow up" at minor infractions and have no "reserve threat" for exploratory moves beyond the minor. For the new teacher, a good sound start can save an unpleasant first year!

Now—you're in the car. Your students are in a dual-control driver education car for the first time. Here, yours is the psychological advantage in establishing the pattern of student-teacher relationship. A good opening is to describe the course and its requirements. Once you (the new teacher) find that you have their full attention and acceptance as the unquestioned leader (and it doesn't take long under these circumstances), you can start putting the more nervous ones at ease with light humor and reassurances that there are no penalties for learning difficulties. Some students will be nervous at the thought of driving for the first time (at last!).

## *The Course*

The preceding advice was directed to the new teacher. Many who take the qualifying courses in driver and traffic safety education have had teaching experience in other subject fields. From this point on, this text applies to both new and experienced teachers.

Although the organization of the course will differ among high schools, several items are worth mentioning to students in the orientation period. Suggested are the following (in your own words, of course):

1. We have (as you see) four students in a car group. When one is absent from school, his driving time will be taken by another. When he returns, he will have the opportunity to make up the lost time. Don't feel hurt if you don't drive on some days. By keeping all students as near together in progress as we can, we save time we would otherwise lose by going from one location to another for suitable practice conditions.
2. Some students will learn the skills more quickly than others. This is quite natural, and no one is penalized for not learning as quickly as another. Learning more slowly doesn't mean that you will not be a good driver. Many factors enter the learning picture—even having ridden a bicycle a good deal can make a difference.
3. Most students complete all the steps (or projects or lessons) in the course. Sometimes, because of a slower skill-learning rate, a student will not complete every advanced step in the time allotted. This does not mean that he will automatically fail the course. We will take him as far as his skill-learning rate will allow.
4. Occasionally we find people, sometimes very bright people, who just do not easily become skilled drivers. This is no great problem. We just take them as far as we can in the time we have. Sometimes, when it is just a case of very slow learning, that person will become a skilled

driver in time. Sometimes he or she becomes what we may call a "station driver." Some women drivers fall into this category, often because they drive only in town, perhaps to local stores, during the day, and (perhaps) drive their husbands to and from the commuting station. Then, on weekend or other trips, the husband customarily drives. These women are not poor drivers. They are safe, dependable drivers, but limited in experience to certain types of driving situations. Being a station driver for any reason does not mean that you don't have as much right on the public highway as any person.

5. Be sure to come to class on time. You can't depend on running fast enough to catch up to this "classroom."
6. Leave your books at . . . (or on, or place them on the floor in the back, on in the trunk—a safe place).
7. When the weather is cold, we will try to keep the car at approximately classroom temperature. In this way we will avoid the necessity for wearing overcoats, scarves, etc. It is much easier to learn to drive when you can move freely. If you find the temperature uncomfortable, let me (the teacher) know.
8. In addition to our regular lessons (or projects), there is some opportunity for practice driving to and from our school parking place. We will take turns to keep this extra practice well distributed among the group.
9. Your student permits are good only for . . . . (This statement tells the student the pertinent ruling of his state law. It may be that the student learner's permit is valid only when accompanied by a driver education teacher, and only in a dual-control car.)
10. You will be in the car "observing" when others are driving. Please don't bring to class homework assignments to do or books to read. You may miss some points of instruction or some special traffic situation and the action of our driver at the time. Many such situations we can't have repeated (and frequently wouldn't want to), but many of them are excellent learning opportunities when they occur.

The procedures for obtaining a driver's license or regular permit should be described if a student is likely to be eligible for either while the course is in progress. In some states this is common, because of age eligibility. In any case, if it does take place, the student should notify the teacher and the new license or regular permit number should be recorded. In some states the school permit is recognized after completion of the course in lieu of the regular learner's permit. In any case, the student should be advised of any state and school regulations which may apply during the course.

## *"This Is an Automobile"*

The initial introduction to the car may be fairly brief if all students have previously completed the classroom course. Even in that case, however, each item should be mentioned, to be sure that every student recalls what he learned. (All through the course, especially concerning matters of hazard, the teacher should take nothing for granted as being within the student's knowledge. This principle should be remembered when teaching. Every item should be checked as it becomes pertinent to existing conditions. The new teacher will be surprised at the number of basic items many students will have forgotten.)

Normally, the first procedure is to have one of the students sit in the driver's seat (with the instructor beside him, of course) and the rest of the

FIGURE 14-2  A car becomes a laboratory.

students sit in the back of the car, but with their attention concentrated on the "driver" and the teacher's instructions. The driver is first instructed in, and performs, what may be called "predriving habits." If the first five procedures are repeated each time a person enters the driver's seat, they will soon develop into a habit pattern.

These *predriving habits* are:

1. Adjust seat
2. Lock doors
3. Adjust inside and outside mirrors
4. Fasten seat belt
5. Adjust ventilation

Next, identification should be made of the following *informational devices* and the functioning of each explained:

1. Speedometer
2. Odometer
3. Ammeter or generator charge light
4. Oil-pressure light or indicator
5. Temperature indicator
6. Fuel indicator
7. High- and low-beam indicator light

Then the *operating switches:*

1. Ignition switch
2. Starter switch

And the *auxiliary switches or controls:*

1. Headlights
2. Taillights
3. Brake lights
4. Back-up lights
5. Instrument-panel lights
6. Dome light
7. Horn
8. Windshield wipers

And the *operational control devices:*

1. Clutch pedal (if present)
2. Gearshift or selector lever, or push-button selector

FIGURE 14-3 Students should be warned never to place the outside mirror at the eye level of anyone who will drive the car.

3. Accelerator pedal
4. Foot brake
5. Parking brake

And some *additional safety features:*

1. Turn, or directional, signals
2. Sun visors
3. Defroster
4. Padded dashboard

From this list it can be seen that following the classroom course, only a brief identification of each item and a brief mention of its function are necessary. It should be remembered, however, that if this orientation is entirely new to the students, as is sometimes the case, *it is then too long and diversified to be learned in one presentation.* Repeated description of each item is then indicated at appropriate times *during the course.* When this introduction is taught as a continuous lecture, any students to whom the information is new are simply "lost."

In presenting the lesson, it is a good practice to attempt to sense any recognition on the part of the students of items and/or their functions. Those items should then be approached by means of questions, to hold attention.

## PRINCIPLES AND PROCEDURES OF INSTRUCTION

Available driver education textbooks are listed at the end of this chapter. The list includes the four most widely used high school textbooks. It would not be constructive use of text space to repeat here in detail all the *student* movements described in the various high school textbooks. In almost all schools, one or more of those books are available to the teacher, and in all teacher preparation courses such is the case. For the prospective driver education teacher to possess the student textbook and to have to purchase again the same material, raising the cost of this college textbook, is not considered desirable. Therefore, *treatment of the subject of* **in-car instruction** *here will be within the frame of reference of the driver education teacher and will consist of matters of instruction, rather than those specific directions given the students in the standard student textbooks.*

### Skill Teaching

After the orientation meeting, a number of lessons follow in an off-street area, a driving range, or possibly a large parking lot. Where such an area is not available, quiet streets where traffic is light are sometimes used. Obviously, the primary objective of this phase of the course is achievement of specific neuromuscular coordinations. This procedure is not only reasonable, but neurologically sound.

When a child learns to walk, he goes through the same learning process as the beginning driver. His first learning movements are consciously directed by *cerebrally initiated*[2] motor impulses. He shifts his weight for-

---

[2] See Chapter 4, "Attitude and Behavior."

FIGURE 14-4 During the course it is well for the students to see one "ordinary gas stop" properly performed.

ward, then moves a foot forward, shifts his weight again, moves the other foot forward, etc. He consciously directs every movement, including some movements to retain balance. It is quite obvious that during this time he could not simultaneously do this well and keep close track of a complex traffic picture. This is the stage of skill learning in which the beginning driver learns best (and, of course, more safely) when free of conflicting traffic. The situation is similar to concentration on study, without attention-distracting disturbances.

FIGURE 14-5 Offstreet practice area. Skills are first taught where there is minimum distraction.

During this phase of the student's learning, it is important that the teacher not distract the conscious learning process by too much verbal direction or by talking of other things that will come later in the course. When learning a skill, it is important that the student consciously direct his neuromuscular action accurately, since the neural pathways used in practice will be those used (in the same manner) in the learned skill. The nature of the cortically directed practice actions will be mirrored later in the cerebellar-coordinated learned skills. It is important, therefore, that the practice actions be correctly patterned. The neural tissues involved will become patterned in accordance with the patterns of the practice movements. Simply expressed, use of these principles delineates "coaching" from "heckling."

The objective of this stage of practice, neurologically speaking, is to develop by use new functional nerve pathways under the control of the *cerebellum*, the "hindbrain," the neural center specifically patterned to coordinate motor function. To "develop by use" means to "practice"—not merely to perform a coordination once or twice, not merely to be *told* how to do it, but to *practice* correctly, as directed, again and again—enough to establish a new pattern of neural pathways.

When a person first starts to practice, the initial pathway is *corticospinal*—from cerebral cortex directly through projector neurones inward and downward through the brain stem, and down the anterior horns of the spinal cord to the muscles to be used. Then, when practice has had its effect, a more complex neural network is formed, a *cortico-pontin-cerebellar-rubrospinal combination,* involving these other centers apparently better adapted to this function. Thus the neuromuscular skill is better coordinated after practice. Now, in addition, the learner can (consciously) initiate an impulse from the cerebral cortex—as when he decides to start to walk (after the skill of walking is well learned). Then he can continue walking *without conscious direction of each movement.* He can engage in a conversation on a complex subject, or a number of subjects, while the act of walking is carried on automatically.

FIGURE 14–6 Developing automatic skill movements.

This procedure is parallel to the learning process of the beginning driver. He is developing new motor patterns with cerebellar control, which will become automatic, needing only voluntary initiator impulses from the cerebrum. Then the student will be able to perform the necessary steering, accelerating, and braking movements while concentrating on the traffic, needing only initiator, conscious impulses to translate his desires into action, action which is coordinated more efficiently by the appropriate centers of the nervous system than it could be by conscious control under detailed direction by the cerebrum.

Occasionally a teacher is encountered who takes pride in moving his students into traffic situations more quickly than other teachers. Once in a (great) while one boasts of purposely starting them in heavy traffic. (If a school is so situated that this is necessary, it is, of course, unfortunate.) Although perhaps deserving of a citation for courage, the teacher is not operating in the most efficient manner. Each activity should be appropriate to the current need.

Where the manual-shift driver education car is used, for instance, the skill-learning process is more complex and therefore requires more (specifically planned) skill-practice time. One sign of insufficient basic skill practice is discernible when students who have performed the basic skills (of clutch and shift lever, steering, braking, etc.) successfully in the practice area fail to do so as soon as they find themselves in traffic. When this occurs, it is more economical of time to give them more drill on the skills in the practice area than to expect the far-less-frequent practice of the skills in traffic—*with attention partly on that traffic*—to cure the trouble. With experience, the teacher learns to recognize when the student is ready for advancement. There is no set time in terms of hours. When individual differences in learning rates would put one student far ahead of others, some practice-time adjustment within the group may be indicated.

## *The Practice Field*

Many schools have off-the-street practice areas where students are given instruction in the basic skills of driving. Some schools arrange with local police to block off a street (except for local traffic) for a practice area. Some have complete driving ranges.[3]

For best adaptability to the greatest number, the following suggestions for instruction will be arranged for the practice-field-and-street combination. Most can be adapted to other situations. They are not the same step-by-step instructions found in student textbooks, but points of *instructional procedure* to supplement the high school textbook material.

## *Be Ready*

If your practice field is at a distance from the school—and certainly in all cases before taking the driver education car on the road—a set of emergency procedures should be formulated. Local conditions, of course, will determine their nature and number. The following are suggested as desirable in driver education cars:

1. Phone numbers in glove compartment:
    a. The school
    b. The police headquarters
    c. The school physician

---

[3] See Chapter 16, "Driving Ranges, Routes, and Practice Areas."

2. Emergency equipment in trunk:
   a. First-aid kit
   b. Flares, cloth for distress signal, tow line, pry bar, shovel (sand and other winter-weather gear, as appropriate), battery-booster cable
   c. Spare tire, jack, jack handle
   d. Wire mats or sand
3. Procedures listed (with phone numbers, where appropriate):
   a. For road breakdown or accident
   b. For injury
   c. For tire repair
   d. For gasoline, if operating Saturdays, during school vacations, etc.

## *In-Car Teaching Cues*

1. Be ready for the student who, in starting the engine, holds the key in the starting position too long or who—thinking the engine is not running—reengages the starter. Prior emphasis helps to avoid such a possibly damaging error.
2. Use the term "press the brake" in describing the use of the foot brake, rather than letting the student have the common concept of "hitting" the brake.
3. Be alert for the student who begins to "walk the wheel," i.e., to keep both hands in practically the same position, while he turns the wheel by passing it around, hand to hand. This procedure sacrifices the advantage of the kinesthetic feeling, in arm movements, a valuable addition to visually based judgment and necessary to keep the car on a desired course. This tendency may appear at the beginning of the course, or later, on the road. It can be stopped easily, as long as it is not allowed to become a habit.
4. The student who has the tendency to nosedive the car violently at each brake application can be helped by knowing that:

    At 25 miles per hour there is need for a certain amount of brake power. (This is obvious even to the beginner, who applies approximately the proper amount of force to the brake pedal for that speed.) When the car has slowed to almost a stop, say to $\frac{1}{2}$ mile per hour, the same braking force will lock the wheels, causing a sudden, very abrupt stop—and the nosedive tendency.

    At that point just before the car stops, the student should partially release pressure on the brake pedal. It takes some practice to learn just how much. Sometimes the student will release too much and the car doesn't stop as intended. With practice, though, the fault can be overcome.
5. Have "observer" students sit properly so that they won't fall to the floor in the event that the new driver applies the brake with too much force. Occasionally this happens when the new driver unintentionally makes a "crash" stop (if the rear seat is not equipped with belts).
6. When backing the car is first taught, this demonstration will help students to understand the way a car turns while moving backward.

    The teacher has the car stopped with the wheels turned right as far as possible. He places markers on the ground to show the position of the car at that time. He then explains this procedure to the students and tells them that the next move—backward with car wheels turned right—is what a driver does when backing into a parallel parked position at the curb or when backing out of an angle-parking position. The car is then backed slowly a short distance, until the front end is at the farthest left part of its arc. There it is stopped. The students then get out, see by the markers where the car started and how far *left* the front end moved (although the car was backing to the *right*). The teacher then calls to their attention what might happen if the driver didn't realize this tendency when he was performing the maneuvers mentioned, and that accidents are frequently caused by such lack of knowledge.

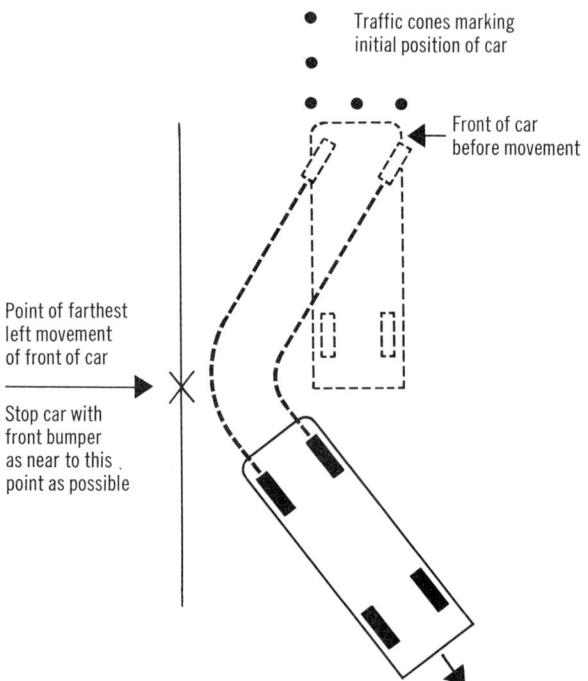

FIGURE 14-7  Cones are placed to show line of front bumper and line of left side of car (extended), before backing. Car is backed very slowly with steering wheel turned fully right. Front of car swings widely to the *left*.

7. Zigzagging (slowly) in reverse through a line of traffic cones spaced about ten paces apart is an excellent drill for getting the "feel" of backing and turning. Because of the wide wheel motion, both hands must be used on the steering wheel.

8. In driving backward in a straight line there is not the same need of both hands on the steering wheel as is present in item 7. Here we can place priority on vision instead. The driver turns partly to his right and braces himself in position by having his right arm on the back of the front seat. His left hand is on the top of the wheel. If he started well, maintaining a straight course should require only slight correcting movements, moving the top of the wheel in the direction the car is expected to go. Looking

FIGURE 14–8  The teacher explains that in this move vision takes priority.

straight backward, the driver has a much wider range of vision than he would have by using mirrors.

## The Automatic Wheel Recovery

Everyone who drives a car recognizes the tendency of the front wheels to straighten out automatically from a turn. Many drivers take advantage of this tendency to allow the wheel to slide through their hands while they maintain a light controlling contact, stopping the movement as needed. The driver education teacher is often asked whether this practice is advisable. Under appropriate circumstances it is, and many teachers use and teach it. (They advise maintaining light contact with the wheel as it "recovers," and not letting it spin freely.)

However, it should be noted that sometimes, after learning and using this procedure on the practice field and on wide, clear streets, students depend on it in the turning situation shown in Figure 14–12. The student should be told that whereas the rate of this recovery varies with the speed of the car, the tires, the degree of turn, and possibly other factors, the turn into a narrow lane in traffic *must be accurate* in timing, in rate, and in degree of turn. The experienced driver sometimes starts the automatic recovery with a push on the wheel to be sure that it does not operate too slowly. The teacher should be ready for the time when a student will depend on the automatic recovery and it does not respond as he expects.

## Traffic Cones and Stanchions

For many years teachers have given skill exercises using portable, flexible markers. Occasionally one hears that such equipment is "obsolete." However, the many who still use these markers do so knowing that they are establishing space limitations within which students must perform skill practice with greater accuracy than would be needed without the markers. This includes weaving in and out through a line of markers, forward and backward, and other steering exercises. (The cones and stanchions are similar to some of the testing equipment used by some motor vehicle authorities in driver license examinations.)

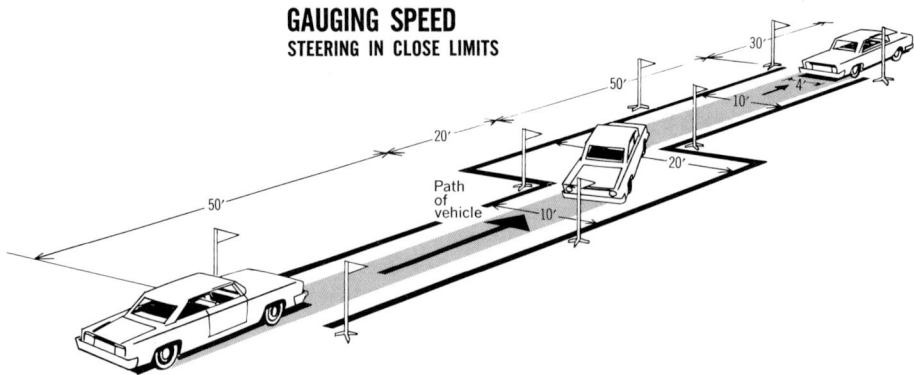

FIGURE 14-9 Some teachers use stanchions to define practice patterns; some use a single line of traffic cones ten paces apart.

The point here is that the new teacher should avoid accepting unsupported individual opinions on professional procedures. Driver education literature, professional associations, workshops, courses, and conferences are sources of reliable information on teaching. Many experienced teachers have returned from professional meetings with new and better ideas and procedures.

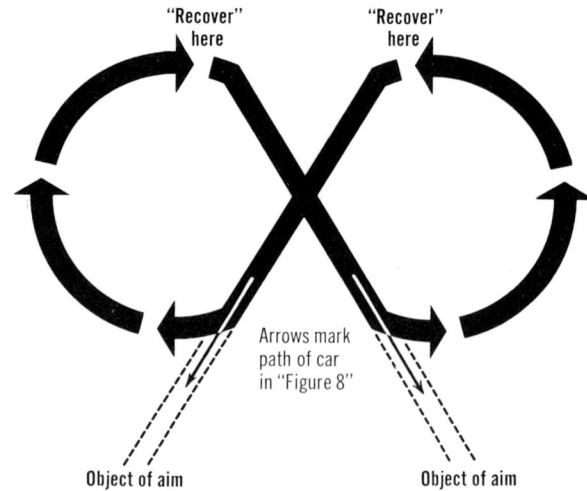

FIGURE 14-10 "The Figure Eight."

### The Figure Eight

This is an old, standard steering exercise. It is commonly used where schools have sufficiently wide practice areas. It has value, varying greatly according to how the exercise is done. Minimum value is achieved by having the student drive in a rough figure eight. He practices the hand-over-hand steering wheel movement, and he feels some response in the car as he uses

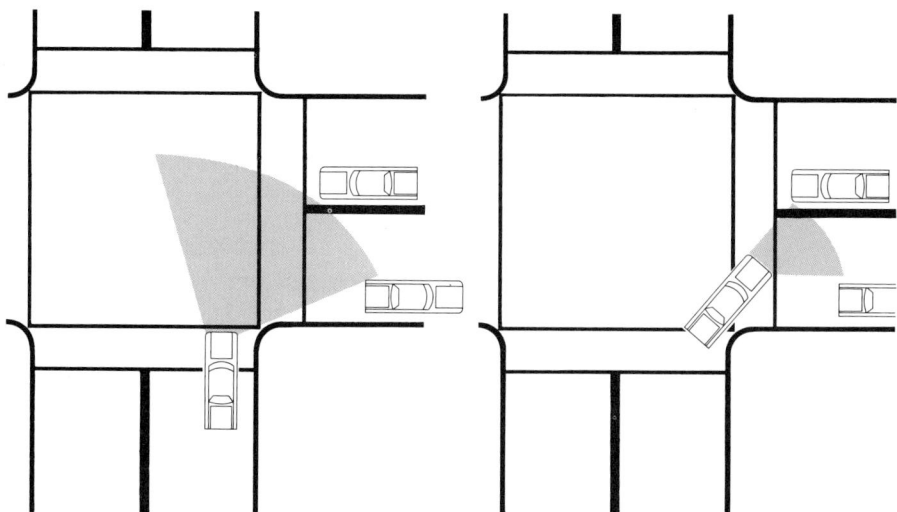

FIGURE 14–11  As the car begins its move into the right turn, there is a wide clear space ahead.

FIGURE 14–12  Recovery from the turn must be made in a considerably narrower space.

the wheel. However, he does not develop the accuracy in "recovery" from turns which is necessary in traffic.

Recovery from a turn requires *more* accuracy than starting the turn. Notice in Figure 14–11 how, when the car *starts* the turn, there is a fairly wide span of open space ahead. As long as the driver didn't start turning too soon and strike the curb with his right rear wheel, he has a widening margin of space ahead of him. Note how, in Figure 14–12, *when he starts to recover from the turn* he is driving into a very narrow space between car A and car B. This is a place where the beginner is likely to encounter trouble when he starts driving in traffic. *The teacher should be ready to brake and perhaps to help with the wheel when the student is learning to recover from turns, especially right turns, in traffic.* When you read newspaper accounts of accidents attributed to drivers "losing control" in turning, this is frequently the situation—only there was no teacher to anticipate it and to take corrective action.

In teaching turning skill, the figure eight is very effective when it includes appropriate drill in accurate recovery. The method of drill is to sight objects well beyond the practice area ("objects of aim"), in line with the straight stretches of the figure eight (see Figure 14–10). The exercise is performed so that each time the driver recovers from a turn into one of the long straight lines of the "eight" (also Figure 14–10), he practices stopping the steering wheel *accurately* so that the car points *directly* toward the appropriate object of aim. When the recovery is performed correctly, the driver does not "oversteer," necessitating turning the wheel the opposite way to get in the proper aimed path, nor does he "understeer," requiring him to turn the wheel again in the original direction to get on the proper path

## 190   IN-CAR INSTRUCTION

NOTE: The definite aim requires greater accuracy than simply performing the figure eight through a number of traffic cones. In the latter case a gradual "feeling" process can be used in "recovery," making a gradual correction sufficient as one approaches the cones. In the traffic situation, the recovery must be immediate and complete. (This does not discredit the use of cones and stanchions in other training exercises.)

### Tires

You may wonder what has happened to those fine front tires on that car that was new last fall. If you don't know, people may think you were a little careless. Of course, it is possible that at some time the right front wheel did strike the curb a bit hard, and you didn't have the wheel alignment checked. But, more likely, you have had many students doing figure eights on the practice field, winding in and out of cones, and making many more turns than one does in normal driving. When the car is turning, especially turning sharply and continuously, there is a considerable wearing of the front tires. These exercises can wear out a pair of tires well within a school year. It needn't have been anybody's fault—just good teaching. It's a good idea to keep track of tire wear and rotate tires as needed.

### The Manual Shift

Whatever textbook or guide is used in the school, step-by-step procedures for starting, shifting, and other movements will be prescribed. Here are eight hints to help teaching in the practice area with the manual-shift car:

1. Give students a paper drawing of the shift pattern when they meet for the orientation class and tell them to memorize it before coming to the next class—meanwhile, they should practice the shift with a pencil.
2. Have each student practice shifting, very slowly and gently at first, with the car stationary until he "gets the feel of it."

FIGURE 14-13 "The Figure H." Students should memorize these positions before starting in-car practice.

3. Be ready for the beginning driver who confuses clutch foot and brake foot and who hits the brake with clutch force. This is especially important if it is a power brake.
4. Watch for the "drag" that some drivers experience in shifting which usually results from making an accelerator movement precede the accompanying clutch movement. It is corrected by depressing the clutch each time an instant *before* the accelerator.
5. Caution students to maintain a slight *downward and forward* pressure on the shift lever, so that it doesn't slip up into reverse.
6. Be alert for the student who, to be ready to start forward again after a stop, will try to shift from high to low before the car stops.
7. Show students how they can shift into second ("synchro-mesh") when they cannot shift into low. (This may be significant later for engine braking on a downhill grade.)
8. Emphasize that the car must be completely stopped before shifting from a forward gear to reverse or from reverse to a forward gear.

## Practice on the Road

When the students have achieved the basic skills on the practice field, the next step is usually practice on a street or road where traffic is light and conditions are favorable for the beginning driver. It is well to choose practice-driving locations well ahead of time, each one picked for features appropriate to the type of practice to be done. A good policy is to consult the police agency having jurisdiction. Often the police will have excellent suggestions for practice areas. Once in a great while an individual policeman or crossing guard may decide to reroute the car without consulting anyone. These mistakes are easier to prevent than to correct. In the event of changes due to construction on or near the practice streets, instruction areas may need to be changed. Again, agreement and understanding of all concerned should be reached.

## Criterion for Procedure—Experience

Following are some teaching tips for instruction:

Perhaps the first safety-connected procedure to become significant when the car is used on the street or road is that of *entering and leaving* the car. This procedure is most economically taught from the viewpoint of instructional time when the students are learning to drive in and out from the curb. Two obvious considerations should determine the method to be adopted: safety during the course and safety during the rest of the student's life. The original, traditional method of requiring student drivers to enter and leave via the door on the curbside seemed to fit both considerations. This method was used for some years and did serve as a protective feature during the course. There is no doubt of its safety.

However, after students completed the course, they took the line of least resistance. They did not slide across the seat to get in and out on the curbside of the car. Very few people do. When entering or leaving the car, it is much easier to open the driver's door and step in or out. This is the method

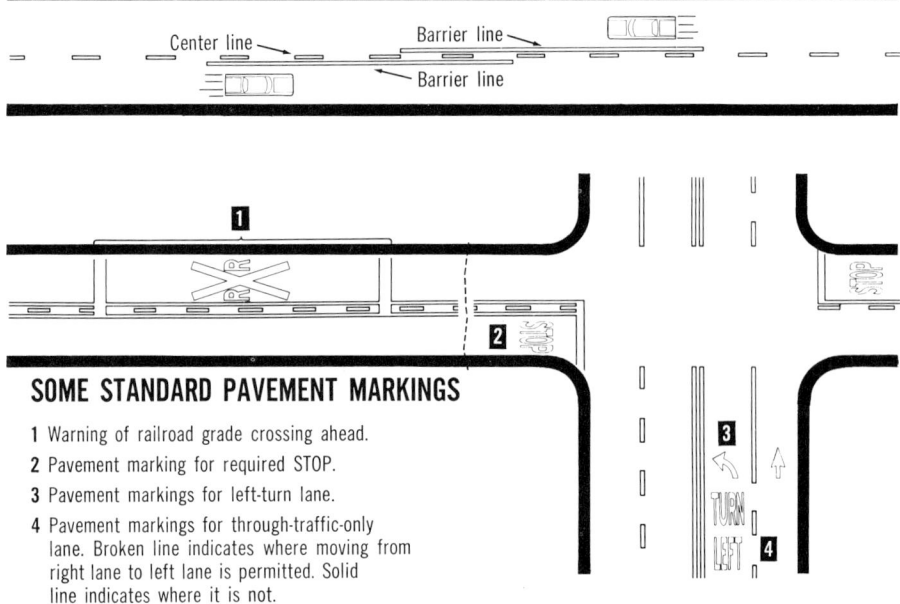

FIGURE 14–14 Try to include at least one practice area where the students can see and react to pavement markings.

people use, including our trained drivers who, after finishing the course, are free to choose. We might note also that driver and traffic safety education experts do the same, with their own cars. Since this is the true situation, it would be less than realistic to continue to require students to use the curbside of the car during the course, only to have them use the driver's side *in a haphazard, untaught, possibly hazardous manner* the rest of their lives.

Another factor has appeared in recent years in the form of floor-mounted gearshift levers or the console and bucket seats in many cars. These discourage any attempt by the driver to slide across the front seat in order to use the curbside door. Some driver education people have expressed alarm also at the danger of any possible attempts to do so without stopping the engine, possibly inadvertently engaging the gears.

As recommended in one of the standard high school textbooks in 1961, a revision of professional thought is indicated in the direction of a procedure more realistic than the hitherto unsuccessful attempt to condition drivers to slide across the front seat of a car to use the curbside door. The alternative would be to condition them to do safely, as a strongly entrenched habit, what they will do anyway when free to do as they choose.

## *Leaving the Car*

Entering and leaving a car is one of the most frequently performed actions in connection with driving. It has definite implications for safety. In view of this, an appropriate lesson outline is suggested here. Because of identical components, it is economical of instructional time to combine this activity with that of driving into and away from a parallel parked position at a curb. The combination of the new concept of leaving the car and that of moving the car away from the curb will be outlined as a natural, single lesson:

1. The curbside door is recommended for use when feasible.
2. The hazards of using the traffic-side door are explained.
   a. Mention is made of the frequency of accidents due to drivers opening the traffic-side door absentmindedly, without looking. Damage may occur:
      (1) To self, if stepping out.
      (2) To a passing bicyclist who has no warning that the door will be opened (a common type of accident).
      (3) To a passing driver who may shy away or brake suddenly.
      (4) To the opened door.
   b. Contributing cause: The driver looks at the inside rear-view mirror and misses the left rear blind spot. Then he opens the door. Sometimes, of course, he doesn't look at all!
3. The following procedure is to be *developed as a deep-seated habit:* The student is taught to look over the left shoulder *first, then* to open the door, *then*—still looking—to step out when it is safe. From this point on, students are told to help each other in habit formation—every time a student is seen to open the door without turning his head left and looking first, the others "sing out." (The teacher sings out, too.) Before long the over-the-left-shoulder look becomes similar in predictability to a conditioned reflex. Students enjoy singing out at each other's expense.

FIGURE 14–15 Some teachers call this "The Three L's." (Adapted from Figure 12–17, *Sportsmanlike Driving.*)

## Moving Away from the Curb

The lesson, still at the curbside, has taken little time up to this point. It is then a natural sequence to teach how to move the car away properly from the curb. Item 2b under *Leaving the Car* is cited as a cause of accidents here also. Then students are taught to:

1. Look in the inside rear-view mirror (for vehicles well down the road).
2. Signal with the left directional signal. Add a hand signal if the former is screened by a larger vehicle close behind.

194  IN-CAR INSTRUCTION

3. Look over the left shoulder for a wider field of vision than the outside mirror. Since the car is stationary, the hazard of driving forward with the head turned is not so significant as it would be on the road. The order 1–2–3 is important, and procedure 3 should *immediately* precede pulling away from the curb. If it is done too early, an approaching car may be missed.
4. Drive the car obliquely from the curb out into the near traffic lane.
5. Practice approaching the curb (not described here) and leaving the curb. As the course progresses, each student will have an opportunity to practice these maneuvers when changing drivers.

## SURPRISES

Year by year the driver education teacher learns what to expect in the nature of surprise moves by his students. New ones will probably always be appearing; yet it is advantageous to know as soon as possible what may be expected.

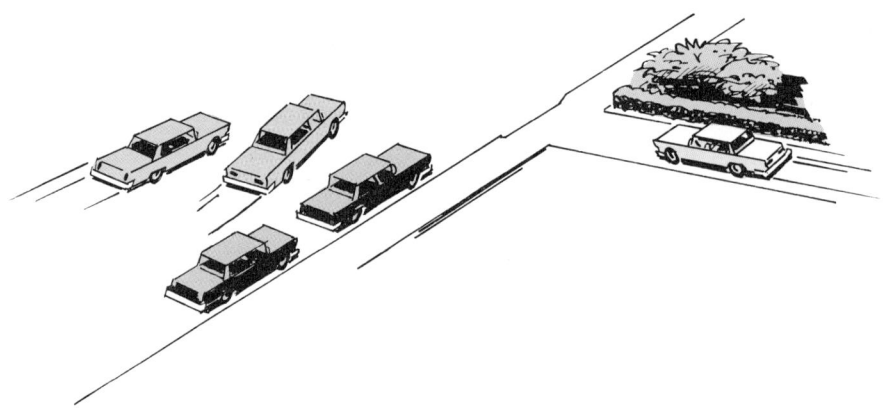

FIGURE 14–16  Be ready for the student to shy away from a hazard on the right. (Adapted from Figure 23–4, *Teacher's Handbook for Sportsmanlike Driving*, 5th edition.)

### Left and Right

It doesn't seem likely that senior high school students would have any difficulty in distinguishing between left and right; yet many an experienced driver education teacher can testify that some do. Occasionally a student, perhaps watching an approaching vehicle, will be told to turn right, may even signal right, and then—entering the intersection—go into a left turn! As always, the teacher must be ready. However, some instructors minimize this error by accompanying the word "right" or "left" with a slight pointing motion of the left hand, indicating the desired direction. Some teachers believe that unless this motion is very brief it may divert the driver's attention. When used regularly, it should be done directly in the view (ahead) of the student driver so that he does not develop a tendency to look downward or to the side for hand directions when approaching an intersection.

The teacher should note, with a very brief glance, which directional signal is flashing. Sometimes this gives warning of a wrong turn coming. He should be ready for this left-right error because some students will assume that following directions must be safe, and make the turn in a hazardous position not anticipated by the teacher. Fortunately this is usually a consistent individual characteristic. Most students do not have it. Students who make the error do it with sufficient frequency to become known for it.

## *The Early Turn*

If the car is about three to five feet from the curb when approaching a right turn, the driver starts turning the steering wheel when the front wheels are opposite the point where the curb begins to turn. (Of course, the rate of turning of the steering wheel and the distance of the car from the curb when the turn was started make a difference.)

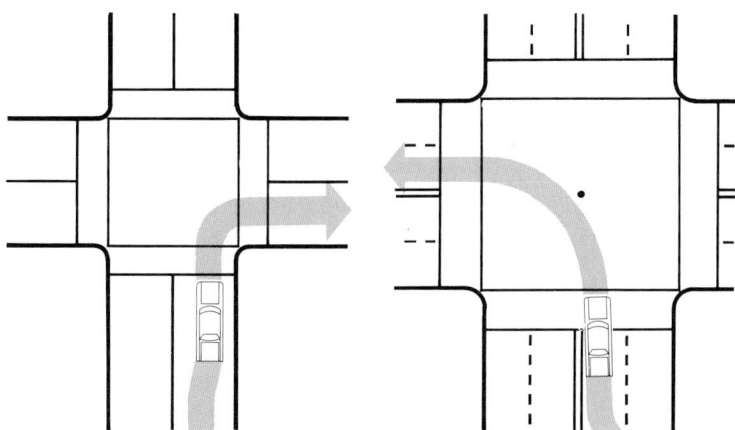

Start turning the steering wheel when your front wheels are opposite the point where the curb begins to curve. Follow the general curve of the curb as you turn. Arrive in the right-hand lane of the street or road into which you are turning.

Start the turn as your front wheels reach the pedestrian crosswalk. After the turn, arrive in the lane on the cross street corresponding to the lane you left.

FIGURE 14-17

The teacher must be ready for students who start turning right too soon. The right rear wheel turns in a shorter radius (describes a shorter arc) than the right front wheel, and students should be told of this. A handy technique to use in stopping the early turn is for the teacher to grasp the steering wheel very quickly with the left hand (palm down) and check the turning motion. It is much easier to check the motion from the teacher's position than to turn the wheel. With a little practice without the students in the car, the teacher can learn to stop the turning of the wheel in a fraction of a second, and without taking his eyes from the road.

Sometimes students will try to correct the too-early turning by feinting far out to the left before turning right. They should be advised of the danger in deceiving other drivers that way. Correction of the original fault of turning too soon and hitting the curb with the right rear wheel is simple. *Don't turn wider—turn later* is the answer.

### Backing Out

Whether it is from a driveway or an angle-parking space, the driver of today has many occasions to enter his car and start backing. The student should be reminded of the not-infrequent accident in which a man leaves his house by a side or back door, gets directly into his car parked in the driveway, and backs out over his own child.

When a person approaches his car from the front, he should walk to the rear and see if there is anyone or anything in back of it. Many a person has approached his car from the front, where it was angle-parked at a shopping center, and backed out over a shopping cart which somebody had emptied and left there.

### Brief-glance Technique

This technique was featured in the 1961 edition of a high school textbook, but it is not yet universally known in the profession. It is very important for both student and teacher and is therefore included here with these teaching tips.

A very common type of accident is one in which a driver "loses control" of a car and runs off the road, or into something, often without being able to account for it. Many of these accidents are of the one-car type. Reports may indicate that the driver was not speeding or drowsy at the time. A great many are the result of "captured attention." The driver had looked at a side road, down a merging road, or at a directional sign for too long a time.

The point is that "driving" really means guiding and controlling a car *continuously*. Have the students watch a driver and see how often he must move the steering wheel just to keep the car on a straight road. He must make corrections constantly. Many young people come to the driver education class falsely believing that steering a car consists of turning the steering wheel when you want the car to turn and holding it straight at all other times. This, of course, is far from correct, and a few have trouble with the car "wandering" until they understand that they must steer continuously.

Even on a straight road, a car will not "hold the road" unless the driver is looking ahead, recognizes each movement of the car away from the desired path, and makes corrections for each such movement. If the driver allows his attention to be diverted from the road ahead, he can no longer make the necessary corrections and the car moves out of line, left or right. If he looks away from the road ahead for too long a time, the car will go out of control. Sometimes it is necessary to look away, as when merging with traffic from another road. This is when the "quick-glance technique" is vital.

The driver gives a *very brief* glance in the direction of the traffic approaching from the side or merging road, then returns his eyes immediately to the road ahead. The one glance didn't tell him everything he should know, such as the speed of the approaching vehicles. He then gives another brief glance, followed again by looking ahead. It may take four or five such brief glances to tell him what he wants to know. Between each two glances to the side, he takes a new look at the road ahead. His mind puts together the intermittent views of the road with an effect like that of the succession of "still" frames of a motion picture. With this *continuous* awareness of the road ahead and the position of his car in relation to it and to the conditions on it, he can guide his car effectively. *At the same time* he has had a number of brief glances at vehicles approaching to merge, and his mind has put those views together to give him the picture he needs of that scene (whether it is actually of vehicles, of guide signs, or of any other object). With this brief-glance technique that very dangerous condition known as "captured attention" can be avoided.

## A Warning

Captured attention is something that does not occur very often (fortunately!). However, the teacher should always be on the alert for it, especially when the student is not yet accustomed to highway driving and highway speeds and especially, also, during a period in which the teacher has emphasized speed control.

A typical example is when a student starts moving the car (possibly to the left) to cross the center line of the road and in the direction of oncoming traffic. Depending on how critical the situation is, the teacher either says "steer" or reaches over quickly and "corrects" with the wheel. The student is usually surprised. He should be asked at once what he was looking at, to take advantage of the incident to teach him and the other students the extremely important implications of captured attention—and of the need for the brief-glance technique.

Frequently it will be found that the student had been looking at the speedometer. This, too, should be done in very brief glances if the first small fraction of a second of looking doesn't tell the driver the story. (Sometimes it doesn't.) The accomplished teacher takes full advantage of these "teachable moments." It is usually desirable, each time, to emphasize the principle, "Whenever it is necessary in driving to look in *any* direction other than straight ahead, it should be done in series of very brief glances. *Between each two glances, look at the road ahead.*"

## The "Lost" Skill

As mentioned before in discussing skill learning, there is one phenomenon in that area that should be anticipated. Occasionally a student who has performed skills very well on the practice field will, during his early experience in traffic, seem to have lost much of his recently acquired ability. In such a case it is highly probable that on the practice field he still depended to some extent on conscious direction of each individual movement. He hadn't yet achieved the formation of neural patterns which have the effect of "automatic" coordination of neuromuscular movements. When he had to direct his attention to the traffic environment, he couldn't concentrate on the skills. Common symptoms are stalling from rough use of the accelerator in the automatic-shift car and jerky starts or stalling from misuse of the clutch in the gear-shift car. More drill practice is indicated.

Loss of control in "recovery" from turns is one symptom for which the teacher should be prepared. Figure-eight practice as described in Figure 14–10 is designed to correct this steering deficiency. The phenomenon of lost skills is not a matter for either discouragement or loss of patience, but merely a symptom of a need.

*Know Your State Customs*

It is obvious that the driver education teacher should know the traffic laws of the state in which he teaches. Customs and policies also may exist which are less obvious but which have definite implications for his teaching. Assuming that he knows the license and permit qualifications and the application procedures, he should make sure that he is acquainted with all regulations and customs pertinent to his work. Examples are:

Some state motor vehicle authorities prefer a certain type of braking. Some insist that only the right foot be used. Some merely prefer the right. Some permit use of either foot, as long as the operation is smoothly performed and the car kept under control. A few encourage left foot braking. Some will not give the driver license road test if the applicant brings for the test a car in which a floor-mounted gearshift lever would obstruct the examiner's movement in reaching the service (foot) brake. Some favor a certain method of stopping and starting on an upgrade.

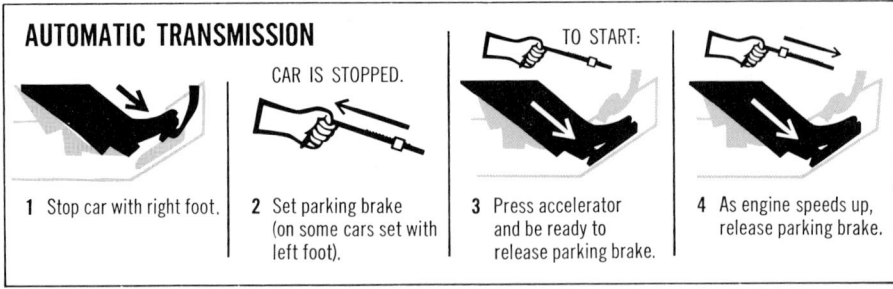

FIGURE 14–18 Some licensing authorities require the applicant to stop and start on an upgrade using this method.

Whatever state policies or preferences may be, the teacher should know them. One could be teaching a perfectly sound procedure only to find that it was not the one favored in that state.

*Early Braking*

It isn't often that brakes fail without warning, but they can. If a driver makes it a practice to brake *early*, when he knows he must stop or slow down, he is less likely to be surprised at the very last moment if he has to use the parking brake, or to maneuver.

There are two other reasons for early braking: (1) It is smoother and safer and (2) it flashes on the stoplight sooner, which, of course, tends to give a following driver earlier warning.

## *Power Equipment*

Whether or not the driver education car is equipped with power brakes and steering, students should be told of the effect of a stopped engine on the power aspects of these functions. Not having been warned, people have "panicked" and failed even to try to use sufficient braking force on the pedal to stop the car. Usually, power failure in steering is surprising but need not be dangerous, since the normal tendency is to continue to steer even though the wheel seems "stiffer." The difference between power failure of brakes and failure due to loss of brake fluid should be explained clearly.

## *PROFESSIONAL JUDGMENT*

Following the theme that the needs of the teacher will be best met with data not already available in standard high school driver education textbooks, or in the literature of general safety education, additional items dealing with *instruction* follow. Though lacking in the surprise element heretofore cited, these are items of professional knowledge that will improve the teacher's competence in the in-car instruction phase of the driver education course.

## *Time Brackets*

In reference to the curriculum of the modern high school, the point has been made how that curriculum has been expanding for generations but the school day has been contained by rigid time brackets. There is much more to teach, but no more time in the day to teach it. A parallel tendency has developed in driver education. From time to time suggestions for additions to the course have been made and followed. Much of the new material improved the subject field. However, the teacher is faced with an ever-increasing time problem. He still is limited, in most cases, to the minimum of thirty hours of classroom instruction and six hours behind the wheel for each student.

It is not intended here to infer any implications of blame. Here as in the curriculum as a whole, a new addition may have more merit than a traditional practice. The important consideration is to emphasize caution in expanding content within the existing rigid time limitations, lest the practice hours become so thinly spread that nothing may be taught well. Fortunately, driver education hasn't reached that point, but the caution is in order. One of the motivating forces in this direction is the need to prepare for driver license examinations. This is not an objective of the course; yet it cannot be ignored as a factor in the public image of driver education and in the image of the program held by state authorities.

Care must be exercised not to spend too great a proportion of the student's six hours of driving practice on parallel parking and other similar maneuvers. These should be taught—at least to the point that the student can carry on with the proper practice procedures—when he has finished the course. They should not, however, take a disproportionate time from the road, street, traffic, and modern highway instruction that carries a life-and-death significance.

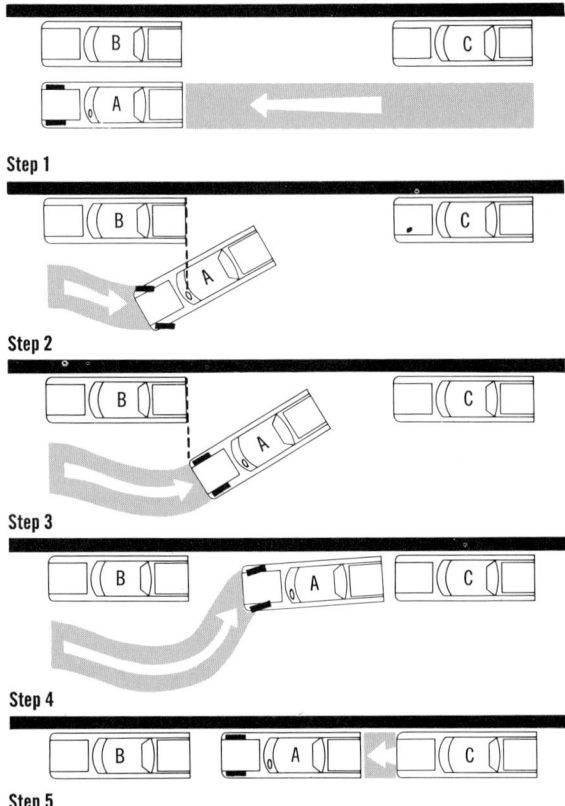

FIGURE 14-19 The student should be taught how to practice these skills correctly, but the share of in-car course time spent on them should be assigned a definite maximum limit.

The time allotment for each skill, or project, should be determined by two criteria:

1. Its difficulty in terms of learning time required
2. Its value to the student in his future life

The danger is that the former may be stressed without modification by the latter. If any part of the course must be reduced or eliminated, item 2 should be the predominant factor in choosing.

### Don't Fear Negatives

Popular sayings to the contrary, a "don't" here and there can be valuable. When teaching maneuvers such as the three-point turn, the U turn, backing into a parallel parked position, and others, the student should be told that there are conditions under which an intelligent driver just *doesn't do them!*

## A Diagnosis

A human being is complexity itself. Many of the diverse factors of that complex universe that is a person enter into the student's behavior in the driver education car. Professionals in this field do not indulge in oversimplifications such as shrugging off individual students as being uncoordinated and therefore hopeless. The teacher, understanding the principles of skill learning, recognizes many of the symptoms of atypical conditions that mean superior or inferior neuromuscular ability. His teaching is *individual, adapted to ability.*

Occasionally a student is encountered who appears to have symptoms of very poor coordination or vision. The student allows the car to "wander" left and right and seems to spend quite a bit of practice time not in a normal path, but heading toward parked cars or toward the opposite side of the roadway. The usual practice of having the student "aim" at distant objects on a practice field doesn't seem to help in this case. The teacher may suspect vision difficulty, but vision tests do not bear this out.

This simple test may help. Each time the student steers off the correct path, the teacher says, "steer"—just the one word, with no indication of direction. *If* the student responds immediately and in the right direction every time, it is apparent that neither his vision, his coordination, nor his judgment was at fault. He *knew* the car was headed out of its lane and in which direction—yet he failed to act at all to correct until told to steer.

Sometimes another symptom is noticed accompanying the steering problem. The student appears to brake late at intersections. It may seem at times that he isn't going to brake at all, although the conditions call for braking. Told to brake earlier, he puts his foot on the brake pedal in time but doesn't actually apply braking force any earlier than he did previously. This helps to identify the problem in steering.

Occasionally a person, through some factor unknown to the teacher, finds it very *difficult to make a decision.* This is a psychological problem and should not be written off as "poor coordination." At least as far as driving is concerned, the teacher can help this student a great deal. Probably the best approach is to convince the student that *steering is a full-time job.* If he can be made consciously to *keep steering all the time,* he doesn't face the obvious decision problems of getting the car back on course after its movements off course have become sufficiently pronounced to take on the *identity* of problems. He really has no trouble recognizing which way to steer. It is simply that *the later he corrects, the greater is the problem that confronts him.* The braking is easier to correct. He can be taught to *press down immediately when his foot touches the brake pedal* and "feel" the response of the vehicle as he brings it to a smooth stop.

Perhaps the main point that emerges from studying cases like this is that a defeatist acceptance of a student as being too poorly coordinated to drive well is not indicated until all other possibilities are explored. There are, of course, limiting factors of coordinative ability, but they should be tested to the limit of the teacher's ability, never assumed. "Poorly coordinated" is a fact of nature that may at times become an unintentional rationalization—if permitted.

## "Our Car Has . . ."

Automobile manufacture is a highly competitive business. No matter how much similarity appears in style trends, manufacturers offer different types of devices and gadgets. It would be wasteful of money and of the highly critical in-car time to attempt to give every student instructions in every kind of car. And, since changes are made from year to year, it could hardly be successful. It is a good practice, however, to mention the most common variations when teaching the use of devices, such as the parking brake. How much detail to include is a matter for the professional judgment of the individual teacher.

A vital item like what to do if the brakes should fail on a long, steep downhill grade should include instructions as to the comparable procedures in other cars. When using an automatic-transmission driver education car, engine braking by use of second gear in the manual-shift car should be explained. In stopping and starting on a hill, the main types of parking brakes should be described. The principle of the "kickdown" shift should be noted, even though the school car may not be so equipped.

The teacher should, as far as practicable, familiarize himself with the features of the various common makes of cars. He may, even then, be surprised by a student whose parents have just bought a new model. This helps, for he can soon make a trip to the showroom and see what "our car has. . . ."

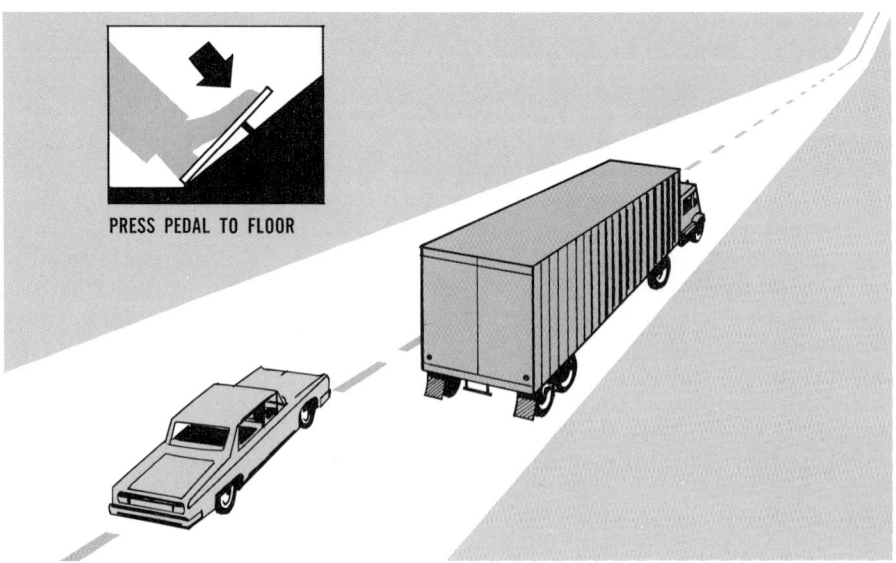

FIGURE 14-20 Limited by local driving conditions, teachers sometimes forget to teach the "kick-down" shift. (Adapted from Figure 21-8, *Sportsmanlike Driving*.)

## Semantics

This subject may at first seem somewhat unrelated to in-car instruction in driver education. Actually it is an important consideration in the self-improvement process of the teacher.

It is quite common for students to have heard and read the expression "hit the brake." It may even have been used at times in classroom discussions. In introducing the student to the car and the course, to use the expression "pressing the brake" gives a better concept of the feel of braking and how brake pressure should be applied.

The expression, mentioned before, *"don't turn wider,* **turn later**,*"* indicates the correct way to avoid the tendency to "jump the curb" with the right rear wheel. *"Keep steering*—steering is a full-time job—you must steer **constantly**" helps to overcome wandering. *Gently and gradually* applies to accelerating, braking, and turning when road surfaces are slippery. It should become a *feeling* on the part of the student as he starts driving on that kind of day—gently and gradually. When using the automatic-steering-wheel recovery, it is easier to understand "let the wheel *slide* through your hands," than "keep control" or "maintain contact with the wheel," although both the latter may be used in addition to the former.

With experience, the alert teacher can develop a set of terms which will be a great asset to his teaching if he carefully notes the effects of his words over "generations" of students. Also, if the teacher brings up appropriate items at the same time in the course to each group of students, he will be less apt to forget to describe or to stress specific points.

## "Used to that Car"

As stated before, although passing the driver license examination is not a basic objective of driver education, many people—including some parents and state authorities—think of it as a criterion of the quality of the course.

It is highly desirable that the course be completed before the student is licensed. After the student finishes the course, he should have an opportunity to practice before going for his examination. With a learner's permit and accompanied by a licensed driver, he can then practice the things he has learned. It might be said that in the course he "learned how to learn." If, during the course, he learned a formula such as backing into a parallel parked position at the curb, and if he practiced it just enough during the course to be able to apply it, he is now ready to spend sufficient time in individual practice to develop this skillfully. This situation is ideal in that he used as little as necessary of course time on this skill and had, therefore, *correspondingly more time for normal street and highway traffic driving.*

The post-driver education course prelicensing practice is important. The student has had very little opportunity to try different cars and may not realize how different characteristics of cars affect smoothness in driving—especially with a new driver. For the convenience of the student and of the licensed driver who accompanies him, for economy in state testing, and for the reputation of the driver education program, it is well that he pass the driver license examination the first time he tries. One thing the

204  IN-CAR INSTRUCTION

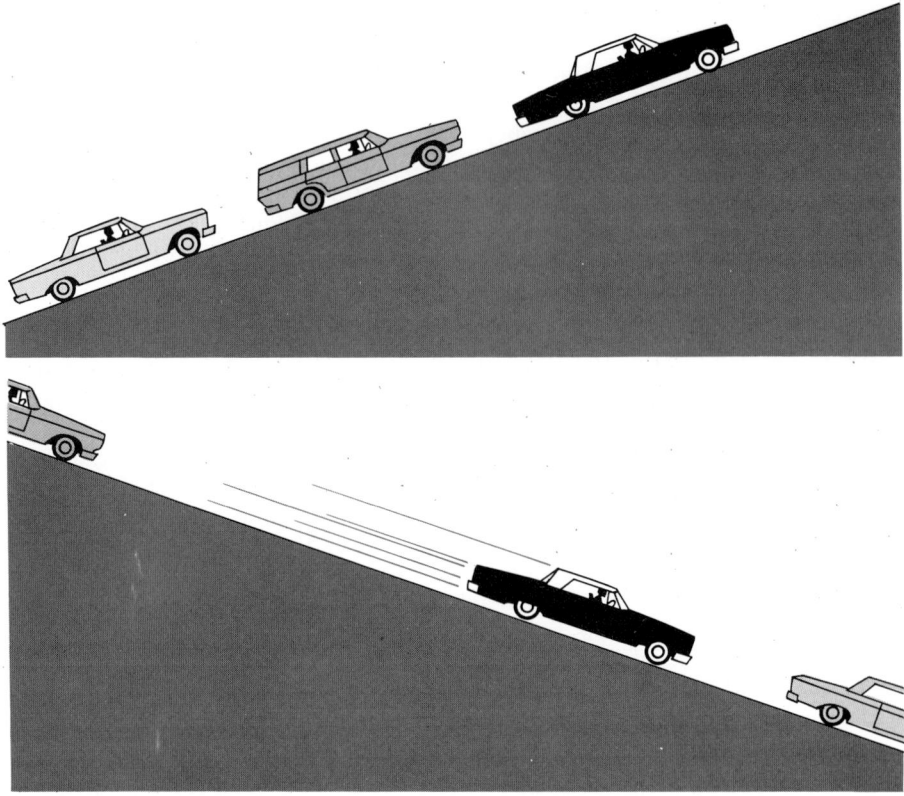

FIGURE 14-21 Call attention to *deadfoot drivers,* who keep the same pressure on their accelerators, uphill and down, varying their speed from **30** to **70** miles per hour. (Adapted from Figure 10-9, *Sportsmanlike Driving.*)

driver education teacher can do very easily is to emphasize the following during and at the end of the course: *When you practice with your permit for the license test, use the same car you intend to use in the test!*

### Lest We Forget

The six hours are so short! Good organization places as much of the content of the total driver and traffic safety education course as possible in the classroom phase. Yet, if some important item has been missed there, it should be covered during in-car instruction—making note to have it put in the classroom course for the next cycle.

Some of the items sometimes missed are: how to change a tire (including how to use the jack handle to lift the tire), how to put on snow chains (including how to do it without jacking up the car), how best to block the wheels of the car to prevent it from rolling, how to push and to tow a car, and how to use battery jump cables. Some may ask how to teach these procedures in the classroom phase of the course. The fact is that there are two very distinct advantages to doing so:

1. Valuable in-car instruction time of students is saved.
2. Car time is saved for scheduling in-car instruction groups, since *any car can be used in the school area for demonstrations,* usually the teacher's own car, while the dual-control cars are in use for practice driving.

## "Snow Days"

Much has been written about driving under adverse conditions. Certainly it is a responsibility of driver education teachers to teach this subject as far as it is practical. The conditions vary considerably in different parts of the country, and with the seasons. There are times, for instance, when students who have progressed sufficiently far in the course can gain valuable experience in driving on snow, in "rocking" the car to get out of deep snow, and in other phases of winter driving. There are other times when conditions are such that it would not be reasonable and prudent to expose students to the risk involved in being on a public highway. Some schools use the practice field or driving range during times of hazardous road conditions. Sometimes it is possible to have a short section of street blocked off by the police department for practice in bad weather.

Wherever and whenever climatic conditions may make it impossible to give in-car instruction, an arrangement should always be understood (and any equipment that might be appropriate ready) for holding class indoors. Occasionally such a "break" helps the teacher to "catch up" on information that should be given the students, but hasn't been for lack of time.

The best rule, from the administrative standpoint, is: The driver education teacher is the qualified expert. He knows the abilities of the students in the class at the time. He knows how far they have progressed. His must be the responsibility of deciding whether or not the car (or cars) go out, and where the driving will be done. From the teacher's standpoint: Can we control our car? Are the students ready for it? Will they be safe from *other vehicles* that may be out of control? The subject of "Winter Driving and Skid Factors" is covered in detail in Chapter 15.

## The "Gas Stop"

*Time* is the critical element in planning the driver education course. It is most critical in making best use of the precious six hours each student spends behind the wheel of the dual-control car. Although there is some educational value in having students observe *one* "gas stop" properly conducted, the routine servicing of cars, including fueling, should be planned so as not to take student driving time. Before and/or after regular school hours is the time for it. Also, remember the great emphasis on *cost* in driver education. Public reaction to cars with teachers and students waiting for fueling on "school time" is not favorable, unless the former is actively teaching.

FIGURE 14–22 Putting on tire chains without using a jack. (This may not be described in the high school textbook used. Adapted from Figure 14–11, *Sportsmanlike Driving*.) *Step 1* (above). Spread the chains on the ground behind the back wheels to remove tangles. Place the chain-reinforcing bars so that they will not touch the tire. *Step 2* (above). Put the end links of the side chains on the "applier" and push it on the tire. *Step 3* (below). Gather the chains up close to the tire.

*Step 4* (above). Drive the car forward until the side chain fastener is near the fender. Remove the applier. *Step 5* (below). Hook the chain together. Fasten the inside hook first, then the outside hook. *Step 6* (below). After driving a few miles, stop and tighten the chains. This is important.

FIGURE 14–23  When teaching students to drive on snow, it is well to call their attention to the small amount of tire surface available to control the car.

### *"Look Out"*

If you saw one of your school's driver education cars heading for a broken bottle or a sharp-edged hole in the road, you would call a warning if you could. There should be some standard method among the driver education staff of warning of such obstacles and of new construction, traffic jams, slippery spots, accidents, or any hazards not yet known to all the staff. Experience has shown that chance word-of-mouth warnings often fail.

Providing a regular place for posting such warnings, perhaps a small chalkboard or a bulletin board with 3 by 5 inch cards where the teachers will look for and see it, can be of help in avoiding flat tires, broken springs, excessive losses of time in traffic, and even a possible accident. The broken bottle you just missed on the way back to school last period might just "catch" the next car on the way out, especially if a student is driving and if it is hidden from his view until very close. You might have stopped and moved it but, under the circumstances of the moment—traffic, and a student driving—it might have been hazardous to do so—so you know that the broken bottle is still there, and you post a warning on your way to your next class.

### *Where Are They?*

Your state may require that school learners' permits be kept in the possession of the school. It is *very* embarrassing to lose them or other official documents, and it sometimes supplies critics of driver education and its teachers with ammunition. A standard custodial procedure, perhaps merely a clipboard (and *not* leaving them in the car) may make the difference.

### *The Owner's Manual*

One recommendation commonly made to high school students in the course is to study the owner's manual of any car they may buy in the future. Sometimes teachers feel that this would hardly apply to the professional—but it does. Frequently new driver education cars arrive without manuals, and it may seem to be an imposition on the dealer who supplied the cars to request them. Actually it isn't. The more you know about a particular car, the better you can drive it as well as take care of it. For instance, a family had two automatic-transmission cars of different makes. The owner's manuals indicated that one should not be downshifted from D to L at a speed greater than 60 miles per hour and that the other should not be so downshifted at a speed greater than 18 to 20 miles per hour. You can see the importance of knowing the facts. Many drivers don't know that fast idling speed can be reduced by just "kicking" the accelerator.

Any year, in any make car, changes may be made. It can be embarrassing, when a student who is just learning about a car, tells the teacher about some feature in the (new?) driver education car of which the teacher was unaware. It isn't serious, but it does lessen the confidence of the students in the teacher's knowledge "of cars," especially if it occurs before they really get to know him and his true competence. *Know the car.*

## *"Do You Have to . . . ?"*

Occasionally the question comes up when turns are made at certain intersections. Approaching an L intersection, it may be possible to make only a left (or a right) turn. The teacher says, "Signal left." The student driver does so, and then executes a left turn. Either he or one of the student observers then asks, "Did we have to signal there? There was only one way we *could* go." A reasonable answer would be first to quote the applicable law, then to say, "We knew that place. We knew we would have to turn left. Maybe the driver of a car in back of us might not know. Maybe our car would hide the view of the intersection from him. Perhaps he would think we were going on straight ahead. Remember, we signal for others, not ourselves."

There is another point of instruction behind this. The traffic safety education problem concerning signaling is to get people to signal, and to do so correctly. There is no general, over-all problem of stopping people from signaling when they happen to believe a signal isn't legally necessary. Like many phases of traffic law, observance cannot depend on whether each driver thinks it necessary (as in the case of stop signs).

We serve our mission best by giving a reasonable answer and by conditioning student drivers to an almost reflexive response in signaling turns. It must also be remembered that signaling for a turn is not only for drivers to the rear, but also for drivers and pedestrians who may be ahead, waiting to drive into the intersection or to walk across the street.

## *"There Are Places"*

Fenders, tailpipes, doors, and bumpers are expensive. When the driver education car is damaged, it can also be embarrassing. It is possible for a dual-control car to be damaged through no fault of the teacher. Obviously, another vehicle could hit it. However, it *may* also be damaged by striking a stationary object, and still the contact could have been beyond the control of the teacher. The most common such incident is striking a curb with the right front tire. A last instant, too strong turning of the steering wheel to the right when approaching a right-hand curb can do it. Since human behavior can never be made perfectly predictable, such incidents cannot be completely eliminated.

There are, however, precautions that can be taken to minimize the probability of such incidents. One of them is to choose appropriate locations for the various maneuvers to be taught. In general there are practice fields, blocked-off and/or quiet streets, and driving ranges, all mentioned elsewhere in this textbook. In-car instruction requires preplanning for specific maneuvers and movements in which some connotation of "minor" car damage is a possibility.

## Curbs

The height of a curb should be noted when selecting practice areas. Backing toward it, as in the second (backing) movement of the three-point turn, may result in the rear of the car extending over the curb. If the curb is too high, damage (most often to tailpipes) may be done. Or, in moving forward into a parallel parked position at the curb, the rear section of the right front fender and the chrome and other metal at the bottom of the side of the car may be bent or torn.

## Obstructions Beyond the Curb

The front and back ends of the modern car extend well beyond the curb before the wheels reach it when moving toward it. In choosing a place to practice the three-point turn, the teacher should note the presence of any obstructions. He should call his students' attention to them, emphasizing the danger of "losing" to vision such an object (even one as big as a tree or pole) when backing toward it in the second movement of a three-point turn and hitting it.

Experienced teachers sometimes predict that they will have at least one student whom they will have to stop from backing into such an object. In car groups of four students, they usually prove to be right if the practice is done where such objects are nearby. Probably the best introduction to such maneuvers is, "Choose a suitable place—or don't try it." (Of course traffic, limited visibility, and other factors must also be considered.)

## Backlash

This property of vehicles varies according to the distance from the back wheels to the farthest rear part of the vehicle. Obviously it is of greater importance in the case of a vehicle like a bus. Pleasure cars, however, have it too.

A high curb or an object not far beyond the curb may be unexpectedly hit by the rear fender or rear bumper in pulling *away* from the curb. If the car is very near the curb and (1) the curb is very high or (2) the object is sufficiently near the curb, the rear of the car may "backlash" to the right into the curb or object when the car is being steered left away from the curb.

When driving in the lane to the right of a bus which is about to turn

## BACKLASH

When you drive away from a parallel-parked position at the curb, this part of your car moves TOWARD the curb.

When a bus turns away from you, this much of the bus moves TOWARD you.

FIGURE 14-24

left, one should remember this backlash principle and not drive too close to the bus. Bus drivers are aware of this but cannot prevent others from driving too close.

### Traffic and Vision

Sites for practicing maneuvers should be selected so as not to impede the normal flow of traffic. There are four reasons for this:
1. It is unreasonable to obstruct traffic.
2. The driver education program is a publicly supported enterprise. Making enemies for it is not the best way of strengthening it.
3. Where there is traffic, one vehicle may tend to hide another. For example, when a number of vehicles are moving around a driver education car which is being backed into a parallel parked position at the curb, it is very likely that the school car will be hidden from approaching vehicles, at least part of the time. This means hazards for that car and possible liability for damage to other cars which may collide.
4. It is not desirable to set an example for the students of maneuvering under these circumstances.

From a safety standpoint, it is not desirable to practice movements like the three-point turn near an intersection or on a hill. Another vehicle may come rapidly around a corner, or over the crest of a hill, and it may be moving too fast to stop. Students should be advised of this hazard for their future driving.

### The Skid

Well-informed drivers know that when the rear of a car skids to one side, you "steer in the direction of the skid." The driver education classroom teacher, knowing the need for clarity in expression, will probably say, "steer in the direction the rear end of the car is skidding." Both statements are correct, but for the driver in the skidding car there is another important element to be considered, *time*. Every experienced teacher, in any subject field, knows that some students' responses are very slow. Even the response to "turn right" or "turn left," simple as the choice is, may sometimes seem very long in coming.

It is not desirable to slow down a naturally quick and correct response (as in recovering from skids) by making the response complex. Although the instruction to "steer in the direction in which the rear of the car is skidding" is an excellent way to describe an action to be remembered, something else should be added. The student should be told that his natural steering reaction is correct. *Just steer to straighten your car out,* tells him that he can go ahead and do the obvious.

When the rear of the car has skidded to the right, the car is headed to the left of its normal course or direction along the road. In his effort to recover from the too-far-left heading, the driver will tend to steer right to correct the skid. This is normal, and it is correct. It is helpful to tell the student about this and to let them know that the skid—when it comes—allows no time for recall and analysis of a complex wording. *Don't wait—just steer to straighten your car on the road* is advice which may save the shy, hesitant, uncertain new driver—or perhaps a not-so-new driver.

WARNING:—Some drivers compensate correctly for the first skid movement, but tend to hold the turn too long, forcing the car into a counterskid. A series of short movements of the steering wheel after the first movement helps.

In spite of our ability to reason, there are many people—even among the most intelligent—who cannot effectively "think under fire" in an emergency. Add these to the ones who normally think slowly, and you have many thousands of people who, when their cars skid, cannot recall to mind the instruction, "Steer in the direction in which the rear end of your car is skidding," interpret it, and execute it in time. *Trying to recall a complex instruction and interpret it may delay much too long the correct reaction they normally would perform in time.*

Where and when weather and practice-area conditions permit, the teacher can take advantage of them so that his students can practice reacting to slow, controlled skids. (There should be no obstructions and no spots of bare pavement in an ice-covered area to "trip" the skidding car.) Direction of steering can be checked at that time.

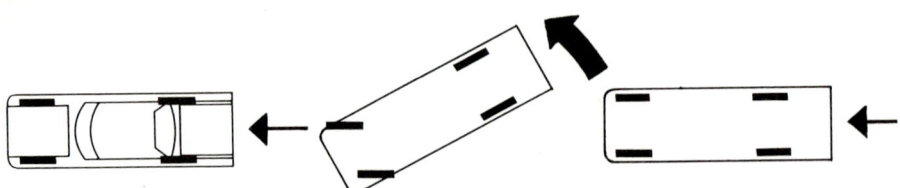

FIGURE 14–25 *The conditioned reflexive reaction is to turn the steering wheel to the right to "straighten the car out" in the road. Any delaying interpretive, mental action may prove costly.*

## Choice of Words

This section on skidding calls attention again to the importance of choice of words and methods of expression. There may be two or more ways of describing a procedure to be taught. Accuracy of statement is not the only criterion for the choice of wording of instructions. The main consideration is the reaction of the students. The good teacher, like the good public speaker, is constantly alert to the *effects* of his words. He modifies his statement until, by observation, he knows how his students respond. For the driver education student to *know* a fact is not enough, if the fact will always be retained somewhere back in the memory to be used only after a slow process of recall and interpretation.

This "hidden" psychologically based factor emphasizes the urgent need that exists for the in-car instruction phase of the course. *Data "stored" in memory in word form must be "translated" in specific physical environments into spatial concepts to result in appropriate action on the part of the driver. This leads to two conclusions:*

1. *It is highly desirable that the initial translations be carried out under the supervision of an appropriately prepared educator.*
2. *The most readily translatable wording should be used in preparing the data for storage.*

While teaching, the driver education teacher's verbal expression should be the subject of a constant process of experimentation, observation, rejection, and modification. This process is important in making a person a *teacher!*

## Supervision of In-Car Instruction

It is recommended that each school or school system assign responsibility for supervision of the entire safety education program to a qualified member of the professional staff. He, or a regularly assigned assistant supervisor, would have the duty of supervision of the driver education program. It is recognized, of course, that in small school systems and in one-car schools, there may be but one driver education teacher. He may also serve as supervisor of safety education.

Whether the actual, physical supervision of a driver education teacher is feasible depends upon two things. (1) An administrator or supervisor qualified to evaluate this teacher's work in the car, and (2) physical opportunity (space) for him to accompany the teacher and students on the road.

Providing an effective method of observation by the supervisor is possible, as on multiple-car ranges, special practice areas, and with car groups of less than four students, procedures can be devised for this supervisory function. This phase of department organization is often cited as a weakness of driver education. Actually it is a difficult problem in all subject fields. There is no general agreement today on optimum student examination procedures or on the amount or methods of supervision of instruction.

In-car instruction in driver education presents greater difficulty of supervision than most areas of the curriculum. The very nature of the course, often organized with three student observers in the back seat of the car, may require student absence and supervisor availability for direct observation of teaching.

Staff time for supervision is not authorized in many—perhaps most—school systems in this subject field in which there is so much emphasis on cost. In school jurisdictions where a person is designated to supervise, the many duties assigned and the number of driver education teachers often make the process spotty. Too, there is necessarily an amount of subjectivity in judging the quality of the driving process itself. It follows that the teaching of that process cannot be rigidly prescribed in detail and accurately graded in objective scores. This point is of considerable moment to the person charged with responsibility for supervision.

Probably the best answer to the problem is the natural leader. He has patience and tact with the teacher. He is modest and self-effacing before the students. He is a well-experienced teacher of the subject and an excellent teacher and superior driver. No equipment, device, process, or invention will substitute for this individual, just as none can replace the gifted, devoted teacher at any level of education.

Teachers who have coached athletic teams may, at this point, recall descriptions of players to be "selected" for various team positions, as often cited in athletic literature: "A . . . should be big, strong, fast, intelligent . . . etc." The experienced coach knows that he doesn't always get the type of "material" which is ideal in every quality; so he does the most practical thing. He gives each player all the help he can to make him as efficient as possible.

The potential supervisor of driver education may not have as many years of experience as desirable. He may, at first, lack sufficient self-confidence to do his best on the job. Obviously, no area of teaching, supervision, or administration can wait for perfection in personnel. So, while the subjective judgment of the gifted supervisor is probably the best criteria we have today to evaluate the teaching process, aids are being developed to furnish some objectivity to the evaluative process. One of these aids is described in the report of a study conducted at Teachers College, Columbia University, *The Effectiveness of Teacher Performance in Behind-the-Wheel Instruction in Driver Education.*[4] The report includes a *Manual for the Administration of the Driver Education Teacher Performance Inventory.* The inventory described in the *Manual* is an instrument for use at supervisory level. The method of using the inventory is described.

Other measurement devices are being developed. Some will be helpful. Some will be of limited or no value. The supervisor of driver education should very carefully analyze any such instrument before relying on it for evaluating the quality of instruction. The field of measurement in this area is new, and the mistakes will be many. Reading Chapter 22, "Research," may help in making decisions.

Perhaps the best criterion in this decision is also subjective. First, reason carefully to see if all factors and variables are provided for in the instrument. If any one isn't, beware of the whole process. Then, consider

---

[4] William G. Anderson, and James L. Malfetti. *The Effectiveness of Teacher Performance in Behind-the-Wheel Instruction in Driver Education,* The Safety Research and Education Project, Teachers College, Columbia University, New York, 1963.

TEACHING TECHNIQUES 215

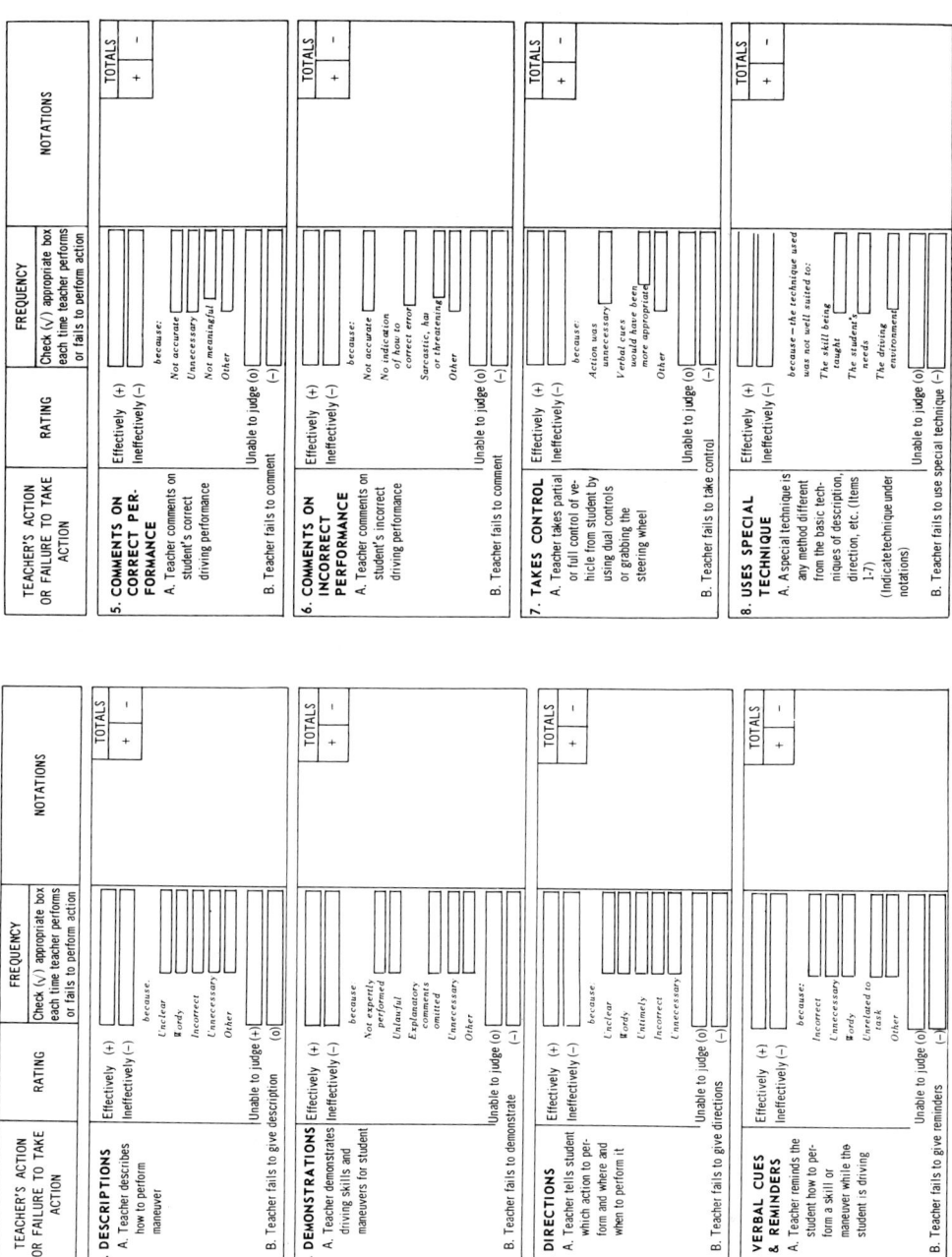

FIGURE 14-26 Driver Education Teacher Performance Inventory. (© 1963 by Teachers College, Columbia University. Used by permission.)

this. Being a good teacher of driver education requires all the qualities of a good teacher in any subject field. It requires some other qualities, also. The responsibility for the life and limb of students under conditions unique in education means that certain qualifications are vitally needed.

It would not be fair to the individual teacher who accepts this difficult job to grade his or her work with an instrument of measurement which contained any weak point or doubt as to its accuracy. It would not be fair to the profession or the students to err in this measurement process. In this new area of driver education, proceed with extreme care and caution. The driver education teacher in the dual-control car is a pretty special kind of teacher. Measurement of the quality of instruction is desirable, but only when it *helps* that teacher perform his difficult task. It should never be a "grading" instrument merely to put some sort of "efficiency rating" in a personnel file. In driver education, we're too busy for that!

## SELECTED BIBLIOGRAPHY

American Automobile Association: *Practice Driving Guides for Use with Sportsmanlike Driving,* 4th and 5th ed., McGraw-Hill Book Company, New York, 1965.

———, *Sportsmanlike Driving,* 5th ed., McGraw-Hill Book Company, New York, 1965.

Anderson, William G., and James L. Malfetti: *The Effectiveness of Teacher Performance in Behind-the-Wheel Instruction in Driver Education,* The Safety Research and Education Project, Teachers College, Columbia University, New York, 1963.

The Center for Safety Education, New York University: *Man and the Motor Car,* 6th ed., Prentice-Hall, Inc., Englewood Cliffs, N.J., 1959.

Driver's manual for your state

Halsey, Maxwell, and Richard Kaywood: *Let's Drive Right,* 3d ed., Scott, Foresman and Company, Chicago, 1964.

*How to Drive,* 2d ed., American Automobile Association, Washington, D.C., 1962.

Owner's manual for driver education car

Strasser, Marland K., John R. Eales, Cecil G. Zaun, and M. Eugene Mushlitz: *When You Take the Wheel,* Laidlaw Brothers, Publishers, River Forest, Ill., 1961.

# Winter Driving and Skid Factors 15

IT WOULD be uneconomical of space and of the reader's time to treat the subject of skidding on ice in one chapter and skidding on a rain-wet road in another, with perhaps snow cited in still another. There are too many common factors which would necessitate repetition. Hence, *winter driving* and *skidding* are both covered under the common title. The subject is complex, involving more than the obvious physical factors. There is need for an understanding of the school's responsibilities and for a *realistic* concept of them on the part of the driver education teacher and of the nonschool safety expert.

Seasonal conditions which prevail at times in large areas of the United States during the winter months bring characteristic hazards that require specific measures—educational, protective, and administrative. Traffic safety experts agree on the needs, and state, municipal, and private agencies operate in all three areas to meet those needs.

## When Winter Comes

Those who teach in areas where winter brings hazardous road conditions have an opportunity, a responsibility, and a handicap: an *opportunity* to teach in the driver education car the knowledge and skills of winter driving, the *responsibility* of doing so when possible, and safe, and the *handicap* of losing car time if weather conditions so require.

As winter approaches, each driver education car should be properly inspected, serviced, and equipped with snow tires, reinforced tire chains, a chain applier, a snow shovel, flares, a box of sand or ashes, a wire mat or Trac-Tred for traction, a tow line, and a windshield-and-window scraper. Of course, the heater, defroster, and windshield wipers should be in perfect order and the exhaust system free of leaks.

FIGURE 15-1 There is no substitute for being ready.

Administratively, all plans for winter driving in the dual-control car, and for alternate, indoor classes if conditions prevent driving, should be made definite in advance, not left to the first storm day. Policies should be written and approved. Included should be definite procedures for all emergencies, such as cars stuck in the snow, mechanical trouble, accident, and sudden worsening of conditions while the car is away from the school area. If the car is being operated after school or on Saturdays, the teacher should have definite places he can call for certain emergencies. (The latter should be the case all year round.)

Some driver education teachers are well informed and highly skilled in winter driving. There is no substitute for the November-to-April winter driving experience common to drivers in our northern and mountainous states. It is significant that many from those areas are amazed when, visiting places having milder climates, they observe the disruption of traffic flow caused by what they consider very light storm conditions. A great deal of the efficiency of winter traffic movement to which they are accustomed lies in the knowledge, skill, and confidence (*but not overconfidence*) of the drivers who are experienced and skilled in driving under those conditions. Driver educators face a complex problem in the matter of winter driving. The nature of the problem is rarely, if ever, truly defined and expressed. Perhaps the most needed item of all is a clear-cut account of just what the needs are and just what and how much high school driver education can do to meet them.

The driver education teacher often finds himself in the position of being "all things to all people." The subject matter of the course he teaches includes law, engineering, physics, marketing, purchasing, economics, insurance, enforcement, citizenship, mechanics, psychology, government, and other subjects—*all of which contribute to making students good citizens of the highway*—and all within the time bracket of thirty hours or more in the classroom course. In the car, he starts with absolute beginners, teaches steering, braking, reversing, turning, use of mirrors, signaling, all types of parking, following other vehicles in traffic, speed control, recognition and avoidance of hazards, city and highway and whatever other kinds of driving the environment permits, changing a flat tire, driving on ice, "rocking" out of snow, and just about anything he thinks his students will face in the future—all in six hours.

## *Limitations Imposed by Nature*

*There comes a time when a realistic approach and a clear statement in defense of the course and of the teacher is urgently needed.* In introducing the subject of *winter driving*, we enter one of several areas in which a critical, comparative, and *realistic* view is needed, and perhaps overdue in publication. The driver education teacher is "on the firing line." Regardless of the excellent intent of all those who prescribe his activities, the results of those activities and the responsibility for them are on *his* shoulders—his and his administrator's and the school board members'. The policy suggested here recognizes this and places first in its considerations the teacher, the school administrator, the board members, and the students. Whenever their welfare appears to conflict with theories of course inclusion, however intellectually conceived, the policy should be firm. The new teacher may be surprised by apparently conflicting professional opinion.

First, we must face the fact that, whether we like it or not, *most* students in the United States, including those north of the Mason-Dixon line, the "snow line," or any line, aren't going to have *winter driving practice* in their driver education courses! Even if every student who finished the course under the usual high school plans during the calendar year were *recalled* to practice when snow and ice came, there would be very little time for each. Learning complex skills takes a good deal of time. Of course, the regular program would have to be suspended for this also, reaching fewer students

220  IN-CAR INSTRUCTION

during the year. This recall procedure, of limited value, is unlikely to become widespread, and as long as some students in a school aren't getting the course at all, it would be unfair and highly undesirable to adopt it.

To have in-car instruction of perhaps six hours spread over the full school year to permit each student to experience all weather conditions might to a small degree accomplish that objective, but it would be extremely inefficient from the standpoint of effective teaching and learning in the over-all course. We must, then, face the "facts of life" as they are. Most students do not get in-car instruction with practice driving under winter conditions, or driving after dark, another recommendation sometimes offered. *These phases of driving must be taught those students as knowledge,* in the classroom.

## "Positive versus Negative"

Traffic safety specialists from outside the school "world" are anxious to help. They give us valuable data on winter driving derived from time-consuming and expensive research. They offer to aid us in every way they can. We appreciate this, and our work profits greatly from their contributions.

We in driver education, however, are part of the world of secondary

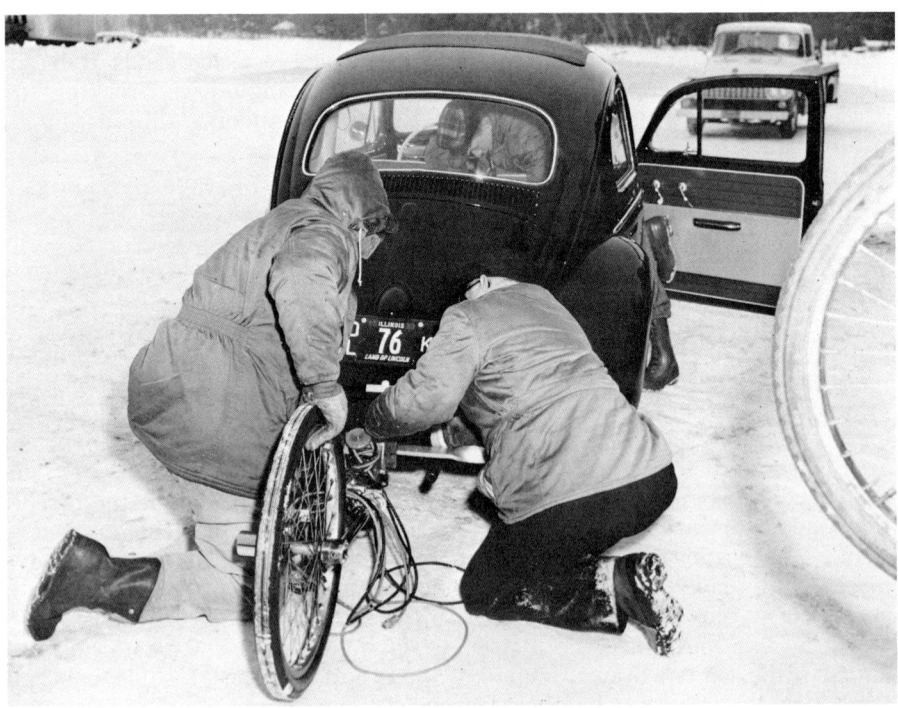

FIGURE 15-2 Test engineers mount a fifth wheel on a test car for measuring speed and braking distance during the Winter Test Program of the National Safety Council's Committee on Winter Driving Hazards. Driver education profits greatly from the work of these traffic safety specialists.

education. We must operate within the framework of that world. We belong in it. To remain there, we must conform to its philosophy, and operate within its basic structure. Otherwise we will not be able to remain, and the young people will then completely miss what we *can* give them. It should be recognized also that we in public education operate within *community* and local "regional" worlds. We are close to the parents of our students and, especially in driver education, work directly before the eyes of the citizens who are the true owners of the schools which employ us. It would be unrealistic, and probably dishonest, for us to operate in a manner which would meet disapproval on the part of a significant segment of the community in which we work.

We may be condemned by some who do not understand, as taking a "negative" approach toward some recommendations. We can only reply that we do not live in a simple universe of all "positive" or "negative" things, "positive good" and "negative bad." Every human situation should be judged in the light of its own unique character. We should not permit ourselves to be intimidated by simple clichés which tend to stop the thought processes of some otherwise intelligent human beings. We must hope that those outside our subject field will understand our problems and will continue to give us the support, assistance, and technical advice we need to do an efficient job.

The treatment here of the subject of winter driving and skidding is one respecting the professional environment and commitments of the teacher of driver education, performing his duties within the philosophy of education, and within the physical and time framework of the school and in accord with the customs and beliefs of the community.

## *The Supplementary Reading Plan*

Conforming to the basic plan of this teacher textbook, the detailed account of student in-car practice of driving under adverse conditions will not be repeated here from the standard high school textbooks. Obviously such repetition would add to the cost of the book to the teacher and to the teacher in training, who already have immediate access to student texts. All good high school driver education textbooks include comprehensive coverage of this subject. *The teacher, especially the new teacher, is urgently advised to study this material.*

The teacher should be thoroughly familiar with methods of starting, stopping, braking, and rocking the car out of deep snow. Also to be noted are oversteering, overpowering, and overbraking, with the caution "gently and gradually" an overriding theme for snow-and-ice driving. Effects of temperature changes are also important to know, as is the matter of visibility.

## *A POLICY FOR INSTRUCTION IN WINTER DRIVING*

Some general principles to be considered follow:
1. It is highly desirable to teach the subject of winter driving and skid control in the classroom course.
2. It is also highly desirable to give students appropriate practice under typical winter conditions in the dual-control car.

3. It is not within the right of the teacher to place any student in physical danger in order to accomplish that practice.
4. Under controlled conditions, such practice may be safe.
5. No matter how much we want to teach our students to drive under characteristic winter conditions, there are many students—in most cases, *most* students—who will not get practice in such driving. This is beyond our control.
6. There *are* negative things in life, whether we like it or not. When a fog grows so dense that drivers cannot see, they should pull slowly off the traveled portion of the road and *stop driving*—leave the car and walk home *off the highway*, if conditions make that the sensible thing to do. We should let our students know this.

    "What if another vehicle runs off the road and strikes yours?" a student may ask. Tell him, "Be glad you weren't in it! You wouldn't help the keep-going-blindly drivers by guiding *one more* moving vehicle blindly about the roads. It might have been worse—it might have been head on. You might have been hurt too, instead of only the fool who kept going until he ran off the road and hit your car. *You can't protect him by keeping your car on the road.*"

    When weather conditions are so bad that you know it would be dangerous (if only because of other vehicles) to take the driver education car out—*don't!* Be sure your students know that there *are* conditions under which intelligent people don't drive. For the driver education teacher, especially with some immature, "daring" colleagues nearby, it sometimes requires much more courage *not* to go out. Such a decision offers a very good *teaching* opportunity to show that driving is a matter of *intelligence* and not, as many young people believe, a sort of modern version of the old tribal tests of *courage* (see Chapter 14, "Teaching Techniques").
7. Winter weather practice is desirable, but no teacher, however highly skilled, can control *other* vehicles on the hazardous highway on which he may consider taking students. This point should be stressed in support of off-street practice areas for early skill teaching and for hazardous weather conditions. Use of such areas can save valuable time under certain adverse conditions and permit in-car instruction at times when it would be foolhardy on traveled streets or roads.

## *SKIDDING*

Most collisions occur because the driver cannot stop quickly enough. The driver may apply the brakes and lock the wheels as soon as a hazard is sighted, but the tires will slide or skid on the road surface for some distance before the car comes to a stop. If the road is slippery, the car will skid a greater distance and the likelihood of a collision will be increased.

When roads become slippery because of rain, snow, ice, or foreign material on the road, skidding becomes an important factor in a potential accident situation. There are no exact figures on the number of accidents caused by skidding since speed is also involved. In many cases, an accident would have been prevented had the speed been slower or the surface less slippery. With modern brakes it is possible to skid the tires even on good

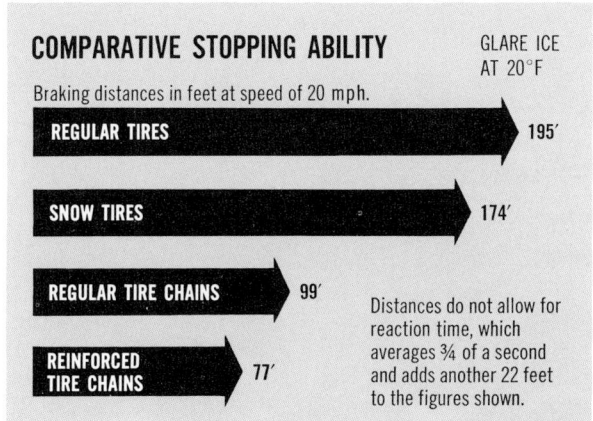

FIGURE 15-3 (Data: National Safety Council.)

dry concrete surfaces. For the purposes of this discussion, only accidents involving skidding on slippery surfaces will be considered. Where accidents involve skidding on normal dry surfaces, other factors, such as speed, are more likely to be the major cause of the accident.

Some years ago, a study of 34,139 rural accidents revealed that in 41 percent skidding was involved. Another study showed that 27 percent of personal injury accidents on wet road surfaces involved skidding, and on icy surfaces the proportion was 82 percent. Increased speeds on the freeways and other well-constructed highways of the future, plus increased traffic volume, indicate intensification of the skidding factor in accidents. Obviously, it is an area for concentrated educational effort, both in the high school course and in general public information programs.

High school textbooks have long included the subject of tire-and-road-surface friction, the effects of inertia on curves being opposed by that friction, and the factors which affect the amount of the friction. Friction between tires and road surface is, of course, necessary for acceleration, braking, turning, and control of the car in its movement on the road. The *amount* of friction between tires and road surface is expressed as the *coefficient of friction.* If the wheels of a 3,000-pound car were locked and a force of 3,000 pounds is required to drag the car forward, the coefficient of friction would be 1.00 (3,000/3,000). A dry pavement surface may have a high coefficient of friction of about .80. A dry dirt road has a low-coefficient of friction, about .50. This means that 1,500 pounds would be required to drag a 3,000-pound car. The material, design, and condition of tires are factors in determining the amount of friction at the command of the driver, as are road-surface *conditions.*

## Skid Data

Without direct reference to all the elementary data on tire-and-road friction cited in high school textbooks, certain little-realized facts should be emphasized:[1]

1. Friction between tires and road is usually reduced when the road surface

[1] From *Subcommittee Report, First International Skid Prevention Conference,* University of Virginia, Charlottesville, Va., 1961.

FIGURE 15-4 Engineers inspect a special tire on a skid test trailer during the National Safety Council's 1964 winter test project at Gaylord, Michigan. Sponsored by the Council's Committee on Winter Driving Hazards, this annual test program has evaluated a wide variety of vehicles, equipment, and driving techniques. Its findings have formed the basis of a public education program aimed at informing all drivers of the extra hazards of winter driving and how to minimize them.

is wet, increasing stopping distances very greatly. The effect of wetness on slipperiness varies greatly with different road surfaces.

2. Such friction for an emergency stop on most wet road surfaces is much lower in high-speed stops. In a quick high-speed stop on a wet road, such friction is almost as low as that on ice.
3. Some road surfaces, which when dry look very nonskiddy and are, become treacherously slippery when wet.
4. When a road surface is wet, its slipperiness cannot be judged at all by looking at it.
5. A shower after a dry spell on a heavily traveled highway may cause the highway, due to oil drippings and road film, to suddenly become very slippery . . . even on the best of roads.
6. Even the slightest swerve, brake application, or speed-up can "trigger" a skid on wet or icy road surfaces. The higher the speed, the greater the probability of a skid.
7. Unevenly or badly worn tires may result in skidding and loss of control even on wet roads the conditions of which are otherwise excellent.
8. Because of greater pavement wear, etc., friction coefficients are often much lower and hence skidding is especially likely to occur at curves, near intersections, on steep hills, and at traffic circles on heavy traffic highways.

Lengthened stopping distance is not necessarily the greatest hazard on wet or icy pavement. The tire-and-road friction of all four wheels may not be equal. Even when the road is perfectly straight, the car may turn and skid into an object well within the braking distance—sometimes an oncoming vehicle in an "opposite" lane, head on. The danger of skidding and increased stopping distance is by no means limited to stopping a vehicle in the line of travel, resulting in a rear-end collision. The braking action may trigger any kind of skid. There are, of course, skids due to acceleration, braking, turning, and combinations of these.

## Skid Practice

Some experts have expressed the belief that practice in actual skidding and recovery is desirable in *advanced* instruction.[2] Practice in slow, controlled skids is feasible when and where *ice* conditions make it safe, and away from (preferably out of sight of) all other traffic. Obviously this practice could not be given to all students in all driver education courses, throughout the year and the nation.

Practice areas have been used on which a dual-control car can be made to skid with comparative safety. These range from simple, chance-flooded and frozen parking lots to elaborately planned courses on frozen lake surfaces. With proper design and ice surfaces free of obstructions and of rough spots that might "trip" a skidding car, such areas permit practice with reasonable safety. Procedures must, of course, be definitely prescribed and rules strictly observed.

A plan used for in-service training of teachers in this area has been published under the title of *Winter Driving Skill Exercises for Teachers*.[3]

In high school driver education, of course, such practice is necessarily seasonal, has geographic limitations, and is appropriate only when the student has achieved sufficient basic skill to profit by it. Like any other phase of in-car instruction, it should not be given any more than its logical share of the six-hour total of behind-the-wheel practice.

Perhaps the first thing, after the safety regulations, taught the student about to practice recovering from skids is to "turn in the direction of the skid," or "turn in the direction the rear of the car is skidding." The procedure is correct, but a word of caution is in order. The teacher, in the classroom and in the car, should consider this point when teaching the subject of skidding: There is a definite danger of *slowing* the naturally correct movement of a driver by superimposing a worded "rule." Read carefully the topic The Skid, in Chapter 14, "Teaching Techniques."

## Snow Walls

Drivers who are well-experienced in "far" northern sections of the country recognize the value of ploughed snow at the side of the road. The early winter or late fall ice storms, with rain making the ice almost unbe-

---

[2] *Ibid.*
[3] *Winter Driving Skill Exercises for Teachers,* National Safety Council, Chicago, Ill., 1960.

lievably slippery, are dreaded partly because there is nothing to stop a skidding car until it strikes a solid obstruction. Road ice, with rain falling on it, has an extremely low coefficient of friction. Drivers whose cars have skidded crosswise in the road often find that they can simply push on one end of a car, and straighten it out on its original path. The only problem is to stand upright while pushing! Like those icy roads, areas used for skid-recovery practice are made much safer by being bounded by high banks of soft, ploughed snow.

### The Wet-pavement Skid

A few traffic safety people recommend skid practice on *wet-pavement* surfaces all year. This is quite different than winter practice on ice, and should be considered separately. From the standpoint of *high school driver education*, such practice is not recommended for the following reasons:

1. Greater speed is required to skid sufficiently for such practice on wet pavement than on ice, especially wet ice.
2. A rough spot in the pavement where the coefficient of friction is comparatively high may, at the speeds involved in this practice, "trip" the car and cause it to roll over.
3. If teen-agers, especially boys, could learn to skid cars on wet pavement in the driver education class, or if they *see* it done and it appears safe, the teacher may start an "epidemic" of skidding. The ability to "peel out" is less spectacular, but the practice is widespread and popular among those who want attention, and what they think is admiration. A possible similar flood of wet-pavement skidding, *possible all year,* would result in many accidents and in a public censure of the driver education course in which it originated.
4. Those who advocate the practice assume an inevitability of the wet-pavement skid situation in normal driving. *Few who practice reasonable driving when the pavement is wet ever skid sufficiently far for corrective steering to be effective.* It appears that this is one of those cures which far exceed in severity the condition for which they were evolved. *Prevention* is the key word here, and in the case of the wet-pavement skid, the fault lies in *speed too fast for conditions,* not lack of practice in recovery. Also, the basic six-hour course in the car *should not be expected to include "practice" in getting into and out of all the hazardous situations it is possible for the driver to face in his future.* This is one of the "facts of life" that should be recognized and frankly admitted. We place emphasis on *avoidance* of the danger, rather than on extricating oneself from it. This is especially important in the case of the wet-pavement skid and of skids on wet leaves, sand on the pavement and ridged and bumpy road surfaces.

## SIX POINTS IN PLANNING FOR PRACTICE ON ICE

Although not in disagreement with the theory of skid practice on ice, it is strongly recommended that the following items be very carefully considered before such practice be initiated in the regular high school course:

1. *Complete* safety must be provided for. The area selected should be

smooth, preferably wet ice, free from any spots of dry pavement which might "trip" a skidding car, and free from obstructions, so as to permit safe practice at slow speeds. Soft snow boundary walls are desirable.

2. Students must be *ready*. Having a student practice recovery from a skid early in the course before he or she has learned the basic movements of steering (etc.) is like having a beginning swimmer try to swim the

FIGURE 15–5 The National Safety Council's Committee on Winter Driving Hazards has studied the performance of cars and trucks on snow and ice for more than twenty-five years. Here a professional test driver takes a passenger car through a passing maneuver test on glare ice. Note careful preparation of the test area.

English Channel. It is extremely important to decide whether to have a student practice skidding during any part of the course. Some students are not ready either psychologically or neuromuscularly until they have driven much more than six or eight hours. Careful research is needed to determine when a student is ready for this practice and the amount of time warranted by *the value of the practice at this point of learning*. Meantime, it is the teacher who must decide.

3. Under no circumstances, should students practice skidding on the public highway. Regardless of the skill of the driver or the instructor, a car is not under maximum control when skidding. The psychological effect on students of the teacher permitting less than maximum control on a public highway breaks the rigid inhibition against "taking chances" there. Inhibitions are neither strained nor "bent," they are retained or broken. Enforcement authorities would be justified in treating such practice as a violation, and might be forced to do so by complaining witnesses.

Also, other motorists or pedestrians or parents of small children (or even a parent of one of the students) might *exaggerate* the danger of the highway skid and start a community-wide reaction which could penalize driver education far more than the practice on the highway could benefit the students. A man might be very highly skilled in shooting, but he would encounter considerable objections to his practicing with a hand gun in a crowded street, even though *he* knew he wouldn't hit anyone.

All personnel in driver education should keep in mind that the public image of the course depends on what people see and think about it, not what justifications exist in the mind of the teacher. Above all, the teacher should never be tempted to display "courage" to avoid being thought "shy." Activities should be chosen objectively on the basis of professional knowledge and reason. Courage must be taken for granted, and *driving should be completely divorced from it, especially in the minds of teen-age boys.* This point is very important in high school driver education.

4. Some schools may have an area where proper conditions can be found or produced. It is possible that under such conditions sufficiently skilled driver education students might gain from the practice. To be justifiable, this would have to be *in addition to* the basic instruction which would be offered to *all* students. On an "either-or" time basis, of course, the highly skilled student driver capable of gaining from such practice would need the car-and-teacher time less than the average or below-average students learning the basic skills.

5. Although research is lacking on the subject, the possibility of psychological damage exists in skid practice. It does look like "fun." When the irresponsible among teen-agers see the driver education car going into a series of purposeful skids, *it may take a genius to prevent the practice from spreading, even if it can be prevented.* This would hardly endear the course and the school to the community. No reliable data are available on this point; so the teacher will have to exercise judgment and exert leadership to discourage the practice. Many traffic safety experts condemn automobile racing, saying that many automobile races stimulate a rash of reckless highway driving by irresponsible people who imitate to show off. There may be a parallel here.

There are, also, good students who are afraid as beginning drivers. They often become good drivers in time, adjusting *slowly* to the emotional impact of driving. Thrusting them into a skidding experience within the first six hours of their driving life could be more traumatic than educational. In view of the absence of any documented policy, the conclusion must be drawn that skid practice on ice for the sufficiently skilled would be desirable in their training, but that the high school driver education course in most places is at present seldom in a position to offer it. In some areas and under some circumstances, however, this activity may form a regular part of the driver education program during the winter. It is in these areas, of course, that there is greatest need for this instruction and practice.

For teachers who will be looking for subjects for graduate level research, this subject is a challenging one. What should be practiced in the driver education car in relation to recovery from skids? How much? When? How? With which students?

6. One approach open to study, which might conceivably yield the most appropriate answer to the problem, is simulation. One of the chief reasons for simulation of aircraft and motor vehicles is to be able to

(1) offer *training* and (2) perform *research,* without the amount of risk that would be inherent in these acts with the vehicle itself. Skid training is a natural subject for simulation. It could instill both skill and confidence, and do both in the classroom phase of the course—another advantage in point of time. Research is strongly indicated here to achieve simulation of driving under hazardous conditions, including nonprogrammed, laboratory reproduction of skidding and the recovery process.

There is no need to await further research on the *preventive* process. The most important phase of it is *emphasis on the dangerous slipperiness of wet and icy roads,* and recognition of the hazard, as the "ounce of prevention." It is not necessary to have the learning driver experiment to "learn" at just what point a car will skid, if he will keep well under that point in acceleration, braking, turning, and speed. The great majority of drivers do just this and *don't* skid. Smallpox and other diseases resisted cure over the ages, but succumbed to preventive techniques. It is highly likely that the best answer to the skid problem is the traditional approach, instruction in *prevention.*

## Classroom Preparation

The classroom teacher can prepare the student by citing data on friction, emphasizing the "realization" phase of the learning (beyond numbers and "feet"), using case studies and photographs, and bringing into being a *respect* for the wet highway. The word "respect" is used here, but an emotional reaction is inferred as well as one of reason.

## The Science Teacher

Suggested by the driver education teacher, the science department can devise units on this subject appropriate to its own subject content. Some-

**Table 15.1.** Reduced speed required on ice and snow to keep the 133-foot braking distance which you have on dry concrete roads at 50 miles per hour.

|  | *Speed on hard-packed snow* | *Speed on glare ice* |
|---|---|---|
| Average rubber tires | 28 mph | 16 mph |
| Winterized tires | 29 mph | 17 mph |
| Mud-snow tires | 31 mph | 16 mph |
| Winterized mud-snow | 32 mph | 17 mph |
| (Reinforced) tire chains | 37 mph | 26 mph |

source: *Sportsmanlike Driving.*

times this combination lends a little "authority" to the data in the eyes of some students.

## On the Road

Whenever and wherever conditions are appropriate, the driver education teacher can caution the students about *that area ahead* (wet pavement, sand or leaves on the pavement, wet pavement on a curve, etc.). *Approaching the hazard of which they have been warned is a teachable moment* for students. If necessary, appropriate conditions may be sought by the teacher and not left to chance encounter. The theme of this part of the lesson is: "accelerating, braking and turning—*gently and gradually.*"

## SELECTED BIBLIOGRAPHY

*Instructor's Outline for Safe Winter Driving,* AAA Foundation for Traffic Safety, Washington, D.C., 1965.

*Manual of Brake Service,* Weaver Manufacturing Company, Springfield, Ill.

*Subcommittee Report, First International Skid Prevention Conference,* University of Virginia, Charlottesville, Va., 1961.

# Driving Ranges, Routes, and Practice Areas     16

ALTHOUGH EACH school situation is unique in some features, and requires on-the-spot study and judgment, we can learn by the experiences of others in many things. This is, of course, the process we call "education." Whereas geographic features vary greatly, some general principles are known which can aid in planning the areas in which in-car instruction will be given. Some of those principles, derived from the experience of many people over many years, are described in this chapter.

## ROUTES AND PRACTICE AREAS

The in-car instruction phase of driver and traffic safety education developed around the concept of one teacher, with one dual-control car, and two to four students as a group of learners. While one student is at the wheel, the others observe, listen, and receive the benefit of the instruction given the student who is driving. The period is divided to permit each student to have his turn at driving. In this method emphasis is placed on a step-by-step technique of acquisition of skills and knowledge. It is the most common method in use today and is usually termed the "traditional" method. In this method most of the driving is done on the streets and highways. The beginner usually starts in a parking lot or practice area, and then "graduates" to little-used streets or city park roadways. Later, with the basic skills learned, the students drive in normal traffic on city streets. Finally, when students reach the point of "readiness," they advance to driving at highway speeds.

Teaching techniques for the traditional method of in-car instruction are described in Chapter 14. Selection of street driving routes should be made after due consideration of the following:

1. Coordination of policies and plans between school and police authorities is highly desirable. One value is psychological. An esprit de corps which includes both the police officer and the driver education teacher not only is of great advantage to the teacher, but impresses students with the desirability of a good driver-and-police relationship. It is one of the almost intangible factors of attitude conditioning that defy analysis except in great depth.
2. For the early stages of practice driving, a minimum amount of traffic should be the criterion. This is not only a matter of safety, but it enables the new driver to concentrate his attention on learning the basic skills. This is important for the beginner.
3. The specific objectives of each lesson should be the determining factors, to a great degree, in the selection of streets or roads. Planning for these lessons is just as important as planning for classroom instruction. The teacher needs to be thoroughly familiar with the locality where the lessons will be conducted, so as to determine the best areas for various maneuvers and to provide the desired variety of driving experiences.
4. The school administration should be advised of the routes to be used during the in-car instruction. The common method is to include this information in a formal course of study, similar to those of other subject fields. However, teachers should be permitted later substitution of streets and roads, even changing within the school day or period. Traffic and other conditions may change, and individual students' needs vary. Student absences may require last-minute switches.
5. If possible, streets where young grade school children cross near their schools should be avoided as driving routes. Although the driver education car is a safely driven vehicle, the car identification sign alarms some people.
6. Driving routes should be as near the school as practicable. Although

driving to and from them is "practice," it is not always the kind of practice the student needs.
7. All driving projects on all routes should not be required of every student. Some just do not progress as fast as others in the prescribed time of the course. Determination in individual cases should be the prerogative of the teacher.

Experienced teachers have found that an away-from-traffic practice area is particularly important in the beginning phase. Students not only are in the safest possible environment, but also can exert full attention to the development of basic skills without the distraction and interference of other traffic. If possible, such an off-street practice area should be near, or on, the school grounds. It is at the beginning of the course that this is most needed, to develop the basic driving skills. To have the teacher drive to and from the off-street practice area is wasteful of driving time. To have the beginning student do it is to have him practice in a place not suited to his current needs.

Many secondary schools have sufficient campus space for development of athletic fields, parking lots, and for future expansion. If during the planning stage arrangements were not made for a practice area, it is still possible to use parking areas or unoccupied playground space. It is entirely within the framework of the ideals and objectives of education to assign a portion of the school grounds for a driving practice area. Where it is not at all possible to secure an off-street practice area, it may be possible to arrange with municipal authorities to have a suitable street closed to through traffic for these early phases of instruction.

## *MULTIPLE-CAR DRIVING RANGES*

The traditional driver and traffic safety education program includes six hours of driving by each student. Although one, two, or three other students may *observe* at the same time, the *driving* involves one teacher to one student. Obviously when large numbers of students are involved, a method providing for the teacher to instruct and supervise several students driving cars at the same time will reduce the cost per pupil, in terms of teacher salary.

Such a method is the multiple-car plan. This plan is primarily intended to increase the pupil-teacher ratio in driving instruction without sacrificing quality. The multiple-car plan utilizes an off-street driving facility commonly called a *driving range*. Through use of mass-instruction techniques, one teacher is able to instruct two, four, six, or more learners at the same time, each operating a car. The number of students taught per period is dependent upon the size and design of the driving range. The average size of ranges in present use is approximately 200 by 500 feet. Such a range will accommodate six to twelve cars. Teachers experienced in this range technique feel that twelve cars is the maximum for safety, always assuming adequate space for the number used. It can easily be seen that even a small number of cars used on a range would enable a teacher to teach more students.

Regardless of the advantages of the multiple-car plan from an economic viewpoint, "Under all circumstances, it is recommended that the laboratory

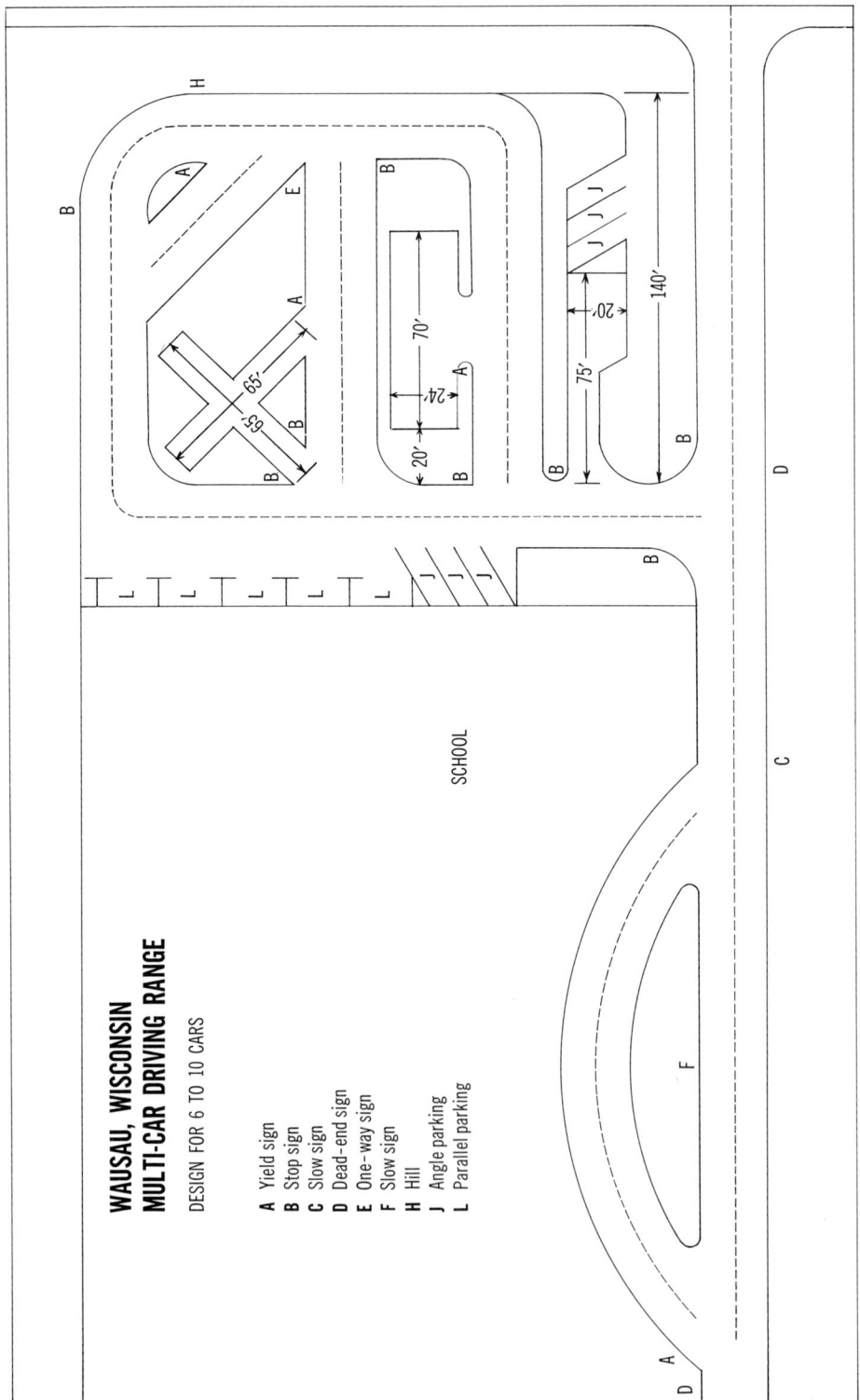

FIGURE 16-1 Typical multiple-car driving range on school grounds.

phase include supervised practice in a dual control car under real traffic conditions."[1] The National Commission on Safety Education further indicates, "Several school systems are experimenting with a four-phased program consisting of experience in the classroom, in simulators, with multiple-car driving ranges, and with on-street practice in the car. This approach appears to take advantage of the benefits of each type of instruction."

No uniform pattern has yet become evident among states in the matter of how many hours of range driving may be substituted for one hour of driving with one student driver being taught by a teacher in the car. There are many unanswered and controversial questions[2] concerning communication between teacher and students in the car, teacher-pupil rapport, creation of an artificial situation, direct supervision, and effectiveness of the instructor in attitudinal development. Nevertheless, it must be appreciated that in most of the schools using this technique, the problems have been recognized and efforts are directed toward increasing efficiency without sacrificing quality.

## Instruction Techniques

Experience with the multiple-car-range plan has brought about a change of in-car instruction techniques. In one method[3] used in Florida,[4] all the students receive step-by-step instruction in the preliminary phases of driving. After the second hour on the range, all pupils operate cars alone following a predetermined traffic pattern which is adjusted in its complexity from time to time to meet the improving skills of the students. As pupils master successive steps, they progress to more complex skills requiring higher degrees of proficiency. From time to time, the instructor will ride with individual students to check on incorrect driving practices. As they move about the course, students devote extra time to practicing those exercises which prove most difficult, as may suit their individual needs.

As a further aid to the instructor in handling the group, a portable public address system or other method of communication enables him to caution or give instructions to pupils anywhere within the area, even while the cars are in operation. Some ranges include a control tower with radio communications to each car. Caution should be used in giving instructions to the students while they are in the process of maneuvering the vehicle. The tendency of the student will be to look in the direction of the instructor, which could create a hazard. Ideally, students should be trained to keep their eyes on the road ahead, even when instructions are being given. Radio communication has great advantage in that it can be heard above car noises and isn't affected by wind which, if blowing from a car toward the control

---

[1] *Policies and Practices for Driver and Traffic Safety Education,* National Commission on Safety Education, National Education Association, Washington, D.C., 1964.

[2] Committee Reports—College Driver Education Instructor's Workshop, Michigan State University, East Lansing, Mich., 1964.

[3] From the presentation at the 1964 National Safety Congress by Dr. Richard W. Bishop, Florida Institute for Continuing University Studies, Tallahassee, Fla.

[4] "Driver Education in Florida Secondary Schools," *Florida State Department of Education, Bulletin 6,* Tallahassee, Fla., 1963.

FIGURE 16-2  Range car with control tower in background in Montgomery County, Maryland.

tower, can prevent the student from hearing the teacher. In addition, it greatly lessens the probability of the student looking toward the tower when the teacher speaks.

(The question is frequently asked as to the degree of hazard involved in permitting students to operate the vehicles alone on the driving area at such a relatively early stage in their instruction. Where the plan has been in operation, the property damage has not been excessive.)

## Details of Instruction

For the initial experience on the range, the cars are placed parallel to each other and 15 feet apart. Following a briefing of the lesson plan for the day, students go to their assigned vehicle and wait with key in hand for further instruction. The teacher then directs the students to enter their cars and execute preparatory steps such as adjusting seats and mirrors, checking doors and windows, and checking the brakes. For efficient use of range time, students should be familiar with these steps beforehand through reading assignments and class discussion. When the preliminary steps have been completed, the teacher "talks through" the steps for starting the engine as the students execute them. The students then repeat this phase of the lesson a few times on their own.

Now the students are ready to learn to drive the car forward and backward and stop smoothly. The teacher guides one student at a time through the steps of moving the car forward and stopping. After each learner has driven his car forward about 50 to 75 feet (depending on the space available) so that all cars are again in line, the teacher directs the students to move forward again all at the same time. After this, the same procedure is followed for backing. Next, the students are directed to repeat the forward and backward procedure on their own for about ten minutes. During this phase of instruction, the teacher watches the student drivers closely in order to spot those having difficulty and those progressing satisfactorily.

The teacher determines which students are ready to start driving around the periphery of the range. Learners needing additional practice in driving forward and backward remain where they are. The others are directed to drive around the range in a counterclockwise direction at slow speed, with an interval of at least three car lengths between cars. The teacher stations himself near the most difficult turn so that he can alleviate potentially dangerous situations. After ten or fifteen minutes, the pattern of traffic should be reversed to a clockwise direction. When the learners who remained at the forward and backward practice are ready, they join the circular traffic pattern. Usually by the end of the period all cars are moving in this pattern.

After the first lesson, at least one new maneuver is introduced each period. If the streets are wide enough (12-foot lanes), the group is divided after the second lesson with one-half of the cars going clockwise and the other half going counterclockwise. After ten or twelve minutes they reverse

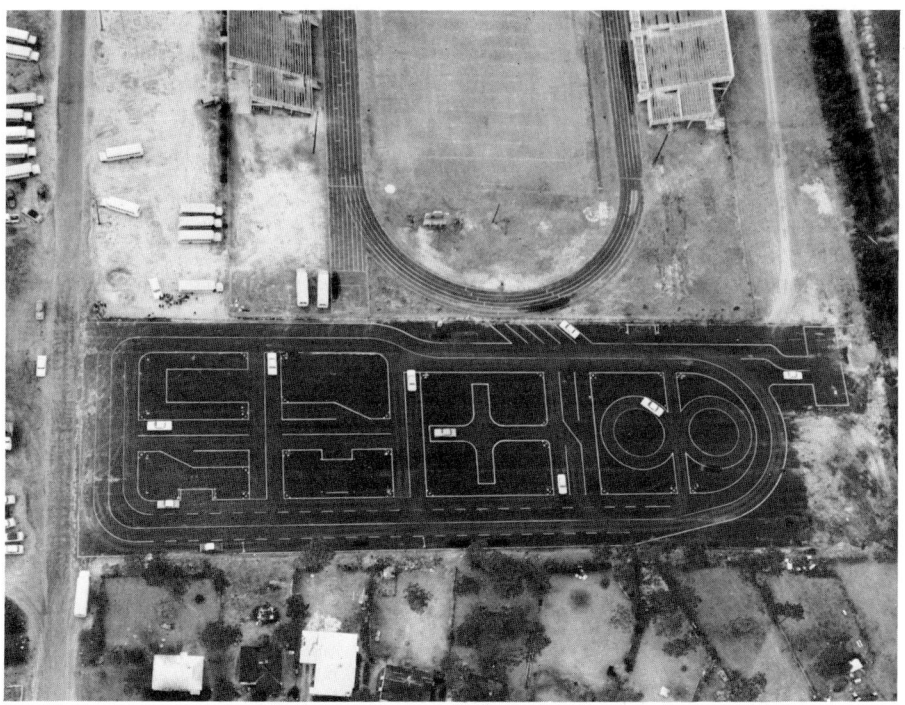

FIGURE 16-3 Aerial view of a driving range at Panama City Florida.

directions so that students get equal time making right and left turns. Halfway through the second period another maneuver is introduced. Entrance into and exit from multiple lanes and lane changing are appropriate early experiences if facilities permit. New maneuvers and traffic patterns are introduced rapidly enough to challenge advanced students.

### Range Maneuvers

The nature and sequence of maneuvers practiced on the range depend upon the size and layout, plus the teacher's imagination and ingenuity. The more comprehensive ranges include two- and four-lane streets, some intersections, a dead-end street, a hill, a simulated garage, a figure eight, and angle- and parallel-parking facilities. Smaller ranges may include only a few of these facilities.

### Pro's and Con's

Proponents[5] of the range method indicate that it:

1. Makes for efficient use of teacher time
2. Permits increased practice of manipulative skills
3. Provides extra instructor time to students with special problems
4. Allows advanced students to progress rapidly
5. Promotes an increased sense of responsibility and self-reliance by permitting early solo operation
6. Enables the teacher to control the environment to meet pupil needs
7. Enhances quality, increases quantity, and reduces cost

Those who have doubts or reservations concerning the program point out that emphasis seems to be entirely toward the reduction of costs.

They list the negative aspects as follows:[6, 7]

1. The range is an artificial and atypical situation.
2. Learning does not usually include normal traffic, curves, or driving at a normal speed. Variety is limited.
3. Several unskilled drivers are confined in a limited area. The pattern followed could be monotonous.
4. It is physically impossible to supervise a number of cars at the same time. Constant inspection is deemed necessary to prevent damage and vandalism.
5. Emergency situations which arise may leave the teacher in a helpless position.
6. The instructor cannot recognize and correct mistakes immediately.

---

[5] From the presentation at the 1964 National Safety Congress by Dr. Richard W. Bishop, Florida Institute for Continuing University Studies, Tallahassee, Fla.

[6] *A Comparison of Various Behind the Wheel Training Methods,* Dr. Robert E. Brazell, The Safety and Traffic Division, Automobile Club of Michigan, Detroit, Mich., 1962.

[7] Committee reports, College Driver Education Instructors Workshop, Michigan State University, East Lansing, Mich., 1964.

7. Vehicle maintenance is more difficult than when one car is assigned to one teacher.
8. Communication between the instructor and the cars, unless the cars are radio equipped, can cause objections from nearby classroom teachers and neighbors.
9. Mechanical repairs are excessive because of low speeds, stalling, and frequent starting.
10. Lack of personal contact with the student driver makes constructive attitude effect less likely, perhaps nonexistent.

FIGURE 16–4 Airport-type tower at state-operated driver license test area, Glen Burnie, Maryland.

## Range Types

There are four types of driving ranges, each designed for a different purpose:

1. HIGH SCHOOL. These ranges are the most numerous. They are designed to expedite the instruction and practice of beginning drivers.
2. HIGHER EDUCATION. Several colleges and universities have developed ranges for their driver education teacher preparation programs.
3. PUBLIC. These ranges are developed as a public service, usually by some civic group to be used for beginning drivers and for those wishing to improve their driving skills.
4. DRIVER LICENSING. Some states use special areas for testing in the driver license examination.

In designing a driving range, the limiting factors are space, funds, knowledge, and the ingenuity of the planners. Some areas have a dirt surface, a simple intersection, and space for few cars. Others are elaborate, have paved surfaces, specially built nearby classrooms, garages, and communication systems. Maximum consideration should be given to the elimination of hazards in the layout. Adequate signs, markings, and lane widths should be of first consideration. Traffic patterns, controls, and movements can be adjusted to minimize inherent hazards.

Regardless of the type of plan used for in-car instruction, it is plainly evident that the success of the program depends on the teacher. His competency to instruct and to adapt his instruction to the problems and characteristics of his students is all-important. His enthusiasm for this work, as well as his ability, will determine his effectiveness.

## *SELECTED BIBLIOGRAPHY*

*Driver Education for Illinois High Schools,* Office of the Superintendent of Public Instruction, Springfield, Ill., 1964.

*Driver Education Program,* Brevard County Board of Education, available from The Florida Institute of Continuing Studies, Tallahassee, Fla., 1963.

*Driving Ranges,* Safety Department, Wisconsin Division, American Automobile Association, Madison, Wis.

*Driving Ranges—Multiple Car Plans for Driver Education Courses,* American Automobile Association, Washington, D.C., 1961.

*Kinds of Ranges and Their Specification in Michigan, Instructional Lessons; Multiple Car Off-street Driving Range,* Highway Traffic Safety Center, Michigan State University, East Lansing, Mich.

*Teacher Preparation—Multiple Car Driving Range Method,* Florida College and University Instructors, Institute of Continuing Studies, Tallahassee, Fla., 1964.

# V ORGANIZATION AND ADMINISTRATION

MANY TEACHERS of driver and traffic safety education, in their first positions in the field, are required to plan the course and to set up a system of scheduling students to fit in with the general pattern of the school program. The school administrator may be highly efficient and yet never have encountered the difficulties specific to this part of the curriculum.

Surprisingly, some schools which have had driver education for many years have clung to their original methods of scheduling which were simply the result of lack of experience, and which should have been replaced long ago.

Most surprising, perhaps, is to hear some well prepared, highly intelligent members of the profession mildly boast that they schedule their entire driver education programs "outside of regular school hours" and "... don't take any time from the students' other classes." Those colleagues of ours need *so* badly to form a philosophy of our *time to teach*—a firm claim to taking six hours from the traditional classroom concept of school, of the student's school life of 10,000 to 12,000 hours—to keep him *alive* to be able to enjoy life, including the fruits of all the rest of his education. Must we fear to claim six, or thirty-six, out of those thousands?

Then, too, we admire the rugged strength of the people who took wagon trains across the nation. We wonder, also, how the pioneers of driver education achieved so much in advancing the subject so successfully throughout that nation. We wonder if we could have done either of those things. We'll never know the answer to the former doubt, but we may learn more about the latter. Part of the answer to the latter will be how successfully can we *keep* the gains made to date. Driver education is still growing, but not nearly so rapidly in proportion to population growth as formerly. We won't gain, we won't hold our own, unless we keep the public informed about the truth of our mission—not last year's board of education or PTA—but today's and tomorrow's. Community support is essential to our mission.

# Scheduling Procedures 17

DRIVER education is an accepted part of the modern secondary school curriculum. Even were it not for the overwhelming statistical evidence that it saves lives and property and prevents needless suffering, common sense would tell us that a properly taught driver is a safer and more efficient driver than the one who has not been so instructed. No one would question the fact that people who have been taught science are better versed in science than others.

Who would engage a doctor, an airplane pilot, or an engineer who had never been instructed in his profession? Imagine coming in for an instrument landing in a curtain of mist and learning that the man at the plane's controls had never been taught the use of the complex instruments before

246    ORGANIZATION AND ADMINISTRATION

him, or flight patterns, or communications, or emergency procedures, or even how properly to check the speed of the plane on the runway—but was operating on his own, self-formed opinion of how to fly a plane. This would be about the time that even the most skeptical passenger would come to favor formal instruction as opposed to trial-and-error learning!

Few intelligent, informed people cling to a preference for the latter method in learning to drive an automobile. One occasionally meets evidence of high school driver education being opposed by some vested interest, but the grounds offered are not at all convincing.

Occasionally, however, some educator, well-meaning but misinformed on the subject, voices concern about driver education being in the curriculum. Aside from a concern about costs, the reason for the worry seems to be the matter of time "taken from" other subjects. Consideration of this time factor is apropos in dealing with scheduling the course. The driver education teacher, and the school administrator or head of department who is responsible for scheduling, should have a clear philosophy in regard to the justification for assigning student time for this subject, as well as knowing how best to assign it.

## *THE TWENTY-FIVE-HOUR DAY*

Regardless of the amount of work to be done or of its urgency, no well-run industry would plan to operate its plant twenty-five hours per day. The twenty-four-hour day is the constant maximum.

FIGURE 17-1

In public education, however, a sort of haphazard growth of curriculum has tended to expand within the fairly rigid, hours-in-the-school-day, limiting brackets. This has been chiefly due to the increasing complexity of modern life and to changing concepts of the scope of primary and secondary education. Making the problem more acute is the demand on the part of many colleges for a type and degree of preparation best suited to college custom and traditional education.

A hundred years ago, public education aimed at giving the student a proficiency in a number of subjects which were believed to fit him for the 1860s and 1870s. During this past century, many new subjects have been added to the curriculum. The trend continued to gather headway. Since Sputnik focused public attention on science and education, we have been adding still more new course material to the curriculum year by year. Traditional subject fields are enlarged with "advanced" courses, all courses are "enriched," and our young people have new subject names on their report cards which were unknown in the last generation.

The resulting problem, as every person charged with the responsibility of scheduling students knows, stems from the fact that nothing is ever removed from the curriculum to make room for the additions. It is a *time* problem now. "Tool-subject" demands, plus traditional demands, plus college preparatory demands, plus space-age demands have made the new, *different* subject driver education frightening to some educators. However important to the welfare of the student, its quality of being different has made it the most obvious "threat" in their time fear. The person directly concerned with driver education, and especially with scheduling it, should know the answers to those doubts and fears.

First, let us look at the cry for "basic education," which has occasionally been raised specifically against driver education. What is *basic education?* Who determines what is *basic* to the welfare of the student? Though not to impugn the sincerity of those who raise the cry, we do owe it to the students and to the future of the nation to refute the idea that that which is *traditional, academic,* and *old* is necessarily better for the most important component of our educational system, the *student.* Let us look at the facts.

What is a *fact?* A fact is always what *I* believe (if you don't take the trouble to analyze it).

What is an *opinion?* That is what *you* believe.

What is *basic education?* That is what *I* believe the school should teach.

What is a *frill?* That is what *you* want to include in the curriculum.

In short, there is pressure to make important decisions on the basis of impressive trigger words which mask mere personal opinion.

If the time dilemma means that something must be reduced in scope or left out of the curriculum, what criteria should be used to determine what it will be? It should *not* be blind acquiescence to trigger words (see Chapter 4, "Attitude and Behavior"). It should not be tradition. It should not be decided according to the number of exponents of a subject who are entrenched in the profession. (With the constant population expansion, we need *all* good teachers. There is no need for concern for personal security.)

*The choice should be based upon the* **needs** *of the student, present and future.* If some thing or things must be removed from the curriculum for lack of time, let them be chosen on the basis of a careful analysis of the student's needs in conjunction with all the subject fields. Let us not simply shake up a trayful of subject names and let the newest, the latest added, the least entrenched (having fewer entrenched exponents) fall off. Let us not remove anything solely because it is different and not traditional. A further analysis is indicated, one which seems not to have occurred to those who would teach only basic, or academic, or traditional subjects. *Just exactly how much time does driver education take—and from where?*

## The Paper Tiger

The *time fear* which some entertain in relation to driver education in the secondary school curriculum has been magnified out of all proportion by an unconscious coalition of some educators who fear encroachment on the time of their subject fields and some other people who have their own personal reasons for wanting to eliminate high school driver education. The time fear is groundless. Actually, comparatively few responsible educators suffer the acute withdrawal symptoms that seem evident in some of the fear-inspired writing on the subject.

Let us first determine the actual student time used in driver education and then consider from where it is "taken." Thirty hours of classroom instruction is the recommended minimum. It is not difficult to attain or surpass this time unit, since classes may be comparable in size to those of any other subject field. The six-hour recommended minimum for behind-the-wheel practice driving is the general standard, with very few fortunate ones having more than that for reasons of economy. Some schools schedule student "observation" time of six to eighteen hours in the car, depending on whether there are two, three, or four students assigned to the driver education car at a time. With a six-hour schedule of actual driving, and four students in the car, each student would have the maximum of eighteen hours of observation. The general practice then is to schedule thirty hours of classroom instruction, six hours of driving, and anywhere from no time up to eighteen hours of observation—a total of thirty-six to fifty-four hours for all three phases of the course. Some schools allot more time for the course where it seems desirable.

In most cases, the student spends roughly 900 to 1,000 hours in school per year, or 10,000 to 12,000 hours in grades 1 to 12. (This does not include kindergarten, "extra" instructional time, or cocurricular activities such as sports, etc.) *We find that the total driver education program usually takes the equivalent of about six and one-half to less than ten school* **days** *out of twelve* **years!** This program includes both classroom and in-car instruction and has been reliably estimated—with less than half the eligible students in the country yet reached—to save about a thousand lives a year, 30,000 injuries, and perhaps $150 million dollars—in addition to other values in education, citizenship, and more efficient use of our vital traffic arteries—a very small *time* tempest in an academic teapot!

## PRINCIPLES OF SCHEDULING

The next point of policy is to determine from what part of the curriculum should the student time be "taken" for driver education—the basic consideration in scheduling. Quite obviously, assignment of students from

SCHEDULING PROCEDURES 249

FIGURE 17–2 Speaking of paper tigers . . . "We can't afford all that TIME."

free, study, or activity periods avoids taking instructional time from any other subject classes. The course can also be given at times outside the rigid time brackets of the school day. Should there then exist pressure of "too much homework" (occasionally a valid complaint by students and parents), the administrative remedy lies in corrective action concerning an individual teacher or teachers, and not in excluding something of value from the curriculum. Since assignment for in-car instruction is primarily individual, a free, study, or activity period in a student's schedule would ideally serve for his in-car instruction. Six to twenty-four hours of that time (depending on observation time) would suffice. Six would be sufficient for his actual behind-the-wheel instruction and practice.

Of course, driver education should not be limited to students who have free periods. Here we face the need for determining policy. Philosophically, students with no free periods should be assigned from subject areas which have objectives similar or identical to those of driver education and some elements and procedures in common with it. A subject field may be looked upon as a tool or a device for achievement of desired objectives. Sometimes by the substitution of one such device for another, some of the same elements are retained and some of the same objectives continue to be achieved. It is possible to obtain this situation in both classroom and in-car instruction in driver education.

Continuing with assignment for the latter, we know that practically all public school systems include physical education on the secondary level. It is usually required by law. In-car instruction does not include the "big muscle," organic activities of physical education and is not designed to improve and maintain cardiovascular efficiency. Other objectives, however, are common to both subject fields. Both use physical activity, i.e., use of the larger muscles of the body (as opposed to those used in writing, for example), to educate. Citizenship is a prime objective of both. Both rely upon, and develop, neuromuscular coordination. Both include the split-second timed reaction which is not characteristic of most other school-taught, neuromuscular skills, such as those in industrial arts, painting, etc. Both furnish rapidly changing environments to which the split-second reactions must often respond, made more complex by requiring a choice of learned reactions. The split-second choice of learned reactions forms a test of a type of cerebrocortical action not yet generally recognized in other areas of educational and intelligence measurements.

In short, by assigning students to the in-car phase of the driver education course from their physical education classes, certain advantages may be gained. They are:

1. Some of the basic objectives of physical education can continue to be achieved during the in-car instruction.
2. Much of the well-intended adverse criticism can be silenced, aiding the public image of driver education by not taking any student at any time from any academic course.
3. Since physical education is customarily scheduled for all students, all may be reached there for assignment in the car.
4. A significant number of present and former physical education people are now teaching driver education. This situation offers a framework for liaison and understanding between the two.
5. State and other jurisdictions which define a minimum time requirement for physical education often label the requirement "physical education, health, and safety." This designation permits the school to use the same weekly time block for all three and meet the standards for full-time accreditation. Included is the time the student spends in the car, *as well as that in the classroom course* which can—and often is—offered as part of the secondary school health education program.

However, regardless of scheduling procedures, *driver education is a distinct subject field in the curriculum, requiring special teacher preparation. Its teachers come from many different subject fields. Driver education has a separate identity, requires special knowledge, and should not be subsidiary to or dependent upon any other subject.*

## MECHANICS OF SCHEDULING

### Schedule Plan A

One of the simplest and most effective methods of scheduling driver education is based on the five scheduling principles described above. Under this plan all students are given *classroom* driver education (so titled) as their health education course *for one year or the appropriate fraction thereof.* The grade level selected would depend on the licensing age in the state. The course should be planned to precede fairly closely in-car instruction in the case of most students.

Since it is highly desirable that students receive in-car instruction before being licensed and since age is a factor in obtaining a learner's permit, birth dates form the most appropriate criterion for priority in selection. The mechanics of selection can follow this pattern:

At the beginning of each school year, all students of the appropriate age level are required to fill out a card as shown in Figure 17–3. The cards should be filed *in order of birth date* in the office responsible for assigning students to the course. Being in touch with groups completing the in-car instruction, the driver education department can conveniently handle student assignments. Students are called for in-car instruction *in order of birth date* as nearly as the availability of car space and the students' programs permit. This system provides advantages in obtaining student permits, in having students complete the course before obtaining a license, and also in having a clear-cut criterion for priority in the selection of students.

Date of Birth_____
                Month             Day             Year

Name_____ Home Room _____

**Check Periods Available for Driver Education**

|   | Monday | Tuesday | Wednesday | Thursday | Friday |
|---|---|---|---|---|---|
| 1. |   |   |   |   |   |
| 2. |   |   |   |   |   |
| 3. |   |   |   |   |   |
| 4. |   |   |   |   |   |
| 5. |   |   |   |   |   |
| 6. |   |   |   |   |   |

FIGURE 17–3. Student availability card.

The length of each cycle of in-car instruction depends, of course, on the number of times per week the group meets, the number in the car group, the length of the class period, and the time requirements of the state for the course. As each group finishes, each student is given a signed and dated pass to be given to the teacher from whose study, free, activity, or physical education class he came. A duplicate of the slip (with the date and time on it also) is placed in the mailbox of that teacher. This procedure ensures continuing control and avoids any unauthorized time lapse between finishing in-car instruction and returning to the original class. This is necessary because of the individual nature of the assignment, delayed progress due to absences, etc.

When one student is absent from the car group, another is given his driving time. The former makes it up when he returns. The number of students assigned to the car at one time depends on state requirements and local policy.

## Schedule Plan B

The in-the-car instruction is the laboratory phase of the driver education course. The following general principle of planning may be utilized in various forms. Its advantage lies in the possibility of having the student assigned to the same teacher for both phases of the course, with both phases occupying the same portion of the school year. The chief disadvantage is the requirement for two available periods during the same day in the individual student's program. The length of the school period will determine the length of the cycle of the driver education course.

Depending on the hours of the school day, additional time may be utilized before and after regular school hours. In this way, the classroom course could be regularly scheduled during the school hours, and only one free or available period during or after school would be needed in the student's schedule for instruction in the car. Also, the pupil-teacher ratio may range from 20 to 28 students to one teacher for each driver education cycle. If there are four cycles per school year, one teacher could instruct 80 to 112 students per year, both in the classroom and in the car.

The sample plan in Table 17–1 is based on one-hour periods and extends through thirty-two school days. It provides thirty-two class periods of in-the-car instruction with four students in the car. Each student spends eight hours, or one quarter of the time, behind the wheel. For shorter periods, the number of days in the class cycle should be proportionately lengthened to make up the difference. If the school has a six-period day, twenty students are assigned to each teacher for each driver education cycle during the year. Seven periods would allow for twenty-four students. The twenty-student classroom group is divided into five car groups of four students each, groups A, B, C, D, and E.

There are many possible variations of this plan. The general method of scheduling students in a school is a determining factor in choosing a plan and perhaps modifying it to fit the situation.

## Schedule Plan C

In some cases, classroom driver education has been given as part of a course in general safety. In others, it has been presented as a unit or units of work in another course or courses. Because both plans tend to relegate driver education to the status and time limitations of a comparatively minor part of the curriculum, they are not recommended.

Because of restrictions of time and space, however, it is necessary for some schools to offer the course as a classroom course during the school year and schedule the in-the-car phase during the summer vacation. The same disadvantages are inherent in this system as there would be in a science course similarly offered, with laboratory only during the vacation period. If such a program is necessary, care should be taken to provide motivation with appropriate devices during the classroom phase. Every effort should also be made to assure full opportunity for the student to avail himself of the in-the-car phase when it is offered. Naturally, some reteaching will be necessary to recall essential classroom presentations, and adequate time should be allowed for it.

Table 17-1.  STUDENT SCHEDULE FOR DRIVER EDUCATION COURSE

| Period | Monday | Tuesday | Wednesday | Thursday | Friday |
|---|---|---|---|---|---|
| 1* | | Classroom (groups A, B, C, D, and E) | | | |
| 2 | A | A | A | A | A |
| 3 | B | B | B | B | B |
| 4 | C | C | C | C | C |
| 5 | D | D | D | D | D |
| 6 | E | E | E | E | E |

* The classroom work may be scheduled during any class period or during an activity period, not necessarily in the first.

## Maximum Use of Facilities

Many schools find their road instruction facilities overtaxed by the size of the student enrollment. Many have found it possible to keep up with the large numbers, giving the course to all students, by adding *in-car instruction* after school hours, on Saturdays, and during all school vacations. This system makes an excellent adjunct to the program, but it should *not* be an out-of-school substitute for it. All regulations and requirements that apply to the program during the regular school day should be continued in effect. Another advantage of this arrangement is a saving in the cost of the course per pupil.

## *ADAPTATIONS*

No system of scheduling will apply equally well to all schools. The plans described here can be modified to fit many school needs. Still other methods may be devised which will be ideal for the conditions in a particular school. Obviously, for permit and license eligibility to be timed with the course, and to have an unassailable criterion for priority in student assignment to the course, *plan A* has distinct advantages. Where, as in most cases, free, study, and activity periods are constant and health education and physical education classes are scheduled for the same period in the weekly time block of the student, each meeting on specified days, any grade can be chosen for the classroom course (in the health education period). Permit and license age in the state would be considered in choosing the grade level for the classroom phase of the course, as well as the in-car phase.

Since "health" periods usually alternate with physical education periods, the in-car and the classroom phases of the course can be kept concurrent. This is true also, of course, when free periods are used for in-car instruction. The exceptions will be those of atypical age, such as the seventeen-year-old tenth grader and the fifteen-year-old senior.

When used under the "pattern-day" schedule in place of the regular weekly class schedule of most schools, the plan has been equally successful. With the "seven-pattern-day" system, one to six students can be assigned as a car class. Six provides for more "observation" time, but requires some repetition of explanations, since only four-student combinations will be in the car at any one time. With four or less in the total group, one or two absent on the same day may cause cancellation of the class. The pattern-day system is not yet in widespread use.

*Plan B* has the advantage of perfect coordination of coverage between classroom and in-car instruction, but requires two available periods per student per day. In addition to this, those periods must be evenly distributed through the day among the students in the class. The plan becomes less feasible as we approach total student body involvement in both phases of the course, and as individual student program characteristics affect it. Also, many schools now have comparatively few students with free periods. Most students would have only the physical-and-health-education period available. Plan A would then apply, rather than plan B. Even if only part of the student body could be accommodated, free periods would not be an ideal criterion for student *selection*.

Although in general the mechanics of scheduling driver education must be adapted to the individual school program, sometimes, too, the latter can with no difficulty incorporate features which will improve the former. An example would be in the large school where two or more gymnasiums (boys' and/or girls') house different physical education classes simultaneously. Scheduling two or more *different grades* at the same time, rather than the same grades (in schools where the in-car instruction is given in physical education time), prevents concentrating the age eligibles at the same hours. Such concentration prevents best use of the driver education cars throughout the day, especially later in the school year when the periods with the older eligibles are exhausted of candidates while others have a surplus.

Properly scheduling the course is important and time-consuming. If individual learner's permits must be secured by the school, more time is needed. Appropriate time should be allocated for the scheduling responsibility. In states where the individual permit application and securing process is unwieldy and time-consuming, it is suggested that state driver education associations work toward correction of the condition. Granting a single group permit to the school would continue the state authority for licensing and would not change the school's responsibility for the eligibility and control of students.

Dedication of the equivalent of six and one-half to ten days of the student's school life to driver education will be, in many cases, the means of saving him the fruits of all the rest of his education—not to mention his life. Not only is the use of student time thoroughly justified, but the person whose efforts and skill in scheduling make maximum student participation possible contributes immeasurably to the future of his students.

## *SELECTED BIBLIOGRAPHY*

*Policies and Practices for Driver and Traffic Safety Education,* National Commission on Safety Education, National Education Association, Washington, D.C., 1964.

Your state course of study, state department of education.

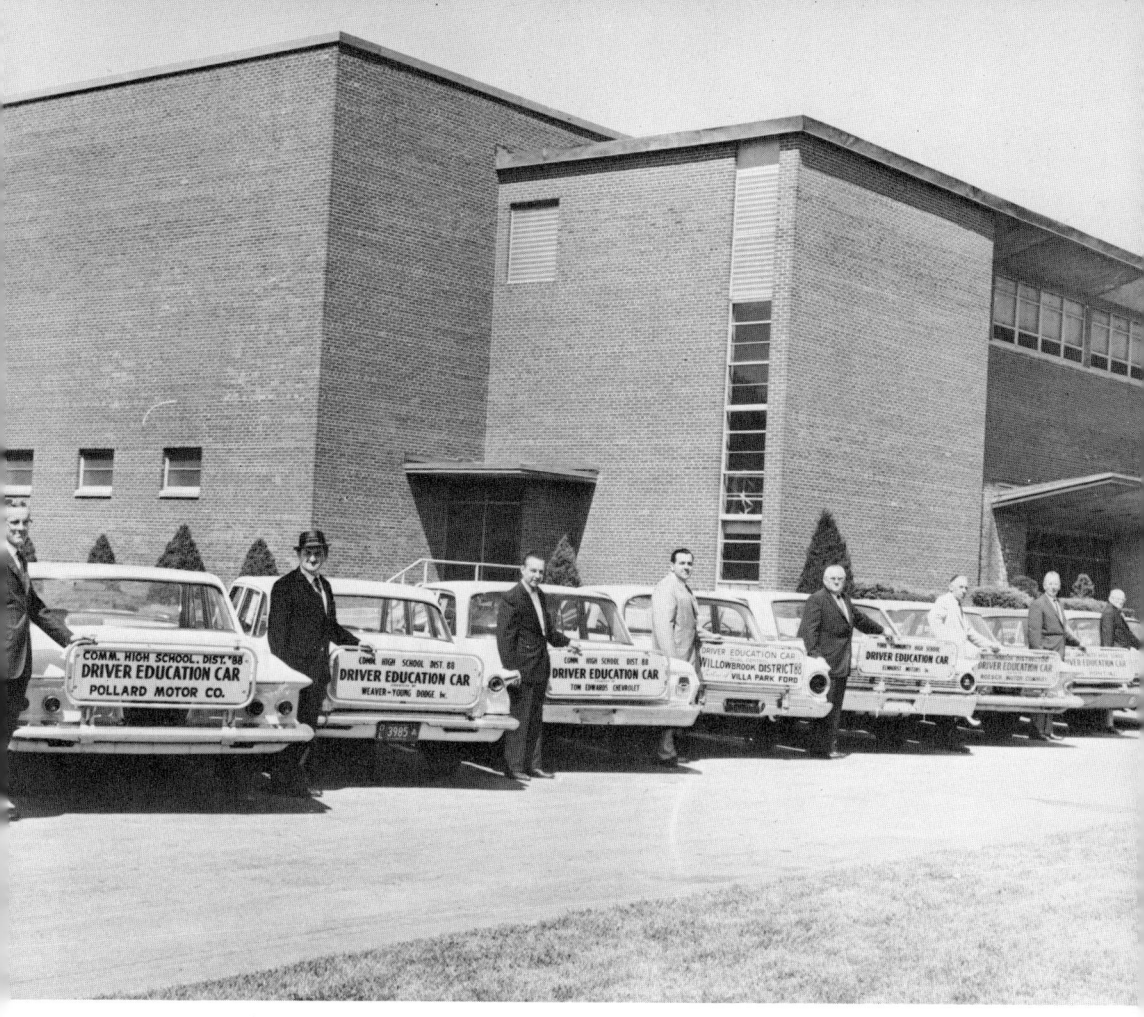

# Dual-control Cars  18

THE IN-CAR instruction phase of the driver education course requires special equipment by which the teacher can control the car when necessary for safety. The major item of such equipment is the dual-control brake. There is a separate brake pedal in front of the teacher. In the case of manual-shift driver education cars, there is usually a separate clutch pedal for the teacher's use. Automatic-transmission cars are usually equipped with an instructor's engine cutoff switch also. A recent survey indicates that about **78** percent of the high school driver education cars have automatic transmissions. Occasionally a second steering wheel is found in cars operated by commercial driving schools, but rarely, if ever, in a high school car.

Experience with well over **12** million high school driver education stu-

## 256 ORGANIZATION AND ADMINISTRATION

dents has shown that the brake and clutch dual controls used in the high school driver education cars are fully adequate for safety. The other steering wheel for the instructor, once thought by some to be necessary, was one additional psychological "pacifier" to the nervous student. Unnecessary for safety, its "disappearance," when the nervous student is being weaned from the dual-control car, can create a void in the environment of overprotection that can be difficult for psychological adjustment.

FIGURE 18-1 Mechanical dual controls. Pedals on the right side permit the instructor to operate both clutch and brake.

There are two types of dual controls, mechanical and hydraulic. The mechanical dual controls, which are used in manual-shift cars, usually consist of a bar inside a tube connecting the instructor's controls with those of the student driver. The design is necessarily determined by the location of the pedals, steering column, and heater. It is important that the dual controls be carefully installed and frequently checked. The hydraulic control consists of a single pedal which is connected to the regular hydraulic lines on automatic-shift cars. There is no clutch control accompanying this hydraulic brake pedal, so it is used only with automatic transmissions.

### Caution

An important point to note in installing the instructor's brake pedal in driver education cars for a large school is the importance of identical location in all cars. A teacher may switch cars regularly according to schedule or occasionally because of car maintenance. He is accustomed to a very

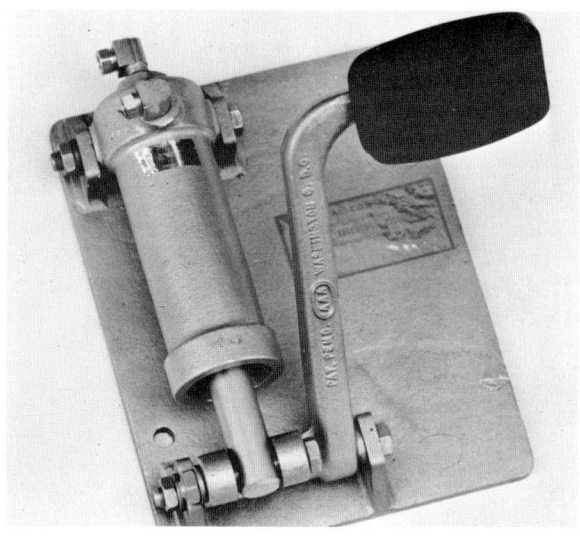

FIGURE 18-2 Hydraulic dual controls. A special hydraulic cylinder connected to the hydraulic brake lines permits the instructor to apply the brakes.

specific coordination in using the dual-control brake. In an emergency, with the traffic situation to consider as well as the action of the student driver, the teacher should not have to look down to find the brake. Neither should there be a risk that he will miss it or have his foot slip off it because it is in a different place than the one to which he is accustomed. The design of the mechanical controls limits the location of the instructor's brake pedal, but with the hydraulic control the pedal can be located as desired. Even if a school operates only one car, when changing the dual control brake to a new car the pedal should be located as nearly as possible in the same spot in relation to the teacher.

Both mechanical and hydraulic dual controls are used on automatic-shift cars. The hydraulic dual control is more expensive, but can more readily be transferred to later model cars, whereas, because of car model changes, mechanical controls sometimes become obsolete.

## *Car Identification*

Cars used for high school driver education should be easily recognizable as such. Most drivers are patient with learners and respect the need for care in avoiding sudden moves close to the school car, moves which might startle an inexperienced driver. Occasionally one meets a driver who seems to suffer a powerful compulsion to pass any car marked "student driver" or "learner." Even with only a few hundred yards to go, it seems that these individuals must show the world that they drive faster than learners. There are, also, the occasional reckless drivers who just don't care. However, most drivers are accustomed to rigid enforcement of school bus laws and are aware of the public's protective attitude toward school children. It does help to have it known that the driver is not only a learner, but a student in the care of school authority.

FIGURE 18-3  Door signs. Decals or lettering on the door panels identify the car as a driver education car.

Several forms of identifying signs and decals are available. Water-applied decals are very effective and are usually applied on the sides of the car. Their chief drawback is that they must be sanded off and the doors repainted when the car is turned in. A little less permanent but quite satisfactory are the vinylcals. They are held in place by a gummed backing. At the end of the year they can be peeled off without damaging the finish, though the surrounding area may be slightly faded.

Signs are available which may be attached to the bumper and readily changed from car to car. There are also signs which are mounted on the roof with suction cups. These have the advantage of being visible from all direc-

FIGURE 18-4  Bumper signs. These identification signs are easily removed from one car and placed on another.

tions and can be seen from beyond intervening vehicles. In some cases the identification is painted on the sides of the car. This is expensive both to apply and to remove, consequently is not generally used.

The content of the sign varies but usually reads:

DRIVER EDUCATION CAR

Frequently the name of the high school is included on the sign.

The sign may also provide acknowledgment of the dealer's donation of the car, when such is the case. *Policies and Practices for Driver and Traffic Safety Education*[1] recommends that no commercial advertising or identification be placed on the school cars, other than the company names that ordinarily do appear on, and in, stock automobiles. It does, however, mention a courtesy credit identification for the dealer where state or local conditions seem to so require. It recommends using only a single line, with letters that do not exceed 1½ inches in height.

FIGURE 18–5  Roof top signs are visible in all directions and over intervening traffic.

## OBTAINING A DUAL-CONTROL CAR

One method for obtaining cars is by outright purchase by the school district, in the same manner as any school equipment. (During the 1963–1964 school year, 21 percent of the cars used in public high schools were

[1] *Policies and Practices for Driver and Traffic Safety Education,* National Commission on Safety Education, National Education Association, Washington, D.C., 1964.

purchased.) The exact cost varies with circumstances and should be investigated locally. Cost data should be sought also from other schools in similar circumstances in the same state.

## Cars on Loan

To date, dealers have loaned many thousands of cars for use in driver education. Nearly 10,000 cars were loaned during the 1963–1964 school year, or 64 percent of all cars used in public high schools. This has added impetus to the program, not only because of the investment of school funds saved, but also because of the psychological effect among the tax-paying public. The school board that is considering offering a course in driver education has strong support in this evidence that the automobile industry favors driver education. Also, the public—like most individuals—likes the idea of getting a good bargain. The free loan of a car, or cars, is just that.

FIGURE 18–6 About 10,000 dual-control cars a year are loaned by dealers.

In every case of car loan, public acknowledgment of the dealer's contribution should be made. Some schools have a ceremony featuring the presentation of the keys of the new cars, with a "thank you" to the dealer, and possibly with photographs and press coverage. This is not an advertising campaign but an acknowledgment of a public service and an example of courtesy for the students of the school. If a number of dealers in the town want to donate cars, the school district may use one car of each make, or it can alternate makes each year or so.

To obtain cars on loan, direct contacts can be made with local dealers or original contacts made through the dealers' association. State authorities sometimes provide advice on the subject. Affiliated clubs of the American Automobile Association also assist. The state driver education association members can give the benefit of their experience to those who are new in the field. To continue the loan program it is especially important that the cars be given excellent care and returned to the dealer with an appropriate "thank you."

## Insurance

Before completing arrangements for the loan of a car or before purchasing a car, the subject of insurance should be explored in depth. Are there any state laws or requirements to be fulfilled? In the case of loan of cars, what is the best method of handling the title of the car and registration?

Insurance should cover the school, the dealer (if the car is loaned), the teacher, the students, and anybody else who may have occasion to drive the car. Insurance coverage should include, but need not be limited to: (1) state requirements, (2) $100,000 to $300,000 public liability, (3) $10,000 property damage, (4) $100 deductible collision, (5) comprehensive fire, theft, and tornado insurance.

## Transmission Types

Automatic-transmission cars now outnumber those with manual transmission by 3 to 1 among American cars manufactured today. This is one factor which would favor the use of automatic-transmission cars in driver education. Another point is that the more time that is taken to learn manipulation of the controls of the car, the less of the so-limited in-car time is available for the vital highway and traffic practice. It is very important that the latter be given under the direction of a qualified driver education teacher, and as much of it during the course as possible.

Also, we learn skills most efficiently by progressing from the simple to the complex. Learning the automatic shift first is this type of progression. Many students will never drive manual-shift cars, and learning with them would take valuable instruction time from traffic and highway practice to learn to use clutch and shift lever. Those who learn on automatic-transmission cars have little trouble later in learning to shift manually, if they have reason to.

## School-Dealer Agreement

When cars are loaned to a school, a definite understanding should be reached in regard to their use and to the administrative and maintenance procedures.

The following is a suggested form for a written agreement:

*The school agrees to:*

1. Conduct a high-quality driver education course with in-car instruction, meeting the requirements of the state department of public instruction

(... education) where such requirements have been established; otherwise the following *minimum* requirements will be observed:
30 clock hours per student of classroom instruction
6 clock hours per student of in-car instruction (exclusive of time spent in the car as an observer)
2. Provide an instructor who has completed special driver education teacher preparation of a minimum of forty clock hours and is otherwise approved by the state department of public instruction (... education). In states which have minimum requirements in excess of forty clock hours, the state requirements will be considered as a minimum for car assignment. *Policies and Practices for Driver and Traffic Safety Education*[2] recommends that a teaching minor be required as the minimum requirement for teacher preparation in driver education, certification standards seem to be moving in this direction.
3. Use the car exclusively for driver education activities and have a qualified driver education instructor present at all times that the car is in operation.
4. Make certain of adequate insurance coverage (as specified in the preceding paragraphs under the heading "Insurance").
5. In the event the car is damaged, report promptly any such damage to the dealer and to the insurance company.
6. Identify the car as a "driver education car," with a dealer courtesy line, if desired, not over 1½ inches high.
7. Have vehicle maintenance done to the satisfaction of the dealer and pay all operation and maintenance expenses.
8. Maintain properly the appearance of the car.
9. Provide garaging for the vehicle to the satisfaction of the dealer.
10. Return the car to the dealer on expiration of assignment and pay for servicing or repairs necessary to put the car in the same condition as received, except for normal wear and tear.

*The dealer agrees to:*

Provide the school for its exclusive use, a current-model car(s) to be registered in the name of the school (or) dealer, equipped with dual controls to be paid for by the school (or) dealer, outside mirrors on both right and left, heater and defroster where required, and an instructor's rear-view mirror inside the car [to be paid for by the school (or) dealer].

## Use of the Car

The person in charge of the driver education program should formulate rules and procedures for use and maintenance of the cars. These rules and procedures should be approved by the school district administration, and also the board of education if local circumstances warrant. Maintenance schedules for all cars should be formulated and followed. If more than one teacher uses a car, each should be assigned definite responsibilities.

[2] *Ibid.*

Cars purchased by the school should be used only in accord with an approved standard operating procedure. Cars used on approved nondriver education school business should have the "driver education" and "student driver" signs covered. *Cars on loan from dealers should be used only in driver education instruction, and as provided in writing in agreement with the dealer.* Driver education cars, loaned or purchased, should never be seen in unusual places, at unusual times, or driven by unauthorized persons. Many driver education people have had experiences like the following one:

Teacher X left his own car at the dealer's when he picked up a school car there each day. At the end of the day, he took the school car back to the dealer who garaged it and then drove his own car home. One day at school he received a phone call at noon from his wife telling him that their baby was sick. His car was at the dealer's, some distance from the school. He drove home in the driver education car (which was idle during his twenty-seven-minute lunch hour) and drove his wife and baby to a hospital. He then returned to school, all in the twenty-seven minutes. The board of education office called the school that afternoon about phone calls they had received, complaining about a teacher's family using a school driver education car for their own personal business. A driver education car is *always* in the public eye when on a public thoroughfare!

## *Equipment*

Driver education cars should have seat belts, sun visors, padded dashboards, and other safety equipment as it is developed and accepted by safety authorities as practical. A first-aid kit, fire extinguisher, flares, reflectors, reinforced tire chains where such may be needed, Trac-Treds, and a separate, interior, wide-angle rear-view mirror for the instructor should be standard equipment.

## *Allowances for Dealers*

Manufacturers have always been wholeheartedly behind the high school driver education program. The initial six high school courses started in 1936 were made possible by six cars loaned by the Pontiac Motor Division of General Motors. As the program expanded, cars were loaned through the dealers of the various automobile manufacturers. After World War II, above-quota cars were provided dealers as an incentive. When this was no longer effective, an allowance of $125 was given the dealer for each car loaned. This allowance has been increased to $250 and now, in some cases, to $500, depending on the make and model of car and the accessories provided.

## *Adult Schools*

When boards of education conduct adult school driver education, prior written arrangement with the dealer should be made if loaned cars are to be used. All pertinent state regulations and possible additional insurance needs should be studied.

## SETTING AN EXAMPLE

Maintenance procedures and the type and condition of equipment are important not only for the obvious, practical reasons but because they set a pattern for the students. It is overly optimistic to believe that students can be taught proper procedures in the classroom, and then see that they are not carried out with the driver education car—and that those students will then believe and respect what they were taught. The *educational* value of proper maintenance and proper equipment is extremely important. The student must know that the driver education teacher *practices what he preaches.* Otherwise the student may come to believe that what he was taught in the classroom was "kid stuff" and not practiced "for real" in real cars with professionals in charge.

## SELECTED BIBLIOGRAPHY

*Achievement Program, National High School Driver Education,* Insurance Institute for Highway Safety, Washington, D.C. Annual publication.

*Agreement for Use of Dual Control Car,* American Automobile Association, Washington, D.C.

*Aids for Dealers,* American Automobile Association, Washington, D.C.

*Policies and Practices for Driver and Traffic Safety Education,* National Commission on Safety Education, National Education Association, Washington, D.C., 1964.

# School and Teacher Liability 19

PROBABLY the most important concept for the driver education teacher to understand in connection with the subject of liability for pupil injuries is *negligence*. Simply defined, it is a failure to use that degree of care which a careful and prudent person would exercise under similar circumstances. An example might be a teacher permitting a student to open the car door and, without looking, step out into the path of an oncoming car.

## WHO MAY BE LIABLE FOR PUPIL INJURIES?

A teacher is said to stand *in loco parentis* to his pupils. Literally, this means acting in the place of a parent. This status confers a legal right of control, restraint, and correction as is reasonable and necessary. The driver education teacher is also affected by the law in his state which deals with civil liability. Originally the common law concept was that a school, in exercising a governmental function as a state agency, was therefore immune from civil suit. This was considered by many an unjust principle dating back to the "divine right of kings." The government, being the successor of the kings, "could do no wrong."

Legislation in some states has wiped out this immunity of the school district from civil liability as an agency of government. In others it has been practically invalidated by court decisions. In some states, the general principle holds, but permissive legislation allows civil action against a school district under some conditions and not under others. Because of wide variations in this matter, the practical course for the interested teacher is to learn about statutes and court decisions in his own state which deal with negligence liability. The best information could obviously be obtained through the office of the attorney who handles school district matters.

In some states and under certain circumstances, school districts are required by law to pay the sum for which a teacher is held legally liable in a negligence suit. Some states permit school districts to purchase from public funds *liability* insurance to protect the professional staff. Some require it. *Accident* insurance is purchased by the school district in some states to protect pupils. Insurance doesn't alter liability under the law, however.

The group accident policy, paid for by the individual pupil, has become quite widespread. Many such policies cover the student from the time he leaves his home until he returns, provided that his travel is within a reasonable, direct route and time. Physical education activities and athletics, usually excluding interscholastic football (covered by a separate premium), are usually covered by the same policy. The important point for the teacher is that this insurance does not change the matter of liability at all, for school or teacher, and it is purely *accident* (and not liability) insurance.

Although the concept of *negligence* as a basis for liability under tort law is generally recognized, the matter of *who* is liable and *under what* circumstances is extremely varied throughout the country. Perhaps the best statement possible in answer to the question, "Who may be liable for pupil injuries?" is this:

1. Depending on the law of the state, the school district may or may not be held liable.
2. When negligence is established, the teacher may be held liable; in certain states, some of them with limitations, provision is made to protect the teacher from being required to pay the damages.

For more detailed coverage of the subject, a publication of the National Education Association, *Who Is Liable for Pupil Injuries?*[1] is recommended.

---

[1] *Who Is Liable for Pupil Injuries?* National Commission on Safety Education, National Education Association, Washington, D.C., 1963.

## LIABILITY IN THE DRIVER EDUCATION COURSE

The simplest formula for determining such liability is to think of driver education in its true role as an integral part of the school curriculum. As such, the teacher of this course has the same responsibility as any prudent teacher to exercise care in protecting his students (and others) from injury. In the classroom he doesn't permit disorder, and *he doesn't leave his class unattended to perform other duties in connection with the driver education car.* It is not necessarily true that anything that occurs in the classroom in the absence of a teacher can be charged to negligence on his part. Nevertheless, it is recognized by educators that the practice of leaving a class unsupervised is an open invitation to trouble. Performance of an assigned duty elsewhere might (or might not) relieve the teacher from liability, and it might involve the administration also.

Two important points for teachers to remember are these:

1. The outcome of a possible civil court action cannot be surmised and taken for granted by the teacher who takes the risk of leaving a class unattended or absents himself from some other area of responsibility for pupil safety.
2. A civil suit, regardless of outcome, with attendant publicity, cannot help but harm the teacher and the school. The idea (even though without foundation) that "where there's smoke there's fire" can be very damaging to professional reputations. One or two such cases could just about ruin a driver education teacher's chances for future positions in his field in competition with others. The administrators may just not want to take the least possible chance that something may have been wrong with his performance in the past. This is another hazard of any *involvement* in litigation, rarely expressed, but worth consideration if one is tempted to take a chance on the basis that one is not legally liable for a specific act. Publicity is not limited to the guilty, and many who read of the charges never happen to read of the later-established innocence of the defendant.

### *Parental Signatures*

The practice of getting "notes from home" is a very old one in public education. No doubt it has served some purposes very well. Undoubtedly a close liaison between home and school is highly desirable. However, the parental signature as a method of avoiding liability for pupil injury, although of possible psychological value, does not abrogate liability. Some years ago the practice became widespread in the case of student participation in interschool athletics. Students on field trips under school supervision also are often required to bring written permission from their parents. More recently, many schools have required parents' signatures prior to assigning students to instruction in the driver education car.

Psychologically, the practice is sound. The parent *should* be aware of the student's school activities. Also, there may be some condition of which the teacher is not aware that would make the activity inadvisable for that particular student. Too, the suit-conscious parent (and there are a few, apparently a growing number in recent years) may be deterred from instituting a doubtful suit by the fact that he has signed a "permission slip." But the fact remains that such permission does not relieve either the school or the teacher (or administrator) from liability for injury to the student.

It is a principle of law, generally observed, that one cannot waive the liability that may be involved in the event of an injury before that event occurs. Also, the parent couldn't waive the child's rights, even though the parent or an appointed guardian would have to institute the suit for the child. The parental signature, then, is of some value but does not absolve the school or the teacher from liability.

## Course of Study

The subject of "course of study" should be given consideration. This is particularly important in states where it is considered evidence of official approval by the board of education of the described teaching procedures. In driver education, the course of study should include a complete description of course content, including practice areas. It should not attempt to define when each activity and area will be utilized, since there are many variables in weather conditions, student learning, student absences, etc., which would make a time schedule impossible to maintain. The course of study in driver education, however, if only a document of approval, can have value, especially in those states and school districts where official recognition may be given it.

## IN THE CAR

This is the area of greatest concern for liability on the part of the teacher new to driver education. Although negligence suits have been filed against teachers, to date there seem to have been surprisingly few. This may chiefly be due to two reasons: (1) There have been few cases of injury to students in driver education courses. (2) Since it is customary to carry liability insurance for driver education cars, some accidental injury cases may have been settled by the insurance companies concerned without being referred to the courts. There have been exceptions, of course. The point here is that there is no need for alarm on the part of the prospective teacher as long as three conditions govern:

1. The teacher exercises and requires reasonable care in car operation.
2. All legal requirements are met, including possession of student permits when necessary, car registration, maintenance of safe operating condition of all driver education cars, and no driving violations are permitted.
3. Automobile insurance policies are procured (in accordance with state law, of course) which will protect the teacher in the event he is held liable in connection with accidental injury arising from operation of the school driver education car. The amount of coverage should be high enough to take care of any foreseeable judgment, however high. A point important to note here is this: The teacher should make sure that, whatever the custom or ruling may be in the school district, there actually

SCHOOL AND TEACHER LIABILITY 269

*is* a policy in force which covers him in the event of injury to persons or property damage which may result from operation of the driver education car (see "Insurance" in Chapter 18, "Dual-control Cars").

## SOME GENERAL PRINCIPLES PERTAINING TO LIABILITY

In general, to be considered negligence, it would have to be shown that there was a lack of the reasonable care a careful and prudent person would exercise to protect the student. Reasonable care cannot be interpreted as the equivalent of omniscience or more than normal human foresight.

FIGURE 19-1 Decorating for social events is a common scene in the modern school. Any teacher may be assigned to supervise. Very close, careful, and constant supervision is necessary.

Negligence on the part of a person making a claim, which is legally referred to as contributory negligence, is involved in cases of suits for damages when the victim's own lack of reasonable care contributed to the event of the damage or injury. Contributory negligence on the part of the claimant usually prevents him from recovering damages. For example, a pedestrian stepping out from between two parked cars immediately in front of a moving car which struck him would probably be considered guilty of contributory negligence.

In cases of injuries due to automobile accidents (including fingers caught in car doors, etc.), the teacher is expected to render the proper *first aid* in the absence of medical services. Within the limit of the layman's knowledge of first aid, he must not neglect to take proper action, nor must he take any improper action—either of which condition could result in his being held liable for aggravation of the injuries. The physical education teacher and the athletic coach have far more occasions to face this responsibility than does the teacher of driver education. An obvious conclusion is that every driver education teacher should know proper first aid procedures. A very practical "ounce of protection" is described under the heading Be Ready in Chapter 14, "Teaching Techniques."

Leaving a driver education car unattended, with the engine running, especially adjacent to a school where young pupils are present, might make a teacher guilty of negligence, if young pupils got into the car and were injured on account of its being left in that condition. One would not properly leave a car with the key in the ignition switch and the engine running (although it does happen). Certainly a driver education teacher would be unlikely to do so on any public street. However, it has been done on school grounds, particularly in cold weather, to permit the heater to warm the car.

If the car were to be taken by a high school student, and he were injured in an accident, the school and the teacher would probably not be held liable. (Some criticism might follow, however.) On the other hand, if a small child were to climb into the car and release the brake, the negligence principle might be involved.

## Purpose of This Chapter

It should be obvious by now that no complete knowledge of pertinent law can be imparted in the teacher preparation curriculum. The *general principles* of school and teacher liability should be recognized, however, so that all concerned understand the responsibilities imposed on the school and the school personnel for the physical protection of the students.

### SELECTED BIBLIOGRAPHY

Podesta, Victor J.: *Student Accident Insurance,* The State Federation of District Boards of Education of New Jersey, Trenton, N.J.

*Policies and Practices in Driver and Traffic Safety Education,* National Commission on Safety Education, National Education Association, Washington, D.C., 1964.

*The Pupil's Day in Court,* Review of 1963, Research Division, National Education Association, Washington, D.C., 1964 (annual).

*The Teacher's Day in Court,* Review of 1963, Research Division, National Education Association, Washington, D.C., 1964 (annual).

*Who Is Liable for Pupil Injuries?* National Commission on Safety Education, National Education Association, Washington, D.C., 1963.

# Costs and Financing   20

MUCH HAS been said and written about the cost of driver and traffic safety education. Although the program has grown at an almost incredible rate since its inception a few decades ago, it is still not available to a sizable proportion of eligible high school students.[1] This is chiefly due to budgetary considerations. Among them one finds a great deal of misinformation, most of which exaggerates the cost and tends to discourage the much-needed expansion of the program. Every driver and traffic safety education teacher and every school administrator should have a clear-cut understanding of the costs involved.

[1] *Seventeenth Annual Achievement Program, National High School Driver Education,* Insurance Institute for Highway Safety, Washington, D.C., 1964.

Driver education is recognized as an integral part of the secondary school curriculum and, as such, should be included in the budget of the public school system in the same manner as any subject. It should be recognized also that there is no logical reason for singling it out for special tuition charges. The need of a young person for this course does not necessarily correspond with the ability of his parents to pay tuition. It is suggested that the reader review this subject under Professional Opportunity in Chapter 1, "The Profession—Opportunity and Challenge."

The National Commission on Safety Education makes the following recommendation under "Financial Support" on pages 18 and 19 of *Policies and Practices for Driver and Traffic Safety Education:*[2]

> When local and state funds for the foundation program of education are not adequate to provide the minimum standard course for all eligible students, it is recommended that the state provide the additional funds. The appropriation procedure should provide the desired degree of permanent fiscal support. About one-half of the states now reimburse local school systems for a substantial part of the cost of driver and traffic safety education through special financial support legislation.
>
> Courses for adults and out-of-school youth should be tax-supported to the same extent as other offerings in the public school adult education program. This would not preclude the charging of enrollment or laboratory fees in states where this is common practice in adult education programs.
>
> For college students preparing to teach this subject, the course should be of the same length and should be financed in the same manner as any other comparable college course. This would not preclude the charging of reasonable tuition and/or laboratory fees.

Generally speaking, there is little concern about the cost of the classroom phase of the program, since class groups are comparable in size to those in the other subject fields. Actually, in many places, there is still another condition favorable to the classroom program. In states where there is a minimum time requirement for "physical education, health and safety," the driver education classroom course can be designated as the recognized safety course, fulfilling part of the state time requirement and adding nothing to the budget. It should be understood that the crediting of the course time in fulfillment of this requirement in no way affects the identification of the course which is *driver and traffic safety education.* This is a separate and distinct course in itself, and *time is administratively assigned to it from the total school day.* It is not a "replacement" for any other subject in the curriculum, regardless of where it is placed in the weekly time blocks.

In considering the program of in-car instruction, many people are unduly prejudiced by erroneously applying the simple "pupil-teacher ratio" criterion to this part of the course. The fact is that this is not an appropriate measurement since it emphasizes one factor and completely ignores another equally important one.

---

[2] *Policies and Practices for Driver and Traffic Safety Education,* National Commission on Safety Education, National Education Association, Washington, D.C., 1964.

## THE FALLACY OF THE P-T-R

We often hear, "How extravagant to have one teacher for only four students." Some even ignore the three observing students in the car and call it 1 to 1 ratio, considering only the student who is driving. This is equivalent to classifying all recitation time in a class of thirty students as "1 to 1," since only one is reciting at a time.

The full driver education program, at present almost universally based on a minimum of thirty hours of classroom instruction and six hours of actual driving, has been established beyond reasonable doubt as successful in the accomplishment of its vital mission. All who logically analyze the exceedingly comprehensive and easily available data on the subject recognize this and the moral obligation it implies.

In computing the cost of fulfilling this obligation, the significant factor of the length of the course—the actual *time*, the *man-hours*—is somehow missed. What industrial organization would estimate labor costs by citing the *number of men* on a project and completely ignoring the *time* they worked—the man-hours? Yet this has been the manner in which the in-car instruction phase of the driver education course has been compared with the other courses in the high school curriculum.

*The complete, proved-to-be-successful in-car instruction* course requires six hours of teacher time per student. Computed by the school year, with six hours of teaching per day (the time equivalent of the behind-the-wheel course for one student), each teacher gives the entire in-car phase of the course to 180 students in the common 180-day school year. ("Observation," of course, requires no additional teacher time.) Assuming the same six-hour teaching day, with 30 students in a classroom in any subject field, a teacher gives a course to a total of 180 students in a school year. With any other length of school day the comparison is made using the appropriate numbers. With a day of 5 one-hour classes, he would teach 150 students per year.

Since the students are normally taken from a regularly scheduled study period or activity period, or from physical education class, there is no increased supervising or teaching assignment for a "balance" group, those who would be left of a normal 30-student group scheduled for "driver education, classroom and in-car," with four in a car at a time and a balance of twenty-six requiring supervision. The number of the school teaching staff is unchanged except for the driver education teacher in the car *who teaches the full, recognized effective course to the same number of students per school year (180 six-hour teaching days) as does the classroom teacher of any other subject*. In spite of the quite common concern about the teacher-salary cost of the in-car instruction in driver education, it can be the same in the 180-day school year as for the normal 30-students-per-class courses. (In a shorter school year, it would seem that the latter courses would prove to be more favorable in terms of pupil-teacher ratio. However, this would actually be a lesser number of *hours* of instruction in the 30-students-per-class courses.) The number of *hours of instruction* is a legitimate criterion *as judged by appropriate standards in each subject field*, and should not be ignored in computing costs or in considering course standards. Similarly, if the in-car driver education teacher teaches six *periods* of fifty minutes each, rather than six *hours* per day, he will not cover the equivalent of one student per day. In this case he will give the complete in-car course to 150 students in the 180-day school year. Five 50-minute periods cover 125 students.

Shortening of the school day or school year will have the apparent effect of increasing the cost of in-car driver education without affecting the cost of the classroom subject courses. Obviously, the disparity results from maintaining the time standards of the former while lowering those of the latter. In any case, because of the shorter time required for the complete, proved-to-be-effective driver education course in comparison with the much greater time required for most "classroom" courses, there is little cost difference between the two. The simple "1-to-1 pupil-teacher ratio" ignores the very significant *course time* factor in cost computation.

## COST FORMULA

Still on the subject of the cost of teachers' salaries, the chief determinant of the cost of the in-car instruction, it should be realized that it must be computed with regard to the level of the teachers' salaries in the area in question. Assignment of all young, new teachers to the subject also means a great difference with salary costs—low *at first*, rising across the salary scale over a period of years, until abnormally high at some time in

FIGURE 20-1 In computing costs, only . . .

the future. Obviously, this assignment practice is not a sound one in school administration since, if a general policy, it overbalances a school staff in favor of inexperience, and it is either a temporary deception, or—if carried to extremes and teachers are replaced by new, inexperienced ones, each after a few years—it penalizes the students and the school and debases the teaching profession.

In the case of each individual school situation, however, the actual salary or salaries to be paid the teacher candidates chosen must be considered. Geographically, cost varies widely with the rates of teacher pay. An "average" estimate of teacher cost, or a statement as to the "range" of such costs, has less meaning than would a formula for computing the cost *under the conditions that prevail in the school district where the program is being considered.* Assume a teacher salary of $6,000 per year. (It could be $5,000, $10,000 or any other.) *With a teaching load of six hours per day for 180 school days* per year, this teacher gives the in-car instruction to 180 students per year at a teacher-salary cost of $33.33 per student. *Any deviation from those hours and days would, of course, change the per-pupil cost correspondingly.*

FIGURE 20-2 . . . the true number of course hours, in-car and classroom, should be used.

In a school where driver education properly has status equal to that of all other subjects during the regular school day and year, it is often necessary, because of the size of the student population, to schedule additional in-car instruction after school, on Saturdays, and/or during school vacations. Where this is the case, it is no hardship or downgrading of the teaching profession to pay the teacher on an hourly wage basis. This can be well above the normal pay for most jobs the teacher would obtain for part-time work and still keep the per-pupil-cost low. Obviously, it does not lower professional standards of living.

Again, just assuming the hypothetical figure for comparison of $5 per hour for the overtime portion of the teacher's pay, this would lower the cost to $30 per student. (It would be equivalent to $5,400 per year on the basis of the assumed six-hour day, 180 days per school year.) On the basis of a *five*-hour school day, the normal teacher-salary cost would be $40 per student, with a proportionately greater saving in the number taught outside the regular school day (at $30 per student). With a teacher salary of $8,000, the salary cost of in-car instruction would be $44.44 per student, modified downward in the total school year budget by the reduction resulting from the overtime rate of pay for teaching *part* of the student population after school or during school vacations.

This per-pupil cost of in-car instruction based on teacher-pay cost for a six-teaching-hour school day is the same as for any 30-students-in-a-class, 180-days-per-year classroom course in any subject. If school policy grants one free hour of the six to each teacher on the school staff, then the cost per pupil is elevated correspondingly. Obviously, the fewer the teaching hours per dollar of teacher pay, the higher the cost of any course of standard time commitment.

Teacher assignments are expressed in both whole numbers and fractions, of course, for accuracy where teachers are assigned in driver education for some periods and in other subject fields for others. The standard procedures and regulations governing the conduct of the course during the regular school day and school year should apply to after-school, Saturday, and vacation instruction also.

## *Additional Cost Factors*

For the great majority (65 percent) of driver education courses, automobile dealers lend cars to schools. When a school buys its own car, it often gets the advantage of a special bid price and tax exemptions—plus a trade-in allowance when the car is exchanged for a new model. The net cost to the school is not great. When the driver education cars are exchanged for new ones each year, maintenance costs are low. When a school leases cars and pays a monthly fee, the cost is also not excessive when compared with the original cost and depreciation of some other school equipment. *It is usually possible to obtain cars on a free loan.*

Some boards of education maintain gasoline pumps for school district vehicles. Fuel costs for driver education are somewhat lower when this is done. In communities where municipal vehicles are so fueled, an arrangement can be made between school and municipal authorities for fueling driver education vehicles at the same pumps to reduce cost. The possibilities of all such procedures should be investigated before reporting the projected cost of the program.

In view of the wide disparity among the costs of two items throughout the country, i.e., teacher salaries and car insurance premiums, any "average costs" cited for them would be meaningless to the school administration considering instituting a course in driver education.

Table 20–1 outlines a formula for computing the costs in an individual school district. The figures given are an average of costs in 1,208 schools, as reflected in responses to a survey conducted during the 1957–1958 school year. Obviously, they would have to be raised to reflect the change in money values since that time. The items cited in parentheses in the table do not vary so widely throughout the country and may be used for purposes of estimate. Teacher salaries and car insurance figures are not quoted since any "average" figure given would be fictitious and extremely wide of the mark in many places.

The costs derived from using Table 20–1 are based on the assumption

Table 20–1. Cost of driver education courses

*Car cost*

| | | |
|---|---|---|
| Lease fee, if leased | | $_____ |
| Depreciation, if owned | | _____ |
| Insurance | | _____ |
| Gasoline | ($113.44 per year)* | _____ |
| Oil | ⎫ | _____ |
| Greasing | ⎪ | _____ |
| Washing | ⎬ ($59.81) | _____ |
| Storage | ⎪ | _____ |
| Dual-control installation | ⎪ | _____ |
| Repairs | ⎭ | _____ |
| Other expenses | | _____ |
| Total car cost | | $_____ |

*Text materials*

| | | |
|---|---|---|
| Textbooks: | | |
|   Total number used | _____ | |
|   Total cost | _____ | |
|   Estimated life | _____ years | |
|   Cost per year | | $_____ |
| Text materials consumed during the year: | | |
|   Tests | ⎫ | $_____ |
|   Workbooks | ⎬ ($17.79) | _____ |
|   Driving guides | ⎪ | _____ |
|   Other | ⎭ | _____ |
|   Total cost of text materials for year | | $_____ |

\* Figures in parentheses are averages based on a survey of 1,208 high schools during the 1957–1958 school year.

*(continued on next page)*

## Table 20-1. COST OF DRIVER EDUCATION COURSES *(Continued)*

### Films

| Film | Cost new | |
|---|---|---|
| | $ | |
| | | |
| Total cost | $ | |
| Useful life in years | | |
| Cost of films per school year | | $ |

### Teaching aids and devices

| Teaching aid | Cost new | |
|---|---|---|
| | $ | |
| ($9.94)* | | |
| | | |
| | | |
| Total cost | $ | |
| Estimated useful life in years | | |
| Cost per school year | | $ |

### Teacher salary

| | | |
|---|---|---|
| Teacher salary for school year for driver education | $ | |
| **Total cost of driver education course** | $ | |
| Total students enrolled | | |
| Cost per student enrolled | | $ |

* Figures in parentheses are averages based on a survey of 1,208 high schools during the 1957–1958 school year.

that all behind-the-wheel instruction is given by the teacher seated in the car beside the student. This is the method most commonly used, but other methods are being used to increase the number of students trained per teacher. These methods are discussed in detail elsewhere (see Chapter 9, "Simulation and the Driving Simulator," and Chapter 16, "Driving Ranges, Routes, and Practice Areas.")

1. Simulators allow one teacher to supervise the practice of a number of students at a time. Four hours on a simulator are usually considered equal to one hour behind the wheel of the driver education car.[3]
2. Multiple-car ranges also permit one teacher to supervise the practice driving of several students at one time. So far there is no agreement as to how many hours of driving on a range are equivalent to one hour in a car with the instructor.

Although both driving simulators and driving ranges reduce the salary cost per pupil, this is offset, at least in part, by the cost of the simulators and the driving range. This fact should not be overlooked in comparing the costs of different systems.

[3] *Policies and Practices for Driver and Traffic Safety Education.*

## Reporting

When reporting on projected costs of a prospective driver education program, data cited herein should be obtained and the report composed to apply to the school system concerned. Citing costs as "average" or "ranges" is likely to be met with doubts on the part of administrators and legislators and with contradiction by opponents of the program, with no basis of confirmation available. Such figures compare with an answer to the question, "What is property worth?" Obviously, "where" and "what property" must be considered in answering.

Acceptance of a cost estimate based on experience elsewhere may result in a budgetary appropriation which is too little or too big and damaging to the new program and embarrassing to its proponents. Accurate computation can be made and supported.

## SELECTED BIBLIOGRAPHY

*Policies and Practices for Driver and Traffic Safety Education*, National Commission on Safety Education, National Education Association, Washington, D.C., 1964.

*Seventeenth Annual Achievement Program, National High School Driver Education*, Insurance Institute for Highway Safety, Washington, D.C., 1964.

*Special State Financial Support for Driver Education*, National Commission on Safety Education, National Education Association, Washington, D.C., 1963.

# Maintaining Community Support

# 21

IN DISCUSSING the broad concept of driver and traffic safety education, identification of the subject as an *instrument* of education was stressed. This frame of reference is not understood by those who see it as "different" from "schoolwork." Industrial arts, home economics, physical education, and other subjects met with the same reaction when they were first introduced. There are still critics of all of them, of course, who think of the pen as the only instrument of learning. The well-informed educator of the twentieth century has long since discarded this archaic view. We now educate by a wider variety of means with different emphasis in each area and achieve a wider variety of values than we could with the pen alone. Our formerly "special" subjects are now an integral part of the curriculum. In addition to being an instrument or tool of education, the course content in driver education has an intrinsic value to be found in few fields of study in which the high school student could engage. Although in general this value is known, the driver education teacher should have the facts "at his fingertips."

Experience has shown that introduction and continuation of the program requires community support. Most school people are well aware of this fact. An equally important fact is often missed, however. Most people in the community are not so well informed on the subject as are the professional people directly concerned. A great many who once passively accepted the evidence in favor of the program are still susceptible to arguments against it when advanced, as they sometimes are, by ill-informed or self-interested parties. In addition to this, there are many people in communities who remain aloof from school matters entirely, unless urged to take part by individuals or printed articles. Then they act on the information (or misinformation) immediately at hand. Also, personnel changes in school boards sometimes change established policies.

The point is this. There have been instances about the country—too many to be ignored—where good, well-conducted, and successful driver education programs have been discontinued when pressures were brought to bear on boards of education, unknown to the driver education people in the school. In some cases, the program was restored later when the public awakened to the loss. In others it was not.

The average citizen favors good education for his children. He is sometimes misled in the matter of driver education by those who identify themselves as "budget cutters" (who are "against" almost anything), "purists" in education who sincerely believe that their subject fields are sacred (and others profane), and still others who may be termed "vested interests." Under such pressures our "average citizen" is sometimes misled, and he isn't going to come to the driver education teacher to get the facts. A seed of suspicion has been implanted in his mind. Until then, he probably would have listened attentively to what the driver education teacher would tell him on the subject.

Although all this may appear to be a "negative" view, it points to a definite need. It is not enough to perform a good "public relations" job when the driver education program is being introduced and while it is still new. *Continuing activity is needed to keep the public image of driver education alive, correct, and accurate.*

It is often said that if a good program is in operation there need be no fear of loss of public support. It would be fine if it were so, but all too often good programs *have* been penalized. This is also true of the general functioning of a school. Many a fine school has been penalized by adverse criticism. *It is the **public image** of a school or of a program that influences community action, not the knowledge and judgment of the professional people who know the criteria on which to base judgment.* When we, in the field of driver education, have taken years to develop criteria for evaluating a program— and all do not agree yet—we cannot depend upon unfounded public opinion to create its image. We have to provide the facts. We must create the image.

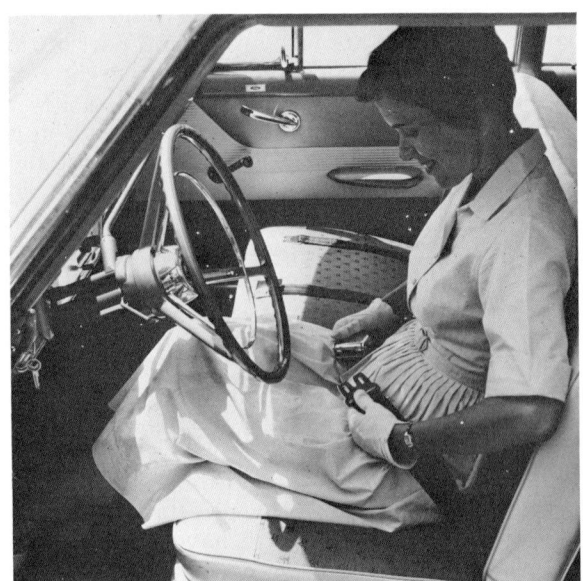

FIGURE 21-1 The news photograph can be used subtly to advocate a good driving practice used regularly in the driver education course.

## THE TRUE IMAGE OF DRIVER EDUCATION

The first and foremost mission of driver education is accident prevention. This is the basis on which communities have "bought" the program. Although professionals in the field know that there are other important values to be gained, the basic fact the public wants to know is whether we are succeeding in reducing highway accidents and fatalities. To this we can give an affirmative answer and an impressive one. A wealth of research data is available to support this answer, far too many studies to be enumerated here.[1] However, forming a conservative estimate based on the data assembled in these studies, the computations in Table 21-1 tell the story.

### Personal Approach

Tabular data can be very clear from a statistical viewpoint but, like many other true pictures, they have much greater effect when the implications are personally identified with individuals.

Most parents of high school students favor the driver education program, especially when their children approach driving age. This is not a matter of selfishness but a human characteristic in which interest becomes intensified with involvement. It springs from self-identification with an object. The latter state can be used honestly and in the best interest of the program by reaching *all* the people of the community, especially the parents of very young children, with facts showing that they *are* involved—*now*, and not only when their children reach driving age.

[1] *Driver Education Reduces Accidents and Violations,* American Automobile Association, Washington, D.C., 1964.

Table 21-1. RESULTS OF THE DRIVER EDUCATION PROGRAM 1936–1960

| (1) School year | (2) Cars in use | (3) Persons trained | (4) Accumulated total trained end of year | (5) Total trained with 5 years or less experience | (6) Estimated deaths had drivers not been trained | (7) Lives saved | (8) Economic loss prevented during year | (9) Saving per person trained during year | (10) Injuries prevented |
|---|---|---|---|---|---|---|---|---|---|
| 1936–37 | 3 | 450 | 450 | 450 | 0 | 0 | $ 0 | $ 0 | 0 |
| 1937–38 | 5 | 750 | 1,200 | 1,200 | 1 | 0 | 0 | 0 | 0 |
| 1938–39 | 25 | 3,750 | 4,950 | 4,950 | 3 | 1 | 50,000 | 13 | 35 |
| 1939–40 | 25 | 3,750 | 8,700 | 8,700 | 5 | 2 | 100,000 | 27 | 70 |
| 1940–41 | 50 | 7,500 | 16,200 | 16,200 | 10 | 5 | 250,000 | 33 | 175 |
| 1941–42 | 50 | 7,500 | 23,700 | 23,250 | 14 | 7 | 350,000 | 47 | 245 |
| 1942–43 | 10 | 1,000 | 24,700 | 23,500 | 14 | 7 | 350,000 | 350 | 245 |
| 1943–44 | 10 | 1,000 | 25,700 | 20,750 | 12 | 6 | 300,000 | 300 | 210 |
| 1944–45 | 10 | 1,000 | 26,700 | 18,000 | 11 | 5 | 250,000 | 250 | 175 |
| 1945–46 | 75 | 3,750 | 30,450 | 14,250 | 8 | 4 | 280,000 | 75 | 140 |
| 1946–47 | 1,500 | 75,000 | 105,450 | 81,750 | 48 | 24 | 1,920,000 | 26 | 840 |
| 1947–48 | 3,000 | 150,000 | 255,450 | 230,750 | 136 | 68 | 6,120,000 | 41 | 2,380 |
| 1948–49 | 4,000 | 200,000 | 455,450 | 429,750 | 254 | 127 | 12,700,000 | 63 | 4,445 |
| 1949–50 | 4,500 | 225,000 | 680,450 | 653,750 | 386 | 193 | 17,370,000 | 77 | 6,755 |
| 1950–51 | 5,500 | 275,000 | 955,450 | 925,000 | 546 | 273 | 24,570,000 | 89 | 9,555 |
| 1951–52 | 6,000 | 300,000 | 1,255,450 | 1,150,000 | 678 | 339 | 33,900,000 | 113 | 11,865 |
| 1952–53 | 6,300 | 315,000 | 1,570,450 | 1,315,000 | 776 | 388 | 38,800,000 | 123 | 13,580 |
| 1953–54 | 7,234 | 418,443 | 1,988,893 | 1,533,443 | 830 | 415 | 47,000,000 | 112 | 14,525 |
| 1954–55 | 8,079 | 467,925 | 2,456,818 | 1,776,368 | 870 | 435 | 54,000,000 | 115 | 15,225 |
| 1955–56 | 9,024 | 527,440 | 2,984,258 | 2,028,808 | 1,030 | 515 | 60,500,000 | 115 | 18,025 |
| 1956–57 | 10,411 | 649,885 | 3,634,143 | 2,378,693 | 1,140 | 570 | 72,000,000 | 111 | 20,000 |
| 1957–58 | 11,964 | 738,408 | 4,372,551 | 2,802,101 | 1,260 | 630 | 87,000,000 | 118 | 22,000 |
| 1958–59 | 12,249 | 870,338 | 5,242,889 | 3,253,996 | 1,462 | 731 | 104,000,000 | 119 | 25,600 |
| 1959–60 | 13,098 | 892,965 | 6,135,854 | 3,679,036 | 1,650 | 825 | 135,000,000 | 151 | 28,800 |
| 1960–61 | 12,036 | 874,532 | 7,010,386 | 4,026,128 | 1,770 | 885 | 150,000,000 | 172 | 31,000 |
| 1961–62 | 11,895 | 1,036,581 | 8,046,967 | 4,412,824 | 1,890 | 945 | 170,000,000 | 164 | 33,000 |
| 1962–63 | 12,983 | 1,114,177 | 9,161,144 | 4,788,593 | 2,150 | 1,025 | 184,000,000 | 166 | 36,000 |
| 1963–64 | 14,997 | 1,256,000 | 10,417,144 | 5,174,255 | 2,430 | 1,215 | 204,000,000 | 171 | 42,500 |
| Total | 155,033 | 10,417,144 | | | | 9,640 | $1,404,810,000 | | 337,390 |

Young children and old folks are by far the most numerous pedestrian victims of traffic accidents. Any family which includes a young child or an old person has a definite stake in the manner in which drivers of the community, including teen-agers, operate their cars. This fact is well worthy of mention.

FIGURE 21-2 Parents also appreciate safety education for the very young.

## The PTA

The facts just mentioned should be presented to parent-teacher associations, because these are groups of people who have the interest of the children and their schools at heart. When truly informed about driver education, they are among the best friends of the program. The new teacher should enter the community with this fact in mind: *The PTA is not an unfriendly critic of teachers and schools, but a very sincere ally of both*. It can also be the voice of the driver education program in the community, when properly informed on the subject.

The accomplishments of driver education in saving lives and property and reducing the number of injuries are by far its greatest virtues in the eyes of the public. Its value has been cited as an instrument for achieving the aims of education. Some additional benefits accrue which will be of interest to parents.

## Insurance Benefits

Insurance companies recognize the value of driver education by granting a reduction in premiums to young drivers who have completed the standard course of (at least) thirty hours of classroom instruction and six hours of behind-the-wheel in-car instruction. This has long applied to male drivers under twenty-five years of age, whose premium rates have been higher than average. In 1965, female drivers in the young age group became subject to higher premium rates and can take advantage of the rate reduction.

Since insurance rates are based on accident experience, the driver education teacher is well advised to keep his knowledge of the insurance implications of driver education up to date. He will be asked many questions by students and parents, and sometimes by administrators and board members who are concerned about public support of the program. He should keep current data on whether the reduction is still in effect. Is it, currently, for both boys and girls? What are the age brackets? Roughly, by what percentage, is the premium reduced?

For a number of years there has been a reluctance on the part of some driver education people to mention this insurance item. Some say that it is not an objective of driver education and, therefore, they will not discuss it. Some censure the parent or the prospective course candidate who inquires about it, and a few have even excluded such students from the course when the course was elective, on the grounds that they did not "have the proper attitude." The one assumption is correct. It is not the purpose for which we have the course in schools. However, it is an existing fact—an incidental side benefit. It has helped to gain support for the program. Driver education people, as well as others, have cited it many times in pointing out how much of the cost of a proposed program would be regained by the community. Parents and students have a right to inquire about it. Answers should, of course, be in very general terms, referring those who inquire to their insurance agents for definite information on company policy.

On the basis of research by the Insurance Information Institute, it has been calculated that on liability coverage alone the loss of the premium reduction allowed for driver education would cost two to five times as much as the cost per pupil of a standard course. Without influencing the basic philosophy of driver education, the insurance premium item is favorable to the program not only by substantially reducing the cost to the community, but by recognizing the effectiveness of the course. This statistically based endorsement by this informed and significant segment of industry is highly constructive in its effect.

## License Age

In some states the special high school student learner's permit may be obtained at a specified age below that required for the driver license. This is a great advantage, enabling the school to give the course to students before they can get licenses on their own. The advantage in learning correct procedures at the very beginning is obvious. Also, some states permit licensing of those who have completed an approved course in driver education at an earlier age, usually a year or two. This tends to increase community interest in providing the course for all high school students. Michigan is one example; here the minimum licensing age is eighteen, but those who have completed an approved course may obtain a license at sixteen.

Since the safety record of those who have completed the course is much better than that of others, the individual driver has a year or two more of the driving privilege without contributing to what some might fear would be a higher accident rate due to immaturity. This privilege is valuable to families in which a son may drive a delivery truck after school or during summer vacations to help family finances or to earn money for college. He may also help with family transportation.

## Future Citizen Voters

"The railroad is coming!" These were words which once electrified whole communities, and even states. Today, the building of a modern highway can mean as much to many thousands of people. It is no longer a concern only for some level of government, some long-distance shippers, and the rest of us on vacation trips. When the building of a highway is proposed, questions arise as to how it can best be coordinated with the road networks of the counties and municipalities through which it passes. Then comes the problem of traffic engineering on all the public thoroughfares in the area, enforcement, parking, maintenance of roadways and traffic controls, and all the services that make efficient traffic movement possible. All these services of government have one essential element in common. They all need the support of an informed citizenry. In a phase of modern living as important as highway transportation and safety, the final authority—the electorate—should be able to base its decisions on a good understanding of the complex problems involved.

Such understanding is one of the features of a comprehensive course in driver education. It is another phase of the citizenship-education aspect of the subject field. It is quite the opposite of the man who, as many traffic authorities complain, "wants a stop sign at his street and no other street in town." In the modern world, a successful democracy requires *informed* citizens in each community.

## Part of Living

One of the great advantages of driver education is seldom mentioned, perhaps because it is so obvious and so simple. Granting the important role that the subject field plays in the vital matter of traffic safety, and granting its implications for citizenship and other important values in education, we should still remember how much *more pleasant and easy* it is to drive to the store, the job, or anywhere, when one is justly confident of one's driving skill, knows traffic law, and knows how to "get along" with the many other people moving about on the same streets on their own errands. It just makes living more enjoyable.

## PUBLIC INFORMATION

The foregoing "image" of driver education is a true one, and one well worth presentation to the public. Just as in driving itself where the person who just "picks up" his procedure and his knowledge without proper instruction tends to be a poor driver, the member of the community who acquires his opinions on the local schools (and on the driver education program) from chance hearsay can hardly be expected to give intelligent support to either school or program. For those who are employed as professional experts it is *part of the job* to inform him.

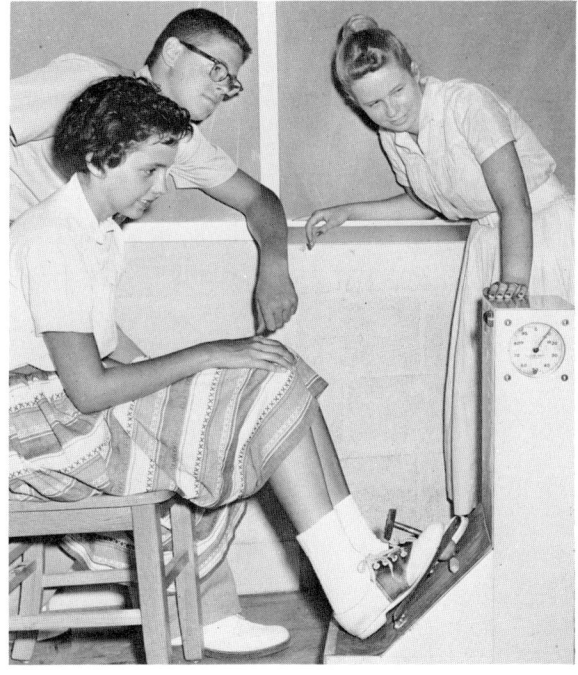

FIGURE 21-3 An occasional photo in a local paper creates interest by showing phases of driver education not familiar to most adults.

Parent-teacher associations were mentioned as one excellent media for public education on the values of the driver education program. They welcome members of the school professional staff who have a message for them on the schools and the students. As indicated, the message is not solely for the high school PTA, but for those of all the schools. Service clubs constitute another community support institution. Composed of civic-minded men representing a cross section of business, industry, and the professions, the very nature of the clubs makes them natural leaders in community enterprise and policy. They welcome speakers at their meetings. The subject of driver and traffic safety education and the school would be very appropriate to their mission of community service. There are groups such as women's clubs, the League of Women Voters, and others who would welcome having the driver education teacher explain the program and its meaning for the student and the community.

Student panels at civic meetings and on radio and television programs can be used effectively. It is desirable, of course, that students be chosen for their knowledge of the subject, maturity of views, and ability in expression. A confused presentation does not do justice either to the student body as a whole or to the subject under discussion—not to mention to the students taking part. Reports to parents of students who are taking the course form another channel of communication with the community, reaching those who are immediately and vitally interested.

In addition to the fact that community support for driver education is very important, and that the school itself belongs to the community, there is yet another point worthy of consideration. Although the association of mathematics, English, science, and many other subjects with community welfare is real and important, it is tenuous in the daily thought processes of most people. Where *traffic safety* is concerned, however, the *community* is interested in it as a community "property." This interest, properly directed, can be a tower of strength to the high school program.

## SELECTED BIBLIOGRAPHY

*Driver Education Reduces Accidents and Violations,* American Automobile Association, Washington, D.C., 1964.

Driver's manual for your state, from state motor vehicle department.

"Penny Wise, Pound Foolish," *The Journal of Insurance Information,* Insurance Information Institute, New York, 1962.

"Right Rate for Every Driver," *Journal of American Insurance,* American Mutual Insurance Alliance, Chicago, Ill., 1964.

## VI ELEMENTS OF THE PROFESSIONAL KNOWLEDGE COMPETENCY

IN THIS PART of our text it is important that the plan of teacher preparation be understood. The subject field, driver and traffic safety education, has long outgrown the mere teaching of how to manipulate the controls of a car. It would be tragic not to make maximum use of the teen-ager's intense interest in the automobile to teach him some things he needs very much to understand. These things are in addition to those which will help him to be a safer and more efficient user of the highway. For both these areas, however, the teacher must have a comprehensive background—must know well the *body of knowledge* of the subject field.

This is not a meager, limited, poor field. It is more than enough to warrant a concentration in college study comparable to the traditional college "minor." Perhaps the point to be remembered is that the body of knowledge of this subject field is *more than a textbook*. It is partly the familiar high school driver education textbooks. It is also the literature of some other professional fields. It is the varied literature of traffic safety, and engineering, and education, and traffic law. And it is the college textbook—this book. Any effort to compress all of it between the covers of one book would be futile—hopeless.

The purpose of this textbook is to present that information which the teacher should know but which is not readily available to him by studying the high school textbook he already has, or by the normal college procedure of going to the library. This book is intended as a *contribution* to the field, not as a reprint of what is already at hand.

The "elements" herein are not excerpts. They are designed specifically to meet the needs of the teacher. They should be considered and studied in that frame of reference. "Keep your high school textbook at hand for reference. Make use of the 'Selected Bibliography' at the end of each chapter herein. And study this text." With these three practices, you can acquire a worthwhile degree of mastery of the *knowledge competency* of the subject field.

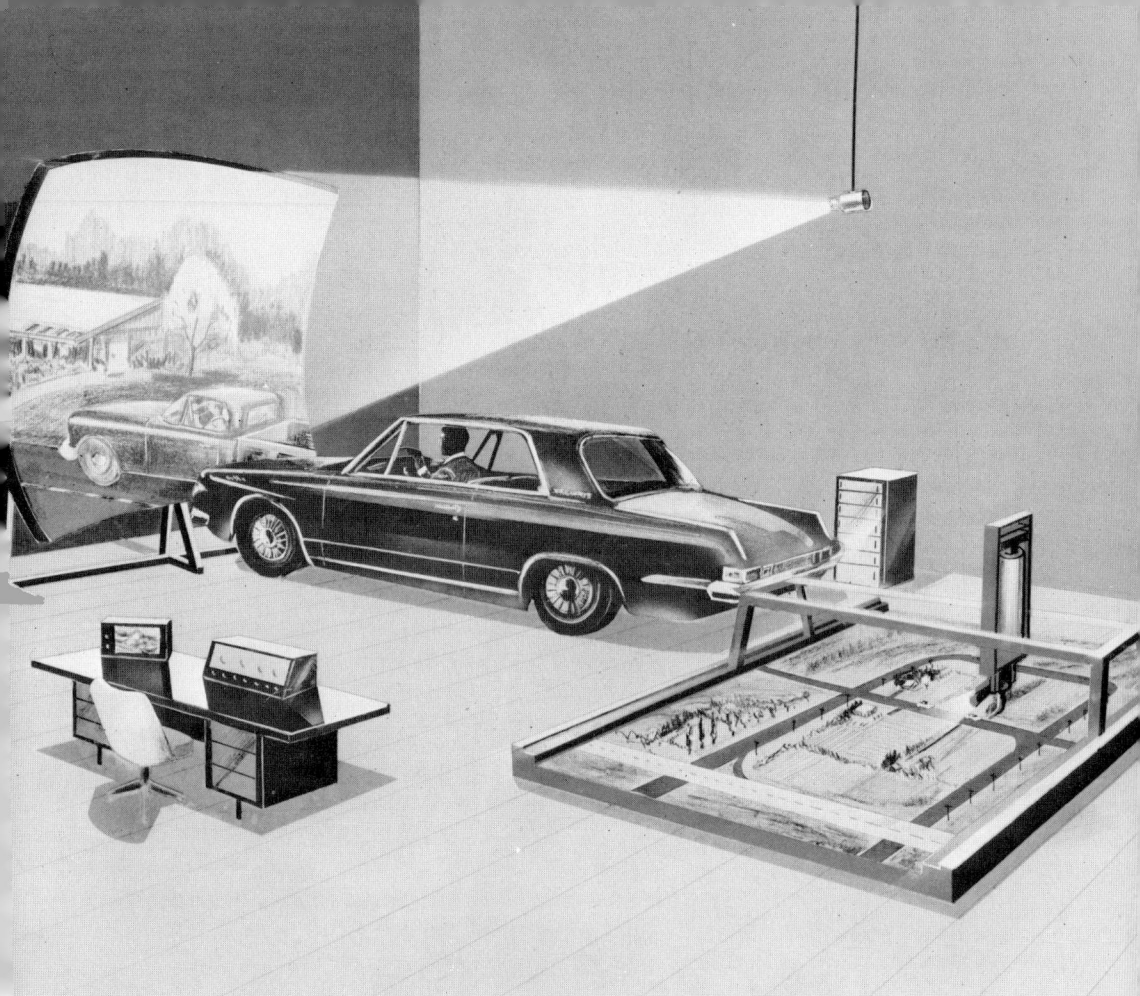

# Research 22

RESEARCH keeps driver education new and vital. Every educator should understand research procedures. Students and parents will have more respect for the teacher who is well informed on recent developments in the field. Professional advancement is more likely to come to the person who keeps abreast of the times. New information will enrich the course. Teachers with a knowledge of research methods are in a good position to evaluate the results of research and to identify conclusions which are not justified by the research reported. Knowledge is not gained automatically like a sponge soaks up water. It takes work and study to absorb and digest information. A teacher should have an open mind, willing and anxious to absorb every bit of information that will improve the driver education course.

Many people in the profession find themselves so occupied with teaching, lesson preparation, grading, courses, lunch duty, various activities, and duties in general, that they feel they have no time to learn about new developments. It is easier to repeat the lessons from the textbook they may have been using for several years. Many feel, also, that they don't have time to conduct research, therefore, it is a waste of time to learn more about it. Every educator should understand research methods. Research in the field of driver education has been done for two major reasons: first, to determine if, in general, driver education is worthwhile, and second, to determine what should be taught and how it can be taught most effectively.

## THE RESEARCH STUDY

In theory, a perfect research study would involve a comparison of the driving records of two identical groups of students, with the exception that one group had completed a driver education course. Obviously this is impossible; so the investigator does the best he can in securing comparable groups. This does not mean that his results are worthless, but in evaluating the results the uncontrolled factors must be kept in mind. The critic too frequently points to weaknesses in a given study and uses that as a basis for ignoring the conclusions. If driver education waits for the perfect study, little progress will be made. The best data available must be used, and considering all factors, a reasonable conclusion should be drawn which can be used as a basis for future action.

In analyzing research studies one must carefully evaluate, perhaps subjectively, uncontrolled factors which may have influenced the results. The more the factors are controlled, the more valid will be the conclusion of any particular study. In comparing the records of a trained group of drivers with an untrained group, we need to know if the two groups are comparable with respect to age, education, sex, driving experience, attitude, amount of driving, nature of driving, etc.

In some of the earlier studies the records of trained drivers were compared with the records of untrained drivers, but no consideration was given to the percentage of girls in each group. It soon became apparent that girls had much better accident records than boys. Consequently, a group of trained students consisting largely of girls would probably have a better record than a group of untrained students consisting largely of boys, even if driver education had no effect. Thus it is evident that without comparable groups it is easy to arrive at false conclusions. Fortunately, this factor has been taken into consideration in most recent studies by separating the boys from the girls or by using balanced groups.

Interpretation of data is highly important. Assuming that the investigator has assembled and reported accurately all the data he has gathered, the teacher can then review it and draw his own conclusions, which may or may not agree with those of the investigator.

In an attempt to evaluate the high school driver education program, one investigator selected two towns within one state, one of which had a program and the other did not. The accident and violations records of the young drivers who had been graduated from the high school in one town were compared with those from the other.

The investigator failed to recognize two very significant factors. In the matter of violations, no mention was made of the strictness of enforcement in the two towns, or the completeness of accident reporting. The other very important factor was that the actual driving conditions in the two towns were overlooked. Many traffic safety people are aware of the inequity of granting awards to some municipalities for no traffic deaths during a year, while adjacent towns (served by the same newspapers which have openly lauded the traffic agencies of the award winner) have had traffic fatalities in spite of excellent accident-prevention programs. The difference between the two may be simply geographical. Heavily traveled state and county highways may cross one municipality, whereas the other may have practically nothing but quiet residential streets. Sometimes one municipality has, within its borders, a large shopping center located on a main state highway having heavy, fast-moving traffic, while its neighbor is residential, with the mass shopping being done in the former community.

Confronted by publicized awards for "superiority" in handling traffic and reducing accidents given to adjoining residential-type towns, officials sometimes despairingly say, "They come over here to have their accidents." Comparing the accident experience of the driving populations of two towns without studying all the driving *conditions* in each town may easily lead to wrong conclusions.

## The "Involvement" Formula

One point should be recognized in planning studies and in reviewing accident data which are cited in research reports. Use of the simple "involvement" formula tends to contaminate the data. For instance, suppose that three expert drivers, all in excellent physical condition, happen to be legally stopped, waiting in line for a traffic signal to change. A fourth vehicle approaches, driven by a drunken driver. The latter fails to stop and strikes the rear of the third car in line, forcing it forward and "telescoping" the three stopped cars. On the simple "involvement" basis, we find that three sober, expert drivers are involved in an accident, and only one drunken driver. Would you say that those who drive while drunk are involved in accidents only one-third as much as sober, expert drivers? Statistically, in this case, this is so.

"Too infrequent to be significant?" Not at all. Isn't it possible that the number of drivers who are *responsible* for causing accidents *may* be about *half* of all accident-involved drivers? (Of course, sometimes more than one driver is to blame.) What about the rest? Are they all, or necessarily even nearly all, equally culpable? Why should the latter be thus included in an accident-involved group when such identification is for the purpose of associating accident experience with personal characteristics or educational backgrounds of drivers? What has innocent involvement to do with a driver's background, or his personal qualities?

Some say, "It is difficult to fix responsibility in accidents." Sometimes it is. Sometimes it isn't. In the case cited it isn't. In many cases it isn't. Why, then, include those cases in the type of study cited? If responsibility can't be determined, or if there is doubt, *include* all the drivers involved. However, by excluding those who are known not to have been culpably involved, the data are less contaminated and the conclusions of the study can be made to conform more closely to the truth.

Individual accident analysis and establishment of responsibility is strongly indicated in research designed to use accident experience as a criterion for evaluating the driving qualities of a group, or of one group to be compared with another. All significant factors must be considered when interpreting research data. The teacher should acquire this ability by a continuing study of driving and traffic safety education research. With a good professional background, this ability is merely an exercise in logical thinking—in common sense.

## REPORTING OF RESEARCH

Many research studies are reported in the popular press, newspapers, and magazines. Every professional person who reads these accounts should reserve decision until he can obtain an accurate account of the study itself, or a thoroughly reliable abstract. Too often a newspaper account of a research study emphasizes the findings of popular interest and fails to present clearly the more important basic findings of the study.

One good example of this is the publicity given to a report recently issued by the U.S. Bureau of Public Roads. The summary in this report[1] reads, in part, as follows:

> The accident-involvement, injury, and property-damage rates were highest at very low speeds, lowest at about the average speed of all traffic, and increased at the very high speeds, particularly at night. Thus, the greater the variation in speed of any vehicle from the average speed of all traffic, the greater its chance of being involved in an accident.
>
> The severity of accidents increased as speed increased, especially at speeds exceeding 60 miles per hour.
>
> The fatality rate was highest at very high speeds and lowest at about the average speed.
>
> Pairs of passenger car drivers involved in two-car, rear-end collisions were much more likely to be traveling at speed differences greatly in excess of those observed for pairs of cars in normal traffic. For example, fully one-third of accident-involved pairs of drivers were traveling at speed differences of 30 miles per hour or more, compared to only 1 per cent of pairs of cars in normal traffic.

To the professional traffic safety man and to a well-informed reader, this would have one clear meaning. *Driving at about the same speed as the bulk of the traffic is safer than driving faster or slower.*

This confirms the conclusions developed under the heading of "Speed Differential" in Chapter 23 of *Sportsmanlike Driving*, 5th edition. The facts were learned, as is so much about the driving task, by careful analysis of available data. To have the confirming evidence of objective research strengthens the position of driver education principles and procedures.

---

[1] *Accidents on Main Rural Highways Related to Speed, Driver and Vehicle*, U.S. Department of Commerce, Bureau of Public Roads, 1964.

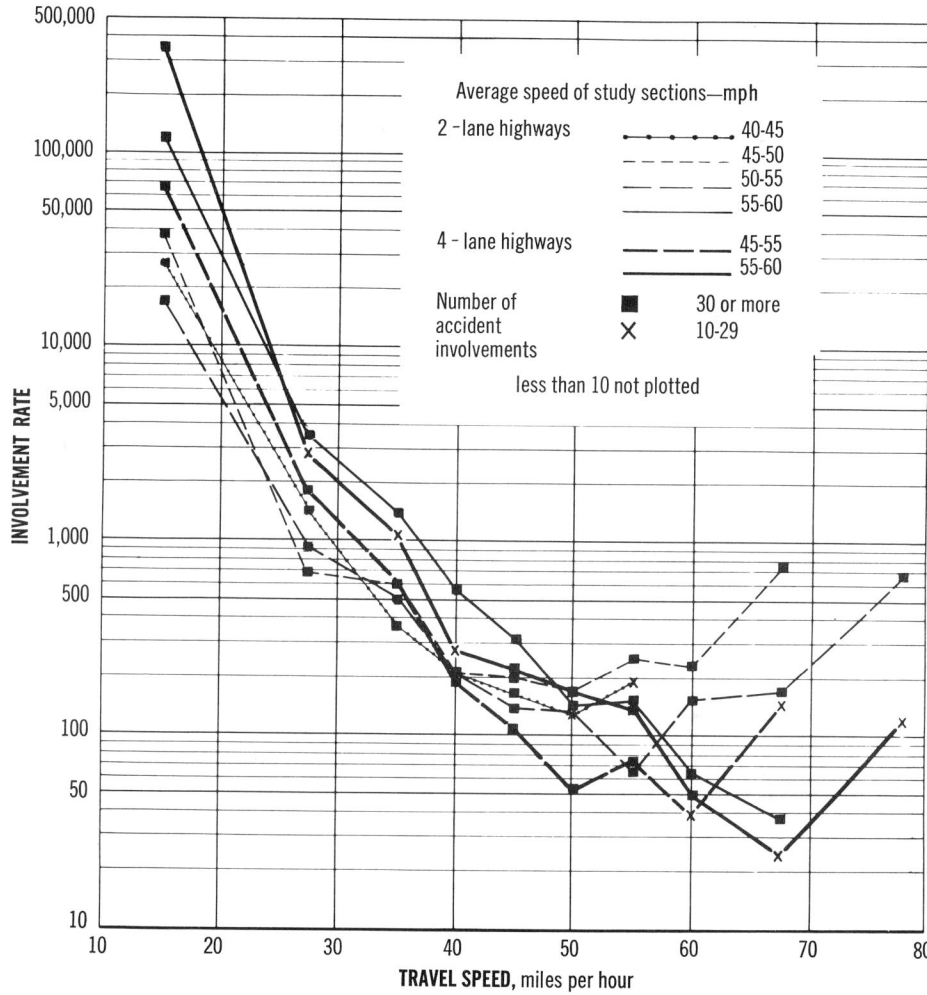

FIGURE 22-1 Involvement rate by travel speed and average speed. (Adapted from *Accidents on Main Rural Highways,* Bureau of Public Roads report, U.S. Department of Commerce, Washington, D.C., 1964.)

## Varying Interpretations

Following the public release on this same study, the popular news media publicized it. Unfortunately, some of the stories were written more for public interest than for accuracy. Featured were headings and claims that fast driving is safe and that moderate or slow driving is dangerous. Eighty miles per hour was said to be safer than forty miles per hour. The most significant item, the "speed differential," was either missed completely in some of the accounts or, in others, lost in generalizations about fast driving being safest.

Such generalizations not only obscure the true significance of a study but, publicized, conceivably may lead to driving at speeds too great for existing *conditions*. Unfamiliar with the road conditions involved in the study, possibly due to incomplete and inaccurate reporting, drivers may adopt the numerical speeds they *believe* were adjudged safest by competent authority. Such speeds, on roads other than the rural highways studied, or under other conditions, could be hazardous.

The situation is somewhat similar to the sensational reporting which announced "discoveries" of miracle medical cures which were never claimed by those who performed the research. For the public good, this calls for intelligent, informed reporting on the part of both professional people in the pertinent fields and the news media.

Young drivers are condemned for their bad accident record. No one will argue about the fact that they do have a bad record, but are we justified in jumping to the conclusion that the cause of the bad record is youth? It could be inexperience. Perhaps the record of the forty-year-old driver with one year of experience is just as bad as the seventeen-year-old driver with one year of experience. Maybe it is inexperience, rather than youth, that is the cause of the bad record. The facts are just not known. The answer would come only if drivers of all ages, but with the same amount of experience, were studied.

Driver education teachers are frequently confronted with comments and questions on the subjects of new "discoveries" in driving, traffic safety, and the automobile. This occurs in and out of class in the case of students, and just about anywhere with fellow staff members and other adults. As a specialist in traffic safety, the driver educator should be ready with the "answers." Developments in the field should be covered in class, and discussion often originates in student reading and reporting. Students should be encouraged to report new information they read in magazines and newspapers. It is very important that the teacher be in a position to interpret and evaluate all data pertaining to his area of specialization. This requires the ability to evaluate a study and form logical conclusions which are firmly based on the data presented. This is an ability which improves with practice.

## *RESEARCH TRENDS IN DRIVER EDUCATION*

Over the years much effort in research in this field has been devoted to studying the effect of a driver education course on the subsequent driving performance of the student. This may be due, at least in part, to adverse criticism which appears to demand documentation of worth in this subject alone, of all courses offered. Other areas of the secondary school curriculum established long ago do not face the concerted attacks which are directed at this new, different, and, therefore, more vulnerable target. As the true worth of this new phase of education for the 1960s and 1970s gains recognition, the need for the evaluation-type study diminishes and the direction of research effort should change.

Many studies have been made comparing the driving records of students who have completed approved driver education courses with others who have not. Usually, the course included at least thirty hours of classroom instruction and at least six hours of road instruction. Practically all studies have pointed to superior driving records, i.e., significantly less accident involvement and fewer violations, on the part of those who have completed a high school driver education course.

The existence today of such extensive data supporting driver education indicates need for research to turn elsewhere. Actually, the data support the subjective but quite obvious conclusion that a properly trained driver is a more efficient and safer driver than one who is not trained, just as students who have completed a mathematics course will score higher in a pertinent examination than similar students who have not taken such a course.

Needed now is concentration on *what* should be taught and *how* it should be taught. For this, further research is needed in analysis of "the driving task," with special emphasis on the human factors. This need is vital because it affects not only driver education but all areas of traffic safety. Once research has defined *what* should be taught, then additional research is needed to determine *how* it can be taught most efficiently; this in turn will involve college courses where high school teachers are being taught to do an efficient job. Some research is being done in this area, but much more is needed.

## *PROFESSIONAL LITERATURE*

The driver education teacher should be conversant with the professional literature in his field. This includes reports of studies which pertain to traffic safety in general and driver education in particular. It includes evaluation studies, status studies, behavioral research, current data on vision and hearing—especially as specifically applied to the driving task—advances in development of principles and procedures in driver education, and all traffic safety material published by recognized agencies in the field. The driver education teacher may be called upon to serve as coordinator or director of safety education—perhaps for a school system. It is greatly to his advantage to keep fully informed *in all areas of safety education.* Even if his current position would not so indicate, knowledge of the broader field which *includes* driver education is very worthwhile.

At the end of this chapter a selected reference list will serve as a guide to the reader of professional literature. The teacher should see that these publications are available in the classroom or the school library. In view of the fact that the driver education course occasionally comes under fire, the teacher should have at hand the data necessary to defend the program. Publications such as *Driver Education Reduces Accidents and Violations*[2] and *Summary of Results of Studies Evaluating Driver Education*[3] are especially important. These summaries constitute an ever-valuable *case for driver education.* In this field, under present conditions, the teacher not only should know the worth of his work but should be in a position to defend and promote it among both professional and lay groups and individuals.

---

[2] *Driver Education Reduces Accidents and Violations,* American Automobile Association, Washington, D.C., 1964.

[3] *Summary of Results of Studies Evaluating Driver Education,* National Commission on Safety Education, National Education Association, Washington, D.C., 1964.

There is a good deal of research data in areas related to traffic safety, to (general) principles of education, to mental, physical, and emotional characteristics, to engineering, to physics, and to other fields—*in addition to that of the specific driver education evaluation research*—which demonstrates the worth of the subject. These data, properly interpreted, also point the way for improvement of the subject field. It is strongly recommended that the teacher and the future teacher of driver education carefully review the "Research"[4] section of the Action Program of the President's Committee for Traffic Safety. A ready knowledge of the professional literature not only benefits its possessor in the obvious ways, but also enables him properly to refute the claims of opponents of driver education who sometimes cite research studies to support erroneous and misleading criticisms of the program.

## *Be Ready*

One example is a commonly repeated reference to the Skokie, Illinois, study conducted by the Allstate Insurance Companies, reported in January, 1960. This report is described as "a study of the effects of car use and ownership upon the scholastic standings of junior and senior students at Niles Township High School, Skokie, Illinois." In the conclusions of the study, *car ownership* is associated with lower academic standing. Some opponents of driver education distort this to mean that driver education results in lower scholastic grades and cite the study as evidence that driver education is *undesirable*. The study does not indicate this in any manner. In reference to driver education, the report[5] reads as follows:

> Where the study touched on driver education, the results would seem to upset the assumption that those likely to be attracted to driver training would be the brighter students with mature attitudes toward safety. The Niles Township survey revealed that driver education classes were made up, to a large extent, of those students in the bottom quarter of scholastic standings.
>
> ### *Trained drivers have better records*
> These lower scholastic standings, however, were not reflected in the behind-the-wheel performance of driver education students. As a group, they had less than half the accidents and violations of untrained students.
>
> Of the 72 percent of the student body which had learned to drive, 19 percent were taught in the high school driver training classes. The others were instructed by parents, relatives or friends. The high school trained drivers had only 27 accidents per hundred students as compared to 41 accidents per hundred students who learned to drive in other ways.
>
> Only 8 out of 100 high school trained drivers collected traffic violation tickets of the students who took part in the survey, while 25 out of 100 parent-trained students received tickets.
>
> ### *Driver education effective*
> The better driving records of the high school trained students offer a tribute to the effectiveness of the high school driver education classes. Although

---

[4] "Research," a section of The Action Program for Highway Safety, President's Committee for Traffic Safety, Washington, D.C.

[5] *The High School Student and the Automobile,* Allstate Insurance Companies, Skokie, Ill., 1960.

driving classes are largely made up of students *whose grades were in the lower quarter of their classes,* these students nevertheless have a fine record on the streets and highways, where responsibility is essential. Thus, we must conclude that *high school driver education courses not only teach the techniques of safe driving, but develop a sense of responsibility in those students most in need of it.*

Teachers have occasionally been embarrassed at public meetings when confronted with questions, comments, and even deliberate misstatements about driver education studies of which they, themselves, had no knowledge. The misstatement may impress the audience, while the teacher later learns the true facts—alone. Intelligent documentation of the subject field is one more ability which stems from a knowledge of the professional literature.

The teacher should beware of docile acceptance of a process, a method, a technique, or a device on the basis of its being cheaper, plus the fact that it has *not* been successfully established by studies to be inferior. True, it may not be, but *failure* of studies to verify this does not positively establish equality as a fact. Currently, some deep-thinking educators are facetiously—yet meaningfully—referring to "the phenomenon of no significant differences." The implication is that very real differences may exist (in either direction) but that the study methods, and especially the evaluative criteria, may be too weak to detect and properly identify them. In many cases they *are* that weak.

Another caution—the term "significant" in a statistical sense should not be confused with its alter ego which might infer that the subject is practical for application to individuals in the real physical world. A test may reasonably measure a driving-related characteristic among a large population, yet it could be a grave injustice to an individual to disqualify him from driving on the basis of his score on that same test.

The need for research in driver education is great today and will be so throughout the foreseeable future. Teachers now entering the field will soon be carrying on this mission. The sooner each individual prepares himself for the task, the greater can his contribution be, and the greater his satisfaction and his own professional advancement in the field.

## SELECTED BIBLIOGRAPHY

*A Critical Analysis of Driver Education Research,* National Commission on Safety Education, National Education Association, Washington, D.C., 1957, 60 pp.

*A Teenage Pattern,* Allstate Insurance Companies, Marketing and Research Division, Skokie, Ill., 1960.

*Driver Education Reduces Accidents and Violations,* American Automobile Association, Washington, D.C., 1964, 16 pp.

*The High School Student and the Automobile,* Allstate Insurance Companies, Safety Department, Skokie, Ill., 1960, 21 pp.

McFarland, Ross A.: *Human Variables in Motor Vehicle Accidents,* Harvard School of Public Health, Boston, Mass., 1955, 203 pp. Bibliography.

"Research," *The Action Program for Highway Safety,* President's Committee for Traffic Safety, Washington, D.C.

*Research Needs in Traffic Safety Education,* National Commission on Safety Education National Education Association, Washington, D.C., 1956, 20 pp.

*Research Review,* National Safety Council, Chicago, Ill. Quarterly.

Stratemeyer, Clara G.: *Accident Research for Better Safety Teaching,* National Commission on Safety Education, National Education Association, Washington, D.C. 1964.

*Summary of Results of Studies Evaluating Driver Education,* National Commission on Safety Education, National Education Association, Washington, D.C., 1961.

*Tests and Evaluation Methods Used in Driver and Safety Education,* National Commission on Safety Education, National Education Association, 1959, 48 pp.

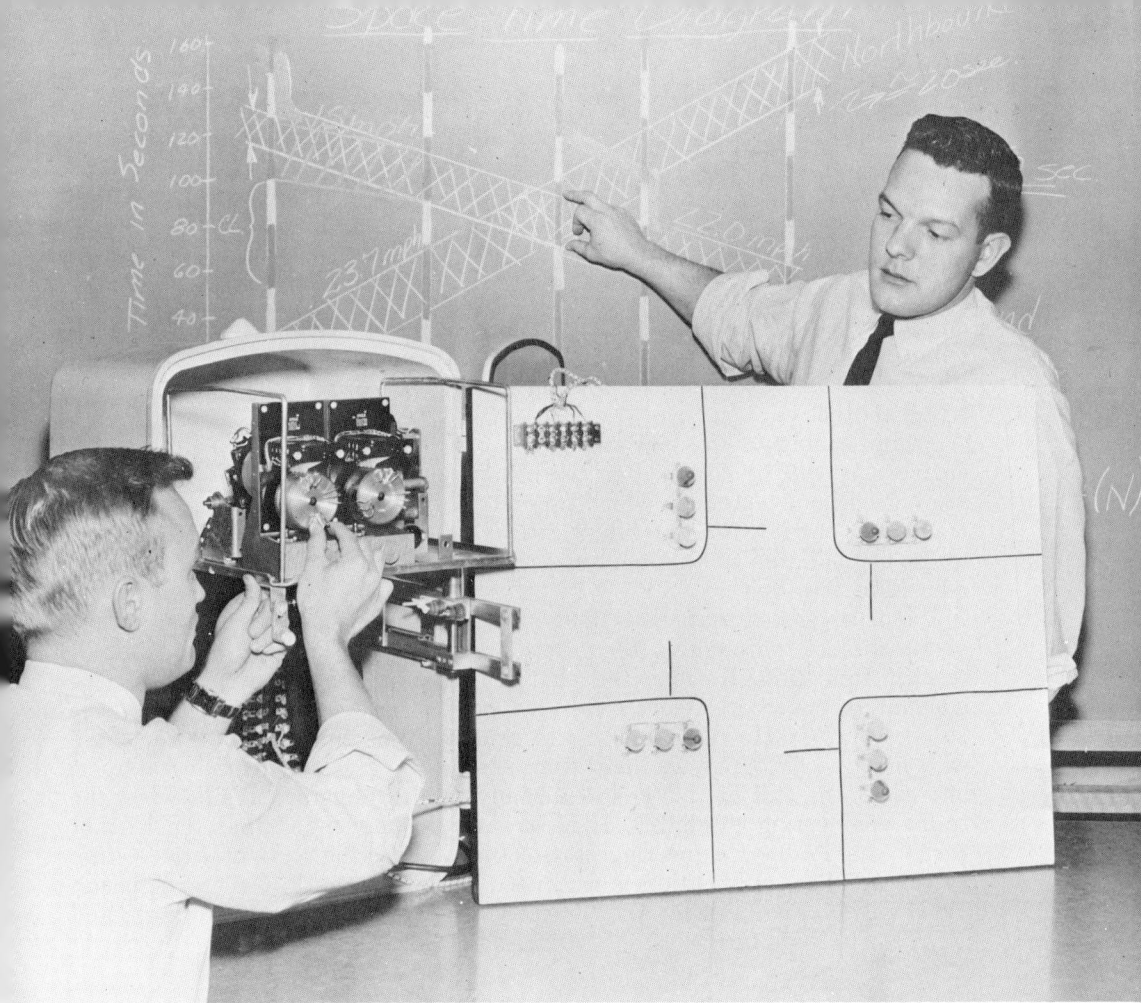

# Traffic Engineering                                   23

THE DEPTH of this competency to be mastered by the driver education teacher is not defined by a clear-cut policy of any identifiable segment of the profession. Opinion varies of the amount to be included from just enough to instruct students in the meanings of traffic control signs, signals, and pavement markings, and perhaps a general description of the role of traffic engineering in the "three E's," to a course (seemingly) almost suitable to an engineering degree.

Probably the answer is another of those "in-betweens"—enough of the engineering background to give the teacher confidence in his ability to cover the subject adequately, yet with not too much time invested so as still to permit acquisition of an all-round background in the numerous competencies needed to teach driver and traffic safety education.

The diversity of backgrounds of our professional personnel in this subject field is one of its strong points. It should be expected that with this diversity there must be conflicting opinion on the direction of emphasis in the preparation of those who enter the profession. Perhaps the best policy lies in the recognition of the fact that this new, very comprehensive discipline which we call driver and traffic safety education welcomes all contributing disciplines, but in its own internal teacher preparation procedures it remains balanced—not to develop deficiencies in any area nor to overstress another.

Conforming to this philosophy, our treatment of the subject of traffic engineering will be designed on the pattern of a *teacher competency*. There are high school textbooks which present a quite comprehensive coverage of traffic engineering for the future *citizen-driver*. There is no need for him to go beyond this in this one phase of the many-faceted course of driver education as a *driver*.

It is suggested that the teacher study the high school textbook coverage of the subject thoroughly. Then there are two paths ahead of him, as in all teacher education. He may feel that for his purposes the subject has been adequately covered. He may feel the need of a deeper knowledge of the subject matter. He can go as far in this study as time permits. For those who may wish to pursue their study in depth, a selected bibliography is offered at the end of this chapter. Many publications are available on the traffic engineering discipline. It is strongly recommended that the teacher review the Traffic Engineering part of the Engineering section of the *Action Program*.[1] This publication is organized in four parts: I, General Aspects; II, Highway Engineering; III, Traffic Operations (traffic engineering); and IV, Vehicle Engineering.

## Ten Points to Remember

A capsule summary of traffic engineering can well be taken from an address given before the First Inter-American Traffic Seminar in September, 1961, by D. Grant Mickle, Executive Director, Highway Research Board. The driver education teacher should fully understand these basic facts about the profession:

1. It is a relatively new science, a specialized branch of civil engineering.
2. Its mission is to apply engineering principles and methods to achieve safe, orderly, and expeditious movement of people and goods on the highways.
3. It operates on the self-evident principle that official responsibility for our roads and streets does not end with the building and physical maintenance of the road structure—that efficient operation of those facilities to the best advantage of the public is a responsibility of government.

---

[1] *Engineering Section, Action Program for Highway Safety*, The President's Committee for Traffic Safety, Washington, D.C.

4. It seeks to relate the geometric features of road and street design to the character, amount, and speed of the traffic the facilities must accommodate.
5. It tries to understand the desires and abilities of drivers, the characteristics of their vehicles—and the limitations of both.
6. It aims not only to obtain the best possible service from existing roads and streets, but to ensure maximum operating efficiency from new facilities.
7. With the advent of modernization of major roadways into controlled-access highways, the planning and design of the new features will depend heavily on the traffic data provided by the traffic engineer.
8. Traffic engineering is essential if the potential benefits of our system of modern freeways are to be realized. Experience has demonstrated that professional level planning of operations is necessary.

FIGURE 23-1 Attaining maximum operating efficiency requires analyses by professionally trained specialists.

306  ELEMENTS OF THE PROFESSIONAL KNOWLEDGE COMPETENCY

9. Traffic engineering helps to coordinate transportation planning and community development.
10. It provides leadership in effectively correlating street transportation, public transit, and parking.

It would be a good practice here, when teaching the 10 points, to call attention to their importance by analyzing the economic implications of the single, last word—parking.

Many businessmen believe that some areas, and even some major cities, are having their business potential strongly affected, even strangled in some cases, on the basis of that one factor alone, *parking*. Mass department-store shopping, once centered in the shopping districts of cities, has been at least partly diverted to outlying shopping centers, primarily because of the factor of available parking space. City department stores have been practically forced to abandon the old central city merchandising concept and open branch stores in outlying shopping centers which are convenient for automobile transportation.

FIGURE 23-2  Parking—a problem that haunts cities.

## DEVELOPMENT OF METHOD

Let us assume that by this time the new teacher is at least moderately oriented in the subject of general teaching methods. Let us assume also that he is sufficiently versed in college-type study to be able to learn the "ten points" and the data contained in the Traffic Operations part of the Engineering section of the *Action Program*—and that he *has* learned both. Let us assume also that he has read and studied the quite comprehensive coverage of the subject to be found in a good high school textbook and has supplemented that knowledge with reference reading from the Selected Bibliography at the end of this chapter.

Let us make one more assumption about this professionally educated person we call a "teacher"—that he has a good command of the conventional classroom methods and materials of his profession. He is now ready to learn the special methods which have been found effective in teaching the subject of traffic engineering. Some of these methods have several advantages, such as:

1. They aid in motivation by being *different* from conventional classroom procedures.
2. The students work *outside* the physical environment of the place which they associate with their experience as a captive audience.
3. The students see traffic engineering in action—and its results.
4. For at least the first few times, the *teacher* will probably have a profitable learning experience.

## *Accent on the Human Story*

It may be said to be a basic principle of teaching that at the two extremes of student life—the kindergarten and the primary grades at one end and the university graduate school at the other—*method* and *content* reverse their roles. "Course" content is far easier for the teacher to master in the lower elementary grades, but the "how" or method of teaching may well be at its peak of importance in the first grade. Conversely, the graduate student is supposed to be capable of assuming much of the responsibility for his learning, but the teacher on that level should be a highly competent master of the content of the discipline he professes.

The reversing role of method and content is not an even progression. One point in the student's life where the change is abrupt is the step from high school to college. *It is important for the teacher to realize that the teaching-and-learning procedure with which he has become familiar in college may be quite foreign to the experience of his high school students.* Although the content of some of the advanced courses in the modern secondary school are of college caliber, it would be impractical to attempt to repeat the teacher-preparation driver education course in the high school.

The subject of *traffic engineering* is not likely to be looked forward to eagerly by the high school student whose primary interest is in *driving*. The girls in the class will probably view it as many do the study of the mechanical aspects of car maintenance—not for them! This is a challenge to the ingenuity of the teacher. Like the professional traffic safety speaker, he must *make them like it*. It can be done.

The best introduction to the subject of traffic engineering for the high school student is one which will give it a human-interest characteristic. The unfamiliar term *traffic engineering* is not one which is likely to stir enthusiasm in most students. Slide rules, mathematics, and the building of bridges and dams will come to some minds. Probably a few will even envision a traffic engineer as one who runs a train. Many of the girls in the class will anticipate boredom while the class studies this subject (as they do when the subject of the automobile engine is announced). This introductory period is an important one in teaching any subject.

*Making a Start*

One might start by simply defining traffic engineering as that phase of engineering which deals with:

1. Planning and geometric design of streets, highways, and abutting lands
2. Traffic operations thereon, as their use is related to the safe, convenient, and economical transportation of persons and goods

Basically, it is a science of traffic *operations*.

When did it begin? Well, the first traffic engineers recognized as professionally trained specialists came on the scene in this country about 1922. A point of interest might be made of one of the Caesars forbidding vehicles in the business districts of Rome and decreeing one-way streets and parking regulations for chariots—which might qualify him or some of his "boys" as traffic engineers.

Highway engineering was highly developed in ancient times, and some of the old Roman military highways can still be seen today. It is quite likely that traffic problems plagued some of the cities of the ancients as they do us today. The demand for a professional specialization in the *operation* of highways is an old one. A little imaginative discussion of the traffic conditions of ancient Greece and Rome, Shakespeare's England, our "colonies," the "road" West and "horse-and-buggy days" can enliven student's imaginations—and their interest.

With the advent of the motor vehicle, 85 million of them and 180 million people now dependent on them not only for personal transportation, but for the essentials of life, motor vehicle traffic has become a very significant support of our way of life—and has brought some problems to solve.

At this stage of the introduction to what—to the student—had threatened to be a mechanical, not particularly human subject, excessive definition, technical aspects of the field, and general austerity of approach should be avoided. If the class hasn't for some time been in touch with the meaning of the traffic accident to its *victims*, it might be well to inject that. The creation of a dragon, in this case reference to a real one, the *Accident*, often paves the way for ready acceptance of a dragon-slayer, the *Traffic Engineer*, (a technique not unknown to many in the political arena).

There are many true cases of high accident locations where good traffic engineering has slain the "dragon." Several are cited in the Traffic Operations part of the Engineering section of the *Action Program*. It is very effective to select such a location familiar to the teacher, and if possible one the students also know, where this has happened. Inquiry of the police department or traffic engineer may bring forth such examples, the stories of which can be interesting. Then—where to go next?

Obviously we're leading to student involvement in a traffic engineering project or two. This procedure has resulted in some very enthusiastic student participation in many cases. There actually have been student projects

FIGURE 23-3  Traffic engineering safeguards *people*.

which brought about some dramatic improvements in safety or traffic movement.

## PLANNING THE STUDENT INVOLVEMENT PROCESS

An important consideration comes to mind. The teacher should make certain that no student project will bring discredit to any agency of local government. The driver education program in a high school needs all the friends it can get. Friends are not necessarily made by implications that official community agencies are inefficient, or that a high school project has identified glaring deficiencies not recognized by the local authorities. This procedure has been carried out on a few occasions. To encourage the community to hire a traffic engineer by publicly demonstrating in a high school project that the police or other official traffic direction was bad is highly undesirable, even though it might achieve some objectives.

Let the students conduct their project at a place and in a manner that may even point a need, but *not* a place where incumbent responsible officials will stand condemned. The teacher can report flagrant mishandling of traffic in much better ways than to get the student body excited about it. If conditions are found to be bad, the students are not going to keep it a secret!

The very police official who might be unfamiliar with traffic engineering principles would be a very welcome sight approaching in a patrol car when a reckless driver was endangering the students in the driver education car.

Another point to be carefully considered is the element of danger to the students. The alert teacher must anticipate, see, and forestall any danger when directing students in a project. However, the teacher is still responsible, morally and often legally, for the safety of students who are carrying out an assigned or suggested project "on their own." He should be able to foresee, at least reasonably well, what hazards exist. He should know, for instance, that a group of boys will occasionally engage in horseplay. He should not, then, approve a project where such behavior is likely to be more than normally hazardous.

A young person who has grown up playing in the streets of a big city *might* have a well-developed self-protective mechanism which would allow him to concentrate on a study of traffic and yet be aware of the approach of any threat to his physical safety. Such a mechanism is not a congenital gift, at least not in a way that would break the individual's concentration on the task at hand and immediately and unfailingly direct his attention to the threat to his safety. When assigning or suggesting a project to be conducted in the presence of (not *in*, of course) motor vehicle traffic, one point is good to remember. Each of those students is *only a few years* past being the "small child" playing at the curb, who drivers are afraid *may* unconsciously dart out into the traveled roadway after a ball. The "ball" in this case could be a tape measure to determine the width of a traffic lane. It could be any learning task to be performed on or near the traveled portions of roadways. Students sometimes have a tendency to attempt projects at the most obviously hazardous traffic locations.

In short, the teacher should first utilize his own professional background in safety education and visit any site being considered for a student project and assess it for possible hazards. Also, before assigning or suggesting any project, the appropriate civil authorities should be consulted and a complete understanding achieved. All project assignments should be scheduled for daylight hours for two reasons. Hazards are greater after dark, and some parents strongly prefer that their children remain at home evenings. Where *courses of study* are used in a school system, any out-of-school project should be described in the appropriate one and approved by the school and district administration and the board of education where such approval of courses of study is customary.

## Nature of Projects

The primary purpose of the project method is to *teach*. It is not an end in itself, although there are cases in which it has been permitted to become so. First, *the conventional class-time work is the primary body of the course.* It should also be the pacemaker. Assignments of all kinds, including the traffic engineering project, are only instruments for teaching the current component of the course. The keyword is "current," because the outside activity is only an extension of the classroom work, to be carefully developed and later reported in class at the time the appropriate course material is being covered. The out-of-school project should *never* be used as busy work or merely to add prestige to the course.

Let us suppose that a popular high school textbook is being used in this part of the high school driver education course. One well-known book covers twenty-three pages of material on the subject of traffic engineering, a far more comprehensive, better planned and directed understanding of that subject than that possessed by even the well-informed adult driver. There is no need here to seek "new" knowledge to "enrich" the high school course, unless there is infinitely more than the "30-and-6" (hour) time allotment available to teach the great amount of material in the *total* driver education course.

Rather, when subjects such as the *accident spot map* and the *collision diagram* are reached, the enrichment of the course can be this device of direct, personal *involvement* of the student in the real activity. This is not to extend the subject matter indefinitely, but to teach what is reasonable—*well.*

*When* shall the project be planned? There is no inflexible rule. If available *course time* permits, the out-of-school project is best done during that time *with the teacher present.* There are a number of good reasons for this:

1. The teacher is responsible for the orderliness of the group, as well as for the safety of the individual students.
2. He can readily see the conduct of the project and its results.
3. He knows what has been covered.
4. He is the person specially educated to *teach*. He may have to add his teaching ability to the well-meant explanations of those who talk to the students.
5. If conditions permit, he can take his class out for some projects during that regular class time and avoid clashes with assignments from the "5-point" college-associated courses, and also avoid loss of students to athletic teams and other after-school activities.
6. He can add to his own competency with the experience gained.

The best project, then, is one (1) in which *class* time is used (if it can be afforded), (2) at which the teacher is present, (3) in which no other subject is penalized (or believed by parents to be penalized), (4) in which the project is appropriate to the current course coverage, and (5) that is well done by the host agency.

## *For the Teacher-in-training*

The best way for the teacher-in-training to learn the details of the project method is to experience it himself. This has a double objective. He is not merely learning one method of teaching, but he is learning *his course content lesson* from it in the same way as his high school students will in the future.

Assume that, in covering the subject of traffic engineering, the college student of driver education has been taught the principles of the vehicle count, the accident spot map, the collision diagram, and the speed survey. Here is an opportunity for experience in application of the project method to his own learning procedure. Starting with observance of every principle and procedure desirable in planning and arranging a high school project, the following class projects are examples of what can be done at college level.

FIGURE 23-4  A graduate student takes data on traffic speeds for his research project.

## *Class Project 1: Study of a Hazardous Location*

1. Check with the local police department and obtain accident experience for at least the past year, preferably the last two or three years.
2. Obtain the following information:
    a. Date of accident.
    b. Time of accident.
    c. Type of accident:
        (1) PD (property damage), (2) NF (injury), (3) F (fatal)
    d. Indicate number injured or killed.
    e. Describe type of accident:
        (1) Rear-end, (2) right angle, (3) side-swipe, (4) pedestrian, (5) bicycle, (6) any other
    f. Indicate direction of travel of vehicles.
        (See accompanying sample report form, Figure 23–5.)
3. Draw a collision diagram for each accident.
4. Determine the most prominent type of accidents occurring at the intersection.
5. Visit the location to determine if any visible evidence is present indicating hazards.

TRAFFIC ENGINEERING 313

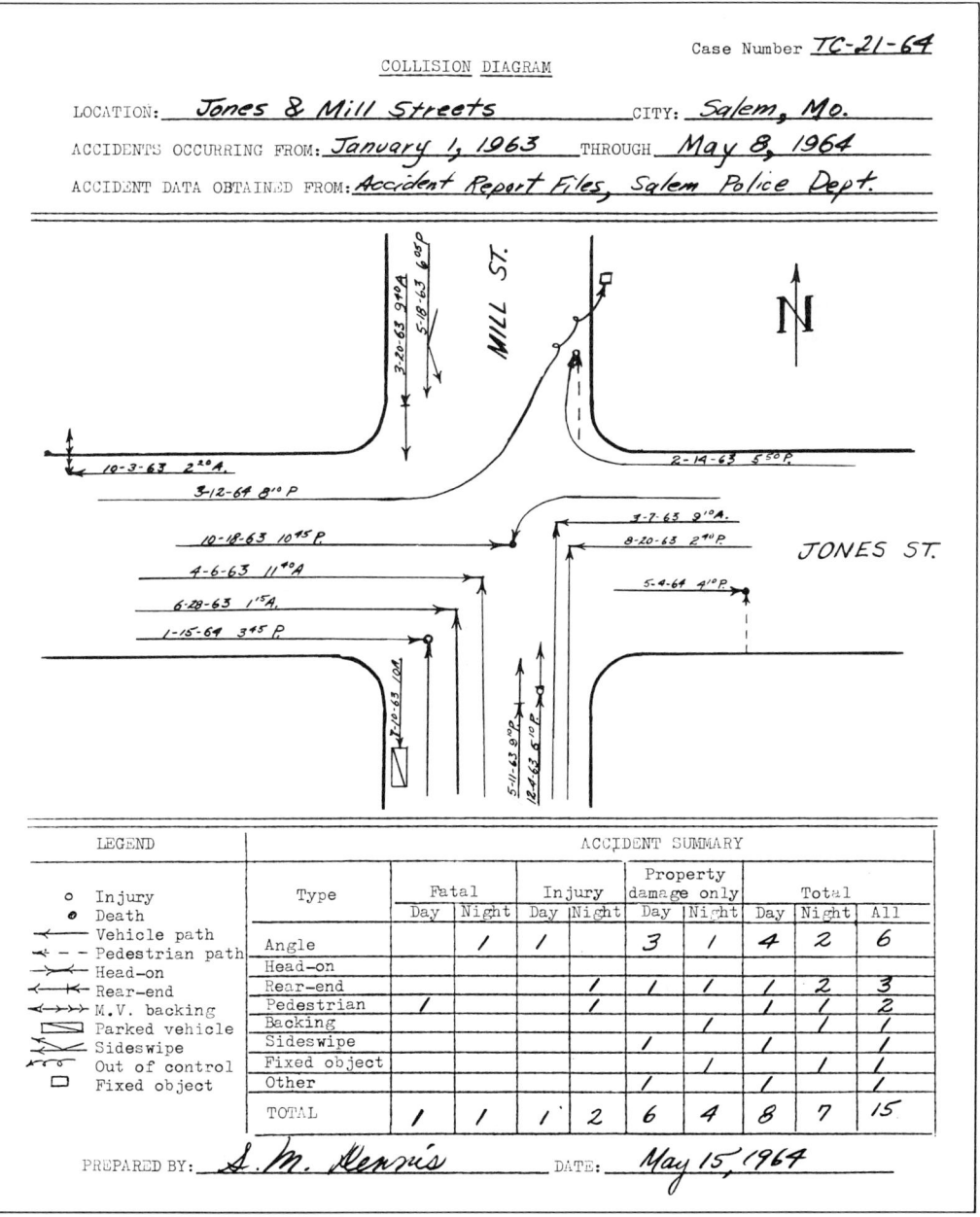

FIGURE 23-5

6. Suggest possible means that should be considered for reducing the most serious hazards.

## Class Project 2: Vehicle Counts

In this study, the object is to determine the number and actions of the vehicles that pass through an intersection. For the purpose of this demonstration, use four students to count vehicular traffic at an intersection. Each student is to tabulate the vehicles approaching the intersection on a particular street. Here is the procedure:

1. Fill in the information on the top of the field sheet (Figure 23–6).
2. Each student is assigned to one approach to the intersection.
3. Each student will tally the following:
   a. Number of vehicles turning left.
   b. Number of vehicles turning right.
   c. Number of vehicles going straight through.
4. Record this information each half hour.
5. Continue study for one hour.
6. Tabulate results on summary sheet (Figure 23–7).

## Class Project 3: A Simple Speed Survey

1. Pick a location where vehicles move freely, such as an open stretch of road.
2. Place one student at one point where the view of the road is good, but where he is not easily visible to drivers.
3. Place a second student exactly 176 feet forward of the first student and also in an inconspicuous spot.
4. The first student signals with his (or her) hand when a vehicle reaches his (or her) location.
5. The second student starts a stop watch when the hand signal is given and stops the watch when the vehicle reaches his (or her) location. *Example:* If the recorded time is 4 seconds, the speed of the vehicle is 30 mph (see Figure 23–8).
6. Determine the speed at or below which 85 per cent of the vehicles traveled. This is known as the "85 percentile speed" and is the primary factor in determining what a speed limit should be.

## THE POST-PROJECT LESSON

This is one of the most important elements of the method. To have students "hand in" their reports after a field trip solely for grading and to neglect the post-project discussion is like keeping the container and throwing away the food! (Unfortunately it has been done.) For the teachers-in-training the discussion is especially important. Not only is a clarifying interchange of comments, reactions, and ideas indicated, but a detailed and comprehensive discussion, guided by the college course director, should cover an *evaluation of the procedure for a hypothetical high school driver educa-*

TRAFFIC ENGINEERING 315

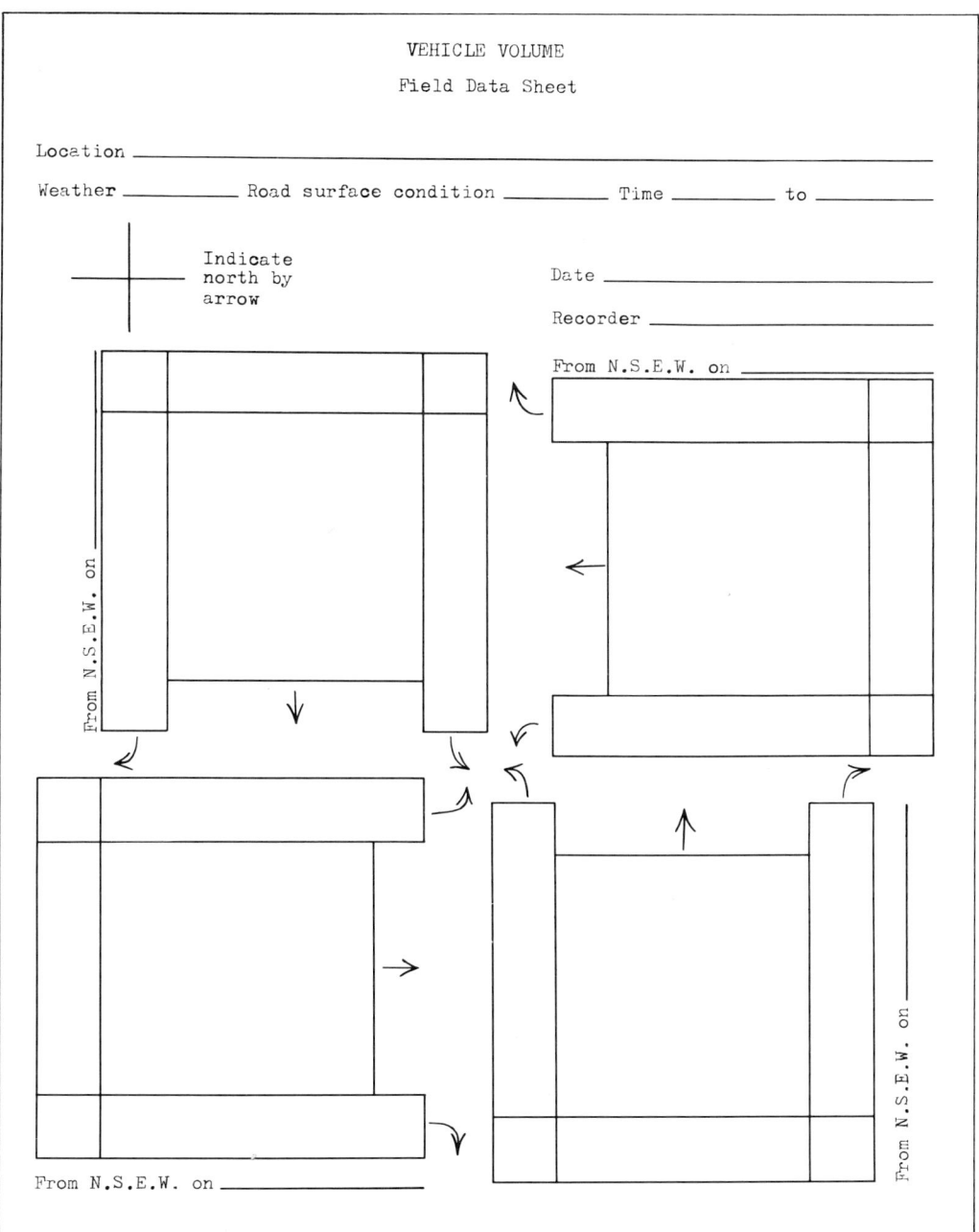

FIGURE 23-6

# TRAFFIC COUNT
## SUMMARY SHEET

Location _____ Date _____

Weather _____ Road Surface Condition _____

| TIME STARTS ........M. | from North on _____ St. | | | from South on _____ St. | | | from West on _____ St. | | | from East on _____ St. | | | HALF HOUR TOTAL |
|---|---|---|---|---|---|---|---|---|---|---|---|---|---|
| | L | S | R | L | S | R | L | S | R | L | S | R | |
| | | | | | | | | | | | | | |

TOTAL

TOTAL

COMPILED BY _____ DATE _____

FIGURE 23-7

# MOTOR VEHICLE SPOT SPEED
## FIELD SHEET

Date_____ Location_____ Direction_____
Time_____ Weather_____ Road Surface Condition_____

| SECONDS | M.P.H. for 88 ft. | M.P.H. for 176 ft. | PASSENGER VEHICLES | No. VEH. | BUSES | No. VEH. | TRUCKS | No. VEH. | TOTAL |
|---|---|---|---|---|---|---|---|---|---|
| 1 | 60.0 | 120.0 | | | | | | | |
| 1-1/5 | 50.0 | 100.0 | | | | | | | |
| 1-2/5 | 42.8 | 85.7 | | | | | | | |
| 1-3/5 | 37.5 | 75.5 | | | | | | | |
| 1-4/5 | 33.3 | 66.6 | | | | | | | |
| 2 | 30.0 | 60.0 | | | | | | | |
| 2-1/5 | 27.2 | 54.5 | | | | | | | |
| 2-2/5 | 25.0 | 50.0 | | | | | | | |
| 2-3/5 | 23.0 | 46.1 | | | | | | | |
| 2-4/5 | 21.4 | 42.8 | | | | | | | |
| 3 | 20.0 | 40.0 | | | | | | | |
| 3-1/5 | 18.7 | 37.5 | | | | | | | |
| 3-2/5 | 17.6 | 35.2 | | | | | | | |
| 3-3/5 | 16.6 | 33.3 | | | | | | | |
| 3-4/5 | 15.7 | 31.5 | | | | | | | |
| 4 | 15.0 | 30.0 | | | | | | | |
| 4-1/5 | 14.2 | 28.9 | | | | | | | |
| 4-2/5 | 13.6 | 27.2 | | | | | | | |
| 4-3/5 | 13.0 | 26.1 | | | | | | | |
| 4-4/5 | 12.5 | 25.0 | | | | | | | |
| 5 | 12.0 | 24.0 | | | | | | | |
| 5-1/5 | 11.5 | 23.0 | | | | | | | |
| 5-2/5 | 11.1 | 22.2 | | | | | | | |
| 5-3/5 | 10.7 | 21.4 | | | | | | | |
| 5-4/5 | 10.3 | 20.6 | | | | | | | |
| 6 | 10.0 | 20.0 | | | | | | | |
| 6-1/5 | 9.6 | 19.3 | | | | | | | |
| 6-2/5 | 9.3 | 18.7 | | | | | | | |
| 6-3/5 | 9.0 | 18.1 | | | | | | | |
| 6-4/5 | 8.7 | 17.6 | | | | | | | |
| 7 | 8.5 | 17.1 | | | | | | | |
| 7-1/5 | 8.3 | 16.6 | | | | | | | |
| 7-2/5 | 8.1 | 16.2 | | | | | | | |
| 7-3/5 | 7.8 | 15.7 | | | | | | | |
| 7-4/5 | 7.6 | 15.3 | | | | | | | |
| 8 | 7.5 | 15.0 | | | | | | | |
| 8-1/2 | 7.0 | 14.1 | | | | | | | |
| 9 | 6.6 | 13.3 | | | | | | | |
| 9-1/2 | 6.3 | 12.6 | | | | | | | |
| 10 | 6.0 | 12.0 | | | | | | | |
| 11 | 5.4 | 10.9 | | | | | | | |
| 12 | 5.0 | 10.0 | | | | | | | |
| 13 | 4.6 | 9.2 | | | | | | | |
| 14 | 4.2 | 8.5 | | | | | | | |
| 15 | 4.0 | 8.0 | | | | | | | |
| | | TOTAL VEHICLES | | | | | | | |
| | 85-PERCENTILE SPEED | | | | | | | | |

DATE _____ RECORDER _____

FIGURE 23-8

*tion class.* Each detail of the experience should be analyzed in the light of its theoretical occurrence with a group of high school students.

When the project method is used with high school groups, the post-project lesson would, of course, be of a different nature. Normally, the only value-limiting factors of the method are the availability of appropriate agencies and facilities, the ingenuity of the teacher, and the *time* in the course.

## TRAFFIC ENGINEERING IN THE HIGH SCHOOL COURSE

In summarizing the coverage of the subject, a few points should be kept in mind. The title of this chapter could have been "Traffic Engineering Education," were the term generally recognized. There has been no intent to repeat the engineering field *content* which is abundant in the literature, including in the better high school driver education textbooks. Rather there is a minimum of engineering data, with emphasis on *presentation*—how to gain interest in a "dry" (to students) subject, how to devote student driver education time to activities beyond those traditional in the classroom which are known to teachers, and how to avoid interdepartmental time conflicts which could do the program (and therefore the students) far more harm than good.

A final caution is in order for the driver and traffic safety education teacher-to-be. The citizen of the future will be better equipped to give intelligent support to that important responsibility and function of government—*traffic engineering*—if he has a good understanding of what it is. He will also be a better informed driver. Therefore—it is a valuable part of the driver education course.

However, it is only one phase of a very comprehensive course which has been approved by the public primarily as a lifesaving measure to protect their children. The volume of course content should never be permitted, where time is a rigid, limiting factor, to replace and exclude the basic essentials necessary to the student's safe operation of a motor vehicle. *The skeletal framework of the high school course in driver and traffic safety education is* ***time.*** Apportionment of time should always be made on the basis of an *intelligently planned priority.*

Finally, the teacher and the future teacher should not leave this subject of traffic engineering with the impression that the *project method* is the only—or even the basic—method for teaching the subject. It is featured herein as an *additional* technique to be used whenever feasible, in terms of time and conditions, above and beyond the other teaching methods which the well-prepared teacher should command.

In this chapter, *traffic engineering*—a discipline particularly well adapted to the project method—was used to develop an understanding of the *method*—just as both method and content would be taught the college student in carrying out the three projects suggested in this chapter.

TRAFFIC ENGINEERING 319

FIGURE 23-9 The high school student will recognize good examples of traffic engineering. Above: A modern, attractive overpass eliminates hazards to crossing pedestrians. Below: Overhead signs help drivers to position their cars in proper lanes well in advance of the intersection, aiding traffic movement and safety.

## SELECTED BIBLIOGRAPHY

*A Career in Traffic Engineering,* Institute of Traffic Engineers, Washington, D.C., 1960, 24 pp.

Hurd, Frederick W., Theodore M. Matson, and Wilbur S. Smith: *Traffic Engineering,* McGraw-Hill Book Company, New York, 1955, 647 pp.

*Maintaining Accident Records* (Procedure Manual 3E), Public Administration Service, 1313 East 60th Street, Chicago, Ill., 1958, 24 pp.

*Manual of Traffic Engineering Studies,* Institute of Traffic Engineers, Washington, D.C., 1964, 167 pp.

*Manual on Uniform Traffic Control Devices,* U.S. Government Printing Office, Washington, D.C., 1961.

*Measuring Traffic Volumes* (Procedure Manual 3A), Public Administration Service, 1313 East 60th St., Chicago, Ill., 1958, 48 pp.

*Traffic Engineering Guide for Cities under 50.000,* National Safety Council, Chicago, Ill., 1955, 28 pp.

*Traffic Engineering Handbook,* Institute of Traffic Engineers, Washington, D.C., 1950 (new ed., 1965).

# Police Traffic Supervision     24

THE FIRST question that should come to mind in citing the competencies needed by the teacher of driver and traffic safety education is *"Why?"* It would be foolish to take the precious course time in a high school to teach a mass of data which are of no value to the student—either as knowledge or as a means to a valid educational objective. Similarly, with teacher preparation time so limited and with so much to be learned, we cannot justify inclusion of masses of special professional knowledge of other disciplines which will be of no use to the teacher-to-be in his future. Rather, we should ask, *"What* should he know, and *why?"* All too frequently we hear perfectly sincere opinions that "the teacher should know . . ." followed by many minor details of the field in which the speaker has specialized.

*Enforcement* is one of "the three E's." Properly oriented, the driver education teacher should be extremely well versed in Education and should know enough about Engineering and Enforcement to give his students a desirable appreciation of them and enough knowledge to warrant the student's future support of them as citizens. It is neither necessary nor desirable to create a citizenry motivated to attempt to tell the traffic engineer where traffic signals should be placed nor the police officer how to make out a report. Occasionally one encounters this kind of concentration of time and effort on an area of special interest to the teacher or college instructor. The loss caused by this practice occurs in an unrealized stealing of time from the all-around preparation that requires all the course time that is available.

*Why*, then, teach about police traffic supervision? When we answer this question, we are guided to answer the question, "What should we teach in the high school?"

## PLANNING TOWARD OBJECTIVES

Why teach police traffic supervision? Well, first, the study of law enforcement has two objectives for the good of the community:

1. Voluntary observance of law by citizens
2. Citizen support of adequate enforcement agencies and policies

These, then, become two of the citizenship-developing objectives of the high school driver education course.

"Observance and Enforcement" is the title of a chapter in a popular high school textbook. The need for *voluntary observance* should be made an important part of the student's understanding of law and law enforcement. It should be noted by all school people concerned with elementary and secondary education, however, that the *attitudinal conditioning (and the factual instruction) of the student in regard to law enforcement agencies should not be left to the secondary level*. Attitude may be strongly patterned before the student reaches the driver education class. The attitude of a person as it relates to the agencies and personnel of law enforcement is a factor in determining his voluntary observance of law. It is an important factor of citizenship.

What to teach—and how much should be taught—in regard to *voluntary observance* of law requires a well-thought-out decision in each case. Considering the citizenship objective, this part of the course is an attitudinal entity. A rapport between students and police is a path to achievement of the objective. In general there are two phases to development of this rapport, an *understanding* of the difficult and even dangerous problems faced by police officers and a *feeling* of sympathy and friendliness for those who protect the students and their families—one phase *intellectual* and one *emotional*.

The former, a matter of *knowledge*, is taught as factual course content. The latter will tend to follow, in part, from this knowledge, and can be strengthened by a more emotional association of a constructive kind. The latter can be organized in two phases. Probably the best initial contact, for most student groups, would be a visit of a police officer or two to the classroom. Students are normally more "at home" and at ease there than they

FIGURE 24–1  The familiar environment fosters rapport.

would be on a visit to police headquarters, and the atmosphere is more favorable to their responding to the visitor's presentation in a friendly manner.

Later, with the same officer or officers acting as hosts, a conducted, instructional tour of the police headquarters would be the second, or follow-up, project. There is a subtle effect in this "home-and-home" plan. In the somewhat forbidding (to the student) atmosphere of the police headquarters, the sight and the hospitality of their former guest or guests as friendly hosts *is* reassuring. It is the emotional rapport with those former guests and the subtle *association with the visual symbol of the uniform these former guests and now friendly hosts wear* (Chapter 4, "Attitude and Behavior"). Facetiously, the college student may refer to this method as "sneaky." The fact is that it *is* an example of using in a constructive manner what we know of emotion association as a determinant of attitude.

The teacher of driver and traffic safety education may know the policeman who is regularly assigned to school work. Normally he is a person who has demonstrated an aptitude for working with children. However, the teacher should see to it that only an officer who is able to get along well with children is invited to work with students. An overbearing, threatening, stern, or gruff one might have just the opposite effect on his assigned mission —without intending or realizing what he is doing. The nonspeaker should also be avoided. In school, children are keenly aware of lapses in grammati-

FIGURE 24-2  The friendly host becomes the teacher.

cal construction that they might not notice elsewhere. Most police officers today do an excellent job on school assignments.

In planning experiences for the students, the teacher should be highly selective. In what should normally be a desirable educational experience, an element of discord could raise havoc with the objectives of that part of the driver education course. The teacher is well advised first to make the acquaintance of the police department. The cooperation of the police officers will make his task easier and more successful. Perhaps less realized, his success will make their task easier and more successful also, in the long run.

### The Goal Is within Reach

Perhaps the first thing the teacher should know about this subject is that the attitude objective *is* within reach. It *can* be done, and it *has* been done. A few years ago the author visited a school in a poor, depressed area of a large city. It was a place in which one would expect to find crime running rampant and the police hated. The most startling feature of that visit resulted from the fact that a poster contest was in progress, and the walls of the hallways were covered with posters. The theme of the contest was to show the student's own vocational ambition—what he or she most wanted to be.

There, in this industrialized "slum" area, more than half of the many posters drawn by boys showed a policeman! Many of the rest of the posters pictured firemen in action. Most of the girls' posters showed nurses and teachers. Something had happened here. It was too "pat" to be chance. Somebody had done a remarkable job of getting the police officer *accepted* in the type of environment that often breeds hate for law, for authority, and for anyone who represents them. *Somebody* (or some people) *is building in that school—building people, good citizens.* It can be done.

The driver education teacher who meets some students for the first time and recognizes in one or more an obviously troublesome attitude may be inclined to accept the "percentage" as inevitable, beyond his control. It may be so; yet it may not. As a member of the school staff, and possibly as a member of the state and local educational associations, the teacher has a voice that can be heard. Elsewhere in this book the admonition, "Join 'em" is expressed, and it can mean teaming up with our classroom teachers here too. No need to decry the fact that students coming to the driver education class are arriving with a poor attitude toward driving behavior, toward police, toward the law, etc., at least not until a remedy has been tried. Some pupils may have been yielded to the "enemy" by default.

The teaching profession outside the fold of driver education is not insensitive to the need for protecting children against traffic and other hazards. Much is being done in the safety patrol movement. Uncounted thousands of primary grade teachers are showing children how to respond to traffic signals, to use police-protected intersections, to choose the "safest way" to school, etc. This is *safety education,* the parent discipline of which driver and traffic safety education is a part.

The teachers who are devoted to this mission, and many others who need only guidance, have the potential of being a major force in the constructive conditioning of the student. They can play a big part in the formation of his attitude toward traffic law, toward enforcement, toward police, and toward a mature and civilized view of operating a motor vehicle with respect for the rights, life, and limb of his fellowmen.

## *Association—A Two-way Street*

It is probable that many thousands of these classroom teachers have been devoted leaders in teaching citizenship, without having fully realized the importance of the policeman-and-pupil *symbolic* relationship. All teachers advocate good citizenship and respect for the "law." The fact that the enforcement officer in uniform represents the law is often mentioned. However, the two-way nature of a mental association is not usually considered. We don't know how many cases there have been of an unpleasant or a distasteful experience, or even an impression obtained by word of mouth of police as "authority," in which dislike or hatred of the police—the symbol—may have engendered a dislike, a disrespect, or a hatred for law. Such transference of emotion by association can result in serious and lasting mental reactions. Of course an "undeserved" traffic ticket or seemingly or actually unnecessary gruffness on the part of a police officer may trigger a similar reaction in a driver.

FIGURE 24-3 "Traffic safety education" must not await the driving phase.

The law-enforcement mission of police is one which often makes their role seem to be that of the aggressor. Rebellion in any form tends to be against authority, the "establishment." The need is for positive action in building a constructive image of law, enforcement, and enforcement personnel. So we should not wait until the first day the boy walks into the driver education class and bemoan the fact that he already has a bad attitude toward law, police, driving, driver education, etc.; recognition of the trouble should precede an attempt at remedy. If his previous teachers have failed to recognize a need, we return to the same old maxim—don't fight 'em, join 'em.

Get yourself on the agenda of a staff meeting, a school or district teachers' meeting or a meeting of the local education association. Prepare an appealing presentation of the case of action to build the kind of attitude necessary to live well in a world crowded with people. Give a few tips on how it's done. It is not necessary to "talk down" to one's colleagues. Educated people listen well to a specialist telling of his own field. Start with a description of the boy who came to your class with the obviously poor, perhaps vulnerable or dangerous attitude, and then tell the need which the school can meet—this is the language and the mission of the true teachers. You can start action.

Here is where the principles you learned about introducing the student to the police officer can be passed on to others, a process which should start in the lowest grades. The teachers should know that a uniform is more than a blue (or gray, or green, or brown) suit. It is a symbol of the *law*, the *authority of society,* and the *government* as represented by the police officer. The customary approach of teaching that one should respect the police officer because he represents those things recognizes only the "traffic" on one side of the street. As mentioned before, *mental association can be a two-way street. The impression the child gets of the uniformed figure can determine his reaction and his attitude toward law and society!* This is something you know—something your subject field can contribute to your colleagues. Share it with them. Charge them for it. Make their cooperation the price of your convincing presentation, so that you will find your new students more susceptible to your teaching during the comparatively short time you have with them. Their preceding eight or ten years of school should not be neutral in this part of citizen behavior. Enlist as much of it as you can in your mission. There may be little you can do in the matter of constructive home influence on the student in the cases which need it most. In a school so organized and so minded that cooperation and coordination of effort are possible and encouraged, a significant portion of the students' time can be well planned toward specific attitudinal objectives. If you feel that your school and its

FIGURE 24-4 The police officer merits the respect due a well-trained professional. Driving skill is but one of the many phases of the training of an efficient officer.

staff are apathetic (and usually such a state is only a result of nobody taking initiative) don't join 'em—fight 'em. *Take* the initiative.

## THE TRUE PHILOSOPHY OF LAW AND LAW OFFICERS

So far we have dealt with attitude building toward police agencies and personnel and of a dual outcome of such attitude, namely, a desire to support this function of government and a motivation toward voluntary observance of law.

The high school student's understanding of these needs is covered in his textbooks. Beyond that coverage, the teacher should know and be prepared to teach as circumstances may warrant (in the school and elsewhere) what is good enforcement of traffic law. What is the best thinking of responsible police administrators about the responsibility of government to regulate traffic to operate in a safe and orderly manner?

The International Association of Chiefs of Police, in 1963, issued a position statement on police traffic management. It presents to the citizen the official position of police administrators. The statement follows:

## POSITION STATEMENT ON POLICE TRAFFIC MANAGEMENT, INTERNATIONAL ASSOCIATION OF CHIEFS OF POLICE

### Introduction

Police administrators are charged with the responsibility of protecting life and property and providing police services which will provide the citizens of their communities maximum protection with a minimum of interruption. By far the greatest public safety losses to the people of the United States and most other countries stem from street and highway collisions and congestion.

From this perspective, the International Association of Chiefs of Police believes that a statement of its policies in this field is necessary and desirable. The Association strongly recommends the adoption of each of these policies by all police agencies. It recognizes that local conditions will require adaptation in details. At the same time, however, the IACP believes that the general principles contained in these statements are essential for maximum reduction in traffic losses.

The police have a wide range of interests in highway transportation. They have a direct responsibility for traffic law enforcement, traffic direction, accident investigation, and traffic records. They also have an auxiliary interest in other aspects of traffic safety and regulation, for there is practically no street or highway traffic activity that does not to some degree affect the police in the pursuit of their objectives.

1. The police administrators of this Association accept the fact that police efforts alone will not provide the utmost in safe and efficient highway transportation. They recognize the need for: sound, realistic, and balanced programs of traffic laws; highway, automotive, and traffic engineering; driver licensing and driver improvement; traffic courts and prosecutors; safety and driver education; collection, analysis, and use of traffic records; coordination of effort in states and communities by all

POLICE TRAFFIC SUPERVISION 329

FIGURE 24-5 ". . . protecting life and property . . ." means that some forms of driving behavior must be eliminated.

agencies with traffic responsibility; responsive community climate developed by public understanding and support.

2. In the enforcement of traffic laws, ordinances, and regulations, the rights and privileges of the people, as stated in the several constitutions and statutes and subsequently interpreted by the courts, will continue to be faithfully observed and respected by the police, taking heed specifically of the following:
   a. The constitutional protection of every individual against unreasonable searches and seizures.
   b. The right of a person to bail.
   c. The right of a person to be informed specifically of the charge or charges filed against him.
   d. The right of a person to counsel.
   e. The right of an accused to appear and defend himself in a duly constituted court of law.
   f. The right of a person to a fair and impartial trial.
   g. The right of a person to be presumed innocent until proven guilty.
   h. The privilege of every person to the use of the public highways when conforming with existing laws and regulations.
3. Traffic laws should be enforced at a sustained level, with uniform interpretation in all jurisdictions. The quantity of enforcement should be sufficient to produce maximum safety in each locality.
4. Equally as important as the amount of traffic law enforcement is the quality of enforcement. To be effective, enforcement must be directed at

the violations known to be accident causative. In addition, it must be applied in those places and at those times shown by experience to have a disproportionately high percentage of accidents. There will probably never be enough policemen to apprehend all violators for every violation; therefore, enforcement personnel and enforcement effort must be used to the best possible advantage.

5. Every police officer on the streets and highways—regardless of his specific assignment—should, when he observes a traffic violation or non-traffic offense, take appropriate enforcement action.
6. The enforcement of traffic laws solely for revenue purposes is as abhorrent to the police as it is to the public. The practice should be eliminated wherever it exists.
7. The salaries, pensions, and other fringe benefits of police officers should not by legislative, budget, or other provision be dependent upon fines or costs assessed in criminal or traffic adjudications. The fee system should be abolished in law enforcement and in criminal prosecution and adjudication.
8. The enforcement of traffic laws for the sole purpose of building an activity record is as repugnant as enforcement for revenue purposes.
9. There should be one enforcement policy for all street and highways users and not one that gives preference to either local residents or non-residents.
10. The effect of police traffic law enforcement is to a very important degree dependent upon the disposition of charges by other official agencies. It is incumbent upon the police to establish and follow sound policies in the amount and quality of enforcement action taken by them and produce in the courts proper and sufficient evidence. The police must also keep sufficient records and report all necessary data to appropriate central agencies. Having carried out these duties appropriately, their responsibilities are completed, but the enforcement process is not. Police enforcement action is affected by the soundness of policies of driver examination and licensing; by the efficiency of court administration; by the prompt and complete reporting of all dispositions to the driver licensing administrators; and by the resultant actions taken by the licensing administrators.
11. Traffic law enforcement is affected by the "community climate." Public understanding and support is essential to this vital function of police service. The effectiveness of state and local public support organizations will determine to a great degree public understanding and support. Police agencies should provide leadership in the development of a sound public safety education program.
12. The police are also responsible in a substantial degree for public attitude toward traffic law enforcement. Traffic law enforcement and traffic direction must be performed in a uniform manner to be understood and acceptable. But even more important, this must be done in an efficient and courteous manner.
13. The police are definitely and unequivocally opposed to the "fixing" of traffic cases in any manner by any agency, official, or person. It should be eliminated if and wherever it exists.
14. The police administrator must seek, and should be requested, to advise and consult in the construction or reconstruction of trafficways and facilities, including the use of signs, signals, and markings. It must be recognized that the police cannot correct inadequate streets, highways, and parking facilities. At best, the police can by control and direction only alleviate inadequate physical situations.

15. Police should be consulted in the drafting of new traffic legislation which, if ultimately enacted into law, would require enforcement by the police. Police should be asked about the need for proposed legislation, whether it is enforceable, and if so, whether the enforcement of it will require any additional manpower or equipment.
16. The enforcement of traffic laws by the police should not be regarded as a sports contest. Competition has no place in modern-day traffic flow on public streets and highways. The police are committed to a policy of traffic patrol which normally will be conducted by uniformed officers using easily identifiable vehicles, supplemented when necessary by officers using equipment not readily identifiable as police equipment. The IACP also believes concealment for traffic law enforcement is justifiable when necessary to bring under control a situation that cannot be controlled by usual methods.
17. The use of scientific devices such as mechanical, electronic, photographic, and chemical equipment is justifiable when required to enhance the law-

FIGURE 24-6 The radar speed meter—one of the scientific aids to efficient police traffic supervision.

ful efforts of the police. The limits to the use of devices by the police should be determined by their legality and scientific soundness.

18. The violation of traffic laws has nothing to do with the intent of the violator; therefore, it is incumbent upon the motorist or pedestrian to obey. If he does not obey, it should not be necessary for the police officer who apprehends him to prove that he intended to violate. It should only be necessary that the officer prove that the offender did in fact commit that violation.

19. The words "entrapment" and "speed trap" are frequently used in the public press. Both of these terms imply that by some inducement or action the police have caused or enticed a person to violate the traffic laws. The police deplore the use of these or similar terms. The police do not entice people to violate traffic laws. In this connection, there has been and possibly are, today, some isolated instances where there is existing traffic legislation which the public generally neither approves nor considers necessary but which the police through legislative process are required to enforce. If and where such undesirable and unnecessary traffic laws do exist, they should be repealed by legislative action.

20. The police do not feel that the ultimate in safe speed for motor vehicle transportation has been reached. They recognize that increased safe speed for every form of transportation is a means of progress. Regularity of vehicular movement, however, must be recognized as an essential of efficient transportation. Comparatively low speeds are as disruptive as high speeds. Varying conditions such as traffic, road, and visibility affect the safe speed. The wide range of skills and capabilities of individual operators is a factor to be considered.

In light of these several factors and the need for reasonable, specific, understandable speed regulations it is, therefore, believed that the following considerations should be given in the formulation and enforce-

FIGURE 24-7 An elevated vantage point for police traffic supervision.

ment of legislation designed to control undesirable effects of too great or too little speed for existing conditions.

  a. Absolute maximum speeds should be established for rural and urban driving after consultation of police and engineers.
  b. Empower the appropriate agency, after consultation with police, to legally raise or lower these limits in specific zones after engineering and traffic accident studies establish that the proposed changed limit is reasonable and safe for that zone provided that the zone affected is properly and adequately signed.
  c. Make it incumbent upon drivers to drive at speeds lower than the absolute maximums when consideration of existing conditions indicates a safe speed is lower than that of the existing maximums.
  d. Legislation based on prima facie limits which allow the individual driver to exceed these limits, when within his judgment it is safe to do so, is undesirable.
  e. Minimum speed laws based on consideration of the speed for the most rapid, lawful, and efficient movement of traffic should be formulated after appropriate surveys determine the relationship of the need for rapid movement to its effect on the safe movement of traffic.
  f. Review to determine the need for establishing or adjusting speed regulations should constitute a continuing program.

## *The Citizen's View*

The truly law-abiding citizen finds no fault with the expressed policies of this highly respected organization of professional police administrators. The interests of police personnel and of drivers are best served when the welfare of the public is held paramount. There is no division of interests between the police officer and the driver. As an example of this, one might cite twelve basic enforcement policies advocated by an association of 9 million motorists:[1]

1. Proper enforcement of traffic laws is of the highest importance in the promotion of traffic safety.
2. Every enforcement program should be selective in its approach, concentrating on the worst violations, places, and drivers, and thus making the most valuable use of limited enforcement personnel.
3. Investigations by specially trained accident investigation squads are strongly recommended, with arrests made only when necessary.
4. There should be power to suspend and revoke drivers' licenses when warranted by the driving records. Provisions for mandatory suspensions or revocations should be determined by legislative action.
5. Enforcement officers should not be subject to efficiency ratings or have to depend for promotion on the number of traffic arrests or citations they make.
6. Legislation should be enacted wherever and whenever needed, removing as far as possible from political influence all traffic courts and traffic law enforcement agencies.

[1] American Automobile Association.

7. Courtrooms should be clean, adequately equipped, and dignified in appearance.
8. Judges should be professionally trained in law. Where such persons cannot be obtained, those in their place should have special knowledge of traffic laws, police procedure, and traffic engineering.
9. Proper records of court procedures should be maintained.
10. The traffic court should be a place of justice and never an agency operated primarily to collect fines.

It is quite obvious to the discerning, and should be pointed out to the teen-ager, that there is no conflict between the police officer and the *driver*. Actually, the conflict of interest exists with the good driver and officer on one side and the traffic violator on the other—a lesson in placing visual, physical symbols with their proper associations (Chapter 4, "Attitude and Behavior").

FIGURE 24–8 Traffic duty has many risks—a fact that should be cited in guiding the development of the student's attitude toward police.

### *A Well-meant Discord—The Drag Strip*

In quoting the IACP Position Statement, another quotation from the same source comes to mind. Many driver education teachers have been questioned (and even pressured) on the subject of "drag-strip" activity. Sometimes, in view of the nature of their mission of safety, they are accused of being prejudiced against a constructive, harmless activity if they disagree with some of the thinking behind it. Some well-meaning advocates of that activity theorize that young people "have to get speed out of their systems" and that this is a good way to do it.

Of course, on analysis, that theory doesn't stand up. After countless generations, since long before the beginning of history, man traveled no faster than the speed of a running horse. Comparatively few human beings ever moved faster than they could on foot. Only in the last hundred years or so have men, in a small minority, a very small part of their lives, moved faster. Even today a very few of the many millions of people have traveled faster on the earth than the ordinary speeds of the automobile. Perhaps most, even today, haven't approached that. In view of the facts of the natural phenomenon we call heredity, it is ridiculous to claim that man has speed "in his system," which he must "get out." It is, of course, a shallow rationalization.

In some areas of the country, drag strips became popular and were endorsed and even supervised by police agencies. Both the drag strips and the surrounding areas, including the streets and highways, were known to, and observed by, the police. It is significant that the responsible voice of police leadership, the IACP, has taken the following well-considered stand on the subject:

## RESOLUTION

### Expressing Policy That Law Enforcement Agencies Refrain from Participating in the Establishment and/or Operation of Drag Strips

*Whereas,* speed is recognized as the leading contributing cause of major traffic accidents, and

*Whereas,* law enforcement agencies in their efforts to contain this element of the traffic problem emphasize enforcement and education directed toward the elimination of excessive and unsafe motor vehicle speed and unwise competition of motor vehicle operators in highway traffic, and

*Whereas,* the establishment and use of drag strips as a facility for individuals to compete in speed events and driving practices generally considered unsafe in normal traffic tend to inspire the participants and non-participants at these events to attempt duplication of such unsafe practices in normal traffic streams, and

*Whereas,* sensible motor vehicle operation does not permit the driver to entertain a belief that he must compete with his fellow driver but rather that such safe driver must possess the quality of cooperation, and

*Whereas,* if the personal enthusiasm and public support now directed to approval of "drag strips" were harnessed with elements of high school driver training and public education there should be more rapid growth and development of this basic approach to the traffic problem which is believed to have the greatest potential insofar as eventual solution is concerned;

*Now, therefore, be it resolved,* that the International Association of Chiefs of Police, in Conference assembled in the City of Chicago on September 13, 1956, does hereby adopt an expression of policy that law enforcement agencies refrain from participating in the establishment and/or operation of drag strips or other similar activity designed for speed contests, and that participaton of law enforcement agencies in the encouragement of high school driver training would better serve the public interest.

336   ELEMENTS OF THE PROFESSIONAL KNOWLEDGE COMPETENCY

## THE TRAFFIC COURT

The average citizen thinks of the police as the agency which "enforces the law." There is, however, another phase to the governmental function of requiring obedience to law, and that is the judicial branch of government. Truly they "interpret" the laws. But their actions must be such that enforcement of law is effective. Obviously it would do little good for the police to bring law violators into court if they were all to be dismissed at once without some action which would have some deterrent effect on future crimes against society.

Number 10 of the IACP Position Statement states that it is incumbent upon the police to "produce in the courts proper and sufficient evidence." It also states that police enforcement action is affected by (among other things) "the efficiency of court administration." Here is recognition of a need for a total support of law which cannot be achieved by one branch of government without the efficient operation of the others concerned. Number 19 of the IACP Position Statement cites sound legislative action as one of the factors of the cooperative venture we call *law*.

FIGURE 24–9   ". . . produce in the courts proper and sufficient evidence."

A great deal of effort has been directed to improve the quality of traffic courts since the days when the country was spotted with "roadside courts" which fined motorists wholesale, with very little resemblance to either justice or judicial dignity. Some states have taken definite action to eliminate these tribute-extracting agencies which had for their frank purpose fund raising from out-of-town motorists. Some are still operating openly today. As a matter of fact, about half of the 50 states now have some form of the "fee system"; that is, the justice of the peace receives a portion of the fine imposed on motorists. More reform is needed in this area of justice before the motorist can feel certain that even his basic constitutional rights will be respected wherever he may go in this—his own—country. Courts dealing with traffic law must be as dignified and fair as any, and of course, most of them do operate in just that way.

This brings us to the point of the visit of the driver education class to the traffic court, a fairly common procedure. If it can be done without penalizing the balanced program in point of time, and without intraschool conflict, it can be beneficial. Like any other field trip, it should be well planned and the teacher should perform a reconnaissance mission in advance. To the high school student, the well-conducted traffic court is a good lesson in justice. Too, the traffic court is the only court which a great many people see during their entire lives. It may easily be, in many cases, *legal justice, the court, the judicial branch of the American government* in the eyes of those who visit it, especially during an impressionable age. It is a serious responsibility on the part of the teacher to see that it is a constructive learning experience.

There have been instances in which court visits have been unfortunate. Poorly conducted courts, miscarriages of justice, lack of respect for defendants or witnesses or police officers, failure to impose suitable penalties—these do not build a proper respect for our system of justice. The teacher should make sure in advance that any court visit he may plan will leave his students with the feeling that "the place of justice is a hallowed place." The young person's *attitude* toward our system of justice is more important than his learning about the mechanics of a court, especially a poor one.

Many judges cooperate fully with the high school program and explain to the students the operation of our court system. Even more than this, the strict, fair, and impartial dispensing of justice can make a lasting impression on the teen-age visitor. *Fairness* includes fitting each penalty to the offense, making each a deterrent to future violation, fairness to the police officer who testifies as his duty, *and inclusion of some educative process where such seems to be needed*, as well as a just decision as to guilt or innocence of the defendants. Elsewhere in this book, in Chapter 26, "Driver Improvement Activities," some educative processes of the court are described.

It is suggested that, in this area of law enforcement, the driver education teacher-to-be become familiar with the Police Traffic Supervision section of the *Action Program* of the President's Committee for Traffic Safety.

As in all school field trips, detailed planning is necessary. The judge who will preside should be contacted in advance and his advice sought. Of course, all school rules for field trips should be observed, including parent permission slips, and administrative approval should be obtained.

## "Why Don't the Police . . . ?"

The classic cry of the traffic violator, "Why don't the police concentrate on catching criminals instead of watching for a law-abiding citizen like me to pass a stop sign?" The answer is simple, "They would, Mister, and effectively, if they didn't have to keep you from killing yourself and others by just such juvenile conduct." "Why don't the police . . . ?" This is a question one hears at times, sometimes directed to the subject of crime and sometimes to regulation of traffic. Perhaps an indication of the answer lies in the almost unbelievable apathy shown by witnesses of certain publicized crimes. Even slow, cruel murders have been witnessed by numbers of people who wouldn't even telephone the police because they didn't want to "get involved." These instances, not traffic-involved, are sufficiently emotionally associated to be used effectively as attitude-affecting examples of what we might identify as citizenship failure and a form of inhumanity. The association here is constructive.

FIGURE 24-10 This should be identified as a symbol of *protection*.

This is not a characteristic of our people in general, but it is characteristic of far too many who think of themselves as law-abiding citizens. *Your students of the future must understand that certain requirements are needed for effective law enforcement, entities without which the law cannot protect them either as drivers or as human beings. Citizen backing or "support" is a necessity. Since in any society people must depend on law, they must also support it. A citizen's rights are earned rights.* Some of the "facts of life" about law and enforcement which the teacher should see that his high school students of the future know are these:

1. There will never be enough policemen to observe the behavior of all people at all times, nor even to detect all violations of law.
2. The policeman has a number of "bosses." One is the *law*. The citizen must see to it that the law is sound, just, and *enforceable*. As a voter, the lawmakers work for him.
3. Another "boss" of the policeman is the level of government by which he is employed. If the orders of that governing body are wrong, and the citizen is not getting proper protection from law, let him, collectively, make his wants, his *demands*, known—he holds the vote.
4. Since we can't put a policeman in every motor vehicle (and on every corner), the basis of effective law is *voluntary observance*. It should be only the hoodlum, the criminal, the insane who need enforcement action. Each time a person who doesn't believe he belongs in that category vio-

lates the law, *he is on their side* against the forces of law and order. We could do a great deal more about controlling crime if we didn't have to devote so much of our enforcement effort to the childish actions of a comparatively few adults who often complain about not being properly protected against criminals.

FIGURE 24-11 By the taking of six or eight "still" photos at two-second intervals, the photographic record will show that the camera car followed at a constant distance and therefore its recorded speed was the same as that of the lead car. In this case the speed was 62 miles per hour in the 15-mile-per-hour school zone (see sign).

5. The citizen who neglects his duty because he doesn't want to "become involved" should get a few books that tell what some people *have* done to make this country a good and safe place in which to live and to bring up children. Then he should letter in the word *coward* below the mirror before which he combs his hair—and keep it there until such time as he recognizes a duty and *acts* without fear of becoming involved. Of course, nobody will do this, but the association of the trigger-word "coward" with an act has been implanted in the mind of the impressionable young person. This is the sort of association indicated by what is known about attitude and behavior (Chapter 4).

You don't *hire* a soldier to go into combat and then forget him while you do—or fail to do—what you can to defeat the enemy. The student should be shown the policeman as a protector, rather than as one who

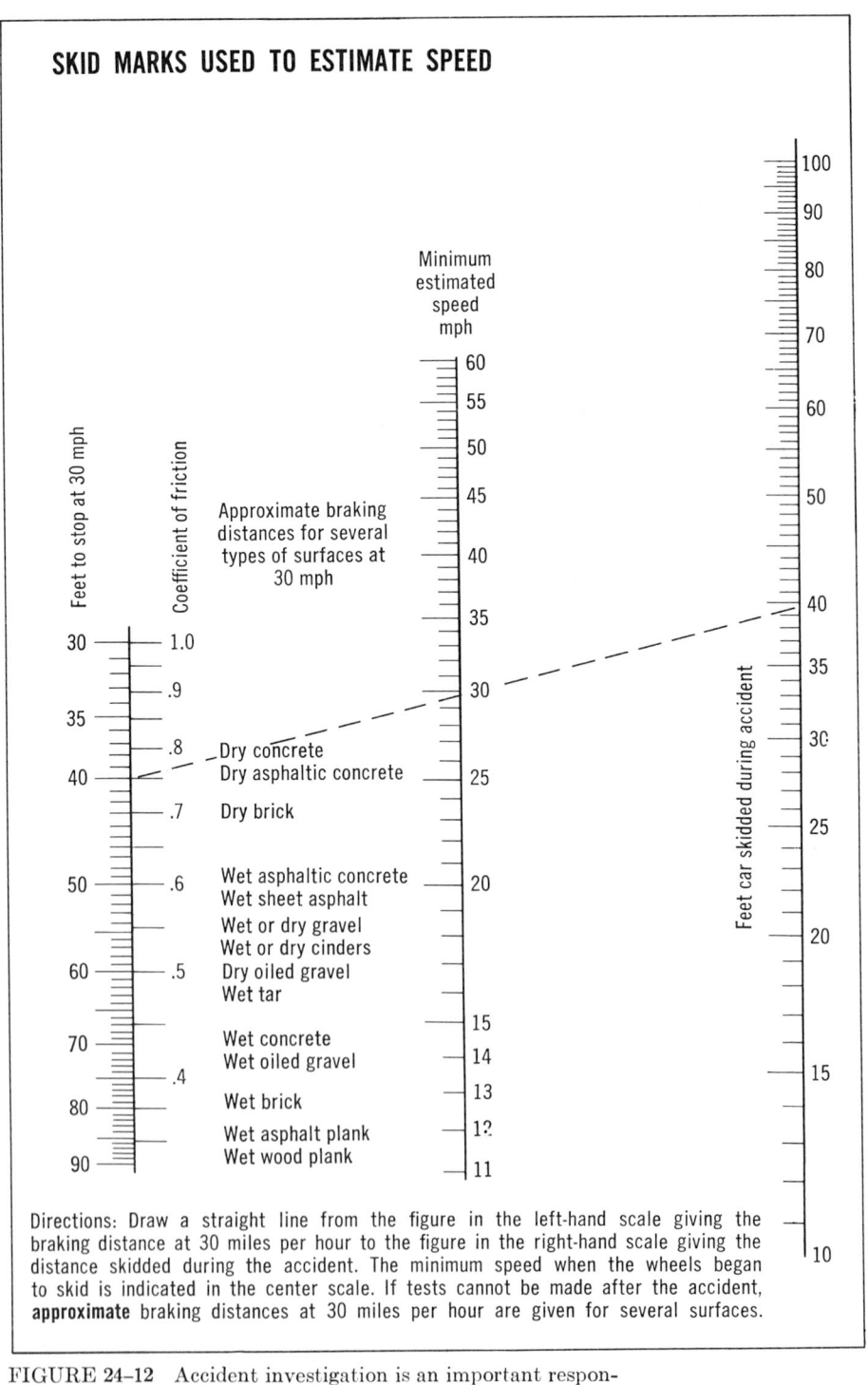

FIGURE 24-12 Accident investigation is an important responsibility of police departments.

helps regulate his, the student's, conduct. The latter association helps break down his rapport with school, parents, etc., and should be countered with *other* associations.
6. Finally, as long as there are thousands and thousands of policemen, there will be a few "bad cops." The young person *must* be made to know that, having seen or met one who is objectionable, to generalize on such a fact is ridiculous. There are bad students, and teachers, and soldiers (and textbook writers)—but this does not reflect on all members of any of those groups.

Perhaps a little golden rule of citizenship might be taught for use by the adult citizen of the future: "As long as I see that something is wrong, each time I think about it I will ask myself, 'What have *I* done about it today?'"

## SELECTED BIBLIOGRAPHY

"Police Traffic Supervision," *A Section of the Action Program for Highway Safety,* President's Committee for Traffic Safety, Washington, D.C.

Tamm, Quinn: "The Police: Pivot for Highway Safety Efforts," *Traffic Quarterly,* Eno Foundation for Highway Traffic Control, Saugatuck, Conn., April, 1964.

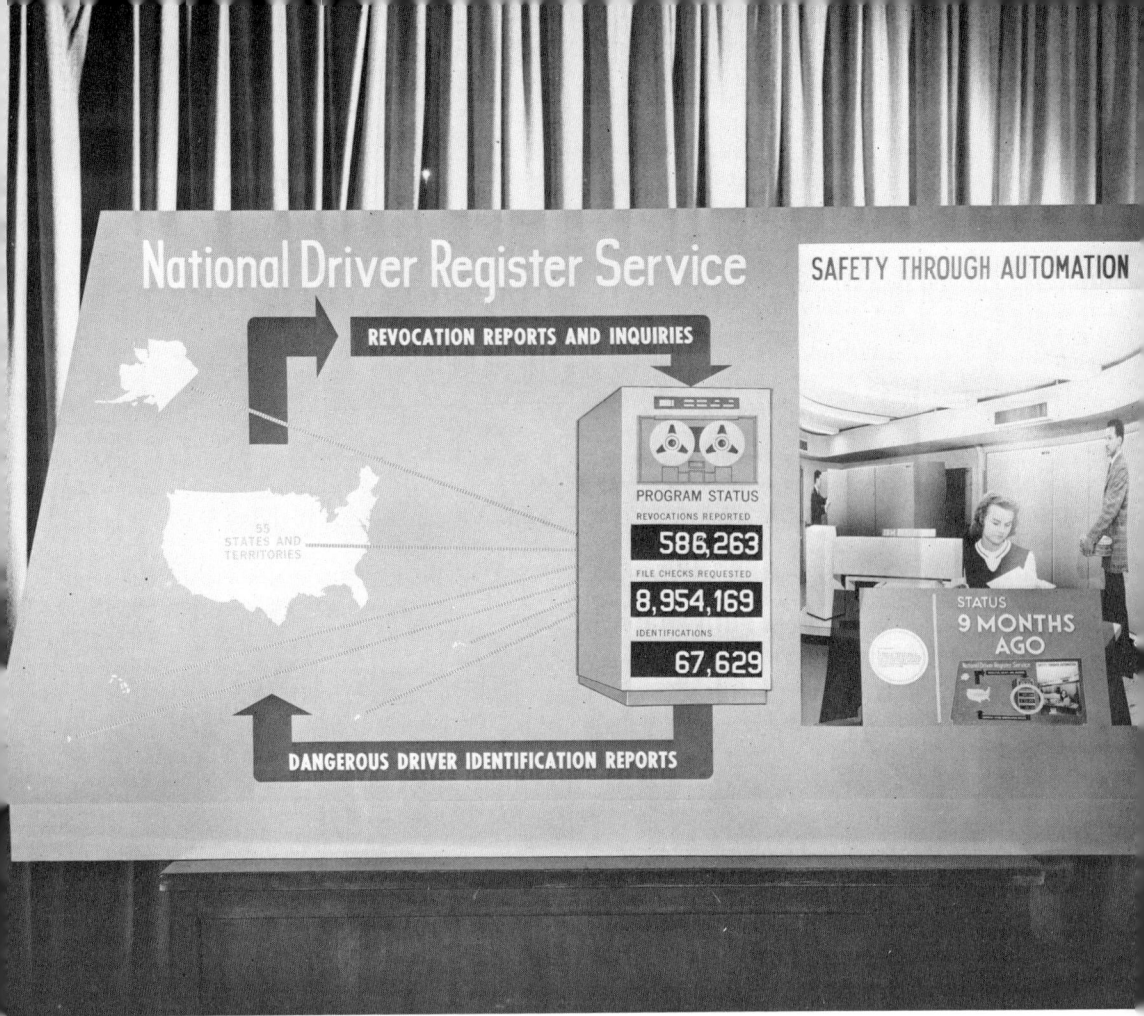

# Motor Vehicle Law and Administration  25

MOTOR VEHICLE administration is recognized as a state function. State laws and regulations governing motor vehicles are neither uniform nor permanent in detail, and no constructive purpose would be served by a reprint of the traffic codes of the fifty states and the District of Columbia. However, the driver education teacher is strongly advised to obtain a copy of traffic laws and regulations in the state in which he teaches and to keep himself informed of all changes as they occur. In fact, it is well worth the time to make a very careful study of them. Not only will they strongly affect his normal occupation, but he will face questions on the subject from many sources. Knowing the correct answers not only will enhance his professional prestige but will do the same for driver education in the community.

High school textbooks in driver education furnish adequate elementary coverage of the principles of state control of motor vehicles and the part played by the *Uniform Vehicle Code* and the *Manual on Uniform Traffic Control Devices* in the design of that control. (The *Model Traffic Ordinance* is a companion guide for municipalities within the state.) It should be understood by the new teacher that these three publications have no legal status in themselves. They serve as *guides* or patterns for state and local action.

Obviously the extent to which the states, counties, and municipalities conform to national standards and guides determines the degree of uniformity of traffic controls throughout the country. In principle, although specific controls such as speed limits must logically vary between city street and rural freeway, general variations at state borders are an anachronism. The unifying tendency of these codes, then, is a force in the direction of meeting an urgent need of a nation's motor vehicle traffic which itself knows no state boundaries. It is important to realize that the national guides represent the experience and judgment of foremost authorities in all fields of highway transportation.

In referring to motor vehicle and traffic regulation as primarily a state responsibility, it should be understood that this is not a totally inviolate or sacred principle. The driver and traffic safety education teacher should have a flexible outlook on the subject. The purpose of such regulation is street and highway transport with safety. Each function of traffic safety should be performed by the government agency best suited to the task. Many aspects of safety are the concern of nongovernmental associations and groups.

The Interstate Commerce Commission has long been concerned with regulation of vehicles engaged in commercial transportation of goods and persons across state lines. The history of state legislation gives no indication that such regulation, if left to the states, would have the uniformity necessary to avoid handicapping or possibly stifling interstate trade with different and conflicting requirements. The ICC is an accepted institution.

Occasionally one hears of "pronouncements" by elected officials that if the state legislatures do not enact certain motor vehicle safety laws, the Federal government will step in and take over jurisdiction in the interest of traffic safety. There has been no strong tendency toward such action, although a few instances of Federal enactment of motor vehicle legislation have occurred. In 1962, a Federal law was enacted providing that hydraulic brake fluid sold or shipped in interstate commerce for use in motor vehicles shall meet certain specifications prescribed by the Secretary of Commerce.

In the Senate Commerce Committee Report on this bill (H.R. 2446), it has been stated: "Although 27 states and the District of Columbia have enacted legislation to protect motorists from sub-standard brake fluid, only 10 states have put sufficient teeth in their legislation to prevent the marketing of spurious products." Considering the safety implications of the product, the need for uniform standards and enforcement is quite obvious.

In 1963, the President signed into law Bill H.R. 134 which directs the Secretary of Commerce to prescribe and publish in the Federal Register

FIGURE 25-1 Publications for the professional library of the department of driver education.

minimum standards for seat belts sold or shipped in interstate commerce for use in motor vehicles.

## THE NATIONAL DRIVER REGISTER SERVICE

In 1960, the Driver License Register law was enacted, establishing in the Department of Commerce a National Driver Register Service, which is a Federal clearinghouse containing information on persons whose driver licenses have been revoked in cases of:

1. Driving while intoxicated
2. Conviction for a traffic offense resulting in a fatality

Though it is completely voluntary, all fifty states participate in the program. In addition to sending to the service, for recording, the names of drivers whose licenses were revoked on these grounds, the names of new applicants for licenses are also submitted. The latter are checked, and if their prior licenses have been revoked in another state, that information is furnished the state where the application was made. The original law was broadened by subsequent legislation to expand the term "revoked" to cover any person whose license or privilege to operate a motor vehicle has "been terminated or temporarily withdrawn," for either of the two offenses mentioned. Further amendments to broaden the scope of the service have been proposed and are awaiting legislative action.

Prior to establishment of the register, it was a simple matter for a driver to have his license revoked in one state, and to apply and obtain a license in another state. No state could check with all the other states on every license application, whereas it and every other state would also be beset by inquiries from all the others on their license applicants.

The probability is that we may expect more Federal motor vehicle laws in the future. Indicated is an urgent need for the automotive industry to redouble its efforts in the development and installation of safety devices for the protection of automobile drivers and passengers. Also, it is highly desirable that all state legislatures work to bring their motor vehicle laws in conformity with the *Uniform Vehicle Code,* so that maximum uniformity may be achieved among the laws throughout all states. The measure in which these goals are accomplished will probably be a major factor in determining the extent of the future Federal role in motor vehicle legislation.

## *STATE CONTROL*

In spite of the evidences of Federal interest cited, motor vehicle administration has remained primarily a state function. State motor vehicle laws comprise the basic legal control of motor vehicles and their operation throughout the nation.

There has been a commendable tendency among the majority of states toward improvement of their motor vehicle laws and toward uniformity, in conformance with the recommendations of the *Uniform Vehicle Code.* Other states, however, have done relatively little to revise and improve their laws since the earliest pertinent legislation was enacted. Between the two, there are examples of different degrees of action and inaction. Anyone familiar with state legislative action is aware of the necessity for professional leadership and the support of citizens' groups in a continuous effort to achieve modernization of legal codes. Such efforts are a critical need in motor vehicle and traffic regulation.

Another urgent need is one that one rarely sees expressed in print. Motor vehicle administration, based on law and including that responsibility of government known as *traffic safety,* has become a highly complex operation. Not only is efficient administration needed, but departments must be staffed with professionally trained personnel. Though the popular concept of an "administrator" has taken on an implication of very general, nonspecific qualifications, the fact remains that at all administrative, policy-making levels a thorough knowledge of the principles and procedures of the operations is urgently needed. The inference is clear. Administrative and all policy-making levels should be staffed with professional "career" personnel. Unfortunately, current practice doesn't always conform to this principle.

Another current need in many states is the creation of separate, independent motor vehicle departments, free of subsidiary ranking under other agencies of state government. A permanent requirement in every department is an adequate budget. Salaries should be sufficient to attract and hold professionally educated men in appropriate positions. Many a state motor vehicle department has lost key personnel to cities, to prosperous counties, and to private agencies solely because of lower salary scales under the state budget. Another inducement for key personnel to remain would be to place all administrative, policy-making, and supervisory positions under career civil service.

## DRIVER LICENSING AND VEHICLE REGISTRATION

The legal basis for driver licensing is the state's power to enact laws for the welfare of its citizens. All states require that drivers be licensed. Driving has generally been legally interpreted as a privilege and not a right. The state sets the standards for licensing and prescribes, for the safety of its citizens, the conditions under which the driving privilege may be revoked. Most state laws also provide for cancellation or suspension of registration and surrender of license plates of a vehicle, in the interest of public safety. Driver licensing and vehicle registration have been accepted as state responsibilities throughout the country.

Whereas the registration of vehicles is an important function of government, particularly as an aid to law enforcement, it is also a source of state revenue, a fact that makes it highly unlikely that the Federal government will ever be forced to take it over by default. With license tags identifiable by state, and displaying letters and numerals that are individually recorded, vehicle identification is not difficult, and no need for centralization of the function seems evident. In fact, the increasing volume of vehicles, with the bulk of identification "look-up" cases intrastate, further centralization is contraindicated. States are increasingly turning to machine recording and selection.

The subject of driver licensing is extremely important because of its implications for the quality of performance of the *driver*, the basic factor in traffic safety. The truly complex problem in the driver licensing procedure is the examination of applicants to determine their fitness as drivers. Many people driving today recall when no examination was required to obtain a driver's license. Later, the examination was a brief ride with an examiner.

The following principles of driver licensing are quoted from *Driver License Examinations.*[1]

> Driver examining and licensing are based on principles that should be reviewed as an introduction to the material in this manual. Some of the principles involved are so essential to the driver licensing program that they have been enacted into law in most states and have been held to be constitutionally sound. All of these principles should be used to govern decisions of driver-licensing administrators in the formulation of their driver-examining and licensing programs.

[1] *Driver License Examinations,* American Association of Motor Vehicle Administrators, Washington, D.C., 1959.

1. *The state may legislate for the welfare and safety of its citizens.* The legal basis for driver licensing is found in the state's power to legislate for the welfare and safety of its citizens. Such laws may not be discriminatory and must be within the provisions of the state's constitution. Accordingly, all states require that a driver must be licensed before he can operate a motor vehicle on streets and highways. In addition, if the driver, after licensing, becomes a danger to others he may be removed by suspension or revocation of his license. In other words, the state, through its police powers, has provided legislation that permits removing from streets and highways those drivers who threaten the welfare and safety of its citizens.

   Most states require that an applicant demonstrate his knowledge of motor vehicle regulations and ability to operate a motor vehicle safely before granting the driving privilege. Because the state has responsibility for protecting users of streets and highways from harmful acts of others, it may exercise police powers by providing legislation to deny the driving privilege to all who do not pass successfully driver examinations.

   Courts have held that the state's enactment of driver licensing legislation providing for denial of the driving privilege to persons not meeting departmental requirements is a proper exercise of its police power. Adverse decisions of the courts may be expected, however, if the state has not exercised its police power judiciously and in the best interest of the public.

2. *The license to operate a motor vehicle is a privilege granted by law.* The question of the right of a citizen to receive a driver license has been the subject of repeated court decisions. In all cases,[2] the courts have held that permission to operate a motor vehicle on streets and highways is a privilege granted by the state under proper legislation, and is not an inherent right. . . . This concept is not strange or unusual, because if driving were a right, nobody would be able to control undesirable drivers through license procedures. The unsafe or unqualified driver could be prosecuted in courts for his illegal acts on streets and highways, but the state would be unable to exercise its police power for the protection of other users of the highway.

3. *Driver licensing is an administrative function of the state government.* The legislature in each state has required that drivers must be licensed but it almost universally permits an administrator to establish details regulating driver licensing. Under such arrangements, the driver license administrator may develop standards for drivers and types of examinations that would be too detailed for legislation. This right to delegate authority to administrative bodies, in this case driver license administrators, has been upheld consistently by the courts.

   In exercising the administrative function of driver licensing, most states require that each applicant for a license pass an examination to demonstrate that he has the necessary knowledge and skill to operate a motor vehicle. In addition, the state, acting through the administrator, may impose reasonable requirements or limitations on any applicant for the driving privilege. This is the basis for restrictions that are placed on drivers deficient in elements of human personality needed for the driving task.

---

[2] State supreme courts are divided on the question of whether driving is a right or a privilege. Some courts have held that driving is a privilege in the nature of a right.

FIGURE 25-2 These files contain the records of approximately 1,700,000 Maryland drivers.

4. *The state is responsible for the quality of drivers using streets and highways.* If a state grants the driver the privilege to operate on the streets and highways, the state has the responsibility to see that he is reasonably qualified to drive and that he does not become a menace to others. The state gives examinations to detect unqualified drivers, prevents such drivers from operating motor vehicles and removes drivers from the highways who can not or will not improve their driving. To the driver-license administrator, this principle is of utmost importance; the traffic safety program of his state may depend upon how well it is applied.
5. *The driver has a legal right to appeal from action of the administrator.* The driver must have a legal right to appeal from the arbitrary action of the administrator in denying the driving privilege. Driver licensing laws like the Uniform Vehicle Code provide for review of administrative action to determine that the actions of the administrator were proper. This principle is equally applicable to pre-licensing and post-licensing procedures.
6. *The driving task determines what the driver needs to know and be able to do to operate a motor vehicle.* The driving task itself, not the driver-license administrator, establishes what the driver must know and be able to do if he is to avoid arrests and accidents while operating a motor vehicle. This principle must not be disregarded when devising driver examinations or determining standards for the driver.
7. *Driver examinations are given to measure present knowledge and skill.* It is not the object of driver examinations to train drivers or to predict how good future driving will be, but rather to determine how well they

FIGURE 25-3 This part of the driver's license test requires the license applicant to turn the car completely around in the enclosed area.

can drive and understand traffic regulations at the time of the examination. It is true that the driver will learn from the examination but that is not its primary purpose.

8. *Driver examinations contribute to improved traffic safety.* There are several ways in which driver examinations improve traffic safety in areas where they are administered. The standards on which they are based must be high and they must be uniformly administered if this principle is to be realized.

*Examinations encourage drivers to increase their knowledge and skill.* The fact that an applicant will not get a license if he fails usually induces him to study and practice before he appears for the examination. This means that he will at least learn the contents of the driver manual and practice driving until he can perform in an acceptable manner. Such study and practice also creates an awareness of some problems involved in traffic safety and, it is hoped, develops an urge to assist in the solution of these problems.

*The value of the license to the driver is increased after he passes an examination.* Even though the license may not cost much, the driver will value it more if he must pass a stiff examination to obtain it. This sense of value should also cause the driver to make a serious effort to avoid driving acts that might cause loss of driving privileges.

*The driver learns from a good examination.* Often a driver develops his first appreciation of traffic safety during the examination. He learns the importance of increased knowledge and skill and their contribution to safe driving. In addition, he learns to correct errors that are detected during the examination and thus increases his contribution to traffic safety.

*Incompetent drivers are denied the driving privilege.* Driver examining is the only means available for screening out incompetent drivers prior to licensing. Otherwise, we would have to wait until incompetent drivers had difficulties before we could revoke the driving privilege. Denial of the driving privilege to incompetents is a direct contribution to traffic safety.

*Driver examining is the only means of reaching all drivers.* The vast majority of drivers will have no contacts with traffic safety officials other than those at driver examining stations because most drivers do not have arrests and accidents that result in police or court action to correct deficiencies.

9. *One license is enough.* Licensing by one state should be valid in all states. Such validity eliminates the necessity for several states independently licensing the driver and for his carrying more than one driver license certificate at any time. In practice, driver license administrators should require a driver to surrender any valid driver license certificates in his possession from other jurisdictions prior to issuance of a driver license certificate by the new jurisdiction. If an applicant formerly licensed by another state claims that he no longer has a certificate issued by that state, an affidavit to this effect should be obtained before licensing him elsewhere.

Multiple licensing, and corresponding multiple issuance of certificate, causes confusion, makes enforcement difficult, increases paperwork, and creates legal difficulties. A person need not be licensed separately as an operator and also as a chauffeur any more than he needs a separate license for each state in which he travels.

10. *Licenses should not be the same for all people.* Some people use the driving privilege for different purposes than others. Most of us want only a learner's permit at first which lets us drive with an instructor. Some people want licenses to make a business of driving. Such people who want to serve the public should meet higher standards of safety than those who only drive to transport themselves or their families, their friends and their goods. State laws generally recognize at least three kinds of licenses as the Uniform Vehicle Code does.

*Instruction permit*—a driver license issued to one to drive on streets and highways while learning to make the vehicle do what he wants it to do and how to behave in traffic. Necessary instruction must be given by a regular, licensed driver riding in the front seat with the learner, except in the cases of motorcycles and scooters.

*Operator license* permits one to operate an ordinary motor vehicle for his own pleasure or business. Such drivers might be called amateur rather than professional because they do not receive pay for driving.

*Chauffeur license* permits one to operate a motor vehicle for pay, to operate a school bus or to operate any motor vehicle used to carry people or property for compensation. Such drivers might be called professional drivers rather than amateurs.

The qualifications or standards of drivers for different kinds of licenses may also vary. The learner needs only the basic physical ability and knowledge; his license is for the purpose of obtaining skill. Professional chauffeurs can and should be required to meet higher standards. If they expect to drive big trucks with trailers, they should have skill to do so.

Differences in licenses restrict some drivers. The learner is restricted to driving with an instructor; the operator is restricted from driving for hire. Other special restrictions may be put on any driver by the administrator for safety. Such restrictions are authorized by law and may be of great variety. The most common one is the restriction to

## MOTOR VEHICLE LAW AND ADMINISTRATION

FIGURE 25-4 Some of these future drivers will learn that they need glasses to drive safely. This fact will be noted on their licenses.

drive while wearing corrective lenses for people who cannot see well enough to drive without them.

11. *Rules of safe motor vehicle operation and standards for drivers must be published.* Often legislative enactments and administrative regulations are unavailable to the general public. Even when they are available, they are sometimes difficult to understand, especially for people who do not comprehend legal terminology used to state the law or regulation.

To make it as easy as possible for drivers to know the laws and regulations that they should, the driver license administrator should provide a driver manual. It should summarize laws and regulations pertaining to motor vehicle operation, safe driving practices and other information that would help make drivers more proficient. The driver manual should be carefully written to assure easy comprehension by all drivers. Manuals must be distributed without cost for widest use especially in schools, libraries, and driver training classes.

The foregoing eleven principles, quoted from the publication of the American Association of Motor Vehicle Administrators, *Driver License Examinations,* may be considered somewhat similar in function to the *Uniform Vehicle Code*—a guide for state action.

## The Teacher as a License Examiner

Driver licensing is obviously fully accepted as a state function. A proposal has been made in a number of places which is of vital concern to driver education people. Some say that the responsibility for examination may properly be delegated by the state motor vehicle authority to another agency of government in the case of applicants best known and most easily accessible to that agency. The proposal has been made in some states—usually arising from unofficial sources—that the schools, in the persons of the driver education teachers, give driver license examinations to students who have completed the driver education course. The reasons usually given are:

1. The driver education teacher is in a better position to know the skill, knowledge, and attitude of the student than any other person could be as the result of a necessarily brief examination.
2. The driver education teacher is a fully prepared professional.
3. He also observes the driving behavior of students around the school area and has greater opportunity to know how the student behaves when not consciously under observation (as with a learner's permit, perhaps) than would the state examiner.
4. This system would relieve the time pressure felt by many examining agencies because of increasing population, insufficient personnel, and uneven seasonal loads. It would shorten the waiting time for the public and/or permit use of more time for each examination.

There are negative reactions to this proposal:

1. Some examiners have expressed the belief that the training of the examiner and that of the teacher are different, and that one preparation does not necessarily qualify a person for the other work.
2. Some driver education people see a danger of introducing local pressures to force the teacher to pass individuals. (This is hardly valid, since such pressures have failed to dominate the educational system in other subject fields.)
3. The third objection to the proposal is probably the most serious. When a state examiner *passes* an applicant as qualified to drive, he, the examiner, is a "blank face" in a uniform. He has no other identity. To all intents and purposes he *is* the state. If the newly licensed driver becomes culpably involved in a fatal accident the next day, the state's examiner is not thought of as a party to the tragedy. Place a driver education teacher in the same situation and he is a *person,* an *individual,* who put that driver on the road! The victim or victims of the accident may be students of the same school, or relatives of students, and are very likely to be members of the local community.

Even a traffic violation or series of violations by the recently licensed teen-ager could reflect on the teacher who served as license examiner, even though there may have been no way that he could have foreseen the driver's behavior.

TEMPORARY SERVICE. Suggestions have been made also that driver education teachers serve as summer license examiners when seasonal and staff vacation conditions may cause a backlog of driver license applicants at the examination points. Where school and local area people are not involved, except perhaps occasionally by chance, the conditions previously cited do not govern. Here, too, the teacher is a uniformed representative of the state.

That is his public image, not that of a local teacher—a very important difference.

As to ability, a trained specialist who is qualified to teach driver education and evaluate the progress of each student should be qualified to judge the proficiency of the license candidate. A course or briefing on the state examination procedures would be desirable, especially if such course or briefing is normally given to full-time examiners. The temporary examiner should meet the same minimum standards as the full-time personnel.

This subject has been discussed in a number of places. Driver education teachers should be aware of its implications and should be ready, whenever the question arises, to take a constructive stand, possibly through their state associations. In many areas it may never arise, since license examining and driver education are not normally considered bracketed in the same agency or with the same personnel.

In view of the desirability of extending the high school driver education program through summer vacations in order to be able to reach all students, the summer license examining proposal is not likely to be feasible where many school districts are concerned.

## DRIVER LICENSE EXAMINATION COMPONENTS

### Vision

One of the primary requirements for obtaining a driver's license is satisfactory vision. This subject is covered in detail in student textbooks. Additional data are presented for the teacher in Chapter 6, "Impairment of Driving Ability."

### Knowledge

Knowledge of traffic law and regulations and of good driving practices are subjects of written examinations. (Oral examinations may be given.) This includes the shapes and meanings of signs, the meanings of traffic signals, "rules of the road," etc. The written test should be sufficiently comprehensive to ensure that the candidate either possesses the knowledge necessary for safe, efficient driving or is given a period of time to learn it before being licensed. Peculiarly, certain jurisdictions do not inform the candidate which items he missed. In the cases of many of those who pass the test, they never do seek the correct answers to the missed questions. This is, of course, poor procedure. The test should be educational as well as evaluative as far as possible.

### Driving Skill

Driving skill is tested by having the applicant perform the various skills and maneuvers necessary to successful driving. Some states have specially designed testing areas for this "road test." Originally it consisted of a short demonstration drive by the applicant with an examiner in the car with him. In some jurisdictions this road test is still limited by time, the

FIGURE 25-5 A modern driver test range with three individual testing lanes controlled from the rooftop tower shown above the parking lot.

number of applicants often being greater than the capacity of the testing facility and personnel. Both the public and the state legislature should be kept informed of the importance of having adequate, trained personnel and up-to-date facilities for the driver license examination program.

*Psychological Factors*

There is no question about the vital role played by psychological factors in highway safety. Driver behavior is the keystone that supports or destroys the entire fabrication of highway safety. The safest road can be—and often is—the scene of fatal accidents that have no basis but bad driving. This is not to demean the important contribution of engineering, but to emphasize the sometimes unrealized significance of the driver testing function.

Testing for the psychological factors of driving offers a challenge which still defies the knowledge of today's experts. The latter are fully aware of the problem. Some states include items of *attitude* and emotion on their examination forms. In the case of "emotion," it is probable that an applicant may be sufficiently hyperemotional to be so identified by the examiner. A driver who responds to the examiner's directions or drives a car in a certain way may be said to have evidenced a poor attitude. It is, of course, far more likely that a candidate for a driver's license will behave before the examiner in a way which would at least *appear* to show an excellent attitude.

A number of research studies have been conducted over the years in which attempts were made to devise instruments for measuring attitude, including driver attitude (see Chapter 4, "Attitude and Behavior"). Although some degree of success has been claimed, no test yet exists of sufficient reliability to classify or evaluate the attitude of an *individual*. No examiner, however intelligent and well educated in the subject, can determine the attitude and future driving behavior of any reasonably intelligent individual who prefers that it not be known.

Conceivably a candidate for a driver's license can exhibit aberrations that indicate an atypical mental condition. The nature and severity of his actions may be such that refusal of a license or special testing is indicated. In the great majority of applicants for drivers' licenses, however, the mental and emotional qualities significant to driving are not evident to an observer.

CAUTION IS INDICATED. Measurement of "personality characteristics" is often claimed. The teacher is warned against acceptance of test instruments for such measurement when the results are to be identified with individuals' names. Until the subject is much better understood by research personnel and by teacher and examiner, it is a matter for laboratory investigation and not for application to individual citizens to determine their fitness to exercise a common privilege of their citizenship.

This is not to discourage research. Rather, the graduate-student teacher is encouraged to take an active part in research in the behavioral sciences concerned in driving. Just as the courts protect the individual against the weaknesses of interpretation inherent in the polygraph ("lie detector"), so it is the responsibility of *informed* traffic safety personnel to employ only those instruments and tests which have been established beyond doubt as thoroughly reliable in individual application.

In the field of psychological research in relation to driver behavior, the teacher is well advised to adopt an attitude of skepticism. A new device, instrument, scale, or test, may be justified *according to the requirements of educational or psychological research procedures. This does not mean that it can be applied to an individual and yield the truth sought.* The more reliance that is placed on previously, similarly supported instruments or techniques devised in similar research, the greater the chance there is of multiple error. Because something is called "the best we have today" is no valid reason for foisting it on an unsuspecting public. If investigators are not sure, the study should be pursued further. No recording of the names of persons serving as subjects should be made. If the procedure proves not thoroughly reliable and not completely fair to the subject individual, then it should be cast aside and study begun anew in another direction.

The infiltration of highly theoretical and unsound testing and evaluating procedures into the field of motor vehicle administration and driver education must be resisted by all well-informed personnel in those fields. Development of sound procedures, however, is a challenge to all those who are qualified. The well-prepared driver education teacher can accept this challenge and integrate existing needs into his own program of graduate education and into the research requirements for advanced degrees. The field of driver examination and evaluation offers a ready challenge.

## *Restrictions*

Some candidates for drivers' licenses will be found to be capable of driving safely under some circumstances, but not under others. For instance, a person may have his vision corrected by glasses to meet the minimum standard of vision for a driver's license. Without his glasses, driving may be hazardous. In this case, his license would be a restricted or conditional license. A statement like "to operate when wearing corrective glasses or lenses only," or possible just the words "glasses or contact lenses" would be placed on his license. The license would not be valid unless he is wearing them.

There are general restrictions also. The holder of a learner's permit may operate a vehicle only under certain conditions. An operator's license may not entitle a person to drive buses or, in some states, trucks. The purpose of restricted licenses is to permit people to drive within the limit of their ability to drive safely, but not beyond that limit. There are many kinds of restrictions.

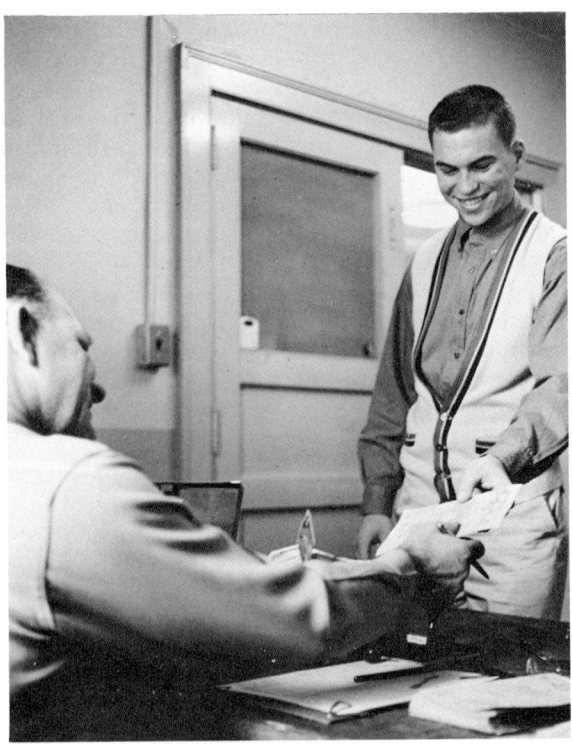

FIGURE 25-6 Big moment on L-Day.

## DRIVER IMPROVEMENT

To understand the broad meaning of the term, one must keep in mind that it refers to improvement of the level of driving by the *total population of drivers*. It ranges from *mandatory* action such as automatic revocation of a license under the law for a certain violation, to a *discretionary* action by a representative of the motor vehicle administration, such as adding a license restriction which seems needed for safety.

In some jurisdictions, driver improvement schools or clinics are maintained for examination and corrective action. Violators and accident repeaters are sometimes referred to these clinics. The various categories of driver improvement schools are described in Chapter 26, "Driver Improvement Activities."

## "Point Systems"

More than half the states have "point systems." Enforcement is better in some than in others, depending largely on the provision for personnel and facilities to implement the program. Reporting and recording all moving violations within a state and taking subsequent action in cases in which a predetermined number of points is exceeded obviously requires a special staff and facilities. A typical point-system scale is shown in Table 25-1.

Table 25-1.   TYPICAL POINT-SYSTEM SCALE*

| Offense | Points charged |
|---|---|
| Driving, or permitting another to drive, under the influence of alcohol or drugs | 12 |
| Involvement in fatal accident (if held responsible) | 12 |
| Leaving the scene of an accident | 8 |
| Reckless driving | 6 |
| Exceeding speed limit | 4 |
| Other violations | 3 |
| Three convictions within 18-month period | additional 3 |

* A driver who is charged with 12 points in a three-year period is called before the director of motor vehicles to show cause why his driving privilege should not be revoked.
SOURCE: Figure 9-10, *Sportsmanlike Driving*.

Operation of point systems varies with different states. In some states, a driver receives a warning letter after accumulating a certain number of points within a specified time. Reaching a higher number, he may be called in for an interview. Usually a maximum figure is set at which the driver is required to present a good case, or his license is suspended. Sometimes the suspension is automatic after receiving a certain number of points. After a specified period of time following a conviction, the points assessed are removed from a driver's record. The equity in this system exists in the fact that the driver "writes his own record."

When introduced, the point system was a great stride forward in driver improvement. Prior to that time the habitual violator who could well afford to pay fines was able simply to buy the privilege of breaking the law as he pleased. With the advent of the point system, a traffic law conviction took on a new meaning.

## Interstate Cooperation

It is highly desirable to report convictions of out-of-state drivers to the motor vehicle authority in the latter's home states. In some states, such reports are made. In some states, points are assigned on the basis of these

FIGURE 25-7 Officers are specially trained in instructional techniques for driver improvement work.

reports. In some, licenses are suspended for out-of-state violations if, had they occurred in the home state, they would have resulted in suspension.

Some motor vehicle authorities recommend a "one-license concept," that a driver may be licensed in only one state at a time. In spite of interstate reporting, a driver who found he was nearing the point limit might obtain another license in another state. He could then exhibit the second license when apprehended for subsequent violations. This would give him a new start in points in a second (or third or fourth) state while making it appear in his home state that he had improved.

In some states drivers are required to surrender unexpired licenses issued in other states when applying as a resident driver. The unexpired licenses are then each returned to the issuing state with a request for his previous driving record. There are, of course, still loopholes in this procedure. In some states all licenses issued to nonresidents are stamped as valid only in the issuing state. Of course, a temporary or false address can defeat this provision. Reciprocity arrangements between states for reporting and acting in out-of-state violations do help some.

## *Financial Responsibility*

All states have some form of financial responsibility laws. Three have compulsory insurance laws. Several others have an unsatisfied judgment fund type of law. Some states have laws that conform to the *Uniform Vehicle Code*[3] which recommends (page 83) that persons who have been convicted or who have forfeited bail for certain offenses under motor vehicle law and those who have failed to pay judgments arising out of ownership, maintenance, or use of motor vehicles must furnish "proof of financial

---

[3] *Uniform Vehicle Code,* National Committee on Uniform Traffic Laws and Ordinances, Washington, D.C., 1962, p. 83.

responsibility for the future." Failure to do so results in suspension of the registration or the driving privilege.

The *Uniform Vehicle Code* also provides that insurance policies or bonds to serve as such proof must cover $10,000 because of bodily injury or death of one person in any one accident, $20,000 to two or more persons, and $5,000 because of property damage in any one accident. In most states the amount of property damage is one criterion for legally required accident reports. The amount specified varies greatly among the states.

## SELECTED BIBLIOGRAPHY

A study in depth may be made with *Driver License Examinations, Motor Vehicle Administration,* and the *Uniform Vehicle Code*. The *Manual on Uniform Traffic Control Devices* and the *Model Traffic Ordinance* show design for uniformity. *Motor Carrier Safety Regulations* defines the ICC motor vehicle regulations.

Anthony, Anthony: *Suspension and Revocation of Drivers' Licenses,* Automotive Safety Foundation, Washington, D.C., 1961.

*Digest of Motor Laws,* American Automobile Association, Washington, D.C., annual.

*Driver License Examinations,* American Association of Motor Vehicle Administrators, Washington, D.C., 1959.

Hyde, Wallace N., Ed. D., Director Driver Education and Accident Records Division: *A Review of Point Systems with Recommendations for Administrative Procedures,* North Carolina Department of Motor Vehicles, Raleigh, N.C., 1959.

*Manual on Uniform Traffic Control Devices,* U.S. Government Printing Office, Washington, D.C., 1961.

*Model Traffic Ordinance,* National Committee on Uniform Traffic Laws and Ordinances, Washington, D.C., 1962.

*Motor Carrier Safety Regulations,* Interstate Commerce Commission, Bureau of Motor Carriers, Washington, D.C., 1961.

"Motor Vehicle Administration," *A Section of the Action Program,* President's Committee for Traffic Safety, Washington, D.C., 1960.

*One License Concept, The,* National Committee on Uniform Traffic Laws and Ordinances and the American Association of Motor Vehicle Administrators, Washington, D.C., 1963.

*Uniform Vehicle Code,* National Committee on Uniform Traffic Laws and Ordinances, Washington, D.C., 1962.

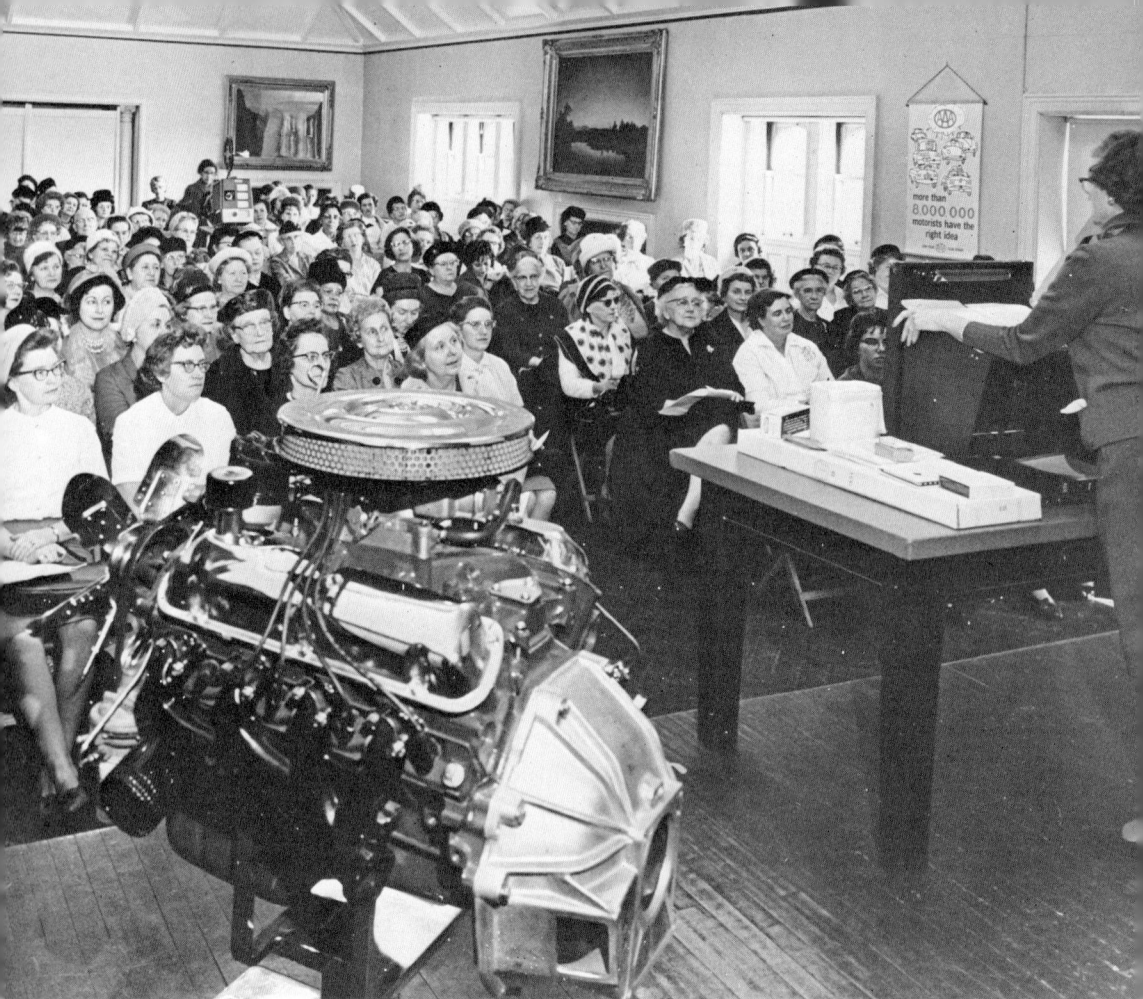

# Driver Improvement Activities 26

TO UNDERSTAND the broad meaning of the term *driver improvement,* one must keep in mind that it refers to all improvement of the level of driving by any or all of the *total population of drivers.* It ranges from mandatory action, such as automatic revocation of a license under the law for a certain violation, to the operation of schools, centers, or clinics attended by licensed drivers for the improvement of attitude, knowledge, and skills of drivers.

These schools are operated by a number of agencies and are designed for different groups of drivers. Some are operated for violators who are referred to them by traffic court judges or motor vehicle departments. Such referral is usually made with the consent of the person so assigned in lieu of a fine or other penalty. There are 200 to 300 schools to which the majority of the students are referred by traffic courts. They operate in almost all states. Other "clinics" are operated for accident repeaters. A third type of driver improvement school is the voluntary type designed for older drivers, handicapped drivers, young drivers, or just any driver who feels the need for competent instruction. These are conducted by adult schools, automobile clubs, and industrial and other institutions, public and private, which are interested in traffic accident prevention.

In the case of violators, it has become recognized that fines alone will do nothing to improve their driving if they remain ignorant of how they *should* drive, or if their attitude is poor and they can go on paying fines. Neither is the accident repeater likely to be *able* to improve his own driving practices very much without some guidance.

A considerable amount of success apparently has been achieved, measured in terms of the post-school driving records, by graduates of driver improvement schools. As yet there is a lack of valid research to evaluate the results accurately.

FIGURE 26–1 Improved driving records follow attendance at the driver improvement school for violators.

The elderly constitute a group which seem to benefit a good deal from both the testing and the instructional phases of driver improvement. Many older women, widows who having driven very little or not at all when their husbands were living, now find driving a necessity because of the location of their homes. Many old people of both sexes, bombarded with articles and stories about their failing senses, impaired coordination, and lengthened reaction time, begin to wonder if they really should be driving. It is very important to them to be able to attend a driver improvement school and learn just how well they are equipped for driving a car in modern traffic. Some leave the school with their knowledge of driving brought up to date. Some learn of previously unrealized deficiencies and how to correct them. Some are warned of serious or even dangerous deficiencies that should limit their driving, possibly to daylight hours. Some, of course, may find that they just should not drive at all.

## THE SCHOOL PLAN

Before studying "plans" of driver improvement schools, it should be recognized that there is no general pattern. The movement is growing in what must be admitted is as yet a disorganized, nonuniform manner. Procedures mentioned in this chapter may apply wholely or in part to one school, center or clinic. They may not apply to another.

Also, although our knowledge of the potential impact of the education of drivers tells us that the principle of the driver improvement school is sound, we must admit that we have no nationwide evaluation objectively established, as yet. As in the cases of practically all techniques of education, the majority of reports emanate from the agencies and individuals who use these techniques. This method does not make for objectivity in reporting. The teacher should keep this in mind when reviewing evaluative reports. Probably a thorough objective analysis of driver improvement schools would show a full curve from the very poor to the highly successful. It is known that one state gives a 1½-hour group lecture and film, and another provides 18 to 24 hours of instruction. Some use certified teachers; some do not.

It should be safe to assume that when sound principles of education are applied, the driver improvement school will be successful. It is simply an extension of driver education to out-of-school populations, keeping in mind that teaching procedures appropriate for adults may differ from those for teen-agers. In many cases, high school driver education teachers serve as instructors in those schools. In some, judges, police officers, motor vehicle department personnel, and civilian instructors do the teaching.

In this and in future reading on the subject of driver improvement schools, these facts should be kept in mind. All schools are not brilliant successes. Neither are all failures. "They," as an institution, are sound in principle and offer a hope of considerable constructive effect, the degree and nature of that effect depending on the soundness of the educational procedures in each school. The principle of the driver improvement school is sound, as education is sound.

### Phases of the Driver Improvement School Course

The driver improvement school concept usually includes three general procedures: diagnostic testing, correction, and instruction. The standard battery of psychophysical tests may be administered. When some deficiency is identified, the student is advised of it and a corrective procedure is recommended. A simple example would be impairment of visual acuity, detected by means of a test such as the Snellen chart. Correction may be made by issuance of a conditional license requiring the wearing of glasses while driving. Another example is the case of a woman who had merely turned her head toward one side or the other when she wanted vision in that direction, until one day—failing to look—she was involved in an accident. After identification of the trouble, she learned to adopt a systematic process of glancing left and right to compensate for the "tunnel vision" deficiency. (Incidentally, in this case the diagnostic procedure led to a later medical diagnosis which detected a serious condition—in time to correct it.)

"Psychophysical" tests measuring characteristics directly concerned with driving have become fairly common procedure in driver improvement. The equipment used is standardized in character and has been used in high school driver education for quite a few years.

## Psychological Tests

"Psychological" testing in driver improvement, however, is comparatively new. Although some psychological testing instruments (Siebrecht Attitude Scale, etc.) have been known for a considerable time, new procedures are in use and others are being developed. This is an area in which a word of caution is in order.

Psychological testing is not an exact science. Some even hesitate to classify it among the sciences at all, at least as yet. Some "instruments" have shown some degree of reliability in measurement of qualities in sizable groups of people. This is not to say, however, that these same instruments can be successfully applied to individual drivers, to classify them in terms of their accident or violations potential. Some people concerned with the handling of problem drivers have expressed hope of a breakthrough in this field. A few have expressed a belief that psychological testing can now identify the future driving behavior of the individual license applicant. Some statements have come very close to wishful thinking.

The driver education teacher should be sure to *avoid endorsement* of techniques which may be rated as having evidenced statistical "significance" but which might easily do great injustice if used to evaluate qualities of individual drivers, by name. This is not to discourage research, but rather to emphasize the principles of true research, requiring that any procedure to be applied to human beings, and designed to be interpreted as a measurement of individuals, *first* be established as thoroughly sound *beyond any reasonable doubt*. We are not justified in placing any discriminatory restriction on the driving privilege of any person, on the basis of a test or rating scale which may identify *group* trends, but which is not surely reliable in every *individual* case.

The effects of driver improvement work, then, are generally successful, but not evenly so in all areas. In the standard psychophysical testing procedures, it has been quite successful. In the matter of instruction, it seems to have been successful also. The purely psychological aspects of the improvement program might be said to be in an experimental stage and should be considered from that standpoint rather than as an established procedure, good or bad.

## *Instruction*

In addition to testing, instruction is an important feature of the driver improvement program. Many of today's drivers secured their licenses when knowledge-type examinations were not required in their states. In some states the knowledge requirement has since been upgraded, in keeping with the increased complexity of the driving task. It is always important to include in the driver improvement activity some instruction in that body of knowledge in which the student's driving record has indicated his deficiency.

One of the features of the driver improvement program is recognition of the attitude factor in driving and an attempt to influence that factor. Various methods are employed. Discussion techniques, films designed for attitude effect, and factual presentation of the traffic and accident picture are used.

FIGURE 26-2 Good instruction is the chief requirement for success in driver improvement schools.

Probably the most critical feature in determining the success or failure of the driver improvement school is the quality of instruction. Regardless of the type of operating agency, the instructors should be selected for their ability to teach and to lead. The best source of instructor material is in the field of high school and college driver education. Such instructors are trained, professional teachers. It is, of course, not always possible to obtain them. Police or motor vehicle personnel are sometimes assigned the teaching duty. When this is the case, selection should be very carefully made. Instructors should *believe* in the activity and should demonstrate a plausible enthusiasm for their mission. They should be selected for their ability to instruct. They should be trained in methods of instruction and the use of teaching aids. No atmosphere of "guarding," punishment, or imprisonment should exist in the schoolroom. A court order can require attendance, but it cannot compel learning or a change of attitude. The instructor must accomplish them. The atmosphere must be favorable to accomplishment of this mission.

Outside resource people may be used to good advantage. The identification of the "specialist" adds to the confidence of the students, and the resource person may also make a unique contribution. Instructors who are not professional teachers of the subject are best prepared for this assignment by completion of the same college courses as teachers preparing for certification in the field. Arrangements for admission of these nonmatriculated students to these courses can be arranged with the college by the agency sponsoring the driver improvement school.

## Policies

Certain features are significant in determining the success of a driver improvement program. In the case of the school for violators, it is considered desirable that attendance be voluntary but failure to attend be penalized. In the case of accident repeaters, attendance is usually required. Care should be exercised in determining the criteria for compulsory attendance of these groups. Some standards have been more appropriate than others.

One state required *all* drivers who had been *involved* in two accidents within a stated period to attend a "clinic." Perhaps the difficulty of determining responsibility for an accident, with a desire to avoid even an appearance of discrimination, caused the authorities to establish this blanket requirement. Obviously, it did little to improve attitude or respect for

FIGURE 26-3 Driver improvement lessons can be broadcast to all television viewers.

authority, to require drivers whose cars were hit while parked to spend their time having their eyes, driving, and knowledge checked. Later, owners of cars struck while parked were exempt, but many whose cars were struck from the rear while properly awaiting a light change were called in. This also had some doubtful results.

In another case, drivers over a prescribed chronological age who were involved in an accident were required to attend driver improvement schools. This procedure was of rather doubtful value in many cases and later had to be discontinued. Great care should be taken in determining who shall be *required* to attend such schools.

Wherever the schools are intended for volunteer students, the name "violators' schools" should not be used, even if two or more schools are being conducted separately. People don't like to *risk* being thought of as violators because of the association of the name. "Schools," too, is more acceptable than "clinics" to most people.

In all, the driver improvement school has become a permanent institution and, properly conducted, it contributes measurably to the many-faceted area of improvement of performance of the driving population.

## The Driver Improvement School of Denver

An example of a driver improvement school is that conducted in Denver, Colorado. The following is excerpted from a description of that school, one of the more widely known, founded by District Judge Sherman G. Finesilver, who serves as its unpaid director:

> The Denver Driver Improvement·School was founded in 1959. Nearly 25,000 students—both violators and volunteers—have attended its classes. Students attend six evening classes held on Tuesday and Thursday evenings from 7 to 9 P.M.; classes are conducted at Opportunity School—an evening vocational school in Denver's downtown district. The school operates without a budget, and instructors serve on a volunteer basis. . . .
> 
> A recent survey completed by the University of Denver Statistical Department indicated that over 90 percent of the graduates of the school enjoyed an unblemished driving record for a four-year period or longer after completing the school.
> 
> The School presents a practical and understandable basic program easily accessible to Colorado residents. Traffic safety and adult driver education are presented in an interesting and thought-provoking manner. Graphic demonstrations and meaningful visual aids are extensively used.
> 
> The course stresses instruction in recognizing the common causes of accidents and how to prevent potential accidents. The course content has proved of value to the beginning driver, the experienced driver, and the would-be driver. The subject matter consists of the techniques of motor vehicle operation, winter and mountain driving, safe driving practices, and extensive review of state and city traffic laws. There is no behind-the-wheel instruction other than the operation by each student of a driving simulator and reaction tester.
> 
> The school is not limited to traffic violators. Many volunteers attend. No class or attendance fee is charged for attendance. The age of those attending ranges from 14 to 86 years.

Students successfully completing the course do not have to take the written examination when applying for Colorado operator's licenses.

As an outgrowth of the success of the Denver school, extensive traffic safety and driver improvement seminars affecting every segment of the driving population have been conducted by the school's faculty throughout Colorado. The effectiveness of the Denver school has been the impetus for formation of other similar schools throughout the state and country.

Among many others, these lifesaving programs have been instituted and regularly conducted on an annual basis for cadets at the United States Air Force Academy and at Lowry and Ent Air Force Bases, and other military installations. Yearly seminars are also conducted at the Federal Correctional Institution (for teen-age offenders of Federal laws). Seminars and traffic safety leadership institutes have also been conducted before public and parochial high school students throughout the State of Colorado. The School was the first in the country to develop an annual driver education program for adult deaf drivers, and for drivers over 65 years of age.

There are many other excellent driver improvement schools throughout the country, including the Driver Improvement Clinics conducted by the North Carolina Department of Motor Vehicles and the Traffic School conducted by the Police Department in the District of Columbia.

## TWO NATIONWIDE PROGRAMS

The National Safety Council instituted a driver improvement program in 1964. A pilot program in Toledo-Lucas County, Ohio, launched the project. Training methods used by commercial vehicle fleets were the basic course techniques. Kinescopes were made during that course which served as the nucleus for the design of the nationwide program. The plan calls for "cooperating agencies," local safety councils or associations, to serve as sources of supply for films and other teaching aids and registries of certified instructors.

Any voluntary local group may become a "course sponsor" in arranging a course for its members and others. Instructors become certified by the National Safety Council by completing the basic Driver Improvement Course. The course is standardized by adherence to a detailed instructor's manual and by the fact that only instructors certified by the Council are used. The course is open to licensed private motorists and to professional drivers of small fleets where training facilities do not exist.

Another already extensive driver improvement program is that conducted by the clubs of the American Automobile Association. Courses for teen-agers, experienced drivers, violators, emergency drivers, other special groups, and for drivers in general are given. Courses in conventional driving are common, and special subjects are offered such as freeway driving, car maintenance (including courses for women), and others. This is one of the oldest and most extensive driver improvement activities existing today.

In all, a great deal of time, money, and effort are devoted to driver improvement activities today, most of it directed to adult groups who are past the age at which the benefits of high school driver education can be given them. As one teacher expressed it, "Even if we reach all teen-agers with driver education, we'll still have to do something to save them from the adult drivers." The "something" is being done in the driver improvement schools of the country.

## SELECTED BIBLIOGRAPHY

Fletcher, Harry D.: *Driver Improvement Schools—A Guide for Their Operation*, American Automobile Association, Washington, D.C., 1963.

*Summary, Conclusions, and Recommendations of a Psychological Comparison of Violator and Non-Violator Automobile Drivers in the 16 to 19 Year Age Group*, Safety Research and Education Project, Teachers College, Columbia University, New York, September, 1960.

Tossell, Richard: "Meeting the Educational Needs of Traffic Violators in Driver Improvement Schools," doctoral dissertation, New York University, New York, 1962.

# Safety Features of Automobiles

# 27

INTENSIVE research and competition among manufacturers have resulted in the production of a car far superior to that built 20 or 30 years ago. This does not mean that the present car is perfect or that there have been no backward steps. For example, stability has been increased by lowering the center of gravity. However, this has lowered the position of the driver so that he cannot see as well over hills.

The major reason for discussing car construction in a driver education course is to impress on students the many safety features that are available or can be incorporated in current-model cars. It is hoped that once a generation of new drivers is impressed with the importance of these features, they will insist on having them when purchasing a new car. In evaluating modern changes in car design and equipment, we must be careful to distinguish between those changes made to sell cars and those changes which make a safer car. Consumer education is necessary, and the driver education teacher is the most appropriate person to give that instruction.

Many safety features necessarily are a compromise. Narrow pillars increase visibility but are weaker in case of a roll-over. Wraparound windshields supposedly increase the driver's field of view. Actually the windshield has nothing to do with this, it is the location of the door pillars, and moving the door pillars only moves the blind spot farther back. Colored windshields reduce the heat transmitted on a bright, hot day but reduce visibility at night, especially if the color is dark. Cost is an important item. A certain device might prevent a few accidents, but the cost of putting it on all cars may be excessive for the good accomplished. The same amount of money spent on some other feature might accomplish much more.

The Federal government is taking an active interest in safety as related to the cars it buys. The General Services Administration bought some 47,200 vehicles for Federal government use in 1964. These do not include military vehicles. Specifications are being revised; a few of the safety features being considered include: (1) seat belts, (2) padded instrument panel, (3) recessed instrument panel and control devices, (4) impact-absorbing steering wheel and column, (5) stronger door latches, (6) four-way flashing lights for disabled vehicles, (7) safety glass, (8) uniform bumper heights, (9) standard gear selector lever positions, (10) better tires, and (11) outside rearview mirrors.

The Federal Trade Commission is also interested in the subject. Specifically the Commission is investigating the possibility of better labeling of tires so that the purchaser will have a more intelligent idea of what he is getting for his money. With the current confusion of names, the buyer is hard put to tell the difference between a $15 tire and a $25 tire. To make an intelligent selection, the consumer needs to know how well the tire will stand

FIGURE 27-1  How best to build a strong box?

up under high-speed driving, how well it will resist rupture, how well it will wear, how resistant it is to skidding, etc. Standardized quality or class ratings might be the answer (class A, B, C, etc.)

In developing a safe car, two major factors must be considered. First, the car should be designed in such a manner that the driver will be better able to avoid accidents. This involves such items as better visibility, better brakes, better maneuverability, sound weight distribution, and mechanical design that will reduce mechanical failure. The safest car is the one with which the driver can most easily avoid accidents.

The second major problem is to design a car that will protect the driver and passengers, when an accident is unavoidable. This means better packaging or the building of a strong "box" that will keep the occupants in the car, and an interior design that will reduce injuries caused by persons being thrown about inside the vehicle. *In almost every accident, there are two collisions.* First, the car collides with another car or some other object. At this point, considerable property damage may result, but the passengers are not affected. The second collision occurs when the passengers are thrown out of the car or against its interior. The resulting injuries are caused primarily by the passengers hitting unyielding surfaces, which results in excessive deceleration of various parts of the body. Restraining devices such as seat belts and harnesses and energy-absorbing features such as padded instrument panels are designed to reduce the severity of injuries.

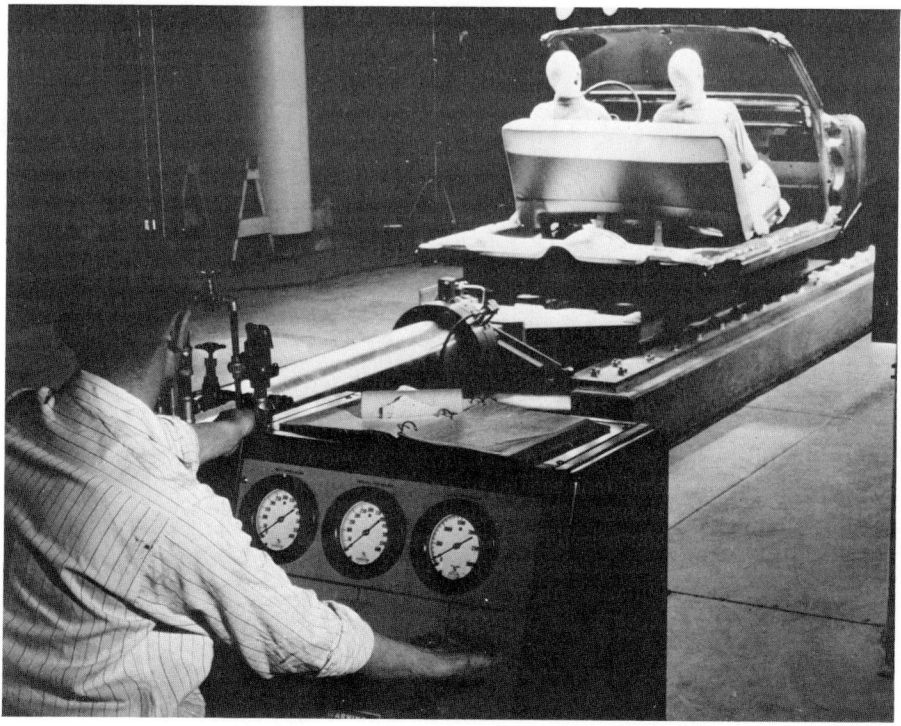

FIGURE 27-2  The impact sled tests the safety implications of the "second collision."

## VISIBILITY

In general, visibility has been greatly improved except that in late-model cars the driver's eyes are nearer the road surface so that his vision over hilltops is more restricted, particularly in low sport cars. Also because of the low position, the driver has more difficulty seeing small objects on the road surface near the car. A good project to emphasize this fact is to place a student behind the wheel of a car while another student outlines on the pavement the limits of the surface which cannot be seen from the driver's position. Other cars can be placed on the same spot for comparative purposes.

Visibility forward has been improved by moving the door pillars back with reference to the driver in order to give a wider view ahead. Pillars have also been made narrower to reduce the width of the blind spot they cause. In this connection, if outside mirrors are used, they should be mounted above or below eye level to avoid adding another blind spot.

The use of wraparound windshields is not an unmixed blessing. The ends produce a certain amount of distortion and are difficult to clean properly by the windshield wipers. Flexible wiper blades have replaced the rigid blade better to clear the curved windshields. Electrically driven windshield wipers provide a constant speed, whereas the vacuum-operated wipers slow down when the engine is under heavy load, as when going up a steep grade. Windshield washers, a relatively new addition, make it possible for the wipers to clean the glass when mud is splashed on it after the rain has ceased.

Unfortunately, body designing has not always allocated adequate consideration to visibility. Long hoods, wide front fenders, and large tail fins leave much to be desired in seeing the ground immediately around the car. This visibility is important when parking or when on one's own driveway where children or their toys are likely to be present.

Higher speeds require greater visibility distances at night. Headlights have been greatly improved, but lighting at night is still inadequate under many conditions. The introduction of the sealed-beam headlights in 1939 was a great advance. The problem of keeping the lamps in focus was eliminated. Aiming was greatly simplified, and deterioration of the reflecting surface was practically eliminated. In 1956, aiming pads on the lamps further simplified the aiming problem. The dual headlighting system introduced on 1957 models provided more light and better beam patterns. Unfortunately, increasing the light intensity alone is not the complete answer. Each time the light intensity is increased, the glare problem is also increased.

Communication among drivers by means of turn signals and stoplights still leaves much to be desired. Amber turn signals in the front of the car represent a step forward. They have greater attention value and are less likely to be confused with other white lights. Taillights and stoplights should give a clear unmistakable indication of the intention of the lead driver to the following driver. These indicators should be uniform and so clearly different that they can be easily understood. The wide variation in taillights and stoplights with respect to shape, size, intensity, and location on modern cars hardly meets these requirements. In too many cases it is

FIGURE 27-3 Headlight improvement. In both photos lights are on lower beam. The photo above shows light from original sealed beam headlamp. The photo below shows light from four-headlamp system.

impossible for the following driver to tell if the lead car is braking unless he is looking at the rear lights of the car ahead at the instant the brakes are applied. All exterior vehicle lights should be designed to see by and to be seen and not as elements of style or decoration.

Narrower front corner pillars in general and a larger rear window in particular have greatly increased the driver's vision. An important added

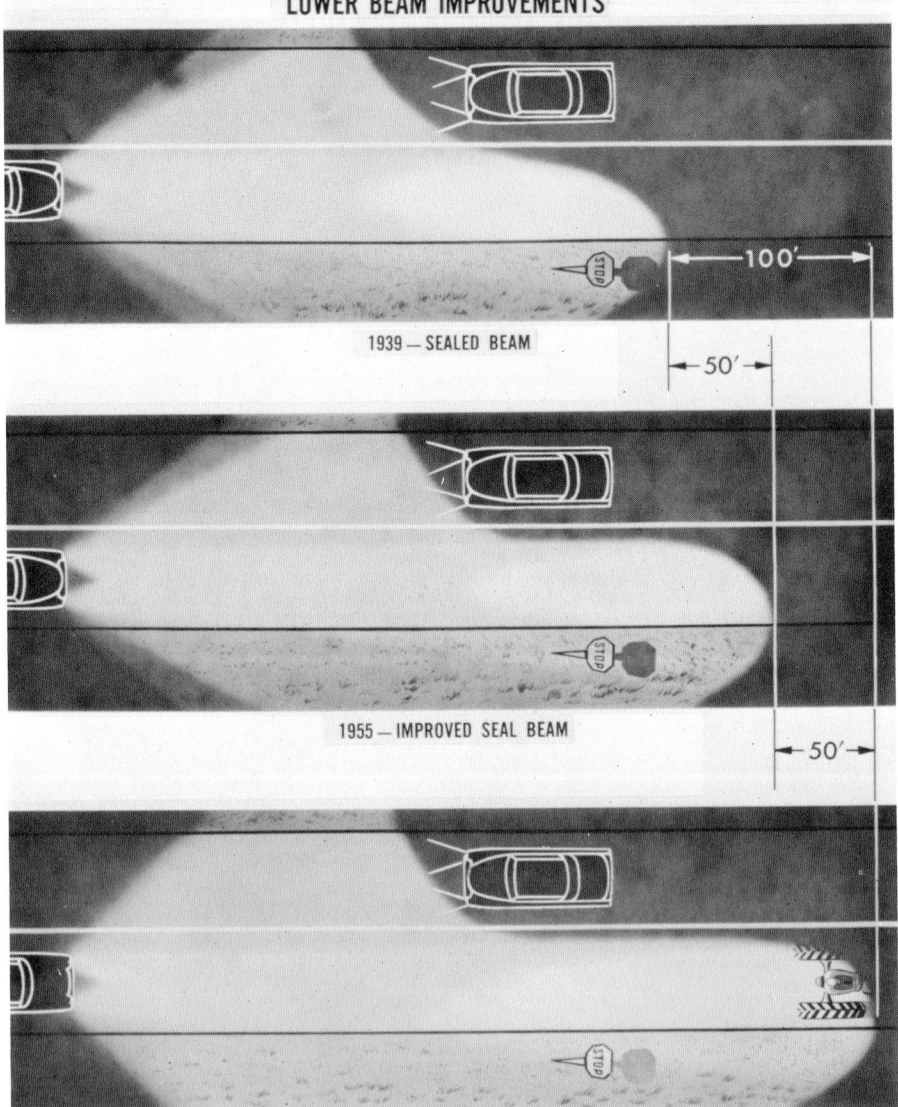

FIGURE 27-4

advantage to the larger rear window is the ability of a driver to "see through" several cars ahead. This is a significant factor in reducing the possibility of rear-end collisions. The driver has more advance warning of a sudden stop since he can observe the actions of a driver two or three vehicles ahead and does not have to wait for the stoplights of the vehicle immediately ahead to come on.

## CONTROLLABILITY

The previous sections have dealt with advances in automotive engineering which enable a driver better to see hazardous situations in the making so that he has more time to take evasive action. Advances have also been made which enable the driver to start, stop, and steer a car more effectively so as to avoid a collision or to decrease the impact if the collision cannot be avoided. Fortunately, a low center of gravity not only makes a better looking car but results in a car less easily overturned when making a sharp turn or going into the ditch to avoid a collision.

The steering mechanism has been greatly improved over the years so that the driver has more effective control and in an emergency can maneuver more readily to avoid trouble. Increased size and weight of the modern car have partially canceled the gains of better steering systems. Partly to overcome this problem, as well as to make driving easier, power steering was introduced in 1951. Although some hazards are involved, especially for the driver unfamiliar with power steering, there are several distinct advantages. It requires less effort and is therefore less fatiguing. Power steering enables the driver to retain effective control when certain forces on the front wheels are greatly increased. This occurs in the case of a blowout, when the wheels drop off the edge of the pavement, or when a front wheel hits a hole or bump in the road. However, the driver education teacher should be sure to emphasize to students the infrequent, but frightening, condition when the motor dies and there is no longer power steering. Immediately it seems as though it is impossible to steer—actually it is very much harder to steer. If this occurs while the car is moving, the driver should avoid panic. He should put the selector level at neutral and restart the engine.

In most cases, an accident could be avoided if a driver could stop soon enough. Unfortunately, physical laws make it impossible to eliminate the stopping distance (reaction distance plus braking distance). However, research and mechanical improvements over the years have greatly reduced the braking distance.

Braking effectiveness was practically doubled when four-wheel brakes were introduced in 1923. Hydraulic brakes, introduced later, further increased braking efficiency substantially. The introduction of power brakes reduced the effort required to apply the brakes, though braking distances were not materially affected. The lower pedal usually used with power brakes reduces slightly the time required to get the foot on the brake pedal. Self-adjusting brakes introduced in recent years help to compensate for the shortcomings of many owners who fail to maintain their brakes properly.

Frequent stops from high speeds with heavy cars put an excessive load on the brakes. To meet these more severe conditions, disk brakes have been developed and were used on ten models of American cars in 1965. The most effective braking and steering control is obtained when the wheels are just at the point of skidding but not actually skidding. Considerable research has been done and devices have been developed which will hold the wheels at the point of impending skid. Probably the major factor preventing the general use of such desirable devices (which are used on airplanes) is the cost.

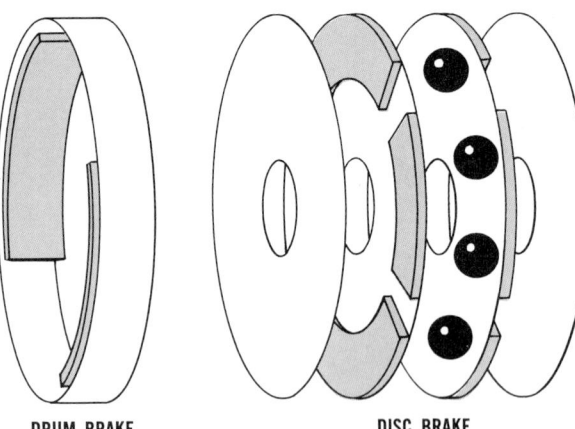

FIGURE 27-5 The "disc" brake permits greater braking surfaces than the older "drum" brake.

Another safety feature recently introduced is the split or dual brake system. At least two American manufacturers factory-install such a braking system. In the more common hydraulic brake system, a rupture in any part of the system will result in the loss of brake fluid and the loss of braking force on all four wheels. Although this does not happen often, it can be very serious if the rupture occurs when a driver slams on his brakes to avoid a collision. Basically, the split or dual system involves one brake system for the front wheels and one for the rear wheels; so that if either fails the other is still intact and brakes are still operating on two wheels. The cost of this split or dual system is not great, but one objection is that one system may fail without the driver being aware of it.

In addition to the ability of brakes to stop the wheels, the braking distance is also controlled by the friction between the tires and road surface. This becomes especially important where wet, snow, or icy conditions exist. Snow tires in use for many years have some advantage over regular tires in snow. A new development has been the use of studded tires. About **80 to 100** tungsten-carbide studs are inserted in the tire tread and protrude about $\frac{1}{32}$ inch to give a better grip on ice. Preliminary tests on ice indicate a substantial improvement over regular snow tires. Because the studs do extend slightly beyond the tire surface and thus may do some damage to the pavement, their legal status in many states is questionable.

## *STABILITY*

Many injuries result when a vehicle overturns or rolls over and passengers are thrown about inside. Developments in car design over the years have reduced the likelihood of overturning. A lower center of gravity and wide track design have increased the side force necessary before a car will turn over. Streamlining and a lower silhouette have reduced the effect of side winds. Softer tires, shock absorbers, and better springs have reduced the bounce effect on the car body itself when going over rough roads.

In some cars, traction on the rear wheels has been increased by placing the motor in the rear and thus increasing the weight on the driving wheels. This is not an unmixed blessing as it brings with it some additional prob-

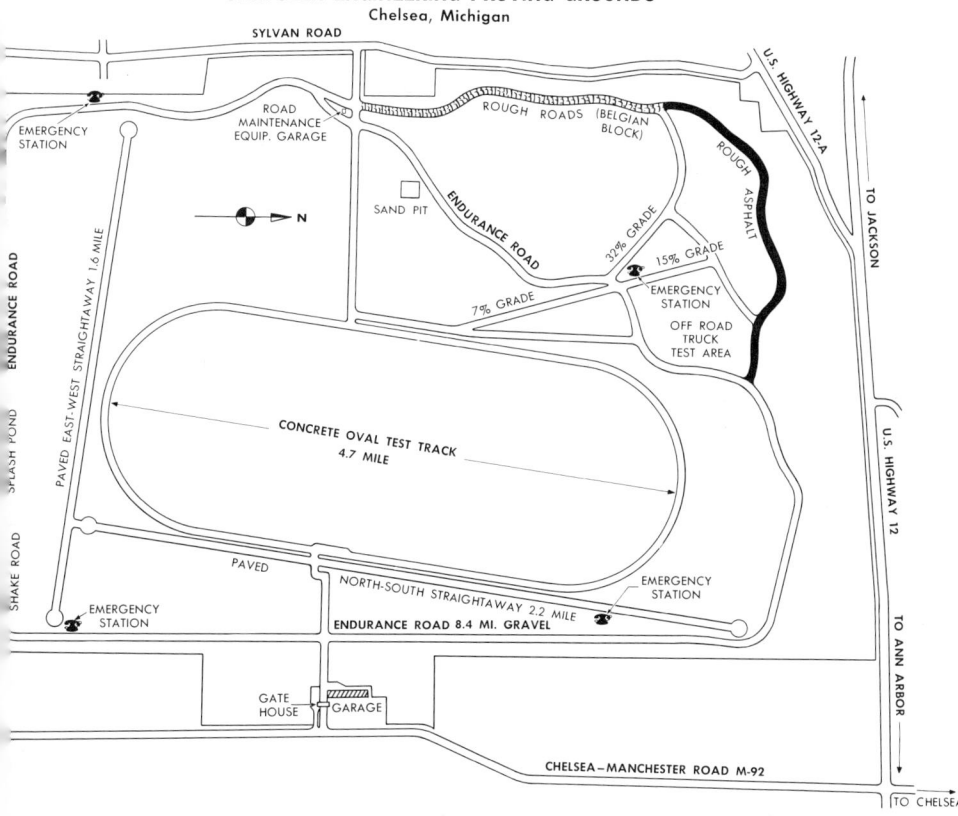

FIGURE 27-6 Extensive testing is done under all types of road conditions.

lems. It makes the vehicle more susceptible to side winds and less stable in going around curves. This difficulty is overcome to a large extent by substantially increasing the air pressure in the rear tires. This again presents another danger, if the tires are rotated and the air pressure is not adjusted accordingly. This hazard should be pointed out so that anyone rotating tires on a rear-engine car can make sure that the air pressures are correct after the tires are rotated.

Roll-over bars are used in racing cars to protect the driver in case the car rolls over. The incorporation of roll-over bars in regular passenger cars would further increase the safety of the car in case of roll-over. This protection is also accomplished, in part, by new designs which strengthen the side pillars and the roof of the modern automobile.

## MECHANICAL DURABILITY

Some mechanical failures are costly and very inconvenient but have little effect on the safety of the car occupants. An example of this is engine failure at midnight in a desert on a road 40 miles from nowhere.

One of the early improvements on the automobile that saved many a broken arm was the electric starter introduced in 1912.

As far as accidents are concerned, it is the sudden, unexpected failure of brakes or steering that is serious. If brakes slowly get poorer, the driver tends to compensate by driving slower and allowing longer following distances. However, if the brakes fail suddenly, there is little he can do to compensate. There have been several developments to reduce the possibility of sudden mechanical failure. The split or dual brake system has been previously discussed. This enables the driver to retain about half the braking effectiveness in case of a failure.

Tire quality has been greatly improved to reduce the chance of sudden blowouts. Safety tires provide an extra fully inflated inner tire or tube to retain air in case of a puncture of the regular tire. Tubeless tires run cooler and thus reduce the possibility of blowout because of excessive heat. In case of puncture, tubeless tires lose air more slowly than tube tires and thus give the driver more of a warning that his tire is going flat. Safety rims reduce the possibility of a tire rolling off or losing air on sharp turns at high speeds. The Rubber Manufacturers Association has adopted minimum standards for tires which include among other items resistance to rupture and the ability to stand up under extended high-speed driving.

Sudden steering failures have been reduced by better design and better facilities for lubrication to reduce wear at critical points. Power steering is so designed that if the power fails the driver can still steer, though much greater effort is required.

## *PROTECTIVE PACKAGING*

The previous discussion has been devoted to design features which help a driver avoid an accident. There are a number of features which affect the seriousness of injuries once an accident has occurred.

The automobile may be considered as a strong "box," built to keep foreign objects from penetrating the car and secure enough to keep the occupants in the car. Research has shown that for comparable accidents it is much safer to remain in the car than to be thrown out. The all-steel body, developed years ago and continuously improved, has done much to provide the strong box. Many controlled crashes have been conducted by Cornell University, the University of California at Los Angeles, and the automobile manufacturers to determine where weak points exist.

Laminated safety glass in the windshield has a plastic inner layer which reduces the flying of sharp pieces of glass in case of collision. But this type of glass still shatters so as to produce sharp daggerlike pieces. Tempered safety glass is not used in windshields in the United States, chiefly because the glass when broken shatters into small irregular pieces which may stay in place and so make it almost impossible to see through.

For years, laminated safety glass was used in the side and rear windows. In recent years, manufacturing processes for tempered safety glass have been greatly improved so that now such glass is generally used in the side and rear windows. Extensive investigations have been made to determine if, for comparable accidents, injuries were more serious with one type of safety glass than with the other. Although the research has been thorough and extensive, there is no evidence to date to indicate that one type of glass is significantly better than the other in reducing the seriousness of injuries.

Since it is safer to remain in a car, considerable work has been done to develop door latches which will keep the doors closed in case of collision. The first designs of an improved latch reduced door openings in collisions by 33 percent. Later, further improved latches reduced door openings by 40 percent.

Assuming that the car is built to prevent external objects from entering and the passengers from being thrown out, the next step is to reduce damage to the occupant in the second collision—the collision of the occupant with the inside of the car. The severity of this second collision can be lessened if the deceleration rate is reduced. Energy-absorbing bumpers would help, especially in head-on or rear-end collisions, but space limitations, mechanical problems, and the cost of suitable devices have prevented the development of anything very effective to date. As the metal collapses in the first collision, the entire front end of the car acts as an energy-absorbing element and reduces the severity of the impact of the second collision.

Seat belts have been found to be an effective restraining device to keep occupants in the car. Since January 1, 1964, they have been included in most new American cars as a delete option. In other words, they are supplied unless the customer specifically states that he wants the car without seat belts. In accidents in which seat belts were in use, serious and fatal injuries were reduced about 35 percent. It is interesting to note that the chief value of the seat belt was to keep the occupant in the car. In later studies of injuries sustained for comparable accidents where the occupant remained in the car, the lap belt did not exert a strong effect on injury reduction. Shoulder harnesses combined with seat belts will probably be more effective, but a lack of pertinent accident data prevents an evaluation of their effectiveness.

As one approach to the injury problem, Cornell University Aeronautical Laboratory analyzed accidents involving 1956–1961 cars, when seat belts were not used, to determine the injury-producing features of the car. The leading causes of injury, listed in order, were:

1. Instrument panel
2. Steering assembly
3. Windshield
4. Door structures
5. Ejection

As a result of this study, several improvements in design were made. Control knobs were recessed and padded instrument panels made available. The deep-dish steering wheel was developed to reduce injuries caused when the steering wheel collapsed and the driver came into contact with the end of the steering column. To date little has been done with the windshield. If seat belts are used, moving the windshield farther forward will help. It is possible that new materials may eventually be developed to replace the glass currently used.

Some advances have been made in the design of doors and instrument

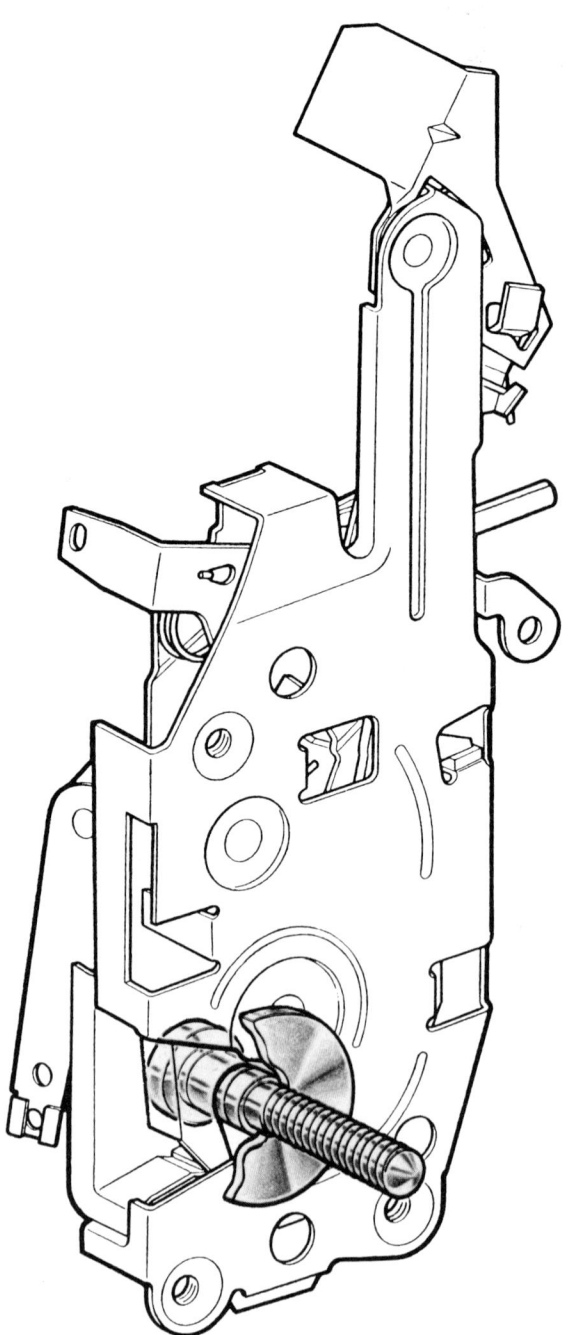

FIGURE 27-7 New interlock device for car doors. The darker or shaded portion on the drawing is the post which is fastened onto the door hinge pillar of the car body. The other mechanism is the interlock device which is located on the door edge. When the car door is closed, the two parts become engaged and the flange on the end of the post is completely interlocked all the way around.

panels to reduce or eliminate projecting knobs. The greatest improvement has been in the development of door latches which are now much more effective in keeping the occupants in the car where the likelihood of serious injury is greatly reduced.

Looking to the future, additional safety features have been proposed. In a serious head-on collision the steering column is sometimes pushed farther into the driver's compartment. Several designs, including a collapsible steering column, have been proposed and are being tested.

Substantial integrated seats, well anchored, would do much to keep the passengers in place in case of a collision.

Even when seat belts are used, many injuries are caused by the passenger hitting the instrument panel or windshield on the right side. Moving the windshield forward and removing the right-hand panel would reduce these injuries.

In summary, much has been done and much more can be done in the design of safer cars. However, these safety features will not be available unless the buying public demands them. The driver education teacher is in an excellent position to give young drivers a knowledge and an understanding of the value of various features which are or can be made available if demanded by the buying public.

## *SELECTED BIBLIOGRAPHY*

Campbell, Dr. Horace E.: *45 Steps to Safer Cars,* Consumer Bulletin, Consumers' Research, Inc., Washington, N.J., 1964, 30–32 pp.

Chayne, Charles A.: *Automotive Design Contributions to Highway Safety,* The Annals of the American Academy of Political and Social Science, November, 1958.

*Consumer Guide to Automotive Safety Features,* Automotive Safety Engineering Office, Chrysler Corporation, P. O. Box 1118, Detroit, Mich., 1964, 46 pp.

*The Safety the Motorist Gets,* Society of Automotive Engineers, Inc., 485 Lexington Avenue, New York 17, N.Y., 1959, 37 pp.

*Today's Motor Vehicle Showcase for Safety,* Automobile Manufacturers Association, 320 New Center Building, Detroit, Mich., 1963, 8 pp.

Wolf, Robert A.: *Four Proposals for Improving Automobile Crashworthiness,* Cornell Aeronautical Laboratory, Inc., Buffalo, N.Y., 1964, 30 pp.

# Automobile Maintenance 28

THE MODERN automobile is a very efficient and highly complex machine. To many people, unfamiliar with its principles and its machinery, it is a modern magic carpet, needing only a continuing supply of gasoline to keep running until its style looks "old." Then it is turned in for a new model, and the new magic carpet becomes a part-of-the-time home on wheels.

On the rare occasions when the engine fails and the power to move is partly or completely lost, the possibility of mechanical failure becomes evident and is recognized. The more significant fact that often escapes recognition is this: *Engine failure that causes automobiles to stop or to lose power noticeably includes only a small part of the great number of mechanical failures that do occur. The most significant failures are those which* affect the parts of the car concerned with safety including those which affect steering, braking, and visibility.

For example, a kink or obstruction in the hydraulic brake line can cause a *delay* in the reaction of the brakes, following pressure on the brake pedal. Assuming a common freeway speed of 60 miles per hour and a delay of half a second, the car will travel *44* feet before the brakes even *start* to grip. This adds 44 feet to the stopping distance. As a point of interest in connection with maintenance and vehicle inspection, this delay has been found to amount to as much as four or five seconds in the case of tractor trailers, or at 60 miles per hour as much as 440 feet, or the length of 4.4 football playing fields before the brakes *start* to act!

This is but one of the lesser known mechanical deficiencies which have very serious implications for the safety of the occupants of a motor vehicle, and of all persons wherever it is operated. Mechanical trouble ranges from a slight maladjustment of a headlight to a sudden brake failure in a "tight spot."

## *FLEET MAINTENANCE—AN EXAMPLE*

The experience of commercial organizations and governmental agencies operating large fleets of vehicles has shown that carefully planned regular vehicle maintenance is essential. Without it, operations would soon become chaotic.

Many driver education teachers personally recall the rigid vehicle maintenance regulations and procedures in the case of military vehicles. The various "echelons" of maintenance, the strict "deadlining" of vehicles for maintenance, and the remarkable record of service of military vehicles under severe conditions are a familiar story to many. Some consider the remarkable service of the "6 by 6," "workhorse" truck an important factor in military successes in the Second World War. Maintenance procedures "kept them rolling."

No individual car owner would personally have the experience of these great truck, bus, and military organizations. This is a point in a constructive "selling job," in which the driver education teacher can use these very obvious examples. Not so well recognized are some contrasting conditions of individual ownership of noncommercial passenger automobiles. The future car owner should recognize them.

## *PRIVATE CAR MAINTENANCE*

The average car owner is not a mechanic, nor is he usually well acquainted with the machine he drives. Even the "old timer" who used to put new "band" linings in the transmission of his "model T" (with string or wire on his wrench to prevent "losing it" in the transmission casing) finds himself lost under the hood of a modern car.

Automobile agencies operate service departments to provide effective maintenance services. Some are better to deal with than others, because of facilities, personnel, and the volume of work at any given time. Really good mechanics are highly sought-after artisans today. The wise car buyer learns

FIGURE 28-1 Very few of today's adult drivers really know their cars.

where the best service can be had at a reasonable price. Many people fall into the common pattern of taking the car in for repair *only when some mechanical trouble interferes with normal driving.* The service department, with a busy work schedule—and usually pressed by each car owner for the earliest possible return of his car—makes only those repairs which the owner specified. Most gasoline service stations perform routine lubrication services but are not staffed or equipped for effective inspection.

Detection of conditions which may lead to failure of any part of the car, then, in most cases, depends on recognition of them by the untrained, unskilled, unequipped owner.

## *The Human Factor*

Add to this failure to get regular professional-type inspection and maintenance, other human factors. When a steering wheel develops a little play or a brake pedal doesn't engage the brakes until pretty close to the floor, it is usually a case of very gradual change. The person who drives the car regularly doesn't readily recognize the slow change. Add to this the human trait of procrastination, the rationalization of "needing" the car (for work, for a trip, or for any reason) and the factor of cost, then the lack of proper maintenance becomes understandable though not justified. These are pitfalls the student should be taught to understand and avoid.

Standard high school driver education textbooks contain detailed information on normal maintenance procedures. Textbooks furnish the details, but the teacher still has the problem of convincing the student of the need for proper maintenance. Contrasting the commercial and military attitude toward vehicle maintenance with that of the average owner driver, the professional versus the amateur, is one approach.

## MOTOR VEHICLE INSPECTION

Because of the weaknesses of voluntary owner-operator vehicle maintenance procedures, it is obvious that there must be a significant number of vehicles being operated with defects that range from mild, nuisance-causing flaws to very hazardous conditions of the braking or steering apparatus. How great a part mechanical failure has played in the traffic accident story to date is problematical. Exponents of compulsory vehicle inspection claim that mechanical failure is responsible for a great many accidents. Opponents state that it is insignificant in comparison with the other factors as a cause of highway accidents.

Causes of traffic accidents may be classified as human, vehicle, and road. Accident investigation cannot establish a definite percentage relationship among the three. The postaccident condition of cars involved usually doesn't permit a positive conclusion as to preaccident conditions. Collision very frequently damages steering mechanisms, brake fluid lines, and other vital controls. Also, individual accident reports are not very reliable. Those who review many of them often detect some wide variations between the reports of two drivers involved in the same collision. Even completely neutral, disinterested witnesses often differ in reporting what they saw. Nobody knows, either, how many drivers, having lost control because of excessive speed or lack of skill, have charged their accidents to "the brakes failed" or "the steering gear failed." That mechanical failure contributes to the accident picture can hardly be denied. Estimates of *how much* it contributes vary so widely, however, that we cannot assess its relative importance very accurately.

The first state effort to cope with this factor was a voluntary vehicle inspection program instituted in Massachusetts in 1926. The following year, recognizing the probability of mechanical failure as part of the accident-causation picture, "save-a-life" vehicle inspection campaigns were proclaimed by the governors of New York, Massachusetts, and Maryland. In 1929, Massachusetts, Maryland, and Pennsylvania enacted legislation providing for periodic inspection of motor vehicles. Since 1930 some eighteen other states and the District of Columbia have followed suit. For obvious reasons, mainly scarcity of parts, civilian vehicle maintenance reached a low ebb during the Second World War.

### The National Safety Check Program

In 1945, the International Association of Chiefs of Police, working with the automotive industry, inaugurated the National Safety Check Program. The current vehicle Safety Check Program for Communities is sponsored by the Auto Industries Highway Safety Committee, *Look Magazine,* and the National Safety Council. This program consists of a complete plan for community support and participation. Committees and subcommittees are formed, literature is prepared and distributed, and newspapers, radio, and TV are used in publicizing the program. Preparations are made months in advance of the actual inspection. Windshield stickers are given for vehicles checked for brakes, lights, steering, tires, exhaust system, glass, windshield wipers, rearview mirrors, and horn, and found to be in good order.

FIGURE 28-2  The whole community is invited to take part.

Perhaps the greatest value of the program is educational, making the community conscious of the pressing need for proper car maintenance. (This is also a responsibility of driver education in the high school, of course.)

## STATE INSPECTION OF MOTOR VEHICLES

The *Uniform Vehicle Code*[1] sets forth model legislation covering on-the-road inspection of any vehicle believed *"upon reasonable cause"* to be unsafe or not equipped as required by law. It also gives a format for legislation providing for *periodic* inspection of all vehicles. Two generally recognized types of the latter system are provided (either to be chosen by the state). They are:

1. Periodic inspection (one or more times per year) at official (state-operated) stations.
2. Periodic inspection (once or twice per year) at official (privately operated, appointed) stations. (These are usually garages so authorized by state permit.)

At this writing, New Jersey, Delaware, and the District of Columbia

---

[1] *Uniform Vehicle Code,* National Committee on Uniform Traffic Laws and Ordinances, Washington, D.C., 1962, chap. 13.

have state-operated systems, and nineteen states have state-appointed systems.

## Legally Required Inspection—Pro and Con

The driver education teacher should be prepared to answer questions on this subject, from students and from members of the community.

The absence of reliable data as to the true impact of mechanical failure as an accident cause makes an accurate evaluation of the program impossible. The National Safety Council[2] states that one out of seven vehicles safety checked in the 1963 National Vehicle Safety-check program was found to be in need of maintenance attention for safe driving. In 1962, accidents reported due to inadequate brakes and improper lights totaled only 1.9 percent of all accidents. The data and the sources are too dissimilar to offer significant comparison. Some experts believe that mechanical failure causes, or is at least partly involved in, about 4 percent of all accidents. Other estimates range from 8 to 20 percent, "or even higher."

Advocates of compulsory vehicle inspection commonly cite the following arguments in support of their position:

1. Many vehicle owners either don't check their vehicles periodically or defer needed repairs. Compulsory inspection assures that major safety features are checked and corrected as necessary at least at certain regular intervals.
2. States can properly carry out their statutory responsibility to see that vehicles on public highways are in a safe condition only through actual vehicle inspections.
3. Existing compulsory inspection programs have found that a high proportion of vehicles presented for inspection fail to meet basic safety standards.
4. Compulsory inspection programs will remove unsafe vehicles from public highways and will discourage use of a state as a "dumping ground" for unsound vehicles.
5. The quality of vehicle repair and servicing is often improved, since garages realize that their work will later be inspected.
6. Inspection systems provide a means for checking correctness of vehicle registration, thereby discouraging vehicle thefts and registration law violations.
7. Periodic inspection creates safety consciousness among vehicle owners.

Opponents of compulsory motor vehicle inspection usually present the following arguments:

1. The substantial amounts of money required for an efficient vehicle inspection program could be used much more productively in other areas of traffic safety.
2. There is no proof that vehicle inspection programs have reduced or prevented traffic accidents.

[2] *Accident Facts,* National Safety Council, Chicago, Ill., 1964.

FIGURE 28-3 The major safety features are checked.

3. The proportion of vehicles found to have an unsafe condition has not significantly changed after institution and operation of a compulsory inspection system.
4. Periodic vehicle inspection creates considerable inconvenience and cost to motorists—and unnecessarily so in the instance of persons who voluntarily maintain their vehicles in a safe condition.
5. Under compulsory inspection programs, there is a tendency on the part of motorists to rely solely upon official inspections for detecting unsafe vehicle conditions and/or to defer repairs until shortly before inspection time.
6. Some motorists must take time off from work in order to have their car inspected, thereby losing income.
7. It is extremely difficult, if not impossible, thoroughly to supervise and enforce inspection station operations.

The most recent comprehensive analysis of motor vehicle inspection programs was that made by the Committee on Transportation and Commerce of the 1961–1963 Assembly of the State of California. In a published report on the results of its study, the Committee states as its first recommendation:

> Based mainly on inconclusive results of the Committee's nationwide survey on the effect of compulsory periodic inspection, the committee recommends that such other approaches to increased traffic safety as increased enforcement and application of currently authorized roadside vehicle inspec-

tions and enlargement of the scope of current headlight and brake inspection requirements should be considered in California prior to compulsory periodic statewide inspection at a potential tremendous cost to motorists and the State.

## Who Should Inspect?

As previously cited, two states and the District of Columbia operate their own inspection stations and nineteen states have officially appointed private stations. Eight other states authorize or require vehicle inspection by all or certain municipalities. There is no active municipal inspection program in two of those states, and some fifteen cities in the other six have programs.

FIGURE 28-4 New Jersey, Delaware, and the District of Columbia have state-operated inspection systems.

The state-owned and state-operated system appears to be practical only in states having a relatively small area and a fairly concentrated population. However, generally cited advantages of this type of system over the appointed garage system are that it (1) produces maximum uniformity in inspection methods and processes, (2) can be more easily and effectively supervised and controlled, (3) provides opportunities for other official activities relating to drivers, (4) eliminates patronage and other problems that can arise in official selections of appointed garages, (5) reduces improper inspection practices for the purpose of commercial gain, and (6) induces inspectors to give primary attention to equipment affecting safety rather than to that which can involve a substantial expenditure for repair.

Asserted advantages of the appointed garage system over a state-owned system are: (1) existing commercial stations can usually be utilized for inspection operations; hence, no substantial outlay of state money is required for new facilities; (2) a greater number of inspection stations can be made available, reducing the inconvenience of inspection to motorists; (3) questions as to governmental competition with private enterprise are eliminated; (4) vehicle owners have a choice of inspection stations; and (5) any needed corrective work usually can be done in the same garage where inspection is performed, often by the vehicle owner's regular mechanic. One of the first states to adopt this system has since changed to state-owned and -operated stations.

Mobile inspection units have been tried unsuccessfully in some states. New Jersey, however, operates such in addition to the regular facilities—usually in drive-in theater areas—and has found them an aid in relieving congestion at the regular inspection stations.

## Conclusions

The actual impact of vehicle failure on the highway accident picture is not known. "Informed" opinion varies. However, one general conclusion which is indisputable is that vehicles should be maintained in safe operating condition—and this requires periodic checking of certain vehicle parts.

It is not known whether the sizable costs of official compulsory, periodic inspection programs might (or might not) be more effectively employed in other traffic safety activities. *On-the-road inspection* of vehicles which police officers have reason to believe defective can also be used—though certain unsafe vehicle conditions are not visibly apparent. Both types of inspection are cited in the *Uniform Vehicle Code*.[3]

In states which do not have geographically concentrated populations, an appointed garage inspection is usually more feasible than a system utilizing state-owned and state-operated inspection facilities.

The teacher of driver education should be well acquainted with all facets of automobile maintenance, both voluntary and compulsory.

## SELECTED BIBLIOGRAPHY

*Accident Facts,* National Safety Council, Chicago, Ill., 1964, annual.

*American Standard—Inspection Requirements for Motor Vehicles,* American Standards Association, Inc., New York, 1956.

*Engineering and Vehicle Inspection,* American Association of Motor Vehicle Administrators, Washington, D.C. Bulletin 10, vol. 21, October, 1956.

*The Federal Role in Highway Safety,* U.S. Government Printing Office, Washington, D.C., 1959.

*Manual of Brake Service,* Weaver Manufacturing Company, Springfield, Ill.

*Motor Vehicle Inspection,* American Association of Motor Vehicle Administrators, Washington, D.C., and Association of Casualty & Surety Companies, New York, 1957.

*State-wide Periodic Motor Vehicle Inspection,* American Association of Motor Vehicle Administrators, Washington, D.C., 1957.

*Uniform Vehicle Code,* National Committee on Uniform Traffic Laws and Ordinances, Washington, D.C., 1962, chap. 13.

*Why Motor Vehicle Inspection,* American Association of Motor Vehicle Administrators and Auto Industries Highway Safety Committee, Inc., Washington, D.C., 1963.

[3] *Loc. cit.*

# Automobile Insurance 29

IF IT WERE necessary to condense this chapter into three words, those words would be, "Read your policy." This advice would apply to every person who owns or drives a car, to driver education students, and to driver education teachers. The policy is the basic document of the insurance industry. *It tells the exact terms of the contract between the policyholder and the company.* It contains a great deal of information. To know one's policy well is to know most of the important facts about insurance. Why, then, teach the subject of insurance and why have the teacher-to-be study it?

There are four main reasons:

1. The wording of the policy is clear cut, but not at all easy reading. The policy is also quite long. The complexity of the format and the wording

of the policy prevent many people from gaining a clear understanding of its provisions.
2. Many people are, of course, capable of understanding the provisions of the policy, but the length of the document and the press of time keep many of them from studying their policies.
3. There are some points about automobile insurance, some interesting and significant points, which affect the policyholder's interests and yet are not terms of the policy.
4. As in other curriculum content, there are some special approaches the teacher may use to make the subject more interesting to the high school student.

The foregoing rationale is offered not merely in justification of including the subject of automobile insurance in driver education, but as a guideline as to what information on the subject is most needed in the literature which is designed for teacher preparation in driver and traffic safety education. If the teacher-to-be carefully studies the insurance policy—and studies the copious material on the subject in the standard high school driver education textbooks, then his further need lies in (1) material not generally covered in those readily available sources and (2) ways of, or "strategies" for, presenting the subject to his high school students.

## The Basic Principle of Insurance

The teacher can present the basic principle of insurance as a *spreading of risk*. Simply expressed, if experience has shown that one person in a thousand suffers a $5,000 loss from fire each year, each of the 1,000 persons faces the risk that *he* will suffer the full loss, an event that might prove disastrous. If each of the thousand donates $5 to a fund to be paid to the one who does suffer the $5,000 loss, an *insurance* fund is formed and the fire risk has been spread over 1,000 individuals at a *premium* cost of $5 each.

Obviously, it would be unlikely that 1,000 people would meet by chance and make such an arrangement. This is the service that the insurance company performs, a very important service in our mode of life. The insurance company gives an identity to the protection fund, an identity which also furnishes the selling of insurance, the bookkeeping, and the investment and disbursement of the money involved. Not only do the receiving and paying functions require services but, obviously, catastrophe doesn't consistently strike an even proportion of 1 in 1,000 persons with an exact loss of $5,000. *Actuarial* data must be compiled which tell just how much of a premium each policyholder must pay. These data serve to establish a *rate* expressed as a percentage of the *face value* of the policy.

Of course, there must be a *reserve* of assets to take care of payments by the company to its policyholders who suffer *losses* which are *covered* by their policies. It would be poor business to simply hold all these assets, this reserve that has been paid in premiums, as cash which would draw no *interest*. Since much more of these assets is possessed by the company than is needed at any one time, the assets are *invested*. Because the public is vitally concerned in the financial stability of the companies in which people hold policies, states limit the types of investments which insurance companies may make to sound ones, such as high-grade bonds, mortgages, limited to 50 percent of the value of the property, and a prescribed amount of stock. Part of the income of the insurance company, then, is from *investment*. Were it not for this, insurance would cost more.

Obviously, the individual policyholder who *purchases* insurance buys a commodity which he cannot weigh on a scale or examine for texture to judge its worth, its monetary value. This is different from clothing, food, real estate, or even stocks and bonds which have an observable *market value*. The cost of the insurance premium is determined by the amount of money the company has to pay to policyholders who suffer losses which have been covered by their policies. Depending on the actual amount of losses, the rate may increase or decrease. Automobile liability insurance rates have risen 41 percent in ten years. Higher costs of repairs, greater court awards for injuries, and an increase in fraudulent claims have been significant factors in this increase.

FIGURE 29-1  Legitimate costs for repairs have risen sharply in recent years.

In view of the necessarily intracompany nature of the computations of costs and the critical importance of insurance to the public, the industry —like the banking industry—is subject to legal controls established by state law, including examination of the companies' books by state insurance examiners.

One of the basic facts the student should know about insurance is that each policy, whatever its provisions, *is only as good as the company that wrote it*. (This is a good point to emphasize in teaching the future consumer about guarantees also.)

## IMAGE OF THE INDUSTRY

Insurance is an old institution with a surprisingly adventurous history. This is a point in the driver education course that calls for a sound, time-based decision on the part of the teacher. It is one of those areas in teaching where *motivation* for learning is readily available in terms of human interest and time is the limiting factor.

One can present the subject of insurance to be learned by high school students in its skeletal form, each contemporary fact to be learned by rote. This method can be used, but it is "dry." It is unlikely that the average student will have any desire to read more about insurance when in the future the popular magazine, the newspaper, or the consumers' publication carries an article on the subject. Though not guaranteed, a bit of motivation may be added by injecting a feeling of interest, enjoyment, pleasure to the student's initial acquaintance with the subject. (This principle, of course, applies to other areas of learning as well.)

The subject might well be introduced to the teen-ager, or better still, to the younger student first, in historical-narrative form. The industry is a contemporary and a close associate of some adventurous years of history. The owners of the *little* vessels which braved storm-tossed, enemy- and pirate-invested seas were some of the earliest customers of the insurance industry. The bloody pirate attacks on ships at sea and on coastal towns, the pillaging of caravans in the desert, the foundering of countless ships in the wild sea storms, these were not figments of the imagination of writers of adventure stories; these were real events that happened to real people; these were the fabric of which the concept of insurance was made. The teacher who cannot make this material into a colorful true story is unfortunate indeed.

This story, if carried into detail, would be one of the introductory procedures which is normally indicated for grades below those of the driver education course. However, this principle of appeal to human interest transcends age categories. Some high school students may know of seacoast communities whose local history contains accounts of the wreckers of many years ago lighting false beacons on beaches to lure sailing ships ashore to be wrecked and pillaged. These are real perils which had direct relationship to the principle of *shared risk*—of *insurance*.

Of course, the opposite of these cases of vessels and crews falling victim to attack and storm were the great majority which brought home the "wealth of the Indies" and the people to the New World. This was the commerce that formed a foundation for the enterprise we call "insurance." The elementary grade teacher can give some excellent background to arithmetical concepts and problems with environments, events, and characters from the past, involving the principle of shared risk.

Fire insurance and life insurance have their own interesting histories,

FIGURE 29-2 At least the financial risk can be shared among many.

and the comparatively new member of the family, *automobile insurance,* comes very close to the world of adventure as envisioned by the teen-ager of the sixties. After a led-discussion approach, bringing out the adventurous history of insurance (pitched to grade level), a present-day form of piracy offers a very interesting approach to automobile insurance, well illustrating the principles of rate determinations, bodily injury liability, etc. The subject is the wholesale swindle being perpetrated on the insurance industry—and *on the policyholder,* part of whose premium payments go to pay the swindlers.

## PIRACY IN THE SIXTIES

Newspapers in Baltimore, Jacksonville, Los Angeles, Miami, Newark, New York, and elsewhere have published series of articles dealing with the reasons for rate increases for automobile insurance. Most accounts cite *fraudulent claims* as being responsible for a significant proportion of rate rises. In November, 1963, the *Los Angeles Herald Examiner* reported that fraudulent insurance claims had become a multimillion-dollar-a-year enterprise in the Los Angeles area alone. The Insurance Information Institute published a 71-page booklet under the title, *The Great Insurance Swindle.*[1] It reprints, with permission, an unusual series of articles written by a team of reporters of the *Miami* (Florida) *News* who studied the wholesale insurance swindling which was rampant in that area. As a reference for student reading on a subject of considerable social and economic importance, this publication is both instructive and interesting. The involvement of people

---

[1] *The Great Insurance Swindle,* reprinted with permission from the *Miami News,* Insurance Information Institute, New York.

other than the principals in the swindles cuts across lines of profession, business, race, and background and is quite startling in itself.

Imagine accident injury cases like the one in which the lawyer received $2,524.27 and the injured person $2,368.63. Imagine forty-one New York City lawyers being disbarred or forced to resign from the bar, fourteen others being suspended for periods of 6 months to 5 years, four others being censured, and action pending against others for "ambulance chasing." (In addition, the State of New York then investigated some 1,400 doctors on the basis of information that came out of the lawyer's inquiry.)

Imagine one doctor having treated 3,000 cases of "whiplash" injury which the orthopedic doctor who coined the term (to denote neck injury from the head snapping backward as when a car is struck from behind) says is rare. So widespread is its appearance in litigation arising from automobile accidents that it is sometimes called "insurance neck." Of course, there are many other types of injury involved in lawsuits arising from automobile accidents.

These cases typify thousands upon thousands of situations in which claims against automobile insurers make up a multimillion-dollar enterprise. They are no more typical of the legal or medical professions than bank robbers typify the American citizen. Yet, they do point out a tremendous drain of insurance dollars which is costing the automobile owner a goodly share of the money he pays for insurance.

Add to this the unknown millions of dollars that are being paid to shady collision repair shop owners who pad their charges when the bill is to be paid by insurance companies. Some even "split" the added amount with the car owner. The public should be made conscious of the fact that it is paying in high automobile insurance premiums for the transgressions of some of its own members. When the subject of insurance costs comes up with driver education students, as it inevitably does about the time they have to pay, this is a *teachable moment* in this subject—their personal involvement makes it so. Some will respond to the fact that cheating an insurance company is cheating *people,* not an inanimate machine, and is just as *wrong* as stealing *directly* from a neighbor. Some will respond to the obvious need for an all-out attack by *education* on the widespread belief that the insurance company is fair game and that cheating it is not *economically* unsound.

The phenomenon of the insurance swindle is not the main current of information which the public needs on the subject. It *is* a facet of it, however, and a subject for public education. *It is also sufficiently sensational to catch the interest of the student.*

## VITAL SIDEVIEWS

The high school textbook tells the student about the different types of coverage of automobile insurance, *bodily injury liability, property damage liability, medical payments coverage, comprehensive physical damage insurance, and protection against uninsured motorists.* The teacher should not be stampeded by critics of driver education into dropping this content from the course as "not related to safety." There is room for at least this much coverage of the subject of insurance in even the minimum 30-hour classroom course. The security of the economic future of the student and his responsibility to others, both require that he become informed in this subject.

Seldom stressed is the matter of *amount* of liability coverage. The student should know:

1. That if he is insured for liability for bodily injury to one person up to the amount of $10,000 and a judgment of $50,000 is obtained by the victim against him—the car owner and/or driver—he will be liable for $40,000 *above the amount that the insurance company will pay the victim*. This could cost him his home, his financial assets, and something of his future well-being plus that of his family.
2. The cost of, say, 25/50 or 100/300 coverage as compared with 10/20 coverage is remarkably low for the additional protection the greater limits afford. Payments as high as a quarter of a million dollars have been awarded to persons for serious injuries.

FIGURE 29-3 Injury and death liability may reach staggering sums far beyond the common 10/20 liability coverage.

The student should know also the minimum limits under the financial responsibility laws of his state. He should know that if he drives in New York State, for instance, he must carry 10/20 liability coverage or he is in violation of the law. He should know what the insurance company would pay him in the event of total loss by collision of his *old car*, to be compared with the cost of the premium. He should know what effects his driving of his parents' (or another's) car would have on the insurance coverage, and what may need to be done about it. He should know that simple scanning of the tables of traffic accident fatalities will not tell him where the premium costs are highest, since nonfatal accidents account for up to 95 percent of all traffic accident costs.[2]

The subject of insurance is an important one in the future of the student —but it can be made an interesting one also. One additional point is well worth considering. Here again (see Chapter 3, "The Student") the student is *fragmented*. In driver education we teach him how important it is that he be covered for liability in connection with his ownership and operation of an automobile. We would be severely criticized for (and subject-oriented time scheduling would rarely permit) explaining to him, while on the subject of liability, that his future ownership of a home carries similar risks—the patch of ice on the walk, the weak plank in the front step, the tree limb that breaks off in a storm, the hired boy who cuts his hand mowing the lawn or clipping the hedge, the swimming pool, and the dog which nips a child in "self-defense" when cornered and frightened by screaming children, the "attractive nuisance"—there are many areas of liability in addition to those concerned with the automobile. When motivated to interest in the subject, the student would be most receptive to learning—were his learning process not fragmented by subject field determination. The answer in this case of insurance may lie in coordination with teachers in other departments (if the subject of insurance and liability is covered elsewhere) and/or enough mention of the other areas of liability to stimulate his interest in pursuing the subject further on his own. We can't justify spreading driver education time too thinly, but we must use all the ingenuity we possess for the benefit of the student. This is one of the qualities of the "teacher" as opposed to the "employee."

## *SELECTED BIBLIOGRAPHY*

*Automobile Insurance,* filmstrip and record (with manual signal and automatic signal), Insurance Information Institute, New York.

*Automobile Insurance for Students in Driver Education,* Insurance Information Institute, New York, 4 pp.

*A Family Guide to Property and Liability Insurance,* Insurance Information Institute, New York.

*The Great Insurance Swindle,* Insurance Information Institute, New York.

*Journal of American Insurance,* American Mutual Insurance Alliance, Chicago, Ill., December, 1964, pp. 9–12.

Richardson, Gayle E., C.P.C.V.: *Behind the Fine Print—The Basic Facts about Insurance,* David-Stewart Publishing Co., Indianapolis, Ind., 1961.

*Sample Insurance Policies for Property and Liability Coverages, Prepared for College Students in Advanced Courses,* Insurance Information Institute, New York.

---

[2] National Safety Council, *Traffic Safety,* April, 1962.

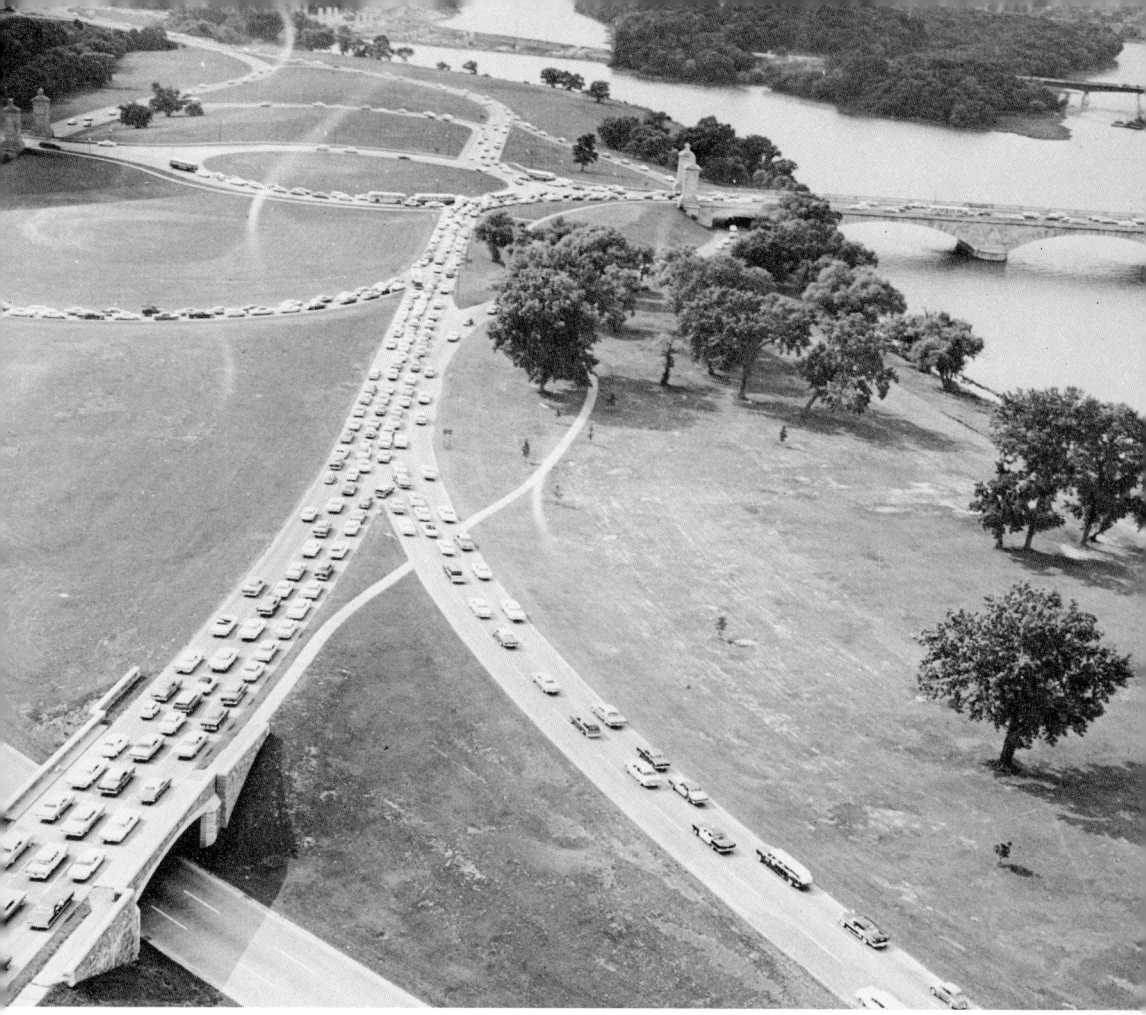

# The Defensive Driving Code  30

"DEFENSIVE DRIVING" is a term long used to denote an over-all state of mind as well as acts of driving. The concept is a good one and has served well. It has been broadly interpreted as a "readiness" to take appropriate action to "defend" yourself and your passengers from any threat to their safety on the highway. Some interpret it as a defense against unexpected actions by other drivers, some against errors of other drivers. Probably the most constructive interpretation refers to defense against any hazard, with the assumption that the defensive driver is ready to *anticipate* hazardous situations and to know the right thing to do either to avoid the hazard entirely, or if that is impossible, to take the action best suited to neutralize it. It can be more than that. It can become a code of human concern for others on the highway.

Recently a high school textbook[1] introduced a new phase to the defensive-driving concept. Recognizing that young people want to be not only drivers but topnotch, expert drivers, it added this new phase to the old concept of defensive driving. This new thought is that the truly expert driver, if he is a decent kind of fellow, defends not only himself and his passengers, but also drivers less expert than he, and others such as their passengers, children, and old folks. The psychological implication is a double one, an appeal to the normal young driver's desire to be an "expert driver," and the concept of the expert driver as one who takes care of others less expert. (A rather common self-identification with expertness in driving promotes this behavior-affecting reaction.)

## Application of the Concept

Described in the textbook, the following is the type of action included in the new concept of defensive driving. Assume that "you" are driving on a city street with a fairly complex traffic pattern, a place where a driver's attention is subject to the many distractions common to town and city driving. A line of cars is parked on your right. On your left is a broken white line, which you may cross to pass, separating the traffic proceeding in the opposite direction. Another vehicle is following yours at a fairly close interval. Unexpectedly, a vehicle in front of you stops, perhaps to double-park. You see a clear path to go around it to pass it properly on the left. You can either pull up closely behind it before moving left (provided that it is not a large vehicle which would obscure your vision), or you can start left well in advance of reaching it, *allowing the driver in back of you a clear view of the stopped vehicle and giving him plenty of time to stop if necessary*, or to follow you if traffic permits when he reaches the point of decision.

Obviously, the latter course of action would be the better one from the standpoint of safety and a humane consideration for others. However, it would never occur to many drivers unless pointed out to them. It is one detailed procedure which illustrates the new, broader concept of defensive driving. Often an act of this kind is accompanied by a feeling of pride, a pleasurable sensation, and a motivation to repeat it in kind.

There are many circumstances in which similar acts are appropriate. The driver who stops for a stop sign and notes that a pedestrian, perhaps a young child or a very old person, is waiting to cross in front of him, from his right to his left, is in one such situation. Many drivers wait and motion the pedestrian to cross in front of them. This is courteous and well intended. However, it may have tragic consequences if another driver comes from behind and either does not see the sign or intends to ignore it by impatiently passing the stopped car. Since your stopped car may easily hide the crossing pedestrian, especially a small child, the passing car becomes a very dangerous factor.

The driver who has been indoctrinated with the broader concept of defensive driving would have a feeling of responsibility for the safety of the

---

[1] American Automobile Association, *Sportsmanlike Driving*, 5th ed., McGraw-Hill Book Company, New York, 1965.

pedestrian, especially if he were to wave the latter across. He would be more apt to look around before doing so, especially since a young child often follows the directions of an adult with confidence.

In spite of the complaints one sometimes hears about truck drivers, most commercial drivers have been practicing this kind of defensive driving

FIGURE 30-1  *Yield*—a defensive driving concept that became law.

for many years. Few people who have driven extensively under all kinds of conditions have not observed instances of this excellent example set by truckers. Whether the high school student wants to drive a truck or not, he usually has a high regard for the driving ability and know-how of those who drive professionally. Their example is good for him to recognize.

## *Passing Signals*

One example of teamwork on the highway has *defensive, cooperative,* and *taking care of the other fellow* implications. It is the code of passing signals used by commercial truck drivers. Whether or not this is taught to high school students is a matter for the judgment of the individual teacher. Some authorities believe that it should not be, because of possible disruption of these safe driving practices that just a few of the "lunatic fringe" of teen-agers might accomplish. This refers, of course, only to the irresponsible minority who "peel out," use illegal noisemakers on cars, and show off. This opinion may be right. However, every driver education teacher should know this procedure. Oddly enough, not many have, in the past. Whenever a student (perhaps one whose father drives a trailer rig or a bus) mentions this in class, the teacher would "lose face"—be embarrassed—if he had to admit ignorance.

When one big commercial vehicle overtakes another to pass it, it has long been a custom to flash on the headlights (or to high beam if they are on) to tell the driver ahead that he is about to be passed. Many dispense with this preliminary passing signal today on multilaned divided highways where the driver about to be passed has nothing to do until the passing is complete.

When the passing vehicle clears the other, it is to the advantage of both that it get back in line before another vehicle comes from behind and cuts to the right between the two, possibly to collide with the passing vehicle when the latter cuts back to the right. The passing driver flashes his right directional signal. The driver of the vehicle being passed, when he sees that the rear end of the passing vehicle is sufficiently far ahead, turns on his headlights (or switches to the opposite beam and back). This is a signal to the passing driver that he is far enough ahead to return safely to the lane on his right. He immediately makes this move. He flashes the marker or identification lights on the back of his vehicle off and on, meaning a "thank you" to the other driver who cooperated in helping him to complete the passing movement efficiently and safely.

This procedure is not a matter of law, but of cooperation and courtesy among professionals, and represents *defensive driving* in the new and best interpretation of the term. Summed up, a helpful, constructive concept of defensive driving includes taking care of others who are less able to care for themselves. The expressed accompaniment of this interpretation as taught to students is that "other, *superior* drivers will help to take care of you when you get in a tight spot"—a team spirit kind of approach.

### SELECTED BIBLIOGRAPHY

American Automobile Association, *Sportsmanlike Driving,* 5th ed., McGraw-Hill Book Company, New York, 1965.

# American Highways                                            31

GENERATIONS of young people have been intrigued by tales of the "seven wonders of the world." Today it would be very difficult to identify all the "wonders" of nature and of man's genius and perseverance. No doubt one would have to include the almost magic machines of transportation—machines beyond the reach of the most powerful kings of world history.

The development of the automobile is a story of intriguing interest and adventure. Few realize that it would have been an impossibility were it not for two parallel achievements of man—the use of liquid fuel in internal-combustion engines and the building of a highway system. Stories are told of the disappointment of men who, digging a well to supply their water needs, found only this messy, evil-smelling petroleum gushing from the earth. Perhaps the steam engine might have taken the place of the gasoline engine in cars if there were no oil, but the conventional fuels, wood and coal, would have severely limited the range and convenience of the motor vehicle.

The second of these twofold wonders is *underfoot*. It is so common that we seldom realize that it is one of the major building achievements of all time—the *highway*—millions of miles of it here in the United States. With the car, came the improved highway. Without its parallel growth, having the automobile would have been akin to owning a great luxury liner and only a small pond in which to use it. The public road is a major factor in the American economy. Losing the services of our highway network would strangle that economy.

Aside from the men who built the highways, few give thought to the tremendous task it has been and to the major effort still under way. Who built the great network of streets and rural roads, freeways and bridges, and all the complex interchanges, grade separations, and other engineering accomplishments? Who paid for them? What planning and legislation were needed to develop them? What new concepts of government responsibility arose? What is happening today? What is being planned for tomorrow?

The facts are not normally assembled and available, as are so many data on automobile production, operation, accidents, etc. They are not available from ordinary textbook sources. For this reason, some detail will be presented in this chapter. It is not intended as material for memorization, but for reference when teaching the economic factors of the development of the automobile and the transportation industry.

More than 3½ million miles of public highways serve the nation's **94** million motorists. These roads and streets consist of just less than one million miles of unimproved and graded and drained earth roads, almost 1⅓ million miles of soil-surfaced and gravel or crushed-stone roads, and about the same mileage with black top or better surfaces and pavements. Currently there are about **838** *billion* motor vehicle miles of annual travel on these facilities— and it is forecast that there will be almost 1.3 *trillion* vehicle miles of travel in **1980**. About **48** percent of current travel is on urban streets, where **70** percent of our population now lives. As urbanization continues, **80** percent of our population is expected to live in urban areas by **1980**. The need for services and goods will increase urban travel so that it may be expected that substantially more than **50** percent of the total motor vehicle miles traveled will occur in urban areas. Urban streets currently constitute about **14** percent of all roads and street mileage.

## THE FEDERAL ROLE IN HIGHWAY CONSTRUCTION

"The Federal interest in highways stems from its constitutional directive to establish post roads, regulate commerce among the states, provide for national defense, and promote the general welfare."[1] Federal participation in road construction dates back to **1806** when Congress appropriated funds for improvement of the national pike extending from Cumberland,

---

[1] *America's Lifelines—Federal Aid for Highways*, U.S. Department of Commerce, Bureau of Public Roads, Washington, D.C.

Maryland, across the Appalachian Mountains to Wheeling, West Virginia. This corresponded with the general alignment of present US Route 40. The modern Federal-aid highway system as we now know it had its beginning in 1916. The 110 years between these developments saw little Federal financial support for road construction. What was accomplished was done by the pioneers forging westward, while in the East hundreds of turnpike companies were formed, and rapid but short-lived toll-road development took place. Between 1830 and 1850, development of railroads as the primary mode of transportation so reduced highway travel and turnpike revenues that many of the turnpike companies went bankrupt. Highway transportation entered a period of neglect that extended almost to the turn of the twentieth century.

In 1902 the Brownlow-Latimer Good Roads bill, among other provisions, proposed a Bureau of Public Roads in the Department of Agriculture and appropriated $20 million for road construction to be matched 50/50 by the states. It was eventually defeated, but it laid the groundwork for future legislation.

In 1912, the first Federal-aid convention was held. It resulted in the appointment of a Joint Committee of the United States Senate and the House of Representatives to investigate and report on the subject of Federal aid to highways. An appropriation of $500,000 was subsequently made for the improvement of post roads under the direction of the Secretary of Agriculture and the Postmaster General. A year later the Committee on Roads was established as a standing committee in the United States House of Representatives.

In Atlanta, Georgia, in 1914, the Fourth American Road Congress fathered the American Association of State Highway Officials and the basic outline of the Federal Aid Road Act of 1916. This Act was a milestone in the development of transportation in the United States. The Act spelled out some important features which have withstood the test of over half a century of progress in Federal-aid highway legislation and which still exist in current Federal highway law. The Act provided that selection of routes to be improved with Federal aid and the choice of projects to be built were a state rather than a Federal responsibility. It established the 50/50 matching ratio principle and made the states responsible for supervising construction and for providing adequate maintenance on Federal-aid highways. In 1921, Federal aid for highway construction was restricted to a limited connected system of principal roads now identified as the Primary System.

Provision was made in 1944 for designation of a Federal-aid Secondary System of principal farm-to-market roads and connectors. In the same Act, specific authorization was made for the first time for Federal-aid funds to be expended on extensions of Federal-aid Primary Systems into the urban areas. Thus was born the ABC program as it exists today, the "ABC" standing for the three subsections of Federal-aid fund authorizations, with "A" referring to the Primary System funds, "B" to the Secondary System funds, and "C" to the funds for the urban extensions of the two systems. As important as was the emergence of the ABC program, the 1944 Act created another system of highways whose impact was not to be felt for another dozen years.

## The National System of Interstate and Defense Highways

The National System of Interstate and Defense Highways was authorized in 1944 as a 40,000 (subsequently revised to 41,000)-mile network of highways to connect the principal metropolitan areas, cities, and industrial centers, serve national defense needs, and connect with routes of continental importance in the Dominion of Canada and the Republic of Mexico. The new system, though distinct, was also designated by law as part of the Primary System.

Although the National System of Interstate and Defense Highways was conceived at least as early as 1939 and was legally born in 1944, no special Federal appropriations were made for it and, of course, no major construction was undertaken during the Second World War. The states had been requested by the U.S. Bureau of Public Roads to recommend routes for inclusion in this new system, and by 1947 the states and the Bureau had come to agreement on the general locations of the main routes for the Interstate System. In 1952, Congress authorized $25 million for each of the fiscal years 1954 and 1955 for work on the Interstate System on a 50/50 (Federal-state) matching ratio. Concerned with the lack of progress on the I-System, Congress, in 1954, authorized $175 million for Interstate work in each of the fiscal years 1956 and 1957 and changed the matching ratio to 60 percent Federal and 40 percent state. Meanwhile, the states were using their 50/50 Federal-aid primary and urban funds on the Interstate System, too, but progress was limited by the relatively meager funds available for so big a job.

With passage of the Federal Aid Highway Act of 1956, the United States embarked upon a highway construction program that has been referred to as the *largest public works program in the history of the world*. The program provided for in the 1956 Act (as amended) is significant, not only because of its magnitude but because of unique features never before included in Federal-aid highway legislation. The Interstate program made it possible for the first time to estimate Federal-aid funds for a number of years in advance and to plan construction schedules accordingly. A Trust Fund method of financing, supported entirely by highway user taxes, assured financing on a pay-as-you-build basis, with expenditures for construction geared to income from certain tax levies. For the first time in its history, this country had a highway construction program, adequately financed, to meet forecasted traffic needs for a date in the future. The cost of these highways is shared—90 percent Federal, 10 percent state.

## Financing of Federal Aid Highways

In the passage of the Act of 1956 the Federal government subscribed to the theory of linkage between taxes collected from highway users and funds spent for highway construction. With the establishment of the Highway Trust Fund, certain but not all the Federal excise taxes were dedicated to pay the Federal share of the estimated $47 billion cost of completion of the Interstate System, and also $35 billion for improvement of other highways on the Primary and Secondary Systems.

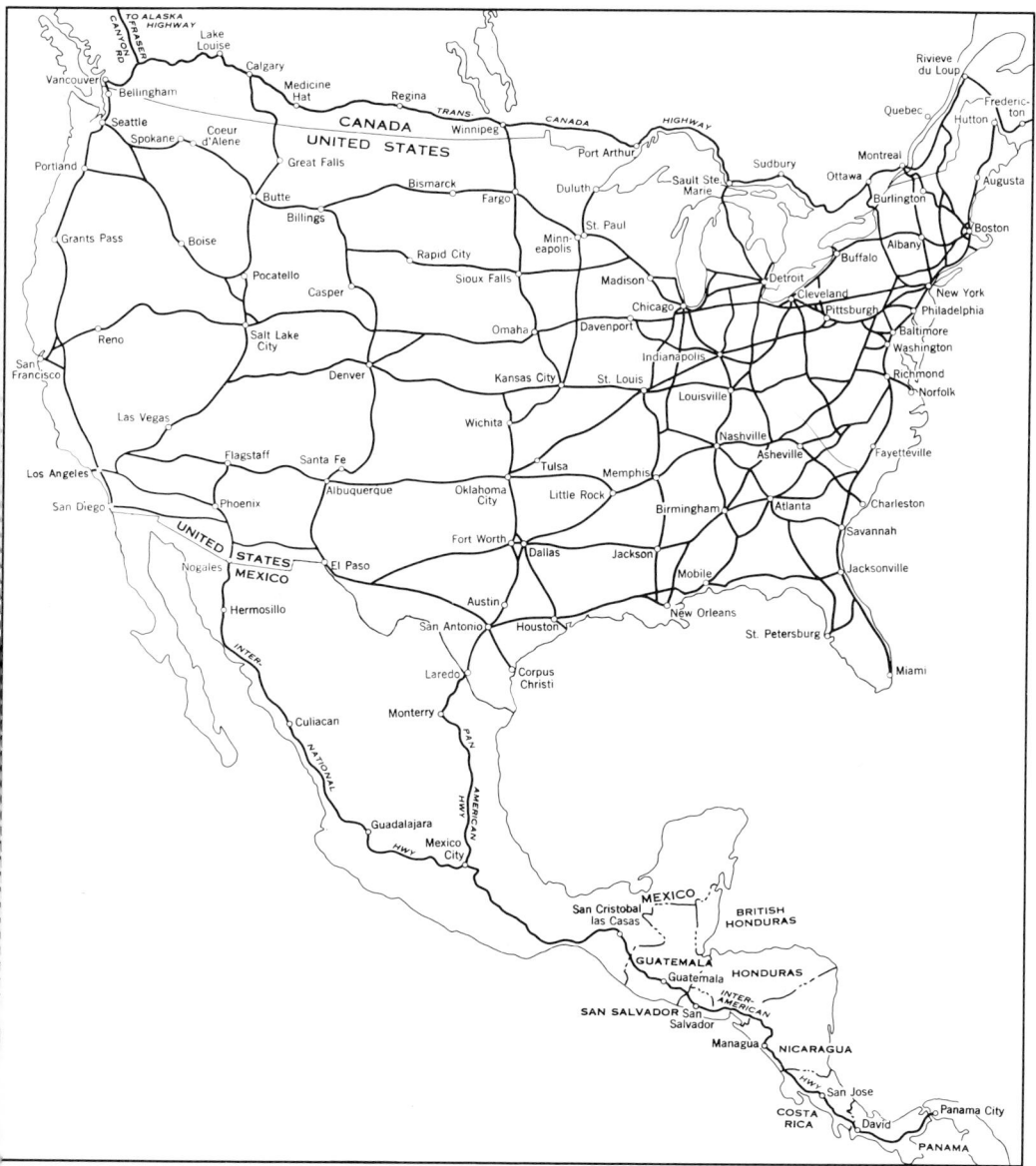

FIGURE 31-1 The National System of Interstate and Defense Highways spans the nation and connects with important routes of our neighbors to the north and the south—coast to coast and from Alaska to Panama City.

The current Federal excise tax of 4 cents per gallon on motor fuel accounts for about three-quarters of all Trust Fund revenue, bringing in over $2.6 billion per year. Other excises dedicated to the Trust Fund include:

New trucks, buses, and tractors—10 percent on the manufacturer's wholesale price

Highway vehicle tires and tubes—10 cents per pound
Other tires and tread rubber—5 cents per pound
Heavy vehicles use—$3 per 1,000 pounds on the total gross weight of vehicles rated at more than 26,000 pounds gross weight

Federal excise taxes on passenger cars, amounting to over $1.8 billion annually, and on automobile parts and accessories, amounting to over $230 million annually, are deposited in the Federal General Fund rather than in the Highway Trust Fund.

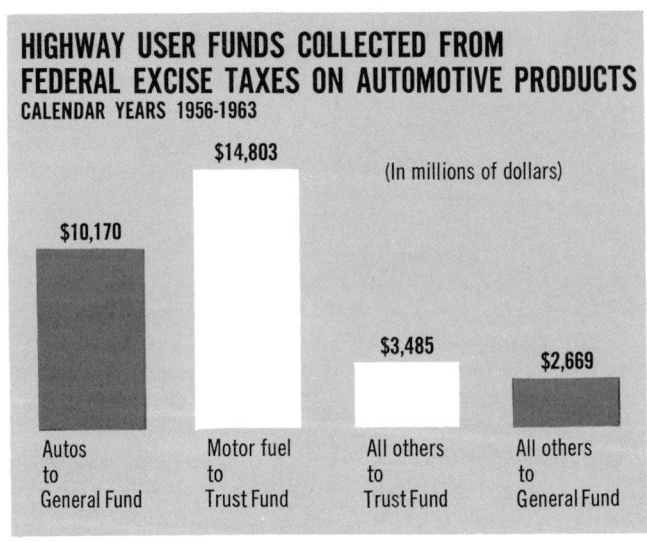

FIGURE 31-2

Between July 1, 1956, and December 31, 1963, receipts from motor vehicle taxes amounting to over $18.2 billion were deposited in the Highway Trust Fund. Over 80 percent of this amount was derived from Federal motor fuel excises. During the period January 1, 1956, to December 31, 1963, receipts from motor vehicle excises deposited in the General Fund of the United States Treasury amounted to over $12.8 billion. Some 79 percent of this revenue was derived from the 10 percent Federal excise tax on passenger cars. Figure 31-2 shows the impacts and relationships between major sources of income to the Trust Fund and other Federal excises paid by users but deposited in the General Fund.

## The Highway Trust Fund

Money in the Trust Fund is used to provide the Federal share (90 percent) of Interstate System costs and the Federal share (50 percent) of ABC program improvement costs. The ABC program has first call upon Trust Fund revenues. Federal-aid funds for the ABC program are traditionally authorized by Congress in alternate years—currently at the level of $1 billion per year. According to existing Federal-aid law, sums made available for the ABC program must be divided as follows: 45 percent for projects

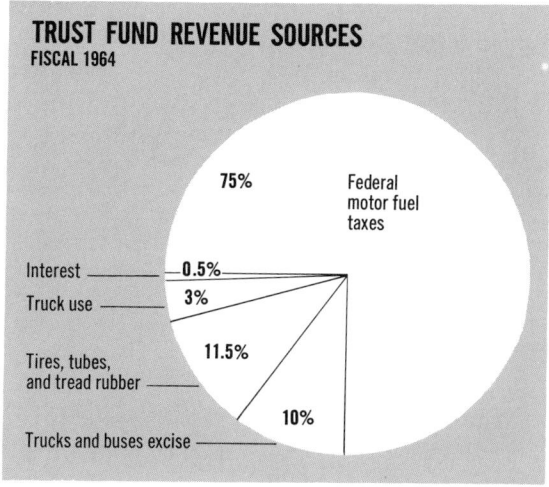

FIGURE 31-3

on the Federal-aid Primary System (rural or urban), 30 percent for projects on Federal-aid Secondary System (rural or urban), and 25 percent for urban segments of Primary and Secondary Systems.

The annual authorized amount for the Primary System is divided proportionately among the states on the basis of land area, population, and mileage of rural mail delivery routes and star routes in each state, compared to the totals for all states. In the case of the Secondary System, the same formula is used, but only that segment of the population which is rural is counted with the other two factors. For urban funds, the sole factor is urban population.

In contrast, Federal aid for completion of the Interstate System is apportioned among the states according to the estimated cost of completion of the system in each state, compared to the total cost of completion in all states. Congressional review of periodic revisions of the cost estimates, which are made by the states and the Bureau of Public Roads, is designed to adjust any inequities as the program proceeds, and to form the basis for adjusting tax schedules, when necessary, to maintain the solvency of the Trust Fund.

## Scope of the Interstate System

The National System of Interstate and Defense Highways, commonly known as the Interstate System, consists of 41,000 miles of limited-access highways. Scheduled for completion about the end of 1972, it links together and serves more than 90 percent of the cities having a population of 50,000 or more, plus many smaller cities and towns. It represents about 1 percent of the total mileage in the United States and is expected to serve more than 25 percent of the total traffic. About 10 percent of the network is planned as six or eight lanes and 90 percent as four lanes. Access will be provided by some 12,000 interchanges, with those in rural areas spaced an average of 4.5 miles apart. Interchanges in urban areas will be considerably

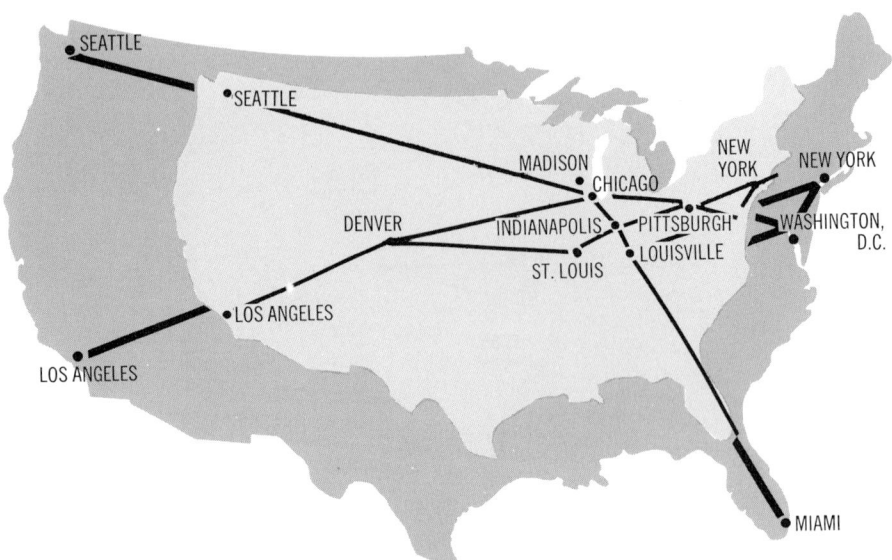

FIGURE 31-4 Substantial shrinkages in driving time are expected to result when the Interstate Highway System is completed. Driving time between Chicago and other major United States cities, for example, will average 28 percent less than at present. The smaller map indicates the relative saving in driving time on the Interstate System compared with present highways. (Adapted from *Highways and Their Meaning to Illinois Citizens*, George W. Barton & Associates, Evanston, Ill., July, 1958, p. 16.)

closer. Federal law does not permit commercial facilities on the Interstate right-of-way; so proper placement of interchanges is of critical importance for serving motorists' needs.

Whereas the Interstate System is being built as a toll-free system, about 2,300 miles of existing toll roads have been incorporated into the System, as permitted by law, rather than building parallel and duplicating facilities in the same travel corridors. 1964 marked the halfway point in time for the construction of the Interstate System. The year closed with 46 percent of the System open to traffic and construction proceeding at the rate (in 1964) of about 2,500 miles per year.

### U.S. System of Numbered Highways

Practically all drivers are familiar with the black-and-white route markers shaped like a shield and bearing the letters "US," a state name, and a route number. These markers appear on roads that are part of the U.S. System of Numbered Highways.

Primarily to guide drivers when traveling outside their home state, the American Association of State Highway Officials, in 1926, selected a system of connecting main routes throughout the country, assigned US

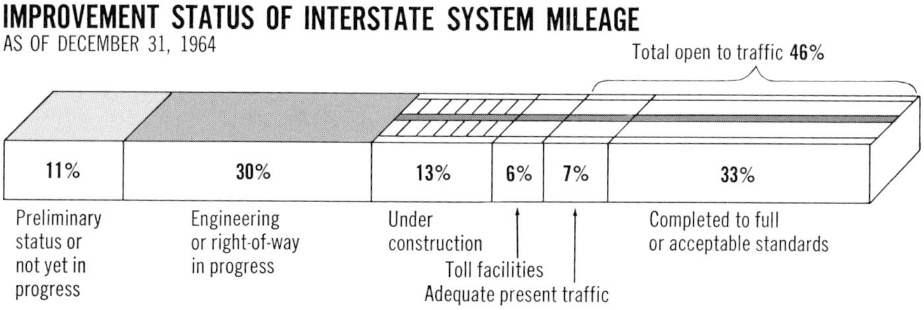

## IMPROVEMENT STATUS OF INTERSTATE SYSTEM MILEAGE
AS OF DECEMBER 31, 1964

Total open to traffic **46%**

| 11% | 30% | 13% | 6% | 7% | 33% |
|---|---|---|---|---|---|
| Preliminary status or not yet in progress | Engineering or right-of-way in progress | Under construction | Toll facilities | Adequate present traffic | Completed to full or acceptable standards |

FIGURE 31-5

numbers to them, and developed a special shield-shaped marker to be posted along them. Such routes now total 170,000 miles. Most of the highways in this network are also parts of state highway systems and of the Federal-aid Primary System.

A carefully worked-out policy has been followed in designating and marking US routes, which with few exceptions connect at least two states. The basic pattern used in assigning route numbers is as follows:

1. Routes which run predominantly east and west have *even* numbers, with the assigned numbers for various routes increasing from north to south.
2. Routes which extend mainly north and south have *odd* numbers, with the lowest-numbered routes in the Eastern part of the country and the highest-numbered ones in the West.
3. Alternate roads for a US route are indicated by addition of a cardinal direction letter or the letter A (for alternate) to the route number, i.e., US 20S, US 30A, etc.
4. Where a US route has branches within or approaching cities, signs with the word Bypass, Business, or Alternate are used in conjunction with the standard US route marker.

Interstate System routes are marked with a distinctive red, white, and blue shield presenting the word Interstate, a state name, and a route number. They, too, have even numbers for east-west routes and odd numbers for north-south routes. However, to help avoid confusion with US System routes, Interstate System routes with the lowest numbers are in the West and South—those with the highest numbers are in the East and North (thus, I-90 is an Interstate System route which runs east and west across the Northern part of the country). Other features of the Interstate System numbering pattern are:

1. Principal Interstate routes have one or two digits in their assigned numbers.
2. Evenly spaced Interstate routes of considerable length have a number ending in 0 (for east-west routes) or 5 (for north-south routes).
3. Parallel or diverging branches of an Interstate route are denoted by

the addition of an appropriate cardinal direction letter (E, W, S, or N) just below the regular Interstate number.
4. In urban areas, the regular one-or-two digit Interstate number is posted along the predominant path of through traffic.
5. Connecting full or partial circumferential routes in urban areas are designated by the appropriate Interstate route number plus an *even* number prefix, and radial or spur routes have the main Interstate number plus an *odd* number prefix.

## *STATE HIGHWAYS*

State highway systems comprise those roads which are usually of greatest importance to the state as a whole, as contrasted with those of primary importance to local areas. State highway departments have responsibility for over 736,000 miles of highways, of which about 59,000 miles are located in municipalities. These highways represent about 20 percent of total mileage in the United States and serve about 60 percent of the traffic. State highway systems incorporate the Interstate System and Federal-aid Primary System. They also include some but not all of the Federal-aid Secondary System, as well as other mileage not on any Federal-aid system.

State highway user tax revenues and Federal-aid payments from the Highway Trust Fund account for most of the funds available for state highways. State highway user tax revenues in 1964 were estimated at $6.5 billion, with 64 percent being derived from motor fuel taxes. Motor vehicle registration fees yielded 28 percent, and the remainder came from miscellaneous revenues, including motor carrier fees. Federal-aid funds paid to states from the Trust Fund totaled $3.9 billion during the same period.

## *COUNTY AND TOWNSHIP ROADS*

About 2.3 million miles of roads are the direct responsibility of approximately 3,000 counties and 15,000 rural towns and townships. Although this constitutes 65 percent of the total mileage in the United States, vehicle miles traveled on these highways represent only about 15 percent of the total travel. The heaviest travel is found in counties contiguous to or within a metropolitan area. Of the total county and local rural road mileage, 1.9 million miles, or 80 percent, are either unsurfaced or surfaced with slag, gravel, or stone. The remaining 20 percent have higher-type surfaces permitting all-weather use.

Only about 10 percent of this county and local rural road mileage serves more than 100 vehicles per day. However, in areas around large metropolitan centers some of these roads are being subjected to the ever-increasing travel demands of mushrooming suburban development. Trips to school, to church, to the shopping centers, and to employment centers more often than not are made partially or entirely on local roads. With 50 million of the 70 million population growth expected by 1980 to be located in suburban areas, county and township roads in these areas can be expected to assume an increasingly important role in providing for traffic service.

## How County and Township Roads Are Financed

Property taxes and other assessments as well as a share of state highway user taxes constitute the primary sources of funds available for expenditure by counties and townships on their roads. Before the advent of the gasoline tax, almost all these funds for local rural roads came from local property taxes. Now, nationally only about 29 percent are obtained from this source. About 54 percent of the revenue is provided as state aid by grants from state highway user taxes and other funds, and the remaining 17 percent by borrowing, general fund appropriations, Federal aid, tolls, and other miscellaneous receipts.

Counties and townships are now spending almost $2 billion per year on their highway plants. About half of this is expended for maintenance, and almost 35 percent for capital improvement. The remainder is spent for debt retirement, interest, transfer to other government levels for work performed on county and township roads, and for other miscellaneous services such as administration and traffic police.

## MUNICIPAL ROADS AND STREETS

There are almost 475,000 miles of roads and streets in municipalities constituting about 13 percent of the total mileage of all roads and streets in the United States. About 88 percent of this mileage is the direct responsibility of municipal authorities, with the remaining 12 percent administered by the state highway department. Municipal roads and streets serve two major functions. They provide access to homes and businesses, and they provide arterial service for the flow of business and commerce. Roadbeds usually provide right-of-way for the major utility services needed to serve the needs of the community. Comprising only 13 percent of total mileage, these highways furnish 48 percent of total traffic service.

All cities need a local system of traffic facilities that will serve their individual respective street transportation needs. New freeways and improved traffic management are helping many municipalities to solve one of their most difficult problems—traffic congestion. In most metropolitan areas with a population of 100,000 and more, the area devoted to streets and alleys amounts to about 30 to 50 percent of the total land area, a proportion which has not varied greatly over the years. Streets must permit motor vehicles to provide services for transportation of people and goods and for police and fire protection and many other public services, as well as furnishing access to adjacent properties, residential and business.

Many of our street networks were designed to serve travel patterns of an era of horse-drawn vehicles. Their inability to serve adequately the travel patterns of a motor vehicle era is the contributing factor to traffic congestion in our metropolitan areas. National traffic studies show that 50 to 90 percent of all motorists using downtown streets in peak travel hours have neither origin nor destination there, but are forced into the area by existing street patterns.

Experience has demonstrated that well-planned freeway systems in large urban areas bring significant relief to overburdened local streets.

Occupying only 1 to 3 percent of urban land area, these facilities can carry about one-half of all urban motor travel, making all areas of the city more readily accessible to those who wish to be there.

## Financing Municipal Roads and Streets

Property taxes account for less than 21 percent of revenues available for expenditure on municipal roads and streets. Local highway user taxes and intergovernmental transfer to the cities of a share of state and Federal highway user taxes accounts for 31 percent. The remaining 48 percent is derived mainly from general fund appropriations, bond sales, investment income, and other receipts.

Expenditures by municipalities have been running about $2 billion per year divided about equally between construction and maintenance. By 1970 it is predicted that expenditures will exceed $2.6 billion annually, with maintenance costs exceeding construction by about $85 million.

### SELECTED BIBLIOGRAPHY

*America's Lifelines—Federal Aid for Highways,* U.S. Department of Commerce, Bureau of Public Roads, Washington, D.C.

*Federal Aid for Highways,* National Highway Users Conference, Washington, D.C., 1959.

*Highway Statistics,* U.S. Department of Commerce, Bureau of Public Roads, Washington, D.C., annual.

*Interstate System Route Log and Finder List,* U.S. Department of Commerce, Bureau of Public Roads, Washington, D.C.

Smith, Wilbur, and Associates: *Future Highways and Urban Growth,* Automobile Manufacturers Association, Detroit, Mich., 1961.

# Driving as a Profession 32

VOCATIONAL training is not the objective of the driver education course. Nevertheless, that which benefits the student, the community, and the nation may well be considered one more advantage of the subject field. In this course students are taught that industry depends on great truck fleets for its existence and that cities depend on them for their food and other commodities. Many thousands of people rely on bus transportation to commute between their jobs and their homes.

In the post-Sputnik era a greatly increased emphasis has been given in schools to mathematics and science. Foreign languages and English also have received their share of attention. Many schools take pride in the high percentage of their graduates who go on to college. Considerable study has been devoted to treatment of the gifted student, and advanced and college placement courses have been added to the curriculum.

The curriculum for the college-bound student has been enriched. Educators recognize, however, the needs of a large segment of the students who will not enter college. Their welfare is also important, and their parents share the responsibility of supporting the educational system. The driver education teacher is in a position to do something special for the non-college-bound young people.

Admittedly there is an unrealistic connotation of prestige associated in the minds of the young (and some of the older) with certain types of employment, whereas other types are held in an entirely undeserved disrespect. Positions associated with what might be called "intellectualism" (to which references are made with words such as "research," "nuclear physicist," "scientist," etc.) comprise one current prestige type. Another type includes highly paid, highly placed leaders of business and industry. Although prestige positions may make excellent goals for the eligible, there is no justification for an association of "failure" with the "ordinary" jobs that make the nation prosperous and strong. Yet such jobs are lacking in status in the opinion of high school students, many of whom will later either have them for their life's work or will be married to young men who do.

There are many good jobs, and businesses, in motor vehicle transportation. Actually, some of the supposedly "menial" type jobs are more highly paid than some in the prestige categories. Certainly they are no less important. These facts should be emphasized in the driver education class, and perhaps in other areas of the curriculum. There was a philosophical laudation of "honest, constructive, manual work" by many parents and educators up to the past generation or so. Possibly because of a more commercial philosophy, possibly partly because of mass media such as television and motion pictures and the trends of fiction, what might be called a vocational caste system has taken form. Though this fictional stratification has little recognition, if any, within our educational system beyond the existence of separate courses of study for the college bound and vocationally oriented ones for others, it does exist in our schools. Also, it engenders opinions and attitudes among students (and parents) which are misleading to many in their plans for the future and a source of a lifetime of discontent for unknown thousands of young couples. Since highway transportation as a career is so closely related to driver education, it can easily be integrated into that area of the curriculum. Not only as a personal career but as a significant segment of American industry, it deserves a place in education.

Although this is true, the driver educator should always keep in mind the element of *course time*. This varies greatly among school systems throughout the country. Many schools provide what might be considered the minimum time needed to cover the essentials of safe, efficient driving. *Where that condition prevails, and wherever time is a limiting factor, a* **priority** *should be set up.* Obviously those essentials should be assigned the time needed. If time permits, however, this vocational and other non-driving but driving-related subject matter is indicated for inclusion.

## OPPORTUNITIES IN HIGHWAY TRANSPORTATION

Motor transportation is a giant of American industry, employing about two and a half million people. Eight million persons in the United States are employed by private and for-hire motor carriers, not including many thousands working in truck and bus manufacture and servicing.

1. Eighteen percent of the total vehicle mileage in the United States is rolled up by trucks, equal to 140 billion miles each year.
2. An estimated 348 billion ton-miles of intercity freight was carried by trucks in 1963, a 60 per cent increase in the past 10 years.
3. Thirty-six percent—approximately 14 million—of all students are transported to and from school by bus.
4. Truck fleets, composed of ten or more vehicles, now number 56,700 in the United States.

The most numerous job opportunities in the field are in driving. Here there are two avenues to student interest. One is the common one of reward. It comes as a surprise to many high school boys to learn that the rates of pay for professional drivers compare favorably with those in other job fields, including many which carry some prestige in the white-collar category. A survey covering this comparison would make an eye-opening out-of-class project for students.

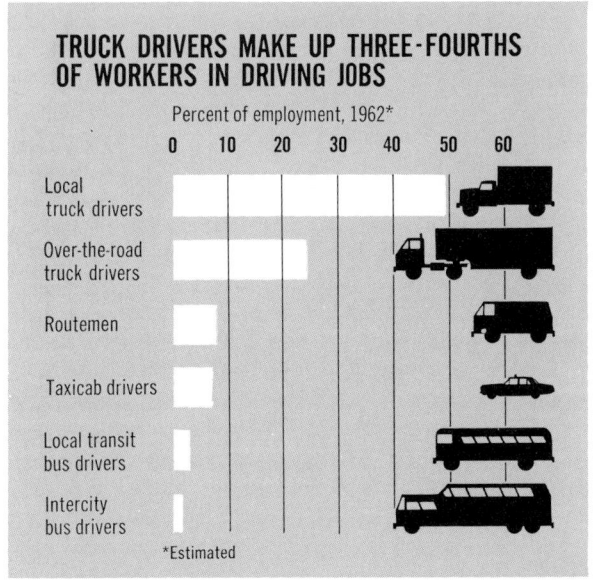

FIGURE 32-1 (Adapted from *1963-1964 Occupational Outlook Handbook,* Bureau of Labor Statistics, U.S. Department of Labor, Washington, D.C.)

Another area of potential interest is the "travel and adventure" appeal this sort of work has for many boys. Combined with the pride of highly skilled performance in driving, the work has for many this potentially strong appeal, as well as satisfying reward. All that is needed on the part of many well-qualified boys (and their future wives) is an understanding of the true value of the work and, for true satisfaction, a debunking of the prestige handicap.

FIGURE 32-2 This skill test is used to determine if the truck or bus driver knows where his front bumper is. Much field work and many demonstrations of practical testing and training methods are included in the training courses sponsored by the National Committee for Motor Fleet Supervisor Training at leading educational institutions.

## No "Blind Alley"

Obviously the highway transportation industry is not operated on one level, type, or classification of jobs. A great variety of assignments is available, according to the abilities, preference, and willingness to learn of the candidates.

The American Trucking Associations[1] list the following:

- Sales
- Traffic
- Terminal management and operations
- Over-the-road operations
- Professional driving
- Public relations
- Accounting and finance
- Insurance and safety
- Equipment maintenance and engineering
- Claims
- Purchasing
- Personnel and employee relations
- Industrial engineering
- Industrial organizations and associations

[1] *Your Future in Highway Transportation,* American Trucking Associations, Inc., Washington, D.C., 1962.

For those who aspire to advancement or specialization, specific training is indicated. Full college preparation is, of course, required for some of these job areas. A list of colleges offering courses in the field of motor transportation is available from the American Trucking Associations, Inc.[2] Motor carrier companies and associations provide scholarships for high school students to prepare for positions in the motor transportation field.[3]

FIGURE 32–3 Properly managed fleets require that the driver carefully inspect his vehicle, following a prescribed routine, before starting on a trip. This demonstration of the step-by-step procedure, including checking condition of tires, is part of the training program given fleet owners and supervisors in the motor fleet supervisor course sponsored by the National Committee for Motor Fleet Supervisor Training.

## Motor Fleet Supervisor Training

The National Committee for Motor Fleet Supervisor Training, composed of twenty nationally known automotive safety, truck, bus, and insurance organizations, has encouraged and assisted some fifty universities and many public school systems in conducting seven types of short training courses. The courses are designed for management and supervisory personnel. Among the subjects studied are selection, training, and supervision of drivers and mechanics. Among the results observed is a marked improvement in the safety record of the truck and bus transportation industry.

Indicative of the progress made by truck fleets which have established safety programs is the fact that although registration of commercial vehicles more than doubled in the past twenty-five years, the accident rate of fleets reporting their accident experience to the National Safety Council per million vehicle miles dropped from 47.10 in 1947–1948 to 13.39 in 1960–1963. In 1948, trucks accounted for 18 percent of the motor vehicles registered and 17 percent of the vehicles involved in accidents. Ten years later and

---

[2] *Transportation Courses in U.S. Colleges and Universities,* American Trucking Associations, Inc., Washington, D.C., 1964.

[3] *Scholarship Programs of Motor Carrier Companies and Associations,* American Trucking Associations, Inc., Washington, D.C., 1964.

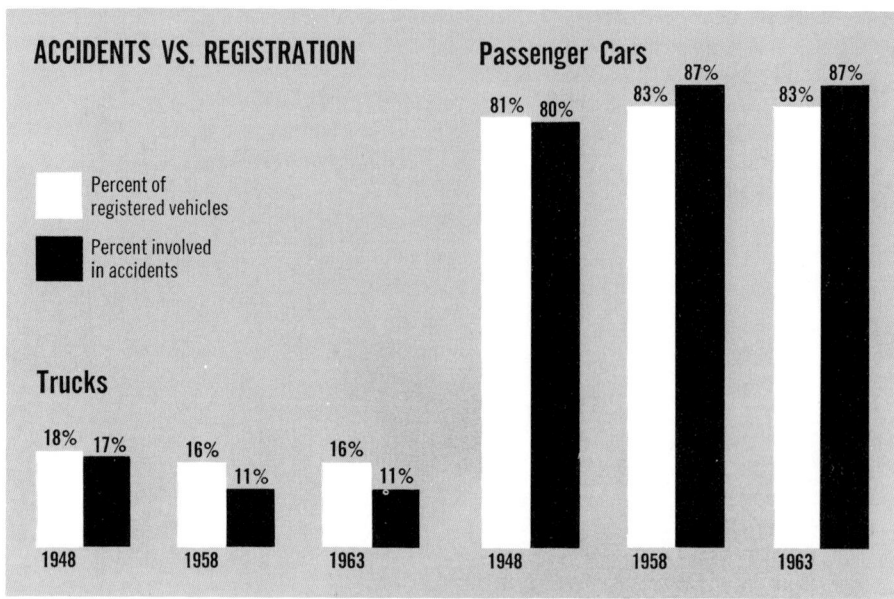

FIGURE 32-4 The accident rate of trucks showed a distinct improvement, while that of cars remained approximately level during the same period.

numbering 16 percent of vehicles registered, trucks accounted for only 11 percent of vehicles involved in accidents, and this record has been maintained since.

Commercial transportation is a subject well worth school time to teach. The one restricting element should be this: the amount of driver education classroom time available "above and beyond" that which is needed to teach the essential features of the course in terms of considered priorities.

## SELECTED BIBLIOGRAPHY

*Careers in Highway Traffic Safety,* National Commission on Safety Education, National Education Association, Washington, D.C., 1959.

*Employment Outlook in Driving Occupations,* Bureau of Labor Statistics, U.S. Department of Labor, Bulletin No. 1375-68, Washington, D.C., 1963–1964.

*Motor Carrier Safety Regulations,* Interstate Commerce Commission, Washington, D.C., 1961.

*Motor Truck Facts,* Automobile Manufacturers Association, Detroit, Mich. Annual publication.

Robinson, W. L.: *Businessmen and Motor Vehicles,* American Automobile Association, Washington, D.C., 1964.

*Scholarship Programs of Motor Carrier Companies and Associations,* American Trucking Associations, Inc., Washington, D.C., 1964.

*Transportation Courses in U.S. Colleges and Universities,* American Trucking Associations, Inc., Washington, D.C., 1964.

*Trucking Industry Careers,* American Trucking Associations, Inc., Washington, D.C., 1963.

*Urban Transportation Issues and Trends,* Automobile Manufacturers Association, Detroit, Mich., 1963.

*Your Future in Highway Transportation,* American Trucking Associations, Inc., Washington, D.C., 1962.

# VII IMPROVING PROFESSIONAL LEADERSHIP

IT HAS BEEN SAID that a leader's only true value lies in what he can do for those who follow him. The story is told of the president of a famous university who was once confronted by a lady deeply concerned about her daughter's chances of getting into college. It seemed that she alone, of all the young people known to mother and daughter, had no recommendations as a leader of her peers. She just wasn't a leader, and her mother said that she despaired of her ever being accepted into college.

"Your daughter will be most welcome as a student here, madam," the college president told the distraught mother. "In fact, we've been looking for her for some time. Everyone who applies for admission brings powerful testimonials as to his or her being the possessor of the quality of leadership in abundance. Now we will have at least one person for them all to lead."

The fact is that one may lead in one field or activity and not in another. One tends to lead in those areas in which one is best informed and/or skilled. It is not necessarily an either-or phenomenon.

The term "professional leadership" has two meanings. We recognize individuals within our profession who lead the rest of us. This is a common and obvious meaning of the term. Less recognized is another, more important implication of "professional leadership." The teacher of driver and traffic safety education is a specialist in a field of vital importance and interest to the students and to the community. This recognized importance and interest brings opportunity for service. The teacher's moral responsibility doesn't end with the last class of his daily schedule. The extent of that responsibility is described throughout much of this text.

Perhaps one other point for the new teacher to understand would be this: The leadership role doesn't require an extrovert or an orator—nor aggressiveness—nor the background of a class president, a team captain, or an honor student. The driver education teacher will be *led to lead*, if necessary, by sincere questions and requests for professional advice. Practice in classroom and elsewhere will give him eloquence. As an informed professional in a critical field, he will find that—*to a degree which he himself will determine*—leadership will seek him out. Improving his own competence for that leadership is his obligation to his students and fellow citizens.

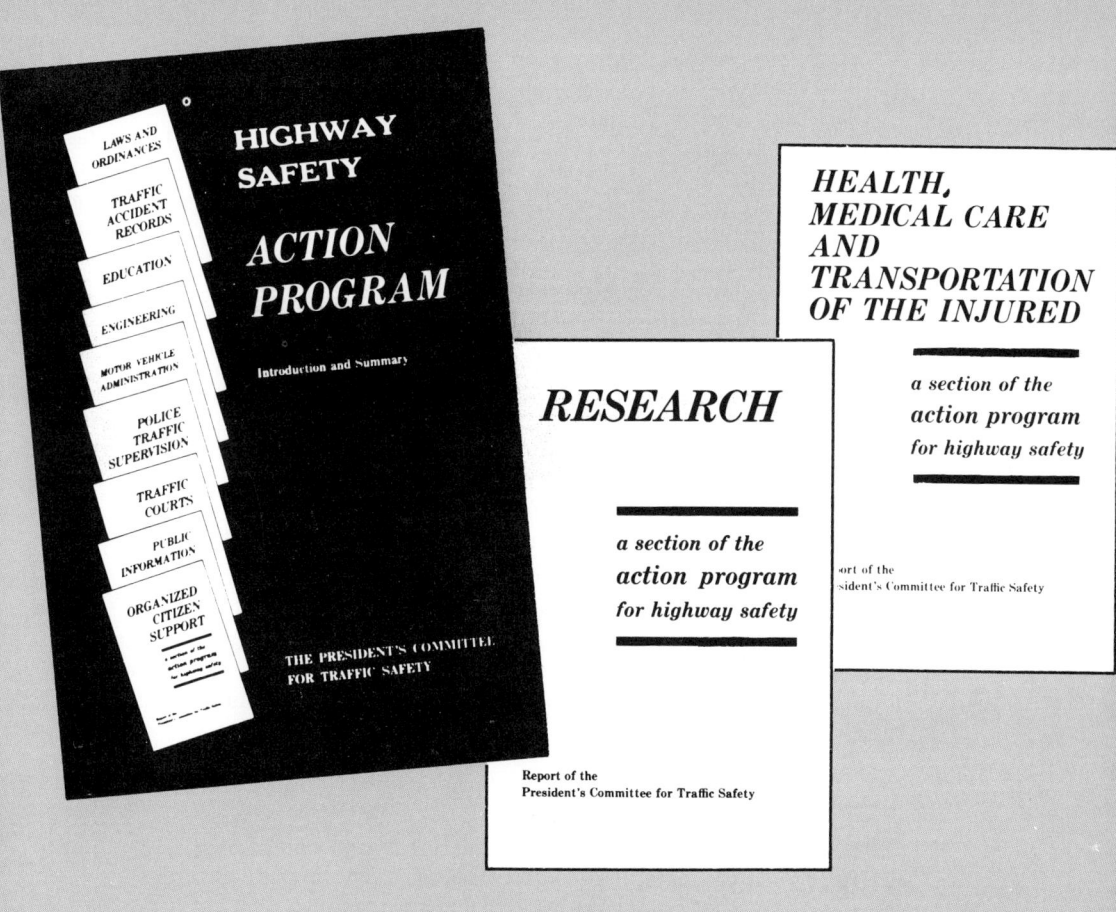

# The Action Program  33

IN THE "auto-oriented" society of today and tomorrow, our educational system will become more concerned with the complex problems of highway transportation. It will have to assume a greater role in the preparation of young people for the responsibilities of citizenship and survival in this motor-vehicle age. In view of our nation's dependency upon and use of the motor vehicle, the role of education is to provide the learning experiences that ultimately will enable society to achieve and maintain a safe and efficient highway transportation system. In undertaking this highly important task, educators themselves must thoroughly understand the nature of the problem and how to use traffic safety measures capable of reducing accidents.

Many factors contribute to the causes of traffic accidents and injuries. Inasmuch as the problem is so complex, it is neither reasonable nor possible to consider any single element of the total problem without recognizing that many other important facets exist. Efforts to classify the relative importance of the factors concerned in traffic accident causation have not been successful. In fact, some efforts have served only to obstruct the reduction of traffic accidents. Three major impediments may be described as follows:

1. Minimizing the importance of a broad, balanced attack such as the Highway Safety Action Program of which the President's Committee for Traffic Safety is the custodian.
2. Oversimplifying the problem by unwarranted and unrealistic emphasis on *single* facets of the total program to reduce accidents, such as safer roads, safer cars, speed-limit enforcement, etc.
3. Refusal to realize that the solution of the multifaceted traffic-accident problem is too complex for any single solution.

The Highway Safety Action Program is the national blueprint that stands today as the finest and most comprehensive compilation of traffic-accident-prevention measures yet developed. It is a guide for states and communities to use in the development of their own "official traffic safety program."

## *The President's Committee*

The President's Committee for Traffic Safety, on behalf of the President of the United States, is charged with the responsibility of stimulating the application of the Action Program of traffic safety measures. It continues to revise and perfect the program in accordance with the findings of research and experience. The committee has established a technical advisory council, representing thirty-six national service organizations, associations of public officials, and Federal agencies as the medium for carrying out its responsibilities.

The Action Program actually had its beginning in 1924, at the first National Conference on Street and Highway Safety, called by President Herbert Hoover at the time when he was Secretary of Commerce. Committees of experts in the various fields of traffic accident prevention were formed to survey and analyze what was being done throughout the country in engineering, law, enforcement, education, and other areas—to learn which approaches were proving most effective, which were not, and what was needed to bring about improvement. Over the ensuing years, the problems of traffic accident prevention and the means of coping with them were studied in depth. Old methods were improved. New ones were developed and tested.

But, it wasn't until 1946 that all this knowledge was brought together for the benefit of the entire nation. It was then that former President Harry S. Truman called his President's Highway Safety Conference in Washington, attended by representatives of every state. Then and there, all the successful methods and techniques that the experts had been developing and testing for more than twenty years were assembled into a single package, and desig-

FIGURE 33-1 President Lyndon B. Johnson receiving a report from the President's Committee for Traffic Safety on the status of the implementation of the Action Program. Seated next to the President is W. R. Hearst, Jr., Chairman of the Committee. Also present (left to right) are William S. Foulis, Executive Director of the Committee, and J. O. Mattson, former Executive Committee Chairman of the Advisory Council to the President's Committee.

nated the "Action Program." This program was revised slightly in 1949, and updated in 1960, to incorporate certain new techniques.

In recognition of the fact that there is no single solution to traffic accidents, the Action Program gives equal emphasis to all the components of accident prevention. When applied, all its elements fit together in a balanced program. These are its major elements: Laws and Ordinances, Traffic Accident Records, Education, Engineering, Motor Vehicle Administration, Police Traffic Supervision, Traffic Courts, Public Information, Organized Citizen Support, Research, and Health, Medical Care, and Transportation of the Injured.

## INTERACTION

If this program is to be effectively applied, it must be borne in mind—by public officials, educators, and private citizens alike—that *all* its elements are necessary, that *each is dependent upon the others*.

### Law

Laws, which are fundamental, give our public officials the authority they need to do their jobs, to set up standards of behavior which protect *us*. But how can the laws protect us unless, in the interest of our safety, they're *enforced* by the police to discourage violations that cause accidents? And how can enforcement succeed, unless our *traffic courts* impress upon violators the necessity for obeying the law for their own safety, as well as for ours?

### Courts

The judges need to know about the past conduct of violators, so that they can pass judgment intelligently.

### Police

The police need to know when and where accidents are happening, so that traffic officers can be assigned effectively.

### Records

Where do we find this information? These facts are reported and collected through what we call *accident record systems,* which show *when* most accidents occur, *where* they happen, the ages of the drivers, direction of

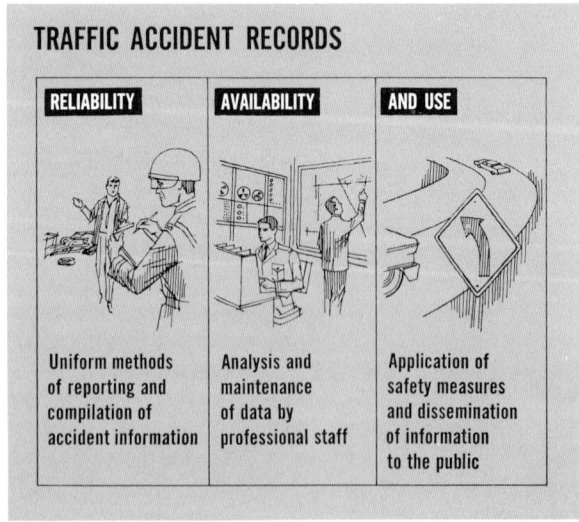

FIGURE 33-2 Interpretation of accident records is an important element of traffic safety research. (From *The Action Program: A Report to the President,* President's Committee for Traffic Safety, Washington, D.C., 1964.)

travel of the vehicles involved, and physical conditions of the roadway. These facts are needed by everyone concerned with traffic accident prevention.

### Motor Vehicle Administration

Consider, for example, a state's licensing authorities, whose job is to regulate the use of motor vehicles in the interest of safety. These authorities must have the facts about accidents to know what needs emphasis in the license examination, to determine whether to grant or withhold a license, and to learn which drivers are conducting themselves unlawfully or unsafely. They may impress upon those drivers that they must do better.

## Education

How best can we prepare the candidate to meet the license examination requirements? How can we train him for good citizenship in our motorized society? By *traffic safety education,* beginning in the elementary grades, and by *driver education* in high school, to teach young people to survive and to let others survive. In their traffic safety education courses, students should learn the *reasons* and the *need* for all the traffic-accident-prevention measures we've been discussing.

## Engineering

Students, in education, learn the role of *engineering* in *designing* safety into our streets, our highways, and our vehicles and in improving traffic flow by strategic use of controls.

## Public Information

What does it take to prevent accidents? It takes *all* these elements, and it also takes *public information* programs to tell us the *facts* on *all aspects* of the traffic-accident problem in our state and community—facts we need to protect ourselves, facts supplied by public officials and brought to us by all media.

## Support

It takes *support* of accident-prevention programs by *organized* citizens. In a free country, our officials can do no more than we, the public, will accept and back up.

## Research

With the rest, it always will take *research* to learn more about people, highways, and vehicles and how these three can be combined to improve our highway transportation system.

## Care of the Injured

Even after an accident occurs, the effects of injuries can be reduced through proper *emergency care* at the scene and during transportation to a medical facility.

The job of helping us to survive in this motor-vehicle age is not simple, there's no simple answer. It takes *all* these elements, and each one depends upon the other. One element, alone, cannot do the job.

## QUALITY STANDARDS

But just any kind of accident prevention is not enough for today's traffic or tomorrow's. That is why our public officials need the guidance of the *minimum standards* of excellence set forth in the Action Program. Laws and ordinances must be sound, realistic, clear, and explicit. Laws must be *uniform* everywhere, so that people will know what's expected of them as they move from one place to another. Laws must do things *for* people, not

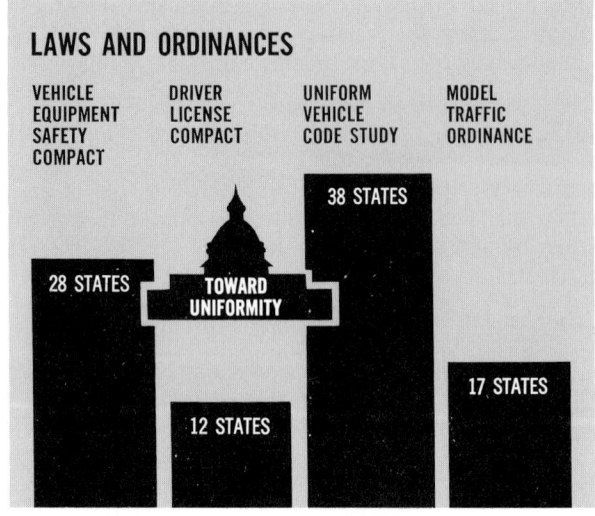

FIGURE 33-3 Uniformity in traffic laws is one of the objectives of the Action Program. (From *The Action Program: A Report to the President,* President's Committee for Traffic Safety, Washington, D.C., 1964.)

just do things *to* them. For our protection we need police supervision by trained officers using modern techniques and equipment, working to assure our safety and convenience on the highways night and day. We need dignified courts, where the goal is not simply to punish violators, but to instill the desire for *voluntary* law observance, to make the streets and roads safer for us and our families. Traffic-accident records must be complete and informative, records that are *analyzed* and *used,* so that accident prevention programs can be based on *fact,* not guesswork. Licensing programs should generate respect for the driving license; regular inspection should reveal hazards before they cause accidents; financial responsibility laws should take many irresponsible drivers off the road. Highway engineering, vehicle engineering, traffic engineering should help make driving comfortable, convenient, and safe.

We need safety education that not only teaches skills, but gives our young people *knowledge* and *mature attitude,* the preparation they need for living in this modern world. Public information programs should build public understanding and acceptance of measures designed to help and protect us, emphasizing the importance of all of us meeting our personal responsibilities. Citizens should be organized in support of public officials with Action Program responsibilities which are based on recognition that our officials can't do the job alone. Research is needed that enlists the best

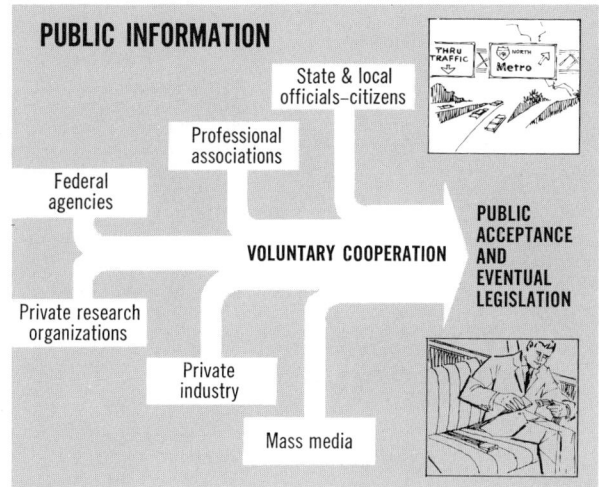

FIGURE 33-4 Public information leads to citizen support and constructive legislation. (Adapted from *The Action Program: A Report to the President,* President's Committee for Traffic Safety, Washington, D.C., 1964.)

minds in the universities and the professions, in business and industry, to work with public officials in the quest for the many needed answers. Adequate medical standards must be set for determining unfitness to drive, to recognize the effects of alcohol and drugs on the driver, and to assure proper emergency care of the injured at the scene of an accident, during transportation, and until professional medical care commences.

What does it take to stop accidents? It takes the principles, procedures, and techniques of *all* this program, which has been endorsed by public officials, educators, and major safety organizations as the best and most complete traffic-accident-prevention blueprint yet developed.

## SELECTED BIBLIOGRAPHY

The President's Committee for Traffic Safety, Washington, D.C.
    *The Action Program, A Report to the President,* 1964.
    *Highway Safety Action Program*
    Sections of the Action Program:* Laws and Ordinances, Traffic Accident Records, Education, Engineering, Motor Vehicle Administration, Police Traffic Supervision, Traffic Courts, Public Information, Organized Citizen Support, Research, Health, Medical Care, and Transportation of the Injured.

* Available from Superintendent of Documents, U.S. Government Printing Office, Washington, D.C. 20025.

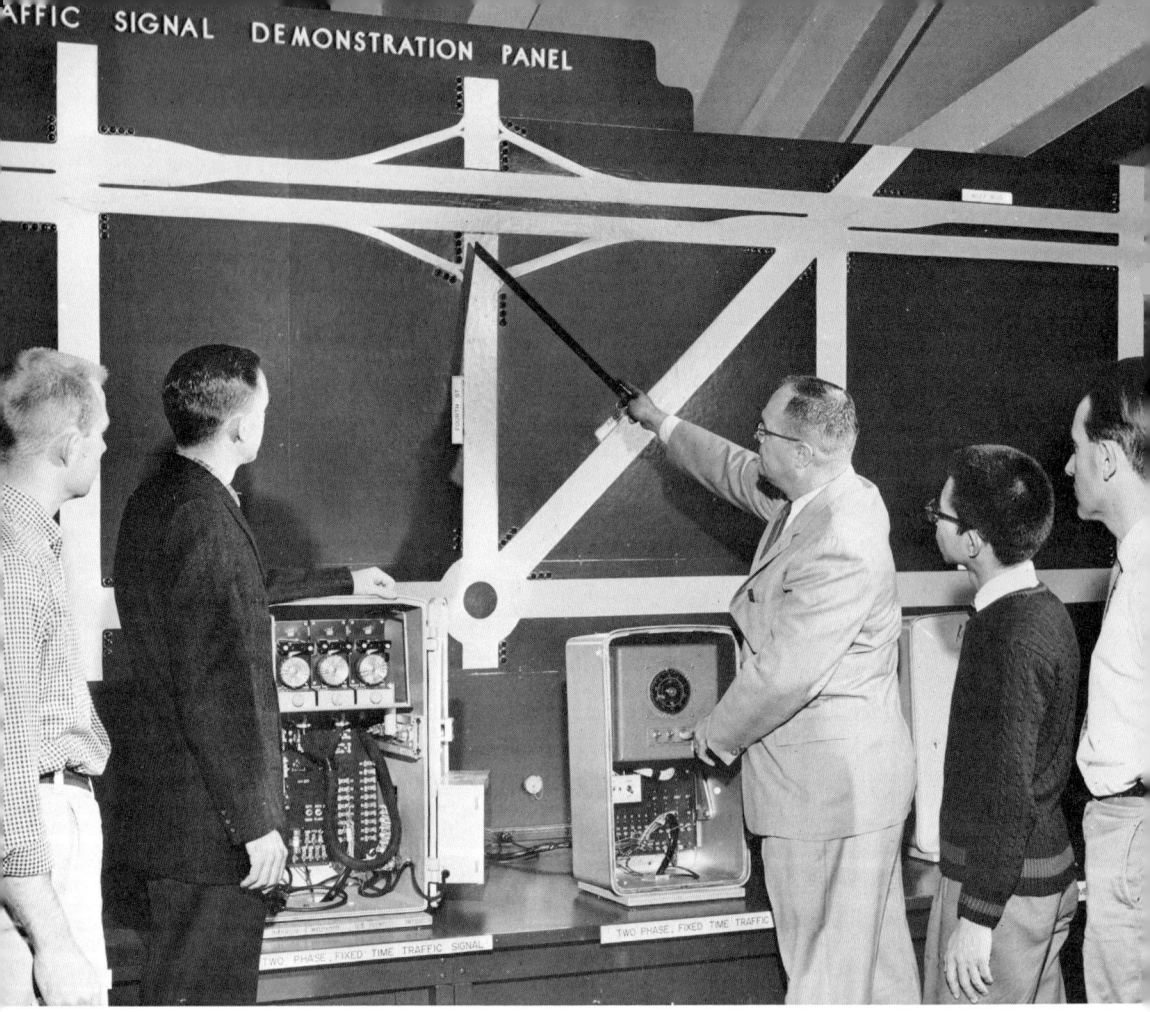

# Traffic Safety Centers    34

TRADITIONALLY, the university is a center of learning and of research. In recent years there has been some criticism that those holding professorships concentrate on research and neglect teaching, to the disadvantage of the college student. Like many contemporary criticisms of education, this is a generalization of what may be observed as an occasional, but by no means common, situation.

The fact is that part of the research contribution of many universities is the result of the faculty-guided work of graduate students. Another very pertinent consideration is the fact that the university staff member who engages in research is in the best position to present to his students *today's* knowledge in his field. Also, contrary to the belief of some, research is not intradisciplinary, pinpoint narrowness. The man who splits the atom sees also the limitless patterns of space. To enter properly, in research, into new areas of knowledge, one must first know the body of existing knowledge. And in whose statements on a subject does the serious student have greater confidence than in the person who stands at the *very source of knowledge* of that subject? It is in the smaller college, isolated from the world of research, that the teaching staff must make an extra effort to keep informed and to present to their students today's body of knowledge.

In traffic safety we recognize an interdisciplinary field. At least three kinds of engineering, as well as medicine, behavioral science, law, and physical science (etc.) are components of the broad entity we call "traffic safety." One can easily see that the university which has departments concerned with these disciplines is in an excellent position both to teach and to investigate traffic safety.

To take advantage of the potential wealth of knowledge and instructional skills and to mobilize them into curriculums for driver and traffic safety education, for highway and traffic engineering, for police traffic supervision, for motor vehicle administration, or for any desired traffic-related professional preparation, an administrative identity with a coordinative function is needed—a "center." This grouping of departmental and other entities of the university into traffic-related curriculums and services is one type of *traffic safety center*.

There is no rigid pattern for such centers throughout the country, although they do operate at New York University, The Pennsylvania State University, Michigan State University, Yale University, Northwestern University, the University of Illinois, Oklahoma State University, the University of California, Purdue University, the Agricultural and Mechanical College of Texas, Southern Illinois University, and others. Teachers College of Columbia University and Iowa State University have programs which prepare teachers and include research, and Cornell University and the University of Virginia operate research-oriented programs. For an account of each of the centers cited, recommended reading is the publication *University Transportation and Accident Prevention Centers*.[1]

A clear concept of the university traffic safety center can be gleaned from the following description:[2]

> In discussing the growth and role of centers in the decade ahead, it is necessary first to identify what is meant by the word "center."
> I shall attempt to define the concept of a center in its fullest sense. In doing so I shall use the terminology Highway Traffic Safety Center since my experience with a center is in that field. The same concept and definition, however, can apply to a center which would embrace other fields of safety as well.
> A university traffic safety center is:
> —An administrative device to effect the liaison with and between many

---

[1] *University Transportation and Accident Prevention Centers*, A Study Conducted by the Traffic Safety Research and Education Committee of the Association of State Universities and Land Grant Colleges and the National Commission on Safety Education, National Education Association, Washington, D.C., 1962.

[2] Gordon H. Sheehe, *Outlook: The Growth and Role of Centers in the Decade Ahead*, presented at the National Safety Congress, 1960.

FIGURE 34-1 Traffic engineering students at Yale University's Bureau of Highway Traffic set up a spot speed check with a radar meter.

teaching departments, service departments, research bureaus, and other special units within the university.
—An organizational device to obtain the multidiscipline attention and effort needed in solving the complex problems of traffic facilitation and accident prevention through research, credit course work, short courses and conferences, field assistance, and information materials and services.
—A means of stimulating interest of university faculty and administrative personnel in helping solve traffic problems.
—A means of utilizing most effectively the resources of the entire university, deciding upon activities deserving priority, and maintaining balance in the total traffic assistance program of the university.
—A manifestation (in terms of budget, facilities, equipment, designated personnel, planned activity program, and accomplishments) of the university's serious dedication to improvement of motor vehicle transportation and traffic accident prevention.
—The center is a clearing house, a referral unit, a central pool of information, a means of communication and avoiding unwanted duplication. The center is a forum which through staff meetings, colloquia, and critiques enriches the thinking of participants having diverse professional and educational backgrounds and experience. This cross fertilization develops staff with broader and deeper understanding of the problems and the contributions from different approaches which can be made by numerous disciplines or sciences working together toward a common objective.
—The center is a fact-finding, problem-analyzing unit.
—It is the liaison unit for the university with the many outside agencies and groups—official, professional, and laymen—who are directly and indirectly active in traffic activities.
—It is the university's "voice" on traffic matters.

—It is the office "outsiders" know about and come to. It is the source of assistance for them.
—It is the contact-making unit in the traffic field.
—It is the service unit of the university in providing traffic assistance off campus.
—It is the source of leadership for much state and local activity. Its staff stimulates activity of committees and commissions and aids in analyzing problems and developing programs. It can enlist scientists and technicians on the university faculty whose skill and specialized talents are needed by groups or agencies outside the university.
—It is the recruiter of personnel for the university program and the developer of career people for the many functions of highway traffic administration and safety.
—It is the seeker of funds for the researcher and of position opportunities for the graduate.

The center can serve in many ways, as the preceding description shows. From the standpoint of driver and traffic safety education, it increases in stature as the standards for teacher certification improve.

The college with the single-course teacher preparation, common throughout the country, still has its function. Driver education teachers are needed, and with increasing high school enrollments and state support legislation, more will be needed for some time to come. As long as these courses meet state certification standards, they will furnish basic specific preparation of some driver education teachers. Many of these colleges have other departments that can add to the educational repertoire of the teacher candidate. When state standards are raised, many of these colleges will add to their staff and facilities and meet the new standards. All candidates, particularly young teachers with families, are not in a position to attend distant universities which have centers; yet they want to *begin* their study. The smaller college which has one, two, or three courses in the subject field is the first step toward their chosen field of teaching. We must be sufficiently realistic to recognize this matter of economics and geography. (It is worth mentioning at this point that every college which prepares teachers of any subject field or grade should include a *required* course in *general* safety education. Every teacher is responsible for the physical safety of his students.)

## Looking to the Future

Eventually all colleges which prepare teachers of driver and traffic safety education must offer curriculums in that field sufficient for certification on improved (in most states) standards. The future of the subject field, however, lies in the *high-quality, comprehensive* teacher preparation which is already in effect in some universities and "on the drawing boards" of leaders in the field in others (Chapter 36, "Design for Tomorrow"). Such teacher preparation can well be the service of the traffic safety center to the schools and students of the country—a *mobilization* of the strong features of a great university into a comprehensive professional curriculum. To these centers will come the in-service teacher who has exhausted the offerings of the smaller college. Here will come the serious student who wishes to emphasize driver and traffic safety education in his graduate study. Here, too, will come the advanced student to perform research in the field.

## Research—A Function of the Center

It has been mentioned that the traffic safety center may be research-oriented. Serving with a staff of highly trained experts in related disciplines, the university can perform very valuable services to the community and the state.

The motor vehicle and traffic administrator cannot be professionally qualified in all the areas related to his responsibility. He cannot personally know the qualifications of all the specialists who are available for research and consultation. Yet he must, conscientiously, make use of the best of today's knowledge, and he must employ research methods to seek out new knowledge that will enhance the capability of his department or agency. To whom can he turn for competent professional services?

FIGURE 34-2 The university traffic safety center has the advantage of staff and equipment appropriate for professional training.

The university offers a reliable source of data and services. Here is centered a competent professional staff versed in a variety of disciplines. Here, too, is a professional integrity that is not guaranteed in every individual or firm which recognizes in traffic safety a potential source of funds for its own profit. Some such individuals and firms are not capable of performing the services they profess to furnish. Of course, all universities are not staffed for traffic safety research. The motor vehicle or traffic administrator or other official who would have research and/or professional writing done would do well to find a university with a center, and then to *study the qualifications of the individuals on the staff*. Not all university research has been of high quality. That which has erred has generally involved well-intentioned attempts to work in the supposedly simple field of driver education and/or traffic safety without an adequate, appropriately prepared staff.

This is another evidence of the need for the regularly organized university safety center.

Universities which pioneered in the safety center concept and the specific fields associated with each are: Northwestern—Northwestern University Traffic Institute (*police traffic supervision, enforcement, licensing, etc.*), 1936; Purdue—Public Safety Institute (*engineering, police, fire, motor vehicle*), 1936; Yale—Bureau of Highway Traffic (*traffic engineering*), 1937; New York University—Center for Safety Education (*teacher and leadership education, research, publications, field services*), 1938; The Pennsylvania State University—Institute of Public Safety (*industrial, home, farm, driver education*), 1938. As evidenced in the previously cited list, the number is growing. It is conceivable that as the broad scope of safety education gains increased recognition and as the state certification requirements in driver and traffic safety education are upgraded, the university center identified as a safety *education* unit will become more common.

This is the situation of the 1960s. By the end of the decade, perhaps a new form may emerge. The *school of education* may rightfully include as an area of emphasis—like the traditional major-and-minor concept—safety education or even, specifically, driver and traffic safety education. Here there would be a thoroughly competent staff of education-oriented specialists, a staff which could teach all the elements of the "major" field, not as engineers, police, or general psychologists, but as safety educators well versed in those fields and/or as professors of those disciplines who have become highly informed "immigrants" in driver and traffic safety education as described under *For the Qualified* and *The Contributing Discipline* in Chapter 36, "Design for Tomorrow." An example of this adaptation was described in recommending a "psychology of safety education" to parallel the development of "traffic engineering," a specialty within the broad world of engineering. Courses in engineering for the engineer, police administration for the police official, and other professional specialties aren't necessarily the same as the courses in those areas which should be presented for the teacher of driver education, any more than *performing* music is the same as *music education* for the teacher.

As the field of driver and traffic safety education becomes larger, both in the number of those interested and in scope of content, increased staff and facilities will be assigned to it in many of those institutions preparing teachers. This may lead to well-staffed *departments of safety education* or of *driver and traffic safety education* very possibly far outnumbering today's *centers*. Such departments may also spring from and absorb some of the present centers, to be guided by the present leadership of the staffs of the latter.

The pattern of organization of teacher education in this field is still flexible, but the force of demand for increase and improvement is observable and firm.

## SELECTED BIBLIOGRAPHY

*University Transportation and Accident Prevention Centers*, Traffic Safety Research and Education Committee of the Association of State Universities and Land-Grant Colleges and the National Commission on Safety Education, National Education Association, Washington, D.C., 1962.

# Resource Agencies     35

DRIVER education courses, practically nonexistent thirty years ago, are now given in three out of five public high schools. This rapid expansion did not occur by chance. Neither was it achieved by any one group or organization. Many organizations, aware of the potentials of driver and traffic safety education, have contributed greatly to its development. Adequately prepared teachers, dual-control cars, films, text materials, and training aids were all lacking at the inception of the program. Fortunately, a number of organizations outside the school recognized the need and came to the aid of the program and the schools by helping to make these necessities available.

One occasionally reads criticisms of the program which are based on the fact that "out-of-school" institutions played a part in its development. Two things come to the mind of an educator when this is mentioned. One, the critics can hardly be aware of the history of public education if they believe this sets any precedent at all! Also, does it really matter? Does it have any bearing on the value of the program to the student? If an insurance company can save money (and charge lower premiums, and *save lives*) by encouraging high school driver education, is it even reasonably intelligent to condemn the course and the company because it does so? Many educational materials on the general subject of health are distributed free of charge by life insurance companies and used to good advantage in schools. Many industries furnish instructional materials free to schools.

The type of thinking that decries the existence of *any* altruism in *any* man or group of men reflects, perhaps, more on the character of its originators than on that of its object or objects. Many of the organizations described here offer aid to traffic safety and to high school driver education. Intelligently directed, the educator's interest is in the aid and in its effect on the program and on the student. The school would not make any financial commitment to any organization because of its aid. The school does not advertise. Similarly, it does not hypothesize *motives*. Were this to be done, there might be some misgivings about some of those who seem to go out of their way to condemn driver education and the institutions which give it support of many kinds. Support of public education, constructively directed, is a public service. It will be noted that most of the groups cited here are nonprofit institutions. Some of them give material aids to driver education, and some provide services to driver education and to traffic safety in general.

## *Continuing Services Are Needed*

Although driver and traffic safety education has grown extensively in both quantity and quality over the years and is still growing, a plateau-like tendency has been evident in recent years. In terms of percentage of eligible young people reached by the course in our growing population, the present growth rate of driver education is not nearly sufficient to achieve the potential effect of education in today's quite dismal traffic accident picture.

A great deal is still needed. There are still many problems to be solved. Courses are still not available to over half of the eligible students. Improvement of the quality of instruction is needed at both high school and college levels. Research is needed on just *what* should be taught and what *methods* of teaching are best adapted to the wide variety of course content. There is much yet to be learned about the use of simulators, driving ranges, television, programmed learning, and other teaching aids.

Some of the organizations listed in this chapter will contribute to tomorrow's knowledge in those matters. Others will provide materials and services directly to schools. Still others will serve to contribute to and to improve traffic safety in general and in doing so will be allies of safety educators engaged in the same vital mission. The teacher should know about these organizations, their natures, and their services. Many useful posters, leaflets, and booklets are available without charge from some of these organizations.[1] They provide much worthwhile information to supplement

[1] *Free Materials and Services for Driver Education Courses,* American Automobile Association, Washington, D.C., 1964.

the text material the instructor would normally have. In the cases of some of the organizations listed in this chapter, the assistance is indirect, consisting of research and publications on accident prevention rather than materials for direct distribution to schools or colleges.

Although these organizations are all interested in driver education, this is only one of their interests. Those interests are much broader and include many other traffic safety activities. They can provide information and help that will enrich and upgrade the driver education course to give the high school student a better understanding and appreciation of the over-all traffic problem. A better understanding will result in better citizens for the future.

### American Association of Motor Vehicle Administrators, 404 Madison Building, Washington, D.C. 20005

This is an organization of officials in the United States and Canadian Provinces responsible for the administration and enforcement of motor vehicle laws. The purposes of the Association are to promote reasonable and uniform laws and regulations regarding the operation of motor vehicles, and reciprocity between and among jurisdictions in all matters pertaining to motor vehicles and their operations. Services provided members include training programs for employees in the various fields of motor vehicle control, advisory and consultant services to members of the Association in the reorganization of motor vehicle departments, and publication of technical manuals and bulletins.

### American Association of State Highway Officials, 917 National Press Building, Washington, D.C. 20004

The Association is primarily interested in the improved location, design, construction, maintenance, and administration of highways. Research is conducted to foster better highways. The Association administers the road-numbering system in the United States and cooperates in the development of uniform signs and control devices. It publishes the quarterly magazine *American Highways*. AASHO publications are confined to administrative and engineering specifications and standards and do not include handout material on driver education.

### American Automobile Association, 1712 G Street, N.W., Washington, D.C. 20006

The American Automobile Association is a federation of 782 motor clubs and branches with nearly 9 million members. As part of its traffic safety program, educational material is made available to elementary and secondary schools. This includes posters, lesson guides, stories, teaching aids, driver education materials, training and testing devices, textbooks, and dual controls for driver education cars.

Schools are given assistance in securing dual-control cars. Instructors are provided for driver education courses for high school teachers. Consultants are provided for conferences and meetings involving driver education.

Technical assistance is also provided on parking and traffic problems and on legislation affecting traffic and safety. An annual inventory of pedestrian safety in cities and states is made and recognition given to the cities and states with the best programs and accident records.

**American Bar Association, Traffic Court Program, 1155 East 60th Street, Chicago, Illinois 60637**

The primary purpose of the Traffic Court Program of this organization is to promote better administration of justice by traffic courts. This is done by promoting national standards, conducting traffic court conferences, serving as a clearinghouse for information on traffic court improvement, and making studies of traffic courts.

Assistance is given for installing traffic courts and training personnel. An annual inventory of traffic court activities is made, and awards are given to states and cities. Assistance is given in the preparation of films dealing with traffic court problems. A number of publications have been prepared on the operation of traffic courts.

**American Driver & Traffic Safety Education Association, Department of the National Education Association, 1201 16th Street, N.W., Washington, D.C. 20036**

This is an association primarily of elementary, high school, and college teachers, school safety coordinators, supervisors of safety education, and others interested in driver and traffic safety education. Annual conferences are held and the proceedings published. Consultant services are provided as well as a graduate scholarship program for driver and safety education personnel.

**American Medical Association, Committee on Medical Aspects of Automotive Safety, 535 North Dearborn Street, Chicago, Illinois 60610**

This committee collects and disseminates information on medical conditions which affect driving. Medical standards for driver licensing are developed and recommendations made for the improvement of safety features of automobiles.

**American Optometric Association, 7000 Chippewa Street, St. Louis, Missouri 63119**

Field service is provided by this Association to improve vision standards for driver licensing. Research on vision and driving is supported. A number of pamphlets on the relationship of vision to highway safety are available.

**American Trucking Associations, Inc., 1616 P Street, N.W., Washington, D.C. 20036**

ATA is a national federation of state trucking associations and conferences with headquarters in Washington, D.C. The Departments of Safety and of Public Relations are the major resource divisions of interest to teachers in the driver and traffic safety education field. Single copies of publications on professional driver selection, training, and supervision, on careers and opportunities in the industry, and on related safety materials are available without cost to teachers on request. Some materials applicable to general traffic safety are available in quantities to meet classroom need without cost.

### Auto Industries Highway Safety Committee, Inc., 2000 K Street, N.W., Washington, D.C. 20006

AIHSC is sponsored by the nation's automobile and tire manufacturers, the National Automobile Dealers Association, and the National Tire Dealers and Retreaders Association.

The nineteen-year-old organization, in its efforts to build grass-roots support for traffic safety, provides a wide variety of materials and services. Its programs include: aid to high school driver education, youth traffic safety activities, the National Vehicle Safety-Check, official motor vehicle inspection, Women's Crusade for Seat Belts, Drive for a Safe Holiday and better highways.

The Committee works with public officials, new car and tire dealers, civic, service, safety, and women's groups in support of the Action Program of the President's Committee for Traffic Safety.

### Automobile Manufacturers Association, Inc., 320 New Center Building, Detroit, Michigan 48202

One of the major functions of this association is the collection and dissemination of information on the manufacture, distribution, and use of motor vehicles. The Association cooperates with other industrial and governmental groups in solving problems resulting from the manufacture and use of motor vehicles. It cooperates with many groups, such as governmental agencies, in furthering the appropriate use of motor vehicles and enhancing their role in our society.

### Automotive Safety Foundation, 200 Ring Building, Washington, D.C., 20036

This foundation is a nonprofit research and educational organization financed by the automotive and related industries to work in the public interest to improve the safety, efficiency, and convenience of highway transportation. The Foundation gives financial support to colleges and universities and to national organizations for research, training, and educational activities. Technical staff services are available on engineering, legal, regulatory, educational, administrative, and public support aspects of highway transportation.

### Highway Research Board, 2101 Constitution Avenue, N.W., Washington, D.C. 20418

The Board is an excellent continuing source of reasonably priced publications dealing with virtually every facet of highway transportation, including economics, design, materials, maintenance, traffic control and operations, urban transportation planning, and legal studies. The information that goes into these wide-ranging books is gathered from several sources, the most important of which is the Board's Annual Meeting at which the nation's top highway researchers from highway departments, universities, and industry present reports on their studies. In addition, more than 100 technical committees sponsor and promote research in highway transportation, and the Board also administers an extensive research program for the states and publishes the results. A list of available publications may be obtained from the Highway Research Board.

## Institute of Traffic Engineers, 1725 DeSales Street, N.W., Washington, D.C. 20036

This is an association of traffic engineers throughout the country. Technical papers on traffic engineering subjects are presented at the annual meeting. A technical library for internal use is maintained. Various technical bulletins are published as well as the monthly magazine *Traffic Engineering*.

## Insurance Institute for Highway Safety, 1725 DeSales Street, N.W., Washington, D.C. 20036

The Insurance Institute for Highway Safety was formed in 1959 to provide assistance to officials and citizens of the states in establishing well-balanced traffic safety programs. Its sponsoring agencies are the American Insurance Association, National Association of Automotive Mutual Insurance Companies, and National Association of Independent Insurers.

IIHS assistance is given in three ways: (1) direct assistance to official traffic safety programs in selected states, (2) indirect assistance through financial support for national traffic safety service organizations, and (3) direct financial assistance to qualified state citizen safety organizations.

A special activity is the Annual National High School Driver Education Achievement Program, through which a yearly survey is made to determine the status of high school driver education in each of the states.

## International Association of Chiefs of Police, Field Service Division, 1319 18th Street, N.W., Washington, D.C. 20036

The IACP, organized in 1893, represents police executives of city, county, state, and Federal law enforcement agencies. Consultants are provided to assist law enforcement agencies in planning for, and direction of, efficient police administration, operation, and methods, including traffic supervision. Continuing programs of research are carried on, and training manuals are developed. The Association has a Highway Safety Division and is very active in all phases of traffic safety. It maintains close liaison with, and provides assistance to, various organizations, both governmental and private, in matters affecting highway safety.

## National Commission on Safety Education, National Education Association, 1201 16th Street, N.W., Washington, D.C. 20036

The Commission conducts conferences on driver education, school transportation, driver and safety education teacher preparation and certification, and other areas of concern. Publications are developed, and research is conducted on safety education. The Commission conducts the National Student Traffic Safety Program in which several thousand high schools are enrolled. Consultation service is provided to state and local school systems, colleges, and universities.

### National Committee on Uniform Traffic Laws and Ordinances, 1319 18th Street, N.W., Washington, D.C. 20036

This Committee, whose members represent various governmental and private organizations interested in traffic law and safety, is the custodian of the *Uniform Vehicle Code* and *Model Traffic Ordinance*, the national standards for state laws and municipal ordinances. The Committee periodically reviews these documents and revises them when necessary to reflect current developments or practical experience.

To facilitate the use of the *Code* and *Ordinance*, the Committee also publishes supplementary materials in the form of the "Traffic Laws Commentary" series and the *Traffic Laws Annual*, analyzing existing laws, pending legislation, and case decisions and their relationship to provisions of the *Code* and *Ordinance*.

### National Highway Users Conference, National Press Building, Washington, D.C. 20004

This organization promotes sound public policies in development, safety, taxation, finance, administration, and use of highways. It also acts as a clearinghouse and disseminates information to affiliated state and public organizations. Consultant services are available to highway user groups, officials, and media. Legislative reporting service, periodical bulletins, and technical publications are also available.

### National Joint Committee on Uniform Traffic Control Devices, 1717 H Street, N.W., Washington, D.C. 20025

This Committee, representing a number of official and professional agencies of national scope, has, since 1931, been responsible for keeping current the *Manual on Uniform Traffic Control Devices*, which has been accepted by all state highway departments and is approved as the standard for application on Federal-aid highways.

### National Safety Council, 425 North Michigan Avenue, Chicago, Illinois 60611

Although the Council is interested in all phases of safety, a very substantial amount of effort is devoted to traffic safety. It administers a Traffic Inventory through which the program of an individual state or community is compared with national standards to determine needed improvement. Field service is available to states and communities. Manuals, standards, and other aids for technical groups and citizen safety organizations are prepared. Consultation on driver education public support programs is available on request.

Statistical and research information is collected and disseminated to interested groups. Periodicals include *Safety Education* and *Traffic Safety*. The *Research Review*, also available separately, is published quarterly as an integral part of *Traffic Safety*. *Accident Facts*, released annually, is described in Chapter 2, "The Accident Problem."

The annual National Safety Congress, held at Chicago, provides an opportunity for a wide exchange of information on traffic safety. Committees constantly at work develop research data on such subjects as alcohol, skidding, and traffic accident statistics.

## U.S. Department of Commerce, Bureau of Public Roads, Office of Highway Safety, Washington, D.C. 20235

The Office of Highway Safety was established in 1961 to plan and conduct an expanded program of highway safety, utilizing the resources and facilities of the Bureau of Public Roads. The Office is charged with supervising a program of improvement in the areas of traffic accident records, traffic laws and enforcement, safety education, and traffic engineering. The Driver Register Service, an operating division of the Office, provides a central clearinghouse to furnish information to state driver-licensing agencies on drivers whose licenses have been suspended or revoked for driving while intoxicated or for a traffic offense resulting in a fatality.

The Office also provides the central staff for the operation of the Interdepartmental Highway Safety Board, which was established in 1961 by Executive order to coordinate the total highway safety effort of the Federal government.

## U.S. Department of Health, Education and Welfare, Division of Accident Prevention, Public Health Service, Washington, D.C. 20201

With the establishment of this Division, the Federal government is expanding its interest in traffic safety. Financial support is provided for the conduct of research. This support should do much to develop needed information on the causes and conditions under which accidental injuries and death occur and lead to development of means by which to prevent the accident or to minimize the injury when accidents occur. Program activities are developed which can be carried out by state and local health departments as part of their regular operations.

### SELECTED BIBLIOGRAPHY

*Directory of National Traffic Safety Organizations with Full-time Field Staffs*, National Safety Council, Chicago, Ill., September, 1963.

*Free Materials and Services for Driver Education Courses*, American Automobile Association, Washington, D.C., 1964.

*Traffic Safety Services Directory of National Organizations*, U.S. Department of Commerce, Bureau of Public Roads, Washington, D.C., July, 1963.

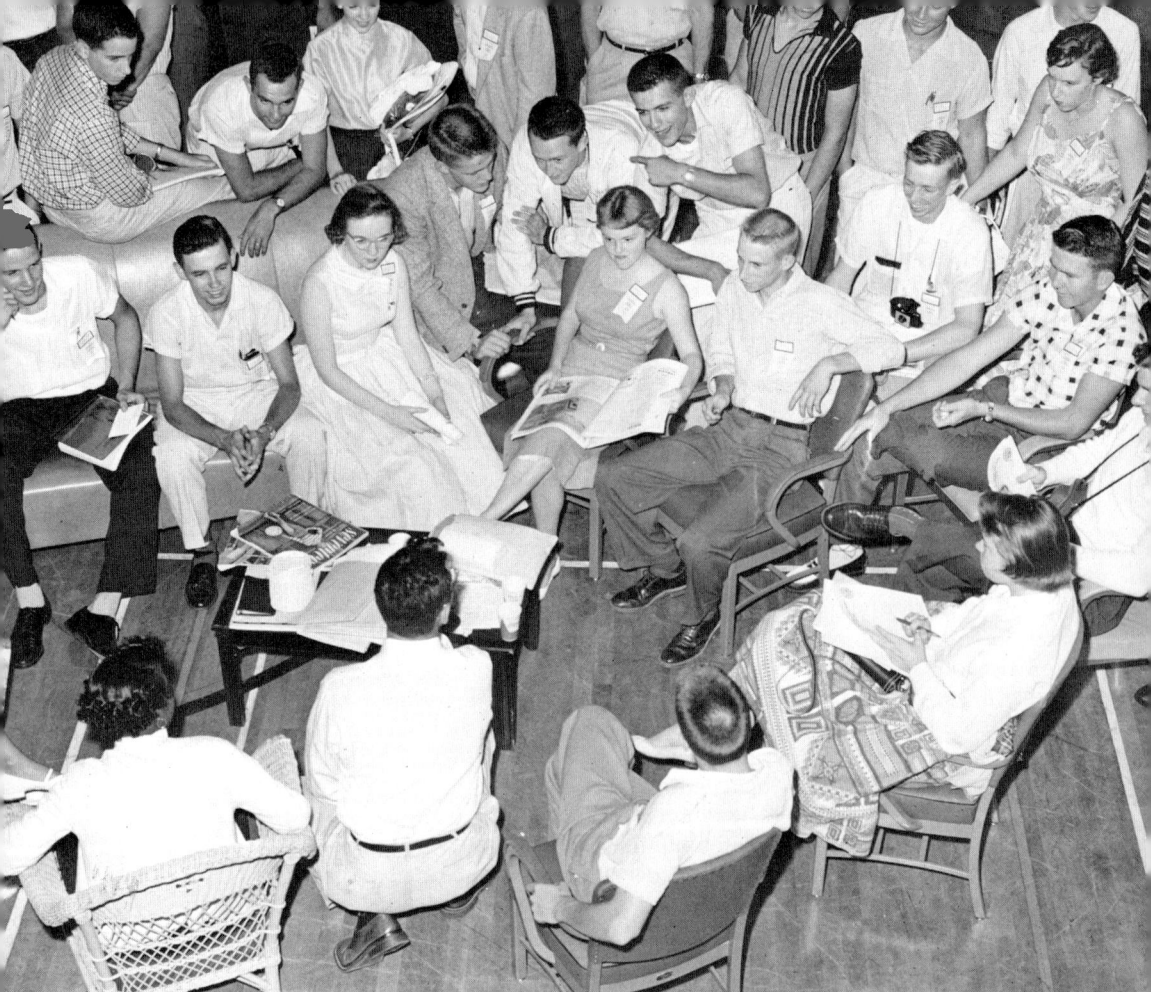

# Design for Tomorrow                                    36

Chapter 1, "The Profession—Opportunity and Challenge," told a little of the past history of driver and traffic safety education. Something more was described of its present role in the development of the citizen of today and tomorrow, and a few indications were mentioned of the probable expansion of the subject field in the future. The latter were based on observable trends and forces already in motion.

Now oriented in the field, the reader can visualize a role of his own and of his contemporaries in this changing picture—not merely as observers of a developing discipline but as *designers* of tomorrow's profession. It should be mentioned that the word "design" used here has the same connotation as when referring to the *design* of a new airplane—a plan for a mobile, measurable entity, one always subject to improvement, in fact one *anticipating* improvement.

The concept of driver and traffic safety education has been changing and building. The forces of experience and thought have been innervating this change from the teaching of safe driving to a multiphased area of education. A visible evidence of the recognition of a new *comprehensive* subject field, and of the needs brought to light by its own frank self-examination, was the creation of a *National Safety Education Conference on Teacher Preparation and Certification in Driver and Traffic Safety Education*. An educational conference is a temporary thing. In mathematics or science, it would be but one move in a history of thousands of years. In driver education, this meeting marked the second significant policy creation in which a definite design for the future development of this new field was drawn. The first was the creation and periodic updating of *Policies and Practices*[1] by the National Conferences on Driver Education.

Sponsored by the National Commission on Safety Education of the National Education Association, the 1965 Teacher Preparation and Certification Conference followed extensive planning meetings of leaders in the field. The main conference, held in the NEA Education Center in Washington, D.C., involved some 150 leading educators from the subject field, from college and university administration and curriculum development, from state departments of education, from contributing disciplines, and from support organizations such as the Insurance Institute for Highway Safety, the Automotive Safety Foundation, the American Automobile Association, etc.

A conference is, of itself, a passing event and not ordinarily a textbook subject. However, a concerted expression by informed leaders of driver education *and* responsible representatives of related areas of education, government, industry, citizen groups, and traffic safety operations—a group expression which points out needs and indicates a design for the future—this marks the coming of age of driver and traffic safety education in the *teacher preparation field*. There is yet much to be accomplished in this area, but the *design for tomorrow* is drawn.

The recommendations featured in the official report of the conference were no surprise to the leaders in the field of driver and traffic safety education. The final recommendations[2] of the interdisciplinary, interagency, interdepartmental, total conference very closely approximated the professional informed opinions of those leaders, tempered, if and when such tempering was indicated, by the advice and counsel of recognized authorities in the areas of education pertinent to each item considered—college administration, curriculum planning, certification, etc. No conflict or difficulty was experienced in the large-group interdisciplinary deliberations—a tribute to the vision and accurate perspective of the safety educators concerned, and also a *recognition of acceptance of the subject field by its colleagues in education*.

[1] *Policies and Practices for Driver and Traffic Safety Education,* National Commission on Safety Education, National Education Association, Washington, D.C., 1964.
[2] *Policies and Guidelines for Teacher Preparation and Certification in Driver and Traffic Safety Education,* National Safety Education Conference on Teacher Preparation and Certification in Driver and Traffic Safety Education, 1965, National Commission on Safety Education, National Education Association, Washington, D.C.

Mention of the fact that the conclusions and recommendations of the conference were no surprise to the safety educators has been made purposely to emphasize two points:

1. The leaders in this field of driver and traffic safety education initially demonstrated a thorough and well-supported understanding of the *appropriate place* of the subject field in the over-all picture of teacher education and certification, as well as of the *body of knowledge* factor which makes even a comparatively new field a mature, soundly based discipline in the universe of higher education.
2. The conference planned implementation of its objectives by involving leaders of all the related areas of teacher preparation and certification in a cooperative project of presentation of its recommendations to educators throughout the country in subsequent regional conferences. These were not offered as recommendations of a new discipline fighting for its place in the sun, but as considered deliberations of leaders of all pertinent areas of education arising in group interaction. Not only is a product so improved, but so, also, is its *acceptance*. These are advantages of the conference approach in our democratic American system of education.

At the time of the National Conference, the writing of this textbook was nearly completed. The broad, comprehensive concept of driver and traffic safety education, so identified in Chapter 1 (The Broad Concept of Driver Education and The Substantive Image of Driver Education) and carried out in content throughout the entire text, was fully supported in the deliberations and conclusions of the conference. This too may be considered in the category of "no surprise," since the concept is one fully supported by the far-sighted leadership in the field and in the past publications of the authorship of this book. There is no schism in the profession on any of the basic principles of the subject field. It is important that this be the case *in both our philosophy and our organization,* for "divided we fall" and with us the welfare of our students. There need be but one *design for tomorrow,* a comprehensive, flexible program. Some important considerations for details of that design are suggested in this final part of this book.

## *ON TREATING THE SYMPTOM*

Some of our very sincere colleagues in education decry any kind of supporting legislation—financial, age differential, or other—in an effort to preserve "education-administrative" principles which have not been inviolate for many, many years. Many people, home owners, municipal government officials, and others oppose increasing real estate taxes because of the hardship it would place on many people, especially retired people, and because they believe that the home owner bears an unfair proportion of the burden of support of public education. This opposition is felt in the form of resistance to driver education in many places solely because, as one more subject in the school curriculum, it increases the cost of operating the school—in the same manner as does any addition to the public school curriculum.

Balance in the tax structure is not going to be worked out by pro-

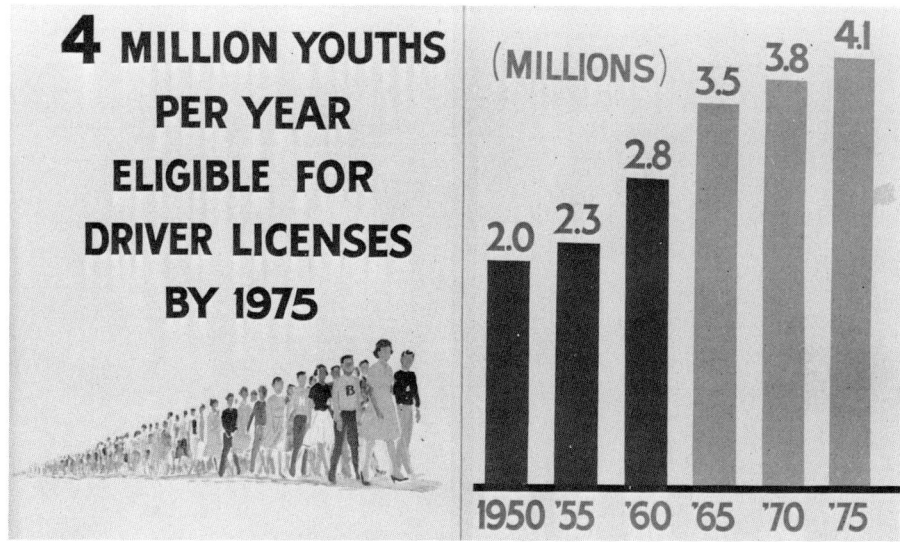

FIGURE 36-1 We aren't increasing our efforts and our support fast enough.

fessional educators. The steady growth of state aid to education, the National Defense Education Act, and the passage of the education bill of 1965 mark a trend toward broad-based taxes in preference to indefinite raising of real estate taxes to meet the rising costs of properly educating our growing population. It is not the mission of this chapter to advocate methods of taxation. It is desired to extend the opportunity for driver education to every boy and girl. Perhaps we should point out certain facts to our colleagues and to other well-meaning people who oppose driver education, not because it is undesirable, but either because they are concerned about methods of taxation to raise the added money to support the program, or because they want no legislation of any kind "prescribing" any specific course, subject, or procedures in education.

For both, here is our request:

Our young people *need* high school driver education. We know, statistically, that *having the course saves life, limb, and valuable property. This is what all concerned must hold paramount*. The kind of financing and the matter of educational legislation *must be held secondary to the welfare of our students and that of the many other users of street and highway*. The poorest possible solution to financing and legislative problems is to penalize the young people so seriously in order to "hold the line" on personal feelings on the other matters.

We must convince our colleagues and others concerned that when they oppose driver education on either basis, they are attacking *symptoms* of the features they don't like in the tax structure or in education-legislation relationships. The "disease," if such exists, lies in an inequitable tax structure or in other conditions which make special legislation *necessary* in order to

FIGURE 36-2   An example of effective earmarking of funds is the Federal support of highway construction.

accomplish this lifesaving mission. The "symptoms" exist in the fact that special measures may be needed for the existence of this, or any other, worthwhile subject in the education of the young citizen. Let those who will attack the disease, but not severely penalize the young people in a narrowly viewed war against symptoms.

## ON INFORMED OPINION

This is an extremely sensitive concept—informed opinion. To be realistic, although in theory every man may "have a right to his opinion," the paid professional has a right (and an obligation) to contribute *only truly informed opinion*. As the contribution of a professional, his statements carry the authority of the diagnosis of the physician. He speaks for a profession. This carries with it an ethical obligation. To be ethical and honest, he must *know* that what he says is true—that the policies and procedures he advocates are surely in the best interests of the people of the school, the community, the state, the nation. The key word is *know*.

The teacher of driver and traffic safety education, prepared within today's broad concept of the profession, is an informed expert. The breadth of concept of the profession is not limited to a body of knowledge. It includes a breadth of responsibilities also. The teacher should be a community consultant in his subject. The professional, with his wealth of experience and

DESIGN FOR TOMORROW 451

FIGURE 36–3 The good, comprehensive school program requires the expenditure of money . . .

FIGURE 36–4 . . . but that money is an investment in youth.

knowledge in his field, should be the consultant on similarly related matters to community, state, and nation. The voice of the informed professional is critically needed in attacking this great social problem—the *behavior* of man newly endowed with the speed and power of the hurricane, but confined in great and ever-increasing numbers to ribbons of roadways. The nation, greatly affected and concerned about this problem, *needs* the contributions of all pertinent disciplines. None is more pertinent than driver and traffic safety education.

The potential contribution of this profession is great yet simple in form. The first obligation we have is to become *thoroughly informed*. The second is to *be heard*. On school and community level we may be heard as individuals. In larger communities and on state and national levels we need an organizational, an institutional voice—the recognized, informed voice of the profession.

## FOR THE QUALIFIED

This nation has been called a "melting pot." People of all nations have come to these shores and, as the years passed, have been absorbed into the American way of life. They acquired the characteristics of an American —language, customs, ideology, dress—and contributed something of themselves, culture, thought, skills. In our educational system, driver and traffic safety education offers a parallel. The professional personnel in this field have come from many subject fields. This has been a distinct advantage to the new field, bringing to it contributions from diversified professional backgrounds.

In the normal, orderly process, the newcomer completes formal college-level study and begins his professional career in the field, usually as a teacher. How far one goes with study, on what level he teaches or supervises, depends on many things. Advancement, when it comes, usually follows professional experience and advanced study. This is the legitimate pattern of a career in driver and traffic safety education.

Both the public and the profession are eager for sound, new knowledge in the lifesaving mission of the subject field. So eager is the public for this phase of our work that sometimes the rewards offered bring an invasion of the professional field by unqualified people and institutions. Informed professionals should be constantly on guard to protect their students and the public against the "research conclusions" of the unqualified investigators. "Studies" are performed, financed by grants or on the graduate level, by people who identify themselves as a "psychologist," or an "educator," or vaguely a "researcher." The true professional, in reviewing the study, finds it full of naïve "discoveries," omission of very significant factors, weird "instruments" devised from ignorance of existing well-designed, tested ones, "related literature" which wouldn't have been complete twenty years ago —a host of items which add up to one word—*charlatanism*. At this moment, "traffic safety" is rife with it.

Well-meaning officials and others, informed in their own specialties, are sometimes impressed with the apparent "scientific" qualifications of the would-be investigators. Freed from the blind, uninformed respect for the

FIGURE 36-5  A conceptual organism created for study—the driver and the vehicle and the road.

"profession" of the "researchers," those officials, or any intelligent person, could easily be shown the flaws and the volume of meant-to-be-impressive, ponderous, ridiculous language which fails, to the trained eye, to cover up the ineptitude of the investigators. This is a problem in traffic safety today. It is also a matter in which the guidance of our well-prepared professionals is needed. Accomplishment of advances in our highly complex field requires more than use of the three familiar incantations, "experimental group," "control group," and "personality traits."

Another, similar matter is the gratuitous article in the popular press which "justifies" a traffic-disrupting or dangerous driving procedure on the basis of the author being a professional in some field other than traffic safety.

Perhaps a general principle is indicated for adoption by professionals in the entire field of traffic safety, including driver and traffic safety education. Whatever the background of the would-be investigator, expert, or writer in other fields, he should be required to prove that he also has a *professional-level background in traffic safety* before being accepted as writer, researcher, or consultant. It is not reasonable to require a fully qualified and possibly experienced teacher of some other subject field to complete additional college study in our field *before facing his first high school class*, and yet to engage another individual who is uninformed in the field to go beyond our present borders of knowledge and bring us new knowledge from "research."

FIGURE 36-6 Students have opportunity to study firsthand the design of many modern traffic facilities.

Like the teacher who comes to driver education from another field, there are many people who have potential contributions which can improve our field. Like the teacher, however, they must know something about the field to be competent to apply these contributions intelligently and constructively. The new "citizen" we want is the one who learns the language, the customs, and the laws so that he can contribute to his new "country."

## THE CONTRIBUTING DISCIPLINE

Like the individual, a number of disciplines have added considerably to the body of knowledge we now possess. Some of these disciplines are extremely broad in content, and only a small part of each is applied and adapted to the frame of reference of traffic safety or of driver and traffic safety education. In engineering, for instance, there are a number of branches. Highway, traffic, and mechanical engineering have each been adapted to a phase of the broad field of traffic safety. Another extremely broad field of study is psychology. Occasionally one encounters a practitioner who, as a self-professed expert in "human behavior," approaches the fictional status of an "all-round expert." This is the opposite of our experience with the practitioners of psychology in our own ranks.

Some of the outstanding leaders in our field came to us from *psychology*. They have brought us a fund of knowledge and have applied it—that which is pertinent—to our mission. After entering and working in the field, they have built up a body of knowledge that we might call *psychology of safety education*. This is an entity (unlike human behavior) with which a person can cope—an area of concentration in which one could be identified as a specialist if he were prepared on a level with other professionals. Here is a case of a *discipline* becoming a "citizen" in our "country," as has enginering, physical science, and others. Just as *educational psychology* became a recognized entity, so can the *psychology of safety education*, a part of which —perhaps a standard course in teacher preparation—could be *psychology of driver and traffic safety education*.

Research and writing in this field would be carried on by its own appropriately informed practitioners—not by general psychologists who "know" our field because it is "human behavior." As indicated in Chapter 4, it is suggested that those joining this field as professionals make additional serious study of the available sound data in the literature of neurology, neuroanatomy, and endocrinology to achieve a better understanding of the extremely complex universe that is driver behavior. So concentrated, so specialized, and so enriched, this area has the potential of being the most challenging and the most valuable of our profession—an "outside" discipline which has become a "citizen."

## YOUR TOMORROW

The teachers and teachers-to-be who read this textbook and who do a conscientious job of supplementary reading and study—a job worthy of a comprehensive discipline—should possess a good basic understanding of the profession they chose. There is one more human point of interest about the profession. "What about the future for my family and myself?" It would not be wise to choose a profession without learning the answer to that question. Too many potentially fine teachers are lost from the teaching profession to business-industry-related curricula or by direct dropping out of college for jobs which seem to offer greater reward than teaching. This is unfortunate, especially since it generally results from misinformation on the true picture of the life of the teacher.

Under Professional Opportunity (Chapter 1, "The Profession—Opportunity and Challenge"), a brief indication of the expanding opportunities in teaching driver and traffic safety education was given. Now, specifically, what are the chances of the qualified driver and safety education specialist getting a job? The chances are good—and improving. Of course, he must take the initiative. In addition to the customary procedures in seeking a teaching position, he should keep well informed on trends and legislation by states. Following the passage of good support legislation in a state, teaching positions in the field are available in considerable numbers. The time of the effective date of the legislation should be noted. One of the problems in implementing good support legislation is to *find* a sufficient number of *properly prepared* teachers. This is in no way advocating state support legislation to provide jobs, but is cited to encourage the teacher candidate with facts. The professional associations should take an active part in communicating position-opportunity-related information to their membership, and in keeping the information current, in this dynamic field.

The better your preparation in the subject field *when the position is open*, the better are your chances of obtaining it. To await professional advancement before starting your advanced study is akin to awaiting the tornado to build the cellar. It's just not practical. With the current trend to upgrade requirements for certification in the subject field, two items should be considered: (1) obtaining positions, initially and for advancement, will require better professional preparation than in the past, and (2) competition for positions on the part of the great number of minimally prepared, 2 and 3 credit-hour, or 40 or 60 clock-hour teacher candidates will be eliminated in favor of those who are better prepared. Your chances increase as your pertinent education increases, but in greater proportion in this subject field at present than in others.

What about your raising the "poor" family among your neighbors and friends? Many teachers have believed this for years, and in many places it was so. It is *not* true today in those states and communities with good school systems. The neighbor with an impressive sounding title may be earning less in 50 weeks per year than the experienced teacher in 35 to 40 weeks. The teacher's salary is the only one that becomes *known* publicly. The inexperienced teacher may not be quite so well off, but his lot is improving *more rapidly* with the competition for his less-expensive services.

Look for the state with good retirement and fringe benefits as well as better salaries. You should be able to retire at the age of 60 with 20 years of service (or younger at a reduced income after perhaps 25 to 35 years of service) with an income that would require an investment of $75,000 to $100,000 to produce in the form of an annuity. Insurance and other benefits should also be included. Also, the security of tenure, where included, has a value to the teacher.

You won't earn as much as your family doctor. You may be surprised, however, if you learn how you do stand in your community in terms of income, security, and benefits. You probably won't learn though, since status is somehow tied to income in popular belief. Many teachers tend honestly to believe that most other workers receive higher wages than they. This is not usually the case, although there are still many places where teachers are not paid as well as other workers of equal educational qualifications. Improvement is the trend. Be assured, your children won't be underprivileged in the average community.

Working conditions? Your fellow faculty members will envy you on nice days in the spring and fall, and pity you in very bad weather. None will have as grave a responsibility for life and property as you will in the car. Each period you teach in the car, however, will be one for which you won't have to grade papers. Your colleagues will envy that! The period in the car, when you try to give each student as much practice as possible, will go with *unbelievable* speed. You will have to use your watch regularly, or time will pass unrealized and that last student will be short-changed.

Remember the fluidity of this new field. The *sooner* you obtain your advanced-degree status in this field, the more "wear and tear" you will get out of it. In other words, city, state, college, and university positions will be opening regularly in this profession. *Be ready—and keep informed.* Be on the lookout for scholarships and for research and teaching opportunities at all levels. Some people who are now initially preparing or furthering their professional education are going to move ahead. The implication is obvious.

Finally, you will be an *educator*. The status of a "safe driving instructor" exists only in the minds of those who have lost contact with today's education. The comprehensive character of the field you represent needs only to be known to be respected on a level with any.

## Again—Join Them

The layman doesn't see much difference between "driver education" and "driver training," or between the "driver education teacher" (or "driver and traffic safety education teacher") and the "driving instructor," but we know that there is a big difference and that the public, and even some of our colleagues on the school staff, need to be made and kept aware of it. As indicated in Chapter 1 and elsewhere in this book, the subject field is both a lifesaving measure and a tool or device of education, with its own specific educational objectives. This latter identity alone would be sufficient to merit for it a place in the curriculum on exactly the same basis as other subjects. It is not desirable to create or maintain a *difference of identity* in the minds of colleagues and observers between this subject field of driver education and the rest of the curriculum.

Very apt for the closing of this text on this challenging field which is a comparative newcomer in the family of Education is the following quota-

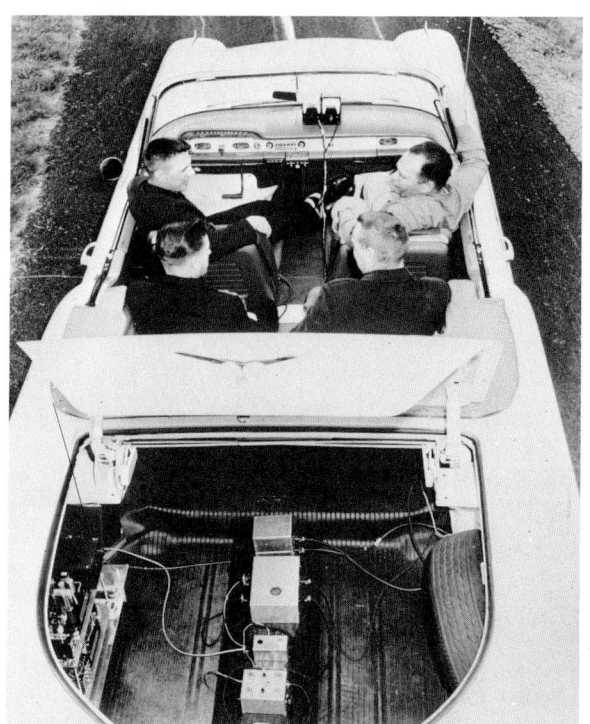

FIGURE 36-7 Design for Tomorrow? Car equipped for automatic driving on full-scale electronic highway at RCA's David Sarnoff Research Center, Princeton, New Jersey. Circuits visible in car trunk include equipment to pick up signals generated in wires in pavement by a car ahead, and control circuits to translate data into automatic operation of accelerator and brakes. Car is steered automatically by signals from cable buried in center of lane, indicated by white line in pavement.

tion[3] presented by Dr. Leon Brody of New York University's Center for Safety Education during the 1965 Conference previously described:

> In 1911, for example, in an inaugural address to students at Oxford University, Walter Raleigh is reported to have said:
> "I am glad to know that you include among your studies here some subjects commonly called technical; I notice especially agriculture and domestic science. . . . These are not poor or narrow studies. Who can be deeply versed in the tillage of fields if he knows no botany, no chemistry, above all, no bacteriology. . . . The management of a home, again, is perhaps the oldest science in the world; it demands all kinds of lore, and leads the way to an intelligent interest in some of the most curious problems of history. These problems have been neglected because historians . . . have lived in Colleges, not in kitchens, and have served on juries, not in dairies. . . . The truth is that there is no considerable kind of human activity . . . which is not a fit subject for University study. The chief danger comes to technical schools when they are divorced from those wider and freer forms of intellectual inquiry which are the sacred charge of a University."

Concurring with this thought, there is no divorce of the technical aspects of driver and traffic safety education from the other contributing disciplines, technical and other, in this interdisciplinary curriculum. The technical needs direct the student and the practitioner to an intensive study of the underlying sciences. At the same time the end product, the teacher, the teacher-to-be and the high school student—each emerges from his broad study a better informed person.

From the outset, this book was planned to guide the in-service teacher and the teacher-to-be into the universe of driver and traffic safety education in the teaching situation in his future. It is a textbook. It is not intended as a total course. Each chapter cites reading references, and it is presumed that the teacher will have available a copy of one of the standard high school driver education textbooks. No mature, comprehensive discipline resides in a single book.

From studying the content of this book, the teacher has learned of trends and indications now observable in the driver and traffic safety education of present and future. *He should see in it also a design for his own, individual tomorrow.*

### SELECTED BIBLIOGRAPHY

Alford, Albert L.: *Non-property Taxation for Schools*, Office of Education, U. S. Dept. of Health, Education and Welfare, Washington, D.C., Bulletin 4, 1964.

*Policies and Guidelines for Teacher Preparation and Certification in Driver and Traffic Safety Education*, National Safety Education Conference on Teacher Preparation and Certification in Driver and Traffic Safety Education, 1965, National Commission on Safety Education, National Education Association, Washington, D.C.

*Policies and Practices for Driver and Traffic Safety Education*, National Commission on Safety Education, National Education Association, Washington, D.C., 1964.

[3] *The Meaning of a University*, An Inaugural Address Delivered to the Students of University College Aberystwyth, Walter Raleigh, Oxford at the Clarendon Press, Oct. 20, 1911.

# PHOTOGRAPH ACKNOWLEDGMENTS

Allstate Insurance Co., Training Division Photo, Skokie, Ill.: Fig. 9–2

American Trucking Associations, Inc., Washington, D.C.: Chap. 32 Theme

*American Youth Magazine:* Fig. 28–2

Del Ankers Photographers, Washington, D.C.: Figs. 6–2, 33–1

Auto Industries Highway Safety Committee, Washington, D.C., Fig. 28–2

Auto Specialties Manufacturing Co., Inc.: Fig. 27–5

Automobile Club of Maryland, Baltimore, Md. (Jack Engeman Studio): Fig. 24–3

Automobile Club of New York, New York, N.Y.: Fig. 8–1

Automobile Club of Washington, Seattle, Wash.: Fig. 9–4

Automobile Manufacturers Association, Detroit, Mich.: Chap. 27 Theme

Automotive Safety Foundation, Washington, D.C.: Chap. 12, 21, 23, 30, 34, 36 Themes; Figs. 1–1, 2–3, 2–6, 3–9, 10–1, 16–3, 23–4, 25–4, 26–3, 29–2, 36–1, 36–6

John E. Baerwald, University of Illinois, Urbana, Ill.: Fig. 34–2

Bureau of Labor Statistics, U.S. Department of Labor, Washington, D.C.: Fig. 32–1

Bureau of Public Roads, U.S. Department of Commerce, Washington, D.C.: Chap. 25 Theme; Fig. 22–1

Don Callander, Washington, D.C.: Chap. 3, 13, 14, 19, 24, 28, 35 Themes; Figs. 1–4, 1–5, 2–1, 3–3, 3–10, 6–3, 15–1, 21–1, 24–1, 24–8, 25–1, 25–6, 29–1, 33–2, 36–2, 36–5

Calvin Productions, Inc., Kansas City, Mo.: Chap. 2 Theme; Fig. 18–6

George A. Campbell, National Education Association, Washington, D.C.: Fig. 1–7

Fred Carter, Seattle, Wash.: Fig. 32–3

Chicago Citizens Traffic Safety Board, Chicago, Ill.: Fig. 24–6

Chrysler Engineering Proving Ground, Chelsea, Mich.: Fig. 27–6

City of Seattle, Engineering Department, Seattle, Wash.: Fig. 23–9

Committee on Winter Driving Hazards, National Safety Council, Chicago, Ill.: Figs. 2–7, 15–2, 15–4, 15–5

Dayton Public Schools, Dayton, Ohio: Chap. 8 Theme

Department of Motor Vehicles, Washington, D.C.: Chap. 1 Theme; Figs. 1–2, 1–3, 3–4, 21–2, 26–1, 28–3, 28–4

Fair Lawn High School, Fair Lawn, N.J.: Figs. 36–3, 36–4

Fisher Body Division, General Motors Corp., Warren, Mich.: Fig. 27–7

General Electric Co.: Fig. 27–3

General Motors Photographers, Detroit, Mich.: Fig. 27–2

General Motors Proving Ground, Milford, Mich.: Fig. 27–1

Heinz Hammer, Zeiss Ikon Camera: Fig. 3–2

Harris & Ewing, Washington, D.C.: Chap. 11, 16 Themes; Fig. 14–6

Hastings-Willinger & Associates, Cleveland, Ohio: Chap. 26 Theme; Fig. 26–2

International Association of Chiefs of Police, Washington, D.C.: Figs. 24–4, 24–7, 24–10

George Kalec, Washington, D.C.: Figs. 3–7, 3–8, 11–1, 11–2, 11–3, 11–4, 18–1, 18–2, 18–3, 18–4, 18–5, 20–1, 20–2, 21–3, 24–2

# PHOTOGRAPH ACKNOWLEDGMENTS

James Karmroot Lightner: Fig. 25-2

Link Division, General Precision, Inc., Binghamton, N.Y.: Fig. 9-3

Louisiana Department of Highways, Baton Rouge, La.: Fig. 30-1

Markel Service, Inc., Richmond, Va.: Figs. 24-5, 24-11

Maryland Department of Motor Vehicles, Glen Burnie, Md.: Figs. 16-4, 25-7

National Commission on Safety Education, National Education Association, Washington, D.C.: Fig. 1-6

National Highway Users Conference, Washington, D.C.: Chap. 9 Theme; Figs. 2-2, 6-1, 16-2, 23-3, 25-5, 27-4

National Safety Council, Chicago, Ill.: Fig. 15-3

New Jersey Division of Motor Vehicles, Trenton, N.J.: Chap. 5 Theme

Dave Packwood, Los Angeles, Calif.: Fig. 2-5

President's Council on Aging, Washington, D.C.: Chap. 7 Theme

Radio Corporation of America, New York, N.Y.: Fig. 36-7

Rockwell Manufacturing Co., Drivo Division, Pittsburgh, Pa.: Fig. 9-1

Safe Winter Driving League, Chicago, Ill. (Laib Photo, Clintonville): Fig. 14-22

Frank A. Spinek, Baltimore, Md.: Fig. 25-3

State of New Hampshire Highway Department, Concord, N.H.: Chap. 31 Theme

Stephenson Corp., Red Bank, N.J.: Figs. 5-3, 5-4, 5-5

Cpl. Jess A. Sullins, North Carolina State Highway Patrol, Asheville, N.C.: Figs. 2-4, 29-3

U.S. Army Photo, Washington, D.C.: Chap. 6 Theme

WTHS-TV—Channel 2, Miami, Fla.: Chap. 10 Theme

Margaret Walker, Washington, D.C.: Chap. 20, 29 Themes

*Washington Post*, Washington, D.C.: Chap. 15 Theme

Yale Bureau of Highway Traffic, New Haven, Conn.: Fig. 34-1

# INDEX

ABC program, 405, 408
Academic standing, car ownership and, 300–301
Accelerator movement, clutch movement and, 191
Accelerator pedal, 180
*Accident Facts*, 24, 26
Accident insurance, group, 266
Accident insurance cases, 396
Accident involvement, 25–26
   aging and, 106–111
   court action in, 267
   drinking drivers and, 76, 295, 344
   "involvement" formula and, 295–296
Accident prevention, 282, 430–431
Accident problem, the, 20–31
   future, 26–27
   human factor in, 21–23
   professional view of, 23–24
Accident rates, analyzing data on, 24–26
   motor vehicle, teen-agers and, 24
Accident records, 428
   research studies and, 294–295
Accident spot maps, 311
Accident statistics, 20
   by age, tables, 107–108
   analysis of, 24–26
     by cause, 25
     motor vehicle fatalities, 1913–1964, 27–28
   estimate of future, 29–31
     inadequacies of, 28–29
Accidents, age and, tables, 107–108
   alcohol and, 76, 107–108

Accidents, investigation of, 333, 385
   responsibility for, 295–296
   from skidding, 223
   speed and, 335
   in winter driving, 222–223
   (*See also* Collisions)
Achievement tests, 160
*Action Program for Highway Safety*, 304, 306, 308, 337
Adjustive responses, 141–142
Adult school driver education, 263
Aetna Drivotrainer, 136
Age, accident involvement and, 106-111, 298
   experience and, 103, 109–110, 167
   pathological v. chronological, 104–105
Aged, the, driving by, 30
   traffic accidents to, 284
Aging, accident involvement and, 106–110
   chronological, 105
   driving and, 97–99, 102–110
   as individual characteristic, 105
   physical and mental changes in, 105–106
Alcohol, drugs and, 88
   effects of, 63–64, 76–86, 431
     degree of, 85–86
   health and, 76
   individual tolerance for, 85–86
   various customs in use of, 89–90
Allstate Good Driver Trainer, 136–137
Allstate Insurance Companies, research studies by, 300–301

American Association of Motor Vehicle Administrators, 351, 440
American Association of School Administrators (AASA), 16
American Association of State Highway Officials, 410, 440
American Automobile Association (AAA), 440–441, 447
 Auto Trainer, 137
 driver improvement program of, 377
American Bar Association, 441
American Driver and Traffic Safety Education Association (ADTSEA), 16–17, 441
American Medical Association (AMA), 110, 441
 Committee on Medical Aspects of Automobile Injuries and Deaths, 92, 94
 statement on medical examinations, 96, 98
American Optometric Association, 441
American Road Congress, Fourth, 405
American Trucking Associations, 419, 441–442
 jobs listed by, 418
Amphetamines, 87–88
Anderson, William G., 214n.
Antihistimines, 87–88
 alcohol and, 89
Asphyxiation, drugs and, 89
Attitude, concepts of, 65, 70–72
 driver license examinations and, 354
 emotional factor in, 58–61
 environment and, 67–68
 foundation of, 57–58
 measurement of, 73
 motion pictures on, 123
 nature of, 61–65, 72
 neural bias mechanism and, 61–63
 simulator training and, 134
 teaching techniques and, 72
Attitude conditioning, advertising and, 59–61, 72–73
 applying principles of, 66–70, 72–74
 method of, 69–70
 "leader" symbol in, 68–79
 leadership and, 68–69, 72–73
Attitude tests or scales, 73

Auto Industries Highway Safety Committee, 385, 442
Automatic skill movements, 182–184
Automatic transmission in driver education cars, 202, 255–257, 261
*Automobile Facts and Figures*, 24, 26
Automobile insurance, 261, 268–269, 277, 285, 358, 391–398
 compulsory laws for, 358
 cost of, 392, 398
 on driver-education cars, 261
 and fraudulent claims, 395–396
 rate increase for, 395
 types of coverage by, 396–398
Automobile insurance policies, reading of, 391–392
Automobile maintenance, 382–390
 private car, 383–385
Automobile manufacturers, allowances to dealers by, 263
Automobile Manufacturers Association, Inc., 442
Automobile ownership, academic standing and, 300–301
 motion pictures on, 124–125
Automobiles, buying of, 10
 damage to, 209
 design, 372–374
 development of, 5–6
 dual-control (*see* Dual-control cars)
 ejection from, injury and, 379
 entering and leaving, 191–193
 maintenance of, 10, 263–264, 382–390
 predicted increase in, 29–31
 safety features of, 180, 369–381
 special features of, 202
 student's introduction to, 177–180
 (*See also* Motor vehicles)
Automotive Safety Foundation, 442, 447

Backing, 185–187
 to park, 211
 practice in, 236–237
Backlash, 210–211
Back-up lights, 179
Bail bond forfeiture, 6

INDEX 463

Barbiturates, 87
Battery jump cables, 205
Beery, Althea, 160n.
Behavior, definition of, 33
  driver, 9, 354–355
  emotion and, 64–65
  foundation of, 57–58
  logical or illogical, 35–37
  nerve impulses and, 65
  pedestrian, 9
  predictable, 58–61
  science and, 33–34
Behavior conditioning, 56–57
  processes in, 4
Behavioral research, 46–47
  conclusions drawn from, 56
  emotional factor in, 63–64
  historical-laboratory approach to, 56–57, 64
Bishop, Richard W., 238n.
Blood-alcohol concentrations, 81, 83, 86
  table of, 83
Blowouts, 375, 378
Bodily injury liability insurance, 396–397
Body fluids, alcohol and, 85
Brain, concentration of alcohol in, 86
Brain action, alcohol and, 78
Brain stem, cerebral cortex and, 70
  dominance of, 63–65
  effect of alcohol on, 78
  emotions and, 78–79
  functions of, 78
Brake failure, 198, 202, 383
Brake fluid, sub-standard, 343
Brake foot, clutch foot confused with, 191
Brake lights, 179
Brake pedal, instructor's, 255–256
  installing of, 256–257
Brake power, speed and, 185
Brakes, and crash stops, 185
  dual-control, 255
  foot, 180, 185
  four-wheel, 375
  hydraulic, 375, 383
  parking, 180, 202
  power, 199
  proper use of, 185

Brakes, self-adjusting, 375
  split or dual, 376
Braking, correction of, 201
  on downhill grade, 191
  early, 198–199
  effectiveness of, 375
  skidding and, 222–224
  state laws on, 198
Braking distance, 375–376
Breath test, 81, 86
Breathalyzer, 82, 84–85
Brody, Leon, quoted, 458
Brownlow-Latimer Good Roads bill, 405
Bucket seats, 192
Budgets, school, driver education and, 272
Bumper signs, 258
Buses, 417–420
  driving too close to, 210–211

California, University of, 378, 433
California State Assembly, Committee on Transportation and Commerce, 388
Carbon monoxide (CO), 89
Cardiovascular disease, 94–95
Cerebral cortex, 183
  brain stem and, 70
  dominance of, 64
  effect of alcohol on, 63–64, 78–79
  effect of drugs on, 63–64
Cerebrum, 61, 63
  inhibitory effect of, 79
  and new nerve pathways, 182–183
Chain appliers, 218
Charlatanism, 452
Charts, use of, 118, 120
Chauffeur licenses, 350
Chemical test laws, "implied consent" provisions of, 83–85
  states having, 84
Cincinnati, Ohio, educational television in, 147
Citizens, apathy of, as witnesses, 338–339
  law enforcement and, 333–334
  and police, 337–339, 341

Citizens, rights of, 338
Citizenship, golden rule of, 341
  good, driver education and, 8–9, 250, 286
Civil suits, accidents and, 267
  contributory negligence and, 269
Classroom instruction, 112–168, 204, 250, 252–254
  aids and equipment for, 115–128
  cost of, 272
  driving simulators used in, 129–144
  psychophysical tests integrated with, 154–155
  television used in, 144–149
  tests used in, 144–149
  on winter driving, 221
Clutch foot, brake foot confused with, 191
Clutch pedal, 179
Coefficient of friction, 223–224, 226
Collision diagrams, 311
Collisions, 211, 371, 379, 381, 385
  avoidance of, 375
  insurance and, 397–398
  skidding and, 222–223
  speed and, 296
Columbia University, Teachers College, 214–215, 433
Commercial driving school cars, 255
Commercial transportation, 415–420
Communities, vehicle inspection and, 385–386
Community support, maintenance of, 280–288
*Comparison of Various Behind the Wheel Training Methods, A*, Brazell, 238n.
Comprehensive physical damage insurance, 396
Conditional reflexes, 36
Conscience, attitude toward safety and, 71
Consumer education, 10
Controllability, 375–376
Coordination, muscular, 130–131, 152
  neuromuscular, 142
    alcohol and, 76, 81
    drugs and, 87
    poor, 201–202

Cornell University, 378, 433
  Aeronautical Laboratory, 379
Corticothalamic pathways, 79
Cost formula, 274–276
Costs of driver education, 271–279
  additional factors in, 276–277
  projected, reporting on, 279
  pupil-teacher ratio and, 273–274
  table of, 277–278
Counterskids, 212
County and township roads, 412–413
Courtesy, value of, 8
Courtrooms, 334
Crashes, controlled, 378
  (*See also* Collisions)
Curb, approaching, 194
  and early turns, 195–196
  height of, 210
  moving away from, 193–194, 210
  obstructions beyond, 210
  striking of, 189–190, 209
Curriculum, and time brackets, 199–200, 246–248
  total, driver education in, 272, 280–281
    expansion of, 199, 246–247
    subject matter content in, 146
Curves, skidding on, 224

Dade County, Florida, educational television in, 147
Damage to cars, 209–210
Danger, bad driving associated with, 67
Dashboard, padded, 180
Deafness, driving and, 99–100
Dealers, cars loaned by, 259–261
  manufacturer's allowance to, 263
  school's agreement with, 261–262
Decision-making, problems in, 201–202
Defensive driving, 399
Defensive driving code, 399–402
Defrosters, 180, 218
Delaware, inspection system in, 386–387, 389
Denver (Colorado) Driver Improvement School, 366–367
  for deaf drivers, 100
Depth perception, tests for, 152–153

INDEX 465

Detonator, illustrated, 116
Devices, informational, 179
  operational control, 179–180
Diabetics, 94
Diagrams, use of, 118
Directional signals, 193, 195
Discipline, 18
Discussion versus lecture method in education, 69–70
District of Columbia, inspection system in, 386–387, 389
Door latches, 379, 381
Door pillars, 370, 372
Doors, curbside, entering and leaving by, 191–193
  locking of, 178
  structure of, 379
  traffic-side, hazards of using, 193, 265
Drag strips, 334–335
  IACP statement on, 335
Drinking, accidents and, tables, 107–108
  common questions about, 85–86
  first stage of, 79
  and sobriety tests, 81–85
  social, 76–81
Drinking customs, religion and, 90
  variation in, 89–90
Drinking-and-driving hazard, 344
  behavioral approach to, 77–87
  examples of, 77–81
Driver education, adult, 263
  aids and equipment for, 115–128
  behavioral research and, 46–47, 73–74
  community support for, 280–288
  concept of, 7–8
  cost and financing of, 271–279
  current status of, 14–15
  curriculum for, 8
  defined, 4
  educational television and, 146–149
  future of, 446–458
  for high school students, 6
  integrated into related courses, 38–40
  need for, 449
  objectives of, 8–10

Driver education, parent's consent for, 267–268
  physical aspects of, 115
  as preparation for life, 10
  psychology and, 454–455
  psychophysical tests used in, 150–158
  public image of, 281–286
  public information on, 287–288
  research on, 16, 293–301, 436–437
  research agencies and, 438–445
  responsibilities associated with, 17
  results of, 1936–1960, table, 283
  science and, 10
  and teacher resource, 166
  for teachers, 7, 15
  team teaching in, 165–168
Driver education associations, state, 16–17
Driver-education cars, automatic-transmission, 202, 255–257, 261
  damage to, 209–210
  donated, 259, 276
  dual-control (*see* Dual-control cars)
  identification of, 257–259
  leasing of, 276–277
  liability for accidents in, 268–269
  manual-shift, 184, 255, 261
  radio-equipped, 239
  repair and maintenance of, 239, 263–264
Driver education courses, 268
  cost of program, 6–7
  in driver improvement schools, 362–363
  for high school students, 8
  objectives of, 173–174
  organization and administration of, 245–288
  scheduling of, 245–254
    mechanics of, 250–253
    principles of, 248–250
  state financial support for, 6, 15
  for teachers, 7, 15
  in traffic engineering, 303–319
*Driver Education Reduces Accidents and Violations*, 299
*Driver Education Teacher Performance Inventory*, 214
  illustrated, 215

Driver education teachers, advantages enjoyed by, 18, 456
  and attitude-knowledge interaction, 72
  certification standards for, 12–14
  competency of, 97–99, 304, 321
  and drinking customs of community, 89–90
  experienced, 33, 50
  family use of driver education cars by, 263
  firmness of, 174
  funds for training, 15
  and the future, 455–458
  in-car instruction by (*see* In-car instruction)
  informed opinion of, 450, 452
  and job satisfaction, 18–19
  leadership by, 4, 12, 102
  liability of, 265–270
  as license examiners, 351–353
  negligence by, 269–270
  new, 174, 176–180, 220, 306
  professional background of, 452–454
  and professional literature, 299–301
  professional preparation of, 166, 250, 432–437, 456
  qualifications for, 3–4, 26, 216
  ratio of pupils to, 273–274
  and research studies, 294–295, 300–301
  and resource agencies, 438–445
  responsibilities of, 4, 17, 267, 310
  salaries of, 33, 273–276, 456
  skill teaching by, 180–184
  students and, 32–34
  students as viewed by, 47–50
  supervision of, 213–214, 216
  and traffic engineering, 304
  and winter driving, 218–221
Driver Evaluator, illustrated, 152
Driver improvement, 356–359
  for all drivers, 360–362
  instruction and, 364–365
  psychological tests of, 363–364
Driver Improvement Clinics, 367
Driver improvement program, 362–367
  courses used in, 362–363
  instruction and, 364–365

Driver improvement program, nationwide, 367–368
  policies for, 365–366
  psychological testing and, 363–364
Driver improvement schools, 362–367
  example of, 366–367
*Driver License Examinations*, 346, 351
Driver license examinations, 100–101
  components of, 353–356
  driving ranges for, 239
  education and, 429
  familiarity with car used in, 203–204
  given by teachers, 351–353
  object of, 348
  psychological factors in, 354–355
  and traffic safety, 349
Driver License Registration law, 344
Driver licensing, 346–351, 428–430
  adverse criticism of, 100
  multiple, 350
  vision and, 99–100
Driver safety, in entering and leaving car, 191–193
  medical aspects of, 92–93
Drivers, adjustment to and compensation for impairments by, 99–100
  deaf, 99–100
  drunken, 77, 81, 295
  future number of, 30, 95–96
  incompetent, licensing of, 349–350
  irresponsible, 25
  out-of-state, 357–358
  physical examinations for, 93–96
  skillful, 24
  sobriety tests for, 81–85
  social drinking by, 76–77
    examples of, 77–81
  vision of, 97–99
Drivers' licenses, 346–351
  information on obtaining, 177
  restrictions on, 355–356
  suspension and revoking of, 333, 344
  (*See also* Driver licensing)
Driveways, backing out of, 196
Driving, aging and, 97–99, 102–110
  defensive, 399–402
  while intoxicated, 344
  movements used in, 131–132
  night, 97, 99, 220

Driving, pleasure of, 286
  as a privilege, not a right, 346–347
  as a profession, 415–420
  psychological elements of, 133–135
  in snow, 205
  vision and, 97–99
  winter, 217–230
  (*See also* Drivers)
Driving ability, impairment of, 91–101
  license examinations and, 353–354
Driving practices, motion pictures on, 123
Driving ranges, arguments for and against, 238–239
  design of, 329
  instruction for practice on, 236–238
  maneuvers on, 238
  multiple-car, 233, 235
    cost and, 278
    illustrated, 234
  types of, 239–240
Driving records, research studies and, 294, 298–301
Driving simulators, 129–144
  evaluation of, 142
  as instrument for research, 143–144
  list and description of, 136–137
  psychology of, 133–135
  use of, cost and, 138–139, 278
    reason for, 130
  in testing, 135, 137–139
Drug addicts, 87
  and withdrawal, 88
Drugs, alcohol and, 88
  dangerous to drivers, list of, 87
  "drivers," 87–88
  effects of, 63–64, 87–89, 431
  illegal purchase of, 87
  prescription of, 87–88
Drunkenness, 80–81, 344
Drunkometer, 85
Dry pavements, skidding on, 223
Dual-control cars, 119, 130, 255–264
  equipment for, 263
  first day in, 174, 176–180
  identification of, 257–259
  insurance on, 261
  maintenance of, 263–264

Dual-control cars, obtaining of, 259–263
  rules for use of, 262–263
  safety of, 256
  winter driving in, 218, 221
Dual controls, hydraulic, 256, 257
  installation of, 256
  mechanical, 256

Economic problems, automobile and, 5
Education, basic, 247
  behavioral function of, 33
  broader curriculum in, 280–281
  definition of, 33
  state aid to, 449
Education associations, state, 16–17
Educational television (ETV), 145–149, 166
  advantages of, 147
  in driver and traffic safety education, 147–149
  methods of broadcasting, 146
  uses of, 146
*Effectiveness of Teacher Performance in Behind-the-Wheel Instruction in Driver Education,* 214
8-mm film cartridges, 119
8-mm motion pictures, list of, 128
Electric starters, 378
Emergencies, behavior in, 35–37
  on driving ranges, 238
  procedures in, during in-car instruction, 184–185
  in winter driving, 218
Emotion, behavior and, 64–65
  driver license examinations and, 354
  driving and, 133–134
  learning process and, 4, 12
  as motivation for safety, 67
  and nerve impulses, 58–61, 78–79
  visual images and, 60–61
Emotional drives, alcohol and, 79
Enforcement (*see* Law enforcement)
Enforcement agencies, 9
  (*See also* Police officers)
Engine failure, 382
Engine starting, 185
Englander, William, 122*n*.
Enrollment, facilities and, 253

468  INDEX

Environment, attitudes and, 67–68, 134
   reaction to, 134–135
   simulation of, 133
Epilepsy, 94
Exhaust system, 218
Experience, age and, 103, 109–110, 167
   teaching, sharing of, 167–168
Experimental groups, control groups and, in programmed instruction, 160

Fatalities, revoked licenses and, 344
Federal General Fund, 408
Federal Road Act of 1916, 405
Federal Trade Commission, 370
Figure eight, the, 188–190
Films, availability of, 119
   effects of, 119
   equipment for showing, 120
   single-concept, 119
   use of, 116, 119–120
   (*See also* Motion pictures)
Filmstrip projectors, 120
Filmstrips, list of, 128
Financial responsibility laws, 358–359, 397
Fines, 6
First aid, 270
First-aid kits, 185
Flannel boards, use of, 120–121
Flares, 185, 218
Fleet maintenance, 383
Fog, 222
Food and Drug Administration, 87
Foot brakes, 180, 185
Ford Motor Company Time-Lapse Filmstrips, 128
Forward driving, practice in, 236–237
Forward gear, shifting into, 191
Free choice, leisure and, 65
Freeways, 305
Friction, coefficient of, 223–224, 226
   between tires and road surface, 223–225
Front seats, sliding across, to use curbside door, 192
Front wheels, in automatic wheel recovery, 187

Gas stops, 205
Gasoline, cost of, for driver education, 185, 276–277
Gears, shifting of, 191
Gearshift levers, floor mounted, 192
Gearshifts, 179
General Motors, Pontiac Motor Division, 263
General Services Administration, 370
Generator charge lights, 179
Glove compartments, emergency phone numbers kept in, 184
Goodyear Aerospace Corporation, 143
Government, highways and, 8, 403–414
   (*See also* States; entries under Federal; U.S.)
*Great Insurance Swindle, The*, 395
Group accident insurance, 266

Habits, predriving, 178
Hand signals, 193
Hazardous locations, class project on study of, 312, 314
Headlights, 179
Health education, driver education and, 250, 253
Hearing, defective, 100
   tests for, 152
Heaters, 218
Heise, Herman A., 75$n$., 77, 89
   quoted, 82–83, 88
High- and low-beam indicator lights, 179
High school driver education departments, 166–167, 438
*High School Student and the Automobile*, 300$n$.
Highway construction, 8, 286
   federal role in, 404–412
"Highway hypnosis," 100
Highway Research Board, 442–443
Highway transportation, opportunities in, 416–420
Highway Trust Fund, 406–410
Highways, 9
   American, 403–414
      financing of, 406–409
      interstate and defense, 406–410

Highways, American, numbered, 410–412
  state, 412
  heavy-traffic, skidding on, 224
  as learning laboratories, 9
  skid practice on, 227
  traffic engineering and, 303–309
  (*See also* Roads)
Hills, braking on, 191
  skidding on, 224
  stopping and starting on, 202
Hoover, Herbert, 426
Horns, 179
Human factors, accidents and, 21–23
  in driving simulation, 129–144
  measured by psychophysical tests, 150–158
  motion pictures on, 124
Hypothalamus, emotion and, 58, 79

Ice, driving on, 222
  practice in, 226–229
Identification signs, 258–259
Ignition switch, 179
Illinois, University of, 433
Impairments, adjustment to and compensations for, 99–100, 109
  driving and, 91
  reporting of, 92–93
  "teacher competency" and, 97–99, 101
In-car instruction, choice of words in, 203, 213
  combined with classroom instruction, 174, 180, 204–205
  cost of, 272–276
  course organization for, 176–177
  cues useful in, 185–187
  emergency procedures and, 184–185
  for first day in dual-control car, 174, 176–180
  in groups of four, 174, 176, 205
  liability for accidents in, 268–269
  for orientation to car, 177–180
  physical education and, 249–250
  and professional judgment, 199–205, 208–214, 216
  scheduling of, 249–252
    adaptations in, 253–254

In-car instruction, supervision of, 213–214, 216
  teaching tips for, 191–199
  techniques for, 173–216
Inhibitions, impairment of, 79–80, 86–87
  against taking chances, 227
Injured, care of, 429
Injury, 20, 185
  car features causing, 379
  negligence and, 265
  protection against, 378–381
Institute of Traffic Engineers, 443
Instruction permits, 350
Instructional television (ITV), 146
  strengths and weaknesses of, 146–147
Instrument panel lights, 179
Instrument panels, 379, 381
  padded, 180, 371
Insurance, accident, 266
  automobile (*see* Automobile insurance)
  basic principle of, 392–394
Insurance benefits, 285
Insurance companies, 392–396
Insurance Information Institute, 395
Insurance Institute for Highway Safety, 443, 447
Inter-American Traffic Seminar, First, 304
International Association of Chiefs of Police (IACP), 443
  National Safety Check Program, 395–396
  statement on drag strips, 335
  statement on police traffic management, 328–333, 336
Intersections, signals for turning at, 209
  skidding near, 224
  vehicle counts at, 314
Interstate Commerce Commission, 343
Intoximeters, 85
"Involvement" formula, 295–296
Iowa State University, 433

Joerger, K., 80*n*.
Judges, 334, 337, 428

Kennedy, John F., quoted, 100
Kerrick, John K., 94n.
"Kickdown" shift, 202
Kinesthetic feedback, 132–133, 135, 140–141
  lack of, 141–142
Kinesthetic memory, 132, 140–141
Kinesthetic sense, 131
Knowledge, "folk," 55–56, 64
  license examinations and, 353
  safety, necessity for and, 70–73
  teaching techniques and, 72

Law enforcement, citizen's view of, 333–334
  facts about, 338–339, 341
  motion pictures on, 123–124
  objectives of, 322
Law violators, 9, 333–334
  table of, by age, 107
  (*See also* Traffic law violations)
Laws, 427–428, 430
  attitude toward, 326
  chemical test, 83–85
  compulsory insurance, 358
  conflict in, 86
  financial responsibility, 358–359
  motor vehicle, 342–359
  motor vehicle safety, 343
  police officers as symbol of, 327
  traffic (*see* Traffic laws)
  voluntary observance of, 8, 322, 328
Leadership, 69
  professional, improvement of, 423–458
  teachers and, 4, 12
Learner's permits, 6, 177, 285–286, 356
  loss of, 208
Learning, 40–44
  auditory versus visual, 41–42
  from experience, 168
  rate of, 176
Left and right, distinguishing between, 194–195
Leisure, and free choice, 65
  vehicle traffic increase and, 30
Liability, in the car, 268–269

Liability, in driver education course, 267–268
  immunity from, 266
  principles pertaining to, 269–270
  school and teacher, 265–276
License age, 285–286
License fees, 6
Licensing (*see* Driver licensing)
Life span, extended, 103
Lights, ammeter, 179
  high- and low-beam indicator, 179
  instrument panel, 179
  switches or controls for, 179
  tail, 179, 372–373
  turn signal, 180, 372
Loaned cars, 259–261, 276
*Look* magazine, 385
Loss of control, accidents and, 196
  in "recovery" from turn, 198
  in turning, 189

McGraw-Hill Driver Education Filmstrip Series, 128
Magnetic boards, use of, 120–121
Mahony, Arthur L., 77n.
Maintenance schedules, 263
Malfetti, James L., 214n.
Manual shift, the, 190–191
Manual-shift driver-education cars, 184, 255, 261
*Manual on Uniform Traffic Control Devices*, 343
Marihuana, 80
Mechanical failures, 377
Mechanics, teaching of, 10
  understanding of, 121
Medical advisory boards, 92
*Medical Guide for Physicians in Determining Fitness to Drive a Motor Vehicle*, 92, 94
Medical payments insurance coverage, 396
Mental condition, driver license examinations and, 354–355
Michigan, licensing age in, 286
Michigan State University, 433
Mickle, D. Grant, 304
Microwave broadcasting, 146

INDEX 471

Mirkin, Abraham J., 96n.
  quoted, 110
Mirrors, adjustment of, 178–179
Model cars, 5
*Model Traffic Ordinance*, 343
Models, cardboard, used in teaching, 119
Motion pictures, 8-mm, list of, 128
  16-mm, on attitude, 123
    on car ownership, 124–125
    on driving practices, 123
    on human factors, 124
    multipurpose and general, 125
    promotional, 125–126
    on skill teaching, 122–123
    on traffic law and enforcement, 123–124
  sources of, 126–128
  (*See also* Films)
Motor fleet supervisor training, 419-420
Motor impulses, cerebrally initiated, 180–184
Motor truck fleets, 417, 419–420
Motor vehicle administration, 92, 342–359, 428–429
  interstate cooperation in, 357–358
  personnel for, 345–346
Motor vehicle deaths, 27–28
Motor vehicle inspection, 384–390
  on-the-road, 390
  personnel for, 389–390
  state, 385–387
    legally required, 387–389
Motor vehicle law, 342–359
  state, 342, 345
Motor vehicle transportation, jobs in, 416–420
Motor vehicles, commercial, 383
  government, 370
  military, 383
  predicted increase in, 29
Movements, adjustive, 141–142
  made in driving, practice in, 131–132
    time element and, 132
  unconscious, 183
Muscles, contraction of, 130–132, 140
Muscular coordination, 130–131
  tests for, 152

Narcotics, 87–88
  (*See also* Drugs)
Nash, Jay B., 11
National Commission on Safety Education, 272, 443–444
National Committee for Motor Fleet Supervisor Training, 419–420
National Committee on Uniform Traffic Laws and Ordinances, 444
National Conference on Medical Aspects of Driver Safety and Driver Licensing, 92
National Conferences on Driver Education, 447
National Defense Education Act, 449
National Driver Register Service, 344–345
National Education Association (NEA), 16–17
  National Commission on Safety Education, 447
National Highway Users Conference, 444
National Joint Committee on Uniform Traffic Control Devices, 444
National Safety Check Program, 385–387
National Safety Council, 77, 367, 385, 387, 419, 444–445
National Safety Education Conference on Teacher Preparation and Certification in Driver and Safety Education, 447
National Symposium on the Deaf Driving and Employability, 100
Negative transfer, 140–141
Negatives, use of, in teaching, 200–201
Negligence, contributory, 269
  injuries and, 265
Nerve impulses, 78
  coded, 62
  emotion and, 58, 65
  triggered, 58–61
Nerve pathways, 79
  new, practice and, 182–183
  patterned, 62
Nervous system, 35–37, 51
  attitude and, 57
  drinking and, 80–81

Nervous system, drugs and, 87
Neural bias mechanism (NBM), 61–62
  as determinant of attitude, 62–63
  emotional association pattern formed in, 64–69
Neural pathways, 133
Neuromuscular coordination, 142, 183
New Jersey, inspection system in, 386–387, 389–390
New York State, compulsory insurance in, 397
  educational television in, 147
New York University, 145, 433, 437, 458
Neyhart, Amos E., 6
Niles Township High School, Skokie, Illinois, 300
North Carolina, Driver Improvement Clinics, 367
Northwestern University, 437

"Observer" students, 185
Odometers, 179
Offstreet practice area, illustrated, 182, 184
  for winter driving, 222
Oil pressure lights or indicator, 179
Oklahoma State University, 433
Old age, concepts of, 103–106
  (*See also* Aged; Aging)
Operational control devices, 179–180
Operator licenses, 350
O'Toole, John F., Jr., 162n.
Out-of-state drivers, 357–358
Overbraking, in winter driving, 222
Overhead projectors, 120
Overpowering, in winter driving, 221
Oversteering, 189
  in winter driving, 221
Owner's manuals, 208–209

Parent Teachers Association, the (PTA), 287
Parental control, 47–48
Parental signatures, 267
Parents, attitude of, toward driver education, 282, 284

Parking, 211, 306
Parking brake, 180, 202
Passing signals, 401–402
Pedestrians, crossing streets, courtesy toward, 400–401
  drunken, 80–81
  hazards to, 319
  and traffic accidents, 284
"Peeling out," 226
Pennsylvania State (College) University, 6, 433, 437
Personality characteristics, measurement of, 355
Phone numbers, emergency, 184–185
Photography, 118–119
Physical education, in-car instruction and, 249–250, 253–254
Physical examinations, 93–96
  frequency of, 95
Physical exercise, aging and, 104–105
Physicians, reporting of impairments by, 93
Pictures, 118
  words versus, 116
Point systems, 357
Police headquarters, visits to, 323
Police officers, 323, 325, 428
  cooperation of, 324
  and efficiency ratings, 333
  pupils and, 325–328, 339, 341
  respect for, 327
Police traffic management, statement on, 328–333
Police traffic supervision, 321–341
*Policies and Practices for Driver and Traffic Safety Education*, 259, 262, 272, 278n., 447
Population growth, accident volume and, 29–30
  driver education courses and, 6–7
Positive transfer, 140, 142
Posters, use of, 120, 324–325
Power brakes, 199
Power steering, 199, 375, 378
Practice, on ice, planning for, 226–229
  neuromuscular actions and, 182–184
  on the road, 191
  skid, 225

Practice, skill learning and, 131
  in winter driving, 222
Practice areas, to avoid car damage, 210
  offstreet, 184
  selection of, 211, 232–233
*Practice Driving Guides*, 174, 180
  typical lesson from, illustrated, 175
Predriving habits, 178
President's Committee for Traffic Safety, Action Program of, 300, 425–426
Procedural responses, 141–142
  definition of, 141
Professional associations, 16–17
Professional driving, 415–420
Professional leadership, improvement of, 423
  action program for, 425–431
Professional literature, 299–301
Programmed instruction, 159–163
  evaluation of, by teacher, 162–163
  research on, 160, 162
  student's reaction to, 163
*Programmed Topics from Sportsmanlike Driving*, 161
Projectors, 120
Property damage, 359
Property damage liability insurance, 396
Proprioceptors, 130, 140
Psychology, driver education and, 454–455
Psychophysical tests, administration of, 156–157
  for driver improvement, 363–364
  equipment for, 152–154
    location of, 156
  integrated with class activities, 154–155
  interpreting scores in, 157–158
  list of available, 151–152
  physical arrangements needed for, 155–156
  purposes of, 150–151
  simplicity of, 153–154
  special student projects in, 158
  time required to administer, 153
  use of, 150–158

Public, the, explaining driver education to, 287–288
Public information programs, 429
Public relations, driver education and, 281
Public schools, budgets of, 272
Pupil-teacher ratio (P-T-R), 273–274
Purdue University, 437
Push button selector, 179


Quality standards, 430–431
Quizzes on films, 119


Rain, driving in, 222, 224
RCA Data Systems Center, 143
Reaction to environment, choice of, 134–135
Reaction time, age and, 105
  alcohol and, 76
  fast, 24
  simulators and, 135
  skidding and, 211–212
  tests for, 152–153, 155, 158
Reading, versus listening, 40–42
Reading ability, 42–44
Rear-view mirrors, 193
Rear windows, 374
Reflex action, 36–37
Reports, research, 296–298
Research, behavioral, 46–47, 73–74
  driver education, 16, 293–301, 429
    trends in, 298–299
  in driving simulation, 139–143
  on programmed instruction, 160, 162
  reports on, 296–298
  simulators used in, 130
  at traffic safety centers, 436–437
Research studies, 294–295, 300–301
Responses, adjustive, 141–142
  procedural, 141–142
  quick or slow, 212
Reverse, shifting into, 191
Road ahead, continuous awareness of, 197, 230
Road conditions, speed and, 298
Road practice, 191
Road tests, 353

Roads, county and township, 412–413
  modernization of, 305
  municipal, 413
  secondary federal, 405
  state, 412
  (*See also* Highways)
Roll-over bars, 377
Roof top signs, 258–259
Routes, street driving, 232–233
Rubber Manufacturers Association, 378
Rules, definable, need for, 168
  for use and maintenance of driver education cars, 262–263

Safety, attitude toward, 70–72
  driver, 92–93, 191–193
  of dual-control cars, 256
  simulators and, 130
  in skid practice, 226–227
  of student, 8
Safety Check Program for Communities, 385
Safety features of automobiles, 369–381
Safety glass, 378
Safety patrols, grade-school, 17
Salaries, in motor vehicle administration, 346
  teachers', costs and, 273–276
Schedules, adaptation of, 253–254
  sample, 250–252
  illustrated, 253
School boards, driver education and, 281
School-dealer arrangements, 261–262
School enrollment, educational television and, 146–147
School-student relationship, 44–47
Schools, liability of, 265–270
  (*See also* Public schools)
Science, behavior and, 33–34
  safety education and, 10
Science departments, winter driving course and, 229–230
Seat adjustment, 178
Seat belts, 178, 344, 371, 379, 381
Seats, bucket, 192
Second gear, shifting into, 191
  used in braking, 202

Sedatives, 87
Sedentary life, aging and, 104–105
Selector lever, 179
Self-confidence, 4
Self-preservation, 71
Senior citizens (*see* Aged)
Service stations, 384
Sheehe, Gordon H., quoted, 433–435
Shell Better Driving Test, 128
Shift lever, pressure on, 191
Shift pattern, 190
Shifting, "drag" in, 191
  from forward to reverse and vice versa, 191
  practice in, 190
Shock absorbers, 376
Siebrecht Attitude Scale, 73
Signaling, 195
  at intersections, 209
  when leaving car, 193
Sim-L-car, 137–138
Simulation, 129–144
  of environment, 133
  research in, 139–143
  and skid practice, 228–229
16-mm motion pictures, list of, 122–126
Skid control, classroom instruction in, 221
Skid practice, 225–229
  psychological damage and, 228
  on public highway, 227
  simulation and, 228–229
Skidding, 211–212, 217–230
  data on, 223–225
  on dry roads, 223
  on wet pavements, 226
Skill, 24
  temporary loss of, 198
Skill learning, 130–131, 176
  factors in, 131
  time limitations for, 199–200
Skill practice, 182–184
Skill teaching, 130
  evaluating potential of, 131–133
  in-car instruction and, 180–184
  motion pictures on, 122–123
Skokie, Illinois, study, 300
Slide projectors, 120
Slipperiness, wetness and, 224

# INDEX

Smoking, driving and, 89
Snow, driving in, 205, 218–230
    illustrated, 208
    rocking car out of, 221
Snow chains, 218
  putting on, 204
Snow shovels, 218
Snow walls, 225–226
Sobriety tests, 81–83
Social drinking, 76–81
Social problems, automobiles and, 5
South Carolina, educational television in, 147
Southern Illinois University, 433
Spare tires, 185
Speed, accident involvement and, 296–298, 335
  brake power and, 185
  and braking distance on ice and snow, table, 229
  visibility and, 372
Speed surveys, class projects for, 314
Speed traps, 332
Speeding, drinking and, 80
  skidding and, 223–224
Speedometers, 179
  glancing at, 197
*Sportsmanlike Driving*, 75n., 77, 296
Stability of cars, 376–377
Stalling, 197–198
Stanchions, 119, 187
  illustrated, 188
Starter switch, 179
State College High School, Pennsylvania, 6
State highways, 412
States, and driver education programs, 6–7
  financial responsibility laws of, 358–359
  and motor vehicle law, 342, 357–359
  and National Driver Registration Service, 344–345
  reciprocity between, 358
  and teacher certification standards, 12–14
"Station drivers," 177
Steering, as an adjustive response, 142
  in backing, 185–187

Steering, as full-time job, 201
  power, 199, 375, 378
  when skidding, 211–212
  test of, 201
  "walking the wheel" in, 185
Steering column, 381
Steering exercises, figure eight, 188–190
Steering gear failure, 385
Steering mechanism, 375
Steering wheels, 379
  accurate stopping of, 189
  mock-up of, 131–132
  movement of, 131–133
    constant, 196
    hand-over-hand, 188
  in turning, 195
Stop lights, 372
Stopping, brake pressure and, 185
  "crash," 185
Stopping distance, skidding and, 225
Street driving routes, 232–233
Streets, 413–414
Stress, emotional behavior and, 64
Student permits, 177
Student projects, in constructing teaching aids, 117–119
  in traffic engineering, 312–318
    post-project lesson on, 314, 318
  for using test information, 158
Students, attitude patterns of, 34–35
  behavior problems among, 48–49
  curriculum design and, 8
  and needs of student, 247–248
  drinking by, 76–77
  emotions of, 4, 12
  fragmented, 45–46, 49–50
    reconstruction of, 47–50
  and homework, 38
  importance of, 32
  liability for injuries to, 266
  logic of, 35–37
  mental and physical condition of, 49–50
  "observer," 185
  orientation of, to in-car instruction, 176–180
  problems of, 49
  psychophysical testing of, 150–158
  ratio of teachers to, 273–274

Students, receptiveness of, 11–12
   relationship with school, 44–47
   safety of, 8, 222, 267
   teacher and, 32–34
   teacher's diagnosis of, 201–202
   teacher's view of, 47–50
   teaching aids constructed by, 117–119
   time of, for driver education, 248
   and traffic engineering, 308
     danger to, 310
     involvement in, 309–310
     projects for, 310–318
*Summary of Results of Studies Evaluating Driver Education*, 299
Sun visors, 180
Supervisors, of in-car instruction, 213–214, 216
   manual for, 214
Switches, auxiliary, 179
   operating, 179
"Syncho-mesh," shifting into, 191
Synergy, 88

Tail lights, 179, 372–373
Taxation, for federal highways, 406–408
   for high school driver education programs, 6
   for state, county, and municipal roads, 412–414
*Teachable Moments*, Nash, 11
Teacher certification courses, 6
   aim of, 3
Teacher certification standards, 12–14
   improvement of, 14, 16
   need for, 15–16
   variation in, 14
Teacher Preparation and Certification Conference of 1965, 447–448
Teachers, in the classroom, 112–114
   cooperation among, 39–40
     driver education (*see* Driver education teachers)
   educational television and, 147
   "master," 165, 167
   new, 168, 174, 176
   secondary school, 45

Teachers, shortage of, 13
   specialization by, 45
Teachers-in-training, traffic engineering and, 311–312, 318
Teaching, 40–44
   in the classroom (*see* Classroom instruction)
   knowing and, 113–114
   "lecture method" of, 40
   psychology and, 201
   team, 165–168
   of traffic engineering, 307–319
Teaching aids and equipment, 115–128
   class-constructed, 117–119
   programmed instruction as, 159–163
   selection of, 117–119
   simplicity and durability of, 117–118
   sources of, 121–122
   use of, principles and techniques in, 119–121
Teaching experience, salaries and, 33
Teaching machines, 160, 162
Teaching techniques, 42–44
   attitude, knowledge and, 72
   in-car, 173–216
Team teaching, 165–168
   shared experience in, 167–168
Technology, 146
Teen-agers, 49
   drinking and driving by, 82–83
   motor vehicle accident rate and, 24, 82
   reaction time of, 24
   trigger words used by, 66–67
Television, 144–145
   commercial, 145–146, 148
   educational (*see* Educational television)
   evaluation of, for teaching, 148–149
   instructional (ITV), 146
Temperature changes, winter driving and, 221
Temperature indicators, 179
Test scores, interpretation of, 157–158
Testing, psychophysical (*see* Psychophysical tests)
   use of simulators in, 135–139
Tests, achievement, 160
   breath, 81, 86

INDEX 477

Tests, psychophysical (*see* Psychophysical tests)
  sobriety, 81–85
  used in classroom, 151–154
    depth perception, 152–153
    hearing, 152
    muscular coordination, 152
    for reaction time, 152–153, 155, 158
    visual, 151–152
Texas, educational television in, 146, 148
Texas Agricultural and Mechanical College, 433
Texas Education Agency, 148
Textbooks for driver education courses, 180
  on defensive driving, 400
  on maintenance, 384–385
  on motor vehicle control, 343
  on traffic engineering, 304, 311
  on winter driving, 221, 223
Thurston, L. L., 73
Time, apportionment of, 318
  limitation of, for instruction, 199–200, 205
  reaction (*see* Reaction time)
  spent by student on driver education, 248
Tire chains, putting on, 204
  illustrated, 206–207
  reinforced, 218
Tire repair, 185
Tires, changing of, 204
  labeling of, 370–371
  rotating of, 190
  safety, 378
  spare, 185
  striking curb with, 190
  studded, 376
  worn, skidding and, 224
Toledo-Lucas County, Ohio, 367
Tow lines, 218
Trac-Tred, 218
Traffic, highway, 18
  attention to, 197
  merging, brief glance technique and, 196–197
  predicted increase in, 29–30

Traffic, too early introduction into, 184
  vision and, 211
Traffic circles, skidding at, 224
Traffic cones, illustrated, 188
  in teaching backing, 186
  use of, 187–188
Traffic courts, 333, 336–337, 428
Traffic engineering, 303–319, 429
  definition of, 308
  hazards of, 310
  in high school course, 318
  human interest angle in, 307–308
  role of, 303
  student projects in, 312–318
  summary of, 304–305
  teacher competency and, 304
Traffic engineers, 308
Traffic lanes, pulling into, from curb, 194
Traffic law violations, 9
  age and, table, 107
  research studies and, 204–295
  (*See also* Law violators)
Traffic laws, 8–9
  motion pictures on, 123–124
  state, knowledge of, 198
Traffic operations, 308
Traffic patterns, for driving range practice, 237–238
Traffic problems, cures for, 96–97
Traffic safety, 345
  driver examinations and, 349
  new developments in, 298
Traffic safety centers, 432–437
  concept of, 433–434
  research as function of, 436–437
Traffic safety education, 33, 325
  implication as psychological device, 67
  and the public, 287–288
Traffic safety specialists, 22–23
  advice on winter driving, 220
Traffic tickets, undeserved, 325
Traffic volume, predictions on, 29–30
Trailers, increase in, 30
Tranquilizers, 87–88
Transfer of training, 140
Transmission, automatic, 255–256, 261
  manual, 190–191, 255, 261

"Trigger words," 58–61
  desirable, implanting of, 67
  familiar to teen-agers, 66–67
Trucks, 417–420
Truman, Harry S, 426
Trunks, emergency equipment kept in, 185
Truth serums, 64
Turn, or directional, signals, 180, 372
Turning, early, 196
  loss of control in, 189
  practice in, 238
  in skidding, 225
  skill in, 189
  in traffic, 189
Turns, recovery from, 189–190
  illustrated, 189
  three-point, 210–211

Understeering, 188
*Uniform Vehicle Code,* 85, 343, 345, 351, 358–359, 386, 390
Uninsured motorists, insurance protection against, 396
U.S., Bureau of Public Roads, 296, 405
  Department, of Agriculture, 405
    of Commerce, Bureau of Public Roads, 445
      National Driver Register Service, 344
    of Health, Education and Welfare, Division of Accident Prevention, 445
Universities, 458
  traffic safety centers in, 432–437

Vehicle counts, class project on, 314
Vehicle registration, 346–351
Ventilation, 178
Violations (*see* Traffic law violations)
Virginia, University of, 433
Visibility, 372–374
  in winter driving, 221
Vision, in backward driving, 186–187
  blocked, 210
  color tests for, 152
  defective, 97
  field of, tests for, 151

Vision, impairment of, by alcohol, 76
  licensing and, 97–99, 353, 355
  location for tests of, 155–156
  night, 97, 105
    tests for, 152–153
  steering and, 201
  traffic and, 211
Visual acuity, 105
  tests for, 151, 153, 158
Visual feedback, 135, 141
  skill learning and, 132
Visual images, emotional reaction and, 60–61
Visual tests, 151–152
Voters, future, citizenship education of, 286

"Walking the wheel," 185
Warnings, method of giving, 208
Washington, D.C., Traffic School, 367
  (*See also* District of Columbia)
Wet leaves, skids on, 226
Wet pavement, instilling respect for, 229
  skidding on, 222–227
Wheel recovery, 187
Wheels, locking of, 222
  rear, increased traction of, 376–377
*Who Is Liable for Pupil Injuries?,* 266
Windshield washers, 372
Windshield wipers, 179, 218, 372
Windshield and window scrapers, 218
Windshields, 381
  colored, 370
  safety glass for, 378–379
Winter driving, 217–230
  inspection of car prior to, 218
  instruction policy for, 221–222
  teaching of, 218–221
*Winter Driving Skill Exercises for Teachers,* 225
Wire mats, 185, 218
Word symbols, emotional reaction and, 58–61
Words, teacher's choice of, 203, 213

Yale University, 433, 437

Zigzagging, reverse, 186